CFPA 320.09 KAI
Marx and modern political theory :
Center for Policy Analysis

Marx and Modern Political Theory

Studies in Social and Political Philosophy
General Editor: James P. Sterba, University of Notre Dame

Social Contract Theories: Political Obligation or Anarchy?
by Vicente Medina, Seton Hall University

Collective Responsibility: Five Decades of Debate in Theoretical and Applied Ethics
edited by Larry May and Stacey Hoffman, Purdue University

Original Intent and the Constitution: A Philosophical Study
by Gregory Bassham, King's College

Patriotism, Morality, and Peace
by Stephen Nathanson, Northeastern University

The Liberalism-Communitarianism Debate
edited by C.F. Delaney, University of Notre Dame

On the Eve of the 21st Century: Perspectives of Russian and American Philosophers
edited by William Gay, University of North Carolina at Charlotte, and T.A. Alekseeva, Russian Academy of Sciences

Democracy and Social Injustice
by Thomas Simon, Illinois State University

Marx and Modern Political Theory: From Hobbes to Contemporary Feminism
by Philip J. Kain, Santa Clara University

Marx and Modern Political Theory

From Hobbes to Contemporary Feminism

Philip J. Kain

Rowman & Littlefield Publishers, Inc.

ROWMAN & LITTLEFIELD PUBLISHERS, INC.

Published in the United States of America
by Rowman & Littlefield Publishers, Inc.
4720 Boston Way, Lanham, Maryland 20706

Copyright © 1993 by Rowman & Littlefield Publishers, Inc.

All rights reserved. No part of this publication may be reproduced, stored in a retrieval system, or transmitted in any form or by any means, electronic, mechanical, photocopying, recording, or otherwise, without the prior permission of the publisher.

British Cataloging in Publication Information Available

Library of Congress Cataloging-in-Publication Data
Kain, Philip J.
   Marx and modern political theory : from Hobbes to contemporary feminism / Philip J. Kain.
     p. cm.
   Includes bibliographical references and index.
   1. Marx, Karl, 1818–1883—Contributions in political science.
2. Political science—History. I. Title.
JC233.M299K35   1993   320'.09—dc20   93-904   CIP
ISBN 0-8476-7865-2 (cloth: alk. paper)
ISBN 0-8476-7866-0 (paper: alk. paper)

Printed in the United States of America

The paper used in this publication meets the minimum requirements of American National Standard for Information Sciences—Permanence of Paper for Printed Library Materials, ANSI Z39.48–1984.

For Stanley Moore

whose student I was privileged to be

Contents

Acknowledgments   xi

Abbreviations   xiii

Introduction   1

1   Hobbes, Political Theory, and Sovereignty   17

    I   Sovereignty by Institution and Its Scientific Deduction   20

    II   Social Theory, Political Theory, and Revolution   25

    III   Sovereignty by Acquisition and Moral Obligation   27

    IV   Philosophy of History   29

    V   Legitimate Revolution   31

2   Locke, Social Theory, and Limited Government   37

    I   Property and Social Theory   37

    II   Social Contract Theory and Its Misuse   41

    III   Social Inequality   50

    IV   Sovereign Power and Property   56

viii   *Contents*

3   Rousseau, Individual Liberty, and Community   65
    I   The General Will   65
    II   Individual and Community   75
    III   The *Social Contract* and the *Discourse on Inequality*   83

4   Kant, Philosophy of History, and the Ideal Society   97
    I   Historical Conflict and World Peace   98
    II   Moral Force in History   102
    III   Particular Interest and the General Interest   106
    IV   The Highest Good and a Beautiful World   109
    V   Sovereignty and Revolution   113

5   Hegel, the State, and Spirit   123
    I   Philosophy of History and *Sittlichkeit*   124
    II   The Development of Custom and Tradition   130
    III   Spirit and the State   136
    IV   Sovereignty and Spirit   143

6   Marx and the Earlier Tradition   153
    I   The Categorical Imperative and Revolution   153
    II   Democracy and the General Will   163
    III   Essence and the Communal Individual   176
    IV   The Highest Good, a Beautiful World, and the Aesthetic Condition   202
    V   Rights and Community   212

7   Marx and Pluralism   235
    I   Pluralism and Umbrella Agreements   235
    II   Pluralism and Community   245

III Capitalism and Diversity   264

IV Ethnocentrism   270

V Ethnocentrism and Historical Materialism   279

VI Ethnocentrism and Historical Stages   296

8 Marx and Feminism   311

I Women and Determinism   312

II Men, Women, and the Species   326

III Housework and Alienation   342

IV The Family and Community   369

Bibliography   389

Index   409

About the Author   429

Acknowledgments

I would like to thank Professor Stanley Moore, to whom this book is dedicated, for the graduate seminars that he offered in the 1960s and 1970s where I first learned Marx and political theory. This book is deeply indebted to Professor Moore. I would like to thank the following for extended discussions and for comments on earlier versions of this manuscript: Don Beggs, Michael Brint, Annette Aronowicz, and Loren Lomasky. I would also like to thank Michael Meyer, Jerry Press, Bro Adams, Peter Minowitz, Peter Heckman, James Felt, and Bill Parent. I would like to thank, at Santa Clara University, all the members of the Philosophy Department, the Political Theory Study Group, the Faculty Critical Theory Group, and, at Stanford University, the members of the Interpretation Seminar.

Various parts of this book first appeared in article form. I would like to thank the journals in which they appeared for permission to reprint them here. The articles appear in slightly changed form.

Chapter 1 first appeared as "Hobbes, Revolution, and the Philosophy of History" in *Hobbes's "Science of Natural Justice"* (International Archives of the History of Ideas, Vol. 111), edited by C. Walton and P.J. Johnson (copyright © 1987 by Martinus Nijhoff Publishers, Dordrecht), pp. 203–18. Reprinted by permission of Kluwer Academic Publishers.

Chapter 2 first appeared as "Locke and the Development of Political Theory" in *Annals of Scholarship* V (1988), pp. 334–61.

Chapter 3 first appeared as "Rousseau, the General Will, and Individual Liberty" in *History of Philosophy Quarterly* VII (1990), pp. 317–36.

Chapter 4 first appeared as "Kant's Political Theory and Philosophy of History" in *CLIO* XVIII (1989), pp. 325–45.

xii *Acknowledgments*

Chapter 5 first appeared as "Hegel's Political Theory and Philosophy of History" in *CLIO* XVII (1988), pp. 345–68. This article has been reprinted in *G.W.F. Hegel: Critical Assessments,* edited by Robert Stern (London: Routledge, 1993).

Parts of Chapter 6 first appeared as "Marx and Rights: A Review of *Marxism and Morality* by Steven Lukes" in *Annals of Scholarship* VII (1991), pp. 397–406.

Parts of Chapter 7 first appeared as "Marx and Pluralism" in *Praxis International* XI (1992), pp. 465–86. Other parts of Chapter 7 first appeared as "Marx, Sahlins, and Ethnocentrism" in *Rethinking Marxism* VI (1993).

Parts of Chapter 8 first appeared as "Modern Feminism and Marx" in *Studies in Soviet Thought* XLIV (1993), pp. 159–92. Copyright © 1992 Kluwer Academic Publishers. Reprinted by permission of Kluwer Academic Publishers. Other parts of Chapter 8 first appeared as "Marx, Housework, and Alienation" in *Hypatia: A Journal of Feminist Philosophy* VIII (1993), pp. 121–44.

International Publishers has given me permission to quote from *Karl Marx Frederick Engels Collected Works* (New York: International Publishers, 1975 ff.); from K. Marx, *Capital,* edited by F. Engels (New York: International Publishers, 1967); and from F. Engels, *The Origin of the Family, Private Property and the State* (New York: International, 1942).

St. Martin's Press has given me permission to quote from Jean-Jacques Rousseau, *On the Social Contract with Geneva Manuscript and Political Economy,* edited by Roger D. Masters and translated by Judith R. Masters (New York: St. Martin's, 1978). Copyright © 1978. Reprinted with permission of St. Martin's Press. Also, St. Martin's Press has given me permission to quote from Jean-Jacques Rousseau, *The First and Second Discourses,* edited by Roger D. Masters and translated by Roger D. Masters and Judith R. Masters (New York: St. Martin's, 1964). Copyright ©1964. Reprinted with permission of St. Martin's Press.

I would like to thank Cambridge University Press for permission to quote from J. Locke, *Two Treatises of Government,* edited by P. Laslett (New York: Mentor, 1965). Copyright © Cambridge University Press 1960. Reprinted with permission.

Abbreviations

AE	Schiller, *Letters on the Aesthetic Education of Man*
Ak	Kant, *Kant's gesammelte Schriften*
CHPL	Marx, *Critique of Hegel's Philosophy of Law*
CHPLI	Marx, "Critique of Hegel's Philosophy of Law: Introduction"
CJ	Kant, *Critique of Judgment*
CM	Marx, "Comments on James Mill"
Corsica	Rousseau, *Constitutional Project for Corsica*
CPCSF	Eisenstein, *Capitalist Patriarchy and the Case for Socialist Feminism*
CPE	Marx, *Critique of Political Economy*
CPR	Kant, *Critique of Pure Reason*
CPrR	Kant, *Critique of Practical Reason*
CWF	Marx, *Civil War in France*
"Dissertation"	Marx, *Difference Between the Democritean and Epicurean Philosophy of Nature*
DS	de Beauvoir, *Le deuxième sexe*
EAP	Schiller, *Essays Aesthetical and Philosophical*

Eighteenth Brumaire	Marx, *Eighteenth Brumaire of Louis Bonaparte*
EPM	Marx, *Economic and Philosophic Manuscripts*
EW	Hobbes, *The English Works of Thomas Hobbes*
F	Kant, *Foundations of the Metaphysics of Morals*
"Free Press"	Marx, "Debates on Freedom of the Press"
GI	Marx & Engels, *German Ideology*
Gotha	Marx, "Critique of the Gotha Program"
GPR	Hegel, *Grundlinien der Philosophie des Rechts*
HF	Marx & Engels, *Holy Family*
IPH	Hegel, *Lectures on the Philosophy of World History: Introduction*
IUH	Kant, "Idea for a Universal History"
JQ	Marx, "On the Jewish Question"
L	Hegel, *The Logic of Hegel*
"Leading Article"	Marx, "Leading Article in No. 179 of the *Kölnische Zeitung*"
LW	Locke, *The Works of John Locke in Nine Volumes*
Manifesto	Marx, *Communist Manifesto*
MECW	Marx & Engels, *Marx Engels Collected Works*
MEGA	Marx & Engels, *Marx Engels Gesamtausgabe*
MEW	Marx & Engels, *Marx Engels Werke*
NE	Aristotle, *Nicomachean Ethics*
OC	Rousseau, *œuvres complètes*
Origin	Engels, *Origin of the Family, Private Property, and the State*

PG	Hegel, *Phänomenologie des Geistes*
PH	Hegel, *Philosophy of History*
Poland	Rousseau, *Government of Poland*
PP	Kant, *Perpetual Peace*
PR	Hegel, *Philosophy of Right*
"Prussian Censorship"	Marx, "Comments on the Latest Prussian Censorship Instruction"
PS	Hegel, *Phenomenology of Spirit*
PW, I	Hegel, *Vorlesungen über die Philosophie der Weltgeschichte*, I
PW, II	Hegel, *Vorlesungen über die Philosophie der Weltgeschichte*, II–IV
SC	Marx & Engels, *Marx Engels Selected Correspondence*
Second Treatise	Locke, *Second Treatise of Government*
SWN	Schiller, *Schillers Werke: Nationalausgabe*
Theory and Practice	Kant, *On the Common Saying: 'This May be True in Theory, but it does not Apply in Practice'*
TSV	Marx, *Theories of Surplus Value*

Introduction

I first began to study Marx some twenty-three years ago. In those days there were many things that made it easy to become interested in Marx: among them the political ferment of the late 1960s and the fact that at the University of California at San Diego, where I was a graduate student, there were several important and interesting Marxists—Fredric Jameson, Herbert Marcuse, and Stanley Moore. The latter two were my teachers in the Philosophy Department, and the latter, to whom this book is dedicated, became my dissertation director. Moreover, the spirit of Marx was in the air and it seemed necessary to read him to understand what was happening in the world.

Despite the political ferment of the late 1960s, there were things that made it difficult for me to accept Marx at first. As an undergraduate, I had studied in a great books program at St. Mary's College of California, and the Philosophy Department at UC San Diego, very much under the influence of Richard Popkin at that time, took a history of ideas approach to philosophy. There were things about Marx that seemed at odds with my whole educational background. Some of his texts, especially the *Communist Manifesto*, made him seem like a sort of communist Descartes, like someone who would sweep aside all past culture, tradition, and morality—as if there were nothing of value to be found there—and start over with a clean slate.[1]

I have come to see that this was not an accurate picture of Marx, and indeed, a great deal of my work over the last twenty-three years has involved exploring the roots of Marx's thought in earlier tradition and rejecting anything like a Cartesian break. This is still a part of what motivates this present book. I would like to show that Marx grows out of and tries to go beyond, that he tries to solve the problems

1

and realize the potential of, the tradition in political theory of Hobbes, Locke, Rousseau, Kant, and Hegel.

Since my years as a graduate student, however, a different perspective on Marx has increasingly developed. Indeed, in many ways, it is a product of the radicalism of the 1960s. I would not say that this new perspective has replaced other perspectives. It exists alongside and competes with them, but it is gaining in power. For this perspective, far from it being the case that Marx is a communist Descartes who sweeps aside all past tradition, Marx is the very opposite. He is all too deeply rooted in past tradition—in ethnocentrism, in sexism, and in a totalizing antipluralism. Far from it being the case that Marx rejects and thereby liberates himself from past tradition, he has not at all freed himself from many of the most oppressive and dominating aspects of our past. Thus, in Chapters 7 and 8, I want to respond to some of the objections that contemporary theorists have raised against Marx, and I want to argue that just as I once was mistaken in thinking that Marx had rejected too much of the past, so these contemporary theorists are mistaken in thinking that Marx has not rejected very much of it. Marx does begin to free himself from these past forms of domination, significantly so for a nineteenth-century theorist, and he does so more than is obvious on the surface of his writings, which, after all, were not aimed at a twentieth-century audience, or focused in twentieth-century terms and categories, or for twentieth-century sensitivities. When Marx is understood, I think he can contribute to contemporary theory that wants to free itself from traditional sexism and ethnocentrism and create a pluralist society.

This book makes no pretense of being a complete history of modern political philosophy. It deals with only a few figures: Hobbes, Locke, Rousseau, Kant, Hegel, and Marx. It leaves out many others. And it makes no attempt to say anywhere near everything that might be said about any of these figures. It is merely a series of limited studies that I hope will bring into focus an interesting and important set of issues and problems.

Given my concern in the later chapters with certain contemporary forms of oppression, domination, and power, one of the issues that I want to discuss in the early chapters is the traditional concept of sovereignty as it develops from Hobbes to Marx. For Hobbes, the government must be sovereign and sovereign power must be absolute. This was so because Hobbes, I will try to argue in Chapter 1, had no social theory, only a political theory. The only power capable of holding citizens together in a civil body, for Hobbes, was a political power—the government or the sovereign. If the government lost its grip, individuals collapsed back into the state of nature.

Locke, by contrast, developed a social theory and thus was able to argue for limited government and the sovereignty of the people. The better your social theory—that is, the more cohesion you are able to find among the citizens apart from the political sphere—the less power the government need have to hold the citizens together. If you have a good enough social theory, then, with Marx, you might even begin to talk about the withering away of the state and, I will try to argue, the dissolution of sovereignty. For Hobbes, since he had no notion of social cohesion, the sovereign had to be absolute. For Locke, there is enough social cohesion to argue that government can be limited and that the people can be sovereign. This social cohesion, for Locke, arises out of property, property interest, commerce, and trade. Unfortunately, I will argue in Chapter 2, Locke does not succeed in making the people sovereign. His emphasis on unequal property shifts sovereignty to the propertied classes and in effect makes them sovereign over the propertyless.

For this reason, Rousseau rejects commerce, trade, and seriously unequal property as incompatible with the common good or the general will. Instead, he focuses on custom, tradition, and community as the forces capable of providing enough social cohesion so that the people can be sovereign and so that they can establish a general will and thus rational freedom. Rousseau is not a totalitarian as so many think. Rather, I argue in Chapter 3, he achieves an ideal but utopian synthesis of individual liberty and community. His views are utopian because healthy customs, traditions, and community simply have to be given in a premodern society, and they are incompatible with wealth, commerce, and trade. Such a society is impossible to realize in the real modern world.

Kant's philosophy of history, I argue in Chapter 4, is capable of explaining how particular, conflicting interests embedded in commerce and trade can lead toward the universal, the common good, or the categorical imperative rather than erode it as Rousseau thought they would. And thus Kant can go beyond Rousseau—he not only has a theory of the ideal society but a theory for how actually to realize it in the modern world. But, on the other hand, Kant has nothing to say about, and no way to realize, community.

Hegel attempts to synthesize much of this earlier tradition. He very clearly rejects a Hobbesian absolute sovereign that stands over society and holds the citizens together from outside. Hegel does have a social theory that explains the internal coherence of society apart from the governmental or political sphere. He sees that property, property interest, and trade in civil society provide this coherence much as for Locke, and he also sees that custom, tradition, and community provide this coherence much as for Rousseau. At the same time, he seems aware that unrestrained commerce and trade would shift power to the wealthy classes. On the other hand, Hegel does not want to eliminate wealth, commerce, and trade as for Rousseau and thus make the ideal state impossible to realize in the modern world. He sees, with Kant, that particular interests can lead to the universal.

Hegel's conception of the modern state is thus very similar to Rousseau's ideal community based upon rational freedom realized through a general will and reinforced by custom, tradition, and community. And Hegel develops a philosophy of history similar to Kant's that will allow him to explain the development of an ideal moral society in the modern world based upon a general will that at the same time is compatible with wealth, commerce, and trade. But, as we will see in Chapter 5, to achieve this synthesis among particular interests, the general will, and community, Hegel must abandon individual consciousness and move to spirit.

The laws and institutions of the state, for Hegel, arise through the historical development of the spirit of a people. Through alienation the citizens create the state as their own objectification and then are disciplined by their state. Through this process, both the state and individuals are molded so that individuals receive rational laws that accord with the universal and also with their own interests, but, for Hegel, the citizens do not democratically control their institutions or give themselves their own laws as for Rousseau. Their laws and institutions just arise through the historical development of spirit.

In order to explain how history can move toward the ideal society, Marx develops a theory of revolution. In many respects this theory is based upon Kant's philosophy of history. Conflicting interests, or in Marx's case, conflicting class interests, lead toward the common good. In fact, the class interest of the proletariat, we shall see, will lead it to act in accordance with the categorical imperative—it will drive the proletariat toward the development of an ideal moral society. Locke was the first to develop a theory of legitimate revolution; except, I will argue, revolution was legitimate for Locke only to defend property, not at all to allow the propertyless to transform things so as to achieve a more equitable society. Kant relies on conflict among nations to achieve the ideal society, and he is even willing to accept the gains in this direction made by revolutions, but he is unwilling or unable to allow that any revolution can be legitimate.

At any rate, Marx develops a philosophy of history in many ways like that of Kant, which will allow him to realize an ideal society that, much like Rousseau's, is a radically democratic and egalitarian community. In these respects, Marx's project is very similar to the project of Hegel, but Marx wants to accomplish all of this while avoiding Hegel's rejection of concrete Rousseauian democracy. Moreover, Marx wants to avoid Hegel's abandonment of individual consciousness and his move to spirit. To accomplish this Marx tries to realize a communal individual and to dissolve sovereignty.

This very brief sketch, which touches upon only a few of the issues that we will take up, nevertheless, I hope, at least suggests how I think Marx's thought grows out of, synthesizes, and realizes the tradition that precedes him. Marx not only develops a theory capable of combining community with rational freedom and concrete democracy, he also moves beyond utopianism. He develops a theory of how actually to bring the ideal society about in the modern world. This is to say, certainly, that he brings to fruition the tradition of Rousseau, Kant, and Hegel. It might be thought that this leaves out, and perhaps is even incompatible with, the tradition that begins in Locke and develops in modern liberalism. In fact, Rousseau, Hegel, and Marx have all been accused of being totalitarians or at least of being on the road toward totalitarianism. I do not think this charge can be sustained. But even if I am right it would still seem clear to most people that a Marxian society would fall far short of what would be considered an ideally open, tolerant, and pluralistic society. Thus, in Chapter 7, I would like to argue something that should be a bit surprising, namely, that the society Marx envisions is very definitely a pluralist society and that pluralism is compatible with community. In Chapter 8, I will also try to argue that Marx envisions this ideal pluralistic community as one that will bring about the emancipation of women, and that Marx, if correctly understood, could contribute more to modern feminist theory than many modern feminists have thought he can.

I have claimed that Marx moves beyond utopianism. We must notice, however, that there are two ways in which one can use the term "utopian." In one of these senses Marx is not a utopian; in the other he very definitely is. In the first sense, political theorists are utopian if they simply describe an ideal society without having any theory of how actually to realize it in the real world. In other words, the theorist has no philosophy of history or theory of social transformation, or at least not one that can explain how to bring the ideal society about. Plato, Thomas More, and, I will argue, Rousseau are good examples of such utopian theorists. Marx, on the other hand, has a very highly developed philosophy of history, an elaborate theory of social transformation, and a complex theory of revolution by which he tries to explain how to realize the ideal society. For Kant and for Marx it is not enough to merely describe the ideal society; a serious political theorist must explain how to realize it. In this sense Marx is definitely not utopian.

Nevertheless, there will always be some tension here. After all, in order to make it easier to develop a theory of how to realize the ideal society, a theorist can always make the ideal a bit easier to realize—the theorist can water down the ideal. The less ideal your ideal society, the less it goes beyond actually existing society, the easier it is likely to be to realize and the less utopian it will be—and, very likely, the less interesting it will be also. On the other hand, the more you emphasize the ideal character of the ideal society, the further it goes beyond actually existing society, the greater and more radical the social transformation it involves, all of this will make it increasingly difficult for the theory of how to realize the ideal to keep up with the ideal. Such a theorist is not utopian in the first sense. Such a theorist *has* a theory of how to realize the ideal. It is just that this theorist's conception of the ideal society is always running a bit ahead of the theory of how to realize the ideal society. Marx is such a theorist and he is utopian in this second sense.

In my opinion this second type of utopianism is acceptable—even desirable. We do not want to water down the ideal to make it easier to achieve. We always want to keep the ideal a bit ahead of what we are likely to be able to realize. If we stripped Marx of his idealism in this area, if we were to accept only what was practically realizable and soberly possible in Marx's thought, we would eliminate a great deal of his power, his brilliance, and his value—or at least I think so. As this book proceeds, the reader will notice that I tend to move through the sober, practical, realizable aspects of Marx's thought as quickly as is reasonably possible and that I tend to focus on his ideal side—on those aspects of Marx's thought that certainly have not been realized and that to some will appear impossible ever to realize. Perhaps this is a failure of mine. Perhaps this is a failure of Marx's. But then perhaps this is what will live when all else is dead in Marx's thought.

Even if Marxism as a political movement is already dead, even if Marx's theory of how to realize the ideal has totally failed, as our liberal journalists now take such great joy in telling us over and over again at every opportunity, perhaps it is only this ideal element in Marx that can remain to inspire us. Marx's thought, as we shall see, always contains a hope—the glimmer, the lure, of a beautiful world, the highest good, the realization of the species' essence.

Despite the fact that most of our liberal journalists seem to believe that Marxism has collapsed in Eastern Europe, it must be said that few Western Marxists—and for a great many years before this collapse—would have accepted the notion that Eastern European societies were Marxist in the first place. This may sound like a cheap way to avoid the issue, but that is very largely due to the news media's ability to make us see reality as they see it. They have us convinced that Eastern European societies were Marxist and that Marxism has now collapsed. But if Western Marxists have been denying for many years that these societies were Marxist, I do not see why we should change our minds now. Moreover, even the most superficial reading of Marx should show that in very fundamental ways Eastern European societies were not Marxist. Marx rejected the existence of a state standing over and dominating society, whereas the Soviet Union had one of the most powerful, dominating, bureaucratic state apparatuses in the world. Marx rejected a standing army attached to the state and held that the only kind of army compatible with democracy was a citizen militia, an army controlled by the citizens that they could use to ensure that the state did not try to stand over and dominate society, whereas the Soviet Union had one of the most powerful standing armies in the world attached to and controlled by the state. And Marx was a radical democrat; he even rejected representatives, who go off and vote as they see fit, in favor of deputies, who are given very strict voting instructions and are immediately recallable by their constituents. The Soviet Union certainly did not have deputies—it did not even really have representatives.

So, whatever has collapsed in Eastern Europe, it was not Marxism—certainly not as Marx understood it, nor as Western Marxists have understood it for quite some time now. The Soviet Union and other Eastern European societies right now are in serious need of some very practical, concrete, technical assistance. They certainly will not get much help in this area from a writer who has been dead for over a century. What they might get from Marx is something different—a hope, a better vision, the lure of an ideal.

Despite our liberal journalists, the abandonment of communism and the embracing of markets in Eastern Europe is not going all that well.

A popular joke in Hungary had it that the Communist government needed forty years to lose the moral support of the people. For its successor, one year was enough.[2] However, I certainly do not wish to try to predict what will occur in Eastern Europe. But one thing—admittedly of a wildly speculative sort—that might be said about Russia is that while it has definitely made very healthy moves toward democracy that everyone hopes will be preserved, at the same time, there are many in Russian society that do not at all want to give up socialism. Is it too utopian to hope that Russia, which has had nothing to do with the collapse of Marxism, might eventually move closer to the realization of truer Marxian ideals? If there is any chance at all of this, perhaps it justifies continued work to uncover this ideal dimension in Marx's thought. At any rate, I in no way apologize for such utopianism.

The charge of utopianism can be very intimidating. One of the most powerful arguments that can be made against moral and political ideals is to call them unrealistic, impossible, utopian. This is usually thought to be a trump. Case closed. Nothing more to say. Moreover, political theorists worry about such charges and try to avoid them. It seems to me that there is a great deal of unthinking that goes on here.

If a theorist makes a sound argument that certain of our social or political institutions are oppressive, unjust, or immoral, what does it amount to to argue that it would be unrealistic and utopian to eliminate those institutions—that you cannot imagine being able to significantly change those institutions? This may merely indicate a failure of *your* imagination. Who could have imagined the collapse of old-style Soviet Marxism twenty years ago? Who could have imagined in 1950 the advances that blacks and women have made in the United States since then, inadequate as these advances have been? What does it mean to call a moral ideal utopian, impossible, unrealistic? Is this intended to eliminate all moral obligation on our part with respect to this ideal? That is often what is suggested by such accusations. But I do not think so. "Ought implies can" has been a truism since Kant enunciated the proposition. But it seems to me we cannot accept this proposition when it comes to political ideals. It may be that we cannot imagine how we can eliminate these immoral, unjust, and oppressive institutions. It may seem impossible to do so. Nevertheless, we still have a moral obligation to remove them. If we cannot imagine how, then we will just have to rely on the imagination of others until we can begin to imagine how ourselves. And we must always remember that what it seems possible to accomplish will change with every step we take.

In three earlier books on Marx I have approached his thought historically in the sense that I have argued that there are different periods of his thought and that he fundamentally changes certain of his views in these different periods.[3] I have not changed my mind about these matters and one will still find references of this sort in the present book, but the last three chapters, which deal with Marx, are not, as my earlier books were, structured to reflect the different periods of Marx's thought. That would simply make matters far more complicated than they already are and it is my purpose to focus on other sorts of historical connections in this book.

One of these, which will become quite central for us in Chapters 6 and 7, has already started to emerge here, namely the tension that exists in the modern world between freedom and community. The difficulty of conceiving, let alone realizing, a society that is both communal and that preserves individual freedom is, I think, one of the major problems, if not *the* major problem, of modern political theory.

As I will argue, especially in Chapter 6, human beings need community; they need it to have a sense of belonging and to be at home in their world. Moreover, community creates a sense of familiarity that makes it possible to work with others smoothly and comfortably, to be close enough to them so that individuals can learn from each other, so that they can develop their powers and capacities, indeed, so that they develop as human beings. Furthermore, community facilitates communication that is necessary for all of these things and that is also, most importantly, necessary to allow us to uncover and overcome any oppressions that hitherto have not been recognized in the community. Community can also combat anomie, aloneness, and alienation. It can give one a sense of place, a sense that what you are and are doing is proper, recognized, meaningful, and significant. It can give one a sense of reality and rightness among the other members of one's community and in one's world. In the past it has even given individuals a sense of being ontologically plugged into the cosmos, rooted in the real and the right. The absence of community in the modern world leaves a cold and lonely abyss.

The trouble, however, before we get carried away with community, is that traditional communities always involved serious oppression—the domination and oppression of women, of other races or religions, of the lower classes, of science by religion, and of progress by custom and tradition, to name only a few. The modern world, on the other hand, has come almost to define itself, at least in very large part, by its concern with freedom, and freedom understood, in very large part, as freedom-*from,* certainly as freedom-from all these traditional oppressions but very possibly as freedom-from the premodern traditional community itself.

As this modern conception of freedom arose and established itself in Europe, it meant rejecting the authority of the Church—its authority over science, philosophy, politics, and morality. The rise of modern science, for example, meant that each discipline carved out its own autonomous area, subject to no authority but reason, and certainly not subject to religious authority.[4] Protestantism even carried this principle into the realm of religion itself. Religious belief should be free from any external authority, certainly of the Roman church, and based solely on individual conscience. With the rise of capitalism, the modern world shed the authority of the community over the economic sphere in favor of individual liberty, competition, and particular interests.

One can almost say that what modernity means, or at least a significant part of what it means, is a continuous, ongoing process of liberation, of emancipating one group after another, of freeing them from one oppression after another. Abolitionists work to eliminate slavery. Socialists try to free the working class from capitalist oppression. Feminists work to free women from traditional male domination. The modern world, we can even say, is out to discover ever-new oppressions embedded in the traditional past and to free individuals from them.

Furthermore, what this ongoing process of liberation also seems to imply is that each attempt at emancipation from traditional authority is likely, sooner or later, to be attacked, in its turn, as an inadequate attempt at emancipation. It will be attacked for failing to get to the root of the oppression and it may even be attacked by more progressive emancipatory movements as itself a new form of oppression. Protestant fundamentalism comes to be seen, by modern liberalism, no longer as a radical form of emancipation but as a closed-minded form of intolerance. The role of capitalism in emancipating us from feudalism is far outweighed, for socialists, by its oppression of the proletariat. And then socialists in their turn come to be seen as totalitarian oppressors. Even modern science, which prides itself on being free of, and freeing us from, all ideology, is now being criticized by modern feminists for its ideological blindness with respect to women.

The real strength of modernity is that it digs deeper and deeper, that it continuously uncovers new forms and layers of oppression, brings them to light, attacks them, and tries to overcome them. And then even this emancipatory process itself is seen as still containing some oppression and is attacked in its turn. This is a powerful dynamic of liberation. At the same time, though, it continuously makes it impossible to establish any tradition, any community, any place, any at-homeness. We never seem to be able to purge our traditions of all oppression so as to finally fit ourselves into them and be at home. We always find further oppressions dirtying our nest.

This drive for freedom, for freedom-from, liberates us from oppression. And without any doubt such liberation is an absolute necessity for achieving the good life. But this liberation does not itself give us the good life. It is a necessary means to the good life. The good life is not possible while any oppression remains. But liberation from oppression is not itself the good life. It is empty. It continuously negates, rejects, eliminates, eradicates, destroys. It not only negates and eliminates external authorities and institutions out in the social world, but it criticizes, attacks, negates, and eliminates within ourselves—attitudes, assumptions, values, feelings, and so forth. It empties us of undesirable qualities, but it does not fill us with anything.

Moreover, this modern form of emancipation, this freedom-from, must at least shy away from itself endorsing anything positive, any substantive form of the good life, any tradition, any form of community, because to do so can and, sooner or later, probably will become something for others to attack, to free themselves from, a new form of oppression. The modern tendency seems to be ever toward pluralism, diversity, difference. Endorsing a single conception of the good is seen as totalizing, as imposing one's views on others, even as totalitarianism. Or at least one more and more frequently hears such arguments these days.

At any rate, community has little chance of establishing itself in the face of this continued and ongoing liberation. And liberation cannot achieve community. The future of any liberation is to be perceived as an oppression that calls for further liberation. Or at least this has been true of liberations in the past. Everyone hopes that it will not be true of their own liberation movement.

I am not poking fun here. I am certainly not dismissing liberation. Liberation, the liberation of workers, of women, of racial and ethnic minorities, and of others, is absolutely essential. Community without such liberation is not acceptable and not possible. Yet continuous liberation that never achieves community, that never roots itself in tradition, that never achieves anything positive and substantive, is ultimately not acceptable either.

Marx, I think, was aware of this problem, at least at the level it had reached in his era, and he was trying to resolve it. He fully endorses, to the level he understands them, to the level that they had materially and ideologically emerged, the liberation movements of his time. He endorses the modern liberation from religious authority.[5] He himself attacked the authority of science, at least the ideological authority of the science of political economy.[6] He wrote many articles in support of the emancipation of slaves in the United States.[7] He endorsed the emancipation of women, as I will argue in Chapter 8. And, of course, he spent his life working for the emancipation of the working class. At the same time, he wanted to regain community and, indeed, saw it as a necessary element of this liberation.

How then is it possible to reconcile, make compatible, community and liberation? It will take a good deal of space to explain this in Chapter 7. Here we can at least say that, in the first place, we must come to understand the ideal community and the good life, not as a static blueprint, a neat and final set of institutions, a finished utopia, but rather as a society that engages in a certain form of activity—free activity, activity that develops powers and capacities, that enriches the individual, activity that is an end in itself. Such activity would leave plenty of room for emancipation, even for ongoing emancipation, for resisting any authority that would try to dominate this activity, make it serve an end other than its own. At the same time this activity would involve interaction with others in a community, an interaction that would create bonds, meaning, connection, at-homeness. This community, then, cannot be static; it has no room for traditional authority, authority that stands over and dominates. Marx rejects a state standing over society, capitalists standing over workers, men over women, whites over blacks. Individuals must empower themselves by interacting with each other in an egalitarian and pluralist community. We will have a great deal more to say about this in Chapter 7.

Yet the Marxian attempt to synthesize liberation and community has not succeeded—it has certainly not been accepted. At least a part of the reason for this is that any liberation movement resents other movements that claim to go beyond it. Capitalism, which begins as a liberation movement and certainly still sees itself as a liberation movement—and Marx would at least agree that it once was[8]—resents the Marxist's claim that capitalism does not go far enough, that it oppresses workers. Either it doesn't like hearing this truth or is unable to accept it as a truth. It feels threatened and counterattacks, at times violently and always ideologically. It accuses Marxism of being even more oppressive. Moreover, other newer liberation movements that have not yet succeeded in their liberation often tend to see Marxism as part of the establishment, as another form of oppression, as a hindrance to their program of liberation.

And without a doubt, a large part of the Marxist movement is guilty as charged. A very large part of the Marxist movement has failed to see the dialectic that Marx envisions between ongoing liberation and community. A large part of the Marxist movement is unable to move beyond its own original notions of liberation, let alone reconcile them with community.

Marxism has real weaknesses. It has weaknesses at the level of practice—the horrors we have seen in communist societies. It also has theoretical weaknesses. It does not have a complete theory for the emancipation of women, less even for races, and, given the development of modern capitalism since Marx, not even for workers. Yet, I want to argue that what we very importantly find in Marx is a recognition of the two sides of this most important and crucial modern tension. We find a recognition of the need for liberation, freedom from domination of all sorts, a continuous, ongoing, emancipation, and, at the same time, the recognition that this is not enough, the recognition that we need community. And Marx has a theory for how to connect these two.

It seems to me that the modern world, if it cannot accept Marxism as it was written by Marx, or certainly as it was played out by the Marxist tradition, which for the most part fell far below the level of Marx, this modern world then needs a new Marxism if it is to solve the problem of reconciling freedom and community. Any solution, I suspect, will have to pay careful attention to Marx and perhaps even launch itself from Marx. This book, it is hoped, will be a modest attempt to bring this problem into focus.

I am sure, though, that some will see the hope of finding anything in Marx that can be valuable for our world as a lost cause and as the greatest naivete. For them, Marx is an old dog that should finally be buried and forgotten. Others might admit that a standard historical treatment of Marx, the old dog, is an acceptable scholarly project, but that linking him with current, "stylish" matters like feminism, ethnocentrism, and pluralism is likely to weaken what might otherwise be a solid study. This problem, however, is not just a problem with the present book. It is a problem in our world. To take just one example, we see the very same tension in the current debate over humanities core courses in the United States.

Many contemporary theorists want to dismiss traditional authors, the canon, great books—which after all were written by white, European, upper-class males. These books should be read critically—*very* critically. They should be called before the bar of modern antisexist, antiracist, antiethnocentric criticism and thoroughly denounced. This is all right. I have no objection to it. But there also are problems here.

Keeping in mind what has already been said about the modern drive toward liberation, one of the things that any decent education should do, it seems to me, is to call into question, force us to reflect upon, our own modern norms, values, outlooks, assumptions, and perspectives. In other words, one of the things that any decent education should do is what those old racist, sexist, and ethnocentric dogs back in the nineteenth century were so good at doing—using history to *undermine*. They used history to show us that our present views, assumptions, and values are not fixed, eternal, and natural, that they had not always been held, that they developed in a specific period under specific conditions, that they thus could very obviously change in the future, and thus that something *better* was possible. Darwin used history to undermine the fixity of species. Marx used it to undermine the fixity and naturalness of capitalism. Nietzsche used it to undermine the fixity and normativeness of Judeo-Christian morality. With a bit of work, one could even argue that Freud used the history of the individual to undermine consciousness.

To simply sift through the great books of the past, denouncing them for being racist, sexist, ethnocentric, and so forth, is all right. It will not sustain your interest for long. To see nothing else in them is a serious mistake. To try to see how a modern antiracist, antiethnocentric, and feminist consciousness arose out of them is more interesting. But to do any of this without calling our own norms, values, and assumptions—yes, even our own antiracist, feminist, antiethnocentric values, norms, and assumptions—into question is to perpetuate what we are trying to overcome.

We should, as Marx and other nineteenth-century thinkers did so well, use history to undermine the status quo. We must see that our values, the ones we accept, our own feminist, antiracist, antiethnocentric values, are not just *our* values, above and beyond all that has preceded us, neat and clean and isolated. Our values are the outcome of earlier history. They are certainly a reaction against, but they also grew out of, and thus in an important sense are dependent upon, our earlier history, which we are so critically sorting through and denouncing. And this certainly would seem to suggest that having grown out of this dirty past there might well be some serious flaws in our own views, unless we think we have reached the Absolute.

We must come to see that our own values, even our best ones, are part of a process, a process that goes beyond but that also grows out of and deeply depends on what precedes us historically. If we fail to see this, the next liberation movement to come along will ruthlessly remind us of it. We must see not only what is no longer acceptable about the past, but how the past made us possible, how we depend upon it, how we are tied to it, how we are stuck with it. We *are* our past to a very great extent. We must see how the past leads to the best norms, values, and assumptions we have and at the same time how our best values, norms, and assumptions, the ones we believe in most deeply, are probably also polluted by our past and therefore need to be improved upon. The past that we continuously reject and undermine also continuously undermines us.

To simply reject the past, to lump it all together as sexist, racist, and ethnocentric, and put it behind us can cause us to forget to question the very values that allow us to dismiss the past in this way. It can cause us to fail to see our own process of development and to rest content with what we are, accept our own values as final: exactly what every liberation movement in the past has mistakenly done, namely, denounce everything but itself.

To bring alive the past, to see our dependence on it, our complicity with it, to see that we have not gotten completely above it or outside it, will cause us to question, reflect upon, our own values—not those of *others* of our contemporaries, but *our* very own values—and to push them further. And, of course, as soon as we develop new values and perspectives and use them to study the past, we will see a new and different past, out of which we now will see ourselves growing in a different way, understand ourselves differently, and so forth.

The past conditions our present norms at least in the sense that we position ourselves to reject precisely what has occurred in our past with the consciousness, perspectives, and tools that our past has made possible for us. We don't reject anything and everything, but our concrete past that conditions, positions, and limits us in a specific way. We do not have an absolute, abstract, disconnected perspective to criticize from. We are the outcome of our specific past. All we can do is to continue to criticize our best values. We can do that by using our past, our traditions, to undermine ourselves and to work toward the sort of community that will facilitate and reinforce this process. I think that Marx can at least begin to help us think about such matters.

Notes

1. *Communist Manifesto*, in *Marx Engels Collected Works* (hereafter *MECW*) (New York: International, 1975 ff.), VI, 499–504 and, for the German, *Marx Engels Werke* (hereafter *MEW*) (Berlin: Dietz, 1972 ff.), IV, 476–81.
2. *The Guardian*, Vol. 43, No. 28 (May 22, 1991), 14.
3. P. J. Kain, *Schiller, Hegel, and Marx* (Montreal: McGill-Queen's University Press, 1982); *Marx' Method, Epistemology, and Humanism* (Dordrecht: D. Reidel, 1986); *Marx and Ethics* (Oxford: Clarendon Press, 1988).
4. See also "Leading Article in No. 179 of the *Kölnische Zeitung*," *MECW*, I, 201 and *MEW*, I, 103.
5. Ibid.
6. *Capital*, ed. F. Engels (New York: International, 1967), I, 14–16 and *MEW*, XXIII, 19–22.
7. See the newspaper articles on this topic collected in Volume XIX of *MECW*.
8. *Manifesto, MECW*, VI, 486–90 and *MEW*, IV, 464–68.

1

Hobbes, Political Theory, and Sovereignty

When approaching the study of Hobbes's political philosophy, one is confronted by several puzzling elements. I wish to take up three of them in this chapter. The most bothersome, perhaps, is Hobbes's claim that there is no significant difference between sovereignty by institution and sovereignty by acquisition or conquest. Both can be legitimate and can be so for the same reason, the consent of the subjects.

One also wonders how to view Hobbes's concept of the state of nature. Is the state of nature to be taken as an actual, presocial, and primitive historical period—the way Locke sometimes understands the concept?[1] Hobbes does speak of "American savages" and of early Germans as examples of peoples in a state of nature.[2] Yet for the most part he does not seem to employ the concept in this way. Among these peoples, as well as in earliest history generally, small family monarchies—that is, small *societies,* Hobbes says in several places—were the norm.[3] The concept of a state of nature can also be understood in a second sense. It can be taken to refer to fully socialized individuals at those moments when the security of well-enforced law is either absent or ineffective. This would be the case, Hobbes suggests, when traveling the highways or even when alone at night in one's home.[4] Hobbes does use the concept of a state of nature in this sense, and also in a third, related, sense. It can refer to the relationship that holds between any two sovereigns, between sides in a civil war,[5] or between a sovereign and some individual in a state of nature. Here too there would be no common power regulating and enforcing relations between the different parties. This sense, while not at all incompatible with the preceding, is nevertheless different from it in that all the parties would not be individuals and they might well be quite unequal in power. The concept of a state of nature might also be understood in a fourth sense, as simply an abstract fiction that serves as the criterion for justice and legitimacy. Thus, an actual law or institution would be just if and only if it can be argued that individuals in such a fictitious state of nature would have consented to the law or institution. As social contract theory develops, this fourth way of understanding the concept comes to predominate. We find the beginnings of this notion in Rousseau and we find it fully developed in Rawls.[6] At first sight we do not seem to find Hobbes employing the concept this way. I hope to show how we do.

I wish to take up one last difficulty. On Hobbes's view, does moral obligation exist in the state of nature or not? Hobbes scholars disagree sharply over this issue. Some argue that there is no moral obligation in the state of nature[7] and that moral obligation does not arise until the sovereign establishes it. However, it is difficult to explain how such obligation could arise at that point. Other scholars argue that moral obligation exists in the state of nature and that if it did not, there would be no basis upon which to establish moral obligation to the sovereign.[8] Each side in this dispute ends up arguing (or at least implying) that certain of Hobbes's statements are to be taken as fundamental and that others are to be discounted.[9] I find it impossible to deny that we find contradictory statements on this matter in Hobbes's writings. For example, in *Leviathan* especially, we find many passages in which Hobbes holds that there is no moral obligation in the state of nature. It is not just that obligation is ineffective or that the validating conditions for obligation are absent; the problem goes much deeper than this. Unaided human reason is incapable of deciding right and wrong. Hobbes says, "for want of a right reason constituted by nature" we must set up an arbiter or come to blows.[10] We even have no "notion" of right and wrong without a common authority.[11] This is so because there is no common rule of right and wrong to be gotten from the object itself.[12] Notions of right and wrong, or good and evil, are simply subjective reactions based upon passions, and passions differ considerably between individuals. Even the laws of nature, Hobbes argues at several points, are not properly laws until the sovereign commands them; it is the sovereign that obliges us to obey them.[13] Nor is it Hobbes's position that the sovereign discovers right and wrong in nature and then simply declares and enforces it; the sovereign actually makes, constitutes, right and wrong. "The makers of civil laws are not only declarers, but also makers of the justice and injustice of actions;

there being nothing in men's manners that makes them righteous or unrighteous, but their conformity with the law of the sovereign."[14]

On the other hand, there are passages in which Hobbes makes it quite clear that there *is* moral obligation in the state of nature. Hobbes tells us that the law of nature is the moral law and that the validity of civil law is based upon the law of nature.[15] Hobbes also admits that individuals as well as the sovereign can violate the law of nature and are answerable to God for such violations.[16]

Hobbes also holds that we are obliged to perform our covenants in the state of nature if the other side has already performed its part. For example, if taken as a prisoner of war or held up by a robber and then released upon promise to pay a ransom, we are, Hobbes holds, even in the state of nature, obliged to pay this ransom.[17] Furthermore, Hobbes explicitly holds that the laws of nature *always* oblige in the internal court of conscience.[18]

If Hobbes contradicts himself in this way, the question to raise is why. Rather than try, as others have, to dissolve this contradiction, perhaps we should simply try to untangle it and to understand it. If we can discover why Hobbes contradicts himself we might discover something interesting about his thought. Perhaps the reason for this contradiction is that Hobbes, to achieve his purpose, is driven to draw incompatible conclusions from the concept of a state of nature. Along these lines, I would like to argue that the three puzzling elements that have been noted might be seen as connected in the following way. The theory of sovereignty by acquisition is Hobbes's model for how political bodies actually and historically come into being. But sovereignty by acquisition depends for its legitimacy upon the working out of a scientific deduction of sovereignty by institution. The latter theory is a totally unhistorical fiction. It serves as the abstract criterion for the legitimacy of sovereignty by acquisition; that is, it operates, as for Rousseau and Rawls, in the fourth sense in which a concept of a state of nature can be understood. Moreover, for the theory of sovereignty by acquisition to work, there must be moral obligation in the state of nature, most obviously an obligation to perform covenants. On the other hand, in order for Hobbes to give a necessary scientific deduction of an absolute sovereign by institution, he must contradict himself and assume that there is no moral obligation in the state of nature. By understanding the interconnection of Hobbes's thought in this way, the germ of a philosophy of history—one that anticipates Kant and Marx—will emerge, as well as an explanation of Hobbes's lack of consistency.

I. Sovereignty by Institution and Its Scientific Deduction

Let us take up sovereignty by institution first. Hobbes's theory of sovereignty by institution per se can be distinguished, at least in thought, from the scientific deduction of this theory. This is so because a theory of sovereignty by institution need not be presented as a necessary scientific deduction. One might simply assume, as Locke or Rousseau do, that for some reason individuals decided to quit the state of nature and to institute society, not that they had to.[19] Since I hope to show that Hobbes's scientific deduction requires the absence of moral obligation in the state of nature, we must investigate to what extent sovereignty by institution can be understood without assuming such obligation. Let us see, then, to what extent it is possible to outline an argument by which Hobbes might, without presuming moral obligation to the state of nature, necessarily deduce a sovereign who establishes such obligation.

Hobbes begins with principles taken from his mechanistic model of natural science. Human appetites (and aversions), like all sense perceptions, ideas, and indeed all causal relations, are determined externally by the motion of objects,[20] and there is nothing in the object that could be a source of common rules of morality. Each individual has a purely subjective and mechanical reaction to the object, a reaction that may well, due to differing constitutions, be different for each—what is good to one person can be evil to another.[21] Furthermore, human will, for Hobbes, is only the last appetite or aversion in the process of deliberation; it is not an independent faculty.[22] Under these conditions, moral obligation is impossible.

Given these principles, conditions of scarcity, and Hobbes's further view that all individuals in the state of nature are equal, rational, and concerned with their own self-preservation, the social contract can be necessarily deduced. Conditions of scarcity plus the fact that reactions are subjective, given normal concern for self-preservation, will produce conflict and selfishness—selfishness in the sense of an increased need to concern oneself aggressively with self-interest and security.[23] Given this conflict together with the fact that all are roughly equal in strength,[24] there is only one possible way out—to establish through agreement a common power that will end the conflict. If some were superior, they might hope to sift to the top of the struggle and establish society (that is, end the conflict of the state of nature) in this way. If all are equal, this is illusion. Furthermore, each is also forced to *desire* a way out. Since the conflict is among equals, each will be threatened, and since motivated by a concern for self-preservation, each will fear for their security.[25] Given the ability of each to calculate rationally their self-interest, the pressure of this situation will eventually force individuals to see the need for long-run security and a social contract instead of immediate security through aggression (which in practice means insecurity). The laws of nature, as Hobbes states them, are simply a description of the steps by which the calculation and the realization of this long-run self-interest will work itself out.[26] Reason is a tool employed by the passions in this drive toward security.

It is still possible, however, that not everyone will be driven to this common end. There could be exceptions because reactions are subjective and different.[27] But at least some would end up fearing all and so contract. Those who will not now risk being left alone in a state of nature vis-à-vis this new political body with its vastly increased strength. Many who were not motivated to join at first will be so now. Those who do not join are simply left weak and isolated in the state of nature.[28] So far this explanation has been purely descriptive. Nothing prescriptive has been introduced.

The next question is how, if at all, moral obligation to the sovereign can arise. In the first place, the social contract establishes a single authority that issues uniform commands—common rules of behavior. Without them individuals would differ and fight. Next, the single authority enforces these common rules so as to cause a similar reaction of the part of each—fear of punishment. Notice that the reaction of each is still externally caused, but that now there are common rules and the reactions of each are at least similar. There is also a further difference between these sovereign-induced reactions and those of an individual in the state of nature. Hobbes argues that the sovereign is an artificial or a public person—an office. The sovereign's power derives solely from the sovereign's ability to use and direct the power of the subjects.[29] As a private person, the sovereign has no more power than anyone else. For Hobbes, the acts of the sovereign are, in the first place, simply the acts of the subjects, and, in the second place, even the sovereign's power to channel and direct these acts derives from the original consent of the subjects given in the social contract. Thus the official acts of the sovereign are our own acts. The sovereign is our representative. Whether we agree or not, it is evident that Hobbes thinks he has shown that the subjects are self-determined—that all laws that a subject must obey are self-authorized.[30] We thus have enforced, self-authorized, common rules and similar reactions to them.

Hobbes wants to go even further. He wants to argue that the commands of the sovereign oblige in conscience. For Hobbes, simply acting in accordance with the law is not enough. It is clear that our intentions must also be in accordance with the law. Furthermore, Hobbes comes quite close to arguing that one must act for the sake of the law. He says that the law should be obeyed because it is law and that the just person should be "delighted in just dealing."[31] Hobbes tries to deduce such full-fledged moral obligation by picturing the political body as a fragile structure ready to collapse back into the state of nature if laws are not obeyed. Subjects thus have a very simple choice: the security of well-enforced, self-authorized law or the suffering and chaos of the state of nature. Insofar as rational calculation of self-interest led individuals to the social contract, they would frustrate their interest if they allowed themselves or others to contradict that decision by disobeying the law and thus raising the threat of a return to the state of nature. To both will and not will a self-authorized law would be absurd; and thus not to will it, Hobbes says, could not be taken as the individual's true will.[32] If subjects do not obey the law at all times, if they obey it only when prudential calculations of interest so dictate, but not when they think they can get away with it, they invite disaster. Each expects this total obedience from others for their own security. Hobbes argues that a consistent interest in one's own security drives each to require of all and of themselves total commitment to the law.[33]

On this interpretation, Hobbes has not gotten beyond a prudential calculation of self-interest to always obey the law. He has certainly not deduced an obligation to act for the sake of the law or to delight in the law. Indeed, in places, he even admits that to delight in something illegal (while not intending to carry it out) is neither a sin nor a crime.[34] Hobbes has at most shown that the acts that a subject intends to carry out, due to fear of consequences, should *accord* with the law. Indeed, to deduce acting for the sake of the law from self-interest (as Hobbes understands self-interest) would be to deduce moral prescriptions from nonmoral premises.[35] However, it is not at all clear that Hobbes grasps this distinction or sees that he has not deduced an obligation that amounts to more than a prudential calculation of interest. As I noted earlier, there are passages in which Hobbes does hold that the laws of nature constitute moral obligations. Why then, it might be objected, don't I just argue that Hobbes bases moral obligation to civil law upon moral obligation to natural law (the third of which is to abide by contracts)? One might argue that since one has contracted, and since contracts oblige morally, one is morally obliged by the civil law even in *opposition* to self-interest. This alternative interpretation is very tempting, but aside from the fact that there *are* those passages that deny the existence of moral obligation in the state of nature, there is another very important reason why Hobbes must avoid this line of argument and thus why we must avoid this line of interpretation.

Hobbes wants to work out a science, or for him the same thing, a philosophy, of politics. By this he means that by beginning with clear definitions gotten by analysis of experience he can deduce (much as one deduces in geometry) the necessity of the body politic.[36] Having sketched this deduction above, we must now notice that the success of this project is incompatible with the existence of moral obligation in the state of nature. If, in the state of nature, individuals could know right and wrong, were morally obliged by it, and acted upon it, then, as Hobbes correctly argues, no political body would *necessarily* result. There would simply be no need for an authority to create and enforce common rules of behavior. Individuals might well be content to remain in the state of nature.[37] Why should they leave it? They *might* leave it, but there would be no *necessity* to do so and thus no science of politics.

We might, however, consider a more complex assumption: for example, that individuals know right and wrong and are morally obliged by it in the state of nature, but do not frequently act morally due either to self-interest or due to errors in judgment. A theorist other than Hobbes might argue that to the extent that individuals know their moral obligations in the state of nature they would possess the criteria by which to judge if and when civil laws, made by a sovereign, were in conflict with natural moral law, and thus situations could arise in which they would have a moral obligation to disobey the sovereign, perhaps even a democratic sovereign. This is to say that subjects would have an obligation higher than that to the sovereign. The sovereign, if it were monarchical, would be limited; if it were democratic, it could be divided. For Hobbes, this would be to say that the sovereign would not be the single, highest authority, which is an absurdity because that is exactly what it means to be sovereign.[38] I do not wish to suggest that moral obligation in the state of nature would pose problems for Hobbes's theory of sovereignty by institution in the sense that such obligation would require that the sovereign be limited. As we shall see, Hobbes can easily get around such problems.

The problem here is different; it concerns the *necessity* of a scientific deduction. If moral obligation exists in the state of nature, even though individuals do not always act morally, would they consent to an *absolute* sovereign in the first place? Moral obligation would not have to be created, but simply arbitrated and enforced. Individuals in such a state of nature might well be willing to do nothing more than establish an arbitrator with just enough (that is, limited) power to enforce decisions. Where do we find motivation for anything more? Hobbes would think this a serious error—an attempt to limit or divide sovereignty and an invitation to civil turmoil.[39] But to argue that individuals in a state of nature would see this would require that we include far more complex presuppositions in our notion of the state of nature. Individuals would almost have to be political scientists who had reflected upon the causes of success and failure in political societies and had come to the same conclusions that Hobbes had. Lacking science, their moral capacity as well as their interest (fear of too powerful a sovereign) would most likely lead them to some form of limited government. As we shall see, in certain places Hobbes himself admits that such limited government is quite possible. To ensure that individuals in the state of nature would not make this mistake it would be necessary to presuppose not just moral disagreement but the absence of morals. This seems to be the only premise that would make necessary the scientific deduction of an *absolute* sovereign.

This last set of assumptions might be modified even further. It might be held that since individuals who can know their moral obligations in the state of nature do not always agree on them, government would be necessary not simply to arbitrate but as an institution capable of bringing individuals into real moral agreement (in the way that, for example, Rousseau's general will unerringly brings about agreement on truly moral laws). In other words, this institution would ensure that errors in moral judgment did not occur and that agreement would follow on these grounds. Hobbes's epistemological principles would not allow for this. No one, the sovereign or anyone else, has access to objective moral truth. The sovereign is an arbitrator who has the power to command arbitrarily.[40] The sovereign does not discover or establish objective moral truth. The sovereign decides which obligations are to be officially established and enforces them. There is no objectively true standard of morality. Moral obligation is simply what the sovereign says it is. For this reason the sovereign must be absolute. This means that the sovereign constitutes what is right and wrong and that the subjects simply have no other standard by which to judge the sovereign or to find the sovereign unjust. Furthermore, the sovereign must be such that it is impossible for it to injure the subjects. The sovereign must be an office such that the sovereign's acts are the acts of the subjects. Thus, if injury were done it would be done by the subjects.[41]

If no one is in a position to argue that civil law is at odds with natural law or that they have been injured by the sovereign, there is no possible ground for legitimate civil disobedience or revolution. This is one of the main conclusions Hobbes wants to reach.[42]

II. Social Theory, Political Theory, and Revolution

At the end of this chapter, I will argue that, despite Hobbes, all of the necessary conditions for a right to revolution are in fact given in his theory of sovereignty by acquisition. But for the present, let us simply try to discover what would be required, within Hobbes's system, to establish such a right. It would be necessary that the subjects have a source of moral obligation independent of the sovereign's commands. They must have a basis for judging civil law against moral law, the law of nature. Were Hobbes to admit, or to the extent that he does at times admit, that there is moral obligation in the state of nature, he seems to open himself to this possibility. But this alone would not be enough to establish a right to revolution. Hobbes has other arguments in reserve. He argues that if the sovereign were deposed, subjects would immediately return to a state of nature—a war of each against all. The sovereign is the essential principle of civil coherence as if the sovereign alone holds a bag of marbles. If the sovereign loses its grip, the marbles fly in all directions. In other words, at least in this area, Hobbes has no social theory, only a political theory.[43] To establish a right to revolution, one must have a social theory, a theory that explains the possible coherence of society, of individuals, apart from the political sphere.[44] For Locke, property and property interest explain this coherence. For Marx, it is class and class interest that do so. The more coherence one finds among individuals in society (apart from the political sphere), the less power one need concede to the political sphere (the government). For Marx the political state will wither away. For Hobbes, the total absence of social coherence requires that the government be sovereign and that the sovereign be absolute.[45]

In order to argue that the government must be sovereign, Hobbes, in *Leviathan,* conflates two contractual stages into one social contract. In Rousseau we find two separate contracts, one by which individuals are constituted as a people and a second by which the people then establish a government.[46] The result of this is that the citizens become and remain sovereign and the government becomes a commission or employee. In *Leviathan,* each contracts with each, not to form a people, but to establish a sovereign.[47] Thus there is no contract between the sovereign and a people that could limit the sovereign's power; indeed, there is not even an independent people that might constitute an authority alternative to the sovereign.

The argument that these two contracts occur at once makes more sense if we examine *De Cive* and the *Elements of Law,* where Hobbes argues that the social contract first results in democracy. In those texts, the act that constitutes a multitude into a people appears indistinguishable from the act that constitutes the people as a governmental power (or sovereign). No second act is necessary to establish government—which for a democracy would mean that as a second step the people would decide that the majority will rule. But this is not a second step; it was already established in the first act and it was even implied, Hobbes argues, in coming together to consider the question of a social contract in the first place.[48]

In *De Cive,* Hobbes takes democracy to be the basic constitutional form. Aristocracy and monarchy derive from it. They do not arise from an original contract, but do require a second act. The people must transfer sovereignty either to a small group or to one person, who then, strange as it may sound, becomes the people. The people need not be sovereign, but the sovereign is always the people. Sovereignty constitutes the multitude as a people and represents them. However, the people may retain sovereignty while simply delegating the function of government to others for a limited period of time.[49] Here the sovereign and the government would be separate.

If one admits that the people can be sovereign, it is then possible to argue for the legitimacy of revolution. In fact, in *De Cive,* Hobbes admits that some revolutions are legitimate. "If in a democratical or aristocratical government some one citizen should, by force, possess himself of the supreme power, if he gains the consent of all the citizens, he becomes a legitimate monarch; if not, he is an enemy."[50]

In *Leviathan,* this argument is simply missing. Moreover, in *Leviathan* Hobbes does not think the people can be sovereign. They would inevitably be divided. If the people are not sovereign, then even granting the possibility of social coherence and of moral obligation independent of the sovereign, disobedience remains illegitimate. It does so, furthermore, because the sovereign's acts are the subject's acts, and thus Hobbes argues that the subjects cannot justify disobedience on the ground that the sovereign is responsible for violations of moral principles. Just as individuals cannot be held to be obliged to themselves, because they are free at any moment to release themselves from the obligation, so the sovereign (because the sovereign is the representative of, because the sovereign *is,* the people) can release itself from any obligation at any time. If the sovereign violates a law of nature, the sovereign is of course answerable to God, but not to anyone else; in particular, not to the subjects.[51] Thus to argue the legitimacy of revolution, besides the need to presuppose an independent moral standard and social coherence, it would also be necessary to show that the sovereign was not the legitimate representative of the subjects, that the sovereign's acts were not their acts.[52]

III. Sovereignty by Acquisition and Moral Obligation

While moral obligation in the state of nature must be ruled out if the scientific deduction of sovereignty by institution is to work, for the theory of sovereignty by acquisition, on the other hand, moral obligation in the state of nature is an absolute *necessity.* Here there is no possibility of leaving it out. Hobbes cannot deduce moral obligation to the conqueror unless he assumes the prior existence of moral obligation in the state of nature.

Hobbes says very little about sovereignty by acquisition. He merely argues that there is no significant difference between it and sovereignty by institution. Thus, all that he has argued concerning the latter is true for the former.[53] The legitimacy of sovereignty by acquisition is not based upon force, but, like sovereignty by institution, requires a compact. It is just that individuals are not driven to contract with equals by fear of those equals as in sovereignty by institution. Instead, all of the conquered fear one person, the conqueror, and covenant with the conqueror as weak to strong.[54]

After the covenant, the conqueror establishes common rules of behavior and enforces them. Hobbes does assert that each authorizes the actions of this sovereign, but the only explanation of this assertion occurs in his discussion of sovereignty by institution and it will not work for the conqueror. Though the conqueror is the representative of the conqueror's own subjects (thus the conqueror's acts are their acts), the conqueror is not necessarily the representative of the conquered. The conqueror's power and acts do not derive from ordering and directing the acts of the conquered, but from ordering and directing the acts of the conqueror's own subjects against the conquered. This would be so except in the unusual case where the conquered actually preferred the conqueror to their own sovereign and were trusted enough to be integrated into the conqueror's administration of power. In the normal case, the conquered would not be self-determined and the laws commanded by the new sovereign would not be self-authorized.

Though the conquered may well be obliged to obey the conqueror due to prudential calculations of self-interest (to avoid death or imprisonment), they would not be morally obliged to obey the conqueror when circumstances allowed their interest to dictate otherwise, and they would certainly not be obliged to the conqueror in conscience. Hobbes is forced to assume that there is moral obligation in the state of nature. The ransom example is crucial here. Just as you are obliged to pay the ransom because the highway robber has completed his or her part of the covenant (by releasing you), so since the conqueror (who, after all, is not that different from a highway robber) has completed the conqueror's part of the covenant (by which Hobbes understands that the conqueror does not imprison or kill you), you are obliged to perform your part of the covenant, to obey the conqueror. This obligation, at least in *De Cive* and the *Elements of Law*, is based upon a prudential calculation of interest. If ransoms were not paid, highway robbers would be fools to trust anyone; they might simply kill their captives—which would not be in your self-interest if ever caught again. In *Leviathan*, however, Hobbes omits this explanation based upon self-interest. One might argue that in *Leviathan* the obligation is moral rather than prudential. At any rate, Hobbes also holds that the laws of nature (the third of which requires abiding by contracts) always oblige in the internal court of conscience. Without such moral obligation, the theory of sovereignty by acquisition would collapse.

Each potential subject can easily foresee that in the event of altered circumstances it would be possible for, and indeed self-interest would demand, renewed struggle against the conqueror. Thus, one's long-term self-interest would be opposed to closing off these future possibilities by taking on at present a binding moral obligation to the civil laws of the conqueror. Such moral obligation might be established if a compact had actually occurred between the conqueror and the conquered. However, if the theory of sovereignty by acquisition is a model for actual history and not an abstract fiction, a serious problem arises in that such explicit contracts rarely occur in history. What about a tacit compact? If obligation and long-term interest are at odds (while only obligation and one's interest in immediate security are in agreement; that is, if one has conflicting interests), how can it be convincingly argued that a tacit compact has in effect occurred? To even begin to argue that a tacit compact has in effect occurred, it must (at the very least) be shown that in opposition to long-term self-interest the conquered are morally obliged to compact. This is the point of the ransom example and of the need to have moral obligation in the state of nature.[55]

To summarize our findings to this point: if Hobbes holds that there is no moral obligation in the state of nature he cannot argue for an obligation to obey the conqueror nor can he derive an obligation to the sovereign by institution (that is, derive moral prescriptions from non-moral premises), though it is not clear that he sees this latter difficulty. If he does assume moral obligation in nature, he might explain obligation to the sovereign by institution but the scientific deduction of his theory becomes impossible. At the same time, while the assumption of moral obligation in nature seems necessary in order to argue for an obligation to the conqueror, as we shall see, it leads to certain other problems—it provides the grounds for a right to revolution.

IV. Philosophy of History

We might ask why Hobbes does not just abandon the theory of sovereignty by acquisition, since, besides being counterintuitive, it requires assumptions that are at odds with his scientific deduction of sovereignty by institution. One answer is that sovereignty by institution is a pure fiction. Hobbes's deductive method, like any geometrical deduction, he says, does not give you the actual generation but simply one of the ways (preferably the shortest) by which the thing might have been generated.[56] In political theory such a method allows you to deduce a theoretical construct and its legitimacy. It does not give the generation of an actual political body. Sovereignty by acquisition, on the other hand, is a model for what can occur and has occurred in actual history. Earliest history, Hobbes says in many places, was a state of war among small family monarchies. Great monarchies arise out of these through war, conquest, and rebellion.[57]

Well, then, why doesn't Hobbes abandon the attempt to give a scientific deduction of sovereignty by institution? Then perhaps he could assume moral obligation in the state of nature without contradiction. The answer is that he would not be able to demonstrate the legitimacy of sovereignty by acquisition. In trying to work out a theory of sovereignty by institution without a scientific deduction demonstrating its necessity, one would only be able to assume that for some reason or other individuals in the state of nature did decide to institute government, not that they had to. Since Hobbes argues for the legitimacy of acquisition on the ground that there is no significant difference between it and institution, it follows that it would not be necessary to accept an actual conqueror unless there were an abstract and general necessity to institute not just any sort of government but an absolute sovereign. If it could be argued at the level of abstraction and generality that individuals might have decided not to institute an absolute sovereign (which, given the existence of moral obligation in the state of nature, we have already argued in Section I, would be quite possible), then real individuals would be free to decide against an actual absolute sovereign, in particular, the conqueror.

To argue that individuals would have an obligation to abide by the civil laws of the conqueror, it must be shown in the abstract that individuals have no alternative anyway but to establish an absolute sovereign, that there is no difference between this particular sovereign (the conqueror) and a legitimate one (as described by an abstract theory of legitimacy, namely, the theory of sovereignty by institution), and, as a third step, that a tacit compact had in fact occurred (which again would mean assuming moral obligation in the state of nature and thus contradicting the scientific deduction of a legitimate absolute sovereign by institution). In the preceding section, I argued that a tacit compact was necessary—I did not argue that it was sufficient—to establish sovereignty by acquisition. A mere obligation to fulfill covenants, even a moral obligation, would not be enough. Such obligation alone would not establish the other party's legitimacy. For example, your obligation to pay ransoms certainly does not establish the legitimacy of highway robbery. Legitimacy must be established independently. Thus all three steps are necessary to establish the legitimacy of sovereignty by acquisition, especially if the covenant is merely tacit.

There is one more possibility. Could Hobbes abandon both his attempt at a scientific deduction as well as his whole theory of sovereignty by institution? He could not do this because it would be impossible to argue the legitimacy of an actual historical occurrence without some sort of abstract theory of legitimacy.

In other words, the two theories of sovereignty should not be taken as alternative views set side by side. The two are inseparable. In order to connect fact and right, actuality and legitimacy, history and philosophy (or science), both theories are required. The scientific deduction of sovereignty by institution operates, as for Rousseau and Rawls, in the fourth sense in which the concept of a state of nature can operate. It serves as the abstract criterion of sovereignty by acquisition. For Hobbes, there are two kinds of knowledge: science and history.[58] Sovereignty by institution is the abstract, fictive, and deductive science of right and legitimacy. Sovereignty by acquisition is the factual historical model for the way things actually occur. Hobbes, and this is part of what makes him a significant modern theorist, does not accept the view (implied perhaps most clearly in Plato and Machiavelli) that political theory either discusses fact or right—one of the other but not both. To accept such a dichotomy would mean either analyzing the dynamics of power struggles (and perhaps offering some advice on how to succeed in them) or abstractly characterizing the just society in utopian fashion (utopian at least in the sense that no explanation consistent with principles of right would be given for how actually to realize such a society). Hobbes attempts to connect these two sorts of theory—an abstract theory of legitimate institutions and a theory of their historical realization. Acquisition is legitimate if there is no significant difference between it and institution. Laws and institutions that actually originate through conquest are legitimate if and only if they are the sorts of laws and institutions that would be agreed to in a fictional state of nature such as that described in the theory of sovereignty by institution.

Hobbes wants to link fact and right by linking history and philosophy (or science), an attempt that, as we shall see, Kant, Hegel, and Marx take up and develop much further and with much greater consistency. Hobbes was limited by the fact that his model for philosophy (or science) was deductive and fictional and by the even more important fact that he had no notion of how to find and explain a directedness in historical development. Thus he has no philosophy of history in the sense of Kant, Hegel, or Marx. He can only connect a historical model to a philosophical deduction in the way I have outlined. Despite the fact that even this project is fraught with contradiction, Hobbes's insight does anticipate these later theorists.

V. Legitimate Revolution

We have seen that the existence of moral obligation in the state of nature is necessary for one theory but poses serious problems for the other. Now, I would like to show that all of the conditions required for a theory of legitimate revolution within Hobbes's system, so thoroughly ruled out by the theory of sovereignty by institution, are given in the theory of sovereignty by acquisition.

First, it is clear that for the theory of sovereignty by acquisition to work there must be moral obligation in the state of nature. Second, I have argued that the conqueror is not the representative of the conquered, and thus, since the conqueror's acts are not the acts of the subjects, the conqueror cannot dissolve obligations simply by releasing himself or herself from them. Third, Hobbes cannot argue that it is impossible for the conqueror to injure the new subjects on the ground that the conqueror's acts are their acts, nor could he so argue on the ground that there is no compact between them to be violated. There is such a compact here as there was not in the theory of sovereignty by institution. Hobbes could only argue this point on the ground that the conqueror has completed the conqueror's side of the covenant (by not imprisoning or killing the new subjects) and thus is obligated no further. But it seems quite unacceptable to hold that the sovereign can complete the sovereign's side of the covenant by such a limited set of acts.

To argue that the conqueror cannot injure the new subjects, it would be necessary to hold that the conqueror must continue to behave in this restricted way. Indeed, in *De Cive,* though not in *Leviathan,* Hobbes admits that if at some later point the conqueror imprisons you, the conqueror voids your obligation.[59] Thus the subjects are in a position to judge the sovereign's acts, they could find that they are unjust, and they could have an uncancellable moral obligation to oppose them. Fourth, in the theory of sovereignty by acquisition the units that make up the state of nature might well be political bodies, not, as would ordinarily be the case in sovereignty by institution, mere individuals. Thus, even granting Hobbes's denial in *Leviathan* that the people can be sovereign (though even more obvious if this possibility exists as in *De Cive*), the conquered could remain a coherent body while rebelling. To throw off the conqueror would not necessarily result in a bag of marbles plunging in all directions. The result would not necessarily be the chaos of a state of nature among individuals, but quite possibly the reassertion of a state of nature between two different political bodies.

If sovereignty by institution is an abstract fiction and if sovereignty by acquisition is a historical model that actually describes the origin of all political bodies (Hobbes says, "there is scarce a commonwealth in the world whose beginnings can in conscious be justified"[60]), then

Hobbes's system could yield a right to revolution in almost any political body.

Indeed, if one is to link fact and right, history and philosophy, without ending up with either a utopia or a mere analysis of power struggles, it is difficult to imagine how to avoid a theory of social transformation that would call (at least under certain circumstances) for a theory of civil disobedience or revolution. One must have some way to explain how history moves toward right rather than just assume that the two will always fit neatly. We find the beginnings of such a theory in Locke, which, however, ultimately backfires. Locke will allow a right to revolution only to the propertied and not to the propertyless, and thus revolution cannot serve to move us toward a more equitable society. We find a further development of a theory that explains how history can move toward right in Kant, who nevertheless rejects all forms of revolution as illegitimate. Finally, I shall try to argue, such a theory will be fully developed in Marx.

Notes

1. J. Locke, *Second Treatise,* in *Two Treatises of Government,* ed. P. Laslett (New York: Mentor, 1965), 378.

2. T. Hobbes, *Leviathan,* in *The English Works of Thomas Hobbes* (hereafter *EW*), ed. W. Molesworth (Darmstadt: Scientia Aalen Verlag, 1962), III, 114. Also, *De Corpore Politico, or the Elements of Law,* in *EW,* IV, 85.

3. Both "American savages" and the early Germans actually belong under the third sense in which (as we shall see) the state of nature can be taken; see *Leviathan, EW,* III, 82, 114–15 and also see note 57 below.

4. *Leviathan, EW,* III, 114. See also *De Cive or Philosophical Rudiments Concerning Government and Society,* in *EW*, II, xv, 6 n.

5. *Leviathan, EW,* III, 115; *De Cive, EW,* II, xv, 6 n.

6. J-J. Rousseau, *Discourse on the Origin of Inequality,* in *The First and Second Discourses,* ed. R.D. Masters and trs. R.D. Masters and J.R. Masters (New York: St. Martin's, 1964), 92–93, 103 and, for the French, *Œuvres complètes* (hereafter *OC*), eds. B. Gagnebin and M. Raymond (Paris: Gallimard, 1959 ff.), III, 123, 132. J. Rawls, *A Theory of Justice* (Cambridge, Mass.: Harvard University Press, 1971), 12–13.

7. See, for example, M. Oakeshott, "The Moral Life in the Writings of Thomas Hobbes," in *Hobbes on Civil Association* (Berkeley: University of California Press, 1975), 95–113. Also J.W.N. Watkins, *Hobbes's System of Ideas* (London: Hutchinson, 1965), 76, 82–83, 86–87, 150 ff.

8. See, for example, A.E. Taylor, "The Ethical Doctrine of Hobbes," in *Hobbes Studies,* ed. K.C. Brown (Cambridge, Mass.: Harvard University

Press, 1965), 41 ff. Also H. Warrender, *The Political Philosophy of Hobbes* (Oxford: Clarendon Press, 1957), 7 ff., 28, 63, 98–99, 102.

9. For a more balanced view, though different from mine, see S. Moore, "Hobbes on Obligation, Moral and Political: Parts I and II" in *Journal of the History of Philosophy* IX (1971), 43–62 and X (1972), 29–42.

10. *Leviathan, EW,* III, 31, 146. *De Cive, EW,* II, 268–69. *Elements of Law, EW,* IV, 255. Also *Concerning Body (De Corpore)* in *EW,* IV, 74.

11. *Leviathan, EW,* III, 115, 130–31, 251. Also *Of Liberty and Necessity* in *EW,* IV, 253.

12. *Leviathan, EW,* III, 41.

13. *Leviathan, EW,* III, 162, 253.

14. *Leviathan, EW,* III, 559. See also *De Cive, EW,* II, 151.

15. *Leviathan, EW,* III, 146, 271, 323–24. Also *De Cive, EW,* II, 49, 190, 200. *Elements of Law, EW,* IV, 111.

16. *Leviathan, EW,* III, 200, 312, 332. *De Cive, EW,* II, 9–10 n, 80 n, 83.

17. *Leviathan, EW,* III, 122–23, 126–27. *De Cive, EW,* II, 23–24. *Elements of Law, EW,* IV, 90–91, 92–93. *Considerations upon the Reputation of Thomas Hobbes,* in *EW,* IV, 422–23.

18. *Leviathan, EW,* III, 145. *De Cive EW,* II, 46. *Elements of Law, EW,* IV, 108–9. Also see Warrender, 53–79.

19. Locke, *Second Treatise,* 375. J-J. Rousseau, *On the Social Contract,* ed. R.D. Masters and tr. J.R. Masters (New York: St. Martin's, 1978), 52 and *OC,* III, 360.

20. *Leviathan, EW,* III, 1 ff., 39, 42. *Human Nature,* in *EW,* IV, 31, 54, 67. *De Corpore, EW,* IV, 115, 120, 124, 390–91, 401, 407, 510. Also "Short Tract on First Principles," in *The Elements of Law,* ed. F. Tönnies (Cambridge: Cambridge University Press, 1928), 162–66.

21. *Leviathan, EW,* III, 41, 61, 146. *De Cive, EW,* II, 47, 196. *Human Nature, EW,* IV, 32, 54.

22. *Leviathan, EW,* III, 48–49. *De Cive, EW,* II, 23. *Human Nature, EW,* IV, 68–69.

23. *Leviathan, EW,* III, 85–86, 111, 142–43. *De Cive, EW,* II, 8. *Elements of Law, EW,* IV, 82.

24. *Leviathan, EW,* III, 110–11, 140–41. *De Cive, EW,* II, 6–7, 12.

25. *Leviathan, EW,* III, 113. *De Cive, EW,* II, 6–8.

26. Hobbes says that the laws of nature are not really laws, but rational conclusions or theorems that dispose, even compel, us toward security [*Leviathan, EW,* III, 133–35, 147, 253. *De Cive, EW,* II, xvii, 44, 49–50. *Elements of Law, EW,* IV, 95, 109. Also *Answer to Bishop Bramhall,* in *EW,* IV, 284–85. See also L. Stephen, *Hobbes* (London: Macmillan, 1904), 208–9]. It is true that in several places Hobbes also says that the laws of nature are more than theorems of reason, they are actually laws, if understood as divine laws "delivered by God in Holy Scripture" (*De Cive, EW,* II, 49–50). This would seem to imply that they oblige morally, but Hobbes holds that scripture can

only oblige us if so commanded by the sovereign (*Liberty, Necessity, and Chance*, in *EW*, V, 179).

27. For Hobbes, passions (e.g., fear or desire) are the same for all persons. But due to differing constitutions, the way in which persons are affected by objects as well as what specifically is feared or desired in the object, can be different for each; see *Leviathan, EW*, III, xi, 28, 41, 61. *De Cive, EW*, II, 48.

28. *Leviathan, EW*, III, 139, 162–63. *De Cive, EW*, II, 74.

29. *Leviathan, EW*, III, 158. *De Cive, EW*, II, 69.

30. *Leviathan, EW*, III, 148–51. *De Cive, EW*, II, 158.

31. *Leviathan, EW*, III, 135–36, 144–45, 277. *De Cive, EW*, II, 33, 46–47, 97, 197. *Bramhall, EW*, IV, 374.

32. *Leviathan, EW*, III, 119–20. *De Cive, EW*, II, 30–31. *Elements of Law, EW*, IV, 96.

33. *Leviathan, EW*, III, 132–34, 141, 260, 703. *Elements of Law, EW*, IV, 108–9.

34. *Leviathan, EW*, III, 277.

35. See Watkins, 76. Also R. Peters, *Hobbes* (Harmondsworth: Penguin, 1956), 170–71. It might be argued that Hobbes neither needs nor attempts to deduce moral obligations as something more than an obligation based upon self-interest. It might, for example, be argued that rule egoism (long-term self-interest as a principle that decides general rules—and which can even be found in the state of nature) is sufficient. But in places, Hobbes certainly wants more than this (see note 31 above). Second, even this sort of obligation in the state of nature, as we shall shortly see, would hinder the scientific deduction of an absolute sovereign, and finally, as we shall see in the discussion of sovereignty by acquisition (Section III), Hobbes needs more than this—individuals must have an obligation in opposition to their long-term self-interest.

36. *De Corpore, EW*, IV, 65 ff., 311 ff., 87 ff. *Human Nature, EW*, IV, 28–29. *Leviathan, EW*, III, 35–37, 52–53, 71–73.

37. *Leviathan, EW*, III, 155.

38. *Leviathan, EW*, III, 179, 312–13. *De Cive, EW*, II, 88, 153–54. *Elements of Law, EW*, IV, 137, 170–71.

39. *Leviathan, EW*, III, 172, 175, 186, 311–13, 316. *De Cive, EW*, II, 95–96.

40. *Leviathan, EW*, III, 706. *De Cive, EW*, II, 151. *Bramhall, EW*, IV, 329, 340–41. *Liberty, Necessity, and Chance, EW*, V, 269.

41. *Leviathan, EW*, III, 147–49, 157–58, 199–200, 203, 235.

42. *Leviathan, EW*, III, 160. De Cive, *EW*, II, 150–53. *Elements of Law, EW*, IV, 200–201, 203–4.

43. See Stephen, 213–14.

44. See *Elements of Law, EW*, IV, 208–9. Hobbes does admit the possibility of factions established by agreements or contracts that could cohere on their own, *Leviathan, EW*, III, 223. *De Cive, EW*, II, 163, 176.

45. The sovereign must even decide its own successor; see *Leviathan, EW*, III, 181.

36   *Chapter One*

46. *Social Contract,* 52, 78–79 and *OC,* III, 359, 396.
47. *Leviathan, EW,* III, 158. *De Cive, EW,* II, 68, 91.
48. *De Cive, EW,* II, 96–97. *Elements of Law, EW,* IV, 127, 139. *Leviathan, EW,* III, 162–63.
49. *De Cive, EW,* II, 99, 103–104, 105, 140, 158. *Elements of Law, EW,* IV, 138–39, 141, 143.
50. *De Cive, EW,* II, 94–95.
51. *De Cive, EW,* II, 83, 98.
52. This argument (that the sovereign can release itself from any obligation) might also allow Hobbes to free the theory of sovereignty by institution from certain contradictions noted earlier. In different places, as we have seen, Hobbes argues both that there is and that there is not moral obligation in the state of nature. If the sovereign can release itself from obligations, then insofar as Hobbes sometimes holds that there is moral obligation in the state of nature, any conflict between this obligation and civil law would evaporate as soon as the sovereign is legitimately established. The people could not accuse the sovereign of violating moral obligations to them because the sovereign, being the people, can release itself from any obligations to itself—that is, to the people, which is itself.
53. *Leviathan, EW,* III, 185–86, 190. *De Cive, EW,* II, 111–12.
54. *Leviathan, EW,* III, 185, 189, 204, 254, 703–5. *De Cive, EW,* II, 109–13. *Elements of Law, EW,* IV, 123–24, 150. A covenant is distinguished from a contract in that for the former at least one party does not actually perform but only promises to do so in the future; see *De Cive, EW,* II, 20. *Elements of Law, EW,* IV, 90. *Leviathan, EW,* III, 121.
55. *Leviathan, EW,* III, 189, 703. *Elements of Law, EW,* IV, 148. *Reputation of Hobbes, EW,* IV, 423. Oddly enough, in the ransom example it is one's long-term interest as opposed to one's immediate interest that makes for obligation.
56. Compare *De Cive, EW,* II, 109 with *De Corpore, EW,* IV, 91 ff. See also *De Corpore, EW,* IV, 66, 312, 388. *Leviathan, EW,* III, 195–96.
57. *A Dialogue between a Philosopher and a Student of the Common Laws,* in *EW,* VI, 147–53. *Leviathan, EW,* III, 82. Also *De Cive, EW,* II, 84 n, 129, 177. *Elements of Law, EW,* IV, 165–66. *Liberty, Necessity, and Chance, EW,* IV, 183–84.
58. *Leviathan, EW,* III, 71. *Elements of Law, EW,* IV, 210. *Human Nature, EW,* IV, 27.
59. *De Cive, EW,* II, 113. *Elements of Law, EW,* IV, 150–52. *Leviathan, EW,* III, 188–89, 190.
60. *Leviathan, EW,* III, 706.

2

Locke, Social Theory, and Limited Government

It has been said that "there are two great themes which men have perceived in [Locke's] *Two Treatises,* the rights of property and the limitations of political authority."[1] These two themes are intimately connected. It is Locke's conception of property and especially the social theory that he develops out of this conception that makes possible the limitation of political authority. Locke's development of a *social* theory, I would like to argue, constitutes a major and lasting advance in the development of *political* theory. In comparison to Hobbes, who had no social theory, Locke is able to argue for much greater equality between citizens and government. This matter will be discussed in Section I of this chapter. But at the same time, I also wish to argue that Locke's conception of property and his social theory end up producing greater inequality between the citizens themselves than was the case for Hobbes and that this finally undermines the equality between citizens and government that Locke had gained over Hobbes. This will be discussed in the following sections of the chapter. The course of political theory after Locke, I will argue in subsequent chapters, attempts to develop social theory further so as to eliminate this inequality between citizens and thus to preserve and strengthen the attempt to limit government. Thus, Locke's social theory leads to significant advance in, yet at the same time sets the problems to be overcome for, political theory.

I. Property and Social Theory

There are three stages to Locke's state of nature and each involves a different form of property. In the first stage, all property is given in common. In the second stage, personal property is introduced that, despite the possibility of some limited degree of inequality, remains relatively equal for all individuals.

Personal property arises in the second stage because "every Man has a Property in his own Person." A person's body as well as the labor of their body are that person's property. Moreover, whatever individuals remove from the common state of nature and mix their labor with becomes their property.[2] This property will remain relatively equal between individuals because, as Locke says, "As much as any one can make use of to any advantage of life before it spoils; so much he may by his labour fix a Property in. Whatever is beyond this, is more than his share, and belongs to others. Nothing was made by God for Man to spoil or destroy." And so also, as much property in land—which is what chiefly concerns Locke—can become a person's property as that person can make use of.[3]

The principle of spoilage is not just a moral prescription based on God's command but a factual description of the way individuals will actually behave. Individuals will not in the long run expend their labor in a wasteful fashion. They will not expend it to produce more than they need, or will not do so for long, because the excess will simply spoil and their labor will have been for nothing.[4] In Locke's view, the principle of private appropriation will not harm anyone else as long as there is enough and as good land left for others, and it is Locke's view that even in his own day there is plenty of good land left in "vacant places of America."[5]

The third stage of the state of nature arises with the introduction of money, which makes vast inequality in property possible. We will discuss this below.

What we must see at this point is that individuals have a natural right to property: a right to property prior to and independent of all political society or government. Moreover, when they enter political society they do not give up their natural right to property—they enter political society only in order to better secure and protect their property. "Government has no other end but the preservation of Property. . . ." In this way government cannot be absolute or unlimited. It is limited by the citizen's natural right to property, which the government must serve.[6] But there is a great deal more embedded beneath the surface here. In Locke we find the beginnings of a social theory that is a part of (but to be distinguished from) his political theory. Moreover, it is this social theory that allows Locke to avoid absolute government.

Locke distinguishes between society and political society. The former exists even between husband and wife or master and servant and precedes political society, which is based upon a compact and involves government. For Locke the state of nature is social. Besides families with masters and servants, there are clearly understood notions of right and wrong and each has the right to enforce them against others in the state of nature. Moreover, there is property. Most political theorists would argue that property as opposed to simple possession requires political society. A *title* to property requires *official* recognition. In Locke's view property as opposed to possession is possible without political society. Equal property does not require the recognition or consent of others at all—it is grounded on God's authority.[7] In the third stage of the state of nature, however, money is introduced and it makes possible the acquisition of vastly unequal property. Money, for Locke, does require the implicit consent or recognition of others,[8] and it implies a good deal of social and economic interaction among individuals. The state of nature contains a rather highly developed social organization, and the consent required for the introduction of money would not be possible without this social organization, but the introduction of money does not require political society or government.

Hobbes, I have argued, had no social theory—only a political theory. He had no theory concerning the cohesion or integration of individuals in civil bodies except a political theory of such cohesion. The only force capable of holding individuals together in this way, for Hobbes, was a political force: the government or the sovereign. Governmental power was the only force holding together what might otherwise be described as a bag of marbles. If the government lost its grip, the marbles would bounce in all directions; that is, citizens would return to the chaos of individuals in a state of nature. It follows from this bag of marbles theory, for Hobbes, that the government must be absolute. If the government is the only force holding individuals together, then anything that interferes with this governmental force raises the risk of a return to the state of nature. There simply can be no interference with this governmental power, no rights against it, and no limits on it, if it is the only power holding the bag of marbles together.[9]

Thus, we can begin to see that if a theorist is able to locate some cohesion—social cohesion—apart from the political or governmental sphere, then the greater this social cohesion, the less power the government need have. In fact, with the development of a social theory that is capable of locating enough social cohesion, we could even begin to talk about the withering away of the political state as Marx does.

For Hobbes, since there is no social cohesion at all, government must be absolute. For Locke, since there is some social cohesion independent of government, government can be limited. Rather clearly for Locke it is property and property interest that produce this social cohesion. Even in the state of nature there is a cohesion centered around property in land, money, trade, the need to defend these interests, and the right to punish offenders against these interests. The task of government when it is constituted by compact is to serve these interests and to provide greater security for them.[10]

Moreover, it is quite clear that Locke was fully aware of this distinction between social and governmental cohesion. He says that we ought "to distinguish between the Dissolution of the Society, and the Dissolution of the Government." It is agreement—the social compact—that transforms society (found in the state of nature) into a political organization with a government. Of society, Locke says, "the usual, and almost only way whereby this Union is dissolved, is the Inroad of Foreign Force making a Conquest upon them." In other words, there is indeed a great deal of cohesion found in society and it is quite difficult for it to be destroyed. Normally, it requires conquest from outside. Locke goes on to say that if society is dissolved then certainly government will be dissolved. But on the other hand, he points out that it is quite possible for the government to be dissolved without at all threatening the dissolution of society.[11] In fact, this happens in any revolution where a society decides to overthrow its old government and set up a new one. What is fundamental and basic here is society and social cohesion, not political or governmental cohesion. If social cohesion is destroyed then certainly the government is destroyed, but government may be destroyed without threatening social cohesion. Social cohesion is more basic, more powerful, and more lasting than governmental cohesion.

Compare this to Hobbes, who even had to insist that the only one capable of appointing the sovereign's successor was the sovereign itself.[12] This was the case because if there was any lapse in governmental power, even a momentary one, there would be no force to hold the bag of marbles together. They would fall in all directions; that is, individuals would return to the state of nature. Legitimate revolution for Hobbes was completely rejected.

Locke, while he has not developed social theory as far as Marx will and thus could not argue that the political state can wither away, nevertheless finds enough social cohesion to develop a theory of legitimate revolution. Society can dismiss its government if it threatens property rights. Society has enough coherence to be able to hold together while overthrowing one government and setting up another.

Nor is this right to revolution likely to lead to chaos in Locke's opinion. Revolution will be very infrequent because "People are not so easily got out of their old Forms. . . ."[13] From the point of view of social theory this makes perfect sense. Social coherence—property interest—exerts a conservative and stabilizing force. People want to protect their property. This will lead them to revolution if it is necessary to preserve their property, but the same interest in the security of property will keep them from revolution unless it really is necessary.[14]

II. Social Contract Theory and Its Misuse

In holding that property is based upon a law of nature grounded in God, Locke is not doing anything unusual. He places himself within a long tradition.[15] But in moving from relatively equal property in stage two of the state of nature to unequal property in stage three, Locke, as Macpherson puts it, removes the limitations and restrictions placed upon property by natural law and God.[16] Locke writes,

> it is plain, that Men have agreed to disproportionate and unequal Possession of the Earth, they having by a tacit and voluntary consent found out a way, how a man may fairly possess more land than he himself can use the product of, by receiving in exchange for the overplus, Gold and Silver, which may be hoarded up without injury to any one, these metalls not spoileing or decaying in the hands of the possessor. This partage of things, in an inequality of private possessions, men have made practicable out of the bounds of Societie, and without compact, only by putting a value on gold and silver and tacitly agreeing in the use of Money.[17]

The principle that restricted individuals to relatively equal property was the principle of spoilage. Individuals ought not and in fact would not appropriate more than they could use—the surplus would simply spoil. With the introduction of money this difficulty is overcome. Surplus can be exchanged for money, which does not spoil and is quite useful. There is then no limit on private appropriation. Dunn argues that, for Locke, money does not *justify* unequal property, but only *explains* its emergence. This is clearly incorrect. Locke says that money "introduced (by Consent) larger Possessions, and a *Right* to them. . . ."[18]

For Locke, property in stage two of the state of nature was not perfectly equal, but it was relatively equal. Small inequalities could arise.

They could arise in several ways. We have seen that mixing one's labor with what is common establishes personal property. It is also the case that labor increases the value of this property. An acre of land planted with tobacco, sugar, or wheat will be much more valuable than the same acre of land lying in common that has not been labored upon. It is labor that produces this increased value.[19] It obviously follows from this that individuals who are more industrious can raise the value of their land or even increase the quantity of land they possess.[20] Moreover, as the size of a family increases, so could their industry increase and thus their possessions.[21] It is also the case, for Locke, that servants can increase one's possessions. The labor performed by a servant increases the property of the master.[22] Those who are free can make themselves servants by selling themselves to a master for a certain time.[23] This, of course, would imply that masters had been able to accumulate more than they themselves could use in order to hire servants. Moreover, for Locke, one can enlarge one's possessions through barter or exchange. To have something to barter or exchange, as well as to have the wherewithal to hire servants, would require that individuals already possess more that they can use, but this is perfectly legitimate, for Locke, because nothing would be left to spoil. The surplus used to pay the servant would be used by the servant, and both parties to an exchange would barter away surplus, which would be used by the other party.[24]

All of this could make for inequality in stage two, but only limited inequality. Locke himself is quite clear about this. He suggests that money first arises out of barter and exchange,[25] and only then does real inequality become possible. He says:

> Where there is not something both lasting and scarce, and so valuable to be hoarded up, there Men will not be apt to enlarge their Possessions of Land . . . For I ask, What would a Man value Ten Thousand, or an Hundred Thousand Acres of excellent Land, ready cultivated . . . where he had no hopes of Commerce with other Parts of the World, to draw Money to him by the Sale of the Product?[26]

Thus, whenever I refer to "unequal property," I mean vastly unequal property made possible by the introduction of money, which for Locke occurs only in stage three of the state of nature. By "equal property" or "relatively equal property," I mean the sort of property that, for Locke, is found in stage two of the state of nature, where a limited degree of inequality is possible but not great inequality.

However, there is a further requirement of the law of nature involved here—that there be enough and as good left for others. It may seem that if in stage three there is no limit on private appropriation, it will soon be the case that there will not be enough good land left for others (unless one travels to America). Locke himself admits as much.[27] Locke argues, however, that active commerce and trade, by increasing the quantity of production, will benefit all.[28] We might interpret this as follows: the development, say, of large estates in the state of nature may make it impossible for some others to become landholders, but yet might make it possible for them to become laborers or servants on these estates in exchange for a wage, and thereby, conceivably by increasing production and trade, even improve their lot. At any rate, whether this is likely or not—and, as we shall see, it is quite debatable—the introduction of money introduces serious inequality among individuals.

All of this takes place in the state of nature. Unequal property for Locke is natural. For Hobbes and Rousseau, property as opposed to possession could only exist in political society. A title to property requires official governmental recognition. Indeed, this is the view of most political theorists. It follows, for Hobbes and Rousseau, that the sovereign's decision is what legitimately establishes the form of property any society is to have. Rousseau envisions the possibility of communal property, but clearly prefers equal property.[29] For Hobbes, it is not likely that the sovereign would decide in either of these ways, but it is a theoretical possibility. For Locke it is not. The government has no say on these matters, nor do the people. The citizens are locked into unequal property—it is natural. It would be unnatural, immoral, and illegitimate for society or government to opt for equal property or communal property. At this level, Locke advocates inequality in political society far more than did Hobbes or Rousseau. Hobbes at least does not dwell on inequality among the citizens and certainly does not justify it as natural. Rousseau, of course, opposes it.

It is my view that Locke's argument for unequal property constitutes a fundamental misuse of social contract theory. Rather than use right as a criterion for assessing the legitimacy of fact, Locke does the reverse. He uses fact to determine right.[30] How does Locke know that at some time in the past—and before the establishment of political society, that is, in the state of nature—individuals consented to the introduction of money and unequal property? It is quite clear that when Locke says in the passage quoted above that "it is plain, that Men have agreed to disproportionate and unequal Possession of the

Earth," he is arguing that since unequal property and money exist and are accepted in his own society, then at some time in the past—and in the state of nature—individuals must have voluntarily and tacitly consented to them. The fact that money and unequal property exist and are accepted show that they were consented to. This is a very bad argument. In fact Locke himself, in arguing against Filmer, says that "an Argument from what has been, to what should of right be, has no great force. . . ." And also, elsewhere, "if what is rightful and lawful were to be determined by men's way of living, moral rectitude and integrity would be done for."[31]

But clearly this is the sort of argument Locke is making. He gives no other reason for the legitimacy of money or unequal property except that individuals consented to them. Money grew out of barter and exchange;[32] individuals consented to the use of money; and this made unequal property possible. There is no argument that individuals were for any reason obligated to accept money or unequal property, or even that they were necessarily driven to accept them. They just occurred and were consented to. When Locke argued that the first two stages of the state of nature involved communal property and relatively equal property, he based his argument for the legitimacy of these forms of property on God's authority.[33] Individuals mixed their labor with what had been common and this was legitimate because God wanted it so. When Locke argues for the legitimacy of money and unequal property there is no appeal to God at all but simply to the fact that individuals must have consented to them. There is no argument for the legitimacy of money or unequal property here except that given the present acceptance of money and unequal property individuals in the past must have consented to them. How does Locke know that such consent occurred? Perhaps unequal property was introduced by force or deceit as Rousseau suggests.[34] If it was not, why would individuals have consented to unequal property? It does not seem plausible that they would have. It is hard to imagine that it would have been in the interest of all. What would lead people, or drive them, to this decision? What is the argument that would convince us that they would have consented other than the fact that unequal property now exists and is accepted? Perhaps we could say that individuals first consented to money—which at first glance seems a more plausible assumption—and that then they had to accept the inequality in property that resulted from the existence of money. But how can we be sure that they consented to the introduction of money? Locke suggests that money arose out of barter. Perhaps it did so as gold or silver, from simply being two among many articles that one could barter, slowly and without notice took the form of a general medium of exchange; and perhaps this occurred before individuals were aware of it or understood it well enough to be said to consent to it. Perhaps, by the time they were aware enough to object, it was already too late. Moreover, even if money and unequal property were introduced by consent, how do we know that this took place in the state of nature and not after the formation of political society?

Social contract theory, even in Locke's opinion, should proceed in a very different way. It should use the concept of a state of nature and the acts of consent (or the social contract) that grow out of this state of nature as a standard by which to *test* the legitimacy of institutions that could or do exist in society. It should use right to test fact. For Rousseau and Rawls, and even, I argued in Chapter 1, for Hobbes, the state of nature is not taken to be a condition that actually existed at some time in the past, but as an abstract standard, a fictional hypothesis, which is used as a criterion to test the legitimacy of social institutions.[35] Social contract theory properly begins by designing a state of nature that depicts human nature, or that at least identifies certain human characteristics as basic and normative. Typically, human beings are at least taken to be free and equal in the state of nature. The next step is to ask what sorts of institutions these free and equal human beings would have consented to as compatible with their freedom and equality. Those that they would have consented to are legitimate institutions. Those that they would not have consented to are not legitimate institutions. And we would have to give reasons, arguments, for why they would or would not have consented to these institutions. To argue that *equal* individuals would consent to *unequal* property would not at all be obvious or easy to argue. Neither Hobbes nor Rousseau, for example, think it could be argued.[36]

So also, one can take actual institutions from one's own society and argue whether or not they would have been consented to by those free and equal individuals in the state of nature and thus decide whether one's own institutions are just or unjust. Locke does not use the concept of a state of nature in this way, at least not when discussing money or unequal property. He does not use it as an abstract conceptual criterion of right to test the actually existing historical institutions of his own society. He does not argue for their legitimacy. Instead, he just accepts the actual institutions of his own society, at least unequal property and money, and assumes that as a historical fact they were consented to in the state of nature.

Social contract theory, even when properly used, is a very risky business. Whatever characteristics are attributed to people in the state of nature can always be questioned. It is always possible that the theorist, consciously or unconsciously, has stuffed into the state of nature those characteristics that, when unpacked and examined, will lead to and justify the sort of society the theorist believed in in the first place. But Locke is even worse. He uses what exists in his own society as the criterion for what must have occurred in the state of nature.

I think it is quite telling that for Locke, unlike Hobbes or Rousseau, the state of nature is taken to be an actually existent historical period. Locke says,

> it is not at all to be wonder'd, that History gives us but a very little account of Men, that lived together in the State of Nature . . . And if we may not suppose Men ever to have been in the State of Nature, because we hear not much of them in such a State, we may as well suppose the Armies of Salmanasser, or Xerxes were never Children, because we hear little of them, till they were Men, and imbodied in Armies. Government is every where antecedent to Records, and Letters seldome come in amongst a People, till a long continuation of Civil Society has, by other more necessary Arts provided for their Safety, Ease, and Plenty.[37]

Indeed, for Locke, it must be the case that the state of nature actually existed in the past. To deduce merely from the present existence of money or unequal property an abstract conceptual right to these things would be absurd. Locke himself, as we have seen, says that "an Argument from what has been, to what should of right be, has no great force. . . ."[38] No, it must have been the case that the state of nature actually existed in history (or prehistory) and that individuals actually consented, at least tacitly, to unequal property and money. What else could establish the right to unequal property? Locke has no argument to show that anything would have obligated, required, or driven people to institute it. He makes no argument that God commanded money or unequal property. The only way he can even begin to justify them, then, is if they were consented to actually and historically. The only trouble is that the only evidence that they were consented to is that they now exist. Locke, it seems, is driven to a position that most social contract theorists would find bizarre and unacceptable.

But let us even suppose, for sake of argument, that money and unequal property were consented to in the state of nature. One might argue, for example, that it is quite plausible that individuals involved in barter, as money arose, came to consent to money because they saw that it facilitated exchange, and thus that they had to accept the inequality in property that money made possible. But even if they did consent in this way, is simple consent, even the sort of consent involved in a full-fledged social contract, ever enough by itself to establish legitimacy? Locke, in his *Essays on the Law of Nature* said, "concerning general consent in matters of morals, we say that it by no means proves a natural law. For if what is rightful and lawful were to be determined by men's way of living, moral rectitude and integrity would be done for." And also in the *Second Treatise* he says, as we have seen, that an argument from what is to what ought to be has no great force.[39]

Can we really say that whatever people consent to—just because they consent to it—is therefore legitimate and moral? Don't they in fact consent to things that are illegitimate and immoral? Certainly, all things done in the state of nature are not legitimate and moral, nor could they therefore be a criterion of legitimacy and morality. It is quite possible to behave immorally in the state of nature. Clearly, more than consent is necessary to establish legitimacy and morality. Consent must accord with some moral obligation, law of nature, or command of God to be legitimate and moral.[40] Or failing that, as for Hobbes, we must be driven to consent such that to go back on our consent would be to contradict ourselves and to return to what we reasonably sought to avoid—the chaos of the state of nature.[41] This latter approach, however, would not work for Locke, as we have seen, because society is not so fragile that it will collapse back into the state of nature over the slightest difficulty. It has considerable social cohesion. Moreover, Locke gives no argument at all to show that we were driven to consent to money or unequal property. He simply holds that we did consent.

Furthermore, to base legitimacy on the bare fact that people at one time happen to have consented, as Locke does, seems rather arbitrary. Since it so happens that they did consent, money and unequal property are legitimate. But if they had not consented, which was just as possible since no argument is given for why they must have or ought to have consented, then money and unequal property would have been illegitimate. This would be all right if, like Hobbes, we were willing to accept the notion that right or legitimacy is also purely arbitrary; that is, that whatever the sovereign happens to decide establishes what we accept as legitimate. Something is legitimate not because it agrees with some higher objective standard of right, but simply because the sovereign decides it. But for Locke this is unacceptable. For him, besides the fact that money and unequal property precede the creation of a sovereign, legitimacy or right should be objective and natural.[42]

Ashcraft has argued that Locke's text *does* contain an argument for the legitimacy of money and unequal property. He points out that for Locke money and unequal property do not violate either the principle of spoilage or the principle that enough and as good must be left for others. But, furthermore, Ashcraft argues that money and the trade it makes possible increase the common stock of all. Ashcraft claims that this accords with God's command to benefit others; Locke says, "God, who hath given the World to Men in common, hath also given them reason to make use of it to the best advantage of Life, and convenience." Locke also says, "The Fundamental Law of Nature being, that all, as much as may be, should be preserved. . . ."[43] Thus, for Ashcraft, Locke is not arguing that money and unequal property are justified merely because people consented to them. That alone, Ashcraft admits, would not be enough to justify money and unequal property. Ashcraft argues that this consent also accords with a law of nature and that this is what justifies money and unequal property. Ashcraft is quite clear that God did not directly authorize or command the introduction of money. Money and unequal property are merely *compatible* with the law of nature, which obliges us to benefit others. Moreover, Ashcraft admits that Locke himself did not actually make the argument that money and unequal property accord with the law of nature that obliges us to benefit others. Locke only made this argument when discussing trade and relatively equal property in stage two before the introduction of money. Ashcraft, however, holds that the same argument *can be extended* to money and unequal property in stage three.[44]

I think it is crucial to see that Locke did not make this argument himself. Perhaps the reason Locke did not do so is because the argument will not work for money and unequal property. And it is even possible that Locke sees that it will not work. In a passage that will be quoted in full below, Locke admits that what laborers earn is "seldom more than a bare subsistence. . . ."[45] It is also clear that Locke admits that the introduction of money and unequal property in stage three implies that land will be scarce.[46] There will not be enough land for all and thus some (unless they are able to go to America) will be forced to labor for others in exchange for a wage—a wage that will seldom be more than a bare subsistence. In contrast to this, in stage two, there was enough land for all and through industry and trade individuals could gain *more* than bare subsistence. All individuals at least had the chance to do so in stage two. In stage three, some do not have this chance while others have a chance to gain a *great* deal more. Thus, it is not at all clear that money and unequal property benefit all—are to the "best advantage of Life, and convenience"[47] for all—and thus it is not at all clear that money and unequal property even *accord* with this law of nature. Perhaps that is why Locke does not make this argument. At any rate, he does not, and I think that my claim that Locke does not give an argument, certainly an acceptable argument, for the introduction of money and unequal property still holds.

Locke, it seems, is caught in a dilemma and he is none too clear about the fact that he is. Since he has no argument from moral obligation, the law of nature, or the will of God to establish the legitimacy of unequal property, he must at least show that individuals did consent to it—and so the state of nature must have existed as an actual historical period. But at the same time it is clear that whatever occurs in an actual historical period—whatever people do or consent to—is not for that reason alone legitimate.[48] Besides actual consent, there must be an actual moral obligation, law of nature, or command of God. But Locke gives no argument of this sort for unequal property. He seems to be running in a circle.

But perhaps we are approaching Locke's state of nature incorrectly. We have already seen that it is not to be taken as an unhistorical abstraction in which we simply imagine isolated individuals to exist. It is historical and social, but prepolitical. Perhaps we should try to understand it more along the lines of what Aristotle was doing in the *Politics* when he discussed the historical development of city-states out of simpler prepolitical societies and family groupings. In certain ways Locke's state of nature does resemble Aristotle's prepolitical society, but I do not think this will help us to argue for the legitimacy of unequal property. Aristotle's way of arguing for the right or legitimacy of any institution was to begin by trying to understand human nature and then to measure the institution against this concept of human nature. However, for Aristotle, we are not able to understand human nature by looking to the beginning of human development in prepolitical society, let alone to a state of nature. Human nature is something that is realized (and thus can be understood) only at the end of a development—at its high point. For Aristotle, human nature is realized in political society and most highly realized only in the best political societies. Once we understand what human nature can become we can use this understanding to measure the right or legitimacy of political institutions—we can see whether or not they foster the realization of human nature.[49] The end becomes the criterion here, not the beginning.

But very clearly we do not find this sort of thing in Locke. For him, it is not what comes later that justifies what comes earlier. Rather what occurs at the beginning, in the state of nature, is intended to justify what comes later. It is just that Locke does not have a good argument for this when it comes to unequal property.

III. Social Inequality

As I have argued, Locke's concept of property constitutes an advance in social theory and by comparison to Hobbes seems to increase the equality between citizens and government by limiting the latter; nevertheless, Locke's acceptance of unequal property actually introduces greater inequality between the citizens themselves than was the case for Hobbes and, as I would now like to argue, this undermines at least for the propertyless the apparent equality between citizens and government and indeed thereby the limited character of government.

The issue of inequality between citizens has been hotly debated in the literature on Locke for many years now. In 1962, Macpherson, in his *Political Theory of Possessive Individualism,* argued in a Marxian fashion that Locke laid the ideological foundation for bourgeois appropriation as well as for capitalist inequality and exploitation. Since then, many Locke scholars have been highly critical of Macpherson's views and have rejected many of them. The careful historical studies of Dunn, Tully, and Ashcraft, for example, reject the notion that Locke intended to be an apologist for capitalism; they argue that Locke was motivated by a commitment to religion, morality, and natural law. More recently, Wood, while critical of Macpherson in certain respects, has argued that Locke *is* a theorist of capitalism, but of early agrarian capitalism, not of later mercantile or manufacturing capitalism.[50]

I do not intend to discuss the question of whether or not Locke was an apologist for capitalism, though I find Wood's revision of Macpherson persuasive. At the same time, while I think that the rich historical studies of Dunn and Tully, and especially Ashcraft's most impressive work, are correct in criticizing certain aspects of Macpherson's argument, and while I agree with their emphasis on Locke's religious and moral commitments, I nevertheless think that they are mistaken about important passages in Locke's texts dealing with inequality. I think that Macpherson and Wood are closer to being correct about these passages. Let me try to bolster their arguments.

For Locke, "The Reason why Men enter into Society, is the preservation of their Property" and "Government has no other end but the preservation of Property."[51] Locke even admits that when individuals enter political society they give up the equality they had in the state of nature in order to preserve their liberty and property.[52] It may seem odd to make property the sole end of government, but Locke tells us that he uses the term "property" in a special and very broad sense. He says that individuals unite in society for the "Preservation of their Lives, Liberties, and Estates, which I call by the general Name, Property."[53] However, it is notorious that Locke does not stick to this definition. He quite frequently uses "property" to mean estate only. Nor do I think it is the case that in doing so Locke is guilty of merely a few innocuous slips. It seems to me that for Locke the aim of government is to protect property in the form of estate far more than it is its aim to preserve property in the form of life and liberty for those without property. As an example of the government's obligation to protect property, Locke says,

> yet we see, that neither the Serjeant, that could command a Souldier to march up to the mouth of a Cannon, or stand in a Breach, where he is almost sure to perish, can command that Soldier to give him one penny of his Money; nor the General, that can condemn him to Death for deserting his Post, or for not obeying the most desperate Orders, can yet with all his absolute Power of Life and Death, dispose of one Farthing of that Soldiers Estate, or seize one jot of his Goods; whom yet he can command any thing, and hang for the least Disobedience.[54]

I suspect that Locke is unaware of what he is letting slip out in this passage, but that only makes it all the more revealing. Here the right to property in the form of estate functions as a restraint on governmental authority far more that the right to property in the form of life or liberty does, and the former seems much more important than the latter. The end of government here is to protect estate far more than its end is to protect life and liberty. Moreover, this is not an isolated example of such an outlook on Locke's part. We find similar views elsewhere. He also says that a lawful conqueror has an absolute and despotical power over the lives of the conquered but not over their possessions. Furthermore, in his essay on poor-law reform, Locke certainly seems willing to restrain the liberty of the poor and unemployed and indeed to advocate rather harsh punishments for them in order to reduce the burden on the propertied classes of supporting the poor; that is, his concern is to protect the estates of the wealthy far more than it is to protect the liberty of the poor.⁵⁵ Here, one certainly feels that there are first- and second-class citizens.

I find myself in agreement with Macpherson here, at least to the extent that I think he is right in claiming that the propertyless are not full-fledged citizens for Locke.⁵⁶ If we keep in mind that "property" often means estate, then when we find Locke telling us that the sole aim of government is to preserve property, we begin to wonder whether here too "property" means estate; and thus whether government's sole, or at least primary, aim is to protect the propertied. It seems to me that this *is* the case for Locke. Consider the following very important passage:

> The Supream Power cannot take from any Man any part of his Property without his own consent. For the preservation of Property being the end of Government, and that for which Men enter into Society, it necessarily supposes and requires, that the People should have Property, without which they must be suppos'd to lose that by entering into Society, which was the end for which they entered into it, too gross an absurdity for any Man to own.⁵⁷

If "property" means estate in this passage, it certainly suggests that the poor or propertyless are at least second-class citizens—if they are citizens at all. And I do think that in this passage "property" means estate. In the second sentence, when Locke says of people entering into society, "it necessarily supposes and requires, that the People should have Property . . .", it certainly seems that "property" means estate—it would be very odd to *require* that people have life or natural liberty, which they have anyway. Slaves, it is true, have forfeited their life and liberty, but it would seem strange to talk of them as *entering* into society at all. They are not allowed to do so. Moreover, in the line that follows the above quotation Locke equates property with goods and substance. "Men therefore in Society having Property, they have such a right to the goods, which by the Law of the Community are theirs, that no Body hath a right to take their substance, or any part of it from them, without their own consent." Later in this passage Locke even uses the term "Estates."⁵⁸ Dunn, however, argues that Locke is not saying that the possession of property is the sole motive for entering political society or the sole condition that allows one to become a member of political society, but rather that it is merely a reason for accepting political society.⁵⁹ But even if this is the way to read the above passage, there are also other reasons for believing that there are first- and second-class citizens for Locke.

Even if, by "property," Locke always meant life, liberty, and estate, still the propertied would have more to gain from government than the propertyless. The latter would gain only the protection of life and liberty while the former would additionally gain the preservation of their property. This in itself would create serious inequality among citizens. But it seems to me that Locke goes a good deal further. Macpherson argues, correctly I think, that the propertyless, for Locke, would not be equally represented in the legislature,[60] or indeed might not be represented at all. Citizens are represented in proportion to the assistance they afford the public; in other words, I think, in proportion to the taxes they pay.

> If therefore the Executive, who has the power of Convoking the Legislative, observing rather the true proportion, than fashion of Representation, regulates, not by old custom, but true reason, the number of Members, in all places, that have a right to be distinctly represented, which no part of the People however incorporated can pretend to, but in proportion to the assistance, which it affords the publick. . . .[61]

Dunn argues that we must read this passage "in the context of incorporated boroughs which do have members of parliament but which no longer have inhabitants, rather than see it simply as an acceptance of property as the sole basis of representation."[62] Clearly, Locke is making the former point, but he is *also* making the latter point. For Locke, taxes are paid out of estates and thus, it would seem, only by estate owners. " 'Tis true, Governments cannot be supported without great Charge, and 'tis fit every one who enjoys his share of the Protection, should pay out of his Estate his proportion for the maintenance of it." Elsewhere, Locke argues that sound economics dictate that taxes should be taxes on land.[63] Furthermore, it was certainly the case in the England of Locke's day that universal manhood suffrage was not widespread, though it did exist in some cities.[64] Ashcraft argues that Locke was a radical Whig and was close to the position of the Levellers on this issue. The Levellers argued for universal manhood suffrage with the possible exception of servants and those who took alms.[65] Tully also argues that Locke wished to extend suffrage to every adult male. If Locke had advocated universal manhood suffrage, we would expect him to indicate that this was his view if he intended to be understood by his contemporaries. He does not do so. In fact, he says the opposite. In his *Fundamental Constitutions of Carolina* he advocates property qualifications for holding various offices, for becoming a member of parliament, for voting for members of parliament, and even for becoming a juryman. These property qualifications start at fifty acres of freehold.⁶⁶

There is another important issue that we must examine here. The ultimate guarantee of limited government, for Locke, is the right the citizens have under certain conditions to overthrow their government. If the people are to be sovereign, they must have the right to replace or overthrow their government under certain conditions. If they do not, they are not sovereign—the government is. We must ask then who has this right—all of the citizens or just the propertied? Macpherson argues that only the propertied would have this right.⁶⁷ Ashcraft argues that all would.⁶⁸

There are various conditions under which the citizens have a right to revolution. Such conditions are given if the government hinders the legislature from meeting or acting or if it tries to alter the legislature or the way it is elected.⁶⁹ It would seem very odd to allow the propertyless a right to revolution on these grounds when they have no right to elect representatives to the legislature in the first place. If altering the way the legislature is elected constitutes a legitimate ground for revolution, it may even be the case that the propertied would have a right to revolution if the electoral procedure were changed to include the propertyless.

There is another ground for legitimate revolution. Citizens have a right to revolution when the government invades their property.⁷⁰ Obviously, the question here is whether or not "property" simply means estate. If so, then only the propertied have a right to revolution and thus the privilege of limited government. Or does "property" also mean life and liberty? If so, then all have a right to revolution as well as the privilege of limited government. Locke claims that he means the latter. He says that citizens have a right to revolution when the legislature attempts "to make themselves, or any part of the Community, Masters, or Arbitrary Disposers of the Lives, Liberties, or Fortunes of the People."⁷¹ No statement could be clearer. The only question here is whether we are to believe that this is what Locke really means. It is quite conceivable that Locke would allow the propertyless the right to take part in a revolution that agreed with and supported the propertied, but imagine a situation in which the propertied and the propertyless disagree. Suppose that the propertyless feel that the legislature has attacked their lives and liberties. Suppose further that the propertied for the most part support the legislature. Would the propertyless have a right to revolt against the legislature supported by the propertied? This would be very odd when the propertyless do not even have the right to vote for representatives in this legislature. Only the propertied have such a right.

Let us push Locke a bit harder. Let us suppose that the propertyless come to feel that the right to property in the form of estate—that is, unequal property—has become a threat to their right to property in the form of life and liberty. Would the propertyless have a right to revolution against the government and the propertied in order to set up communal property, equal property, or at least to reduce the degree of inequality in property? It is quite clear that this would not be legitimate.[72] It would violate the law of nature, which guarantees the right to unequal property. No one has a right against the law of nature—not the government and not any of the citizens. What is very interesting here is that, as we have seen, the natural right to property serves to limit government for the propertied, at least insofar as the government might threaten property or the rights and liberties connected with it. But at the same time the very same principle of property serves to limit the propertyless and to remove the limits on government vis-à-vis the propertyless, at least insofar as the rights and liberties of the propertyless are opposed to property.

But we still have a problem here. If we are to take seriously Locke's claim quoted above that citizens have a right to revolution when the government attacks *either* their life and liberty *or* their fortune, what do we do when there is a conflict between the rights of fortune and the rights of life and liberty? It is obvious that Locke has not thought much about this possibility. He just does not discuss it. However, I think we can identify more precisely exactly what it is that he has not thought about. He has thought a good deal about situations in which the rights of the propertied are threatened and he is quite clear about when they have a right to revolution. He has not thought about the right to revolution of the propertyless against the propertied when the rights of estate conflict with the rights to life and liberty. Moreover, I suspect that Locke simply would not take such a situation seriously. Consider the following passage from *Considerations of the Consequences of the Lowering of Interest, and Raising the Value of Money:*

> for the labourer's share, being seldom more than a bare subsistence, never allows that body of men time or opportunity to raise their thoughts above that, or struggle with the richer for theirs, (as one common interest) unless when some common and great distress, uniting them in one universal ferment, makes them forget respect, and emboldens them to carve to their

56　*Chapter Two*

wants with armed force; and then sometimes they break in upon the rich, and sweep all like a deluge. But this rarely happens but in the mal-administration of neglected, or mismanaged government.[73]

It never occurs to Locke that in the normal course of events the poor concern themselves with anything but bare subsistence. When they do, it does not occur to Locke that it may be for some legitimate reason. It is a problem of mismanagement. For Locke, there does not seem to be room here for legitimate revolution. Locke does not even dignify such uprisings with the name of revolution. They are disrespectful deluges. I find it very hard to imagine that Locke would allow a right to revolution to such individuals—individuals he will not even permit to vote. Moreover, to suggest that in such uprisings the poor forget the respect they owe to the rich is a bit odd for a theorist who when discussing the propertied and their right to revolution never seriously employs the category of "respect" and indeed in his argument against Filmer's concept of patriarchal authority seems to suggest that such a concept has little or no place in political theory.

IV. Sovereign Power and Property

To understand fully Locke's social theory we must also discuss his concept of supreme power or sovereignty. A sovereign is the highest power—the highest power in two senses. It is the highest *legitimate* authority—it is where such authority *ought* to lie. And it is the highest *actual* power—it is, empirically, where the highest power *in fact* lies.

If property is made subordinate to the government or the sovereign, this means that the sovereign can decide to institute communal property or equal property. But at the same time, as we see in Hobbes, this makes the sovereign extremely powerful—it removes a key factor capable of limiting the sovereign. On the other hand, if property is removed from the authority of the sovereign, at least in the way that Locke does it, the sovereign's power is limited; but on the other hand, this rules out the possibility of communal property or equal property.

What if we assume that the people are sovereign? Then subordinating property to the sovereign makes it possible to have communal property or equal property if the people so choose, but it does not subordinate the people to the control of a powerful external force: it makes *them* the highest legitimate authority and power as for Rousseau[74] (which, however, may generate problems of its own). On the other hand, if the people are sovereign and property is removed from the authority of the sovereign in the way that Locke does it,[75] communal property and equal property are made impossible and government is limited but in such a way that government works in the interest of the propertied and against the interest of the propertyless. Sovereignty works for one part of the people against the other part. In effect, the *people* are not sovereign here; one part of the people (the propertied) become sovereign over the other part (the propertyless).

This also makes sense in another way. As we have seen, property and property interest are a cohesive force that holds society together and makes limited government possible. This force, however, would be absent among the propertyless—absent in two senses. The propertyless would not necessarily have any coherence, any solidarity, with the propertied; they could well oppose them. And the propertyless, without property interest or something like it drawing them together, would not have coherence among themselves—they could even be a disorganized rabble as Locke himself seems to suggest in the passage quoted above from the *Considerations*.[76] In other words, Locke's social theory has been developed from his concept of property and applies to the propertied. Locke can try to stretch this social theory to apply to the propertyless insofar as he expects them to identify with property and the interests that grow out of property, but Locke clearly does not have a social theory that applies to the propertyless in the sense that it is capable of locating any other form of social cohesion among them; that is, any cohesion produced by something other than property or property interest. Such a theory remains to be developed by later theorists.

Social cohesion is a tricky business. It may hold parts of society together and produce stability as it does for the propertied while at the same time setting other parts of society in opposition to each other as it may set the propertyless against the propertied. The social and political realms are interconnected in a complex way. The social is the foundation of the political. The social realm can provide coherence so that the political realm need not provide it through force. Yet the social realm can give rise to inequalities, oppositions, and antagonisms that will upset the political realm and lead to tension and strife.

But there is a further problem here that we have skipped over. If the sovereign is actually the highest power, how is it possible to limit the sovereign? How can mere property rights limit the sovereign? One answer might be found in Hobbes. He argued that rights were powers. For example, when individuals in the state of nature decide to establish political society, for Hobbes, they do not and cannot give over to the sovereign their right to self-preservation. The sovereign cannot expect an individual to die willingly, simply because there is no way that the sovereign can have this power. A human being's nature is to seek to preserve itself and there is no way to change this or expect it to be changed.[77]

The social coherence produced by property and property interest *allows* for a limited sovereign, but what *actually limits and restrains* the sovereign? Property and property interest *ought* to limit the sovereign, but how do they *actually* do so? It seems that property rights could work as an actual limit on the sovereign only if it could be shown that there is no way the sovereign can have power over property just as the sovereign can have no power to make an individual die willingly.

In one sense, Locke could make such an argument. He tends to identify the right to self-preservation with the right to property. And this to some extent is acceptable. Without possessions like food, clothing, and shelter, we could not live. Thus a sovereign could no more eliminate this sort of right to property than it could eliminate the right to self-preservation. It has no *right* to do so in the sense that it has no *power* to do so.

But Locke wants to defend *unequal* property. How can he establish a right to unequal property against the sovereign? If the sovereign is the highest actual power and the sovereign is against unequal property, what can the propertied do? We might argue that the wealthy would identify their wealth with their self-preservation to the extent that the sovereign would have no power to expect them to give up unequal property. And this seems to be what Locke does. But to move very far in this direction is to make the wealthy into the sovereign. On the other hand, Locke does seem to expect the propertyless to be content with their lot. Somehow they do not identify self-preservation with property and the sovereign has the power to expect them to accept bare subsistence.

It seems to me, however, that if we take the concept of sovereignty seriously, and hold that the people are sovereign, then all property would belong to the people as a whole. There would be no right way to distribute it except as the people decided. Certainly, the slightest understanding of the concept of sovereignty would show that if the people *in fact* are sovereign, if they in fact are the highest actual power, then they *actually* have the power to distribute property as they see fit. If, counter to this, one were to think that in some way one could establish a legitimate *right* to a certain form of distribution, for example, unequal property (by appeal to the law of nature, the will of God, or whatever), then, it would seem, one would invite disaster for this society. Fact would diverge from right. The actual empirical power of the sovereign would not agree with what is held to be right and legitimate. Unequal property for some means propertylessness for others. If unequal property is held to be a *right,* but sovereignty is controlled by the majority who are propertyless, then fact and right will inevitably conflict.

However, the situation is more complex than this. Property and wealth do give those who possess them greater political power. Wealth gives the propertied classes access to superior weapons, training in their use, and the ability to organize and support an army, not to speak of access to education and a good deal of control over the dissemination of ideas. It may well be that in fact, empirically, sovereign power lies with the propertied. Even if they are a minority, they still may be the greatest power. They have a coherent unifying interest, the means to organize themselves and represent themselves in the government, and their taxes finance the bodies that make the laws as well as execute them. From the point of view of Locke's social theory, then, property and property interest could and possibly would function just as Locke imagines they will. But the stage is set for a different scene. It can easily be imagined that a big enough gap between the propertied and the propertyless or enough oppression of the propertyless, together with a social theory that could explain the possibility of cohesion among the propertyless, would allow them to produce not one of those chaotic and disrespectful deluges that Locke mentions, but an organized and coherent revolution in which they might in fact, empirically, come to have sovereign power.

At that point, it seems to me, Locke's argument for the right to unequal property would crumble. In fact his argument for the legitimacy of unequal property, we have seen, should hardly be dignified by calling it an argument. With this out of the way and the propertyless in power, the sovereign would simply decide how to distribute property as for Hobbes or Rousseau, and for further insight into these matters we would have to look to other theorists, especially to those like Rousseau and Marx who have developed a social theory capable of being applied to the propertyless.

Notes

1. J. Dunn, *The Political Thought of John Locke* (Cambridge: Cambridge University Press, 1969), 100.

2. Locke, *Second Treatise,* § 27. (I cite the section rather than the page when referring to the *Second Treatise.* This will make it easier for those with other editions, and in many cases sections are shorter than pages.)

3. *Second Treatise,* § 31, 32.

4. *Second Treatise,* § 46, 48, 51.

5. *Second Treatise,* § 33, 36.

6. *Second Treatise,* § 94, 95, 131, 135, 139. Tully's reading of § 38 and 45 of the *Second Treatise* leads him to think that for Locke property is not established until after political society has been constituted. These sections are not perfectly clear, but § 28 and 32–34 are, and they tell us that property is established in the state of nature. I think that this is even implied in § 38 where Locke says, "But as Families increased, and Industry inlarged their Stocks, their Possessions inlarged with the need of them; but yet it was commonly without any fixed property in the ground they made use of, till they incorporated, settled themselves together, and built Cities, and *then, by consent, they came in time,* to set out the bounds of their distinct Territories, and agree on limits between them and their Neighbours, and by Laws within themselves, settled the Properties of those of the same Society." (My italics.) Here, Locke is making the claim that fixed property, while it only comes *after* incorporation, nevertheless *precedes laws* which come at an even later date. Thus, if property precedes laws, it would have to precede political society. Moreover, in § 45 Locke says, "the several Communities settled the Bounds of their distinct Territories, and by laws within themselves, regulated the Properties of the private Men of their Society, and so, by Compact and Agreement, settled the Property *which Labour and Industry began . . .*" (my emphasis). This passage does say that political society settles the bounds and regulates some details concerning property, but clearly it is property that had already been established earlier (in the state of nature) by labor and industry. See J. Tully, *A Discourse on Property* (Cambridge: Cambridge University Press, 1980), 98–99, 147–48.

7. *Second Treatise,* § 28, 35.

8. *Second Treatise,* § 50.

9. See Chapter 1, Section II above.

10. *Second Treatise,* § 45.

11. *Second Treatise,* § 211, 212.

12. Hobbes, *Leviathan, EW,* III, 180.

13. *Second Treatise,* § 223, also see 226. Franklin thinks that Locke's argument that revolution will be infrequent is rather weak. It is not, if one understands Locke's social theory. See J.H. Franklin, *John Locke and the Theory of Sovereignty* (Cambridge: Cambridge University Press, 1978), 96.

14. Thus I cannot agree with Wolin who argues that the development of social theory undermines political philosophy. Social theory, in my view, reinforces political philosophy and undermines theories that support absolute political authority; see S. Wolin, *Politics and Vision* (Boston: Little, Brown and Co., 1960), 286–351 *passim.*

15. *Second Treatise,* § 34. See Q. Skinner, *The Foundations of Modern Political Thought* (Cambridge: Cambridge University Press, 1978), II, 153–66, 174 ff. Also P. Larkin, *Property in the Eighteenth Century* (Dublin: Cork University Press, 1930), 5 ff. Also Laslett's Introduction to *Two Treatises,* p. 14.

16. C.B. Macpherson, *The Political Theory of Possessive Individualism* (Oxford: Clarendon Press, 1962), 199–204.

17. *Second Treatise,* § 50.

18. Dunn, 118 n. *Second Treatise,* § 36 (my italics).

19. *Second Treatise,* § 40.

20. *Second Treatise,* § 48.

21. *Second Treatise,* § 38.

22. *Second Treatise,* § 29.

23. *Second Treatise,* § 85, also 24. Slaves are also a subclass of servants; *Second Treatise,* § 85.

24. *Second Treatise,* § 45.

25. *Second Treatise,* § 47.

26. *Second Treatise,* § 48, also 36–37.

27. *Second Treatise,* § 45.

28. *Second Treatise,* § 37, 40, 46. Also *Some Considerations of the Consequences of the Lowering of Interest, and Raising the Value of Money,* in *The Works of John Locke in Nine Volumes* (hereafter *LW*), 12th edition (London: Rivington et al., 1824), IV, 62. Tully's argument that Locke's language shows his moral disapproval of the introduction of money (and thus of unequal property) is quite unconvincing. See Tully, 147–54. For a good critique of Tully, see N. Wood, *John Locke and Agrarian Capitalism* (Berkeley: University of California Press, 1984), 72–92.

29. *Leviathan, EW,* III, 115–16, 131, 165. J-J. Rousseau, *Social Contract,* 56–58, 75 and *OC,* III, 365–67, 391–92.

30. This objection is at least hinted at by Macpherson, 209 ff., 238. Also J.W. Gough, *John Locke's Political Philosophy* (Oxford: Clarendon Press, 1973), 100.

31. *Second Treatise,* § 103. *Essays on the Law of Nature,* ed. W. von Leyden (Oxford: Clarendon Press, 1954), 165.

32. *Second Treatise,* § 46–47.

33. *Second Treatise,* § 25, 32, 34.

34. *Discourse on Inequality,* 141–42, 158–59 and *OC,* III, 164, 176–77.

35. *Discourse on Inequality,* 92–93, 103 and *OC,* III, 123, 132–33. Rawls, 12–13. See Chapter 1, Section IV above.

36. On the other hand, it might be thought that Rawls is someone who would argue that equal individuals in the original position would in fact consent to unequal property—they would do so if it would improve the lot of the worst off. What we must recall, however, is that what is meant here by "unequal property" is *vastly* unequal property, property that means great wealth for

some and, as we shall see, even for Locke, a minimal existence for others. It is not Rawls's view that equals in the original position would agree to this sort of inequality. The only sort of inequality allowed by Rawls would be a limited inequality—limited in that it is allowed only to the extent that it improves the lot of the worst off. This is more like the limited inequality of the second stage of Locke's state of nature (though it involves a different principle of limitation). People in Rawls's original position would not consent to the inequality of Locke's third stage anymore than would Hobbes or Rousseau.

37. *Second Treatise,* § 101. Also all governments are in a state of nature with respect to each other; *Second Treatise,* § 14. Seliger tries to reconcile the concept of a state of nature as a historical period with the concept of a state of nature as an abstract hypothesis, but he does not overcome the difficulties I have raised. See M. Seliger, *The Liberal Politics of John Locke* (New York: Praeger, 1969), 82 ff.

38. *Second Treatise,* § 103.

39. *Essays on the Law of Nature,* 165. *Second Treatise,* § 103.

40. Locke makes this point explicitly in the *Essays on the Law of Nature,* 161, 163, 165.

41. *Leviathan, EW,* III, 119–20. Also *De Cive, EW,* II, 30–31.

42. *Leviathan, EW,* III, 559. *De Cive, EW,* II, 151. In his *Essays on the Law of Nature* (pp. 111, 113, 119), Locke argues that without natural law—which must be decreed by God to be law—there would be neither virtue nor vice, nor fault, nor guilt. Also *First Treatise,* § 124.

43. *Second Treatise,* §26, 183.

44. R. Ashcraft, *Revolutionary Politics and Locke's 'Two Treatises of Government'* (Princeton: Princeton University Press, 1986), 278–79. Ashcraft, *Locke's 'Two Treatises of Government'* (London: Allen & Unwin, 1987), 138–42. A similar argument is made by A. Ryan, "Locke and the Dictatorship of the Bourgeoisie," *Political Studies* XIII (1965), 219–30. Also K. Olivecrona, "Locke's Theory of Appropriation," *Philosophical Quarterly* XXIV (1974), 231–34.

45. *Considerations of the Consequences of the Lowering of Interest, LW,* IV, 71.

46. *Second Treatise,* § 45.

47. *Second Treatise,* §26.

48. Dunn (pp. 102–12) agrees that no historical stage can be normative—an objective criterion of legitimacy—for any other historical stage. But he also thinks that for Locke the state of nature is ahistorical and theological. I agree that this is what it should be, but in fact it is historical and at least in the argument for unequal property the theological dimension is missing.

49. Aristotle, *Politics,* Bk. I, Ch. 2. Moreover, for Aristotle, money, trade, and money making would not be in accordance with natural law as they are for Locke; *Politics,* Bk. I, Ch. 9.

50. Dunn, 134, 212 ff., 222 ff. Tully, 99–100, 136–38, 142–43. Ashcraft,

Revolutionary Politics, 15–16, 150–52. See also Ryan, 219–30. Also E.J. Hundert, "The Making of *Homo Faber:* John Locke Between Ideology and History," *Journal of the History of Ideas* XXXIII (1972), 3–22. Also Hundert, "Market Society and Meaning in Locke's Political Philosophy," *Journal of the History of Philosophy* XV (1977), 33–34. Wood, 7 ff., 13, 15–16.

51. *Second Treatise,* § 222, 94, also see 85, 124, 134, 138. Also *A Letter Concerning Toleration, LW,* V, 10, 43.
52. *Second Treatise,* § 131.
53. *Second Treatise,* § 123, also see 87, 173.
54. *Second Treatise,* § 139.
55. *Second Treatise,* § 178. For the essay on poor-law reform, see H.R. Fox Bourne, *The Life of John Locke* (New York: Harper & Brothers, 1876), II, 377–91. Again, Locke says that a magistrate may "remit the punishment of Criminal Offences by his own Authority, but yet cannot remit the satisfaction due to any private Man, for the damage he has received" (*Second Treatise,* § 11). Here this principle works to the advantage of the criminal, but nevertheless, again we see that the right to property exerts a special restraint on government.
56. Macpherson, 222 ff., 248. Also see Wood, 44. Also see Hundert, "The Making of *Homo Faber:* John Locke Between Ideology and History" and "Market Society and Meaning in Locke's Political Philosophy."
57. *Second Treatise,* § 138.
58. *Second Treatise,* § 85, 138.
59. Dunn, 134.
60. Macpherson, 249.
61. *Second Treatise,* § 158.
62. Dunn, 56. Also Ashcraft, *Locke's 'Two Treatises,'* 178.
63. *Second Treatise,* § 140. *Considerations of the Consequences of the Lowering of Interest, LW,* IV, 55 ff. Also, see Wood, 39. Even John Stuart Mill, in 1860, insists that the assembly that votes taxes should be elected exclusively by those who pay taxes; *Considerations on Representative Government,* ed. C.V. Shields (New York: Liberal Arts Press, 1958), 133. Mill also defends unequal voting to prevent the laboring classes from becoming preponderant in parliament; *Considerations,* 136–43.
64. See Macpherson, 279 ff. Also Wood, 84–85. Also Ashcraft, *Revolutionary Politics,* 148, 152.
65. Ashcraft, *Revolutionary Politics,* 154 ff., 164, 175, 239, 251.
66. *Fundamental Constitutions of Carolina, LW,* IX, 188–90. Wood (p. 84) and Seliger (p. 285) argue that for Locke the masses do not have the right to vote.
67. Macpherson, 224. See also Seliger, 286–87.
68. Ashcraft, *Revolutionary Politics,* 305–9; *Locke's 'Two Treatises,'* 220 ff.
69. *Second Treatise,* § 155, 216.

70. *Second Treatise,* § 221–27.

71. *Second Treatise,* § 221, see also 222. In a political context, words can be used in fascinating and very misleading ways. Consider a political theorist from a past era who discusses and even advocates universal suffrage when the theorist means nothing more than universal *manhood* suffrage. Similarly, I suspect that in the passage quoted, when Locke says that a right to revolution is established whenever the government arbitrarily disposes of the "Lives, Liberties, or Fortunes of the People," what he is thinking when he writes "People" is *"people of property,"* not "people without property."

72. For a different view, see Laslett, 104.

73. *Considerations of the Consequences of the Lowering of Interest, LW,* IV, 71. Ashcraft argues that in this passage Locke does not mean to derogate the poor, but to state a complaint about their condition; see Ashcraft, *Revolutionary Politics,* 268. On the other hand, see Wood, 74–75.

74. *Social Contract,* 54–55 and *OC,* III, 362–63.

75. For Locke, the supreme power is the legislature, but its power is given to it by the people in trust. While the government exists, the legislature is the supreme power, but the people can replace the legislature; *Second Treatise,* § 132, 136, 149, 150. However, as we have seen, only the propertied elect this legislature.

76. *Considerations, LW,* IV, 71.

77. *Leviathan, EW,* III, 116, 127, 204.

3

Rousseau, Individual Liberty, and Community

Within Rousseau scholarship there is serious disagreement concerning the correct way to understand Rousseau's social and political writings.[1] Rousseau is thought by many to be a muddled, confused, and inconsistent thinker. I would like to argue that Rousseau's major social and political doctrines are much more consistent than is usually thought to be the case. In my view, Rousseau is a very careful thinker, but his thought is difficult to understand and it is often misunderstood. Also, it is often thought that Rousseau does not allow for individual liberty and, indeed, that he is a totalitarian. This is connected with Rousseau's concept of sovereignty, which is much like Hobbes's, and with the fact that Rousseau rejects Locke's concept of unequal property. I will try to argue that Rousseau does allow for individual liberty, that he is not a totalitarian, and that he is right to reject Lockean unequal property.

I. The General Will

Those who consider Rousseau a totalitarian do so for several reasons.[2] First, because for Rousseau sovereignty—which is the exercise of the general will—is, as for Hobbes, absolute and thus individuals can have no rights or guarantees against it. Second, because Rousseau thinks that those who refuse to obey the general will should be forced to do so and that thus (as he puts it in an infamous phrase) they "will be forced to be free."[3] Third, because Rousseau's legislator is taken to be a totalitarian manipulator. These scholars, I shall argue, are wrong in considering Rousseau a totalitarian and at the heart of their error lies a failure to understand correctly Rousseau's concept of the general will.

There is also another sort of misunderstanding of the general will that one finds from time to time in writings on Rousseau. Since Rousseau argues that the general will never errs, he is held to be saying simply that whenever the general will gives rise to a law that happens to be right or just, then we have a true case of the general will. If, on the other hand, the law turns out not to be right or just, then we do not have a case of the general will. In other words, it is all an empty matter of definition—a tautology. The general will is simply defined as that which tends to right or the common good. When it does not, it simply is not called the general will.[4] It follows from this, for many, that there is no independent and reliable way of actually telling what the general will is or whether it has been realized. This view also involves a fundamental misunderstanding of the general will. I shall argue that Rousseau gives us a clear mechanism—a set of institutions and procedures—which if carried out (and we can tell whether or not they have been carried out) will actually produce the general will, which will be right and tend to the common good.

Thus, I do not think that the general will, for Rousseau, is either totalitarian or a mere matter of definition. But aside from these gross misinterpretations, it seems to me that no one who has written on Rousseau, at least that I am aware of, has really understood the general will with the clarity that is required.

To understand the general will, we must understand the concept of sovereignty. For Rousseau, as for Hobbes, a sovereign is absolute. It is the highest power and authority. There can be no higher authority or power that limits the sovereign—if there is, then the sovereign simply would not be sovereign; the higher authority or power would. The sovereign cannot even be limited by its own earlier decisions. For these reasons, then, great care must be taken before establishing the sovereign in the first place. How is it conceivable to limit the power and authority of the sovereign? Such limits can come only from the nature of the sovereign itself. It can only be prevented from willing what it itself is incapable of willing. So, for Rousseau, the only possible defense against the sovereign is to see to it from the start that the sovereign (which expresses the general will) is constructed so that it can only will what is right.[5] If it can be guaranteed that the sovereign's nature is such that it can only will what is right—and I shall try to argue that given certain conditions this in fact will be the case—then no defense is needed against the sovereign. In fact, to ask for individual rights or guarantees against the sovereign would be to ask for exceptions on behalf of individuals to act contrary to what is right. Far from ensuring individual liberty, this would be to guarantee rights to act illegally, immorally, and against the common good. It might even be to guarantee social chaos. In Rousseau's view, one does not ask for rights or guarantees against the sovereign—that is not only impossible in fact but conceptually incoherent and senseless. Rights or guarantees against the sovereign would imply some power capable of restraining the sovereign, and if this power existed the sovereign would not be sovereign. This other power would be and then we would have the same problem again with this power. Instead, the only possibility is to construct a sovereign that can only do what is right such that there can be no reasonable objection to acting in accordance with it and such that it would be immoral not to.

Indeed, Rousseau makes what seem to be extravagant claims about the general will. He claims that the general will can never harm the individual; that it is always right and never unjust;[6] that it always tends to the common good, public utility, or the welfare of the whole; and that it always tends to equality.[7] But extravagant or not, I will argue that the general will, at least in *theory,* can do all of these things.[8]

Let us begin to explain the general will. In the first place, we must notice that the general will is not what Rousseau calls the "will of all." The general will expresses the common interest, but the will of all expresses the sum of private interests.[9] The will of all is the sum total of the different particular interests of the citizens; it is what is registered in any ordinary majority vote. The general will, then, is not the vote of the majority. The general will is always right, but an ordinary vote of the majority—the will of all or the sum of particular interests—is not necessarily so.[10] It is true that for the general will to manifest itself there *must be* a majority vote, but nevertheless the general will is *not* to be *identified* with an ordinary vote of the majority, as we shall shortly see.

At the same time, we must not view the general will as a disembodied abstraction unconnected to the individual and instead issuing from some mystical entity. The general will is the will of the individual. More precisely, individuals have two wills: a general will and a particular will. There is nothing odd or surprising about this. It is the same as saying that while individuals have private interests they can also be concerned with the general interest. They have two different interests that they care about even in those cases where these interests may be opposed and even in those cases where their private interests outweigh their concern for the general interest.[11]

The general will can manifest itself and do what it is supposed to do (always tend to right, equality, the common good, and so forth) given four conditions that Rousseau lays out in the *Social Contract,* but unfortunately not all in one place. Nevertheless, once we understand these conditions, the general will will be quite clear, not muddled or contradictory as some have claimed. Let us look at each of these conditions.

1. In the first place, all citizens must sit on the sovereign body—the legislature—and must vote on all issues.[12] There can be no representatives—each must vote in person.[13] Moreover, there should be no factions or associations. This is so because "the will of each of these associations becomes general with reference to its members and particular with reference to the State. One can say, then, that there are no longer as many voters as there are men, but merely as many as their are associations." Citizens must vote their own opinions as individuals. Factions, associations, or parties vote corporate interests. If, for example, there were only two parties, it would tend to be the case that there would be only two votes on each question and it would be nearly impossible for the individual wills of the citizens to be generalized. If, however, it is impossible to eliminate factions, then Rousseau wants as many factions as possible and he wants these factions to be as equal as possible.[14] Furthermore, all of the citizens must be adequately informed, but, again, so that factions and corporate interests do not predominate, the citizens should not discuss matters among themselves outside the assembly but only within it.[15]

2. The second condition is that "the general will, to be truly such, should be general in its object as well as in its essence; that it should come from all to apply to all; and that it loses its natural rectitude when it is directed toward an individual, determinate object." We have already seen that the general will is general in reference to its source—all citizens vote in deciding the general will. Now we must add that it must be general in reference to its object. In other words, if we are to arrive at the general will, the only sorts of questions that can be put to the sovereign body must be abstract and universal questions. As Rousseau puts it in the *Social Contract,* these questions cannot refer to individual persons or facts.[16] In the *Geneva Manuscript,* Rousseau implies an even stricter definition of universality. He says, "when a particular object has different relationships to different individuals, each one having its own will concerning this object, there is no general

will that is perfectly unified concerning this individual object." Here, he seems to suggest that abstraction and generality mean that the object must have the same or a similar relationship to all individuals in the state. In fact, in *Emile,* he actually says, "when the whole people makes a statute applying to the whole people, it considers only itself; and if a relation is formed, it is between the whole object seen from one point of view and the whole object seen from another point of view, without any division of the whole." He adds that laws must relate "equally to all the members of the state. . . ."[17]

3. There is a further condition concerning the way all questions must be put to the sovereign body. Besides being abstract and universal, they must have a specific form: they must ask "what is the general will on this matter?" or "what is the common good in this case?" The citizens must not be addressed so as to elicit their particular interests, but so as to elicit their general interest. As Rousseau says, "When a law is proposed in the assembly of the people, what they are being asked is not precisely whether they approve or reject the proposal, but whether it does or does not conform to the general will that is theirs. Each one expresses his opinion on this by voting, and the declaration of the general will is drawn from the counting of the votes."[18] The citizens, in being asked to cast a vote, are not being asked to express their particular interests; they are being asked to engage in a reflective, intellectual inquiry. As Rousseau puts it in the *Geneva Manuscript,* "the general will in each individual is a pure act of the understanding, which reasons in the silence of the passions. . . ."[19] The citizen is being asked to record an opinion as to what in fact is best for the state. If the majority votes differently than a given citizen, it would not be correct to say that this citizen was outvoted in the same way as would be the case if we were considering an ordinary majority vote—it would not be correct to say that an interest contrary to this citizen's prevailed.

Rather, as Rousseau is quite correct to say, "when the opinion contrary to mine prevails, that proves nothing except that I was mistaken, and what I thought to be the general will was not. If my private will had prevailed, I would have done something other than what I wanted."[20] In other words, the question must be put so as to ask the citizen to reflect on an intellectual matter—the citizen must give an opinion on what is right. Such an opinion quite conceivably could be mistaken. But the citizens—insofar as they do seek the common good and insofar as the general will really is their will—are properly concerned with what is right more than with their own vote and they realize that the majority is more likely to be right than any given individual.[21] Thus we see that for the general will to manifest itself, a vote of the majority is required. But this vote is quite unlike an ordinary majority vote where citizens register their particular interests.

4. The final condition is that all laws must be rigorously and equally enforced, and all citizens must realize when they are voting that this will be the case. As Rousseau says, "everyone necessarily subjects himself to the conditions he imposes on others," and, as he puts it in *Emile,* it would be desirable if "the laws of nations could, like those of nature, have an inflexibility that no human force could ever conquer."[22] If each citizen knows that they and all others will be strictly bound by the law they are voting on, they will take great care to see that it is right and equal for all.[23]

If these four conditions are given, the general will can do all that Rousseau says it will. What is required here, as Rousseau puts it in the *Geneva Manuscript,* is "the art of generalizing ideas."[24] The point is to address only a person's abstract, reflective, long-term, rational interest, not his or her personal, particular, immediate, selfish interest. The citizens must be made to reflect about what it would be like if everyone always acted in a certain way. They must be made to consider the action as a universal and necessary principle—as a categorical imperative, to use the language that Kant will later develop.

If the citizens do this, then even thieves (to take just one example) would vote against theft. However, if you were to address only their particular interests; if you were to ask thieves whether a particular act of theft was right; you might very well get some remarkably convincing justifications of those particular acts of theft. But if you address the abstract, reflective, long-term, rational interest even of thieves; if you ask whether in general, in all cases, everyone should be allowed to steal; if you ask them whether theft should always be permitted by laws that are rigorously and equally enforced as if they were laws of nature; then even thieves would vote against theft—or at least a majority would. Some individuals will be unable to put aside their particular, immediate, selfish interests; some individuals will be unable to vote their general interest in the abstract case; but a majority will be able to do so. Here it is very important to remember that individuals have two sorts of interest: a particular or selfish interest and a general interest. This general interest is *not* simply the interest of *others* in opposition to one's *own self*-interest. The general interest, for Rousseau, is the individual's *own* interest. Individuals can obviously be concerned with the common good of the society in which they live and wish to have this common good realized. The general interest is the individual's *self*-interest just as much as is their particular interest.

Individuals can have this general interest at the same time that they have particular, selfish interests that diverge from or even contradict their general interest. Whether they vote their general interest or their particular interest is a complex matter that will depend upon a great many things. One of the things it depends upon is what sort of question is put to the individual—does the question elicit the individual's particular interests or the individual's general interest?

For Rousseau, there is no guarantee that individuals will decide, as they should, for their general interest over their particular interest. Rousseau can only argue that, given the right conditions, which we shall continue to discuss as we go, the *majority* of the citizens will side with their common general interest. Part of the reason for this is that when asked to speculate on what the general interest is, those citizens who fail to vote for the general interest, who instead vote their particular interests, will nevertheless come down on different sides of the issue: in voting their particular interests some will vote yes and others no, and these votes will cancel each other out, thus allowing the general interest to triumph. This is what Rousseau means, I think, when he says concerning the sum of private wills, "take away from these same wills the pluses and minuses that cancel each other out, and the remaining sum of the differences is the general will."[25]

Thus, the vote of a majority is necessary to produce the general will, but the general will is not an ordinary majority vote where each is expected to vote only their own self-interest. The majority must vote their interest concerning what they take to be right in the abstract case if the general will is to manifest itself. The difference between Rousseau's general will and Kant's categorical imperative is that for Rousseau the citizens are expected to vote their interest in the general abstract case—their long-term interest as citizens of a community rather than their immediate interests as particular persons. For Kant, interest must not determine us at all.[26]

Rousseau also says, "the general will is always right and always tends toward the public utility. But it does not follow that the people's deliberations always have the same rectitude."[27] What Rousseau means here, I think, is that if the question posed is abstract and of the form "what is the common good in this case?", the general will can emerge and always be right. But we must notice that there are other types of ordinary issues that the sovereign body must consider and that they cannot be posed in this same form—Rousseau refers to these as "deliberations." For example, one of the questions that the sovereign body must take up at each sitting is, "Does it please the people to leave the administration in the hands of those who are currently responsible for it?"[28] This is not an abstract question—it refers to particular persons and it may well call forth the particular interests of the voters. Thus, there is no guarantee that the answer to it will be right. The answer will not be an expression of the general will; it will merely be an expression of what Rousseau calls the "people's deliberations" or the will of all.

Also we can now see more clearly that Rousseau's opposition to factions and to discussion outside the assembly should not be taken as an attempt to oppress citizens by prohibiting them from organizing to defend or advance their legitimate concerns. Rather, it is an attempt to see that they do such things in and through a body that concerns itself with the common good and is always right instead of through small factions that pursue corporate interests and thereby may oppose the common good. Moreover, factions, associations, or parties can hinder the general will from forming because even when abstract questions of the form "what is the common good in this case?" are asked, corporate interests may well be powerful enough to prevent the individuals' answers from being an expression of their general interest and thus from being right.

However, we must now notice the way in which self-interest is crucial for Rousseau. The general will could not be realized without it. This may seem confusing. But despite all I have said about the fact that citizens must vote their general interest rather than their particular interest, this must be understood in a very specific way. One way to avoid self-interest would be to try to suppress it or eliminate it totally. This we must not do. Self-interest in a certain sense is at the very heart of the general will. One reason that anyone—including thieves—votes against theft is because they know that if theft were allowed they might well be the victim of an act of theft, and their self-interest revolts at this. As Rousseau says, "Why is the general will always right and why do all constantly want the happiness of each, if not because there is no one who does not apply this word *each* to himself, and does not think of himself as he votes for all? Which proves that the equality of right, and the concept of justice it produces, are derived from each man's preference for himself and consequently from the nature of man. . . ."[29] Self-interest must be present—people must think of themselves—but they must consider their self-interest in the abstract case where laws will be rigorously and equally enforced for all.

Self-interest must not be eliminated; it must be transformed. If one's self-interest is considered rationally only in the long-term, abstract case, then self-interest becomes, or at least comes to agree with, the general interest. In answering the question, "what is the general will in this case?", the citizens do, of course, consider and seek the common good in a positive sense; but they also, in a negative sense, consider their self-interest. They reflect upon what harm might occur to them if a law (that would be rigorously and equally enforced for all) were or were not to pass. They try to imagine in the abstract case any possible harm they might suffer—which would be much the same sort of harm that any and every citizen might suffer—if this law were or were not passed. If theft were allowed, then I—or any other citizen—might be the victim of an act of theft. Here, self-interest coincides with the general interest. The fact that I might be the victim of an act of theft would be unacceptable to my self-interest; the fact that others might be victims of an act of theft would be incompatible with my concern for the general interest. If my concern for the general interest or my understanding of it are not enough to cause me to vote against theft, my self-interest will be enough to do so and it will lead me toward the general interest.

It can, of course, be the case that the individual's particular interest differs from the common good or the general interest. One reason for this could be that social conditions are such that laws will affect individuals differently. If there is serious inequality in property, status, or classes, voting to *allow* theft might not only appeal to my immediate selfish interest, but it might even tend to agree with my long-term interest, and if propertylessness and poverty were widespread enough in this society, theft might even agree with the common interest of the majority. Thus, for one's particular interest and the common good to have any chance of agreeing, and for the general interest of all to agree, laws must affect all citizens equally, or at least similarly. For Rousseau, this will require, as we shall see, relatively equal property, as well as a common set of healthy customs and religious views.

At this point, perhaps we can better understand Rousseau's seemingly paradoxical claim that citizens can be "forced to be free."[30] In the first place this simply means that the community can force its citizens to obey the laws. This is certainly not totalitarian—it is not even unusual. All societies do it. But this community is a bit different from other societies. Here each and every citizen has voted on the laws they are expected to obey. In being forced to obey laws that the citizens have given themselves, the citizens certainly should be considered to

74   *Chapter Three*

be freer than would be the case otherwise. But even further, here the general will guarantees, at least in theory, that these laws will be rational and in accord with right. This, in Rousseau's view, ensures that the citizens will be free in obeying them. Rousseau does not understand freedom in the way that the liberal tradition does. Civil freedom does not simply mean being unhindered in the pursuit of one's inclinations or desires. That is to be a slave to one's appetites. To be free requires acting from rational and moral principles. Only in that way is one self-determined.[31] Thus, if inclination leads individuals to make an exception for themselves in violating a law, to force them to obey these laws (as any society would), is to force them, in Rousseau's community, to obey the rational and moral laws they have given themselves, and thus it makes some sense to say that they are being forced to be free.

But what if it is the case that the citizen is forced to obey a law that that citizen originally voted against? Can we still say that this citizen is being forced to be free? If it is the case that in voting on this law, the citizen had been asked to speculate upon what is right rather than record a particular interest; and if it is the case that the majority of the citizens, following the procedures that have been outlined above for the realization of the general will, are more likely to come up with what is right than the individual alone is;[32] and if the citizen really has two wills, one that seeks particular interests and one that seeks the general interest (only the latter of which makes for freedom and which is the one the citizen wants to act upon), then even in being forced to obey the law that the citizen voted against, the citizen, we can legitimately say, is being forced to be free. In other words, if disobedient citizens do believe that a specific law really is the general will, which is to say that it really is rational and right, even if these citizens did not vote for it, then if these citizens are forced to obey this law when inclination would lead them to make an exception for themselves, it is legitimate to say that they have been forced to be free (of course these citizens would be even freer if they were also inclined to follow the law).

The only problem arises, it seems to me, in the case where a citizen is firmly convinced that the law in question is not right; that is, that it is not the general will. This, we must see, is possible. Rousseau is not, in the fashion of Hobbes, simply defining right as whatever the sovereign decides is right. Right is not arbitrarily established by authority. Rousseau is outlining a procedure that if followed will ensure that the sovereign discovers what actually is right. If it fails to do this—if the four conditions necessary for the realization of the general will have not been given—then the citizens are not free in obeying this law whether they are forced or not.[33] This is a problem that Rousseau does not discuss in the *Social Contract*, though he does in the *Government of Poland*. We shall consider it at the end of this chapter.

II. Individual and Community

As I have said, I do not think that Rousseau is a totalitarian. Many of the scholars who label him as such begin by being disturbed that Rousseau does not hold to a liberal model of individual liberty, and since he thus falls outside the liberal tradition—the only acceptable tradition for them—they are led to categorize him as a collectivist or a totalitarian. But Rousseau simply is not a liberal and to try to discuss him in liberal categories—including liberal categories of what is opposed to liberalism—will distort Rousseau's thought. He simply is neither a liberal nor a totalitarian.

For example, one of the mistakes frequently made by these scholars is to take the general will as a collective entity existing on its own and to see Rousseau as requiring that the individual identify totally with this entity—that the individual be totally absorbed into it to the point where the individual's own interests and liberties are annihilated. The only interests and liberties are those of the collective entity.[34] This is hardly the case for Rousseau. It is not the case that the general will is a collective entity that overpowers and absorbs individuals, their interests, and their liberty. Rather, the general will comes about only by, and is nothing else than, the will of individuals themselves reflecting in a rational and almost Kantian fashion on their own long-term interests. This is quite individualistic. Moreover, as I have pointed out above, it is crucial to see that individual self-interest is essential to the realization of the general will. Besides these individualistic elements, we find that as a second step the general will must also be reinforced by a sense of community, a sense of commitment to the common good; as well as customs, traditions, and religion that both make up and support this community.

We might be able to understand this better if we consider a set of concepts that come from the German philosophical tradition. This tradition—represented especially by Tönnies, but also Hegel, Marx, and others—distinguishes between two forms of society: a *Gemeinschaft* and a *Gesellschaft*. In a *Gesellschaft*, individuals are basic, primary, and natural; whereas society is secondary, artificial, and derivative. The nature, the interests, and the liberties of equal, atomic individuals precede society, at least conceptually, and society is established by a contract and regulated by abstract general laws. Society must satisfy the nature, interests, and liberties of these individuals—that is society's purpose as well as the principle of its legitimacy. Here individuals tend to relate to each other externally and often selfishly and competitively. Hobbes and Locke would be good examples of theorists of this sort of society.

In a *Gemeinschaft*, on the other hand, it is the social community that is taken to be basic, primary, and natural. It precedes, at least conceptually, individuals, who only develop as individuals, only become fully human beings, in and through the social community. Human beings are social by nature and they only realize their nature in society. In a community, individuals are linked to each other by internal bonds of feeling based upon custom, tradition, habit, and religion. A good example of a theorist of this sort of society would be Aristotle.

The German philosophical tradition also distinguishes between two forms of morality: *Moralität* and *Sittlichkeit*. *Moralität* is individual, rational, and reflective morality. It is based on individual autonomy and personal conviction. For Hegel, *Moralität* begins with Socrates and reaches its high point with Kant. *Sittlichkeit*, on the other hand, is ethical behavior grounded in natural custom, tradition, and religion. It is based on habit and imitation in accordance with the objective laws and traditions of the community. Personal reflection and analysis have little to do with *Sittlichkeit*. It is best represented, for Hegel, in the Greek *polis* before Socrates.

We find a good example of the difference between *Sittlichkeit* and *Moralität* in Plato's "Myth of Er." There we find a man about to select his next reincarnated life. We discover that in his previous life he had been a good man but only because he had been brought up in a good city. His ethical behavior had been based upon custom, tradition, habit, and upbringing; that is, *Sittlichkeit;* not upon philosophy, reason, or reflection, not *Moralität*. He behaved properly, but it was not the case that he knew what was right nor did he perform actions because they were right. Consequently he chose the life of a grand tyrant without noticing that it would involve eating his own children.[35]

Those who argue that Rousseau is a totalitarian overlook the elements of *Gesellschaft* and *Moralität* in his social theory. They emphasize almost exclusively the elements of *Gemeinschaft* and *Sittlichkeit* that are found there. We must notice that both sets of elements are present and that Rousseau wants to combine these elements. Indeed, roughly speaking, we can say that Books I and II of the *Social Contract* primarily describe a *Gesellschaft* and emphasize *Moralität*, whereas Books III and IV try to supplement and reinforce these elements by building up elements of *Gemeinschaft* and *Sittlichkeit*. For Rousseau, citizens are free only if the customs that shape inclination, feeling, and desire are in accord with reason and the general will. If citizens are to be free and happy, they cannot be forced, or at least they cannot be continuously and systematically forced, to follow reason against their inclinations and desires. Customs and the general will must be in agreement.

In Books I and II of the *Social Contract*, we can see that Rousseau is concerned with a *Gesellschaft* and *Moralität*. We see this in his discussion of individuals in the state of nature, in the way in which they artificially establish society through a social contract, in the rational reflection through which individuals without communicating among themselves outside the assembly reflect abstractly on what is right, in the abstract and equal laws that arise out of the general will, and generally in the individualism that pervades all these elements—most clearly where Rousseau tells us that self-interested reflection (the consideration of how one might be harmed by any specific law) is crucial for the realization of the general will.[36]

But at the same time Rousseau is concerned with building a *Gemeinschaft* and *Sittlichkeit*. As he says, "To these . . . laws is added . . . the most important of all; which is not engraved on marble or bronze, but in the hearts of the citizens; which is the true constitution of the State; which . . . preserves a people in the spirit of its institution, and imperceptibly substitutes the force of habit for that of authority. I am speaking of mores, customs, and especially of opinion—a part of the laws unknown to our political theorists, but on which the success of all the others depends. . . ."[37] For Rousseau, healthy customs are necessary and important: freedom is impossible without them.[38] So also virtue, patriotism, and bonds of solidarity are crucial.

The link between *Gemeinschaft* and *Gesellschaft*, *Sittlichkeit* and *Moralität* might best be seen by looking again for a moment at the third condition required for the realization of the general will. As we have seen, all questions put to the assembly must have a specific form: they must ask "what is the general will on this matter?" or "what is the common good in this case?" Here all the individual, rational, and reflective aspects are present. Each individual citizen is asked to reflect alone. No factions or discussion outside the assembly are allowed.

Each is being asked to engage in an abstract and rational inquiry concerning what is right. And each, at least as a part of their reflection, considers in a self-interested way how they might be harmed by the proposed law. But at the same time each individual is forging a link to the community; valuing the common good above particular interest; trusting that the community is more capable of discovering objective right than the individual alone; and willing to admit that if the majority votes differently, the individual was mistaken. In this way, as Rousseau puts it elsewhere, individuals learn "never to consider their persons except as related to the body of the State, and not to perceive their own existence, so to speak, except as part of the State's" and then "they will eventually come to identify themselves in some way with this larger whole; to feel themselves to be members of the homeland; to love it with that delicate sentiment that any isolated man feels only for himself; to elevate their soul perpetually toward this great object; and thereby to transform into a sublime virtue this dangerous disposition from which all our vices arise."[39]

The ideal is to combine *Gesellschaft* and *Gemeinschaft*. One or the other is not acceptable for Rousseau. We might slip away from this ideal balance in two ways. We might fall away from the ideal by deciding to elect representatives to the legislative assembly. The waning of patriotism, the predominance of private interest over concern for the general interest, the domination of private over public affairs, lack of concern about affairs of state, Rousseau argues, lead citizens to institute representatives.[40] Here elements of *Gemeinschaft*—patriotic sentiment, public commitment, and the concern for the common good that grows out of direct and active political participation—are lost and customs begin to deteriorate; though, on the other hand, elements of *Gesellschaft*—individualism, self-interest, abstract rational law, and moral reflection—may well remain.

On the other hand, we might fall short of the ideal, as the Greeks did, by instituting slavery.[41] Here it would be possible to preserve *Gemeinschaft* at least for the citizens. They would have the free time for direct and active political participation and thus be able to maintain the predominance of public spirit and patriotism over private interests and affairs, but they would lose crucial elements of *Gesellschaft*. They would lose the equality of individuals and abstract equal laws, and thus the general will would deteriorate.

In Rousseau's society, healthy customs, traditions, and public opinion would be maintained by a censorial tribunal that, far from being totalitarian, should not and even cannot attempt to create, change, or reestablish customs and traditions. It merely declares what custom and tradition currently are and thus tries to preserve them by slowing down their corruption.[42] Custom and tradition would also be reinforced by a civil religion that combines a simple, inner, personal commitment, without intolerance or superstition, with a sentiment of sociability and respect for the laws.[43]

There is another crucial matter that we must discuss here and that is Rousseau's view of property. Rousseau rejects unequal private property, a great gap between rich and poor, and extensive commerce or trade. He sees them as serious threats to the general will and to the customs and traditions necessary to reinforce it.

While Rousseau is willing to accept property held in common, he prefers private property that is relatively, though not absolutely, equal for all citizens.[44] All citizens should be self-sufficient—they should have as much as they need, but no more than they need. Moreover, to have a right to hold property, citizens must labor upon it themselves.[45] No one should be wealthy enough to hire another, nor poor enough to have to work for another.[46] Rousseau envisions a society of self-sufficient artisans and farmers. He opposes wealth, trade, and commerce because they involve a most powerful form of particular interest that is capable of drawing the citizens away from the realm of public affairs and locking them into the realm of private ones.[47] Rousseau stands in the tradition of Plato and Aristotle for whom wealth is a corrupting force. Rousseau—always enamored of paradox—even suggests that if a society were unfortunate enough to possess great natural wealth, then it should dump its surplus wealth onto the executive—the Prince. Since wealth corrupts; it is better to corrupt the Prince rather than all the citizens.[48]

Wealth feeds self-interest and erodes the citizen's commitment to the public sphere. It will corrupt customs, tradition, and patriotism, which then will no longer be able to reinforce the general will. Moreover, it can even erode the general will directly. It will mean that many laws will not fulfill the second condition for the realization of the general will; they will not apply to all equally and thus the individuals' particular interests may tend to disagree with their general interest. This will make it all the more difficult for the citizens to transcend their particular interests in order to concern themselves with abstract questions. It will also make it more difficult for them to fulfill the third condition for the realization of the general will—the need to ask "what is the common good?" or "what is the general will?" instead of "what do I want?" It will make factions all the more likely; it will promote inequality; and may even lead to the introduction of representatives.[49] Moreover, while I have tried to argue that it is theoretically plausible that the general will can always reach the right decision about moral matters like theft, it is not plausible to expect that the general will could avoid particular interests and always be right about the sorts of complex, tangled, and difficult property disputes that would arise out of a developed system of commerce and trade. For this reason alone, Rousseau must rule them out.

This ancient conception of wealth—the notion that commerce, trade, property, and wealth feed particular interest and irrevocably corrupt the customs, traditions, and patriotism of citizens—is the key, I think, to Rousseau's utopianism. Rousseau has no theory of how socially to transform and mold customs—for that we will have to wait for Hegel. Once customs become corrupt, all is lost. Healthy customs, capable of drawing citizens out of private interests and affairs, capable of attracting them to public affairs and the common good, and thus capable of reinforcing the general will, must just be given in a society if that society is to have any chance to succeed. Rousseau does not think that undesirable customs can be reformed. As he says, "A thousand nations that have flourished on earth could never have tolerated good laws, and even those that could were only so disposed for a very short time during their entire existence. Most peoples, like men, are docile only in their youth. They become incorrigible as they grow older. Once customs are established and prejudices have taken root, it is a dangerous and foolhardy undertaking to want to reform them. The people cannot even tolerate having their ills touched for the purpose of destroying them. . . ."[50] The ideal state of Rousseau's *Social Contract* is utopian in the sense that it cannot be realized in a modern developed society; such societies have already become corrupt and it is impossible to reform them. The ideal state could only be installed in a relatively "primitive" and undeveloped society if the proper customs just happen to be present there already.

Had Rousseau, like Adam Smith and many others after him, been able to argue that a conflict of private interests leads to the common good, might he have avoided this utopianism?[51] In a market economy with a developed division of labor, Smith argued, each must depend upon others to satisfy their needs. But despite this interdependence, each attends only to their own self-interest. They seek only their own personal profit; they pay little attention to others; they only infrequently cooperate with them consciously; and they do not concern themselves with the common good. Nevertheless, for Smith, this self-seeking not only leads to a common good but does so much more effectively than if individuals had consciously and cooperatively sought to realize the common good in the first place. Active, aggressive, competitive self-seeking, given the economic interdependence of each upon all, produces the common good—the wealth of the nation—out of which each struggles to gain a share. Self-seeking, through an invisible hand, Smith says, produces this common good more effectively than consciously seeking to produce it would.[52]

We must notice that the general will, for Rousseau, involves at least a hint of Smith's model. The general will is after all a procedure for transforming particular interest into the common good. Citizens do not consciously, cooperatively, and altruistically decide upon the good and then act on it—at least they do not do so directly and immediately. Instead they reflect on their self-interest in the abstract case; they imagine how they might be harmed if they were victims of a particular law. This self-interest leads them to the common good, which they only then become conscious of, cooperatively establish, and allow to grow into custom and tradition. But while Rousseau is willing to employ this sort of model for the general will, he does not apply it to the socioeconomic realm, to a theory for the transformation of customs (as Hegel will), or to history (as both Kant and Hegel will). Can we say that Rousseau was simply unaware of the possibilities of this model? And if he had been aware of them, would he have been able to use this model to avoid utopianism and to locate his ideal society in a modern state? I do not think so. Einaudi suggests that Rousseau was aware of notions in the writings of Melon that approximated Smith's model and that Rousseau rejected them totally.[53] Moreover, Smith's model applied to the socioeconomic realm would introduce a competitive market economy incompatible with the strong bonds of community, moral solidarity, and equality that Rousseau desires.

Furthermore, Rousseau, I think, would be very much opposed to the notion of a common good arising behind one's back, unintended, or through an invisible hand. There is, I have said, something of this involved in the general will—self-interest is necessary so that it can be transformed into a general interest—but once the general will has appeared, then the citizens should act on the good for the sake of the good. They should do what is right because it is right. Rousseau wants a community that consciously pursues the common good and he wants customs that reinforce this pursuit. Thus Rousseau is a utopian, not through ignorance, but due to principle.

Rousseau does seem to be more aware of certain aspects of social theory than either Hobbes or Locke were. He is more aware of how customs and traditions depend upon, grow out of, and are crucially necessary to reinforce political institutions. Locke, it may seem, was much more adept in other areas of social theory. Locke was able to use social theory to explain how to limit the political power of the government.[54] The more coherence one is able to find among individuals at the social level—that is, apart from the governmental sphere of political power—the less power one need grant to the government. If one has no social theory at all or is able to find no social coherence among individuals outside the political sphere, then the only power capable of holding individuals together is political or governmental power. Here, as for Hobbes, who has no social theory at all, the sovereign must be absolute. If, on the other hand, one has a highly developed social theory and finds enough coherence at the social level, then one might even begin to talk about the withering away of the political state as Marx does. For Locke, the social coherence provided by property and property interest allowed him to argue for a limited government. Society was even capable of holding together while individuals replaced one government with another through revolution—something that appeared impossible to Hobbes. Rousseau, whether or not he would be willing to admit that property and property interest of the sort found in Locke's social theory are able to limit sovereignty, nevertheless finds property interest and seriously unequal property totally unacceptable. One is tempted to say that here we must just choose between two incompatible possibilities in the area of social theory. One can either allow unequal property, property interest, trade, and commerce and thus be able to limit sovereign power; or one rejects these and decides for community, equality, and customs that reinforce patriotism, public commitment, and a concern for the common good. Rousseau maintains, with the ancients, that wealth is a corrupting force and abhors the rise of particular interest that Locke's society would produce. But it follows from this, then, that Rousseau has no way to limit sovereign power.

It might seem, as I have just suggested, that one must just make a choice here between two options that have equal but opposing strengths and weaknesses. But I do not think this is the case. I argued in Chapter 2 that Locke's social theory, when pushed to its conclusions, does not really limit governmental power in an unacceptable way. It limits governmental power with respect to the propertied classes, but not with respect to the propertyless, and in effect it makes the propertied classes sovereign against the propertyless.[55] Whether or not Rousseau saw this in Locke's social theory, he definitely saw that it was the case in fact—the whole last part of the *Discourse on Inequality* argues this very thesis as we shall see in the next section.[56] Rousseau saw clearly that property and property interest could not effectively limit sovereign power in a legitimate and equal way. Consequently he had to accept an absolute sovereign as Hobbes did. Since sovereign power could not be limited, the only alternative to a Hobbesian sovereign, then, was to take great care in constituting this sovereign so that it could not harm the citizens.

Thus Rousseau developed his theory of the general will as a guarantee that the sovereign would always be right and thus that one could not reasonably or morally object to a power that always acted in accordance with right. It is not that Rousseau is a totalitarian at heart as so many argue; it is rather that he thinks very clearly and takes the only possible conceptually coherent alternative open to him. And once he decides for the general will as the only acceptable alternative, then custom and tradition become all the more important to reinforce the general will. This, however, has the consequence of making Rousseau's theory utopian. All he can do is hope to preserve healthy customs and traditions when they already exist and thus he needs institutions like a censorial tribunal and civil religion to reinforce them. These institutions draw accusations of totalitarianism from some. I have tried to argue that they are wrong about this, but more importantly it seems to me that they have not carefully followed the course of Rousseau's thought and have not understood the options open to him. It seems to me that Rousseau took the proper course as well as the only possible one.

III. The *Social Contract* and the *Discourse on Inequality*

Some scholars argue that the views Rousseau expresses in the *Social Contract* are inconsistent with those expressed in his earlier *Discourse on Inequality*—that in the *Social Contract* Rousseau's views are collectivist and totalitarian whereas in the *Second Discourse* he endorses a radical form of individual liberty.[57] I have already argued that the *Social Contract* is not totalitarian; now I would like to argue that the *Social Contract* and the *Second Discourse* are not inconsistent.

We must begin by noticing that the state of nature, as Rousseau conceives it in the *Second Discourse*, is divided into four stages. In stage one there are no social relations at all—individuals simply live in isolation. There are no families, but only casual mating; there is no communication among individuals, nor even language; there is no property of any kind; and there are no conceptions of good or evil.[58] The human being is basically an animal.[59] Contrary to Hobbes, for whom there are no stages in the state of nature, in this first stage, for Rousseau, there can be no war simply because there is nothing to fight over. There is nothing worth attacking or defending. If you happen to confront someone at one fruit tree, it is just too easy to move on to the next.[60] On the other hand, stage one does resemble the first stage of Locke's state of nature in that no personal property exists.

With increased population and the development of a certain amount of scarcity, we move into stage two. Here we begin to find loose associations established for hunting and simple property in the form of huts.[61] But, as in the second stage of Locke's state of nature, unequal property has not developed yet; and, in opposition to Hobbes, while there may be some fighting in this stage, it does not amount to a war of all against all. These simple huts are not worth attacking or defending when others can be built so easily. Here families develop, as do language, moral sentiment, and customs.[62] Rousseau finds this second stage to be the ideal:

> This is precisely the point reached by most of the savage peoples known to us, and it is for want of having sufficiently distinguished between ideas and noticed how far these peoples already were from the first state of nature that many have hastened to conclude that man is naturally cruel, and that he needs civilization in order to make him gentler. On the contrary, nothing is so gentle as man in his primitive state when, placed by nature at equal distances from the stupidity of brutes and the fatal enlightenment of civil man . . . this period of the development of human faculties, maintaining a golden mean between the indolence of the primitive state and the petulant activity of our vanity, must have been the happiest and most durable epoch. The more one thinks about it, the more one finds that this state was the least subject to revolutions, the best for man, and that he must have come out of it only by some fatal accident, which for the common good ought never to have happened. The example of savages, who have almost all been found at this point seems to confirm that the human race was made to remain in it always. . . .[63]

Stage three arises with the development of agriculture and metallurgy. Rousseau argues that if only one of these arts has developed it is still possible to remain in stage two. But with both, surplus production and division of labor arise; it becomes possible for one person to possess enough for two; unequal private property develops; and tensions arise between rich and poor.[64] Here we have arrived at the third stage of Locke's state of nature, where we find unequal property, and here we now have something to fight over. Individuals will be willing to stand and protect their land or perhaps attack their neighbor's. We are now ready for Hobbes's war of all against all,[65] which we might call the fourth stage of the state of nature. Out of this fourth stage will arise a social contract, but for Rousseau it is an illegitimate one. Some wealthy individual,

> Destitute of valid reasons to justify himself and of sufficient force to defend himself . . . [he] finally conceived the most deliberate project that ever entered the human mind. It was to use in his favor the very forces of those who attacked him, to make his defenders out of his adversaries . . . To this end, after having shown his neighbors the horror of a situation that made them all take up arms against one another, that made their possessions as burdensome as their needs, and in which no one found security in either poverty or wealth, he easily invented specious reasons to lead them to his goal. "Let us unite," he says to them, "to protect the weak from oppression, restrain the ambitious, and secure for everyone the possession of what belongs to him. Let us institute regulations of justice and peace to which all are obliged to conform. . . ."[66]

The question we must deal with here is how we can move from the illegitimate contract of the *Second Discourse* to the legitimate one of the *Social Contract*. There are passages in Rousseau's works that suggest that this is impossible. "Once peoples are accustomed to masters, they are no longer able to do without them. If they try to shake off the yoke, they move all the farther away from freedom because, mistaking for freedom an unbridled license which is its opposite, their revolutions almost always deliver them to seducers who only make their chains heavier."[67] Certainly there are masters toward the end of stage three and in stage four, and if so, it is impossible to remove them effectively. Moreover, these masters would be the very force, Rousseau suggested in the passage quoted above, that would work for an illegitimate social contract in their own interest. Again, in another passage already quoted above, Rousseau argues that once customs have been corrupted it is "dangerous and foolhardy" to try to reform them. "People cannot even tolerate having their ills touched for the purpose of destroying them. . . ."[68]

What is clear, I think, is that it would be impossible to move from stage four of the *Second Discourse* to the legitimate society of the

Social Contract. But, on the other hand, what if the social contract were to arise out of stage two, or even stage three before it had moved too far along toward inequality and the corruption of customs? This again would be quite utopian, but it certainly is a conceptual possibility. Moreover, there is much in the *Social Contract* and the *Second Discourse* to suggest that this is what Rousseau has in mind. He suggests, we have seen, that it was only due to some "fatal accident" (which should never have occurred) that we left stage two.[69] Earlier he spoke of an age at which all would want to stop.[70] Later he tells us that what determines the form of government that will arise once the social contract has been established is the degree of inequality to be found in the state of nature when the society was formed.[71] This suggests that the social contract might arise earlier or later in stage three or perhaps even in stage two. This is suggested again in the *Social Contract,* where Rousseau tells us that if individuals unite before they possess anything, they may even hold land in common.[72] Also in the *Social Contract* he tells us that in Europe there is still one country capable of legislation, namely, Corsica.[73] In the *Constitutional Project for Corsica,* Rousseau describes the "primitive" simplicity of Corsica and his general program is to encourage Corsica to develop its agriculture but not commerce or trade.[74] In other words, his project is to keep it from developing very far into the inequality of stage three and certainly to prevent it from reaching stage four.[75]

But there is a problem here. If, in the *Second Discourse,* a social contract does not arise except out the state of war that develops in stage four of the state of nature, how, when we move to the *Social Contract,* could we expect it to arise earlier? How, at least for Rousseau, could we even expect the notion of a social contract and a general will to occur to "primitive" people? The sort of society described in the *Social Contract* requires highly developed rational abilities if the general will is to be able to function, whereas it is clearly Rousseau's view that reason had not developed yet in the early stages of the state of nature. Even further, when it does first develop it comes as a force of corruption. Rousseau says,

> Reason engenders vanity and reflection fortifies it; reason turns man back upon himself, it separates him from all that bothers and afflicts him. Philosophy isolates him; because of it he says in secret, at the sight of a suffering man: Perish if you will, I am safe. No longer can anything except dangers to the entire society trouble the tranquil sleep of the philosopher and tear him from his bed. His fellow-man can be murdered with

impunity right under his window; he has only to put his hands over his ears and argue with himself a bit to prevent nature, which revolts within him, from identifying him with the man who is being assassinated. Savage man does not have this admirable talent, and for want of wisdom and reason he is always seen heedlessly yielding to the first sentiment of humanity.[76]

Thus, if a people has developed reason, they have already been corrupted and the ideal society of the *Social Contract* would be impossible, whereas if they have not yet developed reason they could not dream up, let alone institute, the general will.

However, Rousseau is quite aware of this difficulty. He speaks in the *Second Discourse* of rules that "reason is later forced to re-establish upon other foundations when, by its successive developments, it has succeeded in stifling nature."[77] In other words, after reason has developed and has stifled nature, it must, at a later period, reestablish itself on other foundations—by which Rousseau means, I think, the general will. Rousseau is aware of the problems involved here: individuals at earlier stages of the state of nature, when they are still capable of having a good society, are at that point incapable of instituting it themselves. What is the solution here? The solution, I think, is the legislator.[78] As Rousseau says in the section of the *Social Contract* dealing with the legislator,

> Wise men who want to use their own language, rather than that of the common people, cannot be understood by the people. Now there are a thousand kinds of ideas that are impossible to translate into the language of the people. Overly general views and overly remote objects are equally beyond its grasp. Each individual, appreciating no other aspect of government than the one that relates to his private interest, has difficulty perceiving the advantages he should obtain from the continual deprivations imposed by good laws. In order for an emerging people to appreciate the healthy maxims of politics, and follow the fundamental rules of statecraft, the effect would have to become the cause; the social spirit, which should be the result of the institution, would have to preside over the founding of the institution itself; and men would have to be prior to laws what they ought to become by means of laws. Since the legislator is therefore unable to use either force or reasoning, he must necessarily have recourse to another order of authority, which can win over without violence and persuade without convincing.[79]

The legislator is not an outcome of Rousseau's totalitarianism, but of his utopianism. The legislator, who is neither a magistrate in the government nor the sovereign,[80] must give laws to a "primitive" people that is unable to give them to itself. The legislator gives laws, not in the sense of particular laws—these can only arise from the general will—but in the sense of a general political constitution and of the conditions necessary for the realization of the general will, which nevertheless must still be approved by the people. As Rousseau says, "He who drafts the laws, therefore, does not or should not have any legislative right. And the people itself cannot, even if it wanted to, divest itself of this incommunicable right, because according to the fundamental compact, only the general will obligates private individuals, and one can never be assured that a private will is in conformity with the general will until it has been submitted to the free vote of the people. I have already said this, but it is not useless to repeat it."[81]

The *Social Contract* and the *Second Discourse* are not inconsistent and the legislator is not totalitarian as so many suggest. The *Social Contract* should be seen as a short chapter introduced by the legislator into the long history sketched in the *Second Discourse*. The tendency of that long history, we have seen, is to move toward the corruption, inequality, and conflict of stage four. The legislator is a means, not of preventing this decline permanently, for, as Rousseau even in the *Social Contract* says, this decline is inevitable,[82] but of slowing it down and holding it off for as long a time as possible. The legislator and the *Social Contract*, far from being opposed to the individual liberty of the *Second Discourse,* are a means toward preserving it beyond its natural term. They are also a means to stave off the corruption that reason inevitably undergoes if it develops on its own in the state of nature; they are an attempt to rechannel it, to allow it—through the general will—to arise in a healthy way and to avoid its natural corruption (but again only for a short time). Thus, the legislator, "One who dares to undertake the founding of a people[,] should feel that he is capable of changing human nature . . . of altering man's constitution in order to strengthen it . . . He must, in short, take away man's own forces in order to give him forces that are foreign to him . . . The more these natural forces are dead and destroyed, and the acquired ones great and lasting, the more the institution as well is solid and perfect."[83]

Moreover, it just is not the case for Rousseau that we find individual liberty only in the state of nature of the *Second Discourse* and not in developed societies like that of the *Social Contract*. In fact, in the *Government of Poland* we find a most extreme form of individual liberty, which, though not mentioned in the *Social Contract,* it seems to me, could be compatible with it. In the first place, we must see that the society described in the *Government of Poland*, in essence at least, is very much like or at least tends to approximate the society of the *Social Contract*. It is true that Rousseau's Poland will have a king, but it is not true that the king (or even the government in general) is the sovereign. For Rousseau, much as for Marx who follows him here, there should be no standing, professional army attached to the government. There should only be a citizen militia that keeps sovereign power in the hands of the people.[84] It is also true that not all citizens sit in the Polish legislative body, but it is not the case that this body is sovereign over against the people. Rousseau proposes that the members of the legislature—the Diet—be deputies rather than representatives and that it be made difficult for a deputy to return to even two consecutive sessions of the Diet. Deputies are not representatives; they are not sent to the Diet to voice their own sentiments as representatives would be. Instead, they are given very strict voting instructions by their constituents and are strictly accountable to them for carrying out these instructions. The deputies will not be returned to the Diet if they fail to carry out these instructions—they can even be punished for failing to do so. These instructions would be drafted and approved by local dietines in plenary sessions.[85] In this way, sovereignty is shifted toward the citizens organized in local dietines. Rousseau also advocates that in the future the masses be enfranchised in stages.[86] Rousseau's proposals for Poland, we might say, constitute a transitional program designed to tend toward the society of the *Social Contract*.

But even before the masses are enfranchised, Rousseau seems to think it possible for the general will to emerge in Poland. He says that the general will is "the product of the interplay of all sectional interests, combining with and balancing one another in all their variety."[87] This seems to suggest that with a proper representative sample of national opinion, the general will can emerge. This may seem odd, but even in the *Social Contract*, where Rousseau disapproved of factions because the will of these associations would be general with respect to the faction but less general than the will of the state as a whole; nevertheless, even there, if it was impossible to avoid factions, then Rousseau thought that the general will could still arise if factions were made as numerous as possible.[88] Sufficiently numerous factions, then, if they represented a general enough section of national opinion, could perhaps allow the general will to emerge in Poland; though clearly if all were enfranchised the will of the nation would be generalized more adequately. On the other hand, Rousseau does not explicitly state that the Diet must consider only abstract questions of the form, "what is the general will in this case?", though perhaps he does imply this.[89]

But at any rate, given the at least very rough approximation of the Polish constitution to that of the *Social Contract,* we can take up another matter. Rousseau goes on to discuss a very interesting traditional Polish institution—the *liberum veto.* Any member of the Diet has the right as an individual alone to veto the legislative decision of the whole Diet. But at the same time, Rousseau suggests, such persons must be made answerable for their veto not just to the local dietine but to a special tribunal that would either reward these individuals or condemn them to death.[90] This veto, it seems to me, could work just as well, if not better, in the society of the *Social Contract* where the general will very clearly exists.

While the fact that individual vetoers must face a tribunal that may condemn them to death is most objectionable and quite unacceptable; nevertheless, mixed up with this is something very interesting and very important. Despite this unacceptable threat of death, the *liberum veto*, one could argue, allows for far greater individual liberty than is conceivable in a liberal society. The *liberum veto* is possible only insofar as individuals are centered in a community and are responsible to that community. Liberal individualism, on the other hand, leaves the individual unfettered, unconnected to others, and not responsible to them in anything like the same sense as in a community. In a liberal society, individuals would not be allowed to assert their wills and affect others to the extent that such a veto allows. But as a committed member of the community, with the highest sense of responsibility to it, because the community is at the heart of the individual's being and concern, the individual can, for Rousseau, veto the will of the community if the individual is convinced that that will is harmful to the community. This is a check against the possibility of the failure of the general will and the consequent misdirection of the community. Individuals, for Rousseau, are free only in acting on rational laws in accord with right; that is, only in acting on the general will. Each individual, as committed member of the community, can veto its will if they are convinced that it is against the true will—the general will—of the community.

But it is crucial here that these individuals not be liberal individuals vetoing on behalf of their own self-interest, with little or no sense of responsibility to the community. They can veto only if the general will, the good of the community, is their highest aim. Hence, for Rousseau, something like a tribunal is necessary. But why should we expect this tribunal to know whether the veto truly accords with the general will any better than the vetoer or anyone else would? This is not Rousseau's point. The tribunal does not know the general will better than anyone else. This is not its function. There is no suggestion, for example, that the tribunal can *reverse* the veto if it decides it is wrong. All the tribunal can do is exert pressure ahead of time to restrain the vetoer from vetoing arbitrarily or for a self-interested reason. It creates another mechanism that can work toward the realization of the general will even when the legislature fails to realize the general will.

The death penalty that this tribunal can hand out is obviously very objectionable, but nevertheless, there is an important point involved here. Rousseau is showing us that a community can allow for much greater individualism, and more heroic individualism, than liberalism can. The liberal individual can neither harm nor benefit the group as much as a member of a community can. The latter's individual liberty can accomplish far more for either good or evil than the former's can. Thus, far from taking individual liberty less seriously than liberalism does, this is to take it far more seriously. I do not see how Rousseau can be called a totalitarian when he will allow individuals to veto the will of the community when they think it is mistaken. But they can veto the will of the community only in the interest of the community and any tendency to do otherwise must be restrained by something like a tribunal—though a death penalty is unacceptable.[91] On the other hand, this is all another example of Rousseau's utopianism.

Notes

1. My views on Rousseau are especially indebted to the graduate seminars that Professor Stanley Moore held and I attended in the early 1970s.

2. For example, F. Watkins, "Introduction" to *Rousseau: Political Writings* (Edinburgh: Thomas Nelson & Sons, 1953), xiii ff., xxix. E. Barker, "Introduction" to *Social Contract* (London: Oxford University Press, 1960), xxxviii. L.G. Crocker, "Introduction" to *The Social Contract and Discourse on the Origin and Foundation of Inequality Among Mankind* (New York: Washington Square Press, 1967), xxi–xxiii. L.G. Crocker, *Rousseau's Social Contract* (Cleveland: Case Western Reserve University Press, 1968). C.E. Vaughan, "Introduction" to *The Political Writings of Jean Jacques Rousseau* (Cambridge: Cambridge University Press, 1915), I, 4–5, 21, 48, 56–59, 112. J.L. Talmon, *The Origins of Totalitarian Democracy* (London: Secker & Warburg, 1952), Chapter 3.

3. *Social Contract,* in *On the Social Contract,* ed. R.D. Masters and tr. J.R. Masters (New York: St. Martin's, 1978), 55, 59 and *OC,* III, 364, 368.

4. See, for example, Vaughan, I, 66. Crocker, *Rousseau's Social Contract,* 69. M. Cranston, "Introduction" to *The Social Contract* (Harmondsworth: Penguin, 1968), 37. G.H. Sabine, *A History of Political Theory,* 3rd edition (London: G.G. Harrap, 1963), 591–92.

5. *Social Contract,* 54–55, 59 and *OC,* III, 362–63, 368.

6. *Social Contract,* 55, 61, 66–67 and *OC,* III, 363, 371, 379–80.

7. *Social Contract,* 59, 61, 63 and *OC,* III, 368, 371, 374. *Political Economy,* in *On the Social Contract,* 212 and *OC,* III, 245.

8. I would not argue that the general will could work in *practice*. Rousseau, in my view, is a utopian theorist. Moreover, Rousseau himself sees to some extent that the general will cannot work in practice, or will not work for long. He explains how particular interest will sooner or later interfere with or triumph over the general interest. The particular interest of the government, for example, will sooner or later undermine the sovereign body and thus the general will (*Social Contract,* 96 and *OC,* III, 421). And, of course, anything that feeds particular interest and causes it to grow more powerful than the general interest will destroy the general will or prevent it from forming (*Social Contract,* 84, 108–9 and *OC,* III, 404, 438). Rousseau envisions the ideal society of the *Social Contract* as a stop-gap measure to stave off this inevitable decline for as long as possible (*Social Contract,* 98–99 and *OC,* III, 424).

9. *Social Contract,* 61 and *OC,* III, 371. *Geneva Manuscript,* in *On the Social Contract,* 168 and *OC,* III, 296–97.

10. *Social Contract,* 67 and *OC,* III, 380.

11. *Social Contract,* 55, 63, 109 and *OC,* III, 363, 375, 438.

12. *Social Contract,* 59 n, 79–80, 118 and *OC,* III, 369 n, 397, 451.

13. *Social Contract,* 102 and *OC,* III, 429–30.

14. *Social Contract,* 61 and *OC,* III, 371–72.

15. *Social Contract,* 61 and *OC,* III, 371. That discussion does take place within the assembly is suggested at *Social Contract,* 109 and *OC,* III, 439.

16. *Social Contract,* 62–63, 66 and *OC,* III, 373–74, 378. *Geneva Manuscript,* 190 and *OC,* III, 327.

17. *Geneva Manuscript,* 189 and *OC,* III, 327. *Emile,* tr. A. Bloom (New York: Basic Books, 1979), 462 and *OC,* IV, 842. *Social Contract,* 66 and *OC,* III, 379.

18. *Social Contract,* 110–11, also 109 and *OC,* III, 440–41, 438.

19. *Geneva Manuscript,* 161 and *OC,* III, 286.

20. *Social Contract,* 111 and *OC,* III, 441.

21. A common practice of journalists is to interview individuals after they have left a union or party meeting that has passed an important common resolution, and journalists are often very interested when these individuals have second thoughts and begin to differ from or even disagree with the common resolution. What this suggests is the view that the individual's opinion when alone and outside the collective group should be taken as the individual's real opinion. One wonders whether this outlook is ideological. Isn't it being as-

sumed that the collective has coerced the individual, even if perhaps only in very subtle ways, and that the collective opinion is somehow secondary and less real than what the individual thinks when alone and outside the group? But why is it so obvious that this is the case? Why isn't it even more plausible that the views arrived at through the give and take of open discussion, criticism, argument, and counterargument in a union or party meeting (or even more so in a sovereign body capable of generating a general will that never errs) should be taken as more objective, fundamental, and real? The experience of academics—it has certainly been my experience—is that opinions reached in discussion with others are to be preferred to the opinions one arrives at alone. This is even the case where after leaving a discussion with others one finds that one begins to disagree with what they had argued and with what one agreed with during the discussion. Why privilege one's present disagreement over one's previous agreement when it is quite clear that if one reentered the discussion one's views would very probably be changed again and might end up closer to the earlier agreement? Even if one finally and fundamentally disagrees with others in discussion, one's disagreement is better founded—better refined through argument—than if one had just disagreed alone and in isolation.

22. *Social Contract,* 63, also 104 and *OC*, III, 374, 432. *Emile,* 85 and *OC,* IV, 311.

23. Of those scholars who are aware of these four conditions, the analysis that comes closest to my own can be found in E.H. Wright, *The Meaning of Rousseau* (London: Oxford University Press, 1929), 76 ff., 97 ff.

24. *Geneva Manuscript,* 161 and *OC*, III, 286.

25. *Social Contract,* 61 and *OC*, III, 371.

26. There are other scholars who note similarities between Rousseau and Kant, but not in the way I have. See E. Cassirer, *Rousseau, Kant, and Goethe,* trs. J. Gutman, P.O. Kristeller, and J.H. Randall, Jr. (Princeton: Princeton University Press, 1945), 32. E. Cassirer, *The Question of Jean-Jacques Rousseau,* tr. P. Gay (Bloomington: Indiana University Press, 1963), 58, 62–63, 104. A. Levine, *The Politics of Autonomy* (Amherst: University of Massachusetts Press, 1976). G.D.H. Cole, "Introduction" to *The Social Contract and Discourses* (New York: Dutton, 1950), xl, xlix. A. Cobban, *Rousseau and the Modern State* (Hamden, Conn.: Archon Books, 1964), 77. Wright, 29. For a discussion of differences between Kant and Rousseau, see S. Ellenburg, "Rousseau and Kant: Principles of Political Right," in *Rousseau After Two Hundred Years,* ed. R.A. Leigh (London: Cambridge University Press, 1982), 3–22.

27. *Social Contract,* 61 and *OC*, III, 371.

28. *Social Contract,* 107, also 105 and *OC*, III, 436, 433–34.

29. *Social Contract,* 62, also 59, 64 and *OC*, III, 373, 368, 376. *Geneva Manuscript,* 175 and *OC*, III, 306.

30. *Social Contract,* 55 and *OC*, III, 364.

94   Chapter Three

31. *Social Contract*, 55–56 and *OC*, III, 364–65. For a good discussion of these matters, see J. Plamenatz, "On le Forcera d'Etre Libre" in *Hobbes and Rousseau: A Collection of Critical Essays*, eds. M. Cranston and R.S. Peters (Garden City, N.Y.: Anchor, 1972), 318–32.

32. This assumption—that the majority of the citizens are more likely to come up with what is right than the individual alone—is absolutely central to Rousseau's general argument. One would have hoped to hear more from Rousseau in defense of this view, but one does not. It is clear, though, that Rousseau, unlike Kant and Rawls, has no way to ensure that the individual alone can arrive at what is right. Kantian individuals can succeed in hitting upon the categorical imperative if they carefully ask themselves whether their maxim can be universalized without contradiction. Rawlsian individuals can discover what is right by operating behind a veil of ignorance—they do not know what their particular interests are. How can Rousseau's citizens be sure that they have voted their general interest rather than their particular interest? Rousseau admits that the individual can be mistaken about this (*Social Contract*, 111 and *OC*, III, 441). The only way Rousseau gives us to be sure we have arrived at what is right is to see how the majority votes—*if*, that is, all of the necessary conditions for the realization of the general will (which we still have to say more about) are given. Also see note 21 above.

33. That this sort of failure is possible, see *Political Economy*, 216 and *OC*, III, 250–51. Hobbes, *Leviathan, EW,* III, 559.

34. See, for example, Crocker, *Rousseau's Social Contract*, 90–92. Vaughan, I, 21, 54.

35. Plato, *Republic*, 619B–619C.

36. *Social Contract*, 62 and *OC*, III, 373.

37. *Social Contract*, 77 and *OC*, III, 394. See also *Geneva Manuscript*, 192–93 and *OC*, III, 331.

38. *Social Contract*, 70–71 and *OC*, III, 385–86.

39. *Political Economy*, 222 and *OC*, III, 259–60.

40. *Social Contract*, 102 and *OC*, III, 429–30.

41. *Social Contract*, 103 and *OC*, III, 430–31.

42. *Social Contract*, 123–24 and *OC*, III, 458–59.

43. *Social Contract*, 125–31 and *OC*, III, 460–69. Rousseau is willing to banish anyone who does not believe the articles of this civil religion (*Social Contract*, 130–31 and *OC*, III, 468). Rather than see this as a sign of totalitarianism as so many do, it seems to me that it should be taken as a reflection of Rousseau's times. Even Locke, whom no one would call a totalitarian, would not tolerate anyone who was not a religious believer (see *A Letter Concerning Toleration, LW*, V, 47). Rousseau is also willing to put to death anyone who falsely proclaims these articles. This is quite harsh and objectionable, but I do not see that it alone makes Rousseau a totalitarian. If it cannot be argued that Rousseau is a totalitarian in other respects, his harshness here is not enough to make him one.

44. *Social Contract*, 58, 75 and *OC*, III, 367, 391–92.
45. *Social Contract*, 56–57 and *OC*, III, 365–66. *Discourse on the Origin of Inequality*, in *The First and Second Discourses*, ed. R.D. Masters and trs. R.D. Masters and J.R. Masters (New York: St. Martin's, 1964), 154 and *OC*, III, 173.
46. *Social Contract*, 75 and *OC*, III, 367; I take this passage to mean that no one should work for another because this is Rousseau's view in the *Discourse on Inequality*, 79, 151 and *OC*, III, 112, 171.
47. *Social Contract*, 76 and *OC*, III, 392. *Discourse on Inequality*, 199–200 and *OC*, III, 206. *Government of Poland*, tr. W. Kendall (Indianapolis: Bobbs-Merrill, 1972), 67–68 and *OC*, III, 1003–4. *Constitutional Project for Corsica*, in Watkins, 283, 303 and *OC*, III, 905, 920.
48. *Social Contract*, 92–93 and *OC*, III, 415–16.
49. *Social Contract*, 101–2 and *OC*, III, 428–30.
50. *Social Contract*, 70 and *OC*, III, 385. Also *Discourse on Inequality*, 80 and *OC*, III, 112–13. *Poland*, 1 and *OC*, III, 953.
51. On Smith and Rousseau, see L. Colletti, *From Rousseau to Lenin*, trs. J. Merrington and J. White (New York: Monthly Review Press, 1972), 155–63.
52. A. Smith, *The Wealth of Nations*, ed. E. Cannan (New York: Random House, 1937), 423.
53. M. Einaudi, *The Early Rousseau* (Ithaca: Cornell University Press, 1967), 57, 96.
54. However, Rousseau himself implies that the more private wills and the general will, customs and laws, agree, the less repressive force the government need use; *Social Contract*, 80 and *OC*, III, 397.
55. See Chapter 2, Sections III–IV above.
56. *Discourse on Inequality*, 151 ff. and *OC*, III, 171 ff.
57. Vaughan, I, 4–5. Barker, "Introduction" to *Social Contract*, xxxi. See also Watkins, ix–xiii. Also see the discussion of Cassirer, *The Question of J-J. Rousseau*, 51–53.
58. *Discourse on Inequality*, 120–21, 128 and *OC*, III, 146–47, 152.
59. *Discourse on Inequality*, 142 and *OC*, III, 164.
60. *Discourse on Inequality*, 139, also 195 and *OC*, III, 161, 203.
61. *Discourse on Inequality*, 143–46 and *OC*, III, 165–67.
62. *Discourse on Inequality*, 146–48 and *OC*, III, 167–69.
63. *Discourse on Inequality*, 150–51, also see 104 and *OC*, III, 170–71, 133. Also *Geneva Manuscript*, 159 and *OC*, III, 283.
64. *Discourse on Inequality*, 151–54, 157 and *OC*, III, 171–73, 175.
65. *Discourse on Inequality*, 157 and *OC*, III, 176.
66. *Discourse on Inequality*, 158–59 and *OC*, III, 177. For other scholars who recognize stages in Rousseau's state of nature, though some of them divide these stages differently than I do, see A.O. Lovejoy, *Essays in the History of Ideas* (Baltimore: Johns Hopkins Press, 1948), 14–37. R.D. Masters, *The*

Political Philosophy of Rousseau (Princeton: Princeton University Press, 1968), 166. Colletti, 152–53. Also J. Starobinski's "Introduction" to the *Discourse on Inequality* in *OC*, III, lxii–lxiv. Also S. Ellenburg, *Rousseau's Political Philosophy: An Interpretation from Within* (Ithaca: Cornell University Press, 1976), 70–82.

67. *Discourse on Inequality*, 80 and *OC*, III, 113.
68. *Social Contract*, 70 and *OC*, III, 385.
69. *Discourse on Inequality*, 151 and *OC*, III, 171.
70. *Discourse on Inequality*, 104 and *OC*, III, 133.
71. *Discourse on Inequality*, 171 and *OC*, III, 186.
72. *Social Contract*, 58 and *OC*, III, 367.
73. *Social Contract*, 75 and *OC*, III, 391.
74. *Corsica*, 282–83, 287, 303–6, 314, 317 and *OC*, III, 904–5, 908, 920–22, 929, 931.
75. Rousseau also says that barbarians can gain their freedom, but that once customs have been corrupted it is most difficult to regain it; *Social Contract*, 70–71 and *OC*, III, 385.
76. *Discourse on Inequality*, 132, also 94–95 and *OC*, III, 156, 125.
77. *Discourse on Inequality*, 96 and *OC*, III, 126. See also *Social Contract*, 56 and *OC*, III, 364.
78. Also see Ellenburg, "Rousseau and Kant: principles of political right," 10–11, who sees that the legislator gives laws to people in earlier stages of the state of nature but claims that there are problems involved here.
79. *Social Contract*, 69 and *OC*, III, 383. Also *Geneva Manuscript*, 182 and *OC*, III, 316–17.
80. *Social Contract*, 68 and *OC*, III, 382.
81. *Social Contract*, 69 and *OC*, III, 383. Also *Geneva Manuscript*, 180–81 and *OC*, III, 314.
82. *Social Contract*, 98–99 and *OC*, III, 424.
83. *Social Contract*, 68 and *OC*, III, 381–82.
84. *Poland*, 81, 84 and *OC*, III, 1014, 1016. *Discourse on Inequality*, 81 and *OC*, III, 113. K. Marx, *Civil War in France* (hereafter *CWF*), *MECW*, XXII, 332 and *MEW*, XVII, 340.
85. *Poland*, 36–38 and *OC*, III, 979–81. Marx, in the *Civil War in France*, also follows Rousseau's treatment of deputies; see note 84 above.
86. *Poland*, 29–30, 43, 82, 97 and *OC*, III, 974, 985, 1015, 1027.
87. *Poland*, 42 and *OC*, III, 984.
88. *Social Contract*, 61 and *OC*, III, 372.
89. *Poland*, 37, 46–47 and *OC*, III, 980, 988.
90. *Poland*, 58–59 and *OC*, III, 997. The Tribunate, which Rousseau discusses in the *Social Contract* (120 and *OC*, III, 454), bears some resemblance to the *liberum veto*.
91. Rousseau's willingness to hand out the death penalty too quickly is too harsh, but again it is not enough to make him a totalitarian.

4

Kant, Philosophy of History, and the Ideal Society

I wish to argue in this chapter that Kant is the first truly great political theorist of the modern period. Let me explain what I mean and try to make the argument.[1]

Traditional political theory (before Kant) almost always did one or the other of two things—never both. One sort of theorist speculated about the ideal state in utopian fashion; that is, without really attempting to explain how such a state might be brought about in the real world. Plato, Thomas More, and Rousseau are good examples of this approach. For Plato it was simply a legitimate and worthwhile philosophical endeavor to try to understand the nature of justice even if it could not be realized in the actual world. For Thomas More, as well as for Plato, such an ideal at least provided a standard to use in criticizing existing society.

The other traditional approach was the opposite. It was relatively unconcerned with ideals and simply sought to examine the actual, empirical dynamics of real-world power struggles. It studied human self-interest and aggression in order to understand political reality adequately enough to be able to act in it with some chance of success. Thrasymachus in Book I of Plato's *Republic,* to some extent Thucydides, and in large part Machiavelli did this.

Until Kant, political theorists tended for the most part in one or the other of these opposed directions. From the perspective of power dynamics, the concern with justice and morality often appeared naive, utopian, or at best hopeless. As Machiavelli says, "how we live is so different from how we ought to live that he who studies what *ought* to be done rather than what *is* done will learn the way to his down-

98   *Chapter Four*

fall. . . ."² After all, what can moral investigations tell us about the actual workings, let alone the stable consolidation, of political structures? What can the moralist hope to do, merely argue that we should get everyone to behave morally, that we educate people, or that we should turn the administration of the state over to a wise and just philosopher? If that is all you have to say, why bother doing political theory? You are hopelessly naive.

But, on the other hand, from the perspective of the moralist, simply to analyze power dynamics is to abandon the most important considerations of political theory, namely, the development of human virtue, justice, and the good life. The ability to manipulate power may gain you your self-interest, may even produce order, but never virtue, dignity, or justice.

What makes Kant the first great modern political theorist is that he seriously attempts to take both of these approaches. Hobbes, as we saw in Chapter 1, also made moves in this direction, but with little success. Political theory, for Kant and for many after him, including Marx, must not only discuss the *ideal* state but must also have a theory of how actually to *realize* the ideal. It must analyze actual power struggles, self-interest, and conflict but in order to show how this empirical dynamic, if properly understood, can be guided toward the realization of the ideal society.³ In other words, it is Kant's philosophy of history that makes for the greatness of his political theory.

For Kant, there are two forces at work in history. One is the empirical dynamic of conflicting self-interests. The other is morality. And both, if understood properly, will lead us toward the same goal: peace, a league of nations, international law, and just societies. Let us examine these two forces that Kant finds at work in history—first the conflict of particular interests.

I. Historical Conflict and World Peace

Kant begins his essay "Idea for a Universal History" by noticing a paradox; namely, that rates of birth, marriage, and death in any given population are stable. This is a paradox because marriages, and at least to some extent births and deaths, depend upon or are influenced by individual choices that involve free will; but nevertheless, we can accurately predict rates of birth, marriage, and death in the population as if they were causally determined in the strictest possible way.⁴ How are we to make sense of this?

One explanation, Kant suggests, is that individuals (motivated by their own inclinations, decisions, or choices) seek only their own particular purposes, but in some way (which will have to be explained) each individual furthers without realizing it some common but unknown purpose or end.[5] In other words, there is some sort of directedness, some sort of purposiveness, operating here behind the scenes—a purpose of which individuals are completely unconscious, a purpose that is not the purpose of any individual. They seek only their own personal, particular ends, but some larger, common purpose is realized without their intending it. If we were able to understand this purposiveness, then perhaps we could direct it. Perhaps we could even direct it so that history progresses toward a state in which human beings are both moral and happy.[6] If we could understand this directedness in history, humans perhaps could control their own destiny.

Kant thinks that human *selfishness* is the key here. More specifically, he thinks that we find two different propensities within human beings. He sums these up as *"unsocial sociability."* Human beings have an unsocial propensity—a propensity to isolation, selfishness, and lack of concern with the interests of others. But they also have a social propensity, a propensity to associate with others in society. They need others just to stay alive. They must cooperate with others to be able to produce enough to satisfy their basic needs. And after all, even aggression would not get very far without someone nearby to attack. As Rousseau pointed out in his *Discourse on Inequality,* selfishness is only possible in a situation where you can compare yourself to others and prefer yourself. In other words, selfishness is only possible in a social setting.[7]

These two factors then—being close enough to others, associating with them, plus our selfishness—produce conflict, competition, and even war. While there is an obvious negative side to this conflict, we must also attend to the positive side, which perhaps is even more important. Conflict and selfishness, even avarice and lust for power, do, after all, awaken our human powers and stir us out of complacency. Selfishness drives us to accomplish things; competition sharpens our abilities. We develop our human potentialities. We are driven toward the fullest development of our powers and capacities.[8]

So we are driven to society by sociability and the need for others. Once in society, antagonism, competition, and selfishness set in and our powers and capacities develop. In fact, for Kant, this development will eventually lead to the society of morality, justice, and peace that he is after.⁹ *Selfishness and aggression will lead toward morality*—that is Kant's argument. We must try to understand how this will occur.

Kant is following Hobbes here. But also in Book II of Plato's *Republic,* Glaucon set out a social contract theory of society that, although much simpler, is very much like Hobbes's theory. Let us look at Glaucon first. Glaucon assumes that before individuals established society they existed alone in relative isolation. Moreover, individuals are selfish and aggressive—they really prefer doing injustice to others and benefiting themselves. And if they were powerful enough, or if, as Glaucon puts it, they had magic rings like Gyges, they would do exactly what Gyges did—seek their own self-interest and injure others. But alas, for Glaucon, such rings exist only in stories; which is to say that Glaucon, at least in part, disagrees with Thrasymachus, whose argument we heard in Book I of Plato's *Republic*. Glaucon and Thrasymachus agree that individuals are selfish and aggressive. But Glaucon does not agree with Thrasymachus that some people are superior. If some people *were* superior or more powerful, they would rise to the top of the struggle and establish order in this way. For Thrasymachus, if all are selfish and aggressive, but some are superior, the superior will gain control and establish justice *in their own interest*. For Glaucon, this is illusion. Much as he might wish for it, it only happens in mythology. All *are* selfish and aggressive, but at the same time, alas, all are *equal*. Therefore, the only way out of this chaos of conflict among bumbling equals is to make a contract that establishes society, order, and justice *in the interest of all*. Nevertheless, for Glaucon, justice is second best. People really prefer doing injustice and pursuing their self-interest, but lacking magic rings, they realize that this is impossible; that they will fail and be hurt; and that others will do them injustice. So they settle for justice, order, and security in the interest of all.¹⁰

As we have seen in Chapter 1, Hobbes's views are similar. In working out a necessary scientific deduction of society, Hobbes begins with the hypothetical notion of a state of nature; which is to say a condition of human beings where no political institutions, laws, or morals have been established or are in effect. In this state of nature, for Hobbes, human beings are selfish and aggressive. They are also equal, motivated by a concern for self-preservation, and rational.

Given their natural selfishness and aggression, they will fight. There will be, as Hobbes puts it, a war of all against all. But since all are equal, no one will be able to impose order by establishing power over the others. All will simply be threatened by this very dangerous state of conflict. Given their concern for self-preservation, they will fear for their lives and begin to seek a way out of this chaos. Given that they are rational, they will eventually discover that since all are equal and thus that none will successfully rise to the top of the struggle, the *only* way out is to come to an agreement and establish a social contract. If we grant Hobbes's assumptions concerning the nature of human beings, we will have to admit that individuals will inevitably be driven to this social contract. They will have to relinquish their power to a sovereign who establishes order, security, and justice.[11]

Kant takes up the Hobbes–Glaucon model but extends it to the relationship among nations. For Kant, the same conflict that drives individuals from a state of nature to society drives societies toward law and morality. Once political societies exist, conflict and war among individuals cease—law and authority put an end to them. Instead, conflict and war take place at a more general (and more destructive) level; they occur among nations. Conflict and war (just as they forced individuals to society, law, and authority) will force nations to a league of nations, lawful regulations, and a common authority. Wars, revolutions, and conflicts will continue remaking the international political map until we get a league of nations and international peace.[12]

Just as at the level of individuals, so at the international level there are two important propensities in operation. There is an "unsocial sociability" among nations. On the one hand, we find the assertion of national self-interest that drives nations toward aggression and war. But there is also an important form of sociability among nations, namely, their interest in commerce, trade, and economic interaction. It is the dynamic interplay between these two factors, this international unsocial sociability, that will lead to a league of nations, peace, and international law. *War, for Kant, will lead to the end of war.*

As wars become more serious, destructive, and expensive, they become more uncertain. They come into conflict with ever-increasing economic interests. Wars, as they become more disruptive, interfere with trade. As world trade grows, as nations become more interdependent, as they rely more and more on each other commercially, war poses an ever-greater threat to the smooth functioning of the international market. At the first sign of war, other nations will intervene to arbitrate, to quash the war, in order to secure their own national commercial interests. This is the first step toward a league of nations.[13]

As commerce continues to increase and as wars become even more expensive and destructive, we move further toward a league of nations. With the establishment of this league, pressure will be put on each nation to establish civil freedom and just internal constitutions. Any domestic threat to peace within a specific nation will be of concern at the international level since it could eventually affect other nations.

Kant's philosophy of history exhibits a mixture of insight and error. In modern times the relations among major powers in many ways have borne out Kant's prophecies. The threat of serious conflict among major powers often drives them to back off, negotiate, and compromise. Kant's model seems to work among major powers that are relatively *equal* in strength. It will not work among powers that are very *unequal* in strength. Commercial self-interest, rather than hindering the outbreak of war, may very well drive a powerful nation to invade a smaller and weaker one; especially if it can be handled so as not to draw other powerful nations into direct conflict and if the powerful nation thinks it can clean things up quickly and get its way economically. From the other side, a weak and poor nation may well find itself driven to almost suicidal revolt in order to attempt to throw out a powerful nation if it thinks circumstances will allow for even a hope of success. And, indeed, we have seen many wars of this sort in recent times. Moreover, the interests of powerful nations may lead them to side with different factions in a weaker nation if the powerful nations think they can avoid direct conflict with each other and if they think the general conflict can be contained.

So Kant's model does not work in all areas. Nevertheless, what is really interesting about it is the notion that selfishness and aggression lead toward peace, law, and morality. This is a secular version of the traditional theological view that God's providence brings good out of evil. Human evil or self-seeking is used by God, or by history, to bring about a good result that humans neither intended nor foresaw. This makes, however, for a radically different picture of the proper relation of morality to self-interest. Traditionally, it was morality's task to suppress self-interest, even annihilate it if possible. Think of Plato or Thomas More. For Kant, morality's task is not to suppress self-interest or conflict. Kant argues that self-interest, conflict, and war are leading to the very same end that moral reflection would have dictated from the start.[14] The task of morality is to use this conflict, guide it, not suppress it, at least not immediately.

II. Moral Force in History

Let us move on to the second force at work in history, namely, morality. For Kant, the categorical imperative is the general form of the moral law. It is not a specific law with a specific content. It is a general form that allows us to discover or test the morality of any specific maxim. What we need, to perform this test, is to know the general form of law—the general form that any law must have if it is to be a moral law. All laws, in the first place, are commands or imperatives. They command us to do something or command us not to do it. It is *necessary* that we do it or not do it. Second, they tell us to do it or not to do it in all cases without exception. They tell us to do it or not to do it *universally*.[15] The general form of law, then, is the categorical imperative—a universal and necessary command.

In any situation where we want to know how to act, we formulate a maxim, then ask whether, if this maxim were given a universal and necessary form, we could will to carry it out. We must act only on that maxim that we could will to be a universal law of nature.[16]

To make a maxim universal and necessary we would say, for example, "Everyone should steal always and under all conditions." We immediately see that this would be impossible—a contradiction. We might decide to steal in a specific situation where it served our particular interest, but we would reject stealing when it is universalized. Universalizing the maxim allows us to see what can be a moral law and what cannot. For Kant, morality is based on reason, not interest. We might feel that it is in our interest to steal in a particular situation, but our reason tells us plainly that stealing in general—universalized stealing—must be rejected. For Kant, we engage in this rational analysis of a maxim in order to separate our interests, feelings, or inclinations about a particular act from our rational, abstract assessment of what is moral in general.

For Kant, to be moral *is* to act rationally. It is not moral to be determined by interest or inclination. Only if we follow reason are we free, self-determined, and moral. If we are determined by our interests, inclinations, or feelings, for Kant, we are determined by natural forces (or by motives determined by natural forces) and thus we are causally determined heteronomously. We are determined by something other. We have not been determined by ourselves. We are only self-determined if we are determined by our reason.[17]

To put this another way, it is not enough to act simply in *accordance* with reason or in *accordance* with the categorical imperative. We must do the act *for the sake of* the categorical imperative, because it is rational, and for this reason alone. The only thing that can determine the action if we are to be free and moral is our own reason—this rational analysis—and nothing else.[18]

If we simply refrain from stealing, we do act in accordance with the categorical imperative—in external agreement with it. But if our actual motive is simply to have a good reputation, or to be liked, or because we like the other person, we are being determined by inclination or feeling and we are not free or moral. We are not acting for the sake of the moral law. We must refrain from stealing for one reason alone, because it is rational, or, the same thing, because it is the moral law, because it can be universalized. Only in this way are we free. Only in this way do we act on reason, not inclination. Moreover, if we are to be moral, for Kant, we must not even by determined by our long-term interests, even the long-term interests of others or of society. If we are, we will be determined by inclination, not reason. Nor can we be motivated by a concern for results, consequences, or outcomes of the act. Utility, benefit, or good to ourselves or to others must not determine us. Or again we would be determined by inclination, not reason.[19]

We must simply analyze; ask if the maxim can be universalized. We must be determined only by this rational analysis if we are to be free and moral. It is only the intention, the volition, the rationality of the act, which makes it moral.

We can easily see that morality, the categorical imperative, would demand fair laws, just constitutions, and an end to wars. We could not will that everyone be allowed to do the opposite. We could not will to universalize war, unjust constitutions, and unjust laws. Morality would also demand a league of nations.[20] And morality, for Kant, is one of the forces at work in history. Moreover, the other force, we have already seen, drives us toward the very same point that morality does. Wars among nations and commercial interests drive us toward peace, law, and a league of nations. Both morality and war converge toward the same end—one consciously, the other unconsciously.[21]

In *Perpetual Peace,* though Kant is not discussing the historical realization of a league of nations but rather the organization of a republican form of government, we see a good example of these two forces at work. Kant argues that selfish inclinations must be arranged so that they cancel each other.

> The problem of organizing a state, however hard it may seem, can be solved even for a race of devils, if only they are intelligent. The problem is: "Given a multitude of rational beings requiring universal laws for their preservation, but each of whom is secretly inclined to exempt himself from them, to establish a constitution in such a way that, although

their private intentions conflict, they check each other, with the result that their public conduct is the same as if they had no such intentions." . . . (A good constitution is not to be expected from morality, but, conversely, a good moral condition of a people is to be expected only under a good constitution.) Instead of genuine morality, the mechanism of nature brings it to pass through selfish inclinations, which naturally conflict outwardly but which can be used by reason as a means for its own end, the sovereignty of law, and, as concerns the state, for promoting and securing internal and external peace.[22]

Both of these forces are necessary for Kant. One without the other is not enough. Reason and morality alone, he says, would never achieve our end. Humans are too corrupt. Our reason alone is not powerful enough to produce a league of nations and just states.[23]

On the other hand, conflict or war alone will never actually and finally make us moral. Conflict and war drive us toward peace, a league of nations, and legality. But this is only to say that our self-interest drives us toward peace and law; and self-interest, we have seen, is not moral for Kant. Nevertheless, if the laws that get established are the sorts of laws that reason and morality demand, and if our external behavior conforms to these laws, though only due to our self-interest—if, then, we act in *accordance* with the law—a great deal has been gained.[24] The next step, obeying the law not through self-interest but because the law is rational and moral, in other words, acting *for the sake of* the law, is a small step, but a step that we must each make for ourselves. Nothing can force us to be free and moral.

The notion that conflict leads to the same result that morality would have demanded from the start, Kant gets, I think, from Adam Smith's model of a competitive market economy—or at least Smith hints in this direction. In a market economy with a developed division of labor, individuals are dependent upon others. No one can perform all of the tasks necessary to satisfy their own needs—no one can produce all his or her own food, clothing, shelter, and tools. So each specializes, performs one narrow task, and relies upon others to perform the other tasks. Then they exchange goods and services in a market. There is a thoroughgoing interdependence of each upon all here—we need others to buy from, sell to, work for, hire, and in a thousand other ways (both domestically and at the international level). But despite this interdependence, individuals in a market economy, for Adam Smith, attend only to their own self-interest. They are selfish. They seek only their own profit. They pay little attention to others and only infrequently cooperate with them consciously.

For Adam Smith, however, this self-seeking not only produces a common good but it does so much more effectively than if individuals consciously and cooperatively sought to realize the common good. Active, aggressive, competitive self-seeking, given this economic interdependence of each upon all, produces a national capital, the wealth of the nation, that common good, out of which each struggles to gain their particular share. Self-seeking, through an "invisible hand," Smith says, produces the common good much more effectively than consciously seeking to produce it would.[25]

Rousseau, I think, remains a utopian moralist largely because he retains an ancient conception of wealth. He thinks, as Plato and Thomas More did, that a complex and wealthy society will irrevocably corrupt its citizens. Wealth turns the citizens away from concern with the common good and feeds their self-interest. This explains that remarkable passage in the *Social Contract* where Rousseau suggests that a society unfortunate enough to have a great deal of natural wealth should be a monarchy. Society's wealth should be dumped upon the Prince and kept away from the citizens. Since wealth corrupts, it is better to corrupt the Prince rather than the whole state.[26]

Smith and Kant, however, were able to see how the self-interested concern for wealth and commerce can lead, if only unconsciously or through an "invisible hand," to a common good. If, for Kant, we are able to locate such an unconscious directedness in history; if we are able to form an idea for a universal history; if we can see with Adam Smith that self-seeking combined with commercial interdependence leads to the common good; or, much the same thing, if we can see that in history the dynamic tension between war and commerce will lead us unconsciously toward the same point that reason and morality would consciously lead us; then Kant thinks that the other force at work in history, our own reason, our own morality, can begin to hasten this historical development toward its goal.[27]

III. Particular Interest and the General Interest

One of the main tasks of any political theorist is to explain how to reconcile particular interests with the general interest. To have order, let alone morality and justice, any society must bring about the common interests of its citizens. If the society is not to collapse, the interests of the citizens must agree and be harmonious at least to some extent. The problem is that the only agents that can be used to realize this harmony of interests are the individual citizens themselves, and they presumably are all motivated by their own particular and selfish interests. The task of the theorist, then, is to explain how these individuals with selfish, particular interests can produce the common good.

What Plato does, basically, is to remove all social institutions that feed particular interest. He eliminates money, private property, and even the family. He then gives certain individuals a philosophical education that will train them to be concerned with the abstract common good, and he puts these philosophers in charge of society. Thomas More does much the same thing though he differs from Plato in interesting ways.

The trouble here is that there is no attempt to explain how we can start with selfish individuals in existing society and move step by step toward the ideal society in which self-interest has been eliminated and the common good realized. For More, the ideal merely exists in a far off land called Utopia—which means "nowhere." For Plato, the whole project is a philosophical exercise to enable us to know what justice is. Moreover, whatever might be said in support of his theory of education, a theory of education is not a political theory. Education, important as it is in other respects, cannot transform existing society enough to realize the ideal.

Machiavelli, despite first appearances, has a more practical theory of how to turn particular interests to the common good in existing society. Anyone who wants to become a Prince will obviously be motivated by an interest in wealth, personal power, and prestige. But despite this, Machiavelli's point, if he is read very carefully, is that Princes cannot be caught up in their own particular interests. If they are, then sooner or later they will fail. Successful Princes must consider only the large-scale map of competing political forces. They must be concerned with the stable consolidation of an overall power structure. To do this, the Prince must be something of a scientist, and, like a scientist, disinterested. The Prince can be committed neither to virtue nor cruelty for their own sakes. Princes must be detached, so that they can *use* virtue or cruelty—use them merely as tools or means—to consolidate a stable balance of power. Just as much, Princes cannot be caught in the grip of their own self-interests, or they will eventually lose sight of the overall constellation of forces. They must be committed to nothing but the stable consolidation of a political power structure. They must be detached from *everything* else so that they can view *all* things *only* as potential instruments—things merely to be *used*. They must have no other commitment to things. They must put aside their own aims and have the consolidation of a stable power structure as their only aim.[28] The pressure of power politics, together with a little advice from Machiavelli, will force the Prince to shift away from personal interest. If not, eventually the Prince will simply fail. The Prince, to succeed, must begin to look beyond narrow self-interest to the establishment of an ordered power structure, and this, if only in a minimal sense, is in the common interest.

In Hobbes, we find that conflict among self-interested equals in the state of nature forces each of them, if they are to preserve themselves in this very dangerous situation, to begin to concern themselves with their long-term common interest in security, a social contract, and law. Their self-interest drives them toward the common interest.

Machiavelli and Hobbes, unlike Plato and More, are not out to eliminate particular interest, but, like Kant, to use it, to allow it to generate the common good. They take a modern view of the relation of self-interest to the common good. Nevertheless, the societies that Machiavelli and Hobbes are able to generate may have order and even security, but they are certainly not moral, just, or ideal.

Rousseau's concept of the general will is also a device designed to transform particular interests into the general interest. He too, takes a modern view of the relation of self-interest to the common good. Self-interest is not to be repressed or eliminated. Rather, individual citizens with particular interests produce the common good by voting on general questions that ask them to speculate upon and register the general will. They register their interest in the abstract, general case. Furthermore, Rousseau's society is just and moral. However, Rousseau, like Plato and More, gives us no realistic explanation of how to realize such a society. He merely describes it and its institutional mechanisms.[29]

It is only Kant who pulls all these elements together such that self-interested conflict among nations leads to just and moral societies. In Kant, we get both a sketch of the ideal state as part of an international league of nations and, at the same time, a theory of the dynamic of power conflicts—a theory that explains not only how these conflicts will lead historically to the realization of the ideal state, but also how we ourselves can begin directing things toward the realization of this ideal. Kant brings together in a single theory the two opposed approaches of traditional political theory, and he outlines the project that later theorists like Marx and others will take up and develop in a more complicated and sophisticated way.

IV. The Highest Good and a Beautiful World

We have explained Kant's attempt to achieve a certain set of reconciliations—the reconciliation of utopian political theory with the empirical study of power dynamics, the reconciliation of the forces of self-interested conflict with the forces of morality in history, and the reconciliation of particular interests with the common good. We must now see that these attempts to link the empirical or natural with the moral in the historical and political sphere are an integral part of Kant's larger attempt to link nature and morality at the level of his architectonic and thus to reconcile the *Critique of Pure Reason* with the *Critique of Practical Reason.*

We must begin by noticing that, for Kant, an "idea" in the historical realm is the same thing as what in the *Critique of Pure Reason* he called a regulative idea or an idea of reason. A regulative idea can neither be proven nor disproven—it cannot be given in experience or known. It is a regulative principle of reason, not a constitutive one. Reason seeks the totality of things organized into a connected whole. It holds before us the goal of finding greater systematic order and unity among phenomena; it allows us to subsume lower-order laws grasped by the understanding under higher-order principles or laws projected by reason; it allows us to treat things *as if* they were intelligently and purposively organized; and it thus assists the understanding in carrying out its task of extending the realm of connected theoretical knowledge—of extending it toward the unconditioned.[30]

Historical ideas, like the idea that conflict and war lead toward peace and morality, are regulative ideas, as Kant himself makes quite clear in several places.[31] We cannot *know* that conflict and war will lead toward peace and morality, but we have reason to act *as if* they do. This assumption, together with the greater systematic order and unity that it makes possible, can allow us to act to hasten historical development toward this goal. But even more importantly, historical ideas, like regulative ideas in general, are also intimately connected with what, in the *Critique of Practical Reason,* Kant calls postulates of practical reason.[32]

In the *Critique of Practical Reason,* Kant tells us that just as theoretical reason seeks the absolute totality of conditions, so does practical reason. It seeks the highest good. It is clear that the moral law and not the highest good must be the determining ground of our will if we are to be free and moral, but nevertheless every volition must have an object.[33] Our ultimate object, then, is the highest good. The highest good certainly involves virtue, but it also requires happiness. A life without happiness simply could not be considered to be the highest good for human beings. The highest good, then, is the combination of morality and happiness. However, this combination involves certain problems. Since virtue and happiness are not identical, and since, for Kant, happiness certainly cannot be the motive for virtue (or we would be determined by inclination, not reason), it can only be the case that virtue leads to happiness.[34]

This is where the difficulty lies because happiness, which is produced by the satisfaction of our inclinations and desires, would require that things in the natural world occur so as to satisfy our inclinations and desires. Therefore, the realization of the highest good, which combines virtue and happiness, would require that the natural world be regulated so that it satisfies our inclinations and desires (and thus makes us happy), but regulated in such a way that we can also act in accordance with the moral law. The trouble is that the moral law demands *rational* motives, motives independent of inclination and desire, and independent of the harmony of nature with our inclinations and desires. There is not the slightest ground, Kant says, either in nature or in the moral law for assuming the possibility of a continuous harmony between happiness (the satisfaction of our inclinations and desires) and morality. But if the highest good is to be possible, and, for Kant, it is necessary that it be possible as the necessary object of a will determined by the moral law, then we must *postulate* the possibility of a harmony between nature and morality. The only way we can do this, Kant thinks, is to postulate the existence of a God who regulates nature so as to make possible the satisfaction of our inclinations and desires (and thus happiness) in harmony with the moral law. The postulate of a God is necessary for the realization of happiness combined with virtue and thus the highest good. This is not something that theoretical reason can either prove or disprove, but, in Kant's view, practical reason must postulate it and is justified in doing so.[35]

In the second *Critique,* it seems to be God who is responsible for reconciling virtue and happiness and for realizing the highest good. But in Kant's writings on politics and philosophy of history we find a slight shift and a further development of this conception. As early as the "Idea for a Universal History" of 1784, Kant is willing to say that human beings themselves must be responsible for creating whatever happiness or perfection they are capable of.[36] As we can easily see from previous sections of this chapter, they do this by transforming the social and natural world so that it fits their morality; they reconcile particular interests with the common good; they hasten the empirical dynamic of self-interested conflict toward an ideal and moral society; and thus, in general, they work toward the reconciliation of nature (that is, the satisfaction of interests, inclinations, and desires—thus happiness) with morality, the moral law, and therefore they work toward the realization of the highest good. It is quite clear that in very important ways human beings themselves are responsible for the realization of the highest good. In *Theory and Practice* (1793), Kant explicitly says that human beings play a collaborative role in realizing the highest good. He even says that in this respect, "man may see himself as analogous to the divinity."[37]

We can say, then, that in the Dialectic of the *Critique of Pure Reason* Kant shows that it is impossible either to prove or disprove the existence of a God. In the Dialectic of the *Critique of Practical Reason* he shows that practical reason must postulate the existence of a God who reconciles nature and morality, happiness and virtue, so as to make the realization of the highest good possible. Then in his writings on politics and philosophy of history, Kant gives us a concrete program—an idea—for how human beings themselves can assist in actually realizing the highest good.

In the *Critique of Judgment,* Kant again deals with this attempt to reconcile nature and morality, and he does so as part of his larger architectonic purpose of linking the first and second *Critiques.* Kant begins by telling us that the concept of nature and the concept of freedom "are entirely removed from all mutual influence which they might have on one another . . . by the great gulf that separates the supersensible from phenomena."[38] Yet, in accordance with the concept of freedom, the final purpose of morality ought to be realized in the realm of nature. Freedom and nature ought to be brought into harmony. But for this purposive transition from morality to nature to be possible we need a ground of the unity of these two realms. It is the faculty of judgment that gives us this mediating link. This is not determinant judgment, which subsumes a particular under a given universal concept, but reflective judgment, which, given a particular, seeks a universal principle under which it can be subsumed.[39] Reflective judgment gives us a concept of purposiveness in nature that allows us to judge the particular to be contained under the universal. It allows us to consider particular laws in nature *as if* they were part of a larger systematic unity designed by a divine intelligence. It links reason and understanding by making possible the transition from the final purpose of morality to the conformity to law of nature.[40] Thus it gives us:

> a formal teleology of nature, which we in fact assume in it [nature] but which is the basis neither for a theoretical knowledge of nature nor for a practical principle of freedom; nonetheless it gives a principle for judging nature and investigating it in search of general laws of particular experiences, according to which we must posit them to bring out that systematic connection needful for coherent experience, and which we have an a priori ground for assuming.[41]

Thus, we can say that the *Critique of Practical Reason* showed that we are justified in postulating the possibility of achieving the highest good. The *Critique of Judgment* then gave us the conceptual apparatus that would allow us to conceive how this final purpose—the highest good—could be realized in nature. It allowed us to understand the role of judgment in mediating between understanding and reason and in linking nature and freedom through a concept of purposiveness. And finally, in the writings on politics and philosophy of history, Kant gives us a concrete program—an idea—for how the final purpose—the highest good—can *actually* be realized in the world.

For the highest good to be realized, we have said, nature must accord with the moral law so as to make happiness in harmony with virtue possible. This harmonization is very much like that discussed in the first part of the *Critique of Judgment,* where Kant discusses aesthetic judgment and beauty. We are led to wonder, then, whether the realization of the highest good in history might also produce a beautiful world. When nature harmonizes with our understanding—that is, when nature is experienced as if it were purposively organized to harmonize with our cognitive faculties—we experience a feeling of pleasure and the object is experienced as beautiful. That is what beauty means for Kant. An object appears beautiful when on its own accord it appears to conform to the laws of the understanding without being determined by a law of the understanding. Nature on its own just appears as if purposively designed for us.[42] Thus, it would seem that if nature and morality were brought into harmony through historical development, then here too we ought to experience nature as if it were purposively designed for us and thus we ought to experience our world as beautiful.[43]

Thus, as nature is brought into harmony with morality through our own historical efforts, we move toward the realization of the highest good: we work toward the harmony of happiness and morality. In this way our historical activity helps to realize a postulate of practical reason. Moreover, this harmonization of nature and morality must be seen as purposive. Nature would progressively come to harmonize with—appear as if it were designed for—our cognitive faculties, and our world would begin to be experienced as beautiful. Beauty as well as morality and happiness would be realized in history—or at least Kant gives us an idea that will help us to work toward this final purpose.

Moreover, for Kant, the experience of beauty involves a harmony and balance between the sensuous and rational faculties of the individual. In an experience of the beautiful we are determined neither by reason in opposition to inclination, nor by inclination in opposition to reason. The two, instead, are in harmony and they reinforce each other. For Kant, this is the freest possible relationship that an individual can have to an object.[44] There is no opposition, tension, or coercion between the faculties of the individual. This is even a freer relationship than that which we find in moral freedom, where we are normally determined by reason in opposition to our inclination. If we are determined by reason, and if our inclinations spontaneously agree with our reason, then we would be even freer.

Thus, in history as we transform the natural-social world to agree with our morality; as we reconcile particular interests with the common good; as we control those natural elements that satisfy our interests, inclinations, and desires and thus produce happiness in harmony with the moral law; we are creating a situation in which the inner faculties of individuals, their sensuous and rational faculties—their inclination and morality—will come to agree and be in harmony. We are creating a situation in which the highest freedom, as in an experience of beauty, will become possible. Our world would then appear as if it were designed for us. It would appear as a beautiful world. The realization of a beautiful world is a theme that is taken up and developed further by Schiller and even, we shall see, by Marx.[45]

V. Sovereignty and Revolution

I have argued in this chapter that Kant is the first great modern political theorist because he has a theory both of the ideal state and of how to realize it. This is not to say, however, that I think that Kant has accomplished this project with complete success. In my opinion there are several things for which he must be criticized. Although his theory of how to realize the ideal state is a most interesting one, his theory of what the ideal state would look like when achieved leaves a great deal to be desired.

In the first place, Kant often tells us that civil laws are to be considered legitimate only if they are the sorts of laws that a people could have given themselves.[46] But it is quite clear, for Kant, that it is not at all necessary, as it was for Rousseau, that the people be the ones who *actually* give themselves these laws. The sovereign can quite well be the one who gives these laws to them. Kant wants a sovereign who rules autocratically but governs in a republican way; that is, who governs in accordance with laws that the people *could* have given themselves.[47]

It follows from this that Kant thinks revolution to be immoral. It is true that if an actual revolution succeeds in bringing about a more just political constitution, then, for Kant, the citizens ought to accept that constitution, but, nevertheless, the act of revolution itself was immoral.[48] Much as for Hobbes, there are difficulties involved in Kant's thought here. We must be able to explain how history moves toward right, not just assume that they will agree. I do not see that one can explain how history moves toward right without a theory of social transformation that at least under certain circumstances calls for a theory of revolution. Kant refuses, or is unable, to develop a theory of legitimate revolution, but seems to be forced to rely on revolution, at least at times, to move history toward right, while nevertheless denouncing revolution as illegitimate. At any rate, the only thing that citizens legitimately may do to further historical development is to criticize their institutions publicly in order to move the autocrat slowly toward reform.[49] It seems to me that this alone would be rather ineffective, but, more interestingly, it seems to me that Kant's arguments against the legitimacy of revolution will not stand up under criticism.

One of his main arguments against revolution is that it is shown to be illegitimate by the principle of publicity. This principle functions in the legal sphere much as the categorical imperative does in the moral sphere. No law, for Kant, is legitimate if it cannot stand the test of publicity. In other words, any maxim is to be considered unjust if it cannot be publicly avowed without risking the defeat of its own purpose by calling forth opposition to itself. Kant thinks this principle shows revolution to be illegitimate.[50] But it seems to me that he confuses a revolution with a coup. A small conspiratorial group seeking to overthrow the government probably would be frustrated if it made public its plans. But a popular revolution supported by the majority of the citizens against an unjust government would not necessarily frustrate its plans by making them public. In fact, revolutionaries often complain that one of the main obstacles to revolution is lack of access to the means of publicity. Nevertheless, for Kant, the principle of publicity, as it has been stated, is merely negative. It will indicate which maxims are unjust. It will not tell us which maxims are actually just. This is so, for example, because a very powerful but unjust government might well be able to make public its repressive plans against the populace without risking the frustration of these plans in the least.[51]

However, at the end of his discussion of this matter, Kant gives us an affirmative principle of publicity: "All maxims which stand in need of publicity in order not to fail their end, agree with politics and right combined." In other words, if these maxims can only attain their end through publicity—if publicity is actually necessary for their success—then these maxims are just.[52] It seems to me that popular revolutions supported by the majority against unjust governments might well be able to satisfy this affirmative principle of publicity and thus serve to legitimately move society further toward the realization of the highest good.[53]

Kant also has another argument against revolution. He says in *Theory and Practice*,

> it would be an obvious contradiction if the constitution included a law for such eventualities, entitling the people to overthrow the existing constitution, from which all particular laws are derived, if the contract were violated. For there would then have to be a publicly constituted opposing power, hence a second head of state to protect the rights of the people against the first ruler, and then yet a third to decide which of the other two had right on his side.[54]

This argument against revolution is persuasive only if we are willing to agree with Kant, who, like Hobbes and unlike Rousseau, is assuming that the ruler (the head of state, the government, or the monarch) is the sovereign. By a sovereign we mean the highest actual power and the highest legitimate authority. It is obviously a contradiction to argue that any group can legitimately overthrow the sovereign because that would imply that the sovereign was *not* in fact the sovereign—not the highest power and legitimate authority. The group legitimately overthrowing the sovereign would be the highest power and legitimate authority and thus *it* would be the sovereign. And then no group could revolt legitimately against this sovereign. If you have a sovereign, then to revolt against it legitimately—whoever it is—is incoherent. If you *can* legitimately revolt against it, it simply is *not* the sovereign. If it *is* to be the sovereign, then you cannot legitimately revolt against it because it is the highest legitimate authority.

But what if, as for Rousseau, the *people* were sovereign? Then they certainly could overthrow an unjust head of state, monarch, or government without any of these contradictions arising, and the constitution could quite consistently contain provisions for this eventuality. Because the *people* and not the government are sovereign, the people could overthrow the government without acting against the sovereign at all or getting involved in contradictions with regard to the concept of sovereignty. Furthermore, if it was the constitution that constituted the people as sovereign, then no small group could overthrow the constitution without giving rise to the same contradictions as discussed above, but the people as sovereign certainly could change the constitution. What could stop them from doing so if they were sovereign? Any claim that there should be a power to stop them would be to claim that there should be a power higher than the people and thus that the people were not sovereign.

Kant also suggests that we could not consistently will to universalize the maxim that it is legitimate to revolt against an unjust ruler. To do so would be to make all constitutions insecure and produce complete lawlessness.[55] Again, this argument works only if we assume that the ruler is sovereign and that without such a ruler, all law, cohesion, and order would be impossible. Kant, like Hobbes, seems to think that the only force capable of providing cohesion and order is a political force—the government or sovereign. Like Hobbes, he seems to have no social theory; that is, no theory of how cohesion is possible in society apart from the political or governmental sphere. The more cohesion one finds in society apart from the political sphere, the less power the political sphere or government need have. Marx, for example, thinks that the political state can wither away. Thus, clearly, if the people are sovereign and if as such they are capable of maintaining order, cohesion, and law, then there would be no difficulty in getting rid of an unjust ruler who was intended to serve the people rather than dominate them. This would be no more inconsistent than firing an incompetent employee.

Kant, at times, wavers and becomes quite confusing on these issues.

There are places where Kant seems to claim that the people *are* sovereign. For example, in the *Metaphysical Elements of Justice,* he tells us that the "legislative authority can be attributed only to the united Will of the people."[56] Here, he seems to suggest that the people must actually make their own laws. He then says, "the sovereign of the people (the legislator) cannot at the same time be the ruler, for the ruler is himself subject to the law and through it is obligated to another, the sovereign. The sovereign can take his authority from the ruler, depose him, or reform his administration, but cannot punish him."[57] Here, it seems that the people are sovereign and that they can even depose the ruler. But for some odd reason they cannot punish the ruler. This is so because, to "punish the ruler would mean that the highest executive authority would be subject to coercion, which is a self-contradiction."[58] Here, one begins to wonder whether Kant is shifting back to the view that the ruler rather than the people is sovereign. Two pages later, at least in the second paragraph of the quotation that follows, it seems clear that the ruler has again become the sovereign:

> if the organ of the sovereign, the ruler, proceeds contrary to the laws—for example, in imposing taxes, recruiting soldiers, and so on, so as to violate the law of equality in the distribution of political burdens—the subject may lodge a complaint about this injustice, but he may not actively resist.
>
> Indeed, even the constitution itself cannot contain any article that would allow for some authority in the state that could resist or restrain the chief magistrate in cases in which he violates the constitutional laws. For he who is supposed to restrain the authority of the state must have more power than, or at least as much power as, the person whom he is supposed to restrain. . . .[59]

Here the ruler is clearly sovereign—the ruler must have at least as much or more power than anyone else in the state. And even if Kant has claimed earlier in this text that the people must make their own laws rather than submit to an autocrat who makes the sort of laws they would give themselves, nevertheless, if the people can do nothing about a ruler who violates these laws, they have gained little.

Notes

1. I would especially like to thank Michael Brint and Michael Meyer for their comments on earlier versions of this chapter.

2. N. Machiavelli, *The Prince*, tr. T.G. Bergin (New York: Appleton-Century-Crofts, 1947), 44 (my emphasis).

3. It might be argued that Aristotle and Locke adopted both of these approaches to political theory before Kant did. But I would argue that this is not so. Aristotle and Locke do empirically consider what goes on in actual societies (Aristotle, for example, collects the constitutions of all the Greek city-states) and they also talk a bit about the best state. But neither has a real theory for how an empirical dynamic will actually realize the ideal state—and certainly no philosophy of history.

4. "Idea for a Universal History" (hereafter *IUH*), in *On History*, ed. L.W. Beck (Indianapolis: Bobbs-Merrill, 1963), 11 and, for the German, see *Kant's gesammelte Schriften* (hereafter *Ak*), ed. Königlich Preussischen Akademie der Wissenschaften (Berlin: de Gruyter, 1910 ff.), VIII, 17.

5. *IUH*, 12 and *Ak*, VIII, 17.

6. *IUH*, 13–14 and *Ak*, VIII, 19–20.

7. *IUH*, 15 and *Ak*, VIII, 20–21. J-J. Rousseau, *Discourse on Inequality*, 222 and *OC*, III, 219.

8. *IUH*, 13, 15 and *Ak*, VIII, 18–19, 21.

9. *IUH*, 15 and *Ak*, VIII, 21. *Perpetual Peace* (hereafter *PP*), in *On History*, 106, 111 and *Ak*, VIII, 360–61, 365. Also *On the Common Saying: 'This May be True in Theory, but it does not Apply in Practice'* (hereafter *Theory and Practice*), in *Kant's Political Writings*, ed. H. Reiss (Cambridge: Cambridge University Press, 1971), 90 and *Ak*, VIII, 310–11.

10. Plato, *Republic*, 358B–361E.

11. See Chapter 1, Section I above.

12. *IUH*, 18–20 and *Ak*, VIII, 24–26. *PP*, 106–8 and *Ak*, VIII, 361–63.

13. *IUH*, 23 and *Ak*, VIII, 28. *PP*, 114 and *Ak*, VIII, 368. *Theory and Practice*, 90 and *Ak*, VIII, 310–11.

14. *IUH*, 18–19 and *Ak*, VIII, 24–25. *PP*, 112–13 and *Ak*, VIII, 366–67.

15. *Foundations of the Metaphysics of Morals* (hereafter *F*) tr. L.W. Beck (Indianapolis: Bobbs-Merrill, 1959), 18–19 and *Ak*, IV, 402–3.

16. *F*, 18–19, 39 ff. and *Ak*, IV, 402–3, 421 ff.

17. *F*, 62–63 and *Ak*, IV, 444. *Critique of Practical Reason* (hereafter *CPrR*), tr. L.W. Beck (Indianapolis: Bobbs-Merrill, 1956), 66 and *Ak*, V, 64.

18. *F*, 6, 14–15 and *Ak*, IV, 390, 397–99.

19. *F*, 10, 14–17 and *Ak*, IV, 394, 397–401. *CPrR*, 122 and *Ak*, V, 117–18.

20. *PP*, 100 and *Ak*, VIII, 356.

21. *IUH*, 18–19 and *Ak*, VIII, 24–25. *PP*, 111–13 and *Ak*, VIII, 365–67. *Theory and Practice*, 90 and *Ak*, VIII, 310–11.

22. *PP*, 112–13 and *Ak*, VIII, 366–67. In Chapter 3, I argued that Kant's categorical imperative and Rousseau's general will are very similar. Notice that Kant himself employs the concept of a "general will" from time to time in his writings and, much like the categorical imperative, the general will "concerns the form of right and not the material or object" to which a person

is related (see *Theory and Practice*, 75 and *Ak*, VIII, 292). Moreover, the general will is incapable of being unjust (see *Metaphysical Elements of Justice: Part I of the Metaphysics of Morals*, tr. J. Ladd (Indianapolis: Bobbs-Merrill, 1965), 78 and *Ak*, VI, 313–14). However, for Kant, the general will does not require that the citizens vote on each law. It is only necessary that they be given laws that they could have imposed upon themselves. Kant wants a sovereign that rules autocratically but governs in a republican way. (See "What is Enlightenment?" in *On History*, 7 and *Ak*, VIII, 39. *Theory and Practice*, 77, 79–81, 85 and *Ak*, VIII, 294, 297–99, 304. *Contest of Faculties*, in *Kant's Political Writings*, 184, 187 and *Ak*, VII, 87–88, 91. Also, *Metaphysical Elements of Justice*, 96 and *Ak*, VI, 328.)

23. *IUH*, 17–18 and *Ak*, VIII, 23.

24. On the difference between legality and morality, see *Metaphysical Elements of Justice*, 19–21 and *Ak*, VI, 219–20. Kant also says that perpetual peace is an ideal that can never actually be realized, but that we can continually approach it as a duty; see *Metaphysical Elements of Justice*, 124 and *Ak*, VI, 350.

25. A. Smith, *The Wealth of Nations*, ed. E. Cannan (New York: Random House, 1937), 423.

26. *Social Contract*, 92–93 and *OC*, III, 415–16.

27. *IUH*, 22 and *Ak*, VIII, 27.

28. *The Prince*, 8, 33, 34, 50, 51.

29. See Chapter 3, Section I above.

30. See, for example, the *Critique of Pure Reason* (hereafter *CPR*), B383–384, A641-B669, A644-B672, A652–653, A677–B706. I have used the N. Kemp Smith translation (New York: St. Martin's, 1965) but cite the standard A and B edition pagination so that any edition, English or German, may be used.

31. *CPR*, B373–374. See also, *IUH*, 22, 25 and *Ak*, VIII, 27, 30. Also, "Review of Herder," in *On History*, 38 and *Ak*, VIII, 54. Also, "End of All Things," in *On History*, 75–76 and *Ak*, VIII, 332–33. Also Beck, in *On History*, xix–xx. Also Reiss, in *Kant's Political Writings*, 28.

32. *CPR*, A633–634, A641-B669.

33. *CPrR*, 34, 111–13 and *Ak*, V, 34, 107–9.

34. *CPrR*, 114–18 and *Ak*, V, 110–14.

35. *CPrR*, 4, 119, 129, 137–39 and *Ak*, V, 4, 115, 124–25, 132–34. *CPR*, A641-B669.

36. *IUH*, 13–14 and *Ak*, VIII, 19–20.

37. *Theory and Practice*, 64–65 and *Ak*, VIII, 279–80. Also *PP*, 106–8 and *Ak*, VIII, 362–63. Also *Religion Within the Limits of Reason Alone*, trs. T.M. Greene and H.H. Hudson (New York: Harper and Row, 1960), 92 and *Ak*, VI, 100–101. See also Y. Yovel, *Kant and the Philosophy of History* (Princeton: Princeton University Press, 1980), 6–7, 29 ff., 72–75, 99, 121.

38. *Critique of Judgment* (hereafter *CJ*), tr. J.H. Bernard (New York: Hafner, 1966), 32 and *Ak*, V, 195.

39. *CJ,* 12, 15–16, 33 and *Ak,* V, 176, 178–80, 196.

40. *First Introduction to the Critique of Judgment,* tr. J. Haden (Indianapolis: Bobbs-Merrill, 1965), 9 and *Ak,* XX, 202–3. *CJ,* 16, 33 and *Ak,* V, 180, 196.

41. *First Introduction,* 10 and *Ak,* XX, 204. See also, *CJ,* 17 and *Ak,* V, 180–81. In the "Idea for a Universal History," Kant asked whether it was "reasonable to assume a purposiveness in all the parts of nature and to deny it to the whole?" (*IUH,* 20 and *Ak,* VIII, 25. See also *PP,* 106–7 and *Ak,* VIII, 360–62). And indeed, in the third *Critique,* he makes it clear that he understands history as a teleological and purposive development. In the second part of the third *Critique,* Kant gives us a brief sketch that outlines much of what we have found in his writings on philosophy of history and politics. For Kant, the human being is the ultimate purpose of nature on earth in reference to whom all other things constitute a system of purposes. To realize this purpose, human beings must use nature as a means. They can attain this final end only in a civil community and a cosmopolitan system of states with a lawful arrangement of relations between persons. Moreover, it is war that leads to this conformity to law and system of states (*CJ,* 279, 281–83 and *Ak,* V, 429–30, 431–33). In this way the highest good—the harmony of morality and happiness—will finally be realized through the activity of human beings themselves. Kant says, "Now we have in the world only one kind of being whose causality is teleological, i.e. is directed to purposes . . . The being of this kind is man, but man considered as noumenon, the only natural being in which we can recognize . . . a supersensible faculty (freedom) and also the law of causality, together with the object, which this faculty may propose to itself as highest purpose (the highest good in the world) . . . If now things of the world, as beings dependent in their existence, need a supreme cause acting according to purposes, man is the final purpose of creation . . . Only in man, and only in him as subject of morality, do we meet with unconditioned legislation in respect of purposes, which therefore alone renders him capable of being a final purpose, to which the whole of nature is teleologically subordinated" (*CJ,* 285–86 and *Ak,* V, 435–36).

42. *CJ,* 23–4, 78, 83, 144 and *Ak,* V, 186–87, 241, 245, 301.

43. However, Kant distinguishes between two sorts of purposiveness in the third *Critique:* subjective purposiveness (discussed in the first part of the third *Critique*), which has to do with aesthetical judgment and beauty; and objective purposiveness or teleology (discussed in the second part of the third *Critique*), which Kant links, in the way that we have seen, to his politics and philosophy of history. The difference between these two forms of purposiveness is that subjective or aesthetical purposiveness does not involve a definite concept. The representation is not subsumed under a concept of the understanding, but simply appears on its own as in harmony with the understanding and thus gives rise to pleasure and an experience of beauty. In this way aesthetical judgment is unlike the good, which must involve the concept of a definite purpose.

Objective or teleological judgment, on the other hand, also requires a concept. It requires a concept of reason that relates reason to the understanding such that the concept of the thing's purpose is regarded as the cause of the thing.

This, however, does not involve necessary connection, but simply makes nature comprehensible by analogy with the causality of purposes. It is a regulative principle for the judging of phenomena, not a constitutive principle (*CJ,* 41, 44, 205–7, 212 and *Ak,* V, 207, 209, 359–61, 366. *First Introduction,* 37–38 and *Ak,* XX, 232–34). Thus, the realization in history of the final purpose—the highest good—requires a concept of the highest good and is a form of objective or teleological judgment. Thus it might seem that the realization of the highest good in history would involve only objective or teleological judgment and not aesthetic judgment or the experience of beauty. However, we must notice that Kant distinguishes between two forms of beauty: free beauty and dependent beauty. Free beauty (found, for example, in a flower or an arabesque) presupposes no concept of what the object ought to be. On the other hand, dependent beauty does presuppose a concept of the object's purpose, though an indeterminate one (*CJ,* 65–66, 160–61, 185–86 and *Ak,* V, 229–30, 316–17, 339–40).

For a fuller treatment of the role of concepts in the experience of beauty, see my "Kant and the Possibility of Uncategorized Experience," *Idealistic Studies* XIX (1989), 154–73. Human beauty, for example, presupposes the concept of such a purpose and its perfection. Dependent beauty also allows for the connection of the beautiful with the good and of understanding with reason. The ideal of human beauty, for example, involves an idea of reason that determines the purpose of humanity and that visibly expresses the moral (*CJ,* 67–72 and *Ak,* V, 231–35). Indeed, at the end of the first part of the third *Critique,* Kant argues that beauty is a symbol of the morally good. Aesthetical ideas or symbols, for Kant, are representations of the imagination that occasion more thought than any concept is able to encompass. They are a counterpart to the rational ideas of the Dialectic of the *Critique of Pure Reason,* which were concepts to which no intuition could be adequate. Aesthetical ideas try by means of the imagination to go beyond the limits of experience. In doing so they bring reason into play and thus try to make rational ideas apparent to the senses and therefore also to the understanding. In the experience of beauty, the imagination attempts to link concrete representations with ideas of reason. Symbols, by means of an analogy, try to supply an intuition for rational ideas. Beauty, in this way, can be a symbol of the morally good. It subjectively links nature and morality as well as understanding and reason (*CJ,* 157–60, 197–200 and *Ak,* V, 314–17, 351–54).

44. *CJ,* 44 and *Ak,* V, 210.

45. See F. Schiller, *Letters on the Aesthetic Education of Man* (hereafter *AE*), trs. E.M. Wilkinson and L.A. Willoughby (Oxford: Clarendon Press, 1967). Also, see my *Schiller, Hegel, and Marx,* Chapters 1, 3, and 4. For a different view of the relation of Kant's philosophy of history to his concept of

the beautiful, see W.J. Booth, *Interpreting the World: Kant's Philosophy of History and Politics* (Toronto: University of Toronto Press, 1986), 78 ff., 91, 115–18, 123–24.

46. "What is Enlightenment?", 7–8 and *Ak,* VIII, 39–40. *PP,* 93 n and *Ak,* VIII, 350 n. *Contest of Faculties,* 184 and *Ak,* VII, 88. *Theory and Practice,* 79–81, 85 and *Ak,* VIII, 297–99, 304. *Metaphysical Elements of Justice,* 96 and *Ak,* VI, 328.

47. *PP,* 120 and *Ak,* VIII, 372. *Theory and Practice,* 77 and *Ak,* VIII, 294. *Contest of Faculties,* 184, 187 and *Ak,* VII, 87–88, 91.

48. *PP,* 120, 130 and *Ak,* VIII, 372–73, 382. *Theory and Practice,* 82 and *Ak,* VIII, 301. *Contest of Faculties,* 182 and *Ak,* VII, 85. *Metaphysical Elements of Justice,* 89 and *Ak,* VI, 322–23.

49. "What Is Enlightenment?", 4–10 and *Ak,* VIII, 36–41. *Theory and Practice,* 84–85 and *Ak,* VIII, 304.

50. *PP,* 129–30 and *Ak,* VIII, 381–82.

51. *PP,* 130–33 and *Ak,* VIII, 382–85.

52. *PP,* 134–35 and *Ak,* VIII, 386.

53. Moreover, it is not at all clear that the second formulation of the categorical imperative, which requires that we treat all persons as ends in themselves and never only as means (*F,* 47 ff. and *Ak,* IV, 429 ff.), rules out the violence against others that might be unavoidable in a revolution. Kant suggests that standing armies attached to the state do treat individuals as means, but that defensive and voluntary citizen militias do not (*PP,* 87 and *Ak,* VIII, 345).

54. *Theory and Practice,* 84 and *Ak,* VIII, 303. See also *PP,* 130 and *Ak,* VIII, 382. Also *Metaphysical Elements of Justice,* 86, 140 and *Ak,* VI, 320, 372.

55. *Theory and Practice,* 82 and *Ak,* VIII, 301.

56. *Metaphysical Elements of Justice,* 78 and *Ak,* VI, 313.

57. *Metaphysical Elements of Justice,* 82 and *Ak,* VI, 317.

58. Ibid.

59. *Metaphysical Elements of Justice,* 85, see also 86 and *Ak,* VI, 319, 320.

Hegel, the State, and Spirit

Hegel's political thought can best be understood if we understand its relationship to Rousseau's political theory and Kant's philosophy of history.

In the first place, Hegel's conception of the modern state closely resembles Rousseau's ideal community. This community was based upon rational freedom realized through a general will and it was reinforced by custom and tradition that shaped the character, interests, and feelings of the individual citizens in support of the general will. However, Rousseau's ideal community was utopian—it could not be realized in the modern world. For it to be possible at all, it was necessary that healthy customs and traditions simply be given in a traditional society. The ideal community was incompatible with wealth, commerce, and trade, which for Hegel are necessary elements of the modern state, but which for Rousseau were thought to promote particular interest, the corruption of custom and tradition, and the erosion of commitment to the general will. These matters will be discussed in Section III.

Thus, in order to develop a political theory that will explain the possibility of the ideal state in the modern world, Hegel turns toward Kant's philosophy of history. Kant argued that conflicting particular interests embedded in commerce and trade themselves lead to what morality—the categorical imperative or the general will[1]—would have demanded from the start. Once we understand this directedness in history, for Kant, our moral action can hasten its development to the final goal. Hegel develops a similar philosophy of history that will allow him to explain the development of an ideal moral society in the modern world based upon a general will that at the same time is compatible with wealth, commerce, and trade. Kant's ideal state, however, completely lacked custom, tradition, and community, which are important aspects of what Hegel calls *Sittlichkeit*. Hegel finds this absence objectionable and tries to rectify it. These matters will be discussed in Section II.

Hegel's goal, then, is to combine three things: (1) rational freedom of the sort realized through a general will or categorical imperative, (2) a theory of historical development in which conflicting particular interests lead to a moral society, and (3) custom, tradition, or *Sittlichkeit*. To do this Hegel will have to reject critically certain aspects of the thought of Rousseau and Kant and he will have to explain how custom, tradition, and community, instead of being corrupted by particular interest, commerce, and trade, can come to be compatible with them. The key to this will be Hegel's concept of spirit. These matters will be discussed in Sections IV and V. Let us begin with Kant.

I. Philosophy of History and *Sittlichkeit*

For Kant, we have seen in Chapter 4, there are two forces at work in history. The first is the conflict of particular interests. The second is morality. And both, for Kant, lead to the same end—peace, justice, and a league of nations. Conflict and war, for Kant, will lead toward morality, the categorical imperative.[2]

The notion that conflicting self-interests lead toward what morality demands, Kant gets, I think, from Adam Smith. As we have seen, in a market economy, each pursues only their own self-interest. Nevertheless, this self-seeking not only produces a common good, but it does so, for Smith, more effectively than if individuals had consciously and cooperatively sought the common good. Aggressive self-seeking, given the interdependence of each upon all, produces a national capital, the wealth of the nation, that *common good*, out of which each struggles to gain their particular share. Self-seeking produces this common good through an "invisible hand"; that is, behind our backs and despite our intentions.[3]

Although Hegel, unlike Kant, does not think that world history is leading toward peace, a league of nations, or international law,[4] and although there are other important differences between Hegel and Kant, nevertheless Hegel, very much like Kant, relies on an invisible hand argument both in his philosophy of history and in his theory of civil society. Just as conflicting particular interests lead toward morality for Kant, so for Hegel particular interest or passion is the active

Hegel, the State, and Spirit   125

force in history that gives rise to the universal. Human passions and the universal Idea are the warp and the woof of world history.[5] Hegel says,

> The particular interests of passion cannot . . . be separated from the realization of the universal . . . Particular interests contend with one another, and some are destroyed in the process. But it is from this very conflict and destruction of particular things that the universal emerges, and it remains unscathed itself. For it is not the universal Idea which enters into opposition, conflict, and danger; it keeps itself in the background, untouched and unharmed, and sends forth the particular interests of passion to fight and wear themselves out in its stead. It is what we may call the cunning of reason that it sets the passions to work in its service, so that the agents by which it gives itself existence must pay the penalty and suffer the loss.[6]

World history, for Hegel, occurs as the universal Idea is realized through the conflict of particular interests—a conflict that produces effects quite different from what the individuals consciously intended to accomplish.[7]

So also, in his discussion of civil society in the *Philosophy of Right,* Hegel, as Kant does, follows Adam Smith. Civil society is a system of economic interdependence where self-seeking unconsciously turns into a contribution to the satisfaction of the needs of all. Competitive self-seeking produces a common capital from which each struggles to gain their share. Conflicting particular interests lead to the universal. Moreover, for Hegel, a state is well constituted when the private interests of the citizens coincide with the general end of the state.[8]

So far, the views of Hegel and Kant are quite similar. Now we must examine the differences. In the first place, for Hegel, we cannot say that there are *two different* forces at work in history—the conflict of particular interests and morality—as for Kant. "The particular interests of passion *cannot* . . . *be separated from* the realization of the universal. . . ."[9] We can begin to understand Hegel's views on this matter if we look to the section of the *Phenomenology* entitled "Virtue and the Way of the World." Most commentators on the *Phenomenology* seem to think that this section refers to Don Quixote. None of them, that I am aware of, seem to see what it really refers to, which is so very clearly Kant's philosophy of history.

In this section, "virtue" is described such that it is quite clear that Hegel has Kant's ethics in mind. Virtue is the consciousness that law is essential and that individuality—which is to say, particular interest—must be sacrificed to the universal and thus brought under the discipline and control of the universal. Virtue wills to accomplish a good that is not yet actual; the universal is an "ought" that must be realized. And it can be realized only through virtue's nullifying of individuality or particular interests.[10] For the "way of the world," on the other hand, individuality takes *itself* to be essential—which is to say that it pursues self-interest. It seeks its own pleasure and enjoyment, and in doing so it subordinates the universal to itself. For Kant, both morality and the conflict of particular interests converge toward the same universal end. So also, for Hegel, the way of the world, through the conflict of particular interests, achieves the universal—the very same universal that virtue seeks.[11] For Kant, it was morality's task to guide the historical conflict of particular interests and to hasten it toward its end. For Hegel, virtue too attempts to assist the way of the world to realize the universal. At this point, however, Hegel's disagreement with Kant begins. Hegel argues that, in fact, virtue's assistance is *unnecessary;* the way of the world is quite capable of realizing the universal on its own. Virtue's assistance is a sham.[12] Virtue wants to bring the good into existence by the sacrifice of individuality or particular interest. But it is individuality, the conflict of particular interests, that actually realizes the universal. Virtue wants to realize the universal as something that *ought to be* rather than as something which *is*. The way of the world is our first dim view in the *Phenomenology* of *Sittlichkeit*—morality that appears not merely as an ought, but which is. Hegel says:

> Virtue in the ancient world had its own definite sure meaning, for it had in the spiritual substance of the nation a foundation full of meaning, and for its purpose an actual good already in existence. Consequently, too, it was not directed against the actual world as against something generally perverted, and against a "way of the world." But the virtue we are considering has its being outside of the spiritual substance, it is an unreal virtue, a virtue in imagination and name only, which lacks that substantial content.[13]

Thus, for Hegel, we must drop the idea that virtue exists only as a principle, an ought, which as yet has no actual existence and which is brought into existence through the sacrifice of individuality, particular interest, or passion. Hegel's objection to Kantian morality, or "virtue," is that it is abstract, outside the world, an ought, and that it believes that only it is capable of realizing morality.[14] It has severed itself from the concrete actual world of interest and passion, and it faces it as an other. From this superior position it wants to direct the world. Instead, morality must be rooted in the world. Or, to put this another way, the point Hegel is making here, as we shall see more clearly in what follows, is that Kant's philosophy of history and his ethics are written from the perspective of individual consciousness—the perspective that there are only individual consciousnesses. Morality, for Kant, is a matter of individual will abstracted from the concrete actual world. Certainly, for Kant, inclinations, interests, and passions are part of the world—the world of natural causality—and are to be carefully excluded and separated from the realm of the individual moral will if the individual is to be self-determined and thus free. It is this separation that Hegel objects to. Kant has no notion of spirit or *Sittlichkeit*, which are beginning to emerge here in the *Phenomenology* and which Hegel is aiming at. *Sittlichkeit* is morality embedded in a concrete spiritual world. For Hegel, virtue and the way of the world, particular interest and the universal, morality and the concrete world, are not separate opposed realities externally related to each other. They are internally related as parts of a single spiritual reality that already exists; it is not something that merely ought to be realized.

For Hegel, we must abandon the perspective of individual consciousness and adopt a perspective in which the concrete world and individual consciousness are seen as two parts of one spiritual unity. Individual consciousness is the internalization of the social world and the social world is the outcome of the actions of individual consciousnesses. Each develops in interaction with the other, and each transforms the other.

Hegel agrees with the Kantian and Smithian notion that a conflict of particular interests leads to the universal. What Hegel does not accept is that this can be understood merely at the level of individual consciousness. It must be understood at the level of spirit. Spirit explains how individual interest—the concrete way of the world—is connected to virtue. This will become clearer in Section IV, but here we can at least say that conflict among particular interests gives rise to a set of institutions, a world, which comes to have a life of its own and which reacts back upon and molds those individual consciousnesses and thus leads them to virtue. Particular interests and virtue are not two eternally separate realms external to one another. They are internally related as two interacting parts enclosed within a single spiritual unity, and each produces the other. Virtue is simply mistaken in thinking itself independent and outside of this spiritual reality, superior to it, and thus able to guide particular interests from above. In fact, for

Hegel, we cannot guide history at all as Kant thinks we can. History is not a matter of individual will, but of spirit. Individuals are unconscious tools of world spirit. Moreover, there is no ought that the individual will can independently set out to realize. Morality already exists as this spiritual unity that encloses us and is our very being. Hegel's task is to reconcile us to what *is* by allowing us to correctly understand what *is*. His aim is to transform our understanding of reality so that we accept it, not to transform reality in accordance with an ought.[15]

To understand this critique of Kant more clearly, we must notice that Hegel distinguishes between two forms of morality—*Moralität* and *Sittlichkeit*. *Moralität* begins with Socrates and reaches its high point in Kant. *Moralität* is individual, rational, and reflective morality. It is based upon individual autonomy and personal conviction. One must rationally decide what is moral and do it because it is moral— because our rationality tells us that it is the right thing to do. This rational and reflective component is absent in *Sittlichkeit*. *Sittlichkeit* is best represented in the Greek *polis* before the rise of Socratic *Moralität*. *Sittlichkeit* is ethical behavior grounded in custom and tradition and developed through habit and imitation in accordance with the objective laws of the community. Personal reflection and analysis have little to do with *Sittlichkeit*.[16] *Sittlichkeit* is ethical life built into one's character, attitudes, and feelings.

Furthermore, *Moralität* involves an ought. It is morality that ought to be realized. This "ought" is also absent from *Sittlichkeit*. For it, morality is not something we *ought* to realize, or something we *ought* to be. Morality exists—it *is*. It is already embedded in our customs, traditions, character, attitudes, and feelings. Here there is no opposition between particular interest and the universal. There is no opposition between subject and object. The objective ethical order exists in, is actualized in, is the essence of, the subject.[17]

What Hegel wants for the modern world is neither traditional *Sittlichkeit* nor modern *Moralität*. He wants a synthesis of *Sittlichkeit* and *Moralität* which, though at times confusing, he also calls *Sittlichkeit*. This higher *Sittlichkeit* combines the rational and reflective side of *Moralität* with the transcendence of the ought characteristic of *Sittlichkeit*. It is rational, reflective morality concretely embedded in the customs, traditions, character, and feelings of individuals. It is a reflective consciousness of the ethical substance.[18]

Sittlichkeit without *Moralität* is inadequate for Hegel. So also, Hegel rejects Kantian *Moralität* without *Sittlichkeit*. This was implied in "Virtue and the Way of the World," but it is made clearer in following sections of the *Phenomenology* in which Hegel goes on to argue that Kantian *Moralität* shorn of *Sittlichkeit* is in fact impossible. Hegel argues that it is impossible to discover one's moral obligation in Kantian fashion simply by analyzing abstract principles to see if they are universal and noncontradictory. For example, private property as well as its opposite (common ownership or the absence of private property) are equally universalizable and noncontradictory. Without *Sittlichkeit*—without an immediately given, objective, ethical substance embedded in custom and tradition that actually *is* rather than merely ought to be—it is impossible to discover through analysis one's moral obligation. *Moralität* gets its content from *Sittlichkeit*.[19]

Moreover, *Moralität* without *Sittlichkeit* would leave us with an inadequate form of freedom. For Kant, individual subjectivity alone is free. Individuals are free when practical reason determines their action. The individual, however, is not necessarily free to realize this moral action. The objective world may well present obstacles to the carrying out of the moral action, without, for Kant, affecting the individual's moral freedom in the least.[20] For Kant, such empirical factors, whether they are obstacles or aids, must be completely ignored. They are irrelevant to freedom. Nor do feelings or inclinations play a role here. They need not support the action for it to be moral or free; nor is our freedom affected if our feelings are opposed to the moral action.[21] For Hegel, on the other hand, freedom is realized only when the objective external world and our feelings fit, agree with, and support the subjective rational freedom of the individual. Laws and institutions, feelings and customs, as well as the rationality of the individual must form a single organic spiritual unity. Thus, for Hegel, freedom requires three things: (1) that the individual be self-determined by universal and rational principles, (2) that rationality have been objectified in the laws and institutions of the state such that in obeying civil laws we obey the laws of our own reason, and (3) that interests, feelings, and customs have been molded so as to agree with and support these rational laws such that particular interests are satisfied and yet lead to the universal.[22]

For Kant, the possibility of freedom required that the transcendental self not be located in the natural, causally determined, phenomenal world. Another—a noumenal realm—was required. A sphere apart from the natural sphere was necessary as the source of self-determined, free action.[23] Hegel, in rejecting the existence of an unknown thing in itself,[24] rejects the existence of this separate noumenal realm. Rather than locate a transcendental self in a realm apart, as "virtue" was opposed to the "way of the world," he denies that there are such different realms and he views reality as a single field with two elements reacting against each other such that ultimately the natural objective element is absorbed into the conscious subjective element. In this way the object is no longer alien or other. There is a single spiritual realm split into two parts: the individual subjective realm and the objective substantial realm. Each side produces the other. Individual action and interests give rise to an objective worldly reality, which then turns upon the individuals, molds them, and lifts them to the level of universality. The subject does not confront the object as a heteronomous other. The object is the outcome of the subject's own activity, the realization of the subject's essence, and thus the object is compatible with the subject's freedom. The subject is not externally related to the object, but internally related to it as its own essence.

Individuals work on their world through history and transform it to fit themselves,[25] just as the world transforms individuals so that they conform to it. In confronting their world, individuals confront and discover themselves. For Hegel, they confront their own rationality objectified in the world. This fit between the subjective rationality of the individual and the objective rationality of the world when it is supported by custom, tradition, and feeling, is the basis of *Sittlichkeit*. To pursue this further, we must now turn to Rousseau.

II. The Development of Custom and Tradition

For Rousseau, there is a natural tendency for the customs and traditions of any community to become corrupted. Rousseau argues in the *Discourse on Inequality* that in simple, healthy, egalitarian communities, as soon as agriculture and metallurgy develop and surplus production occurs, society is plunged into inequality, conflict of interests, and the corruption of customs.[26]

Moreover, it is clearly Rousseau's view that once healthy customs have been corrupted, all is lost. They can never be revived. "A thousand nations that have flourished on earth could never have tolerated good laws, and even those that could were only so disposed for a very short time during their entire existence. Most peoples, like men, are docile only in their youth. They become incorrigible as they grow older. Once customs are established and prejudices have taken root, it is a dangerous and foolhardy undertaking to want to reform them. The people cannot even tolerate having their ills touched for the purpose of destroying them. . . ."[27]

Furthermore, for Rousseau, wealth, unequal property, and commerce are fundamentally corrupting forces. They promote self-interest and erode the citizen's commitment to the public good. They corrupt custom, tradition, and patriotism, which then will no longer be able to reinforce the general will. Moreover, they can even erode the general will directly. They will make it all the more difficult for the citizens to fulfill several necessary conditions for the realization of the general will—the need to transcend their immediate interests and to concern themselves with abstract questions, as well as the need to ask "what is the common good?" or "what is the general will?" instead of "what do I immediately want?" Moreover, it is not plausible to expect that the general will could avoid particular interests and always come to the right answer about the sorts of complex, tangled, and difficult property disputes that would arise out of a developed system of commerce and trade. For this reason alone, Rousseau must rule them out.[28]

Thus, as I argued in Chapter 3, Rousseau is a utopian. His ideal state is impossible in the modern world. It is incompatible with wealth, commerce, and trade, which corrupt custom and tradition; and once customs and traditions have been corrupted, all is lost. For a decent society to be possible, healthy customs and traditions must simply be given in a traditional and premodern society. They cannot grow and develop nor can they be revived in the modern world with its commitment to wealth, commerce, and trade.

Hegel certainly wants a state that realizes the universal or the general will and he wants it reinforced by custom, tradition, and *Sittlichkeit*. But he also wants such a state to be possible in the modern world and thus compatible with wealth, commerce, and trade. He therefore needs a theory that will explain how custom and tradition can change—not in the sense that they become corrupted but in the sense that they develop and can be maintained and preserved in a changing modern society involving commerce, trade, and wealth.

To understand this theory, we must notice that Hegel differs from Rousseau in that for him customs and traditions are not simply given conditions—the groundwork—upon which the institutions of a state are to be established. Rather, Hegel argues that *Sittlichkeit* (that is, custom and tradition, the feelings and attitudes of the citizens) are *produced* by social and political institutions. Patriotism, for example, which Hegel understands as a sentiment that "habitually recognizes that the community is one's substantive groundwork and end," is "simply a product of the institutions subsisting in the state."²⁹ It thus follows that different states or a state as it changes historically will produce different customs and traditions.

This production requires that mind pass through a process of education (*Bildung*)³⁰ and this education is a discipline. For example, in discussing the rise of modern Germany out of the Middle Ages, Hegel says:

> The two iron rods which were the instrument of this discipline were the Church and serfdom. The Church drove the "Heart" to desperation—made Spirit pass through the severest bondage . . . In the same way serfdom, which made a man's body not his own, but the property of another, dragged humanity through all the barbarism of slavery and unbridled desire . . . It was not so much *from* slavery as *through* slavery that humanity was emancipated . . . it is from this intemperate and ungovernable state of volition that the discipline in question emancipated him.³¹

In the *Philosophy of Right*, Hegel puts it in more general terms: "Mind attains its actuality only by creating a dualism within itself, by submitting itself to physical needs and the chain of these external necessities, and so imposing on itself this barrier and this finitude, and finally by educating (*bildet*) itself inwardly even when under this barrier until it overcomes it and attains its objective reality in the finite."³² In the modern state, civil society is one of the most important institutions that provide this discipline or education. In the first place, it produces in individuals the habit of work. At the same time, it makes individuals dependent upon one another for the satisfaction of their needs. Finally, as we have seen earlier, it turns self-seeking into a contribution to the satisfaction of the needs of all such that self-interest leads to the universal.³³

But still, how can commerce, trade, and wealth, which are generated in civil society, avoid corrupting custom and tradition and become compatible with *Sittlichkeit?* Hegel is certainly aware of Rousseau's argument that particular interest destroys custom and tradition. In fact, in the Introduction to the *Philosophy of History*, Hegel's general picture of the historical course of nations is quite similar to Rousseau's (except that Hegel thinks the state produces its customs and traditions rather than presupposes them). For Hegel, nations in their youth create their own ethics, customs, and religion, and individuals assimilate themselves to them. In its youth, the nation actively and vigorously struggles to realize itself in the actual world, to make itself what it is, and to defend its achievements. Once this has been accomplished, the nation then starts to become inactive and self-indulgent; it settles into routine and habit; and it stagnates. At this point, "[i]ndividual interests seize control of the powers and resources which were formerly dedicated to the whole." "Individuals withdraw into themselves and pursue their own ends, and this . . . is the nation's undoing." As the nation declines, a new higher principle emerges, but always in *another* nation.[34] Thus, for Hegel much as for Rousseau, particular interests cause the downfall and corruption of nations.

But in the *Philosophy of Right,* while Hegel admits that the principle of particular interest or subjectivity destroyed the ancient world, he nevertheless insists that the principle of particular interest is an essential part of freedom. He claims that the "principle of modern states has prodigious strength and depth because it allows the principle of subjectivity to progress to its culmination in the extreme of self-subsistent personal particularity, and yet at the same time brings it back to the substantive unity and so maintains this unity in the principle of subjectivity itself."[35] In other words—and this is the key—wealth, commerce, and trade as well as the particular interests they promote do not ultimately erode custom, tradition, and *Sittlichkeit* as Rousseau argued because in civil society particular interest is not only compatible with the universal, it actively generates the universal.

Hegel does not develop a theory of how one can set about changing customs and traditions to produce the ones we want in the future. That would be to guide history and that is impossible for Hegel. Rather, he recognizes that customs and traditions just do change. Even Rousseau admitted this—though he thought they only became corrupted. Hegel develops a theory that allows us to understand this change without concluding that it will lead to corruption. He takes up Kant's philosophy of history, Adam Smith's concept of an invisible hand, and some of the views of James Steuart to show that particular interest and competitive self-seeking as well as the customs and traditions that crystallize around this discipline lead unconsciously to the common good, something Rousseau could not see.[36] Far from leading away from the common good and to corruption as for Rousseau, they lead to and reinforce the universal and thus are perfectly compatible with *Sittlichkeit* in the modern state.

We have seen that Hegel objects to Kantian morality because it is abstract—cut off from the concrete world. He instead wants a morality rooted in the world of custom, tradition, feeling, passion, and interest. He wants *Sittlichkeit,* not *Moralität.* In this respect he is like Rousseau. But, as we have also seen, Rousseau's ideal society is a utopia where healthy customs and traditions must simply be given and where property and particular interest are a main source of corruption. Thus, Hegel also appeals to Kant's dynamic philosophy of history so that he can envision change not as a corruption but as the realization of an ideal state that can be compatible with wealth, commerce, and trade in the modern world. This important connection between Kant and Rousseau is made possible because Hegel is able to see two things: first, that given the socioeconomic interdependence of each upon all, particular interests can lead to the universal; and second, that social institutions, especially civil society, through education and discipline, produce customs and traditions that reinforce the tendency of particular interests to realize the universal. Thus, this Kantian dynamic not only leads to the universal, but it is now concrete. It is tied up with particular interests, passions, and activity that will produce a discipline that shapes customs and traditions as well as molds feelings, sentiments, and particular interests together with the universal common good.

Thus, we have three things: (1) morality that exists concretely in the world tied up with interests and passions. It exists there before us. It is not an unrealized ought. It is *Sittlichkeit*. (2) Yet this *Sittlichkeit* does not just have to be given or presupposed in utopian fashion as for Rousseau. It is developing and dynamic without becoming corrupted. And (3) it realizes the universal—the general will or the categorical imperative—not by a "virtue" that exists outside the concrete but in and through concrete interests and individuality.

While Hegel certainly accepts that part of Rousseau's concept of the general will that suggests that individual interest is transformed into the universal, he is nevertheless quite critical of other aspects of Rousseau's concept of the general will. Hegel says that Rousseau:

> takes the will only in a determinate form as the individual will, and he regards the universal will . . . only as a "general" will which proceeds out of this individual will as out of a conscious will. The result is that he reduces the union of individuals in the state to a contract and therefore to something based on their arbitrary wills, their opinion, and their capriciously given express consent. . . .[37]

Many commentators misunderstand what Hegel is saying here. They think he is criticizing Rousseau for understanding the general will as a particular will.[38] Rousseau certainly does not do this, and this is not what Hegel is claiming. By the term "individual will," Hegel does not mean "particular will." Hegel is here making much the same sort of criticism of Rousseau that, as we saw in Section II above, he made of Kant. Hegel is claiming that Rousseau understands the general will only from the perspective of individual consciousness—that for Rousseau only individual consciousnesses exist. Thus, for Rousseau, the general will is seen as the outcome of individual wills willing the common good rather than as the outcome of spirit. It follows from this that the individual wills must vote, that they are responsible for establishing the laws of the state, and thus that individuals rule. Hegel, as we shall see, does not believe that all individuals should vote and he certainly does not believe that they should rule.[39] He believes that this sort of thing led to the French Revolution. Moreover, while the individual will, for Rousseau, does realize the universal or general will, it sustains only an external relation to the general will much as virtue was external to the way of the world for Kant.[40]

For Hegel to be able to reconcile the Kantian–Smithian principle of conflicting interests with Rousseauian custom, tradition, and *Sittlichkeit,* it is crucial that self-interest not be thought to produce a universal external to itself. Self-interest must be understood to sustain an internal relation to the universal as its own essence. It must implicitly be the universal. For Rousseau, particular interest is seen as external to the universal much as interest or inclination was seen as external to and thus incompatible with morality and freedom for Kant. Thus, for Rousseau, in a society in which particular interest is powerful, it will be impossible to achieve the universal—the general will. Particular interest will appear to erode the ethical basis of the state: it will erode custom, tradition, and *Sittlichkeit.* Since particular interest and the universal are external and opposed to each other, the realization of one excludes the realization of the other. Particular interest is heteronomous. If viewed from the perspective of individual will where individuals sustain an external relation to the universal, Hegel agrees that one would have to come to the conclusion, much as Rousseau did, that particular interest erodes the universal. After all, Hegel himself admits that particular interest destroyed the ancient community.

For Hegel, we must transcend the perspective of individual consciousness. Particular interests and the universal must be viewed as internally related—as two interacting elements of one spiritual reality, each molding and forming the other. The universal must be seen as the essential manifestation of the individuals and individuals as disciplined by the universal. Then particular interests—wealth, trade, and commerce—will not be seen as heteronomous. They will be seen as compatible with the universal and with freedom. Individuals will be related to their own essence within *Sittlichkeit* and community. To make this clearer, however, we must say a good deal more about spirit as well as about its relationship to the state and to the individual citizens.

III. Spirit and the State

Hegel's concept of spirit is most difficult to understand, let alone accept. In this section, I simply wish to explain this concept as clearly as possible without getting lost in details so that we can understand the political and historical views that depend upon it. I do not expect to persuade anyone of, nor am I persuaded by, every single consideration involved here. At any rate, in the *Phenomenology,* Hegel discusses the rise of the modern state, and here we find a most important treatment of how spirit develops through alienation and estrangement.[41] The development of the modern state and of culture occurs through a dialectical interaction that takes place between individual self-consciousness and the objective world. The very existence and development of this objective world, as well as the actualization and development of individual self-consciousness, depend upon the fact that self-consciousness alienates itself. Both sides here, which have become split and self-opposed, are in reality two sides of one spiritual unity. This fact, however, is not recognized by either side.[42] Individual self-consciousness, for Hegel, alienates itself—it gives up its very essence—and thus objectifies itself in the world in the form of the state. The individual must alienate itself; in other words, it must serve, recognize, and obey this state. It must sacrifice itself to the state almost to the point of death. Only in this way does the state become actual. The state is made actual only by gaining this recognition, obedience, and service.[43] The state, for Hegel, is nothing but the objectified essence—the recognition, service, and sacrifice—of individual self-consciousness.

Individual self-consciousness thus creates its world through alienation, but at the same time its world takes on a life of its own and appears independent of individual self-consciousness. The objectified state power turns upon individuals. It becomes estranged. It dominates and controls them. It comes to demand their obedience and recognition. In this way it molds, disciplines, and educates individuals. It demands that they conform themselves to this universal substance. As individual self-consciousness alienates itself, conforms itself, recognizes, and serves this state, the state gains reality; it becomes universal, accepted, and recognized. The more power this state gains, the more power it will have to mold and discipline the individual subjects and make them conform to this universal reality.

The state gains in reality by embodying and institutionalizing the reality, the essence, the service of the subjects. The subjects gain reality in being disciplined by, in conforming to, and in being recognized by the universal reality of the state. The state is the subject's *own* reality—its essence, its *self*. At the same time, the state disciplines its subjects, educates them, and lifts them to universality.

Both individual self-consciousness and the objective world of the state are at the same time parts of, and are constituting, a single spiritual unity—a single cultural world that is divided and self-opposed. But this unity goes unrecognized. Moreover, it is quite necessary that it go unrecognized. If either side were to understand this mutual process, its development would falter. If individual self-consciousness saw that the state was its own alienated essence, it would cease to take the state seriously, as essential, and it would cease to respect and serve it. If the state were to see its dependence on its subjects, the state would also cease to take itself seriously. It would cease to take itself as essential and universal, and thus it would lose the power effectively to mold and discipline its subjects toward this universality.[44]

What is occurring here, despite the fact that it is estranged and goes unrecognized, is that individual self-consciousness is being related to and rooted in the objective substantial world, not in the sense that it is being related heteronomously to something other and outside itself, but rather in the sense that the other, the objective, the state, is its own essence, is itself objectified. Moreover, this other—which is its essence—is the universal. It has the universal and rational form of the state and its laws. Individual self-consciousness is thus establishing itself as the universal.

Ultimately, for Hegel, this estrangement and lack of recognition must be overcome. To be free, individual self-consciousness must come to see that the objective order is its universalized essence, and it must *consciously* will to serve and obey that universal, rational, and objective order rather than be dominated and coerced to do so. This recognition, for Hegel, can be gained only after self-consciousness has been raised to the level of religion. As we see in following sections of the *Phenomenology,* religion, the relationship between individual self-consciousness and God, which embraces the totality of things, develops through a dialectical process of interaction much like that between individual self-consciousness and the state. Each establishes and realizes the other.[45] Religion, for Hegel, is spirit's self-consciousness. Religion is the spirit of a people or of a culture reflecting upon itself, understanding itself, depicting to itself its importance, and committing itself to its mission and its truth. Only at the level of religious consciousness do we gain a consciousness with sufficient scope and universality to see that individual self-consciousness and the objective state are simply two interacting parts of one spiritual unity, and only then can we *consciously* will to serve and obey that objective order that we see is our own essence.

In the last section of the *Phenomenology,* Hegel says, this "alienation of self-consciousness . . . has not merely a negative but a positive meaning . . . on the one hand self-consciousness itself alienates itself; for in doing so it establishes itself as object, or, by reason of the indivisible unity characterizing self-existence, sets up the object as itself." This is the process of alienation establishing the state that we have just discussed. Hegel continues:

> On the other hand, there is also this other moment in the process, that self-consciousness has equally superseded this self-alienation and objectification, and has taken them back into itself, and is thus at home with itself in its otherness as such . . . The cultivated self-consciousness, which has traversed the world of spirit in self-estrangement, has, through its self-alienation, produced the thing as its own self; it retains itself, therefore, still in the thing, and knows the thing to have no independence.[46]

Thus, when self-consciousness realizes that the object has no independence, that it is the result of its own alienation, self-consciousness knows the object as itself and is no longer estranged. Estrangement, from the beginning, meant that the subject and the object were two sides of the same spiritual unity. They had become split and self-opposed such that this unity went unrecognized. When this unity is recognized, the estrangement is overcome. Even objectification has been overcome. The object no longer appears as an independent other. It appears as one's own essence.

Hegel's political aim is not to change or remake the world, but to reconcile us to it by allowing us to grasp it in thought fully and adequately.[47] Estrangement is overcome by recognizing what it is. Individual self-consciousness does not cease to alienate itself; it simply recognizes that it alienates itself. It recognizes that the state is its own essence. It then continues to alienate itself, to serve and conform itself to the state, its own essence, but now it does so *consciously* and thus becomes free.

To understand these matters more completely, we must discuss their metaphysical and epistemological background. Hegel's Introduction to the *Encyclopaedia*, while also interspersed with a discussion of other matters, attempts to review the history of philosophy. Hegel indicates the strengths and weaknesses of past philosophical systems and indicates what in them must be preserved as philosophy develops. Later philosophical systems, for Hegel, are always the result and outcome of previous philosophical systems.[48] This is certainly Hegel's view of his own system.

For Hegel, the strength of traditional (pre-Kantian) metaphysics, and what must be preserved from it, is its lack of any antithesis between subject and object. Traditional metaphysics believes that it brings universal objects before the mind as they really are. It takes the laws and forms of thought to be the laws and forms of things. Thought grasps the very essence of things; it directly grasps absolute, objective, universal reality.[49]

On the other hand, modern empiricism abandons metaphysics and turns to experience. For empiricism, whatever is true must be a particular in the actual world and immediately present to sensation. Individuals must feel themselves present and involved in every fact of knowledge they accept. While the object is merely subjective experience, nevertheless it is immediately present and completely certain to consciousness.[50]

Kant's critical philosophy also considers experience to be the sole foundation for cognition. Moreover, all experience for Kant presupposes a transcendental unity of self-consciousness. The multiplicity of diverse sensations is brought into a unity only within a unified self-consciousness. These sensations are constituted into an object by this self-consciousness.[51] Thus, in part, what Hegel considers Kant's strength to be is the same as what he considered empiricism's strength to be: that an object must be *my* immediate experience for knowledge to be possible. But also Kant's strength lies in the most important notion that the object is constituted by our self-consciousness.

Hegel's philosophical system combines and synthesizes the strengths of these three previous philosophical systems. It combines the direct grasp of universal objective reality characteristic of traditional metaphysics with the Kantian and empiricist principle that all experience is immediately mine within consciousness, and it combines these with the Kantian principle that all objects are constituted within a single unified self-consciousness. Hegel's system is a reorganized synthetic unity of the positive achievements of all previous philosophy.

To achieve this synthesis, which at first sight might seem impossible, Hegel must abandon Kant's unknown thing in itself, which he very clearly finds unacceptable in any case,[52] and he must abandon the perspective of individual consciousness. Since Hegel rejects the unknown thing in itself but still holds that experience is constituted by self-consciousness, he clearly cannot hold that self-consciousness constitutes mere phenomenal appearance cut off from a noumenal thing in itself that remains unknown. If we constitute experience and if the thing in itself is not to be unknown but known, then, for Hegel, we must constitute *reality*.

But if it were only individual self-consciousness that constituted reality we would be plunged into a subjectivist chaos. What is required is an absolute self-consciousness[53]—the consciousness of God, or a consciousness that has raised itself to the absolute perspective of God. Here we have a total and universal consciousness that in constituting reality (as for Kant) would have reality immediately present to itself within consciousness (as for Kant and empiricism). Since it includes *all* reality—there being no reality outside such a consciousness—it would also have that immediate grasp of absolute objective reality characteristic of traditional metaphysics. The subjective principle of modern philosophy is compatible with the objectivity of traditional philosophy only for an absolute consciousness. God's subjectivity, because it is total, is objective and absolute. Thus, in finally overcoming estrangement, as we have seen, cultural or religious self-consciousness faces all of reality constituted by itself and immediately present to itself as its own essence.

We must notice that what we have just said here describes at the metaphysical and epistemological level exactly what we earlier said about freedom in the moral and political sphere. Hegel's view that the subjective rationality of the individual must fit with the objective rationality embedded in the laws and institutions of the state is the same as his claim that the objective reality of traditional metaphysics must be immediately grasped within the subjective consciousness of individuals. This identity of subject and object is possible because the subject has constituted the object, the state, as its own essence through a dialectical process of alienation. Moreover, the fact that freedom requires that this identity of subjective and objective rationality be reinforced by custom, tradition, and feeling is the same as Hegel's insistence that our grasp of objective reality be brought home to the personal and particular experience of the individual that we find in modern empiricism.

Moreover, for Hegel, the realm of particular interests and passions is also the realm in which we have that particular and personal involvement that empiricism demands. Furthermore, as particular interests come into conflict, they lead to the universal—to rationality objectively embedded in our world in agreement with subjective rationality; that is, to the objectivity of traditional metaphysics. That they do so without being external to the universal (as self-interest was external to the general will for Rousseau or as Kantian virtue was external to the way of the world) can now be more clearly understood because it has become clear how individual interests and the universal are two interacting parts of one spiritual unity that constitute each other. The universal is produced as the alienation of the particular actions of individuals. The universal or the state is the individual's essence—its *self*—alienated and objectified. Particular interests and the universal are not heteronomous. They appear to be external to each other only if we adopt the perspective of individual consciousness.

All that we have said so far in this section will also help us to understand the transition from civil society to the state as it appears in the *Philosophy of Right*. Critics often object that Hegel is not a liberal, that he in fact subordinates individuals to a powerful and authoritarian state. This, at least in part, is very misleading. In the first place, civil society is the realm in which individual will has its rights, the realm where particular interests legitimately claim their satisfaction, and this is a crucial element of freedom for Hegel.

In civil society, particular interests are viewed, much as for Kant and Rousseau, from the perspective of individual consciousness, and therefore individual will appears to remain external to the universal. Particular interests do lead to the universal, but they do so only unconsciously. Thus, for Hegel, we must move to the level of the state where consciousness transcends the realm of individual will and enters the realm of spirit. Here the rationality implicit in civil society (the unconscious Adam Smithian tendency of particular interests to realize the universal) is posited and administered as law and thus becomes conscious. It is recognized and made actual.[54] Here individual self-consciousness and the universal are not external to one another. Estrangement from universal state power has been overcome and thus individuals consciously will the universal and become free.

Hegel continuously tells us in the *Philosophy of Right* that the relationship that is established between the individual citizens and the ethical substance—the laws and institutions of the state—is such that individuals are related to their own essence, their own substance.[55] Indeed, we have now seen what Hegel means. The state *is* the alienated essence of the individual citizens. The state is constituted by them, but not as an other—not as heteronomous. It is their own essence objectified and universalized. Hegel does indeed subordinate the individual to the state, but this is only to subordinate individuals to their own essence—to themselves. This, then, is a form of objective self-determination because the subjective reason of the individual accords with the rationality objectively embedded in the laws and institutions of the state.[56]

For freedom to be realized, it is not enough that particular interests lead to the universal unconsciously as they do in civil society. Moreover, it is not enough that the state be one's own essence in an estranged form without this being consciously recognized, and it is not enough that subjective and objective reason unconsciously accord. All of this must occur *consciously*.[57] We must *recognize* that particular interests do lead to the universal and begin to consciously pursue the universal in pursuing our own interests. We must recognize that the state is our own essence and subordinate ourselves to it consciously and intentionally. We must recognize that subjective and objective reason accord and act consciously *for the sake of* objective as well as subjective reason—for the sake of the rational laws as well as our own rational maxims. Moreover, the objective rational laws of the state immediately present to the subjective rationality of the individual give rise to a discipline that molds the customs, traditions, feelings, and interests of the individual so that they too consciously support the universal. Thus we have *Sittlichkeit* in the modern state.[58]

Hegel wants to combine the subjectivity of the modern world with the objectivity of the ancient world. For this reason both civil society and the state are crucially important. Without civil society, there would be no individualism and no realm for the satisfaction of particular interest that is so important as an element of freedom. There would be no conflict of interests as an actual force leading to the universal either within the state or in history. Without civil society there would be no rootedness in concrete interests, passions, property, trade, and commerce. Without civil society, the realm of the state and spirit would float into abstraction. On the other hand, without the state individuals would never rise above particular interests; they would never move beyond an unconscious tendency toward the universal. They would never move beyond subjective reason to reason embedded objectively in their laws and institutions. They would never confront their own essence objectified and thus could not be free in obeying the state. In short, they would not reach spirit.

To reconcile modern subjectivity with traditional objectivity, two things are necessary: (1) the objective must be absorbed within the subjective—it must not exist independently outside subjectivity. And (2) the subjective must gain enough scope and universality to be objective and absolute. It must embrace the totality of things like a God whose subjectivity is objective because it is total.

By lifting individual self-consciousness to spirit at the level of the state we see that the state is our own essence, that subjective and objective reason are identical, that the objective reality of traditional metaphysics is immediately grasped within subjective consciousness. The objective world is not other or heteronomous; it is absorbed within subjective consciousness. But subjective consciousness at this point is no longer merely an individual consciousness. It has been molded and disciplined by the objective substantial power of the state. It has become the cultural consciousness of a people. It has been lifted to the universal, to objective ethical rationality.

IV. Sovereignty and Spirit

Hegel is certainly not an authoritarian, let alone a totalitarian. As Avineri has admirably shown, there is even a strong element of pluralism in Hegel's thought.[59] Hegel advocates pluralism in religion and even the toleration of dissenting sects that are allowed to maintain their own customs, traditions, and religious views. Hegel also endorses freedom of the press and of speech, and he advocates social mobility.[60]

The state, for Hegel, is also very definitely concerned with the security and protection of individuals, their property, and their particular interests; it is just that these are not the *ultimate* aims of the state.[61] The ultimate aim of the state is to lift its citizens to spirit, to their own essence, and to the Divine. Only at this level is the individual fully realized, at home with itself, and rationally self-determined.

It is true that Hegel wants a very powerful state, but this means almost the opposite of what it would mean for an authoritarian or totalitarian. Without this powerful state we would sink into civil society and particular interest. This, for Hegel, would be quite disastrous. Hegel tells us that the tendency of civil society, if left to itself, is to move

144   *Chapter Five*

toward a polarization of classes and the immisseration of the lower class—the polarization of society into a powerful wealthy class opposed to an impoverished and powerless "rabble of paupers" that loses its self-respect.[62] It requires a powerful state to work against this natural tendency of civil society.

Furthermore, if we compare Hegel's concept of sovereignty to that of other political theorists, we will see that he is far from being an authoritarian or a totalitarian. For Hobbes, the government had to be sovereign and the sovereign had to be absolute. This was so because Hobbes had no social theory, only a political theory. The only force capable of holding the citizens together in a civil body was a political force—the government or the sovereign. It was as if the government held a bag of marbles. If the government lost its grip, the marbles would bounce in all directions—they would return to the chaos and suffering of the state of nature. Locke, on the other hand, had a social theory and thus was able to argue for limited government and the sovereignty of the people. The better your social theory—the more cohesion you are able to find among the citizens apart from the political sphere—the less power the government need have to hold the citizens together. If you have a good enough social theory, then, with Marx, you can even speak of the withering away of the state. For Hobbes, since he was unaware of any social cohesion, the sovereign had to be absolute. For Locke, there was enough social cohesion to argue that government could be limited and that the people should be sovereign.

This social cohesion, for Locke, arose out of the connection and integration of interests produced by property, property interest, and trade. Unfortunately, as I argued in Chapter 2, Locke did not succeed in making the people sovereign. His emphasis on unequal property and property interest shifted sovereignty to the propertied classes and made them sovereign over the propertyless.[63] For this reason, Rousseau rejected unequal property, commerce, and trade. Instead, he focused on custom and tradition as the forces capable of providing enough social cohesion so that the people could be sovereign. However, healthy customs and traditions simply had to be given in a premodern society for Rousseau, and they were incompatible with wealth, commerce, and trade. Kant's dynamic theory of historical development, while it had nothing to say about custom, tradition, or *Sittlichkeit,* was capable of explaining how particular interest embedded in commerce and trade could lead to the universal rather than erode it as Rousseau thought it would. Nevertheless, for Kant as for Hobbes, the government had to be sovereign. Kant wanted an autocrat who, however, governed in a republican way—an autocrat who gave the people the sorts of laws they would have given themselves.[64] The citizens do not give themselves these laws as they would for Rousseau, but they get the sorts of laws they would have given themselves.

Hegel very clearly rejects a Hobbesian absolute sovereign that stands over society and holds the citizens together from outside. Hegel does have a social theory that explains the internal coherence of society apart from the governmental or political sphere. He sees that property, property interest, and trade in civil society provide this coherence, much as for Locke; and he also sees that custom, tradition, and *Sittlichkeit* provide this coherence, much as for Rousseau. At the same time, he seems aware that unrestrained commerce and trade would shift power to the wealthy classes—this is certainly suggested in his concerns about polarization and immisseration in civil society that must be contained by the state. On the other hand, Hegel does not want to eliminate wealth, commerce, and trade, as does Rousseau, and thus make the ideal state impossible in the modern world. He sees, with Kant and Smith, that particular interests lead to the universal; and he argues, as we have seen, that this is compatible with changing customs, traditions, and *Sittlichkeit*. But while he rejects a Hobbesian sovereign, he does not wish the people to be sovereign, at least not at the level of individual will as for Rousseau. If we reduce the state to civil society and individual will, then there would be nothing to prevent polarization and immisseration. Sovereignty would then most likely shift to the wealthy classes and, with a polarization of classes, it could not be argued that conflicting particular interests would lead to a common good. Particular interest would erode the universal as well as the possibility of customs and traditions that reinforce the universal.

Hegel wants to slip between Hobbes (for whom the sovereign is external to the citizens and wields power over them) and Rousseau (for whom the people are sovereign) while at the same time avoiding Kant's half measures—a sovereign who is external to the citizens and wields power over them as much as for Hobbes despite the fact that the sovereign gives the people the laws they would have given themselves. For Hegel, the citizens do not give themselves their own laws by voting on them as for Rousseau. The citizens, however, do get the sorts of laws they would have given themselves, but they are not given to them by an autocrat as for Kant. The laws and institutions of the state, for Hegel, arise through the historical development of spirit in which the subjective rationality of individuals accords with the objective rationality embedded in the laws of the state. The laws of the state are the laws that subjective rationality would give itself. Through alienation the citizens create the state as their own essence and are molded by their state. For Hegel the government or the state is not external to the citizens; it is their own essence. For Hegel, sovereignty must be understood not at the level of individual will—the individual will either of a people or a government—but at the level of spirit. Hegel's view of sovereignty is thus quite new.

No one of the powers or agencies in the state is sovereign for Hegel. They have no independent authority, but are grounded in the Idea of the whole.[65] Certainly the monarch is not sovereign. Any state simply requires an agency with the authority of final decision, otherwise disputes could continue eternally. This authority of final decision rests with the monarch. But this just means that the monarch has "to say yes and dot the 'i'. . . ."[66] Generally speaking, Hegel's monarch is rather weak.[67] Hegel does at times speak of the monarch as sovereign,[68] but by this he means that the monarch is a figurehead that represents sovereignty. On the other hand, at least in home affairs, Hegel is willing to say that sovereignty resides in the people, not the people as an aggregate of individual wills but the people as the whole of the state.[69] Sovereignty lies in the organic whole bound together by *Sittlichkeit* at the level of spirit. It does not lie either with the government or the people understood as individual wills. It lies in this spiritual totality as a whole. This is possible because of the cohesion of this whole. It is bound together by the integration of particular interests embedded in property, commerce, and trade, which nevertheless lead to the universal. It is bound together by custom, tradition, and *Sittlichkeit,* which embed this universal in individual feeling and character. It is bound together in that subjective reason and objective reason are identical and in the sense that the state is one's own essence. For Hegel the sovereign is not to be seen as an entity that *wields* power *over* others from outside.[70]

Rather, Hegel is concerned with power and authority that binds people together, makes them cohere, lifts them to their own essence at the level of spirit, and makes them rationally self-determined. They are not ruled by the subjective rationality of either the government or the people, but by the objective rationality embedded in the state as a whole, which, however, accords with the subjective rationality of each. To return to individual will, to insist upon voting or subjective rationality, in Hegel's opinion, would be to break this spiritual whole and to move toward making individual will sovereign, either the individual will of a government or that of the aggregate of the people. If one chooses the latter, then as for Rousseau, we would have to give up wealth, commerce, and trade and thus the ideal society would be impossible in the modern world; or else sovereignty would shift to *some* of the people—the wealthy classes—as for Locke.

Nevertheless, Hegel's views must be criticized. The main trouble lies in Hegel's rejection of popular suffrage.[71] Hegel's goal is not to allow the interests of citizens to be represented at the level of the state; it is to prevent opposition between individuals and the state and thus the consequent isolation of the state.[72] For Hegel, individuals are not represented in the legislature as individuals; they are represented as groups through their corporations. Moreover, positions of responsibility in these corporations are not won by election alone, but rather by a mixture of election and appointment by higher authority. There is even a property qualification for the holders of these positions of responsibility. Furthermore, corporations exclude day laborers as well as casual laborers and include only masters of their crafts.[73] All of this, obviously, would work to shift power toward more elite groups. Given that for Hegel the general tendency of civil society is toward a polarization of classes and the immisseration of the workers,[74] it is clear that the poor and the workers will have little influence at the level of the state. Only the elites will. This, in effect, will tend to shift power toward the wealthy classes in a way that recalls Locke.

Moreover, in discussing alienation and estrangement, we saw that estrangement continued to exist as long as the state power appeared as an independent external authority that dominated and controlled the citizens. Estrangement ceases to exist when the citizens come consciously to recognize that they have created the state and that it is their own essence, that in obeying it they are self-determined, and that subjective and objective reason agree. But to fear popular voting, it certainly seems, is to admit that this estrangement has not finally been overcome[75] and that *Sittlichkeit* has not fully been achieved. It is to admit that the subjective reason of the individual citizens cannot be trusted to agree with the objective reason of the state. It is to admit that the particular interests of the citizens will not lead to the universal, the common good, as they *surely* would not if society is headed toward polarization and immisseration. Moreover, Hegel has no real solution to the problem of polarization and immisseration, a problem on which Marx will focus. If this is so, then *Sittlichkeit,* the universal that is supposed to be embedded in the concrete particular lives of individuals, would not grow out of the actual life activity of these individuals—their particular interests would not lead to the universal.

148   *Chapter Five*

Instead, *Sittlichkeit* would become an ideal imposed by the theorist from outside, and we would move back toward the utopianism of Rousseau.

Moreover, to claim, in such circumstances, that the state is linked to the Divine, that it is absolutely right and justified, which is to suggest that it cannot be questioned by individual subjectivity,[76] would be to begin to eliminate *Moralität,* individuality, and subjective reason, and thus the whole organic unity of the state of which these elements are a crucial part would begin to unravel.

Notes

1. That the categorical imperative and the general will are similar, see Chapter 3, Section I above.
2. *IUH,* 18–19 and *Ak,* VIII, 24–25. *PP,* 112–13 and *Ak,* VIII, 366–67.
3. A. Smith, *The Wealth of Nations,* 423.
4. *Natural Law,* tr. T.M. Knox (Philadelphia: University of Pennsylvania Press, 1975), 93 and, for the German, see *Gesammelte Werke* (Hamburg: Felix Meiner, 1968), IV, 449–50. *Philosophy of Right* (hereafter *PR*), tr. T.M. Knox (Oxford: Clarendon Press,1967), 209, 212–13 and, for the German, see *Grundlinien der Philosophie des Rechts* (hereafter *GPR*), ed. J. Hoffmeister (Hamburg: Felix Meiner, 1955), 280, 284–85.
5. *Lectures on the Philosophy of World History: Introduction* (hereafter *IPH*), tr. H.B. Nisbet (Cambridge: Cambridge University Press, 1975), 71–72 and, for the German, see *Vorlesungen über die Philosophie der Weltgeschichte* (hereafter *PW,* I), ed. J. Hoffmeister (Hamburg: Felix Meiner, 1955), I, 83–84.
6. *IPH,* 89 and *PW,* I, 105.
7. *IPH,* 82, also 75 and *PW,* I, 96–97, 88.
8. *PR,* 127, 129–30 and *GPR,* 170, 174–75. *IPH,* 73 and *PW,* I, 86.
9. *IPH,* 89 (my italics) and *PW,* I, 105.
10. *Phenomenology of Spirit* (hereafter *PS*), tr. A.V. Miller (Oxford: Clarendon Press, 1977), 228–30 and, for the German, see *Phänomenologie des Geistes* (hereafter *PG*), ed. J. Hoffmeister (Hamburg: Felix Meiner, 1952), 274–76.
11. *PS,* 228–29, 235 and *PG,* 274–75, 281–82.
12. *PS,* 230–32 and *PG,* 276–78.
13. *PS,* 234 and *PG,* 280.
14. *PS,* 235 and *PG,* 281. See also *Aesthetics,* tr. T.M. Knox (Oxford: Clarendon Press, 1975), I, 56–61 and, for the German, see *Sämtliche Werke,* ed. H. Glockner (Stuttgart-Bad Cannstatt: Frommann, 1927–40), XII, 90–96.
15. *PR,* 11–12 and *GPR,* 16–17. *IPH,* 170–71 and *PW,* I, 210.
16. *IPH,* 97 and *PW,* I, 115.

17. *PR*, 109 and *GPR*, 147–48. *PS*, 212–16 and *PG*, 256–61.
18. *PS*, 216 and *PG*, 260.
19. *PS*, 257–61 and *PG*, 306–11. *PR*, 36, 90 and *GPR*, 49–50, 120–21. *IPH*, 80 and *PW*, I, 94.
20. *F*, 10, 16 and *Ak*, IV, 394, 399–400. *CPrR*, 71 and *Ak*, V, 68–69.
21. *F*, 10, 13–17, 44, 53–54, 60–61 and *Ak*, IV, 394, 397–401, 426, 435, 442. *CPrR*, 28, 31 and *Ak*, V, 28–29, 31.
22. *PR*, 12, 32–33, 90–91, 163–64 and *GPR*, 16–17, 44–45, 121–22, 218–19. *IPH*, 70, 97, 146 and *PW*, I, 81–82, 115, 177. *Aesthetics*, I, 98, 182–83 and *Sämtliche Werke*, XII, 144, 250–52.
23. *F*, 69–73 and *Ak*, IV, 450–54, *CPrR*, 28, 50 and *Ak*, V, 28–29, 48.
24. *The Logic of Hegel* (hereafter *L*), tr. W. Wallace (Oxford: Oxford University Press, 1968), 91–92 and *Sämtliche Werke*, VIII, 133.
25. *IPH*, 64 and *PW*, I, 74.
26. *Discourse on Inequality*, 151–54, 157–59 and *OC*, III, 171–73, 175–77.
27. *Social Contract*, 70 and *OC*, III, 385. See also *Discourse on Inequality*, 80 and *OC*, III, 112–13.
28. *Social Contract*, 76 and *OC*, III, 392. *Discourse on Inequality*, 199–200 and *OC*, III, 206.
29. *PR*, 163–64 and *GPR*, 218–19.
30. *PR*, 165 and *GPR*, 220.
31. *Philosophy of History* (hereafter *PH*), tr. J. Sibree (New York: Dover, 1956), 407 (Hegel's italics) and, for the German, see *Vorlesungen über die Philosophie der Weltgeschichte* (hereafter *PW*, II), ed. G. Lasson (Hamburg: Felix Meiner, 1968), II–IV, 875.
32. *PR*, 125 (translation altered) and *GPR*, 168.
33. *PR*, 129–30 and *GPR*, 174–75.
34. *IPH*, 58–63 and *PW*, I, 67–73. Also, for Hegel as for Rousseau, learning flourishes as the nation degenerates; *IPH*, 61 and *PW*, I, 71. Also *PR*, 13 and *GPR*, 17. *Discourse on the Sciences and Arts*, in *First and Second Discourses*, 41–42, 54 and *OC*, III, 11–12, 22.
35. *PR*, 161 and *GPR*, 215. Also see *PR*, 10, 123, 160 and *GPR*, 14, 166, 214–15. *IPH*, 70 and *PW*, I, 81–82.
36. Some scholars have argued that James Steuart was a more significant influence on Hegel than was Adam Smith; see, for example, L. Dickey, *Hegel: Religion, Economics, and the Politics of Spirit 1770–1807* (Cambridge: Cambridge University Press, 1987), Chapters 5–8. R. Plant, "Economic and Social Integration in Hegel's Political Philosophy," in *Hegel's Social and Political Thought*, ed. D.P. Verene (Atlantic Highlands, N.J.: Humanities Press, 1980), 59–90. R. Plant, *Hegel: An Introduction*, 2nd edition (Oxford: Basil Blackwell, 1983). R. Stern, "Unity and Difference in Hegel's Political Philosophy," *Ratio* II (1989), 75–88. In one sense this is quite clear. Steuart, unlike Smith, thinks that the government, or the statesman, must to some degree control the economy; it cannot leave it to itself. This is clearly Hegel's view also. On the

other hand, it is also Steuart's view that civil society itself, due to division of labor, interdependence of needs, and exchange, produces its own solidarity, integration, or even community—Plant speaks of "communitarian tendencies" ("Economic and Social Integration," 83). Stern goes so far as to suggest that Hegel's view of civil society anticipates Durkheim's conception of mechanical solidarity (Stern, 84–85).

Whether this view is acceptable or not is a delicate matter of emphasis. I think it is to go too far to say that in Hegel's view civil society on its own can generate as much solidarity, integration, or community as is implied in Durkheim's conception of mechanical solidarity. Durkheim's view, or at least his tendency, is to hold that mechanical solidarity will provide sufficient integration in society to make it possible for a state which stands over society to become unnecessary and perhaps to disappear [E. Durkheim, *Socialism*, tr. C. Sattler (New York: Collier Books, 1962), 56, 189–193; also *Division of Labor in Society*, tr. G. Simpson (New York: Free Press, 1964), 27]. This is certainly not Hegel's view. It is not even Steuart's view. The state is necessary for Steuart as well as for Hegel. It is certainly the case for Hegel that civil society contains some integration and cohesion, but the question is how much, enough so that we can call civil society a community? I would tend to say that civil society is not a community. Hegel says that in civil society "the Idea is lost in particularity." This is only overcome in the administration of justice, not in division of labor, exchange, or the interdependence of needs—the realm of civil society where the universal is unconscious (*PR*, 124–25 and *GPR*, 167–68). The administration of justice brings the universal to consciousness (*PR*, 135 and *GPR*, 181). What is needed is a control that stands above and consciously regulates the differing interest that can come into collision with each other in civil society (*PR*, 147 and *GPR*, 197). Community in its full sense, for Hegel as well as Marx, requires consciousness; and that only occurs fully, for Hegel, at the level of the state, not in civil society (*PR*, 155–56 and *GPR*, 207–8).

37. *PR*, 157, see also 33 and *GPR*, 209–10, 45. Also *Lectures on the History of Philosophy*, trs. E.S. Haldane and F.H. Simson (London: Routledge & Kegan Paul, 1968), III, 402 and *Sämtliche Werke*, XIX, 528–29.

38. For example, M.H. Mitias, *Moral Foundation of the State in Hegel's 'Philosophy of Right'* (Amsterdam: Rodopi, 1984), 42. S. Avineri, *Hegel's Theory of the Modern State* (Cambridge: Cambridge University Press, 1972), 184. C. Taylor, *Hegel* (Cambridge: Cambridge University Press, 1975), 372.

39. *PR*, 157, 202–3 and *GPR*, 209–10, 270–71. *PS*, 357–59 and *PG*, 415–18. *PH*, 452 and *PW*, II, 932–33.

40. *PS*, 358–59 and *PG*, 416–18. *Natural Law*, 85–89 and *Gesammelte Werke*, IV, 443–46.

41. *PS*, 295–321 and *PG*, 347–76.

42. *PS*, 294–95 and *PG*, 347–48.

43. *PS*, 306 ff. and *PG*, 360 ff.

44. *PS*, 310–13 and *PG*, 364–67.
45. *PS*, 329–54, 453–78 and *PG*, 385–414, 521–48.
46. *PS*, 479–81 (translation altered) and *PG*, 549–51. For a further discussion of alienation and estrangement, see my *Schiller, Hegel, and Marx*, 40–56.
47. *PR*, 11–12 and *GPR*, 16–17.
48. *L*, 23 and *Sämtliche Werke*, VIII, 60.
49. *L*, 60–61 and *Sämtliche Werke*, VIII, 99–100.
50. *L*, 12, 76–78 and *Sämtliche Werke*, VIII, 50, 116–18.
51. *L*, 82, 87–89 and *Sämtliche Werke*, VIII, 123, 128–30.
52. *L*, 91–92 and *Sämtliche Werke*, VIII, 133.
53. *L*, 93–94 and *Sämtliche Werke*, VIII, 134–35.
54. *PR*, 134–36 and *GPR*, 180–81.
55. *PR*, 105–6, 155, 160–61, 259 and *GPR*, 142–43, 207–8, 214–15.
56. *PR*, 3, 12, 106, 125 and *GPR*, 5–6, 16–17, 143, 168. *IHP*, 97 and *PW*, I, 115. *PH*, 439 and *PW*, II, 914–15.
57. *PR*, 3, 29–30, 155–56, 163–64 and *GPR*, 5–6, 40–41, 208, 219.
58. *PR*, 105 and *GPR*, 142–43.
59. Avineri, 167–75. See also Stern, 75–88.
60. *PR*, 132, 168–69, 205 and *GPR*, 178, 225, 274–75.
61. *PR*, 71, 156, 209 and *GPR*, 96, 208, 280.
62. *PR*, 149–50 and *GPR*, 200–201. *IPH*, 168 and *PW*, I, 207.
63. See Chapter 2, Sections III and IV above.
64. "An Old Question Raised Again," in *On History*, 146, 150 and *Ak*, VII, 88, 91. *PP*, 120 and *Ak*, VIII, 372.
65. *PR*, 179–80 and *GPR*, 240–42.
66. *PR*, 181 and *GPR*, 242–43. *PR*, 288–89; for the German of this passage, see *Sämtliche Werke*, VII, 388–89. Though, on the other hand, the monarch does command the army; *PR*, 212 and *GPR*, 283.
67. For example, he is bound by the decisions of his counselors; *PR*, 288 and *Sämtliche Werke*, VII, 386.
68. For example, *PR*, 182, 186 and *GPR*, 244–45, 250.
69. *PR*, 182–83 and *GPR*, 244–45.
70. At least not in domestic affairs, though this might be true in foreign relations; see *PR*, 212–13 and *GPR*, 284–85.
71. *PR*, 202–3 and *GPR*, 270–71.
72. *PR*, 197 and *GPR*, 263.
73. *PR*, 153, 189, 191, 198, 200, 202 and *GPR*, 204, 253, 255, 264–65, 267, 270.
74. *IPH*, 168 and *PW*, I, 207.
75. For a further discussion of this issue see *Schiller, Hegel, and Marx*, 61–73.
76. For example, Hegel suggests that it is absolutely justified that advanced nations rule over less advanced nations; *PR*, 219 and *GPR*, 292–93.

6

Marx and the Earlier Tradition

In this chapter, I want to show how Marx grows out of and tries to go beyond the tradition of political theory that we have been discussing. I want to argue that Marx develops a theory of revolution founded upon a philosophy of history in many ways like that of Kant, which will allow him to realize an ideal society that, much like Rousseau's, is a radically democratic and equalitarian community. In these respects, Marx's project is similar to the project of Hegel as described in the previous chapter. However, Marx wants to accomplish all of this while avoiding Hegel's abandonment of individual consciousness and his move to spirit. Let me begin to explain each of these claims in more detail.[1]

I. The Categorical Imperative and Revolution

Marx, like Kant, attempts both to describe the ideal society and to provide a theory for how actually to realize it. He develops a philosophy of history similar to Kant's in which conflicting particular interests drive us to what the categorical imperative would have demanded in the first place, and which allows us, unlike Hegel, to guide history toward this end.[2]

In the Introduction to the *Critique of Hegel's Philosophy of Law* (1843–44) Marx holds that "man is the highest being for man" and he argues for a "categorical imperative to overthrow all relations in which man is a debased, enslaved, forsaken, despicable being. . . ."[3] The proletariat, for Marx, is the historical agent that will realize this categorical imperative—and it will realize it through proletarian revolution.

For Marx, any successful revolution brings particular interest and the universal into accord such that particular interest leads toward the universal. In what Marx calls a partial or political revolution, by which he means a bourgeois revolution, a particular class (the bourgeoisie), to attain political dominance, had to be perceived as a general representative of society as a whole. The particular class interest of the bourgeoisie had to appear as the general interest of all nonruling classes such that the liberation achieved appeared as a universal liberation. Not long after it came to power, however, the class interest of the bourgeoisie ceased to represent the general interest and came into conflict with the interests of those classes whose representative it had been for a time.[4]

On the other hand, the proletariat, for Marx, is capable of making a radical or universal revolution. Its particular class interest, the interest that drives it and makes it an actor on the historical stage, drives it to act in accordance with the universal—the categorical imperative. The point that Marx is making in this essay is quite interesting. Because the proletariat is so oppressed, degraded, and dehumanized, its particular class interests, which definitely are selfish interests, nevertheless are such fundamental human interests that they simply cannot be viewed as *mere* particular interests, as demands for special privileges (as the interests of other higher classes certainly could). The needs and interests of the proletariat are the needs and interests of any and all human beings—needs for food, clothing, shelter, education, normal human development, political participation, and so forth. In other words, because of the proletariat's oppressed condition, its needs and interests are the sort that we would demand be satisfied for all human beings. They are universal needs and interests—needs that would accord with the categorical imperative. Because the proletariat is so oppressed, its particular class interest accords with the categorical imperative and its class interest will drive it to act in accordance with the categorical imperative.[5]

Moreover, Marx thinks that the proletariat cannot emancipate itself without emancipating all others in society. Since the proletariat "is the complete loss of man . . . [it] can win itself only through the complete rewinning of man."[6] Since the proletariat's needs and interests accord with the categorical imperative, if it can establish a society that will satisfy such needs and interests, it will realize the universal; it will satisfy the needs and interests of all human beings; it will emancipate humankind generally.

Thus, much as for Kant, we can say that there are two historical forces at work here: first, the particular class interests, the needs, of the proletariat; and, second, as Marx puts it, theory—by which he means the ideals of German philosophy (that is, morality, the categorical imperative). When these two forces accord, theory grips the masses; it answers the needs of the masses; and therefore it becomes a material force. Thus, Marx says, "As philosophy finds its material weapons in the proletariat, so the proletariat finds its spiritual weapons in philosophy." It is no longer merely the case that thought strives for realization, but now, as Marx puts it, reality strives for thought. Particular class interest drives us toward the categorical imperative.[7]

In earlier writings, before Marx settled on the proletariat as the historical agent capable of transforming society in accordance with the categorical imperative, he was struggling with similar issues. He looked elsewhere for agents able to realize the universal. For example, he first argued that a free press transforms "material struggle into an ideological struggle . . . the struggle of need, desire, empiricism into a struggle of theory, of reason, of form." It transforms particular interests into a general interest.[8] Through the efforts of a free press, particular needs come to be recognized as universal needs. The press causes us publicly to recognize needs and interests that are universalizable.

Also, in discussing a proposed law concerning the theft of wood, Marx argued that the particular interests of the aristocracy were in conflict with the form of law. The form of law, the form that any law properly should have to be a law, is universality and necessity. In general, for Marx, the content of a law must be capable of being given a universal form without contradiction. Laws must represent universal ends, not particular interests. This was not the case with the aristocracy. But, on the other hand, the customary rights of the poor to gather fallen wood, Marx argued, do agree with the form of law. They can be universalized because they are natural needs—needs common to all human beings. Here form and content are not in contradiction. Need and right, particular interest and general interest, coincide.[9]

Thus, in both the free press and the poor, and finally in the proletariat, Marx finds an agent that links particular interest with the general interest so that, much as for Kant, particular interest is channeled toward the universal.[10] In fact, in one early journal article (of 1842), though it is never repeated again, we hear at least an echo of Kant's notion that the conflicting particular interests of nations, given the interdependence produced by commerce, will lead toward a league of nations. Marx speaks of a rational system of states or a congress of nations:

it is precisely in England that the pernicious results come into prominence of a system which is no longer the system of our time . . . based on division and not on unity, which, in the absense of . . . a rational state and a rational system of individual states, had to provide special protection for each particular sphere. Trade and industry ought to be protected, but the debatable point is precisely whether protective tariffs do in reality protect trade and industry. We regard such a system much more as the organization of a state of war in time of peace, a state of war which, aimed in the first place against foreign countries, necessarily turns in its implementation against the country which organizes it. But in any case an individual country, however much it may recognize the principle of free trade, is dependent on the state of the world in general, and therefore the question can be decided only by a congress of nations, and not by an individual government.[11]

In later writings, we find that Marx continues to hold views similar to those he sketched in the Introduction to the *Critique of Hegel's Philosophy of Law*. In the *Holy Family* (of 1845), he argues that since the proletariat has been almost completely dehumanized, the needs of the proletariat will drive it to revolt against this inhumanity. And in emancipating itself, it will emancipate humanity universally. He also makes a similar point in the *German Ideology* (1845–46) and in the *Communist Manifesto* (1847–48).[12]

In the *German Ideology*, Marx rejects Kantian morality,[13] and, in fact, he rejects morality in general as ideological illusion.[14] Nevertheless, much as before, he argues that the particular class interest of any successful revolutionary class must represent the common interest.[15] Moreover, the development of his theory of historical materialism allows him to deepen this notion. The fact that existing productive forces in society have been developed so fully and exist within a system of universal intercourse requires that the proletariat (if they are to be able to appropriate these forces and to make use of them for their own benefit) must develop themselves, their own individual capacities, universally. That is, all individuals must develop their powers and capacities fully if they are to control such complex and highly developed forces of production. Moreover, the proletariat will be driven to this universality merely to safeguard its existence—to safeguard its particular needs and interests, and to avoid crises, poverty, and collapse. Thus, again, particular interests are driven toward the universal, but this time due to the development of the forces of production. Furthermore, Marx argues that given the complexity and universality of the forces of production, they cannot, if crises are to be avoided, be controlled by individuals narrowly focusing upon and competitively pursuing particular interests. They can only be controlled cooperatively by a union (or a community) that acts on a common plan[16]—a plan that would focus upon and pursue the general interest, the universal.

Also, in his discussion of the Communist party in the *Communist Manifesto*, Marx argues that the party does not have interests separate from, nor does it impose sectarian principles upon, the proletarian movement. It acts, in fact, much like Marx's earlier description of a free press. It watches and studies the actual historical movement of the proletariat in different countries. It expresses in general terms the actual relations springing from existing class struggles. And it tries to point out and bring to the fore the common interest of the proletariat.[17] It thus brings to light the universal so that particular class interest can more effectively lead toward the universal.

Marx, in his early writings, again following Kant, also holds to a principle of publicity. Particular interests that contradict the general interest "cannot bear the light of publicity," only the universal can. For Kant, any action that would be frustrated by publicly proclaiming it beforehand, was to be considered illegal.[18] Form and content would be in contradiction.

However, there is a significant difference here between Marx and Kant. For Marx, the principle of publicity would support revolution. For Kant, it rules out revolution. I have already suggested, in Chapter 4, that Kant's argument to this effect confuses a revolution with a coup. A small conspiratorial group secretly planning to overthrow the government almost certainly would be frustrated if its plans were made public. But this would not necessarily be the case for a popular revolution supported by the majority. Often one of the main obstacles to revolution is *lack* of access to the means of publicity. Nevertheless, for Kant the principle of publicity is negative. It will only tell us, and only in some cases, which maxims are *un*just. It will not tell us which maxims can actually be considered just ones. For example, Kant says that a powerful but oppressive government might well be able to make public its unjust plans without risking their frustration.[19] Given the power of this government, its plans would be compatible with publicity but nevertheless unjust.

However, Kant then goes on to give us an affirmative principle of publicity. All principles that stand in *need* of publicity—principles that actually *require* publicity for their success—are therefore just.[20] Popular revolutions supported by the majority might well satisfy this affirmative principle of publicity and thus be just. Nor can it easily be argued that revolutionary violence would be ruled out by the categorical imperative, which obliges us never to treat others merely as means but always also as ends in themselves. Kant rejects standing armies on these grounds when he says that to pay people to kill is to use them as mere means or tools. On the other hand, he holds that a voluntary citizen militia for the purposes of defense is quite acceptable.[21] He also says that a citizen must freely consent to the waging of war in general and also to any particular war.[22]

Thus, the voluntary actions of a citizen militia do not necessarily violate the categorical imperative. As we shall see, Marx, like Rousseau, advocates such a militia, not a standing army. Therefore, if all violence does not necessarily involve treating others merely as means, and if majority revolutions against a repressive government pass the principle of publicity, Marx can argue that such revolutions accord with the categorical imperative.[23]

As we have already seen in Chapter 5, Hegel's philosophy of history is similar to, and in fact is a development of, Kant's philosophy of history. However, in discussing Marx I have followed Kant because there are important respects in which Marx is closer to Kant than to Hegel. In opposition to Hegel, it is clearly Marx's view, as it is Kant's, that we can assist in guiding history through our own rational efforts:

> we do not dogmatically anticipate the world, but only want to find the new world through criticism of the old one. Hitherto philosophers have had the solution of all riddles lying in their writing-desks, and the stupid, exoteric world had only to open its mouth for the roast pigeons of absolute knowledge to fly into it. Now philosophy has become mundane, and the most striking proof of this is that philosophical consciousness itself has been drawn into the torment of the struggle. . . . But, if constructing the future and settling everything for all times are not our affair, it is all the more clear what we have to accomplish at present: I am referring to ruthless criticism of all that exists. . . .[24]

For Hegel, much as for Kant and Marx, the motive force of history was the clash of passions and particular interests that realize the universal. But for Hegel the universal was understood as the Idea, and Hegel was willing to say that the conflict of particular interests allowed the *Idea* to realize *itself*. He was willing to say that the Idea—which is the World Spirit or God—uses human passions as the means to realize its own universal ends. This is not the case for Kant or Marx. To understand history, we do not look to the Idea. We do not seek absolute knowledge. We look to history itself, to the conflict of particular interests, and we proceed through criticism, through rational analysis, of what concretely and mundanely exists.

To put this another way, for Kant an *idea* for a universal history is merely a regulative idea, an "as if." For Hegel, on the other hand, the Absolute Idea works itself out with *necessity*. Kant's regulative idea cannot actually be known, but if it is assumed, if we proceed as if it were true, reason can begin to guide history toward its end. For Hegel, while we can know past history, we cannot guide its future development. Philosophy cannot look to the future.[25] The necessity involved in the Idea precludes our conscious guidance of history. For Kant, it is true that in the past history has proceeded unconsciously and without guidance, but to proceed further, for history to move toward morality, human reason must begin to guide it. The full realization of the human being in a moral society, for Kant as well as Marx, is the goal of history and this goal must be achieved consciously by human beings themselves.[26]

For Marx, it is true, history involves more than a regulative idea. He says in 1843 that criticism starts with existing reality and develops "true reality as its obligation and its final goal." Nevertheless, as for Kant, this process is a purely human and social one. There is no Hegelian God or Idea manipulating passions to realize its own universal ends. In other words, the necessity involved in history is not imposed by God or the Idea and accessible only to absolute knowledge. And in claiming to guide history, Marx is not, as with some Left Hegelian philosophers of his era, claiming knowledge of the Absolute Idea and its necessity such that the "stupid exoteric world has only to open its mouth for the roast pigeons of absolute knowledge to fly into it" and such that the future can be settled for all time. Marx says, "we do not confront the world in a doctrinaire way with a new principle: Here is the truth, kneel down before it! We develop new principles for the world out of the world's own principles . . . The reform of consciousness consists only in making the world aware of its own consciousness, in awakening it out of its dream about itself, in explaining to it the meaning of its own actions."[27]

In the *German Ideology*, as Marx develops his doctrine of historical materialism, he does becomes more of a determinist. He says that "communist revolution will be guided not by the 'social institutions of inventive socially-gifted persons,' but by the productive forces."[28] This does not mean that there is no room at all for human beings to guide history. It only means that revolution will not be guided by the arbitrary and doctrinaire inventions of utopian thinkers. Indeed, as we have already seen in our discussion of the *Communist Manifesto,* the Communist party does in fact guide history by studying and understanding actual working-class movements, clearly expressing the interests involved in those movements, and bringing to the fore the common interests of the proletariat as a whole. In fact, this is quite similar to Marx's view in 1843 that we do not confront the world with doctrinaire new principles, but develop new principles out of the world's own principles. We make the world aware of its own consciousness by explaining to it the meaning of its own actions. This is also very much like the free press which brings particular interests to the light of universality. "It will then become evident that the world has long dreamed of possessing something of which it only has to be conscious in order to possess it in reality."[29] Thus, much as for Kant, human reason guides by clarifying, bringing to clear awareness, the tendency of the conflicts of particular interests themselves. The conflict of particular interests, given the way they are structured by material conditions, by the forces and relations of production, do necessarily tend toward the universal, but they cannot realize this end without being guided by rational analysis and criticism.

I argued in Chapter 4 that Kant, like Adam Smith, relies on an invisible-hand argument in developing his philosophy of history. A common good is produced through the conflict of particular interests.[30] There is also an element of this in Marx's theory of revolution. Nevertheless, there is a significant difference between the views of Kant and Marx and those of Smith. For Smith, competitive self-seeking *unconsciously* produces a common good and does so far more effectively than would consciously seeking this common good. For Marx and Kant, while interests do tend unconsciously toward the universal, we must become aware of this tendency and begin to guide it *consciously* if we are to effectively reach the ideal society. For Hegel, this is not possible.

Furthermore, while an invisible hand has a legitimate place in explaining how we move from existing society to an ideal one, it has no place, for Marx, in the ideal society itself. To act selfishly and allow a good to come about behind your back, to merely produce a good unintentionally, does not amount to morality. Morality requires conscious intent. One must know what the good is and do it because it is good.

In an early school essay Marx says, "man's nature is so constituted that he can attain his own perfection only by working for the perfection, for the good, of his fellow men."[31] In the *Economic and Philosophic Manuscripts* (of 1844), Marx argues that human beings are species beings, which means that to realize themselves they must work for the benefit of the species. A species being is a being capable of making the species the object (or end) of both theory and practice. To be able to make the species the object of theory is to be able to conceive theoretically the species as a whole, that is, to conceive a universal idea—the species. Animals, for example, are only able to conceive particulars. To make the species the object of practice, on the other hand, is to *act,* to *work,* for the benefit of the species—the universal.[32]

To work for the benefit of the species, I would like to argue, is to act not merely in *accordance* with the categorical imperative but to act *for the sake of* the categorical imperative. It is certainly to act to satisfy those needs that are common to the species—common to all human beings. These are needs that would be universalizable and thus demanded by the categorical imperative. We can understand this more clearly if we look briefly at Marx's concept of alienation. Alienation makes it impossible to work consciously for the benefit of the species and allows us to work only for the benefit of particular individuals in opposition to the species. If workers are alienated from the product of their work, if they do not consciously, cooperatively, and directly control the product, they cannot possibly direct it consciously to benefit the species. Instead, it can only benefit particular individuals—the owners of the products (the capitalists)—in opposition to the rest of the species. Since human beings need these products but do not control them, their entire world of products will be estranged from them. They will come to be dominated by these products, by their need for them, and thus by selfish particular interests.[33]

Moreover, if the workers are alienated from the process (the activity) of production, if they do not control their own activity in production, they will hardly be able to direct this activity consciously for the benefit of the species. Again, this activity will only be able to benefit particular individuals, this time the workers themselves—it will gain them a wage. It will not consciously and directly benefit the rest of the species.[34]

Furthermore, if the workers do not control their own activity, this activity will end up being controlled, even coerced, by others (the capitalists), and since for the worker this activity will only serve to gain a wage, it will become merely self-interested. Such coerced and self-interested work, Marx thinks, will become meaningless, at least in a larger sense, because it will not be consciously directed toward the universal—the benefit of others, the species.

Marx claims that species activity itself should be our highest object or end. Activities can either have their ends outside themselves or the activity itself can be our end. Species activity should itself be our highest end because it is a free activity (it is consciously directed toward the universal) and because it is an activity that is itself a self-realization (it is directed toward the realization of the species and the species, as we shall come to see, is our own essence).[35]

Alienation from the product and alienation in the activity of production produce alienation from the species. Neither the product nor the activity of production can be consciously directed for the sake of the species. Thus the species cannot be realized and therefore, as we shall see, since the species is the individual's essence, the individual cannot be realized either.[36]

Clearly, if one is alienated from the species, one cannot act for the sake of the species and thus not for the sake of the categorical imperative. But even if such alienation is overcome and one is able to work for the sake of the species, it still may seem that to work for the sake of the species is to seek an *external* end and thus, Kant would say, to be determined heteronomously and therefore by inclination or interest. If this is so, then to work for the sake of the species would not be to act *for the sake of* the categorical imperative. But Kant, in the *Critique of Practical Reason,* admits that inclinations, needs, interests, and purposes are embedded in any maxim. This cannot be avoided and in itself is not objectionable for Kant. However, we must will to carry out the maxim not because of these needs, interests, or inclinations, but solely because the maxim is universalizable and thus rational. Needs, interests, and inclinations are present, but they do not determine our will. Only the possibility of universalizing the maxim should determine our will.[37] This, I think, is also Marx's view. Though our actions do satisfy the needs and interests of the species, we should not act *merely* to satisfy these needs and interests. That would be to be need driven and dominated by need. That would mean estrangement and heteronomy. We must act for the sake of the species because to do so is to act for the universal, because to do so is universalizable, because it would be impossible to universalize not doing so.

Moreover, to act for the sake of the species is not to act for some *external* end—such activity is itself an *end in itself* and our highest end. It is not an external end because Marx claims that the species is our own essence.[38] Thus to work for the realization of the species is to work for the realization of one's own essence. Species activity is the activity in which one realizes one's own essence. And to realize one's essence requires working for the realization of the species—for the sake of the universal, the categorical imperative. This can only be explained further when we discuss Marx's concept of essence in Section III.

II. Democracy and the General Will

Marx's relation to Rousseau is rather complex. He both agrees with Rousseau and is quite critical of him. In the first place, Marx's philosophy of history presupposes complex societies with developed economies—economies in which private property and exchange predominate and thus in which competition, conflict of particular interests, and even class conflict will prevail. If, as for Kant, it is the conflict of particular interests (or of particular class interests) that drives us to the universal, these conflicting interests must be present. Without them, Marx would become a utopian like Rousseau. He would be able to give us a description of the ideal society, but he could not develop his theory of how to realize this ideal society in the modern world.

Moreover, Marx is clearly opposed to a simple society like Rousseau's—a society that would produce a "poor and crude man who has few needs and who has not only failed to go beyond private property, but has not yet even reached it." Marx does not want a society that reduces need to a common level—to a preconceived minimum. He is opposed to this sort of leveling. Marx wants a "rich human being and . . . rich human need."[39] He wants human beings with as wide as possible a range of needs and the highest development of each need, as well, of course, as the means of satisfying them. Thus, for these reasons also, Marx must presuppose a complex and highly developed economy.

The ideal society, for Marx, as for Kant and Hegel, can only grow out of a complex economy with private property and exchange that will produce a conflict of particular interests and class struggle. This, however, is certainly not what Marx wants for his ideal society itself. Marx, like Rousseau, wants his ideal society to be characterized by community, equality, radical democracy, and a general will; and these characteristics, as for Rousseau, are incompatible with complex exchange, the conflict of particular interests, or class struggle. Thus, to move *toward* the ideal society, Marx needs a complex and highly developed economy with private property and conflict of interests. Moreover, the ideal society itself, to avoid leveling, must *remain* complex and highly developed; but on the other hand it must *eliminate* private property, exchange, and class conflict for community, equality, and democracy to be possible. In the *Poverty of Philosophy* (of 1847), Marx suggests that is it impossible and utopian to want to return to earlier, simpler, and less developed, productive forces. This is what Rousseau wanted—or rather his ideal society was only possible before such development had occurred. For Marx, the solution instead is to keep the highly developed forces of production, but, in opposition to Kant and Hegel, to eliminate individual exchange[40] as well as class conflict.

Rousseau, we have seen in Chapter 3, would have been opposed to Adam Smith's model of an invisible hand, at least ultimately. It is true that Rousseau's citizens do not consciously, cooperatively, and altruistically decide upon the common good and then act upon it—at least not directly and immediately. They reflect upon their self-interest in the abstract case—they imagine how they might be harmed if they were to be the victims of a proposed law. Their self-interest leads them to the common good. There is an echo of an invisible hand here. But once the general will has appeared, the citizens should become conscious of it, cooperatively act upon it, and allow it to grow into custom and tradition. Ultimately, the common good should not arise behind one's back, unintended, or through an invisible hand. Citizens must act on the good for the sake of the good. They should do what is right because it is right. The community should consciously and collectively seek the common good and this should be reinforced by custom and tradition. Furthermore, it is quite clear that Rousseau totally rejects an invisible hand in the socioeconomic sphere.[41]

Marx too, we have seen, is opposed to an exchange economy where the pursuit of self-interest produces a common good that arises unconsciously and unintentionally through an invisible hand. To produce a good accidentally and unintentionally, or to merely act in *accordance* with the good, is unacceptable. One must act for the sake of the good—for the sake of the universal, the species, the categorical imperative.[42]

An invisible hand has a place, for Marx, when discussing revolution; that is, when discussing how to move from human beings as they are to human beings as they ought to be. But even here, like Kant and unlike Smith, human beings must finally become conscious of what they ought to be and begin consciously to guide the process of becoming so.

In the ideal society itself, however, an invisible hand has no place at all for Marx. Individuals must finally be able to work consciously, collectively, and purposively for the sake of others. In such an ideal society, Marx says, "I would have the *direct* enjoyment both of being *conscious* of having satisfied a human need by my work . . ." and I would have "become *recognized* and *felt* by yourself as a completion of your own essential nature and as a necessary part of yourself, and consequently would *know* myself to be confirmed both in your *thought* and your *love* . . . In the individual expression of my life I would have *directly* created your expression of your life, and therefore in my individual activity I would have *directly* confirmed and realized my true nature, my human nature, my communal nature."⁴³ Social relations, for Marx, should be direct, conscious, and cooperative. The common good, the needs of others, should be realized consciously and purposively. Exchange should not be allowed to operate out of the direct, conscious, and collective control of human beings; otherwise it will dominate them, frustrate their needs, and erode their community. In an exchange economy, individuals produce separately, put their products onto a market, and market laws set in which are neither understood nor controlled by these individuals. They come to be dominated by these laws.⁴⁴ They do not consciously control their own products or their own activity in the process of production and thus are estranged from the species—the community. They cannot consciously direct their products or their activity for the benefit of others.

If social interaction is not consciously, cooperatively, and directly controlled, exchange will produce estrangement. If social interaction *is* cooperative, consciously controlled, and purposively directed for the benefit of the species, then society (*Gesellschaft*) will be transformed into a community (*Gemeinschaft*). Conscious, cooperative, and purposive control for the benefit of all is what community means. The distribution of products in such a community should take the form of direct communal sharing purposively designed to satisfy the needs of others. In this way a common bond is formed that will grow into custom and tradition (*Sittlichkeit*) and that will reinforce community and provide stability.⁴⁵ We should consciously recognize and feel the power and importance of others in satisfying our needs. Relationships among individuals would be like the community of friends Aristotle thought necessary for a good *polis*.⁴⁶

For Marx, exchange and especially money will erode the moral virtue necessary for a community. Virtues will no longer appear as ends in themselves, no longer reinforce the universal bonds of the community, but instead come to appear as means we are forced to use to achieve particular interests determined by the market. Conscience and honor, he suggests, will be offered for sale and thus become commodities.[47] After exchange developed, Marx says,

> everything that men had considered as inalienable became an object of exchange, of traffic and could be alienated. This is the time when the very things which till then had been communicated, but never exchanged; given, but never sold; acquired, but never bought—virtue, love, conviction, knowledge, conscience, etc.—when everything finally passed into commerce. It is the time of general corruption, of universal venality, or, to speak in terms of political economy, the time when everything, moral or physical, having become a marketable value, is brought to the market to be assessed at its truest value.[48]

So also, as credit develops, the creditor will come to view trustworthiness in an individual not as a virtue that is an end in itself but as a mere *means* to guarantee the repayment of loans. "The life of the poor man and his talents and activity serve the rich man as a guarantee of the repayment of the money lent. That means, therefore, that all the social virtues of the poor man, the content of his vital activity, his existence itself, represent for the rich man the reimbursement of his capital with the customary interest. . . . One ought to consider how vile it is to estimate the value of a man in money. . . ."[49] Exchange is incompatible with virtue, community, concern for the common good, and working for the benefit of the species.

Moreover, for Marx, in an alienated exchange economy, the political state will be estranged from civil society. The term "civil society" refers to the everyday economic realm of private individuals—the realm of material life and particular interests. The term "political state" refers to the realm of government—the realm that should be concerned with the universal, the common good, the general interest. For Marx, it is the realm of species activity where human beings should consider themselves members of a community and work for the common good. But the political state is cut off from civil society. It is a distant realm in which the ordinary individual rarely participates and thus where the individual is merely an "imaginary member of an illusory" community that concerns itself with an "unreal universality."[50]

Moreover, Marx argues that all uprisings break out in "isolation of man from the community." It is isolation from political participation in the community, from the universal, from species being, that gives rise to revolution. And Marx argues that "however partial the uprising of the industrial workers may be, it contains within itself a universal soul. . . ."⁵¹ In other words, just as the oppression of the proletariat, the deprivation of its needs, drives it to act in accordance with a categorical imperative, so isolation from the political sphere, lack of political participation and power, and the absence of community and empowerment drive the proletariat toward this realm of the universal that it lacks.

The society of Rousseau's *Social Contract* is certainly not as bad as the alienated societies Marx has been discussing here. Marx in many respects agrees with Rousseau. For Rousseau, there is no developed realm of exchange that feeds particular interest, erodes virtue, or isolates individuals from the political community. In fact, all citizens sit in the sovereign assembly; thus are members of the political community; and thus concern themselves with the universal. Nevertheless, Marx thinks that some of the above criticisms apply to Rousseau. Rousseau's society, he says, expresses "the abstract ideal of political man." Individuals, who are complete and solitary as they stand, for Rousseau, must be made a part of a larger whole. This means that these individuals must give up their *own* powers and receive in exchange *alien* powers, which they cannot employ without the help of others.⁵² Individuals, in becoming citizens, are transformed. The citizen becomes a member of a whole, a community, and works for the universal *only* as a member of the political assembly. This need not extend to the everyday life of the individual in society, which, at least at the socioeconomic level, is not communal for Rousseau. There, individuals work for themselves, not for the benefit of the species.⁵³ These two separate realms are certainly present in Rousseau's thought, and this is what Marx objects to. He wants these two separate realms collapsed into one. He wants the political realm—the realm of community, universality, and species being—to be realized in, embedded within, the everyday social realm:

> Only when the real, individual man re-absorbs in himself the abstract citizen, and as an individual human being has become a species-being in his everyday life, in his particular work, and in his particular situation, only when man has recognized and organized his *"forces propres"* as social forces, and consequently no longer separates social power from himself in the shape of political power, only then will human emancipation have been accomplished.⁵⁴

The reabsorption of the political state into civil society does away with the political state as an alienated realm separate from, standing over, and dominating civil society. At the same time, it transforms society (*Gesellschaft*) into a community (*Gemeinschaft*) because concern for the universal, working consciously and collectively for the benefit of others, no longer occurs only at the distant, alienated level of the state but has been brought down to and embedded within the concrete, everyday realm of society.

Furthermore, Marx, like Rousseau, is a radical democrat. In democracy, he argues, the constitution is the people's own work—it is the self-determination of the people.[55] In the sort of democracy that Marx envisions, the political state, the realm of universality and community, would no longer be separate, distant, and isolated from individuals in society. The political constitution would be the work, the expression, the self-determination, of the people themselves in society.

One of the ways in which the separation of the political state from civil society can be maintained is through the election of representatives.[56] Representatives are appointed and only they participate actively and directly in the universal realm of the political community. The people themselves remain isolated from direct participation. Marx, like Rousseau, rejects representatives. Marx wants only the self-representation of the people.[57] Nevertheless, the elimination of representatives is not enough to achieve what Marx is after here. This must be explained.

In criticizing Hegel, who, we have seen, is not a democrat at all, Marx, in the *Critique of Hegel's Philosophy of Law* (1843), discusses two rather obvious ways in which representatives could be eliminated in the ideal democracy. Either all individuals could participate in the legislature themselves (as, for example, in Rousseau's *Social Contract*) or they could participate through deputies (as, for example, in Rousseau's essay on Poland). Deputies, we must recall, are different from normal representatives. Representatives are elected and then go off to vote as they see fit. Deputies are given a mandate or commission—specific voting instructions. If they do not vote as they were instructed, the citizens can remove them immediately. Thus, the citizens, in controlling and directing their deputies, would participate in the political sphere more than if they elected ordinary representatives, but would not do so as directly as they would if they themselves all sat in the legislature.

However, Marx argues that the question of whether all are to participate in the legislature or whether they should do so through deputies is a question that arises *only* when the political state is alienated from civil society, and neither of these approaches will overcome the alienation of state from society. In being cut off from the political community, all naturally desire to participate in it; but in the first place Marx thinks it is clearly impossible for all to participate in the legislature, and, in the second place he thinks that deputies, as normally understood, would not solve the problem either. The problem here is that whether all participate or whether they do so through deputies, the only participants would be *individuals*—the *isolated* individuals of civil society. The choice is only between all or some of these *isolated* individuals. And the only universality that could arise in the legislature from these isolated individuals would be universality as the "full count of individuality"—the sum total of the particular interests of these isolated individuals.[58] In other words, individuals in society have not reabsorbed political power, community, species being, and universality into their everyday, particular lives. Legislative activity has not become a *social* function—a communal function rooted in the everyday, particular lives of individuals in society.[59] It remains merely an abstract *political* function.

Thus, for Marx, the only solution is that representation must come to be understood in a radically new way. If the alienation of the political state from civil society is to be overcome, if community is to be reabsorbed into the particular lives of individuals, then it must be the case that in the ideal democracy:

> the significance of the legislative power as representative power completely disappears. The legislative power is representation here in the sense in which every function is representative—in the sense in which, e.g., the shoemaker, insofar as he satisfies a social need, is my representative, in which every particular social activity as a species-activity merely represents the species, i.e., an attribute of my own nature, and in which every person is the representative of every other. He is here representative not because of something else which he represents but because of what he is and does.[60]

In other words, representatives, even if they are deputies, are isolated individuals representing other isolated individuals who for a limited time go off to a separate realm to cast votes. Even if all sit in the legislature, they do so only as isolated individuals seated in the separate realm of the legislature. Marx finds this objectionable. Those who sit in the legislature should all be members of a community and they should be representatives in the way that any and all members of the community are representatives. It may seem odd to speak of a shoemaker, or any worker, as representing anyone. But if society is collectively organized and commonly controlled according to a general plan, then it makes some sense to think of the shoemaker, or any worker, as a delegate of the community, a representative of the associated workers, handling a specific task for the benefit of the community. The shoemaker represents, serves, and satisfies the needs of the community in making shoes.

Marx is contrasting two forms of representation: one that represents from outside and the other that represents from within a community. Legislators must directly interact with other members of the community within that community and consciously serve their needs in a way that is no different from the way any worker does. Such activity must form a conscious bond among members of this community. Legislators must not stand apart from, sit in a realm outside of, and certainly must not stand over and dominate, other members of society any more than a shoemaker does. Legislators must represent *within* the community and the community must be an equalitarian one. Thus it is necessary, Marx says, to have the greatest possible extension of *voting*—of the right to vote and the right to be elected.[61] If the difference between shoemakers and legislators collapses, this will mean that the difference between civil society (the realm in which we find shoemakers) and the political state (the realm in which we find legislators) will have been overcome.[62] We will have to say a good deal more about this transformed form of representation after we have discussed Marx's concept of essence in Section III. However, there is a bit more that we can say now.

In the *Critique of Hegel's Philosophy of Law*, it remains unclear exactly what one votes for or is elected to in the ideal democracy. Representation is transformed, but within this transformed type of representation is there still something like a legislature? Are there still something like deputies? What are the specific arrangements? This becomes much clearer in the *Civil War in France* (of 1871). In discussing the Paris Commune, which lasted for two months during the Franco-Prussian War of 1871 and which Marx considered to be a communist society,[63] Marx says that the commune, chosen by universal suffrage, "was to be the political form of even the smallest country hamlet . . . The rural communes of every district were to administer their common affairs by an assembly of delegates in the central town, and these district assemblies were again to send deputies to the National Delegation in Paris, each delegate to be at any time revocable and bound by the *mandat impératif* (formal instructions) of his constituents."[64] Here we can see that Marx clearly wants deputies elected to a communal body—a body, he says, that would be executive and legislative at the same time.⁶⁵ But these representatives, must be understood as representatives within a community:

> While the merely repressive organs of the old governmental power were to be amputated, its legitimate functions were to be wrested from an authority usurping pre-eminence over society itself, and restored to the responsible agents of society. Instead of deciding once in three or six years which member of the ruling class was to misrepresent the people in Parliament, universal suffrage was to serve the people, constituted in Communes, as individual suffrage serves every other employer in the search for the workmen and managers in his business. And it is well known that companies, like individuals, in matters of real business generally know how to put the right man in the right place, and, if they for once make a mistake, to redress it promptly.⁶⁶

So, there will be deputies and a legislature, but representation will be understood such that it will not contribute to a political state alienated from and dominating civil society. Marx's views on government in communist society are similar to Rousseau's in the sense that the government is not sovereign. It cannot dominate the people. Governmental representatives are employees of the people and like employees can be replaced at any time.⁶⁷ They represent the way shoemakers do. They cannot stand over society. But then Marx differs from and goes beyond Rousseau. Besides not being able to dominate the people, Marx, in the above-quoted passage, suggests that the legislature or the commune is not even separate from society. It is within society. It is merely a particular part of society carrying out a necessary social function that serves society the way any employee serves an employer. The members of the commune are delegates handling their task the way any member of the community does. They represent the community the way a shoemaker, or any worker does. The commune performs a social or a communal function, no longer a political function. Marx says that the working class, when it comes to power, "cannot simply lay hold of the ready-made State machinery, and wield it for its own purposes." It must destroy this state power that stands over and dominates the nation.⁶⁸ In an earlier draft of this same text Marx, echoing his comments in 1843, also says that what is required here is "the re-absorption of the state power by society, as its own living forces instead of as forces controlling and subduing it, by the popular masses themselves, forming their own force instead of the organized force of their suppression."⁶⁹

Moreover, to ensure that there will be no state standing over society, Marx, like Rousseau in the essay on Poland, advocates the elimination of a standing army attached to the state and the maintenance only of a national guard or civil militia—the armed people.[70] The civil militia, made up of and controlled by the people, could be used against the government if it attempted to become a state standing over and dominating society.[71]

Moreover, to prevent the alienation of state from society, the elimination of classes is required, and this will require that exchange be eliminated. A complex exchange economy, as Rousseau and Hegel had already seen, and as we argued in the chapter on Locke,[72] will, through an invisible hand, shift wealth and power to some (the bourgeoisie) and reduce others (the proletariat) to poverty and powerlessness.[73] Nevertheless, while eliminating private property, exchange, and classes, Marx wants to retain highly developed and complex forces of production—he does not want society leveled to the sort of rigid equality that Rousseau sought.[74]

The attainment of the desired form of equality, for Marx, will require a two-stage transition. In the "Critique of the Gotha Program" (1875), Marx expects the first stage of communist society to be characterized by a strict form of equality. Each will get exactly equal shares of the social consumption fund. People will receive certificates from society in proportion to the labor they contribute—the hours they have worked. Nevertheless, the task of society will be to increase to as high a level as possible this social consumption fund and thus the equal share of each. In the second stage of communist society, this strict equality, despite its high level, will be transcended. As the productive forces of society are increased and cooperative wealth flows more abundantly, each will receive according to their needs.[75]

This, I think, is still a form of equality, but what Aristotle would call geometric equality as opposed to arithmetic equality. Arithmetic equality requires that each receive exactly equal shares. Geometric equality requires that the share of A be to the share of B as the worth of A is to the worth of B. We find a version of what seems to be arithmetic equality in the first stage of communist society, where each receives exactly equal shares (at least insofar as they contribute equal labor time). Actually this is already a form of geometric equality in that the share of A is to the share of B in the same proportion as the labor time of A is to the labor time of B. But insofar as their labor times are equal their shares would be exactly equal. In the second stage of communism, however, the share of A would be to the share of B in the same proportion as the needs of A are to the needs of B.[76] This is a higher form of equality that, unlike Rousseau, would ensure the development of a "rich human being and . . . rich human need."[77] Marx wants human beings to develop their needs as far as each is capable, and he wants these needs satisfied.

We must now discuss the general will. In Marx's writings, there is certainly no discussion of formal procedures like those found in Rousseau's *Social Contract* for the realization of a general will. Marx does not argue that the citizens must reflect only upon abstract questions or that the only questions put to the legislature must be of the form "what is the general will on this matter?" However, as we have seen, the general will and the categorical imperative are very similar, and the young Marx is certainly concerned with realizing the categorical imperative in communist society.

Marx mentions the concept of a general will in the *Eighteenth Brumaire* (1851–52). He says that under the French parliament, the nation "made its general will the law, that is, it made the law of the ruling class its general will."[78] This, of course, was a false general will. Nevertheless, Marx goes on to make an important point. After Bonaparte's triumph over parliament, the French nation renounced "all will of its own" to the executive power and submitted "to the superior command of an alien will, to authority. The executive power, in contrast to the legislative power, expresses the heteronomy of a nation, in contrast to its autonomy."[79] In this text, Marx does not tell us whether or not he wants to realize a true general will. But it is clear that executive power means heteronomy and alienation, which would certainly be incompatible with a general will. Legislative power, on the other hand, at least can involve autonomy and freedom, and thus at least might give rise to a general will. Moreover, elsewhere in Marx's writings, though he does not use the term "general will" (except in a few places), we find that Marx does want laws that at least are very much the sorts of laws that would arise from a general will.

In his early writings, Marx tells us that the state is a "great organism, in which legal, moral, and political freedom must be realized, and in which the individual citizen in obeying the laws of the state only obeys the laws of his own reason. . . ."[80] He also says that the state "educates its members by making them its members, by converting the aims of the individual into general aims, crude instinct into moral inclination, natural independence into spiritual freedom, by the individual finding his good in the life of the whole, and the whole in the frame of mind of the individual."[81] Moreover, as we have already seen, for Marx the content of law must agree with the universal form of law.[82] Laws must be universal and necessary. Particular interests cannot be so universalized. They will contradict the universal form of law.[83]

However, we can find even stronger echoes of Rousseau and the general will. For Marx, in the early writings, the laws of the state are the universal norms in which freedom is expressed. In contrast to executive authority, which, as we have seen, is heteronomous, laws are not opposed to freedom or autonomy. "Laws are in no way repressive measures against freedom, any more than the law of gravity is a repressive measure against motion, because while, as the law of gravitation, it governs the eternal motions of the celestial bodies, as the law of falling it kills me if I violate it and want to dance in the air. Laws are rather the positive, clear, universal norms in which freedom has acquired an impersonal, theoretical existence independent of the arbitrariness of the individual." In obeying the law, one obeys one's own reason. Thus, where "the law is a real law, i.e., a form of the existence of freedom, it is the real existence of freedom for man. Laws therefore, cannot prevent a man's actions, for they are indeed the inner laws of life of his action itself, the conscious reflection of his life." And thus, much as for Rousseau, "only when his actual behavior has shown that he has ceased to obey the natural law of freedom does the law in the form of state law *compel him to be free,* just as the laws of physics confront me as something alien only when my life has ceased to be the life of these laws. . . ."[84]

There is also a strong echo here of a passage from Rousseau's *Emile* in which Rousseau distinguishes between dependence on nature and dependence on persons. The former is perfectly compatible with freedom, but the latter produces masters and slaves. What society must do, for Rousseau "is to substitute law for man and to arm the general will with a real strength superior to the action of every particular will. If the laws of nations could, like those of nature, have an inflexibility that no human force could ever conquer, dependence on men would then become dependence on things again; in the republic all the advantages of the natural state would be united with those of the civil state. . . ." In likening civil laws to natural laws, Marx is following Rousseau. Such laws, he says, are a guarantee against the "arbitrariness of the individual," or, as he puts it later, such laws "must be a guarantee against persons."[85]

Marx envisions a democratic society that is self-determined. It gives itself its own laws—laws that would be rational, universal, and like laws of nature. Very clearly, they would be laws that agree with the general will or the categorical imperative. Thus, much as for Rousseau in the *Social Contract*, to compel citizens to obey these laws (which any society would do anyway) is to compel them to be free.

Nevertheless, if, for Marx, there are no formal procedures for a legislative body to follow, how is the general will to be realized? In the first place, for Marx, the legislature is not to be a separate entity isolated from society, but rather a part of and embedded within the community. The general will, then, will not arise from special procedures followed in the legislature nor even from the legislature itself as a separate entity. The general will will arise from the whole community. Furthermore, Marx, unlike Rousseau, is not out to discuss a utopian society in which all the conditions or procedures necessary for the realization of a general will are merely to be presupposed or postulated. To realize the general will, Rousseau, for example, had to presuppose a relatively homogeneous people with similar life conditions, interests, and customs. The real world, however, is filled with different social classes that have very different interests and life conditions. In the *German Ideology* and in other later writings, Marx begins to argue that a unified, single, general will can only arise out of a class with similar interests and a similar situation in life. In other words, a general will only arises out of and is determined by the material conditions of a given class.[86]

Thus, Marx says that any class—including the proletariat—that is aiming at domination must first conquer political power in order to represent its interest as a general interest. This class must "give its ideas the form of universality, and present them as the only rational, universally valid ones."[87] This is not *simply* to impose an illusion. This class *will* be able to represent the rest of society because its interests at this early date are not that different from the interests of other nonruling classes. Its particular class interests have not had a chance to develop in a particular way against the interests of other nonruling classes. And thus in coming to power, this class really will serve the interests of these other classes.[88]

Nevertheless, there is domination here and it will lead to a state standing over and dominating society in the interest of this new class. This will always be the case, Marx thinks, until classes and class rule have been overcome. Then Marx thinks that it will no longer be necessary, certainly, to represent a particular class interest as a general interest, nor will it even be necessary to represent the general interest as ruling.[89]

To understand this latter claim, we must notice that in the *German Ideology* Marx uses the term "common interest" to refer to interests that are actually shared by all individuals and that are determined by material conditions. The term "general interest," on the other hand, refers to shared interests that are illusory or imaginary. Struggles at the *political* level, for Marx, have to do with this illusory general interest. In other words, struggle over abstract general interests merely at the the *political* level will not succeed in reconciling particular interests with the real common interest. To achieve a real common interest will require struggle and radical transformation of material conditions at the socioeconomic level.[90] Thus, when classes, as well as the alienation of the political state from civil society, have actually been overcome, it will no longer be necessary to represent an illusory general interest as ruling, but it will then be possible to realize a real common interest as the outcome of material conditions and thus the universality of the general will will have been concretely realized. There will no longer be a general interest at the political level—the political sphere will have been reabsorbed into society and the common interest will arise out of the everyday social interaction of individuals. To explain this further, we will have to wait until we have discussed Marx's concept of essence in Section III.

III. Essence and the Communal Individual

Hegel's political project, in many ways, was the same as Marx's. Hegel, too, we have seen in Chapter 5, wanted to combine Rousseau and Kant. He wanted the modern state to be a community based upon rational freedom realized through a general will. Moreover, he wanted this rational freedom reinforced by custom and tradition, which shaped the character, interests, and feelings of the individual citizens in support of the general will. Much as for Marx, freedom required three things: (1) that the individual be self-determined in accordance with universal and rational principles, (2) that the laws and institutions of the state also be rational so that in obeying civil laws you obey your own reason, and (3) that custom, tradition, and therefore feeling and interest, support these rational laws.

Rousseau's ideal community, we have seen, was utopian. It could not be realized in the modern world. Healthy customs and traditions simply had to be given in a traditional society. Thus Hegel appealed to a philosophy of history like that of Kant, whereby conflicting particular interests produce the universal—what the categorical imperative or the general will would have demanded from the start. But then Hegel had to explain how these conflicting particular interests could be compatible with custom, tradition, community, and the general will. This was especially so, for Hegel, since conflicting particular interests were necessary *within* the ideal society itself. A modern society, for Hegel, meant developed commerce, trade, and wealth. Thus Hegel had to explain how particular interests could be present without eroding custom, tradition, community, and the universal.

To do this, Hegel explained how customs and traditions were produced by the state and its institutions—they need not just be given. They were produced by the discipline of civil society. And following Kant, Smith, and Steuart, Hegel showed how conflicting particular interests, far from eroding the universal, in fact, led toward the universal unconsciously and through an invisible hand. But since this movement toward the universal was only unconscious in civil society, and since civil society was the realm in which particular interests had a right to satisfaction, conscious community could only exist at the level of the state—the level of spirit. It could only exist in consciousness where one sees that the state is one's own essence.[91] This is where we find the most significant difference between Marx and Hegel. A community merely at the level of the state, a community merely in consciousness, is not enough for Marx. Individuals must actually and concretely participate in community. Community must be realized in the everyday realm of society and individuals must work consciously for the community, the universal, the species, in society. Thus, for Marx, private property, exchange, and competing particular interests that realize the universal only unconsciously must be eliminated in the ideal society. It is not enough to see that the state is one's own essence and to participate in community at that distant, alienated level. The realization of one's essence requires working for the community consciously in everyday life.

In this way, Marx has no need, as Hegel did, to explain how conflicting particular interests can be compatible with community, the universal, and the general will within the ideal society. The ideal society will simply exclude private property and uncontrolled markets that generate conflicting class interests. However, conflicting interests do play a role in Marx's philosophy of history. They play a role in the realization of the ideal society, but not in the ideal society itself. Thus we must explain how conflicting interests, necessary for the realization of the ideal society, will be able to disappear in that society itself and also how customs and traditions, eroded by the conflict of particular interests in capitalist society, can be transformed and revived in communist society without being further eroded by the process of historical change, which realizes this society and which itself depends upon the conflict of particular interests.

For Marx, historical change in capitalist society quite clearly has eroded past custom, tradition, and community. In the *Communist Manifesto,* he says:

> The bourgeoisie cannot exist without constantly revolutionising the instruments of production, and thereby the relations of production, and with them the whole relations of society. Conservation of the old modes of production in unaltered form, was, on the contrary, the first condition of existence of all earlier industrial classes. Constant revolutionising of production, uninterrupted disturbance of all social conditions, everlasting uncertainty and agitation distinguish the bourgeois epoch from all earlier ones. All fixed, fast-frozen relations, with their train of ancient and venerable prejudices and opinions, are swept away, all new-formed ones become antiquated before they can ossify. All that is solid melts into air, all that is holy is profaned. . . .[92]

Moreover, capitalist exchange fosters possessiveness or selfishness. In an exchange economy, things are securely ours and can satisfy our needs only if we *own* them. In an estranged market economy, where our products, the objects of our need, are not controlled by us, where human beings are unable to work consciously and collectively for the benefit of others, where abstract and impersonal market laws control and dominate our social relations, we are driven to possess the product and to desire to possess it if we are to satisfy our needs. This is the only way we can exert any control over the product.

But if estrangement were overcome, if our productive activity, our products, and our social relations were consciously and collectively controlled, if products were distributed in a communal way rather than bought and sold, then, Marx thinks, the selfish drive to possess would be reduced.[93] If individuals were to recognize that the satisfaction of their own needs depends upon individuals working consciously and collectively for the benefit of others, then possessiveness would begin to disappear.

This is not to suggest, as Elster, for example, argues,[94] that Marx's ideal society depends upon achieving a utopian form of altruism. Marx does not ask for altruism *at all*. We do not deny our own selfish interests in order to fulfill a moral injunction to work for the species. Instead, we come to see that working for the species is the only way we can benefit ourselves. We might say that it is self-interest that drives us to work for the benefit of the species in order that we may benefit ourselves. Yet this is not simple self-interest in the liberal sense. We *do*, after all, work for the benefit of the *species*. In a way that recalls Hegel's treatment of "virtue" and the "way of the world,"[95] Marx is holding that self-interest and the universal are not opposed—not even externally related to each other.

Moreover, one certainly does not pursue self-interest and allow this to bring about an alien universal behind one's back and through an invisible hand. Working for the realization of the species is to work for one's own realization because the individual is a member of the species. The species is one's essence—one is internally related to the species. This, somewhat as for Hegel, requires abandoning the perspective of isolated individual consciousness. But it is also different because in doing so, for Marx, we must not end up with Hegelian spirit. Self-interest and working for the benefit of the species are not unconsciously linked through an invisible hand in civil society and consciously so only at the level of the state, at the level of spirit. They must be consciously linked within the everyday life of the social community. To explain this—and to explain how possessiveness, or selfish particular interests, can be overcome and healthy customs and traditions revived—will be a lengthy process. Let us begin by explaining Marx's concept of the individual and work our way toward his concept of essence.

Marx's concept of the individual is quite different from the typical liberal concept of the individual. For liberals, roughly speaking, individuals are simply given—"individuality" is a primitive concept. Individuals come ready-made. They are the basic starting point of social theory. We don't ask where they came from or how they developed. We merely assume their existence. For Hobbes or Locke, they just existed there in the state of nature and we set about constructing society from these given individuals. Individuals are basic and society is external to them and derivative from them.

Furthermore, these given individuals, certainly for Hobbes and Locke, seem to have interests and desires that just belong to them as individuals. Again, these interests and desires just seem to be there, given, unquestioned. Moreover, freedom on this liberal model basically means that individuals not be hindered in the pursuit of these

180   *Chapter Six*

interests and desires. Freedom is the absence of external constraint. Freedom, in a sense, is also just there, given, assumed—at least in the absence of compulsion or external constraint.

For Marx this is unacceptable. Individuals are not given: they are *produced*. They are produced by society or culture. They are not just there, ready-made—they are not to be assumed. Instead, we must come to understand *how* they are produced. For Marx, human beings take up, appropriate, or internalize the values, aspirations, knowledge, productive know-how, technology, and many other aspects of their sociocultural world. After they appropriate or internalize these things, they work them over, labor upon them, perhaps develop them, perhaps come up with something new, and deposit this back in their sociocultural world where others can take it in and repeat the process.

For Marx, individuals are produced by society or culture. Individuals in different cultures or in a single culture at different stages of its development will be different individuals. They will have taken in different values, aspirations, knowledge, and so forth. They will have been individualized differently. But at the same time that culture produces individuals, individuals also produce their culture. Individuals begin by internalizing existing culture, but then they work it over; they transform and develop their culture. Culture, in fact, is nothing but the outcome of individuals, and individuals are the outcome of culture. Culture produces individuals, which then transform and produce culture. Changed individuals change their culture, and a changed culture produces changed individuals. Individuals and their culture cannot be separated as two externally related entities. They are internally related as parts of a single process, and each creates the other.[96]

This model, I think, accurately describes Marx's view at all periods of his thought. In the *German Ideology*, Marx develops a rather determinist doctrine of historical materialism and begins to argue that the historical development of material conditions—not consciousness, ideas, or values—plays the predominant role in determining the development of the individual and society, whereas in the *Economic and Philosophic Manuscripts* ideas, values, and consciousness played an equally important role.[97] But despite this shift, it is always Marx's view that there is an interaction between individuals and their sociocultural world in which each creates the other.

For Marx, the mutual transformation of the individual and of society is speeded up during a revolution. Revolutions do not merely transform social institutions; they transform individuals. They transform even the interests, feelings, and desires of individuals,[98] which then crystallize into transformed customs and traditions. The sort of transformation that set in after the bourgeois revolution, we have seen in the above-quoted passage from the *Communist Manifesto,* eroded custom and tradition—all that was solid melted into air. But a proletarian revolution, insofar as it leads toward a categorical imperative, tends toward the elimination of possessiveness or selfishness, and establishes community, should, as it molds and transforms feelings, interests, and institutions, begin to form healthy customs and traditions that would reinforce the universal—the categorical imperative. The erosion of custom and tradition under the bourgeoisie due to exchange and conflicting particular interests, the sort of erosion that Rousseau thought would be the natural result of any change in customs and traditions,[99] would be reversed. Healthy customs and traditions would be rebuilt and rebuilt in accordance with a categorical imperative.

Marx's conception of the individual implies that if the individual is produced by the culture it takes in, then individuals are produced by *other* individuals, by the human species, who contributed to the producing of culture which the individual internalizes. The main point here, for Marx, is that a higher development of the individual requires a higher development of others—of the human species. The higher development of the individual *requires* a higher development of *culture*. A richer culture there to be internalized is necessary for the higher development of the individual. Thus, to have a richer culture requires a higher development of others, the human species, who produce this culture.

This is quite clear even in something as basic as language—and it would also be true for art, mathematics, science, and most other cultural disciplines. The individual takes up, learns, a given language or discipline that has already been developed to a certain stage by other individuals through history.[100] What the individual can do with this language or discipline, the ways in which the individual can develop them further as, say, a poet, mathematician, or scientist, are in large part conditioned by the level to which the language or discipline has already been developed by others. The richer the language, the more possibilities there are. Scientific experiments, for example, and thus the discoveries these experiments make possible, are highly dependent upon the given level of development of technology—the level to which technology has been developed by other members of the species. Without linear accelerators, for example, certain sorts of discoveries in particle physics are not possible. It is certainly true that what the individual can do with this language or discipline is also conditioned by the individual's *own* ability to use them, but that too in large part is determined by the individual's culture—how the individual has developed in it and been educated by it.

From this, we can begin to understand more clearly what Marx means when he calls human beings species beings. The essence, the nature, of the individual is the species—the human species as a whole. The human being is not an isolated individual being, but a species being. The human being only develops as the species does. The individual only develops through the development of other human beings who produce a richer culture there to be internalized. To understand human nature, we must not look at the isolated individual as liberals do; we must look instead at culture as it has been developed by the human species and embedded in individuals.

Thus, it follows, for Marx, that to seek your own development as an individual, you cannot close yourself off into yourself and merely seek to realize your own private interests as for the liberal tradition. To seek your *own* development, you must seek the development of *others*—the development of the species. You must seek the development of a richer sociocultural world. Moreover, as we have seen, to work for the benefit of the species is to work for the universal, to act for the sake of a categorical imperative. Thus to seek your own development as an individual requires acting for the sake of the universal.

This certainly requires working for the good of the community. But also, ultimately, it implies that we should work for the benefit of the human species as a whole. This may seem unrealistic. However, it is Marx's view in many places that as history progresses, economic systems become more complex in the sense that they involve more thoroughgoing and widespread interdependence.[101] We are being pushed toward increasing universality where what happens in the Middle East affects our local gas pump and where actions that we take in one part of the world seriously affect what occurs in other parts of the world.

Perhaps it is an exaggeration to say that we always depend upon the human species as a whole for our individual development or that our individual actions affect the human species as a whole. But things certainly tend in this direction for Marx and our development certainly depends upon more than our immediate community—it depends at least upon all past history, which culminates in the development of my community. And my actions may well affect much more than my immediate community: they may through my children and their children even affect the whole future species or at least a large part of it.

Certainly an individual can chose not to work for others, the community, or the species. And indeed individuals might even be better off, in *some* sense, from *some* perspective, if they worked only for themselves. In a liberal society they would probably be better off—they would certainly be better able to satisfy their liberal self-interest. If one adopts a liberal conception of the individual, working for the species will appear absurd and things like free riding may appear sensible. Marx's point, as I understand it and am trying to present it, is to develop a different conception of the individual reinforced by a different conception of society. Once you adopt this perspective, Marx thinks (and I think he is right), it will appear sensible to work for the species and not sensible to free ride.

What might Marx argue against the free rider? Imagine an international group of scientists all working in a certain area (and assume that they are not working on things like weapons or in weapons-related areas). Imagine that these scientists refuse to work for the benefit of the species and refuse to cooperate with other scientists. They free ride in the sense that they are willing to take from others and put to use any new discoveries made by the other scientists, but they are unwilling to contribute anything. They keep their research secret so that no one can benefit from it but themselves. Each of these scientists is heir to all the past science of the human species (at least all that they are aware of or consider valuable enough to study). They take this science up and use it to make new discoveries, but they do not deposit these new discoveries back in a common culture for others to take up and push further. If this continues, sooner or later, the work of each scientist will suffer—it will proceed more slowly than it would if the scientist had access to the advancements of the other scientists. If all this were to go far enough we could end up with the secret cults of magicians and alchemists.

Still, one scientist might hold that, yes, all the *other* scientists should share their work; it is just that I will not. I will free ride. This, of course, would be immoral in Marx's view. But besides that Marx also thinks that it is not likely to be in the true interest of this scientist. It is quite possible that if I do make my work available to other scientists, they might be able to take it up and push it further, even push it further in such a way that, as I progress with my current work, their new development of my past work will become necessary for me to be able to progress further with my own current work. One could easily make similar arguments for most other disciplines and areas of culture, but perhaps the case of science is a bit clearer.

Moreover, if we turn away from the individual free-riding scientist for a moment, we would certainly want to say that the citizens who fund this research would want all the technology, the drugs (think of AIDS), the medical discoveries, and so forth, made public as soon as possible so that other researchers could have access to them and make more rapid progress in related areas. Free riders do not make any sense at all from this perspective. The main issue for Marx is how society in general is structured—whether all have access to the accomplishments, discoveries, and products of others or whether these are privately owned and controlled. If we have a communal society then the problem of individual free riders is a different and smaller problem.

We must now begin to explain Marx's concept of essence. Marx holds that the human species works on its world through history and transforms it to conform to its own essence. In this way, in confronting the world, the human species confronts itself. The object that confronts the subject is no longer alien or other. It is not heteronomous. It is at one with the subject. It is the objectification of the subject's own essence.[102]

The essence of a thing is realized through a process of growth or development in which the full potentiality of the thing is actualized. It fully realizes its form and is able to carry out properly its function or activity.[103] For the highest realization of an essence to be achieved, human activity is necessary. Human beings must measure existence by essence, criticize existence when it falls short of essence, and transform existence to accord with essence. To do this, we must begin by evaluating particular existents. We must measure them against their idea, concept, or proper form—their essence. When existence conforms to its essence, the thing has realized its proper end or good. If it fails to conform to its essence, the result is an evil that must be further transformed.[104] To cite one of Marx's examples, we can evaluate a state by examining the essence of the state and discovering whether this particular state fulfills, lives up to, or can be derived from and justified by its essence.[105] Moreover, for the state to realize its essence, legislators, in formulating civil laws, must discover the actual inner laws of social relations, their essence, and formulate this essence consciously as a civil law.[106]

How do we tell whether essence and existence are in accord? The test of whether existence measures up to essence is to compare content and form. For example, the content of a law must not contradict the form of law. The content of the law arises out of the particular nature, the actual life, of the thing in question. The proper form that the law must have is universality. The content of the law must be capable of being given a universal form without contradiction. The state and its laws must represent universal ends, not private or particular interests.[107] As the essence of a thing develops, unfolds its full potential, realizes its form, it moves toward universality. For essence to be fully realized and universality achieved, human beings must have discovered this essence and consciously formulated it as a rational, universal law. To be free, it is not enough that essence and existence unconsciously accord. Existence must consciously accord with essence. We must consciously act in accordance with essence—in accord with rational and universal principles that we have actualized ourselves. Thus, we can see a bit more clearly why in compelling the individual to obey the law, the state compels the individual to be free. The individual is compelled to act in accordance with the individual's own essence as well as in accord with rational and universal principles established by individuals themselves.[108]

However, to understand these abstract and sketchy notions more clearly, we must push a good deal further. In the first place, we must begin to explain how the essence of an external existent, as it is transformed by human labor, can be said to be, or can become, one with the individual's essence. Marx's concept of essence is intimately connected to his concept of need. Need indicates essence. If something is needed by a human being it is a part of the human essence. Need indicates that an external existent is essential to the human being. It indicates that without the thing, the human's essence cannot be realized—it cannot have a "full, satisfied, complete, existence."[109] If the need is frustrated; if it cannot be satisfied; existence is out of accord with essence and alienation is present. Moreover, we must see in more detail how labor is intimately connected with Marx's concept of need and of essence. We must labor upon the world in order to satisfy our needs—we must transform existence to suit our essence. Only in this way can essence develop and be fully realized, and only in this way does external existence become one with our essence. As we labor upon the world and succeed in satisfying our needs, new needs will begin to be felt. These new needs will then call for a further and more complex transformation of the world to satisfy these new needs. At the same time, engaging in this more complex transformation of the world will cause us to develop to a higher level our powers, capacities, and abilities to labor on the world. Moreover, this development of our powers and abilities will itself give rise to even higher and more complex needs, which will then call for a further and more complex transformation of the world to satisfy these more complex needs. This cycle will be repeated over and over again.[110] Needs always point to the future. They continually indicate at higher and higher levels how existence must be transformed to meet our developing needs and realize more fully our essence. And in the same process, the external world will be increasingly transformed to accord with our needs, our essence—it will increasingly become one with our essence.

But to understand more fully how these external objects become one with our essence, we must see that the labor that satisfies the needs of human beings, for Marx, is understood as an objectification (*Vergegenständlichung*). All objects are the result of an objectification. Objects, for Marx, are existents needed by other beings and thus are a part of their essence. However, objects can be needed in two different ways and thus are related to our essence in two ways. Objects can be needed in order directly to maintain the existence of the human being and are part of our essence in this way. Or objects can be needed by a human being as objects in which and through which to express, manifest, or realize the being's powers and capacities. Objectification, for Marx, is understood as this expression, manifestation, or realization of the powers of a being in an object. It is the objectification of the being's essence in the object, and thus the object is related to our essence in this second way also.

However, these two ways in which the object is related to our essence are intimately connected. It is the fact that we objectify ourselves, our essence, in the product that transforms the product so that it is able to satisfy our needs—our essence. The fact that the object is the objectification of our powers, capacities, and ideas is precisely what allows the product to satisfy the needs of a being with such powers, capacities, and ideas. Thus, the external object is one with our essence because it is the objectification of our essence (this is the second sense in which the object is related to our essence), and this is what allows the object to satisfy our needs, our essence (in the first sense).

In one passage of the *Economic and Philosophic Manuscripts*, Marx discusses these matters more generally. He says that even plants have the sun as their object. The sun is the plant's object because the plant directly needs the sun to exist and to grow. But at the same time, the sun has the plant as its object. The sun needs the plant to express and manifest its life-giving powers in the growth of the plant. The sun objectifies itself in the plant.[111]

So also, for human beings, an object is something needed directly to satisfy their essence and maintain their existence—food, clothing, shelter, and tools would be good examples. But at the same time, human beings need objects in which they can objectify their powers and capacities. They need raw material on which to work. Human beings must labor upon nature in order to transform it into the sorts of objects that will satisfy their direct needs and in doing so they transform existence to suit their essence. But also they express, manifest, or objectify their powers and capacities in the object. To realize the human essence, for Marx, it is not only necessary to realize and satisfy the direct needs of human beings, but it is also necessary to manifest and develop their powers.

There is an intimate connection between powers and needs for Marx. The ability to realize any power would involve certain needs, as, for example, when workers need raw material and tools in which and through which to realize their labor. Moreover, the satisfaction of any need would imply the maintaining, reinforcing, or realizing of a power; as, for example, the satisfaction of the need for food, clothing, or shelter sustains the workers' abilities to manifest their power through labor. Furthermore, the drive to realize any power, for Marx, would itself be felt as a need—not a basic need, but a higher need[112]—as, for example, a need for education or general human development. The need-satisfying object is the outcome of a process of objectification.

But we must also see that our objectification is the outcome of, is transformed by, the development of our needs. Objectification begins with a subject whose powers, capacities, and ideas have developed historically to a given level as conditioned by the subject's social and cultural world—its specific level of technology, organization of production, culture, and so forth. For these subjective factors (these powers, capacities, and ideas) to be realized and developed, they must be objectified; that is, they must be set to work and produce an object. If not, they do not develop—they exist only in potential. With the production of a new object (say, a tool) new powers and capacities will be called into play, exercised, and developed both in producing the tool and in using it.

This can then give rise to new needs and ideas; which can call for further new objects to satisfy these needs and thus again new powers, capacities, and ideas to produce and use them. Needed objects promote the development of powers, capacities, and ideas. And the development of powers, capacities, and ideas promote the development of needed objects. Objectification produces objects that satisfy higher and higher needs, and higher and higher needs call forth higher and higher forms of objectification. In this process, the human essence is increasingly realized—our powers, capacities, and ideas are increasingly actualized. Moreover, external existence is increasingly transformed to fit (made one with) our essence—it is increasingly the objectification of our essence and thus satisfies our needs.

Through objectification, existence is transformed to correspond to essence, not just in the sense that the world is continually transformed into objects that satisfy higher and higher needs, but also in the sense that through objectification, through objectifying our powers and capacities in the object, we can begin to contemplate ourselves, our essence, in the object.[113] We can begin to see the object (our entire world of objects) as our own creation, as something produced by ourselves—the result, the manifestation, of our powers, capacities, and purposes. These objects would not be alien or heteronomous. They satisfy our needs and realize our essence. They are our essence objectified.

Furthermore, for Marx, and this is the important point we are heading toward, human beings need other human beings. They need them to carry on production at anything more than the most minimal level. They need them even to develop language, as well as any other art, science, or cultural enterprise. They need other human beings to develop as human beings. Since need indicates essence, it follows for Marx that we are essentially related to other human beings—they are part of our essence.

A part of this need for other human beings is a need for their products. We have said that labor must transform the natural world to produce objects capable of satisfying human need. In any sort of developed economy, where individuals are unable to produce all that they need themselves, individuals will experience a need for the products of other human beings.[114] But in a society with private property and exchange, individuals will be alienated from their products. Products will not be consciously and collectively controlled for the benefit of the species—for the benefit of other human beings. Products will be controlled by the owners of the products. Since others need these products but do not control them, they will be dominated by these products and by their need for them.

This need for the products of others, for Marx, shows us that we have an essential relationship to the products of others that is frustrated by private ownership and alienated exchange. The products of others are part of our essence—we have an internal relationship to them. We are not particular beings who merely need the particular products that we are the owners of. We are total beings, or species beings, who stand in need of all products produced by other human beings. We are species beings in need of a rich social and cultural world produced by other members of the species—a world therefore that ought to be produced consciously and collectively for the benefit of all members of the species.[115]

Thus, without other human beings, without community, we cannot realize our essence. Moreover, as we have said, human beings become what they are at any point in history by taking in the culture that has been produced as the objectification of other human beings. Thus—and here we are arriving at the central point that we are after—we are actually the product of other human beings. We are their objectification. So also, in our own labor, we ourselves objectify the powers and capacities that have been objectified in us and thus we produce others. We are the objectification of other human beings, and other human beings are our objectification. Thus, if alienation were overcome, we could contemplate the species in ourselves—in our powers, capacities, activities, and needs. And we could contemplate ourselves in the species, in other human beings. Our relationship to others is and would be seen as an internal relationship—an essential relationship—in the deepest sense.

At this point, we can see more clearly that for individuals to realize their own essence, they must work consciously and collectively for the benefit of the human species as a whole. The human essence, we have said, is only realized through the transformation of existence to suit essence. Moreover, the ability to transform existence to suit essence is dependent upon the level to which our powers and capacities are developed. However, the level to which these powers and capacities are developed in us is dependent upon the level to which powers and capacities are developed in the species as a whole and objectified in the culture we take in; that is, objectified in us. Thus, the level to which the powers and capacities of the species will be developed is dependent upon individuals working for the benefit of the species.

Therefore, we can see that to work for the benefit of the species is not, contrary to Elster, to be altruistic in any normal sense, and Marx's social theory need not depend upon a utopian ideal of altruism. To work for the benefit of the species, is not to work for *others*—it is not to work for individuals essentially outside us to whom we are externally related. To work for others, to work for the species, is to work for oneself because the species is part of oneself, is one's essence, is oneself.[116] Yet at the same time, this sort of working for oneself cannot be called self-interested in the traditional liberal sense. The individual's self-interest is not other than, externally related to, or opposed to the benefit of the species. The individual's essence is the species. Moreover, the individual does, after all, work for the benefit of the species, for needs that can be universalized and that thus accord with a categorical imperative. Realizing our essence coincides with acting on a categorical imperative.

Hegel argued that "virtue" and the "way of the world," or particular interest and the universal, were not opposed realities externally related to each other. They were internally related as two interacting moments enclosed within a single spiritual unity. Conflicting particular interests give rise to a set of institutions; a world that comes to have a life of its own, that reacts back upon and molds these particular interests, and thus leads them to the universal. In this way, the subject does not confront the object, the world, as an alien other. The object is the outcome of the subject's own activity, the realization of the subject's essence, and thus the object is compatible with the subject's freedom. The subject is not externally related to the object, but internally related to it as its own essence.[117]

So also, for Marx, working for the benefit of the species is not to work for an alien other, but for the realization of one's own essence. Moreover, working for the benefit of the species produces a more highly developed species, which then can mold, be objectified in, be taken in by, the individual. This develops the powers and capacities of the individual and the individual can then contribute more to the development of the species. The object, the other, the species, is not an alien other. It is the objectification of the essence of individuals, and they are its objectification. The individual and the species, the particular being and the universal, are internally related to each other in essence.[118]

We can now see more clearly that working for the benefit of the species is not to be determined heteronomously by inclination or interest, and to work for the benefit of the species is not merely to act in *accordance* with a categorical imperative. It is to act *for the sake of* a categorical imperative. It is certainly not to be determined by an external end. It is to be self-determined—to be determined by one's own essence. Nor is it to be determined by self-interest or inclination. It is not self-interested at all except in the sense that it is a self-realization, the realization of one's own essence. This is an activity that itself is an end in itself, not a means to an external end. This sort of interest in oneself, in one's self-realization, cannot be called "self-interest" in the normal sense of that term. To pursue the highest virtue, to seek to realize one's essence, however these concepts are understood in any ethical system that contains them, is what the individual *ought* to do. Such activity cannot be called self-interested without drastically distorting the meaning of that term. "Self-interest" means to pursue one's own interest *in opposition* to what one ought to do; or, since this would not hold for an egoist, *in opposition* to the benefit of others. But, to realize one's own essence, because one is a species being, *is* to work for the benefit of others. It is to act to realize the species as a whole—the universal.

In working for the benefit of the species, one does not merely act in *accordance with* the categorical imperative. One acts *for the sake of* the categorical imperative. One works for the benefit of the species for the sake of the species. It is only because human beings are species beings, because the human being's essence is the species, that this is also to realize one's own essence. Moreover, in order to work for the sake of one's own realization, one cannot work for the species merely as a means toward realizing an end external to the species (namely, one's own essence) because the individual is not externally related to the species—the individual's essence is the species. Nor is it possible, in working for the sake of one's own realization, to merely act in *accordance* with the universal, in accordance with the needs of the species, while motivated by some other selfish inclination or interest. To work for the sake of one's self-realization, one must work *consciously* for the sake of the species. Individuals must actually benefit the species consciously and collectively. They must actually cause it to develop and they must do so consciously and collectively if they are to develop themselves. This will become clearer in a moment.

In general, one cannot separate the individual from the species so as to argue that the individual works for one rather than the other or that the individual works for the sake of one and merely in accord with the other. The individual and the species cannot be separated in this way—they are one *in essence*.

For Kant, the possibility of freedom required that the transcendental self not be located in the natural, causally determined, phenomenal world. A noumenal realm, apart from the natural, was necessary as the source of self-determined free action. Marx and Hegel reject the existence of an unknown thing in itself and reject the existence of a noumenal realm.[119] Thus, they must have a different model of freedom. Rather than locate a transcendental self in a realm apart, they deny that there are such different realms and they view reality as a single field with two elements reacting against each other such that ultimately the natural objective element is absorbed into, is seen as internally related to, the conscious subjective element. In this way, the object is no longer alien and other, but essentially related to the subject. They argue that the object is the subject's essence and thus that the object is not heteronomous but compatible with the subject's freedom. For Hegel, this requires an Absolute Spirit or God responsible for creating and molding the natural and social world through history. For Marx, the human species itself, through its labor, molds, purposively controls, and objectifies itself in the objective social and natural realm. The human species works on its world through history and transforms it to conform with its own essence. In confronting the world and other human beings in the world, individuals confront themselves and are free.

The model of the individual that I have been sketching in this chapter does not imply a transcendental self or any sort of Archimedean point standing outside of, or above, culture. Individuals exist within culture—their very being is a cultural being, a species being. They cannot achieve freedom by somehow getting outside culture so as to be self-determined in the sense of being undetermined by culture. What they must do is to understand the dialectical process that takes place between themselves and their culture—the way they are formed by culture and the way they contribute to culture. Once they understand this process (and this understanding takes place immanently within culture and is influenced by culture), they can then organize themselves socially to begin controlling their culture (again completely from within culture). They can begin more effectively to realize their own purposes within culture rather than let culture in a haphazard, impersonal, and estranged way determine them. This does not require a noumenal realm. Culture from the start was the outcome of individual contributions occurring within a culture internalized by those individuals. The point is to become aware of this process, to begin to understand it, and to guide it consciously. And very clearly these purposes, goals, values, and aspirations that individuals decide to realize in culture do not stem from a noumenal realm. They arise from culturally embedded individuals and thus we would have to say that these purposes that are to control culture are themselves determined by culture.

It may seem that this leaves us just as determined by culture—just as unfree—as before. But as culture develops and as alienation is overcome, it becomes more and more the case that our conscious purposes predominate over unconscious cultural processes in determining things. This is to say that culture becomes more and more something that is *consciously* developed and molded by individuals (it was always an unconscious outcome of the contributions of individuals anyway). Still, one might say that if we do not make a jump to a noumenal autonomy, it will always be the case that these conscious purposes with which we mold our culture are themselves an outcome of and determined by culture; and thus that there is no freedom here. At this point it becomes crucial to understand that we are *essentially* species beings or cultural beings. To be determined by culture is not to be determined by something *essentially* other, something heteronomous. Our very being is cultural. To be determined by culture is to be determined by something that is essentially ourselves. We can be free while being culturally determined. To be outside of culture would not make us free—it would mean our nonexistence. We can never cease to be determined by culture.

We can only seek to determine the way we are determined by culture and to do it consciously and purposively. In determining the way we are determined by culture we are still determined by culture, but it more and more becomes the case that we are not determined by something other, heteronomous, and estranged that we do not understand or agree with. Instead, it becomes more and more the case that our conscious purposes are coming to predominate in forming and directing this culture we are embedded in and determined by. This culture is our very being and we are merely increasing the role of the conscious side of our being in determining things. And again, to do this we cannot retreat exclusively into our own projects or selfish concerns. We must become aware of our whole culture, the dialectical interaction that takes place between it and ourselves, and we must cooperatively work together with others to understand it and be able purposively to control it. This is freedom as Marx understands it.

Consciousness is crucial here. In order to become free, we must clearly understand our relationship to culture, to the species, and we must consciously and collectively control it for the sake of the species. It is not possible, in working for the sake of our own realization, merely to work in *accordance* with the needs of the species. We must understand our relationship to the species and work with full consciousness for the sake of the species. If we do not, we will be determined unconsciously by culture, by the species, by others, and we will not realize our essence or be free.

However, despite the fact that both Hegel and Marx reject a transcendental self, reject a noumenal realm, and understand freedom in similar ways, there are serious differences here between Hegel and Marx. Hegel is quite willing to accept the existence of an invisible hand in civil society. Particular interests do not consciously lead to the universal, but do so only unconsciously. For this reason Hegel must abandon the perspective of individual consciousness and move to spirit. Civil society, for Hegel, is the realm where particular interests legitimately claim their satisfaction. Thus consciousness must be raised to the level of the state, the realm of spirit, where citizens confront their own essence objectified and universalized as the result of their own alienation. Only at this level are we able consciously to recognize that particular interests in civil society do unconsciously lead to the universal, and only at this level can we begin consciously to pursue the universal ends of the state in pursuing our own particular interests. Hegel does not eliminate the conflict of particular interests or an invisible hand in civil society. He only transcends them in consciousness.

One of the consequences of abandoning the perspective of individual consciousness and moving to spirit at the level of the state is that democracy of the sort that Rousseau envisioned becomes impossible for Hegel. Hegel criticizes Rousseau for viewing the general will as an outcome of individual consciousness. For Rousseau, the citizens vote, establish the laws of the state themselves, and rule as individuals. In Hegel's ideal society, the citizens get the sorts of laws they would have given themselves—universal and rational laws that accord with a general will—but the citizens do not give themselves their own laws by voting on them as for Rousseau. The laws and institutions of the state arise through the historical development of spirit. Through alienation, the citizens constitute their state as their own essence and are molded by this state such that the subjective rationality of the individual citizens accords with the objective rationality embedded in the laws and institutions of the state.[120]

This is totally unacceptable for Marx. He will not transcend individual consciousness and move on to spirit in this way. He wants to eliminate civil society as a realm of competing particular interests so that conscious pursuit of the universal need not take place only at the alienated level of the political state and only in consciousness. And Marx will not accept the rejection of democracy and voting that result from Hegel's views. Marx is able to avoid Hegel's concept of spirit because of his concept of essence. Individuals should not be related to their essence only at the level of the state. That is to be alienated from one's essence. And Marx does not think that alienation can be overcome merely in consciousness. It is not enough to raise consciousness to the level of the state and see the state as the alienation of one's essence. That does not reconcile you with your essence,[121] especially if voting is eliminated and your actual participation at the political level is minimal. For Marx, the alienation of state from society must actually be overcome. The political realm, one's alienated essence, as we have seen, must be reabsorbed within one's concrete, everyday, particular life in the social community.[122]

Hegel's concept of essence locates our reality, our freedom, and our conscious concern for the universal, at the distant, abstract, alienated level of the state—a realm we do not actually participate in to any great extent except in consciousness. Marx's concept of essence locates our reality, our freedom, and our conscious concern for the universal, in the concrete, everyday relations among human beings; in their labor, in the activity by which they satisfy their own needs and the needs of others. One finds one's essence in concrete other human beings that one daily interacts with in society. We need other human beings and their products, and this need indicates that they and their products are part of our essence. Moreover, we are the objectification of the powers and capacities of other human beings, and they are a product of our objectification. Furthermore, to realize our essence, we must work consciously, collectively, and communally for the sake of the species—the universal, the categorical imperative. And we must do so in our everyday lives in society.

However, at the same time that Marx wants to reject Hegel's transcendence of individual consciousness and his move to spirit, Marx does not want to return to isolated individual consciousness as Rousseau understood it. For Rousseau, the political state is not alienated from civil society to the degree that it is for Hegel. After all, for Rousseau, the citizens actively participate politically. They sit on the sovereign body and they do a great deal of voting. Moreover, it is clearly Rousseau's view that individuals ought to identify with themselves as participants in the political sphere: they ought to identify with themselves as *citizens* concerned with the universal, the general will.[123] And for this reason commerce and trade that foster particular interests must be deemphasized. Nonetheless, there is still a separation between civil society and the political state for Rousseau. There is no community at the socioeconomic level of civil society. No one especially works consciously for the benefit of the species. There should be no developed exchange and thus no invisible hand; but citizens work for themselves, not the species. It is only at the political level, in the sovereign assembly, that they consciously concern themselves with the good of the whole and thus consciously work for the species and the universal.

In other words, Marx, in opposition to Hegel's concept of spirit, wants to return to the individual—the concrete, everyday individual in society. But, in opposition to Rousseau, he wants the individual to be a *communal* individual *in essence*. He wants the individual to be a species being. The individual should be part of a community consciously and collectively working for the benefit of the whole community, the species, in the individual's actual, everyday life—not just at those special moments when the individual goes off to the sovereign assembly.[124]

We find strong objections in Marx's writings to Hegel's concept of essence and to his concept of the state. Marx thinks that Hegel inverts in an idealistic way the real relation between the state and concrete institutions like law, the family, and civil society. For Hegel, these concrete institutions are seen as the result, the manifestation, of the state. They are attributes, phenomenal appearances, products, of the Idea or of spirit.[125] The result is that empirical reality is not expressed as itself, but as another reality. It is not determined by its own nature or essence, but by a nature or essence alien to it—the essence of the state. Thus, Hegel "disregards real man."[126] For Marx, it is the reverse. The state arises from the concrete institutions of civil society and the activity of individuals within those institutions. The state is the objectification of the essence of individuals.

In criticizing Hegel here, Marx tends to blur some of the similarities between Hegel's views and his own. Hegel's views, we have seen, are similar to Marx's. For Hegel too, the state is the objectification of the essence of individuals, and individuals are the objectification of the state. But Marx's criticisms of Hegel ultimately are correct. Despite the fact that individuals and the state reciprocally constitute each other, Hegel ultimately weights things in the direction of the state. In ruling out democracy he backs away from allowing the citizens to objectify themselves directly and consciously at the level of the state.[127]

We can now better understand Marx's new concept of representation. Marx does not want isolated individuals in civil society, either in Hegel's sense, who have representatives appointed for them and sent off to the alien level of the state; or in Rousseau's sense, who go themselves to that alien realm. Society must be communal. The isolated individuals of civil society must be transformed into individuals who are communal beings *in essence*. In such a community, each person represents the others, represents the species, because each is linked to the others in essence. Each individual has been produced by, is the objectification of, the others. Each can contemplate the species in themselves and themselves in the species. Thus, in satisfying the needs of others, as Marx puts it in his "Comments on James Mill," I am "the mediator between [them] and the species."[128] What this means is that I am, in the first place, the objectification of the historical development of the powers and capacities of the species. I have internalized the powers and capacities of the species, and in this sense I *represent* the species. Moreover, in work that satisfies the needs of others, I reobjectify the powers and capacities of the species in my product, and make it available to others.

Thus, I also represent the species *for-these-others*. I link, I mediate between, the universal, the species as a whole, the cumulative, historically developed powers and capacities of the species, on the one hand, and, on the other hand, other particular, individual human beings. I represent in the sense that I serve these particular individuals by making the universal accessible to them. My product makes the powers and capacities of the species available to them either by satisfying their needs directly at the level that the species, objectified in me, makes possible; or, at the same level, I afford them the opportunity to manifest and express their powers and capacities in and through the product I provide them. And, of course, others do the same for me.[129]

In this sort of community, when one sends off a deputy with specific voting instructions, the representative is not an other, alien, isolated being sent off to a different, alien realm. The deputy represents the community in that the deputy is the objectification of the essence of the community both in the general sense in which every individual is the objectification of the species and in the specific sense that the deputy is the objectification of the ideas and purposes of the community embodied in the deputy's specific voting instructions.

Moreover, this is true of the legislature as a whole. The legislature is not a different, alien realm external to the realm of everyday communal interaction. In the first place, it is no longer the case that the universal is consciously dealt with only at the political level and not in the everyday activity of society. In society, too, we work consciously and collectively for the benefit of the species. Work in the legislature, then, is only a specific form of working consciously and collectively for the benefit of the species, just as (and no different from) the way any work is. The legislature is a part of, and within, the social community. It represents the community no differently than any individual or group does. It is the objectification of the community as the community is the objectification of the legislature. The community should be able to contemplate itself in the activity of the legislature and the activity of the legislature in itself. And the legislature should be able to contemplate the community in itself and itself in the community. But this must occur just as all individuals are able to contemplate the community in themselves and themselves in the community.

To work consciously and collectively for the benefit of the species, it is not the case that everyone should be a shoemaker. In fact, that would harm the species if other essential tasks necessary to satisfy the needs of, or to develop the powers and capacities of, the species were neglected. So also, for Marx, everyone need not be a deputy in the legislature. The political realm here has been reabsorbed into society, and thus every social activity is political as every political activity is social—every activity is conscious, collective activity for the benefit of the species.[130]

As we have already seen, Marx wants unlimited voting—voting by deputies in the legislature and voting in local assemblies to work out the voting instructions for these deputies. This certainly distinguishes Marx's views from Hegel's. But they are also different from Rousseau's views (even Rousseau's views in the essay on Poland) because in overcoming the separation of civil society from the political state, social activity and political activity become the same. Both are conscious activity for the benefit of the species—the universal. Voting and representation do not merely occur in the far-off and separate realm of the sovereign assembly, but are essential parts of everyday communal life. Interaction between deputies and citizens is no different from interaction between other members of the community. One need not be a deputy sent off to the legislature to participate in community. Community exists in the everyday realm of society and the deputy as well as the legislature are part of and within that community. They are not outside or above it, but subordinate to it as part of it. The election of representatives is no longer a special activity that occurs from time to time and that links the voters to the alien realm of the legislature. Voting has been universalized. It permeates the community. It goes on continuously in the various local assemblies that work up voting instructions.

But this is only one form of voting or delegation—a small part of universalized voting. The general association of all individuals is continuously engaged in a far wider range of voting and delegation. They also delegate representatives to the task of shoemaking as well as to all other such social tasks. They develop a general plan to control production as well as distribution.[131] They consciously and collectively control their entire social world. The legislature and the deputies are the objectification of the citizens' essence. And the citizens are the objectification of the activity of the legislature and the deputies, but only in the sense that I am the objectification of any other member of the community, not in the Hegelian sense where the state stands above and molds society, nor even in the Rousseauian sense where the legislature stands outside society.

At this point, we can begin to see more clearly how a general will can arise despite the fact that there are no specific formal procedures for the legislature to follow as there were for Rousseau. For Marx, the general will cannot arise out of the legislature alone—and certainly not out of a legislature located in a separate political realm alienated from society. The general will can arise only out of a community as a whole.

If classes have been eliminated and the political state has been reabsorbed into civil society, if all social activities become political and all political activities become social (that is, if individuals consciously and collectively work for the benefit of the universal, the community, in their concrete, everyday lives, because they see that this is the only way to realize themselves as individuals), then it would no longer be necessary, as Marx said, to represent the interests of individuals as an illusory general interest or to represent this general interest as ruling at the political level. Rather, a genuine common interest could begin to arise out of the material conditions of the social community itself— material conditions that could be consciously and collectively transformed and controlled by the community to produce and reinforce a common interest and to reinforce individuals as communal beings.

If the interaction of individuals in this community is such that they have overcome possessiveness and work for the benefit of the community, not because they have somehow become altruistic, as Elster suggests, but because they come to see that this is the only way they can realize themselves; because they come to see that they are the objectification of the community and that the community is their objectification; because they are able to contemplate the community in themselves and themselves in the community; because they come to see that each member of the community represents the others, then the general will or the common interest will have already been embedded in the material conditions of this community. The community will already be acting on the general will.

The general will, then, needs only to be clearly recognized, specifically formulated, and explicitly expressed by the deputies and the legislature who are the objectification of this community, the part of the community delegated to express the general will explicitly. It is their task merely to bring to light the universal, the common interest, the general will, already embedded in the community, not, as for Hegel or Rousseau, so that the general will can be consciously reflected upon merely within the legislature or at the level of the political state but so that it can be consciously reflected upon with the everyday life of the community by the members of the community. This task of the deputies and the legislature would be much the same as that envisioned by Marx for a free press or a party. The deputies do not confront the community with doctrinaire new principles, but bring to light the community's own principles. They make the community aware of its *own* consciousness by showing it the meaning of its own actions. The legislature serves the community by clarifying, bringing to clear awareness, the essence of the community so that the community can consciously reflect upon it within the community.

None of this should suggest that consciousness only exists at the level of, or even that it is only initiated by, the legislature. The process is dialectical. The legislature is the objectification of the community's consciousness, and the legislature assists the community in becoming *more* conscious of its own essence and its general will. Then, as the community elects its deputies, works out their voting instructions, and objectifies itself in the legislature, it will objectify itself more consciously in the legislature. The task of the legislature then will be to refine that consciousness even further for the community, which will then objectify this even more highly developed consciousness in the legislature. As this cycle proceeds, consciousness will develop and be reinforced so as to be able to play its role more and more adequately, so that individuals can better understand their cultural interaction (the way they form their culture and are formed by it); so that they can thus consciously control it for the sake of the species. They can therefore be free, and can thus realize their own essence as individuals.

We might notice that Elster is highly critical of Marx's concept of self-realization. He argues that Marx's "emphasis on creative self-realization comes into conflict with the value of community. If production is to be for the sake of the community, at least some of the members, at least some of the time, must indulge in the passive pleasures of consumption," which Elster thinks are opposed to active creativity and thus self-realization.[132] Elster argues that if "creation is to be valued mainly because it is creation *for others,* then in a sense it is parasitic on consumption and cannot avoid being contaminated by the low value attached to the latter."[133] Moreover, Elster thinks that the emphasis placed on self-realization through creativity will lead to widespread frustration and disappointment in communist society for those many persons who simply do not have the ability to succeed in realizing themselves creatively.

Here, as well as in his argument that Marx must rely upon a utopian form of altruism, Elster, I think, fails to understand Marx's concept of the individual. Quite likely this is linked to Elster's commitment to methodological individualism, which holds that all social phenomena are to be explained in ways that involve only individuals—their properties, goals, beliefs, and actions. This concept of the individual, which is based on the liberal concept of the individual, is radically different from Marx's concept of the individual in the ways that I have been arguing in this section.

In the first place, it should be clear from what has been said about Marx's concept of the individual that we cannot contrast passive consumption with active creation. Consumption simply cannot be understood as passive. Consumption is an *active* appropriation and internalization of one's culture, without which one would not even be a human being, let alone an individual. This consumption is the necessary basis for a creative contribution to one's culture, which then can be appropriated by others. Without consumption there would be no production. Consumption is clearly as important to self-realization as creative production. Moreover, to be able to consume, to be able to appropriate one's culture, one must have developed the powers and capacities to do so; and, as well, one's powers and capacities will be developed in the process of appropriating one's culture. Creating for others does not assume passive consumption on their part. It contributes to their active appropriation and the development of their powers and capacities.

Furthermore, I think that Elster is simply mistaken in thinking that Marx's communist society would expect all individuals to achieve the same high level of creativity and thus would foster widespread frustration and disappointment for those who lack the ability to achieve this goal. Marx does not argue that "each should do the work of Raphael, but that anyone in whom there is a potential Raphael should be able to develop without hindrance."[134] Moreover, this is certainly the point of the slogan, "From each according to his ability, to each according to his needs!"[135] This slogan would be pointless if all abilities and needs were expected to be the same. Marx's point is that it is objectionable if the development of the individual is obstructed, and he also thinks that it is the task of the community to provide the material conditions that will allow for the fullest possible development that the individual is capable of attaining. But, on the other hand, Marx never suggests that all can reach the same level, nor that they should be pushed to do so.

I can see nothing that would lead to widespread frustration and disappointment here, especially if we reject Elster's view that consumption or appropriation of culture (which almost all are capable of) is somehow less satisfying, less meaningful, and less a part of self-realization than creatively contributing something new to culture (which fewer would be capable of). Moreover, to work for the sake of the species, for the sake of others, it is not necessary to be creative at the level of a Raphael. The consumer or appropriator of culture can work for the sake of the species, for others, by representing the species, mediating between the species and other individuals, establishing a link between the species and other individuals, transmitting culture to them (say, as a teacher or by providing one's children with an upbringing). This is certainly creative, meaningful, and satisfying in the sense of working for the sake of the species even if it does not involve creativity in the form of innovation.

IV. The Highest Good, a Beautiful World, and the Aesthetic Condition

For Kant, as we saw in Chapter 4, history is seen as leading toward the realization of the highest good. The highest good requires the agreement of virtue with happiness. To realize the highest good, then, there would have to be an agreement between moral action in accordance with universal rational principles and the feelings or inclinations that produce happiness in individuals. For this to be possible, it would mean that the natural world would have to be regulated so that the natural objects that determine feelings and inclinations, and thus happiness, would always determine them in accordance with the demands of morality—the categorical imperative.[136] Though Marx does not discuss the highest good, I think it can be argued that a view similar to Kant's is implicit in Marx's writings. I will try to argue that the activity of the species realizes the highest good. Since we have already discussed how working for the benefit of the species is to act for the sake of a categorical imperative, we must now discuss Marx's views on happiness.

Classical utilitarians define virtue so as to make it identical with happiness. Virtue consists in acting to produce the greatest happiness.[137] This is clearly not Marx's view. For Kant, on the other hand, one can certainly be virtuous without necessarily being happy or producing happiness. And one can be happy or produce happiness without necessarily being virtuous. It is true that happiness and virtue must accord for the realization of the highest good, but virtue and happiness are not identical. The connection between virtue and happiness is synthetic, not analytic, for Kant. To link virtue and happiness requires further conditions.[138] Though Marx does not discuss these matters explicitly, his view are closer to Kant than to the utilitarians. For example, he says that higher wages for workers would only produce better-paid slaves.[139] Higher wages, and thus, certainly for utilitarians, greater happiness, would be possible without affecting the fact that workers are alienated and unfree. Very clearly, morality—working consciously for the categorical imperative—requires freedom, for Marx,[140] as well as the overcoming of alienation. Thus, we can say that simply producing happiness, for Marx, does not amount to morality. Happiness, without freedom and the overcoming of alienation, is not a morally acceptable goal. Again, in the *German Ideology*, Marx argues that the semiartistic work of the medieval artisan was engaging and enjoyable but that this only made the work even more slavish.[141] To make alienated and unfree work enjoyable would be to tie the worker even closer to such work and thus increase its slavishness. Again, mere enjoyment or happiness without freedom is not morally acceptable for Marx. Morality cannot be identified with producing greater happiness. To link morality and happiness requires further conditions.

How then would Marx link freedom and morality with happiness in the ideal case? To answer this we must first notice that happiness can be understood in two different ways. Happiness can mean pleasure, the satisfaction of inclinations, desires, or needs, as it does for Kant and at times for Hegel. Or it can refer to the satisfaction that accompanies a well-performed activity, as it does, in other places for Hegel and also for Aristotle.[142] Moreover, for Aristotle, the higher the activity—the more it accords with our essence—the higher the satisfaction or happiness it will produce.[143]

Using the first definition of happiness, it is not easy to get morality and happiness to accord. For Kant, at least in the *Critique of Practical Reason,* it required a postulate of practical reason—the postulate of a

God who would align nature and inclination with morality so that happiness could accompany virtue.[144]

For Marx, we might say, the human species replaces Kant's God. The species itself works on and remakes the natural world in accordance with its needs—its essence. In transforming the natural world so as to satisfy needs, interests, feelings, and desires, it would produce happiness; and, at the same time, it would realize the universal and conscious moral purpose of working for the sake of the species. It would realize the essence of the species, both in the sense of satisfying its needs (thus producing happiness) and in the sense of acting for the universal (thus acting morally, for the sake of the categorical imperative). The species, then, would realize the highest good.

At this point, the two forms of happiness could coincide. The satisfaction of needs, interests, and desires would occur as the species transforms the world to suit its needs and essence. But, as we have said, for Marx our highest end is not so much, or not only, the satisfaction of direct needs and desires. It is free species activity itself, which is an end in itself: activity that realizes our essence and that involves the expression, manifestation, and realization of our powers and capacities. Thus the satisfaction or happiness that accompanies this sort of activity—a satisfaction or happiness that would be higher as our essence is more highly realized by this activity—would also be present.[145]

Kant also argued that human beings have to create their own happiness and perfection.[146] In so far as the course of history brings particular interests into accord with morality, happiness as well as virtue, and thus the highest good, are promoted. Thus an idea for a universal history gives us a concrete mechanism for realizing the highest good. We do not just rely on God. Here, Kant's views are quite close to those implicit in Marx's writings.

Moreover, it was implied in Kant's writings, I argued earlier in Chapter 4,[147] that the realization of the highest good would also produce a beautiful world. As nature and morality are brought into harmony through our historical efforts in moving toward the highest good, our world would come to appear as if it were purposively designed for us—for our cognitive faculties. This would produce an experience of beauty: an aesthetic relation to the object. For an experience of beauty to be possible, a harmony between the object and the faculties of the subject must occur. The natural object must spontaneously appear as if it were purposively designed for our faculties.[148]

For Marx, existence must be transformed to suit our essence. Moreover, in the object, which is the objectification of the human essence, individuals would be able to contemplate their essence. Thus the objective world, for Marx, would certainly appear to be designed purposively to harmonize with and confirm the human essence. Our relationship to such an unalienated world would be an aesthetic relationship.

Marx thinks, as we have seen, that the general attitude to objects in an alienated market economy is the attitude of possessiveness, and Marx wants to overcome this attitude. Elsewhere, I have argued that the ideal relationship to the object, for Marx, is to be understood as an aesthetic relationship.[149] Marx says, "The care-burdened, poverty-stricken man has no sense for the finest play, the dealer in minerals sees only the commercial value but not the beauty and the specific character of the mineral. . . ."[150] Kant too argued that the aesthetic relationship, far from being one of possessiveness, must be disinterested in the sense that to experience beauty we must not be drawn to the object and dominated by our needs, interests, or inclinations. The aesthetic relationship, for Kant, involves the freest form of satisfaction. It involves an even freer relationship than does our relationship to the good because in the aesthetic relationship we are exclusively determined neither by reason nor sense.

Moral freedom means being determined by reason and, at least in the *Foundations of the Metaphysics of Morals,* this usually meant an opposition between inclination and duty.[151] We are morally free in the sense that we overcome the determination of our inclinations and obey our reason. The aesthetic condition, on the other hand, is understood as one in which we are determined exclusively neither by inclination nor reason. Feeling and intellect, sense and reason, spontaneously and harmoniously agree. Neither dominates the other. In the *Critique of Practical Reason,* Kant shifts away from the suggestion made in the *Foundations* that duty and inclination should be at odds in a moral act. In the *Critique of Practical Reason,* he admits that duty and inclination can agree and he takes such agreement to be an ideal of perfection ever to be striven for but never completely reached.[152] Thus in the *Critique of Judgment* he can speak of beauty, which involves the harmony of feeling and reason, as a symbol of the morally good.[153]

Schiller tried to draw Kant's aesthetics, ethics, and philosophy of history much closer together by seeking to make the harmony of duty and inclination, or reason and feeling, not a symbol but an actual reality; a reality that Schiller thought had actually been realized in the ancient Greek *polis,* and one that history, understood much as in

Kant's "Idea for a Universal History," was on the way to realizing again in the modern world. Schiller argued that an aesthetic education could synthesize aesthetics and morality. Sense and reason, duty and inclination, could come into harmony not as a distant ideal of perfection but actually in the individual. Feeling in accordance with duty would produce a higher morality, an aesthetic morality.[154] Schiller also tried to connect this aesthetic condition to labor. He argued that if we are able to satisfy our needs through labor, if we are not need driven, then we can distance ourselves from the object and begin to contemplate it as an end in itself.[155] Labor could well become an aesthetic activity since it involves our sensuous faculties (in our needs and activities) as well as our rational faculties (in our planning and purposes). If both sides could be brought into harmony and balance, an aesthetic condition would result. For Schiller an aesthetic education would develop and harmonize the faculties of the individual, which then would transform the individual's activity and world. Marx does not think that an aesthetic education will transform the world. But he does think that if the social world and labor were transformed, then an aesthetic condition could result.

All of the elements necessary for the aesthetic condition discussed by Kant and Schiller are present in Marx. Human beings must be in control of their activity and their product; they must not be dominated by need or interest; and they must not be slaves to the object. They must be able to stand back from the product, make it an object of their will and consciousness, and contemplate it freely as an end in itself. Labor ought to be an end enjoyable in itself. The worker's attitude must not be grasping, need driven, or possessive. It should be disinterested or contemplative. The specific character of the object should be appreciated for its own sake as an end in itself. This would be an aesthetic attitude because sensuous physical activity (labor) as well as conscious intellectual activity (in the form of direction and contemplation) would be in harmony. As we transform the natural world to agree with our essence, as we produce a world purposively designed to harmonize with our essence, as we reconcile particular interest with the common good, as we control those natural elements that satisfy our needs, interests, and desires and thus produce happiness in harmony with morality, we create a situation in which the inner faculties of individuals—their sensuous faculties (involved in their needs, activities, and interests) and their intellectual faculties (involved in their purposes and moral ends) will come to agree and be in harmony. We create the possibility of an aesthetic experience of a beautiful world (both the objective conditions for this possibility, namely, the essential harmony of the object with the subject; and the subjective conditions of this possibility, namely, a harmony between the subject's faculties themselves). Thus, as Marx says, the human being would be able to form "objects in accordance with the laws of beauty."[156] Therefore, I think we can say that, for Marx, the activity of the species could produce a beautiful world.

However, there is an important difference here between Marx and Kant. For Kant, an *idea* for a universal history is merely a regulative idea. It is an idea that cannot actually be known, but if assumed, would allow human beings to begin to guide their history toward morality and happiness. Moreover, in the *Critique of Practical Reason,* Kant argued that we must *postulate* the reconciliation of happiness and virtue—the realization of the highest good. Again, theoretical reason cannot know this, but practical reason is justified in *postulating* it. Furthermore, in calling beauty a *symbol* of the morally good, Kant again is only claiming that the realization of the highest good, the reconciliation of morality and happiness, and thus a world that would appear as purposively designed for us and thus beautiful, is also just an idea—a symbol. Marx, on the other hand, wants to talk about the realization of an essence. He wants to transform the world and to realize "its true reality as its obligation and its final goal."[157] To better understand this difference between Marx and Kant it would be helpful at this point to compare Marx to Hegel.

Hegel, we have seen, wants his philosophical system to combine three things: (1) the ability of traditional (pre-Kantian) metaphysics, the metaphysics of the ancient and medieval worlds, directly to grasp absolute, objective, universal reality—to grasp immediately the very essence of things. Hegel wants this ability combined with (2) modern empiricism's claim that all experience is subjective—that all objects are immediately mine, immediately present, and completely certain, within consciousness. And further, these two elements must be combined with (3) the Kantian principle that all objects are constituted within self-consciousness.[158]

To achieve this synthesis, Hegel rejects Kant's unknown thing in itself and he abandons the perspective of individual consciousness. As we have seen, since Hegel rejects the unknown thing in itself but still holds that experience is constituted by self-consciousness, he cannot hold that self-consciousness constitutes mere appearance cut off from an unknown thing in itself that remains behind. It constitutes reality. However, if it were individual consciousness that constituted reality, a subjectivist chaos would result. Hegel must move to an absolute self-consciousness—to cultural consciousness or spirit. This total and universal consciousness, in constituting reality (as for Kant), would have reality immediately present to itself within consciousness (as for empiricism), and it would have the immediate grasp of absolute objective reality (of traditional metaphysics) because it includes all reality immediately present to itself within consciousness: there is no reality outside this absolute consciousness. When estrangement is overcome by seeing that it is the result of one's own alienation, self-consciousness faces all reality constituted by itself as its own essence.[159]

Marx is doing something quite similar. He agrees with Hegel's first requirement. He too wants to regain the objective grasp of universal reality characteristic of traditional metaphysics. Thus he rejects an unknown thing in itself,[160] as does Hegel, and he also argues that we constitute reality. However, he modifies this third requirement. We do not constitute reality merely in consciousness as for Kant. Reality is also transformed and constituted through labor. This allows Marx to reject completely Hegel's second requirement—the empiricist claim that all reality is completely within consciousness—and thus to reject Hegel's abandonment of individual consciousness and his move to spirit or absolute consciousness. This must all be explained.

As we have seen, the human species through its labor transforms and constitutes the objective realm to conform to its essence. What we have not yet seen is that this also realizes the essence of the object. Nature is the human being's object. Human beings need nature to satisfy their direct needs as well as to carry on the labor process in which they objectify themselves and realize their powers and capacities. But, for Marx, if I have an object, the object has me as its object. Thus we must also say that the human being is nature's object. Nature "needs" human beings. It "needs" them, for Marx, because nature, like any existent, we have seen, can only achieve its highest actualization through the activity of human beings.[161] Through human labor, nature is transformed so that its forces are unfolded and allowed to express further their life-developing powers. Through the labor process nature's potential is actualized. Think, for example, of human beings damming a river. In doing so nature is able to release electricity, to realize a potential that it was unable to realize on its own. Then human beings will use the electricity and develop themselves even further. Nature needs human labor for the realization of its essence just as human beings need nature for the realization of their essence.

> The nature which develops in human history . . . is man's real nature; hence nature as it develops through industry . . . is true anthropological nature . . . History itself is a real part of natural history—of nature developing into man . . . The . . . history of the world is nothing but the creation of man through human labor, nothing but the emergence of nature for man . . . man has thus become evident for man as the being of nature and nature for man as the being of man. . . .[162]

Human beings realize their essence through the transformation of nature to suit their needs. But as nature is transformed to suit our essence, nature's essence is also realized. Nature realizes its essence in and through the realization of the human essence. Nature, as Marx puts it, develops "into man"; the development of nature's essence is simply the development of the human essence. Nature does not unfold its essence independently of human beings. Nature needs human labor as the agency that will release its potential, and the release of this potential has as its end the realization of human beings who make use of nature's realized potential to develop their own powers and capacities. Marx, we have seen, is willing to say that the sun realizes its life-giving powers in the growth of the plant. In the same way, natural objects realize, objectify, their powers in human beings. The electricity released from a dammed river heats the houses, lights the streets, and powers the machines of human beings. Realizing the potential of nature through human labor, realizes the essence of human beings. It satisfies their needs and allows them to realize their own powers and capacities. The realization of nature's essence and the realization of the human essence are inseparable.[163]

We must also see that the realization of nature's essence through labor allows human beings objectively to grasp and know nature's essence. Marx says, "man's feelings, passions, etc., are not merely anthropological phenomena in the [narrower] sense, but truly ontological affirmations of essence (of nature), and . . . they are only really affirmed because their object exists for them as sensual object. . . ."[164] In other words, for Marx, the human senses are not merely an anthropological affirmation of nature, a subjective grasping of nature for-us, but an ontological affirmation of the essence of nature, a grasping of the in-itself. Marx also says that "the real existence of man and nature has become evident in practice, through sense experience, because man has thus become evident for man as the being of nature, and nature as the being of man. . . ."[165] Marx, like Kant, is holding that the object is constituted by the subject. But this constitution involves human labor, not merely consciousness. For Marx, nature can only realize itself, actualize its potential, become what it truly is, through human labor. And Marx is claiming that we can grasp and know the natural object objectively. We can grasp the object's essence—what it is in-itself.

Marx's concept of essence allows him to avoid the gap between mere appearance and an unknown thing in itself of either Kantian phenomenalism or empiricist subjectivism. In constituting the natural object through labor, we do, obviously, transform and constitute the object's appearance. But, at the same time, for Marx, we also realize its essence. For Marx, the higher development of an essence is a higher realization of the thing in itself. An essence *is*, most truly, what it *becomes*. Thus the transformation of nature cannot be seen as a divergence from its truth to mere appearance. It is a realization of its truth—a realization of its essence. And our knowledge of the natural object is an ontological grasp of the essence of the object—of the thing in itself.[166] In damming a river to release electricity, or in releasing nuclear power, and in coming to know and to know how to use that electricity or nuclear power, we do not know mere appearance but nature's realized essence; what it is in itself.

Thus, we can say that Marx regains the objectivity of traditional metaphysics. We objectively know the essence of things in themselves. And Marx achieves this without moving to absolute consciousness or spirit. For Marx, the object is not constituted solely through and within an act of individual consciousness, as for Kant; nor an act of cultural consciousness, as for Hegel. Unlike Hegel, Marx rejects the idealistic claim of empiricism that the object is entirely within consciousness. For Marx, objects are the result of our objectification and exist independently outside consciousness.[167] Marx is not an empiricist, but a materialist—or, as he puts it in his early writings, a naturalist or humanist.[168] Since we constitute reality, but do not do so solely within consciousness, there is no need to move to Hegel's absolute consciousness, which Hegel must do to avoid the subjectivist chaos that would result from holding that individual consciousness constitutes reality and to explain how knowledge can be objective (as for traditional metaphysics) when the object is entirely within consciousness. Rather, Marx regains the objectivity of traditional metaphysics by holding that in transforming the object, labor realizes the object's essence, and in grasping this essence, we objectively grasp the thing in itself. Even in his later writings, after abandoning his concept of essence,[169] Marx still holds that human beings constitute their world through labor and come to know it as it is.[170]

For traditional metaphysics, there was a fit between human beings and their world. Human beings and the world had been purposively designed for each other. And thus the goal of human beings should be to come to know their world, to understand the way they fit into it, and to act accordingly. One finds a radical rejection of this sort of optimism in Nietzsche. For Nietzsche, the cosmos certainly has not been designed to fit human beings. It is alien, hostile, and terrifying. It is a place where human beings can only expect to suffer and where happiness is an illusion. For Nietzsche, the only solution is to mask this horrible reality with an Apollonian veil—a beautiful illusion.[171] Marx does not share the radical nihilism of Nietzsche, but neither can he accept the straightforward optimism of traditional metaphysics. Rather, he adopts a perspective that, as far as I can see, gets going with Francis Bacon. The world is neither straightforwardly designed for us, nor is it alien, hostile, and terrifying. Rather, it is neutral and, most importantly, malleable. Human beings, then, must come to understand their world and work on it—design it themselves so as to make it into the sort of place where they can fit and be at home. This view accepts the modern subjectivist approach, which holds that we constitute our world but its ultimate consequence is a world that, as for traditional metaphysics, fits us and, given Marx's concept of essence, is a world we can know objectively.[172]

If the objective fit between the individual and the world characteristic of traditional metaphysics can be seen as an optimistic extreme, then Nietzsche's radical rejection of this fit and his extreme subjectivism, pushed to the length of the necessity for illusions, constitutes an opposite, pessimistic, extreme. Along with Marx, Hegel stands between these two extremes. And, indeed, so does Kant. Kant's emphasis on realizing the highest good and a beautiful world, a world that appears as if it were purposively designed for us, is also an attempt to regain the fit of traditional metaphysics. But, for Kant, this fit is a matter of appearance—an "as if," a regulative idea, a postulate, or a symbol. The fit is *subjective*. Hegel wants to move more toward an objective fit, not by eliminating subjectivity but rather *through* subjectivity—by understanding objective reality as constituted within absolute subjectivity. But such idealism still only gains a fit within consciousness—within spirit. Marx wants to move further than Hegel toward an objective fit. But still it is an objective fit that is achieved *through* subjectivity. However, it is achieved through concrete subjectivity: through the labor of human subjects who realize a fit not merely in consciousness but concretely and materially, and, at the same time, in essence.

V. Rights and Community

To understand more fully Marx's concept of the individual and community, we must also discuss his view of rights. In "On the Jewish Question" (1843), Marx rejects the concept of the "rights of man." He did this shortly after the *Critique of Hegel's Philosophy of Law* in which he had rejected Hegel's concept of a political state standing over and dominating civil society. For Marx, the rejection of rights follows from the rejection of the alienation of state from society for several reasons. A right would at least in part be a right against the state. Rights to freedom of speech, freedom of the press, and so forth, would be rights the state may not infringe upon and they would be rights that would have to be guaranteed and enforced by the state. If you reject the separation of state from society, rights become problematic because they *presuppose* the separation of state from society. A political state would have to exist if we are to have rights against it and if it is to guarantee and enforce these rights. More importantly for Marx, the political state is the expression of species essence, community, and the universal, though in a distant and alienated way. To demand rights against the state, then, would be to insist upon the isolation of individuals from community, the universal, and their essence.

Marx argues that the right to private property, which he thinks is the fundamental right in bourgeois society, is a right of particular interest against the universal and community. Furthermore, to have the state guarantee and enforce such rights, for Marx, is to turn the community, the universal, and the realm of species essence, which are our highest ends (ends that should be concretely realized in society when alienation is overcome), merely into a *means* to promote particular interests that oppose the universal. It is to invert the proper relation of ends to means and of particular to universal.[173] Marx, in the "Jewish Question," even seems to suggest (though it is not *absolutely* clear that he does) that when the revolutionary government of France violated in practice the very rights it upheld in theory, it was their violation of rights in practice that was correct. It is quite clear that Marx rejects a right to private property, but when he seems to approve the violation of rights by the revolutionary French government he also mentions the right to privacy of correspondence and the right to a free press.¹⁷⁴

It would seem, however, that an ideal society that had done away with an alienated political state, while it might no longer need rights against the state, would still want to guarantee individual rights against violation by other individuals. There should be recognized and established procedures for redressing such violations. This alone would not require the separation of state from society nor would such a state be necessary to guarantee and enforce these rights. In his writings on the Paris Commune (of 1871), Marx himself argues that there should be no standing army attached to the state, but that there should be a citizen militia that could see to it that the commune does not become a state standing over society.¹⁷⁵ If an armed militia would not presuppose, and would in fact serve to prevent, a state standing over society, why would rights be objectionable? A right to a free press, for example, could well be an added means to prevent the rise of a state standing over society.

Marx's view, I suspect, is that if the proletariat does not hold power, rights are an illusion. Rights, for Marx, are expressions of particular class interest. If another class is in power, the proletariat's interests will be respected only so far as they agree with the interests of the class in power. If the proletariat comes to power, since its particular class interests, as we have seen, are expected to coincide with the universal, it would not need rights.

Another way to put this is to say that a right must either involve or imply a power to realize that to which the right makes a claim. If one does not or cannot have this power, then it is not very useful to claim to have a right. However, one might argue that the making of a rights claim should be understood as indicating a moral ideal that ought to be realized even if one lacks the power to do so. The trouble with this is that Marx, as we shall see, thinks that rights fall considerably short of the ideal and that rights may even obstruct the realization of the ideal. However, one might continue to argue that even if rights are not the ideal (that is, that even if one wants more than rights), one still does not want less than rights. In other words, it might make sense to demand rights in that situation where one is not yet able to achieve the ideal (an ideal that would involve more than rights), but where one wants more than powerlessness. And, in fact, Marx says, in the *German Ideology*, that "in reality the proletarians arrive at this unity only through a long process of development in which the appeal to their right also plays a part. Incidentally, this appeal to their right is *only* a means of making them take shape as 'they,' as a revolutionary united mass."[176] This suggests that an appeal to rights can play some role as a means in the process of claiming and gaining power, but that rights are not the final moral ideal. These issues must be explained in more detail.

In the claim that rights must involve or imply powers, we can hear echoes of Hobbes and Rousseau. For Hobbes, the sovereign was an absolute power. Rights against the sovereign were simply impossible because nothing could limit the sovereign's power or legitimate authority. If something could, then the sovereign simply would not be the sovereign—it would not be the *highest* power and authority. If the sovereign is the government, as Hobbes thought it should be, the people could have no rights against it. If the people are the sovereign, we can say that they could have rights against the government, but individuals could have no rights against the people.

Rousseau held the same conception of sovereignty and he fully realized that no limits could be placed upon the sovereign from outside—the sovereign could not even be bound by its own past decisions.[177] He realized that the only limits on the sovereign would have to come from the sovereign's own nature. Since individuals cannot protect themselves against the sovereign once it exists, they must see to it that in creating the sovereign they create something that cannot harm them in the first place. They must create a sovereign that is only able to act in accordance with principles of right. This is what led Rousseau to his concept of a general will. The general will, we have seen, gives rise to laws that accord with the universal. There would be no reason to demand rights against the laws of such a sovereign. To do so would be to demand exceptions to what is right for one's particular interests.[178]

In rejecting the alienation of the political state from civil society, Marx is certainly denying that the government is the legitimate sovereign. At times, Marx holds that the species or the community is sovereign.[179] At any rate, no principle above or outside the essence of the species should limit the species. Rights against the species, against the universal, would be morally objectionable. The only limits that could be placed upon the species must rise from its own nature. Only what is universalizable accords with the essence of the species. Particular interests in opposition to the universal have no place and will be eliminated as the species develops historically.

I think that Marx's rejection of rights as an ideal follows from his concept of essence. To see this more clearly we must contrast Marx with Hegel. Hegel accepted rights while denying that the state ought to be a means to protect particular interests. The state was an end in itself.[180] For Hegel, the state embodied the citizen's essence and civil society was the realm of particular interests and rights. But, as we have seen, the relation of the individual in civil society to the state is very different for Hegel than for Marx. Individuals in civil society, for Hegel, work *unconsciously* for the universal. Each pursues their own particular interests but through an invisible hand contributes to the universal ends of the state.[181] Individuals become conscious of the universal ends of the state as ends in themselves only when they lift their consciousness to the level of the state. Individuals can very well be absorbed in their particular interests and have them guaranteed by rights if their relation to the universal need not be explicit in civil society and if their social activity need not be conscious, communal, and purposively directed toward the universal.

For Marx, on the other hand, to realize one's essence, one must do so consciously within the everyday life of the social community. One must consciously work for the species, the universal, in society. Rights, then, would be rights against others, against the community, and against one's own essence. One's relation to others would become heteronomous.[182] The reabsorption of the political realm, the community, the universal, into society would be undone. Emphasis on rights guaranteeing particular interests would lead toward a society where individuals would work only unconsciously for the community. They would concern themselves consciously with particular interests and rights against others. As for Rousseau, absorption in particular interest is the greatest threat to civic virtue.[183]

Marx identifies rights with particular interests. Insofar as particular interests oppose the universal, they have no legitimate place. Insofar as they agree with the universal, the insistence on rights is unnecessary. Ordinary laws would be quite adequate. Trouble would arise, then, only if the community failed to realize the universal. And indeed, those who argue for rights do so precisely to guarantee against this possibility. But this option is not open to Marx in his early writings because of his concept of essence. To establish rights in order to protect against failure to establish the universal would itself prohibit one from realizing the universal. Hegel's concept of essence allowed him to accept rights. For Hegel, the essence is the Idea, which manifests itself in the state and its institutions. For Marx, essence is located in the individual. For this essence to be realized, it must be recognized consciously and community must actually be produced in society.

Individuals must work consciously and collectively for the sake of the species in their everyday lives. They must see themselves as the objectification of others and others as their objectification. They must contemplate the species in themselves and themselves in the species. Rights and the form of consciousness and activity that would accompany them would frustrate the realization of species essence. Rights would deflect consciousness from the universal, which must remain one's purposive end if essence is to be realized. Individuals would begin to focus on their particular interests and rights as isolated individuals. This would not be the case for Hegel because the state already is one's essence whether one fully recognizes it and acts on it in day-to-day activity or not. For Marx, to defend against the failure to achieve the universal would frustrate the drive to produce the universal.[184]

It is true that in the "Jewish Question" Marx seems to accept what he calls political rights. These are the rights of the citizen as opposed to the "rights of man." Political rights are rights that can be exercised only in association with others: for example, a right to participate in the community.[185] The distinction between these two types of rights is rather close to the distinction some contemporary social philosophers draw between positive rights and negative rights. Negative rights imply duties others have *not* to interfere in certain of my activities or *not* to harm me in certain ways. For Marx, these are the rights of an "isolated monad," based "not on the association of man with man, but on the separation of man from man."[186] On the other hand, positive rights imply obligations others have to *assist* me or *support* me in certain activities, or to contribute to the satisfaction of certain of my needs.[187] This notion is included in Marx's concept of a political right, but political rights go further—they require actual community with others. Political rights could be compatible with working to satisfy the needs of the species.[188]

We must notice that the right appealed to by the proletariat, which Marx mentioned in the *German Ideology,* was a political right—it served to organize the proletariat into a "revolutionary united mass." The rest of the rights we have discussed above were negative rights.[189] Even when Marx in the "Jewish Question" seemed to approve of the violation of rights by the revolutionary French government, if he did approve, it is clear that he approved of their rejection of negative rights, not political or positive rights.[190] After 1843, Marx always opposed negative rights for the reasons we have given.

What then is his attitude toward political rights? It is not easy to be certain about this. In some places he seems to favor them; at other places it is not so clear that he does. There are several possible reasons for this wavering. In the first place, specific rights can be ambiguous. If they are rooted in a well-organized community, they may well function as political rights that serve to reinforce and preserve the community. A right to a free press, freedom of speech, or a right to a citizen militia could function in this way. But in a society that was not communal, in the civil society of an alienated market economy, these same rights could instead function as negative rights and work against conscious community. The point here, I think, is that, for Marx, rights are not the main issue. The main issue is to achieve community. Rights alone will not produce community. Negative rights would make community more difficult to achieve in a way that political rights would not. The appeal to political rights, mentioned in the *German Ideology*, can be part of the process of gaining power and organizing as a united mass or community. And once you have community, you could have political rights. Moreover, these political rights could contain the basic content of negative rights, which should function, however, not as particular interests in opposition to the community but in support of the community. The question is whether or not political rights would then be desirable for Marx.

There is a second and connected reason why Marx is ambiguous about political rights. Political rights require association and community, but the question remains whether they are adequate to, and are able to promote, a *fully* developed community. Marx does not state his views on this matter explicitly, but in the "Jewish Question" he certainly seems to suggest that political rights are most relevant to a situation where civil society is still alienated from the political state, and thus where the citizens will want a right to participate in the political sphere (as, in Marx's view, was the case in the society of Rousseau's *Social Contract*). But, for Marx, this is the right to be an abstract citizen, a "political man," who is an "artificial man, man as an allegorical, juridical person."[191] Whereas what Marx wants is to end the alienation of the political state from civil society and to reabsorb the political, the realm of species activity, into everyday, concrete social life. When this occurs, would it fully realize political rights or would it eliminate them as unnecessary? There is no answer to this in the "Jewish Question."

There is also a third reason why Marx is doubtful about political rights. Rights are abstract, reductive, and thus can produce inequality. In the "Critique of the Gotha Program" (1875), Marx tells us that in the first stage of communist society the same principle would prevail as in bourgeois society, namely, the principle of equal right. Here, it is true, Marx is speaking only about a principle of distributive justice. He does not mention civil rights like freedom of speech or the press, but it would seem that they would be present because Marx tells us that we must understand this first stage of communism "just as it emerges from capitalist society; which is thus in *every* respect, economically, morally and intellectually, still stamped with the birth marks of the old society from whose womb it emerges."[192] At any rate, we must see that the rights that Marx discusses here are understood as political rights. In the first place the workers are associated. They own the means of production in common. Labor is cooperatively and communally delegated according to a social plan and the community distributes goods equally to all. There is no exchange or exchange value.[193] The equal right that prevails here is a political right—a right exercised in association, in community, with others.

We must notice that Marx's approach to political rights in the "Critique of the Gotha Program" is fundamentally different from his approach to negative rights in the "Jewish Question." In the "Critique of the Gotha Program," political rights are realized first, and only then, in the second stage of communist society, do we pass beyond the "narrow horizon of bourgeois right." Moreover, it is clear that the existence of rights in stage one will not frustrate the development of the second stage of communist society—in fact, rights prepare the ground for and are a means to this higher stage. Marx does not argue here that rights cause individuals to turn away from the universal toward particular interests. Instead, rights are held to serve a very important function: they firmly establish a strict form of equality.[194] Only once this equality is established does it become possible to transcend the narrow horizon of bourgeois right and to move to the higher stage of communist society.

Ultimately, then, these political rights are inadequate. This is because equal right ultimately produces an inadequate form of equality, or an inequality. Given individuals with unequal endowments and unequal productive capacity, inequality will result.

> Right by its very nature can consist only in the application of an equal standard; but unequal individuals (and they would not be different individuals if they were not unequal) are measurable only by an equal standard in so far as they are brought under an equal point of view, are taken from one definite side only, for instance, in the present case, are regarded

only as workers and nothing more is seen in them, everything else being ignored. Further, one worker is married, another not; one has more children than another, and so on and so forth . . . To avoid all these defects, right instead of being equal would have to be unequal.[195]

Here, equal right is abstract in the sense that we abstract from all the characteristics of the individual except the fact that the individual is a worker contributing a certain amount of labor time. And individuals are treated equally only with respect to these abstract characteristics. As real concrete beings with different needs they are treated unequally. This form of abstraction is overcome in the second stage of communist society where goods will be distributed according to the concrete needs of individuals. There individuals will be treated as concrete beings, not as abstractions.

What exactly does it mean to pass beyond the narrow horizon of bourgeois right? I do not think that it means that rights are to be *rejected* but that instead they are to be *transcended*. Rights are not rejected from the start. They are first realized in stage one and only then do we pass beyond them in stage two. How would transcending rights be different from rejecting them? Transcending rights could mean that individuals would simply act justly without there being a principle or a set of rights that obligates or constrains them to do so. Elsewhere, Marx says that communism, "far from creating individual moral 'constraints,' will emancipate the 'morals' of the individual from its class constraints."[196] Marx's views could be compared to those of Schiller in his *Letters on the Aesthetic Education of Man*. Schiller there contrasted three types of state. In the first, the natural or dynamic state, each person clashes with others and only in this way is activity restricted and order kept. In the second, the ethical state, individuals are confronted by a general will and with rational duties to which they must subordinate their will. In the third, the aesthetic state, individuals confront each other as ends in themselves, and the will of the whole is carried out spontaneously through the natural inclinations of the individuals.[197] The individuals need not submit to a higher moral authority. Rather, the needs, inclinations, and interests of the individual would spontaneously accord with duty, reason, and morality. There would be no moral constraint here.

Marx's description of capitalist society resembles Schiller's natural or dynamic state, a state in which the common good is realized through a conflict of particular interests, through an invisible hand, and where individuals are coerced by processes which they do not control. The first stage of communist society resembles Schiller's ethical state. Marx suggests that universal and rational principles of equal right, to which individuals would have to subordinate their will, would constrain individuals. The second stage of communism resembles the aesthetic state. Here, moral constraint has been transcended.[198] As we work on the world so as to transform it to fit our needs, as we create a world that appears as if it were purposively designed for us, as we realize the highest good and a beautiful world, our needs, desires, and inclinations would accord with our moral purposes. We would be inclined toward morality and would not find it a constraint or a burden.

We might also compare Marx's views to those of Aristotle. When Aristotle said that between friends justice is unnecessary, he was talking, I think, about transcending justice without rejecting it. Friends fulfill the claims of justice without feeling constrained to do so. In fact, the expectations of friendship are even higher than those of ordinary justice. It would be worse to defraud a friend than someone else. Ordinary rules of justice, as well as rights, specify what we owe to others and what we are obliged to give them as their due. These obligations are felt as constraints, burdensome obligations. This is not the way one feels about a friend. Friends give freely without constraint, without a sense of burdensome obligation, and they give more than is due.[199] Friends fulfill the principles of justice and move beyond them. Friendship is a truer and higher form of justice.

I do not think that Aristotle means that each individual would be the personal friend of every other member of the *polis*. That would be impossible. Rather, he means that the *polis* would be made up of a network of friends. Everyone would either be my friend or the friend of a friend at some remove. However, we could replace this concept of friendship with the concept of solidarity, which does not require that we know personally all those we share solidarity with, but, like friendship, does imply that we would want to give them more than their mere due and would do so without any feeling of burdensome obligation. Again, we would fulfill the expectations of justice and move beyond them.

However, in opposition to this, Joel Feinberg, for example, argues that:

> A world without claim-rights, no matter how full of benevolence and devotion to duty, would suffer an immense moral impoverishment. Persons would no longer hope for decent treatment from others on the ground of desert or rightful claim. Indeed, they would come to think of

themselves as having no special claim to kindness or consideration from others, so that whenever even minimally decent treatment is forthcoming they would think themselves lucky rather than inherently deserving, and their benefactors extraordinarily virtuous and worthy of great gratitude. The harm to individual self-esteem and character development would be incalculable.[200]

I do not think that Feinberg's claims are at all obvious. If rights claims were replaced by Aristotle's higher form of justice as friendship, it would not at all be the case that we could not hope for decent treatment from others on grounds of desert. In fact, individuals could hope for and expect more from friends, better treatment from them, than rights would lead them to expect.

I would argue the very opposite of what Feinberg argues. It would not be a society based upon justice as friendship but rather a society based upon rights that would tend toward "immense moral impoverishment." In the absence of rights, Feinberg contends, we would have to consider those who treat us decently as virtuous benefactors worthy of gratitude. How ugly and demeaning Feinberg seems to find this. To the extent that individuals are motivated by rights, thus to the extent that they feel that specific actions can be demanded of them, their spontaneous virtue could tend to be reduced to something merely demanded of them. And Feinberg seems to find it equally ugly and demeaning that the natural response of the individual who is treated decently should be gratitude or love rather than mere expectation. Feinberg admits this openly. "Rights are not mere gifts or favors, motivated by love or pity, for which gratitude is the sole fitting response. A right is something a man can *stand* on, something that can be demanded or insisted upon without embarrassment or shame. When that to which one has a right is not forthcoming, the appropriate reaction is indignation; when it is duly given there is no reason for gratitude, since it is simply one's own or one's due that one received."[201] To the extent that our society and our consciousness revolve around rights, we replace gratitude and love with demands and expectations; we find gratitude and love shameful and embarrassing and their absence dignified.

Marx would certainly think that it is this world of rights that would be the world of "immense moral impoverishment" in which "the harm to individual self-esteem and character development would be incalculable." In a passage quoted above, Marx suggests that in satisfying the needs of another it would be *desirable* that I "be confirmed both in your thought and your love" because "I would have been for you the mediator between you and the species, and therefore would become recognized and felt by yourself as a completion of your own essential nature and as part of yourself. . . ."[202] On the other hand, for Marx, it is only in an alienated and competitive market economy—in a society, we could add, that is based upon rights—that the need of one individual for the product of another (the need, we could say, for decent treatment from another) would be felt as shame. Marx says that in such a society:

> We would not understand a human language and it would remain without effect. By one side [the need and desire for the product of another] would be recognized and felt as being a request, an entreaty, and therefore a humiliation, and consequently uttered with a feeling of shame, of degradation. By the other side it would be regarded as impudence or lunacy and rejected as such. We are to such an extent estranged from man's essential nature that the direct language of this essential nature seems to us a violation of human dignity, whereas the estranged language of material values seems to be the well-justified assertion of human dignity. . . .[203]

For Feinberg, on the other hand, "No amount of love and compassion, or obedience to higher authority, or noblesse oblige, can substitute for" the dignity and respect that arise from rights.[204] One can well admit that to have to depend upon the benevolence of a government standing over and dominating society would be demeaning. But if such an alienated political state had been overcome and community realized, then to claim, between equals understood as friends, that kindness and compassion that would produce gratitude and love would be shameful, while the right to demand from another one's mere desert would give rise to dignity, is to be buried so deeply in an alienated consciousness as to mistake moral impoverishment for virtue.

Aristotle also distinguished between arithmetic and geometric equality. The principle adopted by Marx for the second stage of communist society—"to each according to his needs!"[205]—is certainly a principle of geometric equality. The share of A would be to the share of B as the needs of A are to the needs of B. When Marx objects to the principle of equal right in the first stage of communism, his objection is that using labor time to determine the proportionality of shares between A and B produces inequality, or, we might say, an undesirable form of geometric equality. Shares are not distributed in proportion to need, but in proportion to labor time. And for equal labor times, individuals' shares would be strictly equal, no matter what their needs. We can also say that for Aristotle the relationship between friends is based on geometric rather than arithmetic equality. One gives to a friend not a mere arithmetic due, but in proportion to the friend's worth—in proportion to one's feeling about the friend or the friend's need.[206]

There is good reason to think that Marx is transcending equal right in this way. He does not reject equal right. He takes it seriously. He shows how it can be realized in the first stage of communist society; he suggests that this is an improvement over capitalism; and he suggests that equal right is a necessary means to a higher form of society. But he does want to transcend the narrow horizon of bourgeois right and to move on to this higher form of society in stage two—to a society that, four years earlier, he thought should emancipate the morality of the individual from constraints.[207]

It is important to see that the transcendence of rights does not mean the elimination of rights. If rights are first realized and only then transcended, then the rights that were realized in stage one would have shaped the customs and traditions of that society. Marx argues that custom and tradition are a necessary part of *any* society and that they can even shape, limit, or forbid the direction of society by a sovereign.[208] Thus as stage one were transcended, rights would continue on in stage two, no longer as formal constraining principles but nevertheless as embedded in the customs and traditions of stage two.

Formal rights would not be compatible with the realization of the highest ideals of communist society. They would hinder the realization of a higher form of equality, which, contrary to the principle of equal right and the abstraction it implies, requires that goods be distributed in accordance with needs and that individuals be treated as concrete beings. Nevertheless, the ideals of stage two should tend to move beyond rights in the way that friendship moves beyond justice. Stage two should respect the claims of right embedded in custom and tradition as at least minimal claims.[209]

So here again, community is more important than rights, and Marx's main goal is to promote community. Nevertheless, his goal is not to eliminate rights. Insofar as such rights will constrain the development of rich human beings and rich human need by insisting on a strict form of equality, such rights must give way to a higher form of equality that will allow for the full development of the needs, powers, and capacities of concrete individuals. Rights, even political rights, will not foster communal individuals who must develop to the fullest in order to contribute to the fuller development of others and who depend upon the fullest development of others for their own fullest development. Nevertheless, political rights, preserved in custom and tradition, remain as a minimum beneath which the ideal society should not fall. Marx does not want less than rights would give us. He wants more than they would give us.

If individuals were to have to actively claim their rights in this society, and thus others were to feel constrained to recognize them, it would remind this society that it was falling short of the ideal of justice as friendship or of solidarity. One should not have to claim rights from a friend, nor should the friend feel constrained to recognize these rights. One should spontaneously act toward one's friends so that the issue of rights need not arise. If the issue of rights does arise, one must respect these rights claims still embedded in custom and tradition, but one should also realize that if such claims increase, the community will begin to erode. Thus, one should work to realize the community more adequately so that rights claims become unnecessary. It is quite possible that there would be a natural, human tendency to want not to hear rights claims, or even a tendency to want to repress them, so as not to be reminded of the inadequacies of the community. For this reason, rights must be *firmly* established in custom and tradition.

In the Introduction, I defended the type of utopianism that wants to keep one's social ideals just a bit ahead of one's theory of how actually to realize them. This is not to say that no risks would ever be involved here. I do think that the ideal of transcending rights is one that should attract us. But at the same time, a society that tries to rise above and transcend rights, given the natural human tendency not to want to recognize one's own failures, may instead end up falling beneath the level of rights and simply denying them. In fact, it may well be that something very much like this is a part of what occurred in the past to the Soviet Union. In other words, such utopianism, at worst, can be more than just an empty and innocuous set of ideals—it may actually be harmful. We cannot, then, rely on ideals alone. We must guard in very practical ways against failure and misdirection. But without ideals we would have nothing but very dull gardens to hoe, no matter how technically developed, scientifically cared for, or how well the produce was distributed and marketed.

Notes

1. This chapter borrows heavily from and repeats a good deal of the material found in my *Marx and Ethics,* but it treats the material somewhat differently and tries to develop it further.

2. For examples of those who think there is a relationship between Marx and Kant, see Max Adler, *Kant und der Marxismus* (Berlin: E. Laub'sche Verlagsbuchhandlung, 1925); Otto Bauer, "Marxismus und Ethik," *Die Neue Zeit*, XXIV (1905–6), 485–99; Karl Vorländer, *Kant und der Sozialismus* (Berlin: Reuther und Reichard, 1900); L. Colletti, *Marxism and Hegel*, tr. L. Garner (London: NLB, 1973); L. Althusser, *For Marx*, tr. B. Brewster (London: NLB, 1977), 35, 158, 223 ff.

3. "Critique of Hegel's Philosophy of Law: Introduction" (hereafter *CHPLI*), *MECW*, III, 182 and *MEW*, I, 385.

4. *CHPLI*, *MECW*, III, 184–86 and *MEW*, I, 388–90.

5. *CHPLI*, *MECW*, III, 186–87 and *MEW*, I, 390–91.

6. *CHPLI*, *MECW*, III, 186 and *MEW*, I, 390.

7. *CHPLI*, *MECW*, III, 180–83, 187 and *MEW*, I, 383–86, 391. For a fuller discussion of these matters, see *Marx and Ethics*, Chapter 1, Section II.

8. "Commissions of the Estates in Prussia," *MECW*, I, 292 and *MEW*, supplemental volume I, 405. "Justification of the Correspondent from the Mosel," *MECW*, I, 349 and *MEW*, I, 190. "Debates on Freedom of the Press" (hereafter "Free Press"), *MECW*, I, 164–65 and *MEW*, I, 60–61.

9. "Debate on the Law on Thefts of Wood," *MECW*, I, 230–34 and *MEW*, I, 115–19. "Comments on the Latest Prussian Censorship Instruction," *MECW*, I, 121 and *MEW*, I, 15. Marx is also critical of Hegel's identification of such a universal class with civil servants—the bureaucracy. Hegel argues that they satisfy their private interest in working for the universal (the state). Marx thinks it more likely that they will subordinate the universal to their private interests; *Critique of Hegel's Philosophy of Law* (hereafter *CHPL*), *MECW*, III, 45–48 and *MEW*, I, 247–50.

10. For a fuller discussion of these matters, see *Marx and Ethics*, Chapter 1, Section II.

11. "Industrialists of Hanover and Protective Tariffs," *MECW*, I, 286 and *MEW*, suppl. I, 398.

12. *Holy Family* (hereafter *HF*), *MECW*, IV, 36–37 and *MEW*, II, 37–38. *German Ideology* (hereafter *GI*), *MECW*, V, 290 and *MEW*, III, 271. *Manifesto*, *MECW*, VI, 495 and *MEW*, IV, 472–73.

13. *GI*, *MECW*, V, 193–97 and *MEW*, III, 176–80.

14. See *Marx and Ethics*, Chapter 3.

15. *GI*, *MECW*, V, 46–48, 60–61, 290 and *MEW*, III, 32–34, 47–48, 271.

16. *GI*, *MECW*, V, 87–88 and *MEW*, III, 67–68.

17. *Manifesto*, *MECW*, VI, 497–98 and *MEW*, IV, 474–75. Also, "Instructions for the Delegates," *MECW*, XX, 190 and *MEW*, XVI, 195.

18. "Prussian Censorship," *MECW*, I, 121 and *MEW*, I, 15. "Thefts of Wood," *MECW*, I, 261 and *MEW*, I, 145. *PP*, 129–30 and *Ak*, VIII, 381–82.

19. *PP*, 129–33 and *Ak*, VIII, 381–85. Also see Chapter 4, Section V above.

20. *PP*, 134–35 and *Ak*, VIII, 386. See also Chapter 4, Section V above.

21. *PP*, 87 and *Ak*, VIII, 345.
22. *Metaphysical Elements of Justice*, 118 and *Ak*, VI, 345–46.
23. For a fuller discussion of these matters, see *Marx and Ethics*, Chapter 1, Section II.
24. "Letters from the *Deutsch-Französische Jahrbücher*," *MECW*, III, 142 and *MEW*, I, 344.
25. *IPH*, 35–43 and *PW*, I, 38–49. *PR*, 12–13 and *GPR*, 16–17.
26. *CJ*, 279, 281, 285–86 and *Ak*, V, 429, 431, 435–36. *IUH*, 13–14 and *Ak*, VIII, 19–20.
27. "Letters from the *Deutsch-Französische Jahrbücher*," *MECW*, III, 142–44 and *MEW*, I, 344–46. Marx also objects to Hegel's philosophy of history on similar grounds in *HF*, *MECW*, IV, 85–86 and *MEW*, II, 89–90.
28. *GI*, *MECW*, V, 381 and *MEW*, III, 364.
29. "Letters from the *Deutsch-Französische Jahrbücher*," *MECW*, III, 144 and *MEW*, I, 346.
30. See Chapter 4, Section II above.
31. "Reflections of a Young Man on the Choice of a Profession," *MECW*, I, 8 and *MEW*, suppl. I, 594.
32. *Economic and Philosophic Manuscripts* (hereafter *EPM*), *MECW*, III, 275–76 and *MEW*, suppl. I, 515–16.
33. *EPM*, *MECW*, III, 272–73 and *MEW*, suppl. I, 511–13.
34. *EPM*, *MECW*, III, 274–75 and *MEW*, suppl. I, 514–15.
35. *EPM*, *MECW*, III, 276–77 and *MEW*, suppl. I, 516–17.
36. *EPM*, *MECW*, III, 275–76 and *MEW*, suppl. I, 515–16.
37. *CPrR*, 34–35 and *Ak*, V, 34. *F*, 15 and *Ak*, IV, 399.
38. *EPM*, *MECW*, III, 275–76 and *MEW*, suppl. I, 515–17.
39. *EPM*, *MECW*, III, 295, 304 and *MEW*, suppl. I, 535, 544. *Capital*, I, 132 and *MEW*, XXIII, 146.
40. *Poverty of Philosophy*, *MECW*, VI, 137–38 and *MEW*, IV, 97–98.
41. See Chapter 3, Section II above.
42. *CHPL*, *MECW*, III, 56–57 and *MEW*, I, 259. "Letters from the *Deutsch-Französische Jahrbücher*," *MECW*, III, 144 and *MEW*, I, 346. *EPM*, *MECW*, III, 275–76 and *MEW*, suppl. I, 515–17.
43. "Comments on James Mill" (hereafter *CM*), *MECW*, III, 227–28 (my italics) and *MEW*, suppl. I, 462.
44. *CM*, *MECW*, III, 212 and *MEW*, suppl. I, 445–46. *Capital*, I, 73–75 and *MEW*, XXIII, 87–89.
45. *CM*, *MECW*, III, 217–18, 227–28 and *MEW*, suppl. I, 451–52, 462–63. *Capital*, III, 793 and *MEW*, XXV, 801.
46. Aristotle, *Nicomachean Ethics (hereafter NE)*, 1155^a, 1159^b–1160^a; *Politics*, 1280^b.
47. *Capital*, I, 102 and *MEW* and XXIII, 117.
48. *Poverty of Philosophy*, *MECW*, VI, 113 and *MEW*, IV, 69.
49. *CM*, *MECW*, III, 215 and *MEW*, suppl. I, 449.

50. "On the Jewish Question" (hereafter *JQ*), *MECW*, III, 153–55 and *MEW*, I, 345–46.
51. "King of Prussia and Social Reform," *MECW*, III, 205 and *MEW*, I, 408.
52. *JQ, MECW*, III, 167–68 and *MEW*, I, 370. *Social Contract,* 68 and *OC*, III, 381–82.
53. See Chapter 3, Section II above.
54. *JQ, MECW*, III, 168 and *MEW*, I, 370.
55. *CHPL, MECW*, III, 29 and *MEW*, I, 231.
56. *CHPL, MECW*, III, 49–50 and *MEW*, I, 251–53.
57. "Estates in Prussia," *MECW*, I, 306 and *MEW*, suppl. I, 419. *Social Contract,* 101–3 and *OC*, III, 428–31
58. *CHPL, MECW*, III, 117–18 and *MEW* and I, 322–24.
59. *CHPL, MECW*, III, 119 and *MEW*, I, 324. Also, in the *Grundrisse* Marx argues that Rousseau, like Smith and Ricardo, projects the isolated individual of modern civil society back into a state of nature and then connects these isolated individuals through a social contract; see *Grundrisse, MECW*, XXVIII, 17–18 and, for the German, *Marx Engels Gesamtausgabe (MEGA)* (Berlin: Dietz, 1975 ff.), II, 1.1, 21–22.
60. *CHPL, MECW*, III, 119 and *MEW*, I, 325.
61. *CHPL, MECW*, III, 120 and *MEW*, I, 326.
62. *CHPL, MECW*, III, 121 and *MEW*, I, 326–27.
63. *CWF, MECW*, XXII, 335 and *MEW*, XVII, 342–43. However, Marx does seem to waver on this matter; see "Record of Marx's Speech on the Seventh Anniversary of the International," *MECW*, XXII, 634 and *MEW*, XVII, 433. Also "Marx to F. Domela-Nieuwenhuis on 22 February 1881" in *Marx and Engels Selected Correspondence* (hereafter *SC*), tr. I. Lasker (Moscow: Progress, 1965), 338 and *MEW*, XXXV, 160.
64. *CWF, MECW*, XXII, 332 and *MEW*, XVII, 340.
65. *CWF, MECW*, XXII, 331 and *MEW*, XVII, 339.
66. *CWF, MECW*, XXII, 332–33 and *MEW*, XVII, 340.
67. *Social Contract,* 67, 67 n, 78–79 and *OC*, III, 380, 380 n, 395–96.
68. *CWF, MECW*, XXII, 328, 332 and *MEW*, XVII, 336, 340.
69. *CWF (First Draft), MECW*, XXII, 487 and *MEW*, XVII, 543.
70. *CWF, MECW*, XXII, 331 and *MEW*, XVII, 338.
71. *CWF (Second Draft), MECW*, XXII, 537 and *MEW*, XVII, 595–96.
72. See Chapter 3, Section II above. Also Chapter 5, Section IV. Also Chapter 2, Section III–IV.
73. *Manifesto, MECW*, VI, 486–93 and *MEW*, IV, 463–71. Also, Marx, like Rousseau, thinks that private property originated through usurpation; *Discourse on Inequality,* 158–59, also 141–42 and *OC*, III, 177, 164. *GI, MECW*, V, 364 and *MEW*, III, 348. *Capital,* I, 713–41 and *MEW*, XXIII, 741–70.
74. See Chapter 3, Section II above.
75. "Critique of the Gotha Program" (hereafter *Gotha*), *MECW*, XXIV,

86–87 and *MEW*, XIX, 20–21. In the *Gotha Program* Marx says, "In a higher phase of communist society, after the enslaving subordination of the individual to the division of labour, and thereby also the antithesis between mental and physical labour, has vanished; after labour has become not only a means of life but life's prime want; after the productive forces have also increased with the all-round development of the individual, and all the springs of common wealth flow more abundantly—only then can the narrow horizon of bourgeois right be crossed in its entirety and society inscribe on its banners: From each according to his abilities, to each according to his needs!" (*Gotha, MECW*, XXIV, 87 and *MEW*, XIX, 21). Such a society might seem wildly utopian. It might seem to depend upon the achievement of an impossible to realize ideal of labor as well as upon the achievement of a society of abundance, which the ecology movement, for one, argues is impossible.

I have discussed Marx's ideal of labor at length in *Schiller, Hegel, and Marx* and, indeed, have argued that in his later writings generally Marx backs off from his earlier ideal of labor, that he develops a somewhat more realistic view, and that the above-quoted passage from the *Gotha Program* should be interpreted in light of his later, more realistic views rather than in light of his earlier, more ideal ones (see *Schiller, Hegel, and Marx,* Chapters 3 and 4, and p. 150). With respect to the issue of a society of abundance, it may seem that the above-quoted passage assumes that in order to satisfy human needs what is needed is a society capable of producing an ever-increasing *quantity* of goods—far more than our shrinking resources would allow. However, if one looks at the Introduction to the *Grundrisse* (*MECW*, XXVIII, 29–30 and *MEGA*, II, 1.1, 29), one finds a different model, namely, of a society that concentrates on the production of higher *quality* goods that stimulate and satisfy higher *quality* needs. I suggest that one's ideal society will be more realistic and possible if it focuses more on the stimulation and satisfaction of needs of higher and higher quality than if it focuses on an ever-increasing quantity of goods to satisfy ever-expanding needs.

76. See also *Marx and Ethics,* 152, 179–80.

77. *EPM, MECW,* III, 304 and *MEW,* suppl. I, 544.

78. *Eighteenth Brumaire of Louis Bonaparte, MECW,* XI, 185 and *MEW,* VIII, 196.

79. Ibid.

80. "Leading Article in No. 179 of the *Kölnische Zeitung,*" *MECW,* I, 202 and *MEW,* I, 104.

81. "Leading Article," *MECW,* I, 193 and *MEW,* I, 95.

82. "Thefts of Wood," *MECW,* I, 231–32 and *MEW,* I, 116–17.

83. Marx, I think, is making much the same point when in the *Critique of Hegel's Philosophy of Law* he makes the claim (which is not very clearly explained) that in "democracy the formal principle is at the same time the material principle. Only democracy, therefore, is the true unity of the general and the particular" (*CHPL, MECW,* III, 30 and *MEW,* I, 231). The "formal

principle" here refers, of course, to the form of law—the fact that law must be universal and necessary. By "material principle" Marx means that actual, concrete, particular people give themselves, in democracy, their own laws. They are thus the agent cause of these laws, and they are the material in which these laws are materialized. Thus, this material (the people) gives itself (through democratic processes) its own form (its laws); and, insofar as these laws are universal in form, they lift the particular people that they inform to the universal. Moreover, insofar as the people, through democratic processes, give themselves universal laws, universal form arises out of the material—the particular people. Thus we have the true unity of the general and the particular because the particular produces the general and because the general informs the particular. The general and the particular—the formal and the material principle—become the same.

84. "Free Press," *MECW*, I, 162 (my italics) and *MEW*, I, 58.

85. *Emile*, 85 and *OC*, IV, 311. "Thefts of Wood," *MECW*, I, 243 and *MEW*, I, 128.

86. *GI, MECW*, V, 330 and *MEW*, III, 312. "Berlin *National-Zeitung*," *MECW*, VIII, 272 and *MEW*, VI, 200.

87. *GI, MECW*, V, 47, 60 and *MEW*, III, 34, 47.

88. *GI, MECW*, V, 61 and *MEW*, III, 48.

89. Ibid.

90. *GI, MECW*, V, 46–47 and *MEW*, III, 32–34.

91. See Chapter 5, Section III–IV above.

92. *Manifesto, MECW*, VI, 487 and *MEW*, IV, 465. *Poverty of Philosophy, MECW*, VI, 113 and *MEW*, IV, 69. Also *Grundrisse, MECW*, XXVIII, 337 and *MEGA*, II, 1.2, 322–23. *Capital*, I, 486 n and *MEW*, XXIII, 511 n.

93. *EPM, MECW*, III, 299–304 and *MEW*, suppl. I, 539–44.

94. J. Elster, *Making Sense of Marx* (Cambridge: Cambridge University Press, 1985), 524–25.

95. See Chapter 5, Section I above.

96. See, for example, "Dissertation Notes," *MECW*, I, 436–41 and *MEW*, suppl. I, 80–91. "Leading Article," *MECW*, I, 193, 195 and *MEW*, I, 95, 97–98. *EPM, MECW*, III, 298–99 and *MEW*, suppl. I, 537–39. *GI, MECW*, V, 87–88 and *MEW*, III, 67–68. *Grundrisse, MECW*, XXVIII, 420 and *MEGA*, II, 1.2, 399–400.

97. See my *Marx' Method, Epistemology, and Humanism*, Chapters 1–2.

98. *GI, MECW*, V, 52–53, 214 and *MEW*, III, 69–70, 195. *Manifesto, MECW*, VI, 494–96 and *MEW*, IV, 471–74. "Communist Trial in Cologne," *MECW*, XI, 403 and *MEW*, VIII, 412.

99. See Chapter 3, Sections II–III above.

100. *EPM, MECW*, III, 298 and *MEW*, suppl. I, 538.

101. *GI, MECW*, V, 87–88 and *MEW*, III, 67–68. *Manifesto, MECW*, VI, 488 and *MEW*, IV, 466.

102. "Dissertation," *MECW*, I, 52 and *MEW*, suppl. I, 284. This is Marx's

view even in the *German Ideology,* though there he no longer speaks of essence; *GI, MECW,* V, 39–42, 81 and *MEW,* III, 28–29, 42–45, 70–71.

103. "Leading Article," *MECW,* I, 195 and *MEW,* I, 97–98. In this section I will focus on the development of the human essence. For a discussion of the development of the essence of natural objects, see Section IV of this chapter below.

104. "Dissertation," *MECW,* I, 85 and *MEW,* suppl. I, 327–28. "Free Press," *MECW,* I, 154 and *MEW,* I, 50. "Dissertation Notes," *MECW,* I, 448–49 and *MEW,* suppl. I, 107–8. "Free Press," *MECW,* I, 158–59 and *MEW,* I, 54.

105. "Leading Article," *MECW,* I, 199–200 and *MEW,* I, 102–3.

106. "Divorce Bill," *MECW,* I, 308 and *MEW,* I, 149.

107. "Prussian Censorship," *MECW,* I, 121 and *MEW,* I, 15. "Thefts of Wood," *MECW,* I, 231 and *MEW,* I, 116.

108. "Free Press," *MECW,* I, 162 and *MEW,* I, 58.

109. "Free Press," *MECW,* I, 137 and *MEW,* I, 33. *CM, MECW,* III, 218 and *MEW,* suppl. I, 452. *EPM, MECW,* III, 336–37 and *MEW,* suppl. I, 578–79.

110. *GI, MECW,* V, 42 and *MEW,* III, 28.

111. *EPM, MECW,* III, 272, 336–37 and *MEW,* suppl. I, 511–12, 578–79.

112. *EPM, MECW,* III, 304, 336–37 and *MEW,* suppl. I, 544, 578–79.

113. *EPM, MECW,* III, 277 and *MEW,* suppl. I, 517.

114. *CM, MECW,* III, 218 and *MEW,* suppl. I, 452.

115. Ibid.

116. *EPM, MECW,* III, 276 and *MEW,* suppl. I, 516–17.

117. See Chapter 5, Section I above.

118. See Chapter 5, Section III above.

119. *F,* 69–73 and *Ak,* IV, 450–54. *CPrR,* 28, 50 and *Ak,* V, 28–29, 48. That Marx rejects an unknown thing in itself, see "Dissertation," *MECW,* I, 63–65 and *MEW,* suppl. I, 295–97. *GI, MECW,* V, 264 n, 273–74, 292 and *MEW,* III, 247 n, 254–55, 273.

120. See Chapter 5, Sections III–IV above.

121. *EPM, MECW,* III, 339–41 and *MEW,* suppl. I, 581–83.

122. *JQ, MECW,* III, 168 and *MEW,* I, 370.

123. *Political Economy,* 222 and *OC,* III, 259–60.

124. L. Colletti argues that as far as political theory goes, Marx adds nothing to Rousseau except for an analysis of the economic basis for the withering away of the state; see *From Rousseau to Lenin,* trs. J. Merrington and J. White (New York: Monthly Review Press, 1972), 185. I think this is incorrect. While I agree that in many ways Marx agrees with Rousseau, I think Marx certainly rejects Rousseau's concept of the individual and of representation and tries to develop the concept of a communal individual.

125. *CHPL, MECW,* III, 7–9 and *MEW,* I, 205–8. Also *HF, MECW,* IV, 57–59 and *MEW,* II, 59–61.

126. *CHPL, MECW,* III, 8, 11 and *MEW,* I, 206, 209. *CHPL, MECW,* III, 181 and *MEW,* I, 384–85. *HF, MECW,* IV, 57–59 and *MEW,* II, 59–61.

127. E.g., *CHPL, MECW,* III, 61 and *MEW,* I, 264.

128. *CM, MECW,* III, 228 and *MEW,* suppl. I, 462.

129. *CM, MECW,* III, 227–28 and *MEW,* suppl. I, 462. As G. Spivak so nicely puts it, "represent" can mean "speak-for," as in politics, or "re-present," as in art or philosophy. To speak-for can often mean speaking instead of, silencing, or excluding those spoken for, in a way that re-present does not. Re-present means to present again, or to present to others, to mediate, what is represented without distorting it; see "Can the Subaltern Speak?" in *Marxism and the Interpretation of Culture,* eds. C. Nelson and L. Grossberg (Urbana: University of Illinois Press, 1988), 275–77.

130. *CHPL, MECW,* III, 119 and *MEW,* I, 324–25.

131. *CWF, MECW,* XXII, 332–35 and *MEW,* XVII, 339–43.

132. Elster, 523, also 84, 86, 522.

133. Elster, 87.

134. *GI, MECW,* V, 393 and *MEW,* III, 377.

135. *Gotha, MECW,* XXIV, 87 and *MEW,* XIX, 21.

136. See Chapter 4, Section IV above.

137. E.g., J. S. Mill, *Utilitarianism,* ed. D. Piest (Indianapolis: Bobbs-Merrill, 1957), 10.

138. *F,* 10–12, 15, 35–36 and *Ak,* IV, 395–96, 417–18. *CPrR,* 96, 115, 117 and *Ak,* V, 93, 111, 112–13.

139. *EPM, MECW,* III, 280 and *MEW,* suppl. I, 520–21.

140. *EPM, MECW,* III, 276 and *MEW,* suppl. I, 516–17. "Free Press," *MECW,* I, 158–59 and *MEW,* I, 54.

141. *GI, MECW,* V, 66 and *MEW,* III, 52. See also *HF, MECW,* IV, 36 and *MEW,* II, 37.

142. *F,* 35–36 and *Ak,* IV, 417–18. *CPrR,* 35, 129 and *Ak,* V, 34, 124. *PS,* 375 and *PG,* 435. *PR,* 83 and *GPR,* 123. Aristotle, *NE,* 1097^b-1098^a, 1174^b–1175^a.

143. Aristotle, *NE,* 1176^b–1177^a. See also *Marx and Ethics,* Chapter 2, Section II.

144. *CPrR,* 119, 128–30, 133 and *Ak,* V, 114–15, 124–25, 128–29.

145. *EPM, MECW,* III, 276–77 and *MEW,* suppl. I, 516–17.

146. *IUH,* 13–14 and *Ak,* VIII, 19–20.

147. See Chapter 4, Section IV above.

148. *CJ,* 58, 64–65, 77–78, 83 and *Ak,* V, 222, 228–29, 240–41, 245.

149. See my *Schiller, Hegel, and Marx,* Chapter 3.

150. *EPM, MECW,* III, 302 and *MEW,* suppl. I, 542.

151. *CJ,* 38–44 and *Ak,* V, 204–10. *F,* 13–17, 22–24 and *Ak,* IV, 397–401, 406–8.

152. *CPrR,* 33, 86–88, 126 ff. and *Ak,* V, 32, 83–85, 122 ff.

153. *CJ,* 198–200 and *Ak,* V, 352–54.

154. F. Schiller, "The Moral Utility of Aesthetic Manners," in *Essays Aesthetical and Philosophical* (hereafter *EAP*) (London: Bell, 1879), 126–32 and, for the German, *Schillers Werke: Nationalausgabe* (hereafter *SWN*), eds. J. Petersen and G. Fricke (Weimar: Böhlaus, 1943 ff.), XXI, 28–34. "On Grace and Dignity," *EAP*, 209 and *SWN*, XX, 287.

155. Schiller, *AE*, 35, 167 n, 185 and *SWN*, XX, 323, 386 n, 395. *On Naive and Sentimental Poetry*, tr. J.A. Elias (New York: Ungar, 1966), 169–74 and *SWN*, XX, 486–90. For a fuller discussion of these matters, see *Schiller, Hegel, and Marx*, Chapter 1.

156. *EPM, MECW*, III, 276–77, 300–2 and *MEW*, suppl. I, 516–17, 540–42. *CM, MECW*, III, 228 and *MEW*, suppl. I, 462–63. For a fuller discussion of these matters, see *Marx and Ethics*, Chapter 2, Section II. Also, *Schiller, Hegel, and Marx*, Chapter 3.

157. "Letters from the *Deutsch-Französische Jahrbücher*," *MECW*, III, 143 and *MEW*, I, 345.

158. See Chapter 5, Section III above.

159. See Chapter 5, Section III above.

160. "Dissertation," *MECW*, I, 63–65 and *MEW*, suppl. I, 295–97. *GI, MECW*, V, 264 n, 273–74, 292 and *MEW*, III, 247 n, 254–55, 273.

161. *EPM, MECW*, III, 336–37 and *MEW*, suppl. I, 578–79. Also see Section III of this chapter above.

162. *EPM, MECW*, III, 303–5, also 296, 298 and *MEW*, suppl. I, 543–46, 535, 537–38.

163. *EPM, MECW*, III, 303–5 and *MEW*, suppl. I, 543–46.

164. *EPM, MECW*, III, 322 (translation altered) and *MEW*, suppl. I, 562.

165. *EPM, MECW*, III, 305 and *MEW*, suppl. I, 546.

166. *EPM, MECW*, III, 322 and *MEW*, suppl. I, 562–63. For a fuller discussion of these matters, see my *Marx' Method, Epistemology, and Humanism*, 21–33.

167. *EPM, MECW*, III, 336 and *MEW*, suppl. I, 578.

168. On materialism, naturalism, and humanism, see *Marx' Method, Epistemology, and Humanism*, Chapter 1, esp. 12–13.

169. See *Marx and Ethics*, Chapter 3, Section I.

170. See *Marx' Method, Epistemology, and Humanism*, Chapter 2, Section III. In *Capital*, Marx argues that once fetishism is overcome, "the practical relations of every-day life [will] offer to man none but perfectly intelligible and reasonable relations with regard to his fellowmen and to Nature" (*Capital*, I, 79 and *MEW*, XXIII, 93).

171. See my "Nietzsche, Skepticism, and Eternal Recurrence," *Canadian Journal of Philosophy* XIII (1983), 365–87.

172. For a discussion of the way in which Marx's ideal society would be like the ancient Greek community, see *Schiller, Hegel, and Marx*, Chapters 3–4.

173. *JQ, MECW*, III, 153–54, 161–65 and *MEW*, I, 354–55, 362–67. *HF, MECW*, IV, 113 and *MEW*, II, 120.

174. Marx says, "its revolutionary practice is in flagrant contradiction with its theory. Whereas, for example, security is declared one of the rights of man, violation of the privacy of correspondence is openly declared to be the order of the day. Whereas the 'liberté indéfinie de la presse' . . . is guaranteed as a consequence of the right of man to individual liberty, freedom of the press is totally destroyed . . . But even if one were to regard revolutionary practice as the correct presentation of the relationship . . ." (*JQ, MECW*, III, 164–65 and *MEW*, I, 367).

175. *CWF, MECW*, XXII, 331, 488, 537 and *MEW*, XVII, 338–40, 543, 595–96.

176. *GI, MECW*, V, 323 (my italics) and *MEW*, III, 305.

177. *Social Contract*, 54–55 and *OC*, III, 362–63.

178. See Chapter 3, Section I above.

179. *JQ, MECW*, III, 168 and MEW, I, 370. Marx's concept of sovereignty will be treated in much greater detail below; see Chapter 7, Section II.

180. *PR*, 156 and *GPR*, 208.

181. *PR*, 124–25, 129–30 and *GPR*, 167–68, 173–75.

182. Moses Hess argued that rights imply heteronomy, see "The Philosophy of the Act," in *Socialist Thought*, eds. A. Fried and R. Sanders (Garden City, N.Y.: Doubleday, 1964), 269 and, for the German, *Moses Hess: Philosophische und Sozialistische Schriften*, eds. A. Cornu and W. Mönke (Berlin: Akademie, 1961), 222.

183. *Social Contract*, 102 and *OC*, III, 429.

184. For a fuller discussion of these matters, see *Marx and Ethics*, Chapter 2, Section III.

185. *JQ, MECW*, III, 160–61 and *MEW*, I, 362.

186. *JQ, MECW*, III, 162 and *MEW*, I, 364.

187. See, for example, J. Feinberg, *Social Philosophy* (Englewood Cliffs, N.J.: Prentice-Hall, 1973), 59–60, 94–95. See, for example, *HF, MECW*, IV, 131 and *MEW*, II, 138.

188. See, for example, *JQ, MECW*, III, 160, 162 and *MEW*, I, 362, 364. "Vienna and Frankfurt," *MECW*, IX, 49 and *MEW*, VI, 338. "Provisional Rules of the Association," *MECW*, XX, 14–15 and *MEW*, XVI, 14–15. "Instructions for the Delegates," *MECW*, XX, 188–89 and *MEW*, XVI, 193–94.

189. E.g., *GI, MECW*, V, 209–10 and *MEW*, III, 190–91. *HF, MECW*, IV, 113–14 and *MEW*, II, 120.

190. This is the only passage where Marx speaks against freedom of the press, if he even does so there. Elsewhere he always approves of a free press.

191. *JQ, MECW*, III, 167, also 160–61 and *MEW*, I, 370, 362.

192. *Gotha, MECW*, XXIV, 85, 86 (my italics) and *MEW*, XIX, 20, 21.

193. *Gotha, MECW*, XXIV, 84–86 and *MEW*, XIX, 18–20.

194. *Gotha, MECW*, XXIV, 86–87 and *MEW*, XIX, 20–21.

195. *Gotha, MECW*, XXIV, 86–87 and *MEW*, XIX, 21. See also "Record of Marx's Speeches on Landed Property," *MECW*, XXI, 392 and *MEW*, XVI, 558–59.

196. *CWF (First Draft), MECW,* XXII, 505 and *MEW,* XVII, 563.
197. *AE,* 215 and *SWN,* XX, 410.
198. For a fuller discussion of this matter, see my *Schiller, Hegel, and Marx,* Chapter 1, Section IV and Chapter 3, Section III.
199. *NE,* 1155^a, 1160^a, 1163^a–1163^b.
200. Feinberg, 58.
201. Feinberg, 58–59.
202. *CM, MECW,* III, 228 and *MEW,* suppl. I, 462.
203. *CM, MECW,* III, 227 and *MEW,* suppl. I, 461.
204. Feinberg, 59.
205. *Gotha, MECW,* XXIV, 87 and *MEW,* XIX, 21.
206. Aristotle, *NE,* 1163^a–1163^b.
207. *CWF (First Draft), MECW,* XXII, 505 and *MEW,* XVII, 563.
208. *Capital,* III, 793 and *MEW,* XXIII, 801. *Ethnological Notebooks of Karl Marx,* ed. L. Krader (Assen: Van Gorcum, 1972), 329–30.
209. For a fuller discussion of these matters, see *Marx and Ethics,* Chapter 5.

7

Marx and Pluralism

I. Pluralism and Umbrella Agreements

Contemporary theorists of many sorts, from Isaiah Berlin to Michel Foucault, have become increasingly critical of ethical universalism. The criticism of many of these theorists, if not always aimed directly at Marx, might be thought to apply to him especially. In one way or another, these theorists hold that ultimate values simply differ and that universal agreement cannot be expected about them.[1] To hold that all should agree about ultimate values leads to totalization or totalitarianism. The only acceptable society for such theorists whether they are liberals or radicals, is one that tolerates a pluralism of values.

In other words, it is not just *particular* interests that lead to difference, disagreement, and conflict—conceptions of the *good* themselves do so. No conception of the common good, the general interest, or the general will, then, can overcome these disagreements. There simply is no single common good or general interest. Individuals legitimately differ about conceptions of the good. Thus, those theorists, like Rousseau, Hegel, and Marx, who insist upon a common good or general will are totalizing theorists and are at least on the road toward totalitarianism. The only free society is a pluralistic one that accepts divergence in conceptions of the good. The tradition of political theory from Hobbes to Marx, I think, is a very good place to begin to assess such claims.

In the first place, contemporary theorists who suggest that Rousseau and Marx are totalitarians, or are heading toward totalitarianism, often tend to use these terms in a loose, sometimes almost metaphorical way, and certainly in a different way than the terms are normally used. The simple belief that a common good ought to arise out of an agreement among the citizens, and that they then ought to act for the sake of this common good, is one thing. And it is a very different thing from holding that there ought to exist a state with the power to enforce from above a single conception of the good and with the ability to manipulate citizens so that they are made to agree, and even to identify with, this conception of the good. The latter would be a more adequate definition of totalitarianism and certainly does not apply to Rousseau or Marx, who clearly reject the existence of such a state. The simple fact that citizens agree upon and identify with a particular conception of the good, by itself, does not produce totalitarianism. Citizens must be manipulated in this direction by a power outside or above them for totalitarianism to begin to exist.

But even if one admits that Marx is not a totalitarian, no one that I know of thinks of him as a pluralist. I would like to argue in this chapter that Marx *is* a pluralist. In order to be a pluralist in an acceptable way, however, it is clearly not enough to merely advocate a pluralism of values—to simply allow individuals to pursue different values, ends, or conceptions of the good. One must also consider the question of *power*. If, as is usually the case in a liberal society, there exists a distribution of power that is not perfectly equal, then certain groups will be able to benefit from pluralism in an unjust way. In a society that tolerates divergent values and thus in which citizens are reluctant to criticize or prevent the pursuit of these different values, such pluralism can serve as a screen behind which those with even a small advantage in power may be able to serve their own interests at the expense of the rest of society; and this can even lead to the oppression of certain sections of society. If we tolerate all attitudes toward women, ethnic or racial minority groups, and workers, even if we carefully and formally regulate legal behavior toward these groups, certain attitudes or values held by those with greater power or strategic position, despite legislation, can lead to serious inequality; for example, in access to employment, education, and housing. It certainly has in the United States, as the statistics will show. And this would certainly hinder the free and pluralistic pursuit of the interests and ends of these oppressed groups.

In other words, a pluralism of values absolutely requires a pluralism of power—an equal distribution of power. If not, those with an edge on power will be able to take advantage of the situation, and the toleration of differences will make it easier for them to do so. Very few theorists, however, think that such perfect pluralism or equality of power is possible or even desirable in society. A pluralism of values together with a pluralism of power, at least for someone like Hobbes, would be called a *state of nature*. In Hobbes's state of nature (at least when Hobbes is concerned with the scientific deduction of sovereignty by institution), values differ, there is certainly no common conception of the good, and all are equal in power. Moreover, it does not even require anyone with an edge on power to take advantage of this situation. Anyone with any power at all is quite capable of harming others with equal power, simply by catching them off guard.[2]

As soon as we introduce the concept of power, we see that to preserve the gains expected from a pluralism of values, we must not only have an equality of power but we must *limit* and *control* the use of this power. The normal way of doing this is to develop conceptions of the legitimate use of power that follow from conceptions of the right and the good, and to try to construct a sovereign with the power to enforce these conceptions—a sovereign that will do so, however, by the *legitimate* use of power (that is, a sovereign who in limiting power among the citizens will not violate those limits itself).

The problem here is that if you deny, as many modern pluralists do, that there can or should be a single common set of values—a single conception of the good—then one serious possibility is that you will be driven toward the acceptance of a Hobbesian sovereign. If you deny that there is a single conception of the good that individuals can and should agree upon, and if, at the same time, you agree that the power of individuals must be limited, then you may well be driven to limit power arbitrarily. You simply let the sovereign (whether it be the government or the people) decide what is right—decide the formal procedures for limiting power. This, of course, does not mean that the sovereign discovers what actually is right. Rather, the sovereign just arbitrarily decides what will be taken as right or, simply, what will be done. The consequence of this, as Hobbes saw so clearly, is that there is no possible way legitimately to disagree with the sovereign. If there is no common conception of the good, and no objective conception of the right, except what the sovereign (whether it be the people or the government) arbitrarily decides, how is it possible legitimately to disagree with the sovereign? To do so would be to establish an authority higher than the sovereign and then the sovereign would simply not be the sovereign. This new authority would claim to be sovereign and you would have the same problem all over again with this new sovereign. Pluralism worked out in this way leads to the elimination of pluralism or at least to its radical limitation to whatever range the sovereign happens to be willing to tolerate. This is not very acceptable.

There is, however, another way to conceive the establishment of a pluralist society. The best example of what I have in mind can be found, if we look beneath the surface, in Locke, and also in Rawls. Both Locke and Rawls want a pluralist society that will tolerate religious differences, different conceptions of the good, and different interests. But even here, pluralism cannot be separated from the question of power. Power will never just disappear. The best that can be expected is that power be decentralized, dispersed, controlled, and shared equally. We must see that the toleration of different values is never possible *tout court*. Pluralism, to be possible, must be limited. A perfect pluralism and a perfect equality of power are only possible in the state of nature. For pluralism to be possible in society, there has to be a common agreement at least about certain basic issues. There has to be what I will call an umbrella agreement. This agreement is not deduced from, or dictated by, a single objective conception of the good. That has been rejected. This umbrella agreement is the result of a merely subjective agreement among the citizens, which, however, they do not take to be arbitrary and certainly not arbitrarily imposed by the sovereign.[3] It is an agreement they are committed to and that they think is right. This umbrella agreement, however, does not commit them to agree about everything, but merely about certain basic issues that are important enough to hold them together through whatever other disagreements they have.

By an umbrella agreement, I do not have in mind the social contract itself nor even the decisions made in Rawls's original position concerning, say, the two principles of justice. Those are specific matters whose details the citizens can continue to disagree about, and perhaps even change, without society coming apart. Rawls certainly believes that he has come up with *the* two principles of justice that are *right*. But at the same time Rawls himself can envision other people sharply disagreeing with his two principles and proposing variations or alternatives, all without society collapsing. This indicates that the citizens have some deeper commitments that hold them together despite these surface disagreements. What I mean by an umbrella agreement involves these deeper commitments—commitments that are capable of causing at least the majority to stick with the social project despite whatever other disagreements they have. It is not possible to specify what these central commitments will be for all societies at all times. Different umbrella agreements are possible—for different societies, at different times, in different historical circumstances, and so forth. A commitment to "free markets" might be enough to constitute an umbrella agreement in one case; a commitment to communism or community in another; or even a commitment to a certain religion like Islam, Judaism, or Christianity, in other cases. An umbrella agreement can be based upon anything that a sufficient number of people are willing to take as so central and important that rough agreement about this matter will be enough to keep them together through all their other disagreements.[4] In Locke's case, all must agree to private property and the things that follow from it: unequal property and wealth, commerce and trade, or, roughly and crudely, to the basic principles of a capitalist market society. For Rawls, all must agree to much the same sorts of things, except that Rawls is much more liberal; he argues for far less inequality; and socialism is left open as a possibility.[5]

Moreover, this basic umbrella agreement must reinforce and be reinforced by the social cohesion that actually grows out of property, property interest, commerce, and trade. Only after this basic umbrella agreement is given and reinforced, and only *within* the bounds of this agreement, are difference, disagreement, and pluralism possible. Within the bounds of this umbrella agreement, differences and disagreements can be worked out nonviolently, through talk, negotiation, and compromise. The umbrella agreement reduces differences to the level where they can be handled in parliamentary fashion. The point here is that individuals are free to differ and disagree—pluralism is possible—only within the bounds of this agreement; only short of calling the umbrella agreement into question and threatening its collapse. Moreover, the social cohesion that arises from and reinforces this agreement will produce a situation such that most will *actually* find it in their *interest* not to threaten the agreement. To do so would be to threaten their own property interests. Disagreement will, in fact, stop short of that point. All, or at least most, must consent to this umbrella agreement and, in fact, *will* consent to it to avoid a destabilization of social coherence that would undermine their own interests. Pluralism is only possible within these bounds. To transgress these bounds makes pluralism, except in a state of nature, impossible.[6]

For example, a perfectly pluralist society made up of capitalists, fascists, anarchists, and communists—each with equal numbers, equal power, each equally active, aware, and organized—is simply impossible. There would be a state of nature among them. Some modern pluralists often talk as if no substantive umbrella agreement were necessary; that only a formal agreement concerning respect for rights, toleration of others, the acceptance of pluralism and difference, and so forth, is necessary. Such theorists overlook the necessary limits to pluralism. A society equally balanced among capitalists, fascists, anarchists, and communists could not sort out its differences over such matters as whether free markets, private ownership of means of production, labor unions, soviets or communes, workers' control, and central planning, among many other matters, ought to be supported, controlled, modified, redirected, or eliminated. Such matters could not be decided in parliamentary fashion. Such a society could not decide what is right, let alone the good. It would be possible for one of these groups, if its umbrella agreement (reinforced by the proper sort of social cohesion) predominated, to tolerate a certain number of individuals from the other groups. In a society, say, with a capitalist umbrella agreement reinforced by the proper sort of social cohesion, a certain number of anarchists, communists, and fascists could be tolerated. It is even conceivable in such a situation that all three groups could for a time be relatively equal at the ideological level—the level at which they are able to influence the ideas, opinions, and values of others. This would be quite chaotic, but perhaps conceivable. But this sort of equality at the level of social cohesion, economic structure, social and political institutions, and general policy is simply not conceivable.

There must be a general umbrella agreement reinforced by the proper sort of social cohesion such that all, or at least a significant majority, will push their differences only within the bounds of this agreement—only to a point short of threatening the collapse of the agreement. Only within this agreement is pluralism possible. Any differences or disagreements that would threaten this agreement would have to be perceived by a significant majority as not worth pushing because doing so would cause society to collapse and thus make it impossible for anyone to gain their particular ends. Or, short of this, any differences or disagreements that would threaten the umbrella agreement would have to be effectively stopped by those who support the agreement. Rawls comes closest to my conception of an umbrella agreement when he argues that those who are tolerant do not have to tolerate those who are intolerant when the latter threaten the security of the former.[7] I simply think it is much more difficult than Rawls seems to think it is to draw a neat line between the tolerant and the intolerant—not that it is so difficult to be sure about the really intolerant, but it *is* difficult to be sure about those who claim to be tolerant when they are not tolerating those they claim are intolerant. In general, almost any group can tolerate those who remain within the bounds of the group's umbrella agreement and no group can tolerate those who threaten or attack its umbrella agreement.

Perhaps what deceives so many theorists of pluralism is that for a society to proceed smoothly and for pluralism to genuinely flourish, this umbrella agreement must be taken so much for granted—it must appear so obvious or natural—that it is never seriously questioned. This, it seems to me, is pretty much the case concerning roughly Lockean principles of property and property interest in the present-day United States. This is not to say that no fundamental criticisms of this umbrella agreement ever occur. Socialists and others criticize it constantly. But these criticisms are not taken seriously by the majority. They are simply not heard, or they are viewed as utopian, at the fringe, or something worse; and they certainly do not cause the majority to seriously question their umbrella agreement. Such a state of affairs is necessary, it seems to me, for such a society to function smoothly and for pluralism to appear total. It appears total in the sense that *all* differences or disagreements that appear "sane," "sensible," or "rational"—that is, those that can be contained within the umbrella agreement—are accepted and have their place. "Non-sensible" disagreements, or those that are *perceived* as non-sensible—that is, those that are not compatible with the umbrella agreement—remain at the margin. For an individual committed to this umbrella agreement, the agreement does not seem to be ideological. It does not seem to be a particular set of substantive values imposed upon others. But it certainly is so and such an agreement is necessary to establish an arena in which a certain degree of pluralism is possible.

Thus, the issue of pluralism is not as simple and clear cut as it is sometimes made to seem. Pluralist societies like Locke's are not as pluralistic as they might at first appear. Hidden beneath the pluralistic surface is a necessary agreement concerning a set of substantive values and procedures enforced and reinforced by a form of social cohesion, all of which establishes a certain distribution of power. Without this umbrella agreement and social cohesion, total pluralism would mean a state of nature or would require a Hobbesian sovereign.

Locke's insight into the necessity of an umbrella agreement reinforced by a proper form of social cohesion constitutes a serious contribution to political theory on his part. But Locke's thought also allows us to see that an umbrella agreement and social cohesion can be either broader and more general or narrower and more restricted. In locating this agreement and cohesion in property, property interest, commerce, and trade, power could very well tend to shift to the propertied classes; and thus the arena in which pluralism would be possible could tend to be limited to this area. Toleration would be possible only to a point short of which property and property interest were called into question and threatened. Serious inequality and even oppression could result from unequal property, yet serious criticism of property and property interest might not be heard.

From this perspective, a theorist like Rousseau begins to look less like a totalitarian and more like a theorist who has thought the issues through more deeply. To insist upon the importance of a conception of the good, to insist that citizens must have a way to discover the common good or the general will, that the citizens must come to agree upon it and be committed to it, we can now see, does not differ so radically from Locke, because, for Locke too, an agreement—a common umbrella agreement—is necessary to avoid a state of nature. If we can see that Locke and Rousseau are similar at this level, then their real differences can begin to be seen more clearly. Rousseau simply wants the citizens to be able to be assured that their umbrella agreement accords with what really is the common good or the general will. And Rousseau thinks—quite correctly in my opinion—that this umbrella agreement, common good, or general will cannot be centered upon unequal property, property interest, or developed commerce and trade. That will narrow the umbrella agreement and in fact eliminate a *common* good. It will shift power to the propertied—to a narrow faction with a particular corporate interest.

Moreover, if we read Rousseau carefully, it becomes clear that even for him it is not necessary that the citizens agree about *all* values. They need only agree about certain fundamental values. For example, with respect to religion, Rousseau insists that the citizens must agree about a certain, few, basic matters—the existence of a Deity, an afterlife, and the sacredness of laws. For the rest, he is opposed to intolerance and open to difference. Even Locke would not tolerate anyone who is not a religious believer.[8] Moreover, in other areas Rousseau could allow for more pluralism than he actually does. Nevertheless, one must admit that there is not enough pluralism in Rousseau's society to make it fully acceptable.

However, once we understand the concept of an umbrella agreement and the social coherence necessary to reenforce it, I think we can see almost immediately, at least in general, that pluralism would be quite possible for Marx; and, indeed, there would be good reason to expect that his umbrella agreement would not be as narrow as Locke's. It certainly would not be centered upon and limited to property, property interest, and the values compatible with these interests. It would be a much broader agreement and thus could allow for a great deal more pluralism both at the level of values and of power.

It is quite clear that Marx is fully aware of the existence, in capitalist society, of what I have been calling an umbrella agreement. For example, he is aware that differences and disagreement can occur within a ruling class and can even proceed to the point of sharp opposition. "Within this class this cleavage can even develop into a certain opposition and hostility between two parts, but whenever a practical collision occurs in which the class itself is endangered they automatically vanish, in which case there also vanishes the appearance of the ruling ideas being not the ideas of the ruling class and having a power distinct from the power of this class."[9] Difference, disagreement, and pluralism can be allowed free reign, but only until the umbrella agreement is threatened, and then they stop. The umbrella agreement cannot allow for the toleration of all values. It only has a certain breadth, which is determined by the interests of a given class—interests that are determined by the material conditions of a given society, that are reinforced by the social coherence that arises out of those material conditions, and that make the particular umbrella agreement of that class possible.

Moreover, if we turn our attention to the proletariat, we find that Marx also recognizes and endorses pluralism for them. The proletariat's class interest will not be perfectly homogeneous; it will contain many diverse and conflicting interests. In capitalist society, these interests are likely to be relegated to the margins of, if they are not altogether excluded from, the umbrella agreement of the bourgeoisie. Thus, for the proletariat, at first, "owing to the frequent opposition of interests among them arising out of the division of labour—no other 'agreement' is possible than a political one directed against the whole present system."[10] In discussing the International Working Men's Association, Marx says, "Since the various sections of working men in the same country, and the working classes in different countries, are placed under different circumstances and have attained to different degrees of development, it seems almost necessary that their theoretical notions, which reflect the real movement, should also diverge."

However, through "the exchange of ideas facilitated by the public organs of the different national sections, and the direct debates at the General Congresses," in other words, through basically parliamentary means, they will "engender a common theoretical programme." They will develop an umbrella agreement or the beginnings of one. Moreover, within the bounds of this agreement, difference, disagreement, and pluralism will be possible. It is not the function of the General Council of this association, Marx says, to subject the views of separate sections of the association "to a critical examination. We have not to inquire whether, yes or no, it be a true scientific expression of the working-class movement. All we have to ask is whether its general tendency does not run against the general tendency of the Int. W. Ass., viz., the complete emancipation of the working class? . . . It suits the principles of the Int. W. Ass. to let every section freely shape its own theoretical programme, except the single case of an infringement upon its general tendency."[11]

Moreover, the umbrella agreement of a Marxist society, once it has been fully realized, would be much broader than that of a Lockean society. It would be based upon the needs and interests of a much broader section of society, certainly, than simply the propertied classes; and would be predicated upon greater equality among individuals. Nevertheless, many modern liberals would still insist that at least at the level of ideas and values a Lockean society or a liberal capitalist society would be more tolerant and pluralistic than a Marxist community. Judging from existing liberal capitalist societies like England and the United States, in comparison to recently existing communist societies, this would appear to be true. But at the theoretical level there is no reason why a Marxist society cannot be as pluralistic and tolerant as a liberal capitalist society. This is what I want to argue. Moreover, given recent developments in previously communist countries, and given the widespread and mistaken view that toleration and pluralism are simply incompatible with Marxist socialism, a careful understanding of Marx's views could also be of some help here.

In the first place, I want to show that there are a great many passages in Marx's texts where it is clear that he wants pluralism and opposes its absence. I will quote many of these passages, some of them fairly lengthy. I feel that I must do this to overcome the general stereotype of Marx as an antipluralist and to show how central pluralism is to his thought; and also because some of these passages are found in writings that are not usually read except by Marx scholars. What will have to be explained here is how such pluralism is compatible with community, which might seem to be opposed to pluralism. I also hope to show that those passages in which Marx says things that are incompatible with pluralism can simply be dismissed by a modern Marxist or Marxist society without violating the basic principles of Marx's thought. I also would like to suggest that modern Marxists, with consistency, can and should go beyond Marx and certainly beyond recently existing communist societies in the direction of pluralism.

II. Pluralism and Community

Marx's concept of the individual, discussed in Chapter 6, implied that individuals appropriate their culture, work it over, perhaps come up with something new, and deposit this back in culture for others to appropriate. Culture produces individuals and individuals produce culture. The way I presented this model in Chapter 6 may seem to have emphasized what was common rather than what was different and diverse, but the point of Chapter 6, after all, was to talk about the communal individual. This model certainly can indicate what is common about culture and thus what will be common in individuals, but it would be a mistake to think that it plays down or eliminates individual differences or diversity. This model is perfectly capable of explaining, and very definitely implies, diversity, difference, and pluralism. One's own development as an individual depends upon what in particular one internalizes from this common culture, what precisely one does with what is internalized, and the particular way in which this develops one's individual powers, capacities, ideas, and values.

What I said in Chapter 6 may have sounded as if individuals take in *all* of their culture—all the past contributions of all members of the species—and then simply transmit, or add to and re-present, this totality to others, such that all individuals would end up roughly the same, but that, very obviously, is impossible. No individual can take in more than a small part of this vast culture, and different individuals will take in different parts, work on them in different ways, and redeposit different results back in culture.

There are many factors that limit and select what one takes in, as well as the perspective from which one interprets and appropriates what is taken in, and also what one does with it—the group, class, gender, nationality, or religion that one belongs to or is influenced by; the group's past history, customs, traditions, and development; different economic, technological, and political conditions; one's education, talents, experience, and so forth. Moreover, the existence of alienation and division of labor will be significant factors that will close individuals off from parts of their culture and influence what they can do with it. This begins to suggest, and we will discuss it further below, that certain factors will produce undesirable differences and diversity—differences that involve limitations or constraints and that ought to be overcome. But even if they are overcome in an ideal society, the sociocultural world will still be so complex that no individual or group will ever be able to internalize more than a part of it—different and diverse parts, interpreted in different ways, valued differently, worked on in different ways, influenced by and reinforcing different customs and traditions. In fact, we cannot speak of a single culture. To be accurate we must speak of cultures in the plural, and even cultures within cultures.

The power of this model is that it shows both what is common, and thus the possibility of working consciously, collectively, and communally for the benefit of the species, as well as what is different and diverse, and thus makes for pluralism. To explain the compatibility of these two aspects of the model will take some time. But at this point we can at least suggest that the more individuals work consciously and communally for the benefit of the species, for a richer species, for a richer and more complex culture, the more diversity they will produce. And, at the same time, the more diversity they produce, the more they will be able to contribute to a richer, more complex, and more diverse culture that will benefit and develop the species. If the sociocultural world, even if only a part of it, is objectified and embedded in individuals, the diversity of that world will be objectified in individuals. And the more diverse individuals become, the more their objectifications will produce a complex, diversified culture and a richer species. The more they work for a richer and more complex culture, the more they will develop as differentiated individuals, and the more they are differentiated as individuals, the more complex their culture will become.

It is clear that Marx thinks that individuals should consciously, collectively, and communally control their sociocultural world, and this certainly would require some degree of agreement among these different individuals and cultural groups. It would require that individuals, as it were, lift themselves out of their different and diverse niches so as to enter a common discourse with each other. Nevertheless, this can still leave plenty of room for pluralism and difference. What would be required, as we have already seen, is a common umbrella agreement that would be as broad as possible and a form of social coherence to reinforce this agreement. Within the bounds of this agreement, difference and diversity could flourish. Some differences and disagreements, as in any society, would have to be excluded. Others would have to be worked out through parliamentary means—through discussion, negotiation, and compromise—by individuals with equal power. Other differences, however, could and should simply be valued as necessary for a rich and diverse cultural world.

There are many passages that drive us to the conclusion that Marx endorses this sort of pluralism. He is very much opposed to what he calls "crude" communism, a communism that "wants to disregard talent," that "negates the personality of man," that wants "to reduce things to a common level," that advocates a "levelling-down proceeding from [a] preconceived minimum," and that oppresses women as well as other groups.[12] In *Capital,* Marx complains that commodity exchange is a "radical leveller that . . . does away with all distinctions . . ." and he claims that money is also.[13] Instead, he wants the "rich, living, sensuous, concrete activity of self-objectification . . ." and a "rich human being . . . in need of a totality of human manifestations of life."[14]

Moreover, it is clear in Marx's texts that to produce this rich individual, a complex and diverse culture is necessary. Marx wants an individual "whose life embraces a wide circle of varied activities and practical relations to the world, and who, therefore, lives a many-sided life. . . ." This depends, as he puts it, on the development of a complex "world intercourse and on the part which [the individual] and the locality where he lives play in it."[15] Diversity is not just something to be *allowed*—it should be *promoted*. For example, in communist society, this complex culture, which Marx refers to as "universal intercourse," will be produced by productive forces that have developed to a "totality." The terms "universal" and "totality" here imply, I suggest, not homogeneity and uniformity, but complexity, range, and diversity. Marx argues that, to avoid crises, individuals must come to appropriate and control these productive forces and that doing so will produce the rich individual:

> This appropriation is first determined by the object to be appropriated, the productive forces, which have been developed to a totality and which only exist within a universal intercourse. Even from this aspect alone, therefore, this appropriation must have a universal character corresponding to the productive forces and the intercourse. The appropriation of these forces is itself nothing more than the development of the individual capacities corresponding to the material instruments of production. The appropriation of a totality of instruments of production is, for this very reason, the development of a totality of capacities in the individuals themselves.[16]

This is explained more clearly by Engels:

> The common management of production cannot be effected by people as they are today, each one being assigned to a single branch of production, shackled to it, exploited by it, each having developed only one of his

abilities at the cost of all the others and knowing only one branch, or only a branch of a branch of the total production. Even present-day industry finds less and less use for such people. Industry carried on in common and according to plan by the whole of society presupposes moreover people of all-round development, capable of surveying the entire system of production. Thus the division of labour making one man a peasant, another a shoemaker, a third a factory worker, a fourth a stockjobber, which has already been undermined by machines, will completely disappear. Education will enable young people quickly to go through the whole system of production, it will enable them to pass from one branch of industry to another according to the needs of society or their own inclination. It will therefore free them from that one-sidedness which the present division of labour stamps on each one of them. Thus the communist organization of society will give its members the chance of an all-round exercise of abilities that have received all-round development.[17]

Here, we must begin to explain an issue that will be further discussed below. There is an important reason why Marx may not *seem* to be a pluralist. He certainly wants a rich, diverse, and plural culture, as we have seen. But this fact can be overlooked, or even obscured, by the fact that he also wants all individuals to have access to the richness, diversity, and complexity of culture. He strongly objects to the fact that some individuals, due to alienation or division of labor, can be cut off from access to this complex culture; thus are not caused to develop by it; and thus cannot contribute as fully to culture's development. Certainly, the fact that different groups are cut off in this way from different parts of a common culture, or complex of cultures, will produce diversity and difference between those groups. But this is the sort of difference that Marx thinks leads to an undesirable sort of pluralism.

Marx instead wants what might be called Renaissance individuals—individuals with access to the totality of their complex and diverse culture. He wants all-round individuals. At first glance, this might seem as if Marx wants all individuals to be the same, each to have appropriated the same, common, homogeneous totality of culture, each therefore a replica of the others, but this, as I have already said, is very obviously impossible. Culture is simply too complex for that. These all-round, many-sided individuals will all be different. Difference should not arise, for Marx, from appropriating a narrow and stunted but different range of culture, but from appropriating a broader, more complex, and more diverse range of culture; even if this cannot be all of culture, by being active in it in more diverse ways, and, therefore, by actively contributing to further diversity. Such all-round individuals, far from being more uniform, would be more diverse, and certainly richer, than individuals who are prohibited from appropriating more than a narrow range of their culture. Thus, for example, in the *Eighteenth Brumaire,* Marx says,

> The small-holding peasants form a vast mass, the members of which live in similar conditions but without entering into manifold relations with one another. Their mode of production isolates them from one another instead of bringing them into mutual intercourse. This isolation is increased by France's bad means of communication and by the poverty of the peasants. Their field of production, the smallholding, admits of no division of labour in its cultivation, no application of science and, therefore, no diversity of development, no variety of talent, no wealth of social relationships. Each individual peasant family is almost self-sufficient; it itself directly produces the major part of its consumption and thus acquires its means of life more through exchange with nature than in intercourse with society. A smallholding, a peasant and his family; alongside them another smallholding, another peasant and another family. A few score of these make up a village, and a few score of villages make up a department. In this way, the great mass of the French nation is formed by simple addition of homologous magnitudes, much as potatoes in a sack form a sack of potatoes. Insofar as millions of families live under economic conditions of existence that separate their mode of life, their interests and their culture from those of the other classes, and put them in hostile opposition to the latter, they form a class. Insofar as there is merely a local interconnection among these small-holding peasants, and the identity of their interests begets no community, no national bond and no political organization among them, they do not form a class. They are consequently incapable of enforcing their class interests in their own name, whether through a parliament or through a convention. They cannot represent themselves, they must be represented. Their representative must at the same time appear as their master, as an authority over them, as an unlimited governmental power that protects them against the other classes and sends them rain and sunshine from above.[18]

Without a doubt, Marx is blind to the cultural richness that is possible in peasant life and he underestimates the diversity that can be found there even under the conditions he describes.[19] Such issues will have to be discussed below. Nevertheless, what is quite clear in this passage is that Marx objects to forces that limit variety and diversity and that produce sameness. Moreover, what is quite valid and important in this passage is his objection to forces that limit intercourse and communication, and thus not merely prohibit access to greater cultural diversity but result in subordination. Conditions that exclude one from power, that isolate one, that silence one's voice, that prevent one from speaking in one's own name, do, of course, make for differences, but not in an acceptable way. Acceptable pluralism, for Marx, requires equality, justice, and community among different groups, cultures, or nations; and this must begin even in the early stages of the attempt to realize the ideal society. Marx speaks of the "bond of brotherhood which ought to exist between workmen of different countries, and incite them to stand firmly by each other in all their struggles for emancipation." They ought to "vindicate the simple laws of morals and justice, which ought to govern the relations of private individuals, as the rules paramount for the intercourse of nations."[20] Moreover, it is clear that the development of powers and capacities in the individual, this all-round development of the individual, not only requires a complex culture but the access to it made possible by *community*. "Only within the community has each individual the means of cultivating his gifts in all directions...."[21] A community means that each must consciously, collectively, and purposively work for the benefit of the species, for the benefit of others. This requires that we must be able to reach, communicate with, and interact with others. They must not be so specialized or localized as to be isolated from this community. They must not be so powerless, and social intercourse must not be so uncontrolled, that they are unable to take part in this community, appropriate what is necessary for their development, or contribute actively to the richness and complexity of the community. The development of rich and diverse individuals requires a complex culture as well as the sort of access a community makes possible to that culture.

It is Marx's view that a close-knit interdependence exits between community and diversity, unity and difference. Marx says, "The unity of man with man . . . is based on the real differences between men...."[22] This must be explained, and to do so we must look at Marx's concept of need. This concept is most impressively able to capture the relationship between unity and difference. In the first place, needs imply difference, and do so in two senses. First, one of the main things that makes individuals different is that they have different needs. To view individuals as the same, to see them all, for example, simply as workers, to overlook their real differences, their inequality, their differing needs, is, for Marx, to reduce them and to dehumanize them. To treat them humanly as concrete persons is to see that their needs differ—thus the slogan "to each according to [their] needs!"[23]

Second, human need is itself a need for diversity and difference. Marx says, "The rich human being is simultaneously the human being in need of a totality of human manifestations of life—the man in whom his own realization exists as an inner necessity, as need."[24] This suggests that human realization requires diversity and difference—requires totality—but also that human need itself is a drive toward, is a need for, this richness, diversity, and difference. Where does this need for richness and diversity come from? For Marx, in the early writings, it is part of the human essence that is produced by the objects we are essentially related to. For Marx, we have seen in Chapter 6, need indicates essence. If something is needed by a human being it is a part of the human essence. Need indicates that an external existent is essential to the human being. It indicates that without the thing, we cannot develop our powers, the human's essence cannot be realized, it cannot have a "full, satisfied, complete, existence."[25] In the later writings, our needs are simply stimulated by production. In both cases, rich and diverse needs are produced by complex, rich, and diverse objects that will stimulate the subjective sensitivity to, the need for, this richness and diversity:

> the object is not an object in general, but a definite object which must be consumed in a definite way, a way mediated by production itself. Hunger is hunger; but hunger that is satisfied by cooked meat eaten with knife and fork differs from hunger that devours raw meat with the help of hands, nails and teeth. Production thus produces not only the object of consumption but also the mode of consumption, not only objectively but also subjectively. Production therefore creates the consumer. . . . Production not only provides the material to satisfy a need, but it also provides a need for the material. When consumption emerges from its original natural crudeness and immediacy—and its remaining in that state would be due to the fact that production was still caught in natural crudeness—then it is itself, as an urge, mediated by the object. The need felt for the object is created by the perception of the object. An *objet d'art*—just like any other product—creates a public that has artistic taste and is capable of enjoying beauty. Production therefore produces not only an object for the subject, but also a subject for the object.[26]

Such objects not only produce, but require, the development of corresponding sensitivities in the subject:

> Just as only music awakens in man the sense of music, and just as the most beautiful music has no sense for the unmusical ear—is no object for it, because my object can only be the confirmation of one of my essential powers—it can therefore only exist for me insofar as my essential power exists for itself as a subjective capacity; because the meaning of an object for me goes only so far as my sense goes (has only a meaning for a sense corresponding to that object)—for this reason the senses of the social man differ from those of the non-social man. Only through the objectively unfolded richness of man's essential being is the richness of subjective human sensibility (a musical ear, and eye for beauty of form—in short, senses capable of human gratification, senses affirming themselves as essential powers of man) either cultivated or brought into being. For not only the five senses but also the so-called mental senses, the practical senses (will, love, etc.) . . . comes to be by virtue of its object . . . The forming of the five senses is a labour of the entire history of the world down to the present. The sense caught up in crude practical need has only a restricted sense.) For the starving man, it is not the human form of food that exists, but only its abstract existence as food. It could just as well be there in its crudest form, and it would be impossible to say wherein this feeding activity differs from that of animals. The care-burdened, poverty-stricken man has no sense for the finest play; the dealer in minerals sees only the commercial value but not the beauty and the specific character of the mineral: he has no mineralogical sense.[27]

Marx clearly wants to multiply needs and, of course, their satisfaction, but, as these passages suggest, he does not just mean basic needs. He also means higher needs. He talks about a need for art or beauty. "Need" is a term that encompasses all sorts of desires, wishes, and drives for Marx. It is almost like the Platonic concept of *eros*—a general yearning that can have, and that can be stimulated by, a multiplicity of different objects. To call such wishes and desires needs, suggests that as the sociocultural world develops and becomes more complex, such wishes and desires can and should come to be felt as necessary, as needs, in the way, for example, that air travel in the course of the last century has been transformed from a mere dream appropriate to science fiction stories into an everyday, indispensable necessity. Marx wants an individual with as many of these sorts of higher needs—diverse, developed, and complex needs—as possible.

But at the same time that need indicates the development of difference and diversity, it also indicates unity. It indicates a need for the *other,* a bond with the *different* other, and thus community and union. "Poverty is the passive bond which causes the human being to experience the need of the greatest wealth—the other human being."[28] In producing a product, individuals satisfy their own needs: the need to express, manifest, and objectify their own powers, capacities, ideas, and values. In doing so, individuals realize their difference, diversity, and uniqueness. They also deposit in their culture something new. They contribute to the difference, diversity, and complexness—the richness—of their culture. At the same time, this stimulates the needs of other, different, human beings.

It either stimulates and can satisfy their needs directly and thus contributes to the richness and diversity of the needs of these other human beings, or it stimulates their need, and can provide them the means to express and objectify their own different powers, capacities, ideas, and values in and through my product. Thus it stimulates them to contribute further to the complexity and diversity of culture and of other human beings. This development of difference and diversity is dependent upon access to culture, to others, and to the objectifications of others made possible by union and community. Community means conscious interaction, interdependence, communication, and access—the mutual stimulation, satisfaction, and development of needs. Without community, difference and diversity would not proliferate. To be cut off from union and community with others would be to stop, or at least slow down, the proliferation of diverse and different needs. Pure difference, difference in isolation, would eliminate community, communication, access to the objectifications of others, and thus the proliferation of complexity, diversity, and difference.[29]

We have seen in Chapter 6 that Marx is fundamentally committed to community. He is also fundamentally committed to a principle of difference. "For each person the 'substantial' that he wishes to achieve in thought is something different, depending on his degree of education, the conditions of his life and his aim at the time."[30] In his early writings, Marx said, "one and the same object is refracted differently as seen by different persons and its different aspects converted into as many different spiritual characters. . . ."[31] Marx even quotes Leibniz approvingly: "every monad necessarily differs from every other; for in nature there are never two things that exactly coincide with each other."[32] He also says in *Capital,* "This does not prevent the same economic basis—the same from the standpoint of its main conditions—due to innumerable different empirical circumstances, natural environment, racial relations, external historical influences, etc., from showing infinite variations and gradations in appearance, which can be ascertained only by analysis of the empirically given circumstances."[33]

Adorno's views are relevant here. He argues in a very Marxian vein that, "The name of dialectics says no more, to begin with, than that objects do not go into their concepts without leaving a remainder, that they come to contradict the traditional norm of adequacy. . . . It indicates the untruth of identity, the fact that the concept does not exhaust the thing conceived."³⁴ Furthermore, "To define identity as the correspondence of the thing-in-itself to its concept is *hubris;* but the ideal of identity must not simply be discarded. Living in the rebuke that the thing is not identical with the concept is the concept's longing to become identical with the thing. This is how the sense of nonidentity contains identity . . . Utopia would be above identity and above contradiction; it would be a togetherness of diversity."³⁵ Or, as Ryan adds in commenting on this passage, the good society would maintain difference without hierarchy.³⁶ Compare this to Marx: "philosophers have declared people to be inhuman, not because they did not correspond to the concept of man, but because their concept of man did not correspond to the true concept of man or because they had no true understanding of man." Marx goes on to say that it is "unavoidable that in each individual there remained a residue which did not correspond to this ideal" concept of man. Earlier, he said, "No moral existence corresponds to its essence [or concept] or, at least, does not have to correspond to it."³⁷

Marx's concept of the party, we must also see, is compatible with his emphasis on difference, diversity, and pluralism. The Communist party does not stand above, dominate, or impose a set of its own totalistic views on the proletariat. It does not even "form a separate party opposed to other working class parties." It has "no interests separate and apart from those of the proletariat as a whole." It does "not set up any sectarian principles of [its] own, by which to shape and mould the proletarian movement."³⁸ Also, in discussing the Paris Commune of 1871, Marx says, "The working class did not expect miracles from the Commune. They have no ready-made utopias to introduce *par décret du peuple* [by the people's decree]. . . . They have no ideals to realize, but to set free elements of the new society with which the old collapsing bourgeois society itself is pregnant."³⁹ The party merely "express[es], in general terms, actual relations springing from an existing class struggle, from a historical movement going on under our very eyes."⁴⁰

In opposition to this, it has been argued by some contemporary radicals that Marxist parties are repressive in that they organize around broad common interests that are imposed upon and exclude the diverse and specific concerns of particular groups. To take just one example, Cherríe Moraga, a contemporary radical who is a feminist, a lesbian, and a Chicana, writes, "I had heard too many times that my concern about specifically sexual issues was divisive to the 'larger struggle' or wasn't really the 'primary contradiction' and therefore, not essential for revolution. That to be concerned about the sexuality of women of color was an insult to women in the Third World literally starving to death."[41] In Marx's conception, however, it is not the business of the party to "dictate or impose any doctrinary system whatever."[42] It studies a complex, diverse, international movement. It allows, as we have already seen, "every section [to] freely shape its own theoretical programme" as long as it does not go against the general tendency of emancipating the working class.[43] And it serves as a medium of communication among these different sections.[44]

Thus, the party should not impose a single line on all; nor, of course, when the goals of the party are achieved, when the ideal community is fully realized, would there be a political state to enforce uniformity. Marx rejects the existence of a separate political state that could stand over, dominate, or impose a totalistic set of conceptions, interests, or values on society. Marx wants the "destruction of State power which claimed to be . . . superior to, the nation itself . . ." and the restoration "to the social body [of] all the forces hitherto absorbed by the State. . . ."[45] Moreover, in the *Civil War in France* Marx's argues for deputies who are recallable at short terms, who are given specific voting instructions, and who can be removed immediately if they do not follow these instructions. This implies control by local communes and thus is a model for pluralism, difference, and diversity that would be limited only by a general umbrella agreement. It is a model intended to disperse and localize power—root it in different, local constituencies. This model, we have seen in Chapter 6, would preserve community; a community, we have seen in the present chapter, that values the difference and diversity necessary for the highest development of the individual—an individual rich in needs—and would work out this pluralism through locally controlled deputies.

To understand these matters more fully, however, we must also discuss Marx's concept of sovereignty. If the political state is to be eliminated, it is clear that neither the political state, the government, nor the executive will be sovereign for Marx. In many places, Marx argues that the people are sovereign.[46] Individuals must reabsorb the abstract citizen into themselves. Political power should no longer dominate; it should no longer even be separated from, these individuals. Individuals must organize their own forces as social forces.[47] In the *Civil War in France,* Marx says that individuals must destroy state power as something independent of and superior to themselves; they must restore to the social body all forces hitherto absorbed by the state.[48] This includes eliminating a national standing army attached to a state and its replacement by a civil militia made up of the people, which can be used to see to it that the commune, made up of locally controlled deputies with specific voting instructions, does not try to become a state standing over and dominating society.[49]

In *Capital,* Marx argues that the form in which unpaid surplus labor is pumped out of the direct producers determines the relationship of rulers and ruled—the form of sovereignty.[50] If unpaid surplus labor is not pumped out of the direct producers by another class, if there are no classes, if production and distribution are consciously, collectively, and democratically controlled by the community, then the community, the people, should be sovereign. Marx also argues that custom and tradition, which exist and are necessary in *any* society, can limit and shape the direction of sovereign power.[51] In a well-developed equalitarian community without classes, custom and tradition could work to keep sovereignty in the hands of the people.

However, despite all this, in the "Critique of the Gotha Program" (1875), Marx seems to change his mind. He suggests that the concept of "sovereignty of the people" makes sense only in a bourgeois democratic republic, not in a fully developed communist society.[52] What does this mean? If Marx objects to the concept of the people as sovereign, he is certainly not suggesting that the government, the legislature as opposed to the community, or even the party, become sovereign. He could only be suggesting that sovereignty entirely disappear. Is this possible?

It would seem not. If, as for Hobbes, Rousseau, and others, sovereignty is at least in part an empirical concept that indicates where sovereign power in fact lies, then presumably a social scientist could discover in any given society whether power is centralized in the hands of a government; whether it is distributed unevenly among different classes, groups, or individuals; or whether it is distributed evenly among all individuals. It would have to be one of these possibilities or some variant on them. If you have a group of people interacting with each other, you have power. It is inescapable. It cannot be eliminated. The concept of sovereignty merely indicates how this power is ultimately organized, distributed, and employed—how it is exerted over others.

If, for Marx, there is no political state, no classes, and no standing army, but only an equalitarian community reinforced by custom and tradition with a citizen militia, the armed people, to see to it that their deputies do not try to reestablish a political state, doesn't this mean that the people have power and thus are sovereign?

It seems that Marx would have to admit that the people have power, but would he have to admit that it is *sovereign* power or *political* power? If there are no classes and if there is no political state that stands over and dominates society, then there is no sovereign power that can be exerted over others at least in these ways. On the other hand, the power of the people, the community, exists to prevent power from becoming sovereign power or political power. In other words, this is not like the concept of sovereignty found in Locke or Rousseau, nor is it like Hegel's concept of sovereignty as a spiritual community where people lack democratic power. Unlike Hegel, the people have power, for Marx, but, unlike Locke and Rousseau, the power of the people is not exerted to see to it that the state acts in accordance with the wishes of the people. It is not a power exerted to control the state or even to limit it. There simply is no political state for Marx and thus no political alienation. For Marx, the power of the people is not a power to control political power and thus it, itself, is not a political power. It is a power to *prevent* political power—a power to prevent domination, to prevent a political state, a legislature, or deputies separate from the people, and to prevent classes. This power is a social power that is not separate from individuals as political power.

What is social power as opposed to political power? Social power, for Marx, is a power that binds a community together. It is power as social coherence. This must be explained. If people interact with each other, power arises. It is inescapable. But as long as it cannot become power that dominates, it can remain a power that empowers individuals. It will be a power that allows them to develop their powers and capacities. As we have seen earlier, any human activity that produces objects, from the production of institutions like the state to the production of a piece of music, influences others. It stimulates needs in others. It can stimulate and satisfy the direct needs of others or their need to produce their own objects. Human beings, we have said, take in their culture, work on it, develop it, and deposit the result back in culture as an object for others to take up. This objectification is clearly a power. It exercises and develops one's own powers in producing the object and it stimulates, develops, and exercises the powers and capacities of others who use your product. If this sort of power is not alienated, if it is kept out of the hands of a political state or of particular classes, if it is organized communally and democratically, it will give rise to a social coherence such that individuals can interact and can have access to the objectifications of others, to the richness of a complex culture, so that they can appropriate it, so that they can develop their own powers and capacities, and so that they can contribute to further developing the powers and capacities of others.

Moreover, as we have seen, this development implies difference, diversity, and pluralism. What this means is that power can become less and less *power-over* (the power of a state, legislature, class, or of individuals *over* others); it means that power can progressively be dispersed, that pockets of power, its coagulation, can be dissolved. The contributions of individuals to culture, to others (in the form of new technology, new knowledge, new institutions, new sensitivities, and so forth), if there is no power to isolate them and keep them from others, keep them for one's class or for the political state, if they are *communicated*, if they are fully *accessible*, then they are not turned into power-over others, but are proliferated, spread to, others. One gains power over others, as Marx suggested in the passage quoted above from the *Eighteenth Brumaire* concerning the French peasantry, when others are isolated from access to power, access to objectifications—and such access dissolves power over others. In a community with such access, power as power-over would tend to wither away. Power as empowerment, the development of powers and capacities, would tend to spread. One could say that this *is* to dissolve sovereignty.

We must now look more closely at the compatibility of pluralism and community. At first glance, they might seem incompatible. For someone like Rousseau, they certainly were. Community required a common set of healthy customs and traditions, as well as a homogeneity of interests, life situations, and values. Rapid change, different interests, or a diversity of values and ends would erode the community.[53] But perhaps this was merely an idealized vision of community. Rousseau, after all, looked back to ancient Sparta, which did exclude difference and diversity. But if we look back to ancient Athens, which for many (though, it would seem, not for Rousseau) is almost the paradigm of community, we find a great deal of diversity, disagreement, and even conflict. Think of the conflict between the sophists and the followers of Socrates, as well as between both of these groups and much of the rest of the Athenian community. Yet who would suggest that either of these groups were not a part of the Athenian community? Their conflict was a conflict within a common community. Think also of the conflict, sometimes even violent, between the democratic and oligarchic parties.

What is necessary is an umbrella agreement that makes possible a community of discourse, or a community of discourses—a common arena in which discourse can occur and stop short of violence that would destroy the community and thus the possibility of discourse. One wants a discourse with as little hierarchy, oppression, or domination as possible, so that all voices can be heard; and so that they can argue about removing any further forms of oppression, domination, or hierarchy that any, from their different perspectives, may discover. A community need not be homogeneous. It can be diverse. In fact, diversity is crucial for the development of a complex culture and the rich individual in the ways we have already discussed above. Perhaps even more importantly, diversity and difference are also crucial to allow us to discover, locate, and eradicate hierarchies and oppressions that remain invisible to some members or sections of the community and are only seen by other members or sections of the community who have different perspectives. Such discoveries are even *facilitated* by community, by access, by communication, by familiarity with other diverse and different perspectives.

Contemporary writers have started to see that communities and traditions are much more diverse than had usually been thought to be the case.[54] MacIntyre is most impressive in this respect. He views a tradition as a group of individuals carrying on an argument over an extended period of time in which certain fundamental agreements (what I would call "umbrella agreements") are defined and redefined through conflict not just with those external to the tradition but among those *within* the tradition as well. Traditions can grow in strength, can split, can merge with, absorb, or be absorbed by other traditions, or they can die.[55]

All need not be uniformity and agreement within a tradition. Members of a tradition can be intent upon amending or redirecting their tradition or even opposing its central contentions. Moreover, this can be quite crucial to the development of the tradition. Traditions can mature in finding their way through these oppositions. They can even develop if the tradition is able to solve problems found insoluble by the earlier tradition, resolve earlier incoherencies, or make available conceptual or theoretical resources not available to the earlier tradition.⁵⁶ Tradition and community are not incompatible with difference, disagreement, and pluralism; they can thrive on them as long as they are held together within a common developing umbrella agreement.

It is not pluralism and community that are incompatible. What is incompatible is community and the *liberal conception* of pluralism and individuality. Liberals, or at least some of them, tend to view individual values, projects, and ends as radically individual. But while the projects and ends of one individual may look quite different from those of another individual, if they have developed within and have been shaped by a particular sociocultural world, there will be deeper level similarities. They will all appear to be, say, twentieth-century American projects rather than, say, eighteenth-century African or sixteenth-century Chinese projects.

All of these projects are the projects of individuals—individuals choose them and develop them. But they are also more common than that. To see this is not to eliminate individuality, but to gain a deeper understanding of the individual and of the individual's essential links to other members of the community. Individuality is not produced by projects or ends that are radically isolated from and radically different from those of other individuals, but by the particular and specific constellation of the common sociocultural factors that the individual internalizes and embodies in a project. Individuality grows out of the specific twist, the configuration, the tone, that the individual gives to these internalized common factors, as well as, of course, the particular innovations the individual comes up with.

Moreover, this model suggests that there is something problematic about individuals conceiving their projects as radically personal or as merely the expression of their own isolated self-interests. There is something problematic about choosing your project without awareness of your sociality and membership in a community. If individuals conceptually cut themselves off from the community, they conceptually (and perhaps actually) cut themselves off from their own individuality. Without recognizing the sociocultural elements that have been internalized, without recognizing and relying on the objectifications of others, and without working to develop a common complex culture, individuals will not develop their individuality or that of others as far.

In Chapter 6, however, I argued that to realize their own essence, for Marx, individuals must work for the benefit of the species, the universal; in fact, they must act in accordance with the categorical imperative; their actions must be universalizable. It has almost become a truism today that the categorical imperative is at odds with pluralism and difference. Nevertheless, I do not think there is any incompatibility here. In the first place, Kant's second formulation of the categorical imperative holds that we should always treat others as ends, never only as means.[57] This is perfectly compatible with pluralism and difference. The projects of different individuals should always be treated as ends valuable in themselves, never only as means to our own ends.

The principle of universalization does not mean homogenization, that all must be the same, that all projects fit the same mold. Kant, himself, in the third example following the first formulation of the categorical imperative, argues that if an individual has a particular talent, we could not will as a universal law that this talent be left undeveloped. The categorical imperative would demand that it be developed, and, we could easily add, be accessible to others.[58] Talents, like powers, capacities, and needs, are clearly not the sorts of things that are the same for all. They imply difference and diversity among individuals. The categorical imperative, then, in demanding the development of talents, or powers, capacities, and needs, would be demanding the development of difference and diversity. If so, the categorical imperative, to be consistent, would also have to demand, both as a result of demanding different and diverse talents, as well as to reinforce them, the development of a rich, complex, and plural culture, which is certainly Kant's goal.[59]

The categorical imperative would rule out the realization of needs and interests that cannot be universalized in the sense that they harm others; for example, an interest in exploiting workers, dominating women, or oppressing ethnic or racial minority groups. On the other hand, the existence of needs that are common to all—for example, the need for food or clean air—as well as needs for those things that could benefit all—for example, the development of a more resistant and productive strain of wheat (or rice) or cures for common diseases—would obviously accord with the categorical imperative. All of this could hardly be objected to by the most radical pluralist. Moreover, between these two poles there are many things that fit in neither category— differences that neither harm others nor are the sorts of things that it makes sense to say everyone wants or should want. Examples would be a certain scholar's need for a particular obscure manuscript or the desire to revive and preserve an old ritual or ceremony within one's particular tradition. Such things, however, are perfectly compatible with, or are simply extensions of, Kant's claim that the categorical imperative would demand the development of particular talents.[60] They will produce a richer and more complex culture.

Working for the sake of the species, acting for the universal, acting for the sake of the categorical imperative, is perfectly compatible with producing a very specific, particular object—a poem, an artwork, something unique, idiosyncratic. It need not be something common, something of universal interest. What gives such particulars a universal value is that they add to the richness, diversity, and complexity of the species. They need not always satisfy existing, common, general needs. They can stimulate *new* needs. No individual or group is going to be able to internalize all of a given culture. Culture can be seen as a huge repository for what Lévi-Strauss calls *bricolage*—a repository for picking up, connecting, constructing, innovating, interpreting in a plurality of different and diverse ways.[61]

It is also perfectly legitimate for certain groups to want to preserve unchanged specific customs and traditions and to exclude and isolate themselves from other parts of a complex cultural world—for example: orthodox Jews, Protestant fundamentalists, the Amish, black separatists, some feminists, and so forth. To want to force such groups into a common culture would be to lose or to reduce valuable differences and diversity. It is often assumed that cultures that do not change, or that resist change, if they are not stagnant, decaying, or dead, are at least not very alive. But this is not necessarily the case. Members of cultures that resist change and shun other cultures construct their culture—that is, appropriate their culture, work it over, and deposit it back in the common culture—just as much as individuals in more complex and changing cultures do. It is just that the former do so to prevent change and the latter do so to allow for it or promote it.

The ancient Greeks often noted the fact—and did so with considerable respect, regardless of which city state they were from—that the laws of Sparta had remained unchanged for 400 years. Can we possibly imagine that these laws just remained unchanged on their own because Spartan culture was stagnant or dead? It seems to me that it took enormous effort—conscious effort—to maintain those laws, certainly more effort to maintain them for 400 years than for 100 years, or fifty years. Culture resides in, is preserved, transmitted, and developed through social, political, religious, educational, and many other sorts of institutions. For all these institutions to work together to resist change, one might argue, would require more conscious effort than simply accepting change. Rapidly changing cultures often view the lack of change in traditional cultures as the result of inactivity or inertia. But inertia need not only mean rest. Objects that continue in motion unless checked are also inertial. It may well be the case that cultures undergoing continual change, especially if this is not consciously regulated, are the truly inertial cultures.

At any rate, no group can appropriate all of culture. It can only appropriate more or less of it. Marx certainly favors appropriating more, and he especially objects to forces that, without our knowing it and behind our backs, close us off from access to a rich culture. But there can be no legitimate objection (despite what Marx at times, we shall see, will say) to those who *consciously* choose to exclude parts of culture or to remain unchanged in certain ways.

Unlike some contemporary pluralists who are opposed to all universalization, Paul Patton makes a valuable distinction between universalization and totalization. A political or theoretical perspective is universalizable to the extent that it can be applied to the whole range of society. He takes as an example, modern feminism, which would be applicable to the family, childcare, education, the workplace, unions, the military, and so forth. It does not claim to exhaust the range of possible kinds of analysis of these institutions or of society as a whole, nor to exclude other perspectives, but it has something to say about all, or at least a wide range of, spheres of social activity.

A totalizing perspective is different. It purports to stand outside or above and to oversee or regulate the conflicting demands of particular movements or the particular analyses of different theories. It attempts to govern a multiplicity of outlooks and interests; to resolve them, establish priorities, and institute hierarchies. It will inevitably enforce or impose interests different from those of some minority movements or specific issue groups.

Patton thinks that traditional Marxism wavers between or straddles these two positions.[62] No doubt it has, but I have been trying to argue that Marx *himself* endorses a form of universalization, not totalization. Discourse within a common umbrella agreement, universalization, a categorical imperative, are necessary to rule out things like the oppression of women, workers, and ethnic or racial minority groups. The umbrella agreement must be concrete enough to do this. Yet the umbrella agreement must be "high" enough, or "loose" enough, to allow for differences and pluralism. Different individuals or different sections of society, like the different sections of the International Working Men's Association, must be free to develop their own programs or projects, but they must not contradict the general tendency, the common umbrella agreement, the categorical imperative—they must not oppress others.

Moreover, universalization is crucially important in another respect.

It tends to force the recognition of inequality, hierarchy, and domination in ever deeper and more subtle ways. Even in the past, when the writers of the American Constitution claimed that all "men" are, or should be, equal, it was only a matter of time before blacks, women, and others, who had been excluded from this equality that was supposed to apply to *all,* began to claim their right to this same equality. In general, universal principles enunciated in public discourse tend to force, sooner or later, discovery, recognition, rejection, and elimination of inequalities, domination, and hierarchy, and tend to do so in ever subtler ways.

There is also another form of universalization that is important here. New needs and perspectives of a more particular sort, ones we would not think of universalizing in the first sense, if they are made universally known and accessible in a common arena of discourse, may influence others, stimulate new perceptions in them, and cause them to raise further demands that, for one reason or another, have not arisen before, or have been prevented from arising. A community that communicates with itself, engages in common discourse, that settles on universals as well as gives rise to difference and diversity, is necessary to proliferate and deepen, to reach more subtle forms of, development and emancipation.

III. Capitalism and Diversity

In writing against censorship of the press in 1843, Marx complains,

> You admire the delightful variety, the inexhaustible riches of nature. You do not demand that the rose should smell like the violet, but must the greatest riches of all, the spirit, exist in only one variety? I am humorous, but the law bids me write seriously. I am audacious, but the law commands that my style be modest. Grey, all grey, is the sole, the rightful color of freedom. Every drop of dew on which the sun shines glistens with an inexhaustible play of colors, but the spiritual sun, however many the persons and whatever the objects in which it is refracted, must produce only the official color.[63]

Marx argues for the wealth of difference and diversity in a similar fashion throughout his life. He thinks, however, that various aspects of capitalist society work in fundamental ways against such difference, diversity, and pluralism. One of his most powerful and continuous attacks against capitalism, made over and over again in different guises, is his attack on its reduction of human reality to abstraction, to sameness, its suppression of the concreteness, the specific and multifarious qualities, of individuals. In the *Economic and Philosophic Manuscripts,* he complains that capitalism reduces the individual to a mere abstract worker,[64] a theme we will see again in the later writings. Capitalist estrangement also produces a "bestial barbarisation, a complete, crude, abstract, simplicity of need. . . ." "For the starving man, it is not the human form of food that exists, but only its abstract existence as food. It could just as well be there in its crudest form. . . ."[65] In attacking utilitarianism in the *German Ideology,* Marx argues in a similar vein. He speaks of the

> absurdity of merging all the manifold relationships of people in the one relation of usefulness, this apparently metaphysical abstraction arises from the fact that in modern bourgeois society all relations are subordinated in practice to the one abstract monetary-commercial relation . . . Hence the actual relations that are presupposed here are speech, love, definite manifestations of definite qualities of individuals. Now their relations are supposed not to have the meaning peculiar to them but to be the expression and manifestation of some third relation attributed to them, the relation of utility or utilization.[66]

Again we find the same sort of argument in 1853. During this period, it is true, Marx had veered toward an extreme form of determinism, a determinism that caused him even to reject the concept of a free will. But leaving that aside, what we want to see here is that he argues in the same vein as above, this time, against the theory of punishment found in Kant and Hegel: "Is it not a delusion to substitute for the individual with his real motives, with multifarious social circumstances pressing upon him, the abstraction of 'free-will'—one among many qualities of man for man himself!"[67]

And most importantly, Marx makes the same sort of argument with regard to the labor involved in producing exchange value, "digging gold, mining iron, cultivating wheat and weaving silk are qualitatively different kinds of labour. In fact, what appears objectively as diversity of the use-values, appears, when looked at dynamically, as diversity of the activities which produce those use-values . . . But as exchange-values they represent the same homogeneous labour, i.e., labour in which the individual characteristics of the workers are obliterated. Labour which creates exchange-value is thus abstract general labour."[68] Concrete, specific, different forms of labor, and thus the expression, the objectification, of different activities, different powers and capacities, different lives, are equated with and are viewed only as undifferentiated, abstract, identical labor. Difference is suppressed. Moreover, this will carry over to the rest of the social, political, and cultural world. In exchange, "persons exist for one another merely as representatives of, and therefore, as owners of, commodities. In the course of our investigation we shall find, in general, that the characters who appear on the economic stage are but the personification of the economic relations that exist between them."[69]

Commentators often interpret this passage as if Marx were merely making a methodological decision to reduce persons, in the writing of *Capital,* to personifications of economic relations; and, at times, they criticize him for doing so. Marx, of course, *is* doing this, but he does it, we should now be able to see from the passages previously quoted, because in capitalist society this in fact is the way persons appear; and it should be clear that Marx finds this deeply *objectionable*. Social relations between persons are reduced in the eyes of these persons to the abstract and fetishized form of a relation between things—a relation between their products.[70] And it is certainly Marx's goal to end fetishism.

Moreover, this abstraction from concrete differences even extends to rights. In a passage from the "Critique of the Gotha Program," Marx says,

> Right by its nature can exist only as the application of an equal standard; but unequal individuals (and they would not be different individuals if they were not unequal) are measurable by an equal standard only insofar as they are made subject to an equal criterion, are taken from a certain side only, for instance, in the present case, are regarded only as workers and nothing more is seen in them, everything else being ignored. Besides, one worker is married, another not; one has more children than another, etc., etc. Thus, given an equal amount of work done, and hence an equal share in the social consumption fund, one will in fact receive more than another, one will be richer than another, etc.[71]

One of the reasons that Marx is skeptical about rights is that he thinks individuals ought to be treated as concrete, specific, different, human beings with different and diverse needs. And thus instead of equal rights, the principle ought to be "to each according to his needs!"[72] Liberals tend to think of the abstract character of rights as a strength. Differences do not count. We abstract from, ignore, the race, creed, sex, wealth, and power of individuals. These things are irrelevant. We treat individuals as abstractly equal bearers of certain rights.

This is fine in that it prevents people from being treated worse than rights would demand. But at the same time it is reductive. It ignores the specific and different needs of concrete, particular individuals. Rights are reductive, limiting, and constraining. Marx, in the ideal society, does not want such "individual 'moral constraints.'" He wants to "emancipate the 'morals' of the individual from its class constraints."[73]

Marx wants social relations to be human relations, relations between persons. In production, I should have "the direct enjoyment . . . of being conscious of having satisfied a human need by my work. . . ." Thus, I "would become recognized and felt by you yourself as a completion of your own essential nature and as a necessary part of yourself, and consequently would know myself to be confirmed both in your thought and your love."[74]

In Marx's opinion, modern liberal society, especially England, is not as diverse, pluralistic, or individualistic as it might seem. He says,

> "Eccentricity" or "individuality" are the marks of insular John Bull in the minds of continentals. On the whole, this notion confuses the Englishman of the past with the Englishman of the present. Intense class development, extreme division of labour and what is called "public opinion," manipulated by the Brahmins of the press, have, on the contrary, produced a monotony of character that would make it impossible for a Shakespeare, for example, to recognize his own countrymen. The differences no longer belong to the individuals but to their "profession" and class. Apart from his profession, in everyday life one "respectable" Englishman is so like another that even Leibniz could hardly discover a difference, a *differentia specifica,* between them.[75]

What this quotation suggests is that in capitalist society there are very undesirable forms of pluralism and difference. The development of the division of labor does produce differences in occupations, skills, powers and capacities, outlooks, and so forth, but at the same time it locks the individual into a very narrow, one-sided development. It eliminates richness and diversity within given groups of individuals, produces monotony within classes and professions; and, without community, it isolates and closes these groups off from other individuals, from the complexity, difference, and diversity of others. Individuals have little or no access to the wealth and diversity of culture.

As Engels put it in a passage quoted at length above, the division of labor produces individuals "assigned to a single branch of production, shackled to it, exploited by it, each having developed only one of his abilities at the cost of all others. . . ."⁷⁶ Marx argues that in the division of labor "man's own deed becomes an alien power opposed to him, which enslaves him instead of being controlled by him. For as soon as the division of labour comes into being, each man has a particular, exclusive sphere of activity, which is forced upon him and from which he cannot escape. He is a hunter, a fisherman, a shepherd, or a critical critic, and must remain so if he does not want to lose his means of livelihood. . . ."⁷⁷ Marx also says, "If the circumstances in which the individual lives allow him only the one-sided development of one quality at the expense of all the rest, if they give him the material and time to develop only that one quality, then this individual achieves only a one-sided, crippled development . . . And the manner in which this one, pre-eminently favoured quality develops depends again, on the one hand, on the material available for its development and, on the other hand, on the degree and manner in which the other qualities are suppressed."⁷⁸ This extends even to the development of talents, even artistic talents: "The exclusive concentration of artistic talent in particular individuals, and its suppression in the broad mass which is bound up with this, is a consequence of the division of labour . . . the subordination of the artist to local and national narrowness, which arises entirely from division of labour, and also the subordination of the individual to some definite art, making him exclusively a painter, sculptor, etc.; the very name amply expressing the narrowness of his professional development and his dependence on division of labor."⁷⁹

Marx's solution to this undesirable form of pluralism and difference caused by division of labor is exchangeability of function. "In communist society, where nobody has one exclusive sphere of activity but each can become accomplished in any branch he wishes, society regulates the general production and thus makes it possible for me to do one thing today and another tomorrow, to hunt in the morning, fish in the afternoon, rear cattle in the evening, criticise after dinner, just as I have a mind, without ever becoming hunter, fisherman, shepherd or critic."⁸⁰

In other words, not the division of labor itself, but its crippling effects, are overcome. There will still be different occupations and different branches of industry; tasks in the factory will still be divided up; and thus the difference and diversity that arise from division of labor will still be present. But individuals will not specialize; they will not be locked into one narrow and crippling task. They will move around and develop a range of different abilities.

Some commentators argue that Marx abandons this rather utopian model of exchangeability of function after the *German Ideology*. But this is not true. He merely describes it in less fanciful language. In the *Poverty of Philosophy* Marx quotes Andrew Ure, who says that as the individual worker "transfers his services from one machine to another, he varies his task, and enlarges his views, by thinking on those general combinations which result from his and his companions' labours. Thus, that cramping of the faculties, that narrowing of the mind, that stunting of the frame, which were ascribed and not unjustly . . . to the division of labour, cannot, in common circumstances, occur under the equable distribution of industry."[81] Marx himself goes on to say that as labor loses its specialized character, "the need for universality, the tendency towards an integral development of the individual begins to be felt. The automatic workshop wipes out specialists and craft-idiocy."[82]

Even in *Capital* Marx says, "Modern Industry, indeed, compels society, under penalty of death, to replace the detail-worker of to-day, crippled by life-long repetition of one and the same trivial operation, and thus reduced to the mere fragment of a man, by the fully developed individual, fit for a variety of labours, ready to face any change of production, and to whom the different social functions he performs, are but so many modes of giving free scope to his own natural and acquired powers."[83] He also says in a footnote,

> A French workman, on his return from San-Francisco, writes as follows: "I never could have believed, that I was capable of working at the various occupations I was employed on in California. I was firmly convinced that I was fit for nothing but letter-press printing . . . Once in the midst of this world of adventurers, who change their occupation as often as they do their shirt, egad, I did as the others. As mining did not turn out remunerative enough, I left it for the town, where in succession I became typographer, slater, plumber, &c. In consequence of thus finding out that I am fit for any sort of work, I feel less of a mollusk and more of a man."[84]

The goal of communist society will be to eliminate specialization in the division of labor and the resulting narrowness it produces. It will provide the material means so that "anyone in whom there is a potential Raphael should be able to develop without hindrance."[85] And also, in "communist society there [will be] no painters but only people who engage in painting among other activities."[86]

These last two quotations, if taken together, indicate that Marx's ideal individual is not, as it might seem, the mere dilettante—the individual who is not a painter but merely dabbles in painting among other activities. The goal, at the same time, is to see to it that anyone in whom there is a potential Raphael should be able to develop without hindrance. The goal, clearly, is not the dilettante but the all-round individual, truly accomplished in a variety of activities.[87] The goal is an individual who requires a complex, differentiated, and pluralistic community with full access to differences and diversity, so that the individual can appropriate a wide range of this diversity and achieve the highest possible development of powers and capacities. Yet, as we said earlier, such all-round individuals will not all be of the same mold. Given the complexity of culture, they will be different and certainly richer than those individuals locked into narrow specializations in the division of labor.

Moreover, in the following passage, Marx suggests that even individuals who are not potential Raphaels can accomplish important things in societies that, even though not ideal communities, are at least more open and less constrained by rigid forms of class structure and division of labor. Marx speaks of Abraham Lincoln:

> This plebeian, who worked his way up from stone-breaker to Senator in Illinois, without intellectual brilliance, without a particularly outstanding character, without exceptional importance—an average person of good will, was placed at the top by the interplay of the forces of universal suffrage unaware of the great issues at stake. The new world has never achieved a greater triumph than by this demonstration that, given its political and social organization, ordinary people of good will can accomplish feats which only heroes could accomplish in the old world![88]

IV. Ethnocentrism

But the crippling narrowness arising from specialization and division of labor, however, is not the whole story with respect to the bourgeoisie. The bourgeoisie does, in fact, produce a good deal of access to a richer and more complex world. For example, Marx says, "The bourgeoisie has through its exploitation of the world market given a cosmopolitan character to production and consumption in every country."[89] This, however, is a mixed blessing. While it works against isolation, against being locked into a crippling narrowness, it also eliminates cultural diversity and it is forced upon others.

Marx and Pluralism   271

> In place of the old local and national seclusion and self-sufficiency, we have intercourse in every direction, universal inter-dependence of nations. And as in material, so also in intellectual production. The intellectual creations of individual nations become common property. National one-sidedness and narrow-mindedness become more and more impossible, and from the numerous national and local literatures, there arises a world literature.
>
> The bourgeoisie, by the rapid improvement of all instruments of production, by the immensely facilitated means of communication, draws all, even the most barbarian, nations into civilization. The cheap prices of its commodities are the heavy artillery with which it batters down all Chinese walls, with which it forces the barbarians' intensely obstinate hatred of foreigners to capitulate. It compels all nations, on pain of extinction, to adopt the bourgeois mode of production, it compels them to introduce what it calls civilization into their midst, i.e., to become bourgeois themselves. In one word, it creates a world after its own image.
>
> The bourgeoisie has subjected the country to the rule of the towns. It has created enormous cities, has greatly increased the urban population as compared with the rural, and has thus rescued a considerable part of the population from the idiocy of rural life. Just as it has made the country dependent on the towns, so it has made barbarian and semi-barbarian countries dependent on the civilized ones, nations of peasants on nations of bourgeois, the East on the West.[90]

Marx's views on such matters are complex, and we will have to examine them in detail. He is clearly opposed to illegitimate force, as we have seen above in his opposition to the way division of labor and specialization force narrowness on individuals and as we can also see here in his opposition to the bourgeoisie forcing "*what it calls* civilization" or "the bourgeois mode of production" on other nations, its forcing them "to become bourgeois themselves." But, at the same time, forced or not, he is clearly in favor of access to a rich and complex cultural world and opposed to cultural narrowness. We will have to see if Marx can extricate himself from this contradiction between the desirability of access to complexity and the undesirability of having it forced upon oneself.

Let us consider another but similar case. In a report of one of Marx's speeches in which he addresses the question of whether education should be local or national, Marx argues, "The fault of the American system was that it was too much localized, the education given depended upon the state of culture prevailing in each district. There was a cry for central supervision."[91] Here, Marx is opposed to local narrowness. Nevertheless, at the same time, he opposes the imposition of educational content or values by the central government.

> Education might be national without being governmental. Government might appoint inspectors whose duty it was to see that the laws were obeyed, just as the factory inspectors looked after the observance of the factory acts, without any power of interfering with the course of education itself . . . Nothing could be introduced either in primary or higher schools that admitted of party and class interpretation. Only subjects such as the physical sciences, grammar, etc., were fit matter for schools. The rules of grammar, for instance, could not differ, whether explained by a religious Tory or a free thinker. Subjects that admitted of different conclusions must be excluded and left for the adults to such teachers as Mrs. Law, who gave instruction in religion.[92]

What Marx is endorsing here is more or less what now exists, or what is thought by many to exist, in schools in the United States. For Marx, governmental inspection is necessary to overcome local narrowness, but the government must not dictate content or values. Marx, it would seem, wants a core education of neutral, nonideological subjects that would make a common, complex culture accessible to all. But at the same time he does not want to destroy local culture—Marx will even accept the teaching of religion on the side. This, I think it is fair to say, is an accurate description of what Marx's intends, and many would find it acceptable. It even seems to be a reasonable solution to the contradiction between his opposition to force and his desire for access to a complex culture. But is it really? The government, in requiring neutral subjects, in Marx's view (and many others would agree with him), does not impose ideology. But in a deeper sense, some would certainly argue, it really does. It imposes *Western science* and, presumably, *English* grammar. These subjects would be imposed upon a local community that, for example, might want education carried out in its own, different, language and would prefer, say, religious instruction to Western science. Marx is no doubt blind to the ethnocentrism that some would argue exists here. One might try to excuse him by arguing that he was well intentioned. Given his understanding of ideology, an understanding many others would share with him even today, he opposes ideology and wants to preserve local culture, again, at least as he understands local culture. Nevertheless, whatever we decide about this example, it is quite clear that elsewhere Marx's views do not even approach being as acceptable as one might try to argue they are here.

Marx and Pluralism 273

For example, in "On the Jewish Question," an early article of 1843, Marx opposed the views of Bruno Bauer, who argued that to achieve civil emancipation, Jews should renounce Judaism and the rest of humankind religion.[93] Marx rejects Bauer's notion that religion is the cause of secular narrowness—rather it is merely the manifestation of it—and, thus, Marx rejects the notion that Jews must renounce Judaism. But he holds instead that if human emancipation is achieved, Judaism, as well as all other religions, will disappear by themselves.[94] Here, Marx seems to think it desirable that different religions, and perhaps even different cultures, disappear. He seems to favor a common culture rather than a plurality of different cultures. In the *German Ideology,* he even says that "nationally evolved differences within the species, such as racial differences, etc., . . . can and must be abolished in the course of historical development."[95] Moreover, and very unfortunately, Marx at times has some ugly and anti-Semitic things to say about Jews and at times he makes racist remarks about blacks.[96]

But perhaps his ethnocentrism is most glaring in his infamous discussion of British rule in India. Marx writes, "England, it is true, in causing a social revolution in Hindostan, was actuated only by the vilest interests, and was stupid in her manner of enforcing them. But that is not the question. The question is, can mankind fulfil its destiny without a fundamental revolution in the social estate of Asia? If not, whatever may have been the crimes of England she was the unconscious tool of history in bringing about that revolution."[97] In another article, he defends British rule in India on the grounds that:

> The bourgeois period of history has to create the material basis of the new world—on the one hand universal intercourse founded upon the mutual dependency of mankind, and the means of that intercourse; on the other hand the development of the productive powers of man and the transformation of material production into a scientific domination of natural agencies. Bourgeois industry and commerce create these material conditions of a new world in the same way as geological revolutions have created the surface of the earth. When a great social revolution shall have mastered the results of the bourgeois epoch, the market of the world and the modern powers of production, and subjected them to the common control of the most advanced peoples, then only will human progress cease to resemble that hideous, pagan idol, who would not drink the nectar but from the skulls of the slain.[98]

As ugly as these comments are, we must see that Marx's views, while they certainly are ethnocentric, are not ethnocentric in any simple, straightforward, or unambiguous way. His views are complex and even contradictory. He is torn between opposing commitments. At the same time that he defends the social revolution in India brought about by the British, he very clearly objects to the loss of an ancient culture and he condemns Britain for causing this. Beginning with the British East India Company, "England has broken down the entire framework of Indian society, without any symptoms of reconstitution yet appearing. This loss of his old world, with no gain of a new one, imparts a particular kind of melancholy to the present misery of the Hindoo, and separates Hindostan, ruled by Britain, from all its ancient traditions, and from the whole of its past history."[99] Marx calls it "sickening . . . to human feeling to witness those myriads of industrious patriarchal and inoffensive social organizations disorganized and dissolved into their units, thrown into a sea of woes, and their individual members losing at the same time their ancient form of civilization, and their hereditary means of subsistence. . . ."[100] Here in 1853, Marx seems to have shifted his views a bit. He no longer seems to think, as he seemed to in the "Jewish Question," that it is desirable that different cultures and religions simply disappear. Something important is lost if they do, and Marx finds this loss "sickening." Here ancient tradition and past history have a value; it would seem desirable that they be preserved.

Nevertheless, in the next breath, Marx moves in the opposite direction. He goes on to say,

> we must not forget that these idyllic village-communities, inoffensive though they may appear, had always been the foundation of Oriental despotism, that they restrained the mind within the smallest possible compass, making it the unresisting tool of superstition, enslaving it beneath traditional rules, depriving it of all grandeur, and historical energies . . . We must not forget that this undignified, stagnatory, and vegetative life, that this passive sort of existence evoked on the other part, in contradistinction, wild, aimless, unbounded forces of destruction and rendered murder itself a religious rite in Hindostan. We must not forget that these little communities were contaminated by distinctions of caste and by slavery, that they subjugated man to external circumstances instead of elevating man the sovereign of circumstances, that they transformed a self-developing social state into never changing natural destiny, and thus brought about a brutalizing worship of nature, exhibiting its degradation in the fact that man, the sovereign of nature, fell down on his knees in adoration of Kanuman, the monkey, and Sabbala, the cow.[101]

Very clearly this is ethnocentric and quite ugly. But ugly as it is, we must notice that less than a month later Marx qualifies his views on

Indian culture, even if he does not totally reverse them. He speaks of India, "whose gentle natives are, to use the expression of Prince Soltykov, even in the most inferior classes, '*plus fins et plus adroits que les Italiens* [more subtle and adroit than the Italians],' whose submission even is counterbalanced by a certain calm nobility, who, notwithstanding their natural languor, have astonished the British officers by their bravery, whose country has been the source of our languages, our religions. . . ."[102] At the same time, we can see in what has already been quoted that Marx very clearly objects to the British use of force—which was "actuated only by the vilest interests"; which Marx describes as a "crime"; and which he likens to "that hideous, pagan idol, who would not drink the nectar but from the skulls of the slain."[103] But then he moves back in the opposite direction. It is plain that Marx values the fact that the British will bring modern civilization to India. It will bring the electric telegraph, a free press, European science, and in general—in Marx's view—a superior civilization.[104]

But, again, Marx qualifies and almost reverses this view. He speaks of the time when "the Hindoos themselves shall have grown strong enough to throw off the British yoke altogether."[105] And fours years later, in 1857, he says, "We have given here but a brief and mildly-colored chapter from the real history of British rule in India. In view of such facts, dispassionate and thoughtful men may perhaps be led to ask whether a people are not justified in attempting to expel the foreign conquerors who have so abused their subjects. And if the English could do these things in cold blood, is it surprizing that the insurgent Hindoos should be guilty, in the fury of revolt and conflict, of the crimes and cruelties alleged against them."[106] Moreover, a month later, Marx defends the 1857 revolt of the Indian Sepoys against the British. And he says, "There is something in human history like retribution; and it is a rule of historical retribution that its instrument be forged not by the offended, but by the offender himself."[107]

Here, Marx casts the Indian Sepoys, the Indian soldiers trained by the British, in the same role as the European proletariat, that weapon forged by the bourgeoisie itself for its own destruction, "What the bourgeoisie, therefore, produces, above all, is its own grave-diggers."[108] There is real tension, if not contradiction, in Marx's thought throughout these opposed passages. He supports and justifies the Indian attempt to throw the British out—he even likens the Indians to the European proletariat. But if the Indians succeed, what will happen to that wonderful Western civilization that they are supposed to get from the British? When it comes down to it, or at least at certain moments, Marx would side with the Indian attempt to resist illegitimate force, to throw out the British, rather than with Britain's attempt to introduce the complexity of Western civilization to India.

What we must see in all of this is that Marx is not simply supporting the British and Western civilization and opposing India and Indian culture. His views are mixed and complex. He both supports and opposes India and Indian culture. He both opposes and supports England and Western culture. And he is not very consistent in doing any of this.[109]

In his discussion of the role of Britain in India, Marx is not saying simply that one side represents a principle of good and the other of evil. Rather, he finds a complex, confused, and tragic mixture of the two. The rhetorical model that Marx employs in these cases is one in which good emerges out of evil. We find this same rhetorical model elsewhere also. In *Capital,* Marx writes,

> It was not, however, the misuse of parental authority that created the capitalistic exploitation, whether direct or indirect, of children's labour; but, on the contrary, it was the capitalistic mode of exploitation which, by sweeping away the economic basis of parental authority, made its exercise degenerate into a mischievous misuse of power. However terrible and disgusting the dissolution, under the capitalist system, of the old family ties may appear, nevertheless, modern industry, by assigning as it does an important part of the process of production, outside the domestic sphere, to women, to young persons, and to children of both sexes, creates a new economic foundation for a higher form of the family and of the relations between the sexes. It is, of course just as absurd to hold the Teutonic-Christian form of the family to be absolute and final as it would be to apply that character to the ancient Roman, the ancient Greek, or the Eastern forms which, moreover, taken together form a series in historical development. Moreover, it is obvious that the fact of the collective working group being composed of individuals of both sexes and all ages, must necessarily, under suitable conditions, become a source of humane development; although in its spontaneously developed, brutal, capitalistic form, where the labourer exists for the process of production, and not the process of production for the labourer, that fact is a pestiferous source of corruption and slavery.[110]

Marx is morally denouncing what capitalism has done to the family. Yet at the same time, he thinks that capitalism is laying the foundation for a higher and more humane form of the family. It is clear, however, that this particular example does not involve the imposition of the values of one culture upon another as it did in Marx's discussion of India and China.

Marx and Pluralism 277

Despite the mixed, ambiguous, contradictory, and qualified character of what Marx says about India, there is a strong and uneliminable strain of ethnocentrism there that is certainly at odds with the principles of the International Working Men's Association that Marx himself wrote, namely, the acknowledgement of "truth, justice, and morality, as the basis of . . . conduct . . . toward all men, without regard to colour, creed, or nationality."[111]

However, we should note in passing that it is possible that Marx overstated his real views in his article on British rule in India. In a letter to Engels, he tells us that the *New York Tribune,* for which the article was written, had been supporting the American economist Henry Carey, who was known for his arguments against centralization, which, as Marx puts it, Carey

> in turn blamed on England, who has made herself the workshop of the world and has forced all other countries to revert to brutish agriculture divorced from manufacturing. In its turn, responsibility for England's sins is laid on the theory of Ricardo-Malthus, and especially Ricardo's theory of rent. The necessary consequence of both Ricardo's theory and of industrial production would be communism. And to obviate all this, to counter centralization with localisation and the union,—a union scattered throughout the land—of factory and farm, our Ultra-Free-Trader finally recommends—protective tariffs. To obviate the effects of bourgeois industry . . . his recourse, as a genuine Yankee, is to speed up the process in America itself by artificial means. For the rest, his opposition to England drives him into Sismondian praise of the petty bourgeoisie in Switzerland, Germany, China, etc. And this is the chap who used to deride France for her resemblance to China.[112]

Marx, here and elsewhere, was very much opposed to Carey's views for various reasons. Thus he tells Engels, "Your article on Switzerland was, of course, a direct swipe at the Tribune's 'Leaders' (anti-centralization, etc.) and their man Carey. I continued this clandestine campaign in my first article on India, in which England's destruction of native industries is described as revolutionary. This they will find very shocking. Incidentally the whole administration of India by the British was detestable and still remains so today."[113] This suggests that perhaps Marx does not really find England's role in India to be as "revolutionary," as desirable, as he earlier suggested. Nevertheless, Marx does not withdraw what he said in the articles on British rule in India, and in this letter he goes on to tell Engels that "however much the English may have Irelandised the country [India], the breaking up of the archetypal forms was the *conditio sine qua non* for Europeanization."[114]

I do not want to excuse Marx's ethnocentrism or even to water it down. It is ugly and we must reject it. But I do want to be clear about the degree of his ethnocentrism. I very much hesitate to try to explain it as the view of his nation and his age, but, in fact, it was the view of his nation and age. This is not to explain it away. As I have said, it is unacceptable and we must reject it. But Marx, at times, is singled out as holding an especially pernicious version of a typical nineteenth-century European notion of the superiority of modern Western civilization and the view that it should be imposed on others. This, I do not think, is very accurate. If we compare Marx's views to those of John Stuart Mill, who was in the employ of the East India Company for thirty-five years and who, nevertheless, is generally considered by modern liberals to be far ahead of Marx as a champion of liberty and toleration, we can see how progressive, how ahead of his time, Marx in fact was. In *On Liberty,* Mill writes,

> The object of this essay is to assert one very simple principle, as entitled to govern absolutely the dealings of society with the individual in the way of compulsion and control . . . That principle is that the sole end for which mankind are warranted, individually or collectively, in interfering with the liberty of action of any of their number is self-protection. That the only purpose for which power can be rightfully exercised over any member of a civilized community, against his will, is to prevent harm to others . . . It is perhaps hardly necessary to say that this doctrine is meant to apply only to human beings in the maturity of their faculties. We are not speaking of children or of young persons below the age which the law may fix as that of manhood or womanhood . . . For the same reason we may leave out of consideration those backward states of society in which the race itself may be considered as in its nonage . . . Despotism is a legitimate mode of government in dealing with barbarians, provided the end be their improvement and the means justified by actually effecting that end. Liberty, as a principle, has no application to any state of things anterior to the time when mankind have become capable of being improved by free and equal discussion. Until then, there is nothing for them but implicit obedience to an Akbar or a Charlemagne, if they are so fortunate as to find one.[115]

Compare Mill's straightforward and unhesitating endorsement of ethnocentrism, paternalism, despotism, and imperialism to Marx's hedged, ambiguous, and contradictory approach to the same issues, which—while not acceptable and which should be condemned—nevertheless, is far in advance of Mill.[116]

V. Ethnocentrism and Historical Materialism

I would like to argue that we can reject Marx's ethnocentrism without this requiring us to reject any of the other fundamental elements of his thought. There is nothing about the basic principles of Marx's thought that requires us to accept the imposition of one culture upon another. It is central to Marx's thought that we work for the development of a complex culture. But all the members of such a culture need do to remain consistent with the basic principles of Marx's thought is to make that complex culture—its science, technology, knowledge, and so forth—accessible to others if those others knowingly choose it and willingly accept it. But if they reject it in whole or in part, it is perfectly legitimate for them to do so.

However, this has not been the view of all. Marx's historical materialist philosophy of history has often been criticized for being ethnocentric. Jon Elster, for example, suggests that it has become a "conceptual straight-jacket for the study of much non-western history."[117] Marshall Sahlins, in his book, *Culture and Practical Reason*,[118] as well as critics like Baudrillard, Balbus, and Aronowitz, have argued that Marx develops a single, necessary historical pattern, worked up on the basis of the historical development of Western societies, which is then conceptually imposed on all societies, including non-Western ones. Also, it is claimed that this pattern of historical development proceeds from "lower," more "primitive" stages to "higher," more "civilized" ones and culminates in modern Western capitalist societies as the highest stage before socialism.

Furthermore, Marx's productivism, especially, has been criticized along these lines. The term "productivism" is shorthand for the claim that material conditions, economic conditions, or the forces and relations of production are the factors that predominate in determining all aspects of a sociocultural world. These critics argue that the productivist claim is true, at best, only for modern societies.[119] It is certainly not true, as some of these critics think Marx holds it is, for earlier or "primitive" societies. In the latter societies, as Sahlins puts it, cultural modes of symbolization predominate and no symbolic scheme is the only one possible given a specific set of material conditions.[120]

If these claims about Marx were true, then ethnocentrism and Western conceptual imperialism would be built into the very structure, the basic principles, of his thought. I do not wish to argue that Marx's thought is *completely* free of ethnocentrism. That is probably impossible for anyone. In studying differences between our own culture and that of others, it is, after all, *we* who conceptualize our own culture, the other culture, as well as the differences; and we do this with whatever conceptual apparatus we have available to *us*. But besides this sense in which anyone is liable to ethnocentrism, Marx was not free of ethnocentrism in far more specific ways—as we have just seen in his discussion of India. And one could easily list other examples. Nevertheless, I hope to show that his thought is not ethnocentric or imperialist in the deeper, structural ways suggested above by his critics.[121]

To understand Marx's views, we must dig in and examine the method that he develops in the 1857 Introduction to the *Grundrisse* and that guides his mature thought. I have described this method at length in two other works, in *Marx' Method, Epistemology, and Humanism* and in *Marx and Ethics*.[122] Let me give only the briefest sketch of it here.

Marx's method does not begin with an empirical and historical study of a given society, but with abstract categories gotten by analysis. It begins by isolating through comparison and analysis certain abstract and general categories common to all, or almost all, epochs of production. However, these common categories or characteristics are determined differently in different epochs. The point is certainly not to focus on these common characteristics as abstract laws independent of history or running throughout history in the same way. The point is to see how these general characteristics are determined differently in specific epochs. The point is to distinguish the specific from the general, so as to more clearly isolate *differences*. For example, Marx says that "all production is appropriation of nature on the part of an individual within and through a specific form of society." But in one epoch this appropriation can take the form of communal property and in another the form of private property. Furthermore, the development of a specific epoch is determined not by those characteristics which are common to all but by those which are specific to the particular epoch in question.[123]

These general categories that are determined differently in different historical epochs undergo transformation as they develop historically. In each epoch, Marx argues, a particular form of production predominates. It assigns rank and influence to all the other elements. It is "a general light tingeing all other colours and modifying them in their specific quality." Each category, as it were, is stamped and molded by the particular structure of the period in which it exists because the economic reality which the category expresses has been transformed in each period. The context of interconnected relations is changed by the development that the particular form of production undergoes, and thus the categories must change and develop in order to be able to express these changed relations.[124]

What Marx calls the "correct scientific method" must begin with these abstract categories that have been developed to express modern capitalist society. The method takes up these general categories, works out in the abstract the relationships that exist between them in modern society, and only then works back toward an understanding of the actual concrete world. It can then grasp the concrete as a "rich totality of many determinations and relations." The concrete, for Marx, is the organized and articulated concentration of many determinations and relations—it is not given at the start *for thought*, but is the outcome of a process of comparison, analysis, and investigation. Marx admits that the actual concrete is the starting point for real historical development as well as for observation, but we can grasp the concrete at the start only as a vague and chaotic conception. For science, the concrete for thought must be constructed through comparison and analysis. Only then do we replace the original chaotic conception with a clear and scientific understanding of the concrete.[125]

In some cases, it is not even possible to grasp a category earlier in history. For example, Marx points to Aristotle, who argued that exchange " 'cannot take place without equality, and equality not without commensurability' . . . Here, however, [Aristotle] comes to a stop, and gives up the further analysis of the form of value." For Aristotle, it was impossible that " '. . . unlike things can be commensurable'—i.e., qualitatively equal. Such an equalization can only be something foreign to their real nature." Aristotle was unable to grasp the category of value; that is, to see that different commodities can be equal to each other in value if they both required equal amounts of labor time for their production, because Greek society was founded on slavery. Human equality and thus the equality of labor had not acquired the fixity of a popular prejudice.[126]

Thus, the correct scientific method must be able to start with abstract categories, work out the interconnections between them, and thereby come to understand modern society. In doing so the method will also (as we see in Marx's discussion of Aristotle's attempt to understand the concept of value) be able to understand past societies through comparison, in a way that they may not be able to be understood without that comparison.

An understanding of categories and their interconnection in modern society is necessary in the way that for some contemporary philosophers of science a paradigm is necessary before it becomes possible to study empirically the phenomena under consideration. Moreover, this paradigm or articulated structure of categories makes it possible to understand and illuminate the specific determinations of categories in earlier societies. One can see differences—one can see what is missing (as in the case of Aristotle) or one can identify elements that have been modified, transformed, or developed.

For many years, one passage in the 1857 Introduction was quite obscure to me. Marx first says,

> Since bourgeois society is, moreover, only a contradictory form of development, it contains relations of earlier forms of society often only in very stunted shape or as mere travesties, e.g. communal property. Thus, if it is true that the categories of bourgeois economy are valid for all other forms of society, this has to be taken *cum grano salis,* for they may contain them in a developed, stunted, caricatured, etc., form, always with substantial differences.

This is all fairly clear from what we have seen already, but then Marx goes on to say,

> What is called historical development rests, in general, on the fact that the latest form regards the earlier ones as stages leading towards itself and always conceives them in a one-sided manner, since only rarely, and under quite definite conditions, is it capable of self-criticism (this of course does not apply to historical periods which regard themselves as times of decline). It was not until its self-criticism was to a certain extent prepared, as it were *dynamei,* that the Christian religion was able to contribute to an objective understanding of earlier mythologies. Similarly, it was not until the self-criticism of bourgeois society had begun that bourgeois [political] economy came to understand the feudal, ancient and oriental economies. In so far as bourgeois economy did not simply identify itself with the earlier economies in a mythological manner, its criticism of them—especially of the feudal economy, against which it still had to wage a direct struggle—resembled the criticism that Christianity directed against heathenism, or which Protestantism directed against Catholicism.[127]

Marx holds that the categories—worked up into a paradigm—that explain modern capitalist society will also help us understand past society, as we have seen most clearly perhaps in the case of Aristotle's attempt to understand the category of value. However, Marx is now suggesting that there is an inadequate and unacceptable way of understanding past society, a teleological way, a way that sees all past societies as leading teleologically to one's own society. And Marx suggests that only rarely and under certain conditions is a society able to avoid this inadequate, teleological, ethnocentric approach. The society must have become self-critical. What this seems to mean is that one no longer assumes in ethnocentric and teleological fashion that past societies are mere stages leading to one's own society, but that nevertheless one can still use the categories—worked up into a paradigm— that explain one's own society to understand past society, whose categories have been carried along and preserved in modern society though in developed, stunted, or caricatured form. The paradigm that explains modern society can also be used to sort out these past categories. The question here is how do we understand these special and rare conditions that allow a culture to become self-critical, to cease being ethnocentric and teleological, and that thus allow it to use its categories to understand past society in an acceptable way. What kind of development is it that makes all this possible?

Althusser, for his part, thinks that all of this is an objectionable Hegelian holdover in Marx's thought:

> in order that the retrospection of the self-consciousness of a present should cease to be subjective, this present must be capable of self-criticism, in order to attain the *science of itself* . . . Why was this self-criticism possible at this point? The logic of this essentially Hegelian interpretation tempts one to answer: they attained science itself in the consciousness of their present because this consciousness was, as a consciousness, *its own self-criticism* . . . But this present has a name: it is the present of *absolute knowledge,* in which consciousness and science are one and the same, in which science exists in the immediate form of consciousness, and truth can be *read* openly in the phenomena. . . .[128]

I would suggest a very different reading of Marx's text. Fabian claims that science, "as T.S. Kuhn and many others seem to tell us, cannot be done critically, that is, reflexively *when* and *while* it is being done . . ." that is to say, I think, during the period Kuhn calls normal science, but rather "[c]ritique needs the extraordinary time of crisis. . . ."[129] In other words, to do any sort of scientific study requires a paradigm. And once a paradigm is achieved people begin doing normal science—articulating their paradigm, extending it, deepening it, and so forth. In normal science, one does not question the paradigm. It is not treated critically. It is accepted uncritically and simply developed. In history, once one has a paradigm that explains one's own world, whether it be modern capitalism, Christianity, Protestantism, or whatever, one looks to the past to see how one's world arose and developed; and, Marx would seem to be arguing, one does this none too critically. One's tendency is simply to assume in ethnocentric and teleological fashion that all earlier stages lead to oneself—at least this was what was often done in the past.

On the other hand, once your paradigm has been developed, and once it has gone through a period of normal science (extended, articulated, and deepened itself), it can begin to find anomalies. Difficulties can arise. It can be thrown into crisis. At this point science becomes self-reflexive and self-critical. The paradigm is open to question. There are competing paradigms. Normal science is not the only thing on the agenda. The paradigm itself has to be defended, examined, reflected upon; alternatives might even be considered. Bourgeois society was certainly going through this sort of period when Marx wrote. Indeed, his own writings were part of the cause of this crisis—which of course was more visible to Marx than to his opponents.[130]

In such a time of crisis, one *still* looks to the past to understand where one's own world came from and how it arose—that is just what one does, in Marx's view—but now one does this more critically. One does not assume in ethnocentric and teleological fashion that one's world is the inevitable realization of past history; after all one's very understanding of one's world, one's paradigm, one's identity, is in question. One can begin to criticize one's own world and begin to use the categories of one's own paradigm to understand the past more critically and carefully. One can begin to use this paradigm to compare and to see differences, see steps and stages, rather than recognize only similarities and assimilate the past to oneself.

We must also see that one *must* start with the categories of modern society. One *cannot* begin with the categories that express earlier forms of society and hope to trace their development to modern society. For example, if one studies the feudal period, one will discover that landed property predominates over other forms of production and that they are dependent upon it—it will also appear that only agricultural labor creates wealth. In capitalism, on the other hand, landed property and agriculture become subordinate forms of production. The relationship becomes inverted. Landed property becomes a branch of capital and industry, and, of course, we finally see that labor in general creates wealth. From the categories of a feudal economy, one will not be able to deduce the categories of a capitalist economy. Marx claims that rent, derived from landed property, "cannot be understood without capital, but capital can be understood without rent."[131] Marx also says that the historically earlier form of merchant's capital "is incapable by itself of promoting and explaining the transition from one mode of production to another. Within capitalist production merchant's capital is reduced from its former independent existence to a special phase in the investment of capital . . . The special conditions that take shape with the development of merchant's capital, are here no longer paramount. On the contrary, wherever merchant's capital still predominates we find backward conditions."[132]

I do not think that Marx is trying to impose a single, necessary, historical pattern on all Western societies, let alone on non-Western ones. There is, in Marx's discussion of method, an emphasis on common abstract categories worked up into a single paradigm that makes possible an empirical study of modern society and aids in the understanding of past societies; but the point of this is to allow comparison, to throw into relief *differences*, to illuminate historical changes, and to make it possible to begin to study these differences and changes empirically. As we saw in a passage already quoted above, the *same* economic basis can give rise to "infinite variations and gradations in appearance, which can be ascertained only by analysis of the empirically given circumstances."[133]

Moreover, in a letter of 1877 to the Editorial Board of "Otechestvenniye Zapiski," Marx rejects a critic's attempt to turn his "historical sketch of the genesis of capitalism in Western Europe" into a "historico-philosophic theory of the general path every people is fated to tread, whatever the historical circumstances in which it finds itself . . . But I beg his pardon. (He is both honouring and shaming me too much)." Marx even thinks that Russia might be able to avoid the development of capitalism.[134] Moreover, Marx goes on to give examples of "events strikingly analogous but taking place in different historical surroundings" that "led to totally different results. By studying each of these forms of evolution separately and then comparing them one can easily find the clue to this phenomenon, but one will never arrive there by using as one's master key a general historico-philosophical theory, the supreme virtue of which consists in being super-historical."[135]

On the other hand, four years earlier in the Afterword (of 1873) to the second German edition of *Capital*, Marx quotes a reviewer who characterizes his method as a search for the laws that regulate historical development and who says, among other things, that Marx seeks to "show by rigid scientific investigation, the *necessity of successive determinate orders of social conditions* . . . In a word, economic life offers us a phenomenon analogous to the history of evolution in other branches of biology."[136] Marx approves of the reviewer's description of his method, but it seems to me that his approval is qualified. Marx says, "Whilst the writer pictures what *he takes* to be *actually* my method, in this *striking* and as far as concerns my own application of it *generous* way, what else is he picturing but the dialectic method?"[137] This does not seem to me to imply acceptance of every detail of what the reviewer said.

Moreover, the reviewer also says that for Marx the general laws of economic life are not one and the same in every historical period, which is a view that Marx himself states elsewhere.[138] Laws change and each period has laws of its own. If whatever necessity we are going to discover will have to be derived from these laws, and these laws *change,* I cannot see how it is possible to arrive at the "necessity of successive determinate orders of social conditions." One might speak of necessity *within* a given epoch after its laws have been realized and established, but, if laws *change* in each epoch, then one cannot explain the necessity of historical development *from* epoch *to* epoch. We must take Marx's rejection of a "historico-philosophic theory of the path every people is fated to tread," in his letter of 1877, as more definitive of his views than the interpretation of the reviewer quoted four years earlier in *Capital.* Marx quotes the reviewer, but he only says that the reviewer's description is "striking" and "generous," which is not at all the same thing as saying that it is completely *accurate.*

Moreover, just as laws change, so do categories. It is clear that for Marx the categories that allow us to understand one historical epoch will not allow us to understand the following epoch. The categories that allow us to understand feudal society will not allow us to understand capitalist society, just as the category of merchant's capital will not allow us to understand later capitalism. From the earlier set of categories we cannot trace or deduce—we cannot explain the *necessity* of—the later set, because the later set will have been molded and transformed by a different form of production.[139]

It follows from this that Marx's method is not teleological. Marx himself rejects the notion that "the latest form regards the earlier ones as stages leading toward itself and always conceives them in a one-sided manner. . . ."[140] Marx's method is a backward-looking method. The paradigm made up of the abstract categories of the modern period will allow us to understand the past by comparison. Nevertheless, this is by no means to impose modern categories on the past. "Bourgeois economy thus provides a key to that of antiquity, etc. But by no means in the manner of those economists who obliterate all historical differences and see in all forms of society the bourgeois forms. One can understand tribute, tithe, etc., if one knows rent. But they must not be treated as identical."[141] The method that works out from a paradigm that grasps modern society can begin to understand the past because it it able to throw into relief *differences*.

Marx's method proceeds by situating itself in the epoch it wants to explain—modern capitalist society. It works the abstract categories that explain that period into a paradigm, which then makes empirical study of that period possible. It then looks to the past to try to understand how we got where we are, how what currently exists arose. This is a perfectly legitimate endeavor. It is simply part of understanding one's own society. But in doing so, one neither projects the categories of one's own society back onto earlier epochs nor does one see earlier epochs as leading teleologically toward one's own. Instead, one sorts out differences, discovers by analysis which developments must conceptually presuppose and which must follow upon other developments. Far from this being teleological, Marx even denies that one should "present the economic categories successively in the order in which they played the determining role in history." After all, what good would this do if it is impossible to deduce later categories from earlier ones. Marx certainly rejects a Hegelian approach to these matters. The way in which the method orders the categories is "simply the way in which thinking assimilates the concrete and reproduces it as a mental concrete. This is, however, by no means the process by which the concrete itself originates," as it was for Hegel.[142] Rather, the order in which the categories are presented will be determined by their relation to each other in modern society and the attempt to explain modern society.[143] Then one looks to the past to understand how we got where we are. Adamson, in commenting on these matters, says,

> Marx seems to be suggesting that there is no "logic" inherent in the totality of historical events themselves, no single and necessary pattern of historical development from primitive to "higher" forms of civilization. The only reason in history is the reason in historical writing. Of course, it remains possible to devise a series of stages of historical devel-

opment through which particular societies appear to have moved up to the present, and one may be able to offer some qualified kinds of generalizations on this basis. But all such analysis is radically dependent on one's present standpoint. Hints about man may be found in the ape only if man is already understood. It follows that as man comes to be understood differently, because of the continual reconstitution of the present, we may find new hints in the past and reshape our dialectical visions accordingly.[144]

For Marx, the past is being understood, interpreted, constructed, from a given perspective. It is quite clear that if this paradigm or perspective were changed, we would see the past differently. If, at some time in the future, in a different form of social organization than the one that now exists, or than existed at the time that Marx wrote, investigators were to work up a paradigm to explain their social organization and then were to look to the past to try to understand how they had gotten where they are, very different aspects of the past would be thrown into relief as significant factors that made possible that development. Their view of the past might look very different from our view, or Marx's view, of the past. It is also clear that many very different paradigms worked up at different points in the future would produce, construct, or interpret many very different pasts.

Furthermore, it is quite conceivable that, at any one point in history, different paradigms could be constructed to explain that point in history—different and competing paradigms to explain the economic order, or either different paradigms or adjustments of the same paradigms to explain other aspects of culture besides the economic (Marx himself either tells us or suggests that his method, besides applying to political economy, can apply to religion, mathematics, anthropology, natural science, and astronomy.[145] I have shown elsewhere how it applies to ethics.[146]) If there are competing paradigms, we could certainly argue about which of these paradigms are accurate or appropriate, but nevertheless, again, different aspects of the past would be thrown into relief by these different paradigms. As Adamson puts it, "Inasmuch as totalizations are always done from a particular present, there can be no 'final' totalization, nor is there any reason to suppose that there is only a single appropriate one at a given moment."[147] We shall return to the discussion of Marx's method—and draw our conclusions from it—shortly.

As I said earlier, it has been argued against Marx that productivism (the doctrine that economic conditions predominate in determining the rest of culture) holds at most for modern society, not for earlier societies, and certainly not for "primitive" ones. In the latter societies, cultural forms of symbolization predominate. It is simply a mistake to think that Marx would disagree with this—that he would hold that productivism predominates in all societies—as many of these critics hold that he does. For example, Marx is very clearly aware that in some "primitive" societies commodity exchange, even barter, did not exist. Barter, Marx argues, generally begins on the borders of the community and, as it does so, exchange value rather than use value comes to be the purpose of production. At this point barter begins to exert a disintegrating influence on the community.[148] And clearly, for Marx, before the rise of barter, before the disintegration of the community, the symbolic realm, the realm, for example, of tradition, values, and virtue, had more power than afterward. For Marx, traditional moral authority in earlier societies was capable even of shaping, limiting, and forbidding the direction of society by its sovereign.[149]

Even in the *Manifesto,* Marx says,

> The bourgeoisie, wherever it has got the upper hand, has put an end to all feudal, patriarchal, idyllic relations. It has pitilessly torn asunder the motley feudal ties that bound man to his "natural superiors," and has left remaining no other nexus between man and man than naked self-interest, than callous "cash payment." It has drowned the most heavenly ecstasies of religious fervour, of chivalrous enthusiasm, of philistine sentimentalism, in the icy water of egoistical calculation. It has resolved personal worth into exchange value, and in place of the numberless indefeasible chartered freedoms, has set up that single, unconscionable freedom—Free Trade. In one word, for exploitation, veiled by religious and political illusions, it has substituted naked, shameless, direct, brutal exploitation.[150]

It is clear in this passage that Marx is not a supporter of the values and ideology, the symbolic order, of feudalism, but, at the same time, that he is even less so of that of the bourgeoisie. Nevertheless, it is quite clear that before the bourgeoisie destroyed the symbolic order of feudalism, the feudal symbolic order did predominate. It shaped and molded culture so as to exclude "naked self-interest," "callous 'cash payment,' " "egotistical calculation," and "naked, shameless, direct, brutal exploitation"—in short, the characteristics of a society in which production comes to predominate. Moreover, in a footnote in Volume I of *Capital,* Marx says,

> In the estimation of that paper, my view that each special mode of production and the social relations corresponding to it, in short, that the ec-

onomic structure of society, is the real basis on which the juridical and political superstructure is raised, and to which definite social forms of thought correspond; that the mode of production determines the character of the social, political, and intellectual life generally, all this is very true for our own times, in which material interests preponderate, but not for the middle ages, in which Catholicism, nor for Athens and Rome, where politics, reigned supreme. In the first place it strikes one as an odd thing for any one to suppose that these well-worn phrases about the middle ages and the ancient world are unknown to anyone else. This much, however, is clear, that the middle ages could not live on Catholicism, nor the ancient world on politics. On the contrary, it is the mode in which they gained a livelihood that explains why here politics, and there Catholicism, played the chief part.[151]

Oddly enough, this passage is often quoted by critics in *support* of the claim that for Marx productivism, not the symbolic, predominates in all societies. They do not seem to notice that in the last sentence Marx *admits* that politics, in Athens and Rome, and Catholicism, in the Middle Ages, did *play the chief part*. He admits that the symbolic did predominate. Moreover, two sentences earlier Marx finds it surprising that anyone would think that he was not aware of this. But he also argues that material conditions explain why the symbolic realm played the chief part. Thus, while Marx holds that production does determine society, it certainly does not determine society in the same way in all historical periods and does not play the chief part in all of them.

Marshall Sahlins argues that all cultures must conform to material constraints, but that they will do so "according to a definite symbolic scheme which is never the only one possible." For Sahlins, practical activity and utilitarian interest do not constitute the grounding of culture.[152] One must certainly admit that Marx does not develop such views as far, or in as detailed a way, as Sahlins and other recent writers do, but what we must see is that Marx certainly agrees with such views:

> Thus, just as production based on capital produces universal industry, i.e., surplus labour, value-creating labour, on the one hand, so does it on the other produce a system of universal exploitation of natural and human qualities, a system of universal utility, whose bearer is science itself as much as all the physical and spiritual qualities, and under these conditions nothing appears as something higher-in-itself, as an end in itself, outside this circle of social production and exchange . . . *For the first time,* nature becomes purely an object for men, nothing more than a mat-

ter of utility. It ceases to be acknowledged as a power for itself, and even the theoretical cognition of its autonomous laws appears merely as a stratagem for its subjection to human needs, whether as object of consumption or as means of production. It is this same tendency which makes capital drive beyond national boundaries and prejudices and, equally, beyond nature worship, as well as beyond the traditional satisfaction of existing needs and the reproduction of old ways of life confined within long-established and complacently accepted limits. Capital is destructive towards, and constantly revolutionizes, all this, tearing down all barriers which impede the development of the productive forces, the extension of the range of needs, the differentiation of production, and the exploitation and exchange of all natural and spiritual powers.

But from the fact that capital posits every such limit as a barrier which it has *ideally* overcome, it does not at all follow that capital has *really* overcome it. . . .[153]

"Universal utility," a conceptual scheme in which nature is "nothing more than a matter of utility," arises *"for the first time"* under capitalism. It then becomes the case, *as it was not earlier,* that nothing "higher-in-itself," nothing "as an end in itself," nothing as a "power for itself," no traditional values or symbolic schemes, are acknowledged. They previously existed, but are destroyed by capitalism. Moreover, capital does not overcome these limits *"really,"* but only *"ideally."*

This is also what Marx argues in his discussion of Greek art in the Introduction to the *Grundrisse*. He admits that production did not predominate in ancient Greek society as it does in modern society. This allowed for Greek imagination, the symbolic, to predominate over, to be more powerful than, production. And this, in fact, is what made for the greatness of Greek art:

> As regards art, it is known that certain periods of its florescence by no means correspond to the general development of society, or, therefore, to the material basis, the skeleton as it were of its organization. For example, the Greeks compared with the Moderns, or else Shakespeare. It is even acknowledged that certain forms of art, e.g. epos, can no longer be produced in their epoch-making, classic form after artistic production as such has begun; in other words that certain important creations within the compass of art are only possible at an early stage of its development . . . We know that Greek mythology is not only the arsenal of Greek art, but also its basis. Is the conception of nature and of social relations which underlies Greek imagination and therefore Greek art possible in the age of Selfactors, railways, locomotives and electric telegraphs. What is Vul-

can compared with Roberts and Co., Jupiter compared with the lightening conductor, and Hermes compared with the Crédit Mobilier? All mythology subdues, dominates and fashions the forces of nature in the imagination and through the imagination; it therefore disappears when real domination over these forces is established. What becomes of Fama beside Printing House Square? Greek art presupposes Greek mythology, in other words, nature and even the social forms have already been worked up in an unconsciously artistic manner by the popular imagination.[154]

For Marx, this is not to *eliminate* the influence of production or material conditions in premodern societies. Even Sahlins admits that all cultures must conform to material constraints. Production and material conditions have an influence. If Greek art, mythology, and imagination work up the social forms in an unconsciously artistic manner, this will obviously be conditioned by the particular character of those social forms. One set of social forms would at least have to be approached and imaginatively worked up in a different way than another set. But nevertheless economic conditions do not predominate. Greek art by no means corresponds to the material basis of Greek society. Not production but mythology, the imagination, the symbolic, predominates. Moreover, Marx is clear that different mythologies, different symbolic systems, are possible in the same period; he compares Greek to Egyptian mythology in this same section.[155] With the rise of capitalism, however, the symbolic no longer predominates in the same way. Greek art and especially the epic become impossible. Production comes to predominate. Before this, the weakness of production allowed imagination in Greece, politics in Athens and Rome, and Catholicism in the Middle Ages to play the chief part.

Sahlins readily concedes the importance that Marx attributes to the symbolic in premodern societies. Sahlins recognizes the fact that for Marx the symbolic can play the chief part but argues that *ultimately* Marx transposes "the symbolic coordinates of social being into the consequence of that being." For Marx, the action of production "escapes a symbolic determination and dialectically overcomes it, to itself determine the symbolic system."[156] In other words, ultimately the symbolic system does not predominate over production for Marx; rather production predominates over and determines the symbolic, and it does so in *all* periods. Production predominates in premodern society, we can say, by *allowing* the symbolic to play the chief part. This is also the view of many of those who follow Althusser—while the economy is determinant in the last instance, it can very well determine the symbolic as dominant.

I do not think this view is correct here. It fails to understand the implications of the method that Marx developed in the 1857 Introduction to the *Grundrisse*. There it is clear that a given epoch cannot be studied until after the investigator has worked up a paradigm, a concrete for thought—a symbolic structure. It follows from this that the effect that economic or material conditions, the forces and relations of production, have on us can only be understood *after* we have that paradigm and *through* that very paradigm. Before we construct this paradigm, we only have a vague and chaotic conception of the concrete. Only after we have constructed this paradigm can we gain a clear and scientific understanding of the concrete. Moreover, if the paradigm, the perspective, were changed, so would our understanding of the effect that material conditions have on us be changed.

Marx's very method grants primacy to the symbolic, not just in premodern societies but in *all* historical periods. The symbolic, the paradigm, is a necessary prerequisite for understanding the effects of material conditions. Material conditions can only be understood within and through the symbolic. The symbolic then is primary and our understanding of material conditions is dependent upon the symbolic. Moreover, it just will not do to go on from here to insist that, nevertheless for Marx, it is, when all is said and done, economic conditions that *finally* determine our symbolic construction of the paradigm and thus that economic conditions *are* ultimately more fundamental than the symbolic. This cannot be Marx's position because, if we can only understand the effect of material conditions *after* we have the paradigm and *through* this very paradigm, it would be theoretically impossible to understand how material conditions determined the symbolic construction of the paradigm *before* we had the paradigm.[157]

Thus when Marx says that a low level of production allowed imagination in Greece, politics in Athens and Rome, and Catholicism in the Middle Ages to play the chief part, he is certainly asserting that production always plays a role in any society. Its symbolic scheme will always be affected by production. This will always be so, if only in the sense that different forms of production would have to be conceived differently, worked up differently, in order to be taken up into any given symbolic scheme. But Marx is not and cannot be dialectically reinserting the primacy of production over symbolic schemes by claiming that production allows, in the sense that it independently and fundamentally *determines*, the fact that the symbolic scheme plays the chief part (as, for example, Hindess and Hirst as well as Rey explicitly claim).[158] Marx cannot be doing this because it is clear that we can understand how production determines anything only after we have worked up a symbolic scheme or paradigm, and we can only understand how production determines anything within and through that very symbolic scheme or paradigm. The symbolic scheme always predominates for Marx. Without it we have no understanding but only a vague and chaotic conception.

Nevertheless, it must be admitted that Marx's *also* claims that production determines *all* aspects of society. And, in fact, that is what his very symbolic scheme, the paradigm itself, claims. How is this possible? Is this a contradiction? I do not think so. We must see that production determines, as it were, *within* the symbolic scheme. Production, we can even legitimately say, determines the symbolic scheme itself, but it does not do so from outside the scheme. It does not do so as an external infrastructure that produces a symbolic superstructure. Production determines the symbolic scheme only from *within* the scheme. What does this mean? It means that certain forms of production will be compatible with, allow for, can be worked up by, and can be taken into, certain symbolic schemes. Other forms of production, however, will not be compatible with, will not allow for, cannot be worked up by, and cannot be taken into, those same symbolic schemes. It also follows from this that as production develops it can eventually destroy a given symbolic scheme.

The symbolic scheme is very definitely primary, yet it can be affected, even destroyed, by the development of production, but only from *within* the symbolic scheme; when a given symbolic scheme is no longer able to infuse a given form of production with adequate meaning, allow us to understand it, when it can no longer provide the conceptual foundation for exerting some control over production, when production bursts the limitations of the symbolic scheme. We can even, in this sense, say that production is finally more powerful than—that it predominates over—the conceptual scheme, but again only from *within* the conceptual scheme, only in the sense that as production develops, the conceptual scheme becomes inadequate to it. Production becomes more powerful than—it predominates over—the conceptual scheme from *within* that scheme. As it does so, it requires us to develop a different conceptual scheme more adequate to understanding and controlling production. The symbolic scheme or paradigm is primary (without it we only have a vague and chaotic conception), and it conceptually encloses, allows us to discover the meaning of, understand the various interrelations and interactions of, and it allows us to control to one degree or another, the realm of production.

Marx and Pluralism 295

The realm of production is not primary in the sense that it encloses, gives rise to, and contains the symbolic scheme.

We must notice, and I think we can see it in the last two passages quoted from Marx above, that he himself does not prefer the predominance of production. He prefers the predominance of symbolic schemes, things higher in themselves, ends in themselves, the greatness of Greek art that is lost to the modern world.

This is even clearer in what Marx has to say about the individual of the ancient world. "During earlier stages of development, the single individual seems more fully developed because he has not yet worked out the fulness of his relations and has not yet set them over against himself as independent social powers and relations. It is as ridiculous to long for a return to that original fulness as it is to believe that the present complete emptiness must be permanent."[159] He also says that,

> Among the ancients, we never come across an investigation into which form of landed property, etc., is the most productive, creates the greatest wealth. Wealth does not appear as the purpose of production . . . The enquiry is always about which form of property creates the best citizens . . . In this way, the old view according to which man always appears in however narrowly national, religious or political a determination as the end of production, seems very exalted when set against the modern world, in which production is the end of man, and wealth the end of production . . . In the bourgeois economy—and in the epoch of production to which it corresponds—this complete unfolding of man's inner potentiality turns into his total emptying-out. His universal objectification becomes his total alienation, and the demolition of all determined one-sided aims becomes the sacrifice of the human end-in-itself to a wholly external purpose. That is why, on the one hand, the childish world of antiquity appears as something superior. On the other hand, it is superior, wherever fixed shape, form and established limits are being looked for.[160]

In one sense, Marx is suggesting that both ancient morality and modern bourgeois society are one-sided. Ancient morality deals only with closed shapes and given limits, whereas bourgeois society breaks down these closed shapes and given limits. It develops human powers and capacities beyond them and completely works out the human content. In this sense the modern world is superior. But at the same time it produces alienation and uses the individual as a means toward the end of production—it allows production to predominate—whereas the symbolic scheme of the ancient world took individuals to be ends in themselves and production as a means to their realization—it subordinated production to human beings. Here the morality, the symbolic scheme, of the ancient world is superior for Marx.

We can also say here that while Marx, as we saw earlier, was unable to appreciate the depth of modern peasant life and could only see its narrowness and isolation,[161] he is certainly able to transcend this sort of blindness with respect to ancient society, which was also predominantly agricultural. Despite their narrowly national, religious, and political determination, he finds in them a fullness and a superiority to the modern, alienated, bourgeois individual. No doubt one of the key factors that makes the member of ancient society different from the modern French peasant, for Marx, is that ancient society was based upon a community that made access and communication possible. What Marx is after, of course, is modern production together with a morality or symbolic scheme like that of the ancient world—a symbolic scheme that makes the communal citizen, the communal individual, the aim of production. Moreover, for Marx, the symbolic scheme, not production, must predominate.

VI. Ethnocentrism and Historical Stages

Lévi-Strauss writes concerning evolutionism: "It is really an attempt to wipe out the diversity of cultures while pretending to accord them full recognition. If the various conditions in which human societies are found, both in the past and in far distant lands, are treated as *phases* or *stages* in a single line of development, starting from the same point and leading to the same end, it seems clear that the diversity is merely apparent. . . ."[162] Marx, without a doubt, conceives of history in terms of stages, and he has often been criticized for devaluing earlier stages of culture. He distinguishes Asiatic, ancient, feudal, bourgeois, and socialist forms of production and he also distinguishes among savagery, barbarism, and civilization. But, for Marx, there is no single line of *development* in which everything leads to the same end. Marx's method looks backward, not forward. The point is to look back from modern capitalist society to understand how we got here. Moreover, development is not toward the *same end*. Russia, we have seen, should even be able to bypass capitalist development.[163] The point is to see differences.

Moreover, all of this is not to see these stages as leading teleologically to *"higher"* stages. Marx says, "To understand a limited historical epoch, we must step beyond its limits and compare it with other historical epochs. To judge Governments and their acts, we must measure them by their own times and the conscience of their contemporaries. Nobody will condemn a British statesman of the 17th century for acting on a belief in witchcraft, if he find Bacon himself ranging demonology in the catalogue of science."[164] He also says, "That duelling as such is not rational there can be no doubt. Nor that it is a relic of a bygone stage of civilization. However, a concomitant of the one-sidedness of bourgeois society is that, in opposition to the latter, certain feudal forms maintain the rights of the individual. The most striking proof of this is to be found in the United States where duelling is a civil right. Individuals may become locked in a mutual conflict so insupportable that a duel seems to them the only solution."[165]

Marx also says, "This fad becomes most ridiculous in history, where the consciousness of a later epoch regarding an earlier epoch naturally differs from the consciousness the latter has of itself, e.g., the Greeks saw themselves through the eyes of Greeks and not as we see them now; to blame them for not seeing themselves with our eyes—that is, 'not being conscious of themselves as they really were'—amounts to blaming them for being Greeks."[166] Moreover, capitalism is certainly not to be seen "as the absolutely final form of social production" but merely "as a passing historical phase. . . ."[167] For Marx, it is most *emphatically* not the case that later stages are to be seen as in all ways higher, better, or more valued than earlier stages. In many respects, as we have already started to see, earlier stages are very definitely superior in Marx's view. And this is a most important reason for wanting to compare them to modern society—so as to see their differences, so as to see what has been lost, and thus what might be regained.[168]

We have seen that Greek art, especially the epic, is, for Marx, the *highest* art. "Greek art and epic poetry . . . still give us aesthetic pleasure and are in certain respects regarded as a standard and unattainable model . . . Why should not the historical childhood of humanity, where it attained its most beautiful form, exert an eternal charm as a stage that will never recur?"[169] But there are also other respects in which earlier historical stages were superior. There was no state standing over and dominating society in the ancient world, and in earlier stages there were no classes.[170] Also, for Marx, there was less fetishism in ancient societies.[171] Moreover, in earlier stages there was greater freedom for women, and they had greater influence.[172] All of these latter characteristics serve as models for what Marx would like to achieve in an ideal society of the future.

Todorov suggests that if we treat other cultures as our equal, we will usually treat them as identical to us and this tends to lead to assimilation, which will involve the projection of our own values onto them. On the other hand, if we recognize their differences, these are usually translated into terms of inferiority. "What is denied is the existence of a human substance truly other, something capable of being not merely an imperfect state of oneself." In other words, what is most difficult to get is an other that is not inferior.[173] Our tendency is either to deny otherness or assert inferiority. Many modern authors who wish to avoid ethnocentrism hold that other cultures have had *other* values, other interests, aims, or symbolic schemes that were perfectly legitimate, *for-them*. Marx, we must see, is going much further than this. In many ways, earlier historical periods were *simply* superior to ours, not just *for-those*-earlier-periods, but *for-us*. Moreover, Marx wants communist society to regain many of these losses. In a letter of 1881, Marx writes, "the rural commune finds the modern social system in a crisis which will end only by its elimination, by a return of modern societies to an 'archaic' type of communal property, a form in which—as an American author [Lewis Morgan] who is not at all suspected of revolutionary tendencies, supported in his work by the government in Washington, says—'the new system' toward which modern society tends 'will be a revival in a superior form of an archaic social type.' "[174] Far from either assimilating earlier stages or devaluing their differences as inferior, Marx, it seems to me, shows the deepest respect for them as other.

Nor is this merely a romantic nostalgia for a simpler past that remains lost to us. Augé writes of those who "are concerned to delineate the phantom of an ideal primitive society, full of meaning, still close to the most basic of desires and removed from the repressions that as yet only haunt it: the negative or lost world of a world (our own) that lives only for writing, axiomatics and capital. Thus the others gradually come to assume no other form in these authors' remarks than that of the shadow of our remorse and anxiety. They are a western product meant for the use of the West. . . ."[175] Fabian and Clifford speak of how "primitive" society is distanced as other and inferior by locating it in a different, distant, past time, when in fact the members of such societies may well be alive today and coeval with us in time.[176] Along similar lines, Hountondji objects to anthropologists who look to a simplified view of traditional thought and culture, and give it precedence over real political and economic conflicts in the national culture of the present.[177] Marx may be guilty at times of distancing other cultures as past, primitive, archaic, or childish, but he very well recognizes that these cultures are coeval with us and, indeed, suffer intensely at the hands of capitalist imperialism, for which "the cheap price of its commodities are the heavy artillery with which it batters down all Chinese walls, with which it forces the barbarians' intensely obstinate hatred of foreigners to capitulate. It compels all nations, on pain of extinction, to adopt the bourgeois mode of production; it compels them to introduce what it calls civilization into their midst. . . ."[178]

Far from banishing other cultures to a distant, inferior, past time, and far from introducing what *we* call civilization into their midst—that is, assimilating them to ourselves—Marx, at least in one case, thinks that the Russian peasant commune could be the basis for bypassing capitalism and laying the foundation for socialism, that is, for assisting us all toward the society of the future.[179] This is hardly to relegate exotic peoples to the past and ourselves to the advancing edge of history, as Clifford puts it.[180] Insofar as other forms of society are older than capitalist society and different from it, they might help us *and themselves* get around capitalism to a better future. This is a nondistancing response to distance, and Fabian tends to agree that Marx's thought contains the theoretical possibilities for a negation of this distancing.[181] It is not at all the case in Marx's view that capitalism is better than earlier or other societies. In many ways capitalism is worse,[182] and earlier stages better. Clifford questions our looking back to "primitive" society,[183] but if socialism is something we must *construct,* then we must understand what we are, where we came from, how we developed, what we have lost, and what we are capable of regaining if we are to have any chance of constructing our future so as to make ourselves what we can be.

Notes

1. Berlin, for example, suggests that in a Marxist society, at least on some interpretations of Marx, there would be no serious disagreement about ends or values—they would be agreed upon. Disagreement would occur only about the most effective path to these goals. For Berlin, on the other hand, the only acceptable society would be a pluralist society where there is disagreement about ends or values. See I. Berlin, "Does Political Theory Still Exist?" in *Concepts and Categories*, ed. H. Hardy (London: Hogarth, 1978), 149–53. Also "Two Concepts of Liberty," in *Four Essays on Liberty* (Oxford: Oxford University Press, 1969), 167–72. For other examples, see Rawls, 29, 127. Also, M. Foucault, *Power/Knowledge*, trs. C. Gordon, L. Marshall, J. Me-

pham, and K. Soper (New York: Pantheon, 1980), 80–88. M. Foucault, *Language, Counter-Memory, Practice*, trs. D.F. Bouchard and S. Simon (Ithaca: Cornell University Press, 1977), 205–8. Also on Foucault, see P. Dews, *Logics of Disintegration* (London: Verso, 1987), 200–201. See also, J. Baudrillard, *The Mirror of Production*, tr. M. Poster (St. Louis: Telos Press, 1975), 47–48. Also I. Balbus, *Marxism and Domination* (Princeton: Princeton University Press, 1982), 114.

2. In the state of nature, for Hobbes, anyone can sneak up on anyone else when they are asleep and do them in; see *Leviathan, EW*, III, 110–11.

3. Locke, in fact, is committed to an objective conception of the good; he regularly speaks of the will of God or the laws of nature. But when it comes to money and unequal private property—which I think are key to his umbrella agreement and pluralism—these matters, for Locke, are not deduced from an objective conception of the good. They arise merely as matters that citizens have subjectively agreed to; see Locke, *Second Treatise*, § 28, 35, 50.

What makes this umbrella agreement *actually right* remains a bit vague for this sort of liberal. He or she would insist that it is not the arbitrary decision of the sovereign, yet reject the notion that this right can or should be derived from an objective conception of the good. The right, as Rawls puts it, is prior to the good (Rawls, 31). The right is what the citizens decide, yet it is not arbitrary. Critics would insist that this conception of the right is subjective and relative—that it will vary for different cultures or cultural groups. The Rawlsian liberal would resist this.

4. An umbrella agreement can also shift and evolve historically. For example, in the early 1950s in the United States, it was very possibly the case that the exclusion of blacks, the notion that they should remain in "their place," was a part of the umbrella agreement of majority society. Yet it has turned out since that the increasing inclusion of blacks has not overturned this umbrella agreement. The disagreement about the rights of blacks has come to be seen as not fundamental—not at the level of the umbrella agreement—such that disagreement would cause society to come apart. There is obviously still *serious* disagreement about the rights of blacks and other racial and ethnic minority groups, but this disagreement can be worked on without calling the whole social project into question and threatening its collapse.

5. Rawls, 7, 61, 66, 258.

6. Locke, *A Letter Concerning Toleration, LW*, V, 34, 40, 43–46. W.E. Connolly, for example, writes, "Pluralism has long provided the dominant description and ideal of American politics. As description, it portrays the system as a balance of power among overlapping economic, religious, ethnic, and geographical groupings. Each 'group' has some voice in shaping socially binding decisions; each constrains and is constrained through processes of mutual group adjustment; and all major groups share a broad system of beliefs and values which encourages conflict to proceed within established channels and allows initial disagreements to dissolve into compromise solutions"; see "The

Challenge to Pluralist Theory," in W.E. Connolly (ed.), *The Bias of Pluralism* (New York: Atherton, 1969), 3.

7. Rawls, 218.

8. *Social Contract*, 131 and *OC*, III, 468–69. *A Letter Concerning Toleration*, *LW*, V, 47.

9. *GI*, *MECW*, V, 60 and *MEW*, III, 47.

10. *GI*, *MECW*, V, 371–72 and *MEW*, III, 355.

11. "The General Council of the IWA to the Central Bureau of the International Alliance of Socialist Democracy," *MECW*, XXI, 45–46 and *MEW*, XVI, 348–49.

12. *EPM*, *MECW*, III, 294–95 and *MEW*, suppl. I, 534–35.

13. *Capital*, I, 132 and *MEW*, XXIII, 146.

14. *EPM*, *MECW*, III, 304, 343 and *MEW*, suppl. I, 544, 585.

15. *GI*, *MECW*, V, 263–64 and *MEW*, III, 246–47.

16. *GI*, *MECW*, V, 87 and *MEW*, III, 67–68.

17. "Principles of Communism," *MECW*, VI, 353 and *MEW*, IV, 376.

18. *Eighteenth Brumaire*, *MECW*, XI, 187–88 and *MEW*, VIII, 198–99.

19. See also, "Reviews from the *Neue Rheinische Zeitung*," *MECW*, X, 245 and *MEW*, VII, 202. Also *Manifesto*, *MECW*, VI, 488 and *MEW*, IV, 466.

20. "Inaugural Address of the Working Men's International Association," *MECW*, XX, 12–13 and *MEW*, XVI, 12–13.

21. *GI*, *MECW*, V, 78, also 292, 439 and *MEW*, III, 74, 273, 424–25. *EPM*, *MECW*, III, 332–33 and *MEW*, suppl. I, 574.

22. "Marx to Feuerbach on 11 Aug. 1844," *MECW*, III, 354 and *MEW*, XXVII, 425. Also *GI*, *MECW*, V, 437 and *MEW*, III, 423.

23. *Gotha*, *MECW*, XXIV, 86–87 and *MEW*, XIX, 20–21.

24. *EPM*, *MECW*, III, 304 and *MEW*, suppl. I, 544.

25. "Debates on Freedom of the Press," *MECW*, I, 137 and *MEW*, I, 33. *CM*, *MECW*, III, 218 and *MEW*, suppl. I, 452. *EPM*, *MECW*, III, 336–37 and *MEW*, suppl. I, 578–79.

26. *Grundrisse*, *MECW*, XXVIII, 29–30 and *MEGA*, II, 1.1, 29.

27. *EPM*, *MECW*, III, 301–2 and *MEW*, suppl. I, 541–42.

28. *EPM*, *MECW*, III, 304 and *MEW*, suppl. I, 544.

29. Also in Marx's earliest writings, he says, "understanding is not only one-sided, but has the essential function of making the world one-sided, a great and remarkable work, for only one-sidedness can extract the particular from the unorganized mass of the whole and give it shape. The character of a thing is a product of understanding. Each thing must isolate itself and become isolated in order to be something. By confining each of the contents of the world in a stable definiteness and as it were solidifying the fluid essence of this content, understanding brings out the manifold diversity of the world, for the world would not be many-sided without the many one-sidednesses" ("Thefts of Wood," *MECW*, I, 233 and *MEW*, I, 118).

30. *GI*, *MECW*, V, 290, also 372 n and *MEW*, III, 272, 355 n.

31. "Prussian Censorship," *MECW*, I, 113 and *MEW*, I, 7.
32. *GI*, *MECW*, V, 442 and *MEW*, III, 428.
33. *Capital*, III, 791–92 and *MEW*, XXV, 800.
34. T.W. Adorno, *Negative Dialectics*, tr. E.B. Ashton (New York: Seabury, 1973), 5.
35. Adorno, 149–50.
36. M. Ryan, *Marxism and Deconstruction: A Critical Articulation* (Baltimore: Johns Hopkins University Press, 1982), 80. Ryan argues that Marx, like Derrida, is committed to difference and heterogeneity. Ryan's views in this text are similar to mine in certain respects.
37. *GI*, *MECW*, V, 430–31 and *MEW*, III, 415–17. "Divorce Bill," *MECW*, I, 309 (words in brackets are my addition) and *MEW*, I, 150. Also, Marx says, "The predicate, the essence, never exhausts the spheres of its existence . . ." *CHPL*, *MECW*, III, 26 and *MEW*, I, 228.
38. *Manifesto*, *MECW*, VI, 497 and *MEW*, IV, 474.
39. *CWF*, *MECW*, XXII, 335 and *MEW*, XVII, 343.
40. *Manifesto*, *MECW*, VI, 498 and *MEW*, IV, 475.
41. C. Moraga, *Loving in the War Years* (Boston: South End Press, 1983), 133.
42. "Instructions for the Delegates," *MECW*, XX, 190 and *MEW*, XVI, 195.
43. "General Council of the IWA to the Central Bureau of the International Alliance of Socialist Democracy," *MECW*, XXI, 46 and *MEW*, XVI, 349.
44. "Provisional Rules of the Association," *MECW*, XX, 15 and *MEW*, XVI, 15.
45. *CWF*, *MECW*, XXII, 332–33 and *MEW*, XVII, 340–41.
46. *CHPL*, *MECW*, III, 24–30 and *MEW*, I, 225–32. "Debate on Jacoby's Motion," *MECW*, VII, 232 and *MEW*, V, 222. *Class Struggles in France*, *MECW*, X, 130–31 and *MEW*, VII, 93. *Eighteenth Brumaire*, *MECW*, XI, 147 and *MEW*, VIII, 159.
47. *JQ*, *MECW*, III, 168 and *MEW*, I, 370. *Poverty of Philosophy*, *MECW*, VI, 212 and *MEW*, IV, 182. *Manifesto*, *MECW*, VI, 505–6 and *MEW*, IV, 482.
48. *CWF*, *MECW*, XXII, 332–33 and *MEW*, XVII, 340–41.
49. *CWF*, *MECW*, XXII, 331–32, 488 and *MEW*, XVII, 338, 543.
50. *Capital*, III, 791 and *MEW*, XXV, 799–800.
51. *Capital*, III, 793 and *MEW*, XXV, 801. *Ethnological Notebooks*, 329–30.
52. *Gotha*, *MECW*, XXIV, 95 and *MEW*, XIX, 29.
53. See also E. Durkheim, *Division of Labor in Society*, tr. G. Simpson (New York: Free Press, 1933), 70–132 *passim*. Also, P.L. Berger and T. Luckmann, *The Social Construction of Reality* (Garden City, N.Y.: Anchor, 1967), 125. Modern liberalism has contributed to the growth of this view. It considered custom, tradition, and habit as oppressive and opposed to liberty, im-

provement, and progress; see J.S. Mill, *On Liberty*, ed. C.V. Shields (Indianapolis: Bobbs-Merrill, 1956), 85–86. Even Berlin speaks of the "mass hypnosis of custom," "Two Concepts of Liberty," 128.

54. See, for example, R. Miliband, *Marxism and Politics* (Oxford: Oxford University Press, 1977), 44–45. Also, bell hooks, *Yearning: Race, Gender, and Cultural Politics* (Boston: South End Press, 1990), 213. Also, P. J. Hountondji, *African Philosophy: Myth and Reality*, trs. H. Evans with J. Rée (Bloomington: Indiana University Press, 1983), 165–67.

55. A. MacIntyre, *Whose Justice? Which Rationality?* (Notre Dame: University of Notre Dame Press, 1988), 12.

56. MacIntyre, *Whose Justice? Which Rationality?*, 326–28, 355.

57. *F*, 47 and *Ak*, IV, 428.

58. *F*, 40–41 and *Ak*, IV, 422–23.

59. See, for example, *IUH*, 20–21 and *Ak*, VIII, 25–26.

60. See also *Marx and Ethics*, 28–29. C.B. Macpherson's argument (against I. Berlin) that positive liberty and pluralism are compatible is relevant here; see *Democratic Theory: Essays in Retrieval* (Oxford: Clarendon Press, 1973), 95–119, esp. 111–12.

61. C. Lévi-Strauss, *The Savage Mind* (Chicago: University of Chicago Press, 1966), 16 ff.

62. P. Patton, "Marxism and Beyond: Strategies for Reterritorialization," in *Marxism and the Interpretation of Culture*, 133–34.

63. "Prussian Censorship," *MECW*, I, 112 and *MEW*, I, 6.

64. *EPM*, *MECW*, III, 285, 317 and *MEW*, suppl. I, 524, 557. Also, *GI*, *MECW*, V, 86–87 and *MEW*, III, 67. Marx makes similar arguments against Hegel's concept of essence; see *HF*, *MECW*, IV, 57–59 and *MEW*, II, 60–61. *CHPL*, *MECW*, III, 14–15, 21–22, 27 and *MEW*, I, 213, 222, 228. Marx also argues that all the mental and physical senses are reduced to the sense of "having"; *EPM*, *MECW*, III, 300 and *MEW*, suppl. I, 540.

65. *EPM*, *MECW*, III, 307, 302 and *MEW*, suppl. I, 548, 542.

66. *GI*, *MECW*, V, 409 and *MEW*, III, 394.

67. "Capital Punishment," *MECW*, XI, 496–97 and *MEW*, VIII, 508. On the extreme form of determinism to be found in the middle period of Marx's thought, see *Marx and Ethics*, Chapter 3.

68. *Critique of Political Economy* (hereafter *CPE*), *MECW*, XXIX, 271, also 272–77 and *MEW*, XIII, 17, 18–23. Also *Capital*, I, 38–41, 58 and *MEW*, XXIII, 52–55, 72.

69. *Capital*, I, 84–85 and *MEW*, XXIII, 99–100.

70. *Capital*, I, 72 and *MEW*, XXIII, 86.

71. *Gotha*, *MECW*, XXIV, 86–87 and *MEW*, XIX, 21.

72. *Gotha*, *MECW*, XXIV, 87 and *MEW*, XIX, 21.

73. *CWF (First Draft)*, *MECW*, XXII, 505 and *MEW*, XVII, 563.

74. *CM*, *MECW*, III, 228 and *MEW*, suppl. I, 462.

75. "English," *MECW*, XIX, 163 and *MEW*, XV, 464.

304 *Chapter Seven*

76. "Principles of Communism," *MECW*, VI, 353 and *MEW*, IV, 376.
77. *GI*, *MECW*, V, 47 and *MEW*, III, 33.
78. *GI*, *MECW*, V, 262–63, also 78–79 and *MEW*, III, 245–46, 75–76.
79. *GI*, *MECW*, V, 394 and *MEW*, III, 379.
80. *GI*, *MECW*, V, 47 and *MEW*, III, 33.
81. *Poverty of Philosophy*, *MECW*, VI, 189 and *MEW*, IV, 156.
82. *Poverty of Philosophy*, *MECW*, VI, 190 and *MEW*, IV, 157.
83. *Capital*, I, 488 and *MEW*, XXIII, 512.
84. *Capital*, I, 487 n, see also 421 and *MEW*, XXIII, 511–12 n, 443–44.
85. *GI*, *MECW*, V, 393 and *MEW*, III, 377.
86. *GI*, *MECW*, V, 394 and *MEW*, III, 379.
87. *GI*, *MECW*, V, 47 and *MEW*, III, 33.
88. "Comments on the North American Events," *MECW*, XIX, 250 and *MEW*, XV, 553.
89. *Manifesto*, *MEW*, IV, 488 and *MEW*, IV, 466.
90. Ibid.
91. "Record of Marx's Speeches on General Education," *MECW*, XXI, 398 and *MEW*, XVI, 563.
92. "Record of Marx's Speeches on General Education," *MECW*, XXI, 398–400 and *MEW*, XVI, 563–64.
93. *JQ*, *MECW*, III, 149 and *MEW*, I, 350.
94. *JQ*, *MECW*, III, 151 and *MEW*, I, 352.
95. *GI*, *MECW*, V, 425 and *MEW*, III, 410.
96. *JQ*, *MECW*, III, 169–71 and *MEW*, I, 371–74. "Marx to Engels on 30 July 1862," *MECW*, XLI, 390 and *MEW*, XXX, 259. And Engels has some racist things to say about Mexicans ("Democratic Pan-Slavism," *MECW*, VIII, 365–67 and *MEW*, VI, 273–75).
97. "British Rule in India," *MECW*, XII, 132 and *MEW*, IX, 133.
98. "Future Results of British Rule in India," *MECW*, XII, 222 and *MEW*, IX, 226.
99. "British Rule in India," *MECW*, XII, 126–27 and *MEW*, IX, 129.
100. "British Rule in India," *MECW*, XII, 132 and *MEW*, IX, 132.
101. "British Rule in India," *MECW*, XII, 132 and *MEW*, IX, 132–33.
102. "Future Result of British Rule in India," *MECW*, XII, 221 and *MEW*, IX, 225.
103. "British Rule in India," *MECW*, XII, 132 and *MEW*, IX, 133. "Future Results of British Rule in India," *MECW*, XII, 222 and *MEW*, IX, 226.
104. "Future Results of British Rule in India," *MECW*, XII, 218 and *MEW*, IX, 221.
105. "Future Results of British Rule in India," *MECW*, XII, 221 and *MEW*, IX, 224.
106. "Investigation of Tortures in India," *MECW*, XV, 341 and *MEW*, XII, 272–73. See also Marx's defense of Sicily, "Sicily and the Sicilians," *MECW*, XVII, 370–72 and *MEW*, XV, 43–45.

107. "Indian Revolt," *MECW*, XV, 353 and *MEW*, XII, 285.

108. See *Manifesto*, *MECW*, VI, 490, 496 and *MEW*, IV, 468, 474.

109. Marx also has negative things to say about China; see "Review," *MECW*, X, 267 and *MEW*, VII, 222. Also "Revolution in China and Europe," *MECW*, XII, 94 and *MEW*, IX, 96. He also has similarly negative things to say about the Turks; see "British Politics," *MECW*, XII, 7 and *MEW*, IX, 7–8.

110. *Capital*, I, 489–90 and *MEW*, XXIII, 514.

111. "Provisional Rules of the Association," *MECW*, XX, 15 and *MEW*, XVI, 15. In a letter of 1864, Marx claims that he was obliged by a subcommittee to insert this passage; he says, "The Subcommittee adopted all my proposals. I was, however, obliged to insert two sentences about 'Duty' and 'Right', and ditto about 'Truth, Morality and Justice' in the preamble to the rules, but these are so placed that they can do no harm" ("Marx to Engels on 4 Nov. 1864," in *MECW*, XLII, 18 and *MEW*, XXXI, 15). This cannot be read as a repudiation of the passage in the "Provisional Rules." It in no way suggests that Marx objects to, or was obliged to insert, the pluralistic and tolerant claim that conduct should not be influenced by "colour, creed, or nationality." His complaint only concerns the terms "Truth, Morality and Justice." Moreover, Marx himself says that these terms are placed such that "they can do no harm." In other words, the basic principle stands for Marx.

112. "Marx to Engels on 14 June 1853," *MECW*, XXXIX, 345–46 and *MEW*, XXVIII, 265–66.

113. "Marx to Engels on 14 June 1853," *MECW*, XXXIX, 346 and *MEW*, XXVIII, 266–67.

114. "Marx to Engels on 14 June 1853," *MECW*, XXXIX, 347 and *MEW*, XXVIII, 268.

115. J.S. Mill, *On Liberty*, 13–14.

116. Also see Elster, 490–93, who cites several passages from Marx's texts where Marx rejects the imposition of Western categories on non-Western societies.

117. Elster, 490.

118. M. Sahlins, *Culture and Practical Reason* (Chicago: University of Chicago Press, 1976).

119. For example, Baudrillard, 59, 65–67. Also, S. Aronowitz, *The Crisis in Historical Materialism* (New York: Praeger, 1981), 67–68. Also Balbus, 33–36.

120. Sahlins, vii–viii.

121. Of course, there are many Marxist theorists, especially those influenced by Althusser, who reject productivism—who argue that economic factors do not simply predominate in determining all aspects of society in all social periods. A good many Marxist anthropologists, for example, have argued for the relative autonomy of the political, the ideological, or the symbolic in precapitalist societies, among them E. Terray, *Marxism and "Primitive"*

Societies, tr. M. Klopper (New York: Monthly Review Press, 1972). M. Augé, *The Anthropological Circle: Symbol, Function, History*, tr. M. Thom (Cambridge: Cambridge University Press, 1982). P.P. Rey, "The Lineage Mode of Production," *Critique of Anthropology* III (1975), 27–79. C. Meillassoux, *Anthropologie économique des Gouro de Côte d'Ivoire* (Paris: Mouton, 1964). C. Meillassoux, *Maidens, Meal and Money: Capitalism and the Domestic Community* (Cambridge: Cambridge University Press, 1981). H. Wolpe, *Race, Class & the Apartheid State* (London: James Curry, 1988). Also, especially Godelier, who has argued that while the economic is determinant in the last instance, it is quite able to determine cultural, ideological, or symbolic spheres as dominant. He also shows how kinship relations can be both infra- and superstructural; that is, how they can both be bound up with the ideological and political, yet function as relations of production. See M. Godelier, "On the Definition of a Social Formation: The Example of the Incas," *Critique of Anthropology* I (1974), 69; also, *Perspectives in Marxist Anthropology*, tr. R. Brain (Cambridge: Cambridge University Press, 1977), 33, 93–95, 123–24.

122. *Marx' Method, Epistemology, and Humanism*, Chapter 3. *Marx and Ethics*, Chapter 4. It is also true that Althusser himself, in *Reading Capital*, was one of the first to explore, and to do so in a thorough and masterful way, Marx's method as laid out in the 1857 Introduction to the *Grundrisse* and as employed in *Capital*; see L. Althusser and É. Balibar, *Reading Capital*, tr. B. Brewster (London: NLB, 1970), 145–57. For further discussion of my views on Althusser, as well as Hindess and Hirst, Resnick, Wolff, and Amariglio, see my "Marx, Sahlins, and Ethnocentrism," *Rethinking Marxism* (forthcoming).

123. *Grundrisse*, MECW, XXVIII, 23–26 and *MEGA*, II, 1.1, 22–26. Moreover, Chapter 1 of *Capital* proceeds in the same way. It does not set out to discuss capitalism exclusively, but any form of exchange or commodity-producing society in general. For example, Marx tells us that we find commodities in precapitalist economies (*Capital*, I, 61, 79 and *MEW*, XXIII, 76, 93. *Capital*, III, 177 and *MEW*, XXV, 187). Marx specifically excludes the discussion of wage labor from Chapter 1; he says "Wages is a category that, as yet, has no existence at the present stage of our investigation" (*Capital*, I, 44 n and *MEW*, XXIII, 59 n). A society without wage labor is obviously not capitalist. Marx explicitly states that fetishism can occur in precapitalist societies (*Capital*, I, 82 and *MEW*, XXIII, 97). Capitalism proper is not introduced until Chapters 3 and 4 where Marx finally distinguishes between two forms of exchange characterized by the two formulas C-M-C and M-C-M', only the latter of which is the capitalist form of exchange. The point is to begin with simple categories, distinguish general characteristics from specific capitalist ones, and discover the interconnections with other categories in modern society. Then one can begin an empirical study of that society as well as its earlier historical development. For a fuller discussion of this matter, see *Marx' Method, Epistemology, and Humanism*, Chapter 3, section 1.

124. *Grundrisse*, *MECW*, XXVIII, 43 and *MEGA*, II, 1.1, 41–42.
125. *Grundrisse*, *MECW*, XXVIII, 37–39 and *MEGA*, II, 1.1, 35–38.
126. *Capital*, I, 59–60 and *MEW*, XXIII, 73–74. Also see Aristotle, *NE*, 1133[b].
127. *Grundrisse*, *MECW*, XXVIII, 42–43 and *MEGA*, II, 1.1, 40–42.
128. Althusser, *Reading Capital*, 122–24.
129. J. Fabian, *Time and the Other: How Anthropology Makes Its Object* (New York: Columbia University Press, 1983), 102.
130. *Capital*, I, 15 and *MEW*, XXIII, 21.
131. *Grundrisse*, *MECW*, XXVIII, 44 and *MEGA*, II, 1.1, 42.
132. *Capital*, III, 327 and *MEW*, XXV, 339.
133. *Capital*, III, 792 and *MEW*, XXV, 800.
134. "Marx to 'Otechestvenniye Zapiski' in Nov. 1877," in *Marx and Engels Selected Correspondence* (hereafter *SC*), tr. I. Lasker (Moscow: Progress, 1965), 312–13 and *MEW*, XIX, 110–11.
135. "Marx to 'Otechestvenniye Zapiski' in Nov. 1877," *SC*, 313 and *MEW*, XIX, 112.
136. *Capital*, I, 18 (my italics) and *MEW*, XXIII, 26.
137. *Capital*, I, 19 (my italics) and *MEW*, XXIII, 27.
138. *Capital*, I, 18–19, see also 632 where Marx implies this himself, and *MEW*, XXIII, 26, 660.
139. For a fuller discussion of these matters, see *Marx' Method, Epistemology, and Humanism*, Chapter 3, section IV.
140. *Grundrisse*, *MECW*, XXVIII, 42 and *MEGA*, II, 1.1, 40.
141. Ibid.
142. *Grundrisse*, *MECW*, XXVIII, 38 and *MEGA*, II, 1.1, 36.
143. *Grundrisse*, *MECW*, XXVIII, 44 and *MEGA*, II, 1.1, 42.
144. W.L. Adamson, *Marx and the Disillusionment of Marxism* (Berkeley: University of California Press, 1985), 27.
145. *Grundrisse*, *MECW*, XXVIII, 42–43, 388–89 and *MEGA*, II, 1.1, 40–41 and II, 1.2, 368–69. Also see F. Engels, *Origin of the Family, Private Property, and the State* (hereafter *Origin*) (New York: International, 1942), 27 and *MEW*, XXI, 38. *Capital*, III, 817 and *MEW*, XXV, 825. *Capital*, I, 316 and *MEW*, XXIII, 335.
146. *Marx and Ethics*, Chapter 4.
147. Adamson, 33.
148. *CPE*, *MECW*, XXIX, 290–91 and *MEW*, XIII, 35–36.
149. *Ethnological Notebooks*, 329–30.
150. *Manifesto*, *MECW*, VI, 486–87 and *MEW*, IV, 464–65.
151. *Capital*, I, 82 n and *MEW*, XXIII, 96.
152. Sahlins, vii–viii, 168.
153. *Grundrisse*, *MECW*, XXVIII, 337 (first italics mine) and *MEGA*, II, 1.2, 322–23.
154. *Grundrisse*, *MECW*, XXVIII, 46–47 and *MEGA*, II, 1.1, 44–45. Marx

also says, "But what distinguishes the worst architect from the best of bees is this, that the architect raises his structure in imagination before he erects it in reality. At the end of every labour-process, we get a result that already existed in the imagination of the labourer at its commencement" (*Capital*, I, 178 and *MEW*, XXIII, 193).

155. *Grundrisse, MECW*, XXVIII, 47 and *MEGA*, II, 1.1, 45.

156. Sahlins, 3, 128, also see 34, 127. A similar argument is also made by Baudrillard, 83–88.

157. For a fuller discussion of these matters, see *Marx' Method, Epistemology, and Humanism*, Chapter 3.

158. B. Hindess and P. Hirst, *Pre-capitalist Modes of Production* (London: Routledge & Kegan Paul, 1975), 79. Rey, 39–40.

159. *Grundrisse, MECW*, XXVIII, 99 and *MEGA*, II, 1.1, 94–95.

160. *Grundrisse, MECW*, XXVIII, 411–12 and *MEGA*, II, 1.2, 391–92.

161. *Eighteenth Brumaire, MECW*, XI, 187–88 and *MEW*, VIII, 198–99. "Reviews from the *Neue Rheinische Zeitung*," *MECW*, X, 245 and *MEW*, VII, 202. *Manifesto, MECW*, VI, 488 and *MEW*, IV, 466.

162. Quoted in Terray, 9. Also Augé, 51. Also see Wolpe, *Race, Class & the Apartheid State*, 60. Terray (35–37) argues that Morgan was not an objectionable evolutionist; that he merely set out models that made it possible to conceptualize stages or spheres that one wants to study. Leacock ["Introduction," in *The Origin of the Family, Private Property and the State*, by F. Engels (London: Lawrence & Wishart, 1972), 14] makes a very similar point for Engels, and presumably for Marx, though she finds some of Engels's stages to be Eurocentric (Leacock, 49).

163. "Marx to 'Otechestvenniye Zapiski' in Nov. 1877," *SC*, 312 and *MEW*, XIX, 108.

164. *Revelations of the Diplomatic History of the 18th Century, MECW*, XV, 56—this text is not available either in *MEW* or *MEGA*.

165. "Marx to Lassalle on 10 June 1858," *MECW*, XL, 322 and *MEW*, XXIX, 562–63.

166. *GI, MECW*, V, 250 n and *MEW*, III, 223 n.

167. *Capital*, I, 14 and *MEW*, XXIII, 19–20.

168. See, e.g., "Elections," *MECW*, XI, 488–94, esp. 491 and *MEW*, VIII, 499–505, esp. 502.

169. *Grundrisse, MECW*, XXVIII, 47–48 and *MEGA*, II, 1.1, 45.

170. *Grundrisse, MECW*, XXVIII, 407 and *MEGA*, II, 1.2, 388. Also see Engels, *Origin*, 86, 158 and *MEW*, XXI, 95–96, 168, which was written based upon Marx's *Ethnological Notebooks*.

171. *Capital*, I, 82 and *MEW*, XXIII, 97.

172. *Ethnological Notebooks*, 121. Also *Origin*, 42–44 and *MEW*, XXI, 53–54.

173. T. Todorov, *The Conquest of America: The Question of the Other*, tr. R. Howard (New York: Harper & Row, 1984), 42.

174. "Draft of a letter to V.I. Zasulich on 8 March 1881," quoted in *Ethnological Notebooks*, 87 and *MEW*, XIX, 386.

175. Augé, 92. Also see J. Clifford, "On Ethnographic Allegory," in *Writing Culture*, eds. J. Clifford and G.E. Marcus (Berkeley: University of California Press, 1986), 98–121.

176. Fabian, *Time and the Other*. J. Clifford, *The Predicament of Culture* (Cambridge, Mass.: Harvard University Press, 1988), 5; also, "On Ethnographic Allegory," 111. Also see Augé, 9–10.

177. Hountondji, 161–62.

178. *Manifesto, MECW*, VI, 488 and *MEW*, IV, 466.

179. "Marx to 'Otechestvenniye Zapiski' in Nov. 1877," *SC*, 312 and *MEW*, XIX, 108. "Marx to V.I. Zasulich on 8 March 1881," *SC*, 340 and *MEW*, XXXV, 167. "Engels to N.F. Danielson on 17 October 1893," *SC*, 464 and *MEW*, XIX, 149–50. Engels, "On Social Relations in Russia," *MECW*, XXIV, 39–50 and *MEW*, XVIII, 556–67.

180. Clifford, *Predicament of Culture*, 16.

181. Fabian, 159.

182. *Manifesto, MECW*, VI, 486–87 and *MEW*, IV, 464–65.

183. Clifford, "On Ethnographic Allegory."

8

Marx and Feminism

Marx has been seriously criticized by modern feminists for his views on women, their liberation, and the role that socialism will play in this liberation. I would like to try, as much as is possible, to break down the opposition and hostility between Marx and feminism. I think that if we understand Marx correctly his thought can evoke far more sympathy from modern feminists than has hitherto been the case. This is certainly not to suggest, however, that Marx, back in the nineteenth century, developed a full and adequate feminist theory, or that he said everything, or even very much, of what it is important to say about the condition of women and their liberation; nor even that he established the foundation from which one could derive all, or even very much, of what should be said in this area. In fact, it would be bizarre to make such assumptions about a theorist who wrote toward the very *beginning* of the historical process that we call the modern feminist movement, and who himself held that consciousness can emerge only out of a long historical process involving a dialectical interaction between theory and practice. Yet such bizarre assumptions are often made about Marx by modern feminists, not seriously, of course, but in order to dismiss him. I would like to try to argue something rather modest in this chapter, merely that Marx has a bit more to say, has fewer shortcomings, and could be of more use to modern feminist theory than is often thought to be the case.

A critic could make one or more of the following claims about the relevance of Marx's thought to modern feminist theory. First, one might claim that some or all of the views that are distinctive and central in Marx's thought are conceptually incompatible, that they are in contradiction, with some or all of the views that are central or fundamental to modern feminist theory. This would be the worst case. I will try to argue that those who hold this view are mistaken in their reading of Marx. Second, one might claim that while Marx's thought does not contradict modern feminist theory, nevertheless Marx's thought is *conceptually* irrelevant to and cannot make any serious contribution to modern feminist theory, either because his thought in this area is trivial or flawed or because Marx simply was not aware of or did not concern himself sufficiently with feminist issues. This is not as serious an accusation as the first, but it is still serious. It is perhaps forgivable not to expend any effort in analyzing feminist issues when writing a theoretical text on astronomy or mathematics, but not in writing as many texts on social, political, and economic theory as Marx did. I will argue that those who make this sort of claim about Marx have not taken the time to conceptually unpack his thought. The third sort of claim that one might make here is that Marx fails to discuss the condition of women or their liberation very often; that is, that by comparison to the other matters that concern him, feminist questions receive radically less space in Marx's writings. This, it cannot be denied, is perfectly true about Marx. And, again, if one is writing social, political, or economic theory, rather than astronomical or mathematical theory, this is a serious charge. Yet, at the same time, we must realize that this charge, while perfectly correct, is also quite compatible with the claim that *conceptually,* when Marx's thought (which is always dense, difficult, and obscure) is carefully unpacked, it may be very relevant to and very useful for modern feminist theory. This, in fact, is what I will try to argue in this chapter.

I. Women and Determinism

Modern theorists like Balbus, Baudrillard, and Sahlins argue that at the very heart of Marx's thought we find a commitment to the primacy of production; that is, to the thesis that economic conditions, the forces and relations of production, predominate in determining all aspects of a sociocultural world and that they do so in all forms of society and in all social epochs. This thesis, which is at best true only for modern capitalist societies, is, they claim, illegitimately projected back onto all earlier forms of society by Marx.[1]

If one holds to this thesis, then one would also have to hold that economic conditions explain and determine the nature, origin, and development of the family, gendered division of labor, male domination, and of all other similar and related matters. Certainly, it would be the case, for Marx, since economic conditions differ from society to society and since they develop and change from epoch to epoch, that their effect on the family, gendered division of labor, and male domination would also differ and change accordingly; but, nevertheless, all of these differences and changes would have to be determined by and explained in terms of economic conditions. For many modern feminists, this view is seen to be incompatible with certain basic and fundamental features of modern feminist theory.

In the first place, it has been claimed that a commitment to such productivism leads Marx to fail to take into account the fundamental importance of many traditional activities of women that are noneconomic, nonproductive, or that traditionally have been excluded from the area of economic production. This would especially be the case with respect to women's activities in the family and in reproduction. Moreover, it has been claimed that the commitment to such productivism leads Marx to reduce women's oppression to just another aspect of economic oppression and to ignore the way that, even in modern capitalist society, women's oppression continues to be connected with noneconomic factors.[2] As Harding puts it:

> family life is structured by a lot more materially based social relations than merely economic ones. The restriction of material causes to economic ones is an unjustifiably reductionist restriction . . . economic relations can not capture most of the social relations in which infants and children participate . . . the marxist explanatory scheme . . . is also sexist in that economic categories such as class and material base (understood in the traditional way as economic base) are not even the appropriate categories with which to understand crucial aspects of the social relations of family life.[3]

Moreover, it has been argued that the thesis of the primacy of production leads Marx to think that since the origin and development of male domination was caused by economic conditions, if these economic conditions were fundamentally transformed, if capitalism were overthrown and the primacy of production overcome, male domination too would automatically come to an end.[4] Many feminists find this absurd. In their view, male domination is not caused by economic conditions alone. It existed well before economic conditions came to predominate, which they do only in modern capitalist societies. This, of course, does not mean that the domination of women has not been influenced by economic conditions, especially in capitalist society. It certainly has been, but economic conditions alone did not bring about the origin and development of male domination, do not explain all aspects of male domination even in modern capitalist society, and the elimination of capitalism and of the primacy of economic conditions will not automatically eliminate all aspects of male domination. Male domination exists even in contemporary socialist societies.

Also, as Michelle Rosaldo put it, an extraordinary diversity of gender roles can be found if one compares different cultures. Anthropologists have even found that attitudes or activities that are associated with women's roles in one culture can be associated with men's roles in other cultures, or can be outlawed for both men and women in still other cultures. Every known society recognizes differences between the sexes, but men's activities as opposed to women's activities are always recognized as more important and of higher value (at least by men).[5] In other words, male domination is found in all cultures.[6] What men do is more important than what women do in all cultures, despite the fact that what women do in one culture men may do in another. It doesn't seem to matter what women do; it will always be less important (at least for men). Rosaldo goes on to suggest that given this kind of diversity it is not very likely that male domination can be explained by a single, universal, or necessary cause. It is more likely to be explained by a constellation of different factors.[7] Though she does not mention it, this would tend to rule out the primacy of economic conditions as a single, universal explanation.

Moreover, as many modern feminist theorists have pointed out, reproduction—taken to include childbirth, nurturing, and childrearing—is a most central and fundamental aspect of the socialization of individuals and therefore of the development of the social world. To ignore this or to subordinate it to economic production is to attempt to erase the role of women in the socialization of human beings and the development of the social world. Despite the fact that both Marx and Engels in several places insist that both production *and reproduction* are to be considered fundamental material conditions that determine our sociocultural world, if one is convinced that Marx holds to the primacy of production, this will mean that his recognition of the importance of reproduction will either contradict the primacy of production or that only lip service will be paid to the importance and independence of reproduction while in fact it will be subsumed under and subordinated to production.[8]

However, as we saw in Chapter 7, it is simply not the case for Marx that economic conditions predominate in all societies and in all epochs. In *Capital*, as we saw, Marx records the objection of a critic who claimed that while the predominance of economic conditions is true for modern society, it is not true "for the middle ages, in which Catholicism, nor for Athens and Rome, where politics, reigned supreme." And, far from rejecting this claim, Marx thought it was obvious. Moreover, he admitted that "it is the mode in which they gained a livelihood that explains why here politics, and there Catholicism, played the chief part."[9] He admits that noneconomic conditions played the chief part. Nor, I think, can it be successfully argued that economic conditions still predominate for Marx, in that they determine which noneconomic conditions predominate.[10] In the 1857 Introduction to the *Grundrisse,* Marx said that art in the ancient world "by no means correspond[ed] . . . to the material basis" of society. Rather it was mythology, imagination, that dominated, and this was what made for the greatness of Greek art—a greatness that became impossible as economic conditions, rather than imagination, finally came to predominate in the modern world.[11]

Moreover, as we have seen in Chapter 7, a careful understanding of Marx's discussion of method in the 1857 Introduction to the *Grundrisse* will show that economic conditions never *simply* predominate even in modern society. Marx tells us that it is impossible to study the economic conditions of any society until the investigator has worked up the categories (which are capable of grasping the highly developed conditions of modern society) into a conceptual structure, a concrete for thought; what contemporary philosophers of science would call a paradigm or what Sahlins would call a symbolic scheme. And it is only after we have this paradigm that we can begin to study an existing society or its past historical development. It follows from this that the effect that economic conditions have in society can only be understood *after* we have this paradigm and *through* this very paradigm. Before we construct this paradigm, Marx says, we only have a vague and chaotic conception of the concrete. Only after we have constructed this paradigm can we gain a clear and scientific understanding of the concrete.[12]

Moreover, if the paradigm were changed, so would our understanding of the effect that economic conditions have on us be changed. Marx's very method itself grants primacy to the symbolic, the noneconomic, the conceptual, not just in premodern societies but in *all* historical periods. The symbolic, the paradigm, is a necessary prerequisite for understanding the effects of economic conditions and the way they predominate in society. Economic conditions can only be understood within and through the symbolic. The symbolic then is primary and our understanding of economic conditions is dependent upon the symbolic. Moreover, it just will not do to go on from here to insist that for Marx, it is, when all is said and done, economic conditions that *finally* determine our symbolic construction of the paradigm and thus that economic conditions *are* ultimately more fundamental than the symbolic. This cannot be Marx's position because, if we can only understand the effect of economic conditions *after* we have the paradigm and *through* this very paradigm, it would be theoretically impossible to understand how economic conditions determined the symbolic construction of the paradigm *before* we had the paradigm.

If we see that Marx, at least in the *Grundrisse* and later writings, rejects the notion of the primacy of economic conditions, at least in any crude sense of such primacy, and that he rejects such primacy altogether in early society, it then becomes quite clear that we do not have to accept the notion that economic conditions are solely responsible for determining and explaining the origin, rise, and development of the family; gendered division of labor; and male domination. Thus, it becomes quite possible to hold that before economic conditions came to predominate, the domination of women by men was personal domination, just as in ancient Greece before economic conditions came to predominate, imagination and mythology were able to dominate culture. Moreover, it becomes quite possible, while remaining consistent with Marx's thought, to argue that other factors besides economic ones—natural or biological factors, cultural factors, different symbolic or mythological schemes, psychological factors—are relevant as explanations here. In other words, the explanation is left open; it is not preestablished that the explanation must be economic.

However, we need not confine ourselves to abstract considerations of Marx's views on method. In the *German Ideology,* Marx very clearly treats the family, reproduction, sexual division of labor, and male domination as independent, natural, extraeconomic factors. Even Marx's discussion of historical materialism in the *German Ideology,* his discussion of how economic conditions determine historical development, sets out from a natural, preeconomic foundation:

> The first premise of all human history is, of course, the existence of living human individuals. Thus the first fact to be established is the physical organization of these individuals and their consequent relation to the rest of nature. Of course, we cannot here go either into the actual physical nature of man, or into the natural conditions in which man finds himself—geological, oro-hydrographical, climatic and so on. All historical

writing must set out from these natural bases and their modification in the course of history through the action of men.[13]

One of these original, natural factors is consciousness. Consciousness, from the beginning, it is true, is inseparable from intercourse with other human beings. Consciousness from the start is a social product, but it is not at the start determined by economic conditions:

> Consciousness is at first, of course, merely consciousness concerning the *immediate* sensuous environment and consciousness of the limited connection with other persons and things outside the individual who is growing self-conscious. At the same time it is consciousness of nature, which first confronts men as a completely alien, all-powerful and unassailable force, with which men's relations are purely animal and by which they are overawed like beasts; it is thus a purely animal consciousness of nature . . . precisely because nature is as yet hardly altered by history—on the other hand, it is man's consciousness of the necessity of associating with the individuals around him, the beginning of the consciousness that he is living in society at all. This beginning is as animal as social life itself at this stage. It is mere herd-consciousness, and at this point man is distinguished from sheep only by the fact that with him consciousness takes the place of instinct or that his instinct is a conscious one.[14]

The further development of consciousness is determined by economic factors, increased productivity, needs, and increased population. And with this, division of labor develops. But originally (that is to say, before the predominance of economic conditions) division of labor was "nothing but the division of labour in the sexual act, then the division of labour which develops spontaneously or 'naturally' by virtue of natural predispositions (e.g., physical strength), needs, accidents, etc., etc. . . ."[15] This sexual division of labor precedes the predominance of economic factors. This is not to say that there was no production, no economic activity, going on at this point. People obviously had to eat. Nor is it to say that sexual division of labor or the family can be cleanly separated, isolated, from economic activity; that they have no connection with, no influence upon, or are not influenced at all by, economic activity. But it is to say that this is a very early stage of history, where, among all the factors that make up a sociocultural world, those specific factors connected with production, the economic, have not yet come to predominate in determining all the rest of culture. And the economic does not come to predominate for Marx, as we have seen in the *Grundrisse,* even as late as the ancient Greek

318   *Chapter Eight*

world, where mythology, the imagination, still predominates. In the *German Ideology,* Marx says,

> The first form of property is tribal property . . . It corresponds to the undeveloped stage of production, at which a people lives by hunting and fishing, by cattle-raising or, at most, by agriculture . . . The division of labour is at this stage still very elementary and is confined to a further extension of the natural division of labour existing in the family. The social structure is, therefore, limited to an extension of the family: patriarchal chieftains, below them the members of the tribe, finally slaves. The slavery latent in the family only develops gradually with the increase of population, the growth of wants, and with the extension of external intercourse, both of war and barter.[16]

Here, as in the previous quotation, it is clear that economic production is so undeveloped that not it but natural sexual division of labor—as it develops spontaneously, naturally, or through natural predispositions—causes division of labor to develop in society. Moreover, it is the family, not economic forces outside the family, which gives rise to an extended social structure at this point. The family, of course, is not completely divorced from economic or productive activity, but the family is not dominated and determined exclusively by economic factors. Marx also says, "The third circumstance which, from the very outset, enters into historical development, is that men, who daily re-create their own life, begin to make other men, to propagate their kind: the relation between man and woman, parents and children, the *family.* The family, which to begin with is the only social relation, becomes later, when increased needs create new social relations and the increased population new needs, a subordinate one. . . ."[17] Reproduction, also, is an original, natural condition that determines the historical development of society. It determines the development of the family, which at first is the only social relation—and, as we saw in the previous quotation, all other social relations are a mere extension of the family. All of this before economic conditions predominate.

Very much in agreement with this, as far as I can see, Engels argues,

> According to the materialistic conception, the determining factor in history is, in the final instance, the production and reproduction of the immediate essentials of life. This, again, is of a twofold character. On the one side, the production of the means of existence . . . on the other side, the production of human beings themselves, the propagation of the species. The social organization under which the people of a particular his-

torical epoch and a particular country live is determined by both kinds of production: by the stage of development of labor on the one hand and of the family on the other. The lower the development of labor and the more limited the amount of its products . . . the more the social order is found to be dominated by kinship groups.[18]

At this point, again, it is not economic production (labor) that predominates, but the family. Moreover, as production develops, it first develops *within* the family or kinship groups, "within this structure of society based on kinship groups the productivity of labor increasingly develops, and with it private property and exchange . . . until at last their incompatibility brings about a complete upheaval. In the collision of the newly-developed social classes, the old society founded on kinship groups is broken up; in its place appears a new society . . . in which the system of the family is completely dominated by the system of property. . . ."[19] In other words, while production eventually comes to predominate over and to destroy the family, it originally developed *within* the family and the family predominated over production.

Moreover, it is not just sexual division of labor, reproduction, and the family that are originally considered natural or extraeconomic factors, it is also the case that male domination is one of these original, preeconomic, natural conditions. Marx says, "The division of labour . . . which in its turn is based on the natural division of labour in the family . . . simultaneously implies . . . property, the nucleus, the first form of which lies in the family, where wife and children are the slaves of the husband. This latent slavery in the family, though still very crude, is the first form of property. . . ."[20] And in a previously quoted passage, Marx said, "The slavery latent in the family only develops gradually with the increase of population, the growth of wants, and with the extension of external intercourse, both of war and barter." Here, it is not merely the case that male domination is a natural, extraeconomic factor, but furthermore that it is what gives rise to the economic reality of property. Here, Marx does differ from Engels, who, in the *Origin of the Family,* is famous for holding that it is absurd to think that at the beginning women were the slaves of men. Engels argues that male domination begins only at a later date with the rise of the patriarchal family and especially monogamous marriage. And these institutions arise for economic reasons—out of the need, as property develops in the hands of men, to safeguard paternal laws of inheritance.[21] For Marx, the domination of women is not brought about by economic conditions, but male domination itself establishes economic conditions—at least the first form of property.

So we simply cannot accept the claim of certain modern feminist critics that for Marx the family, sexual division of labor, and male domination are viewed as determined by and subordinate to economic factors that are taken to be primary in all societies and in all epochs. If anything, it is the reverse: economic factors grow up within and develop out of these natural, extraeconomic factors.

If, however, after getting rid of the mistaken notion that Marx holds to the primacy of the economic in all historical periods, we were instead to take Marx's view to be that sexual division of labor is simply natural in the sense of biological, then, it might be argued, we would be heading for different but equally difficult troubles—because this view would also be fundamentally incompatible with much of modern feminist theory. As MacKinnon puts it,

> To Marx, women were defined by nature, not by society. To him, sex was within that "material substratum" that was not subject to social analysis, making his explicit references to women or to sex largely peripheral or parenthetical. With issues of sex, unlike with class, Marx did not see that the line between the social and the pre-social is a line society draws . . . His work shares with liberal theory the view that women naturally belong where they are socially placed . . . Which sex gets which task is first a matter of biology and remains so throughout economic changes . . . Women are assigned housework by nature.[22]

If it is assumed that sexual division of labor is determined naturally or biologically, this can be taken to imply, and has implied for many nonfeminist theorists, that women's roles are fixed, natural, or biologically destined. But as we have seen in Rosaldo, no roles can be universally or naturally attributed to women in all cultures—the roles of women differ widely in different cultures. One of the most important insights of modern feminist theory is that culture transforms natural, biological, sexual differences into gender-defined roles, practices, and institutions.[23] These roles are not fixed, eternal, universal, natural, biological destinies. They are culturally constructed, socially mediated, and historically determined by different cultures in different ways.

It is a serious mistake to think that Marx, of all people, can be accused of biological determinism. He does say in the *German Ideology*, as we have seen, and also in *Capital*,[24] that division of labor has an original, natural, sexual basis, but this certainly does not mean, for Marx, that there is anything fixed, inevitable, eternal, or destined about women's roles. Marx also says, in the *German Ideology,* that the "production of life, both of one's own in labour and of fresh life in procreation, now appears as a twofold relation: on the one hand as natural, on the other as a *social* relation."[25] Sexual relations are not just natural or biological; they are also social.

And it is certainly not the case for Marx that biology can simply determine the social. In a footnote in *Capital*, Marx mentions Darwin and claims that, "as Vico says, human history differs from natural history in this, that we have made the former, but not the latter. . . ."[26] And, for Marx, it is clear that even if we do not make natural history, the making of human history involves the transformation of biological nature. In *Theories of Surplus Value,* Marx discusses Darwin's views on the biological development of plants and animals, and then says, "Man, who produces in society, likewise faces an already modified nature (and in particular natural factors which have been transformed into means of his own activity). . . ."[27] Elsewhere, it is clear that for Marx human history involves even the change of *human nature.* In *Capital*, he says that one "must first deal with human nature in general, and then with human nature as modified in each historical epoch."[28] This even means that basic biological drives like hunger are historically transformed by human history; in the *Grundrisse,* Marx says,

> the object is not an object in general, but a definite object which must be consumed in a definite way, a way mediated by production itself. Hunger is hunger, but hunger that is satisfied by cooked meat eaten with knife and fork differs from hunger that devours raw meat with the help of hands, nails and teeth . . . Production not only provides the material to satisfy a need, but it also provides a need for the material. When consumption emerges from its original natural crudeness and immediacy—and its remaining in that state would be due to the fact that production was still caught in natural crudeness—then it is itself as an urge, mediated by the object . . . Production therefore produces not only an object for the subject, but also a subject for the object.[29]

In the *German Ideology,* Marx says much the same sort of thing about basic desires, "these desires—namely desires which exist under all relations . . . change their form and direction under different social relations. . . ."[30] Even the human senses are transformed historically, "senses capable of human gratification, senses affirming themselves as essential powers of man [are] either cultivated or brought into being. For not only the five senses but also the so-called mental senses, the practical senses (will, love, etc.) . . . the human nature of the senses, comes to be by virtue of its object, by virtue of humanized nature. The forming of the five senses is a labour of the entire history of the world down to the present."[31]

It is quite clear also that the sexual relation between men and women, which Marx in the *German Ideology* insisted was both a natural or biological relation and a *social* relation, would also undergo change, be mediated culturally, and be modified historically. In fact, as we will see in more detail below, for Marx the relation between man and woman indicates the level to which the human essence has *changed* and *developed*.[32] Thus, despite the fact that sexual relations, reproduction, and sexual division of labor have a natural, original, biological core, this does not mean for Marx that such relations are fixed, unchanging destinies that hold throughout all history. Marx certainly does not develop, with all the sophistication of modern feminist theory, the distinction between biological sex and socioculturally constructed gender roles, but he certainly anticipates, and perhaps even provides some of the groundwork for, this distinction. He certainly draws a distinction between a natural, biologically developed core and the way this is modified socially and historically so as to transform the relations and roles that grow out of this biological relation. As Rubin puts it,

> Marx once asked: "What is a Negro slave? A man of the black race. The one explanation is as good as the other. A Negro is a Negro. He only becomes a slave in certain relations. A cotton spinning jenny is a machine for spinning cotton. It becomes *capital* only in certain relations. Torn from these relationships it is no more capital than gold in itself is money or sugar is the price of sugar" . . . One might paraphrase: What is a domesticated woman? A female of the species. The one explanation is as good as the other. A woman is a woman. She only becomes a domestic, a wife, a chattel, a playboy bunny, a prostitute, or a human dictaphone in certain relations. Torn from these relationships, she is no more the helpmate of man than gold in itself is money. . . .[33]

Thus, while the conceptual distinction between biological sex and socioculturally constructed gender roles, as fully developed by modern feminist theorists like Rubin, cannot be said to be present in Marx's thought, the core of the concept is certainly there and Marx has a lot to say about how biological relations are historically transformed into socioculturally constructed roles, though he does not have very much to say specifically about *gender* roles.

Thus, originally, the family, sexual division of labor, and reproduction are natural, extraeconomic conditions that come to interact with social and economic conditions and are thereby transformed from their natural state. Eventually, economic conditions, especially with the rise of capitalism, become more powerful, predominate over, and come to determine these original natural conditions. But the fact that these conditions were originally natural and extraeconomic leaves room for the fact that even in capitalist society it may not be possible to explain all aspects of the condition of women solely by considering economic factors; and certainly it suggests that the overcoming of capitalism and of the primacy of economic factors will not automatically eliminate all oppression of women. The oppression of women, after all, began before the primacy of economic factors. It has been modified and has been increased in certain ways, though diminished in other ways, by capitalism; and the emancipation of women has been blocked in certain specific ways, and assisted in other ways, by capitalism.

Balbus, in opposition to this, thinks that it is Marx's view that capitalism itself eliminates male domination and sexual division of labor, which implies that there would be nothing left for a socialist theorist to be concerned with in this area.[34] He cites Marx's claim in the *Manifesto* that, "Differences of age and sex have no longer any distinctive social validity for the working class. All are instruments of labour, more or less expensive to use, according to age and sex."[35] But this passage hardly suggests that all oppression of women has been eliminated by capitalism. It merely suggests that, as women and children are drawn into the factory, all are treated, in a certain sense, the same—as workers, as labor power. Capitalism does contribute in some limited sense to the equality of women, but certainly not in all ways. This passage itself suggests that wages will be determined by sex; in other words, that women will receive lower wages.[36] Moreover, it is Marx's view in several places that under capitalism, women are seen as the property, or at least as the possessions, of men.[37] In *Capital* Marx even says that as women and children are drawn into the factory beside men, the workman who previously "sold his own labour-power, which he disposed of nominally as a free agent. Now he sells wife and child. He has become a slave-dealer."[38] This is hardly to overcome the oppression of women in capitalist society. Marx's view is that capitalism both contributes to the emancipation of women and also increases their oppression. He says,

> It was not, however, the misuse of parental authority that created the capitalistic exploitation, whether direct or indirect, of children's labour, but,

on the contrary, it was the capitalistic mode of exploitation which, by sweeping away the economic basis of parental authority, made its exercise degenerate into a mischievous misuse of power. However terrible and disgusting the dissolution, under the capitalist system, of the old family ties may appear, nevertheless, modern industry, by assigning as it does an important part in the process of production, outside the domestic sphere, to women, to young persons, and to children of both sexes, creates a new economic foundation for a higher form of the family and of the relations between the sexes. It is, of course, just as absurd to hold the Teutonic-Christian form of the family to be absolute and final as it would be to apply that character to the ancient Roman, the ancient Greek, or the Eastern forms which, moreover, taken together form a series in historical development. Moreover, it is obvious that the fact of the collective working group being composed of individuals of both sexes and all ages, must necessarily, under suitable conditions, become a source of humane development; although in its spontaneously developed, brutal, capitalistic form, where the labourer exists for the process of production, and not the process of production for the labourer, that fact is a pestiferous source of corruption and slavery.[39]

Capitalism creates the conditions for the development of a higher and more humane form of the family and of relations between the sexes, but in the meantime it oppresses the family and women in a more brutal fashion than before.

Moreover, it does not follow from any of this that Marx's view is that socialism will automatically emancipate women, as is often suggested by modern feminists.[40] Even Engels, who is especially accused of this, only says,

> We can already see from this that to emancipate woman and make her the equal of the man is and remains an impossibility so long as the woman is shut out from social productive labor and restricted to private domestic labor. The emancipation of woman will only be *possible* when woman can take part in production on a large, social scale, and domestic work no longer claims anything but an insignificant amount of her time. And only now has that become *possible* through modern large-scale industry, which does not merely permit of the employment of female labor over a wide range, but positively demands it, while it also tends toward ending private domestic labor by changing it more and more into a public industry.[41]

Engels is not saying that socialism will automatically emancipate women. He merely states some of the conditions achieved—participation in production and a certain degree of freedom from housework—that are necessary conditions (and he does not say they are *sufficient* conditions) for such emancipation to become *possible.* On the other hand, Engels does say, "The supremacy of man in marriage is the simple consequence of his economic supremacy, and with the abolition of the latter will disappear of itself."[42] This may sound as if the emancipation of women is expected to be automatic. But all this passage actually says is that to emancipate women it is necessary to eliminate male economic supremacy. It does not say anything about how easy it will be to do so and it does not suggest that it will be automatic in socialist society.

At any rate, even if one decides to read Engels as holding that the emancipation of women will be automatic in socialist society, this is very clearly not Marx's view. In fact, it would be very strange for Marx to hold that all aspects of the previous domination of women would automatically disappear with the collapse of capitalist society. In the "Critique of the Gotha Program," in describing the first stage of communist society, Marx says that what "we are dealing with here is a communist society, not as it has developed on its own foundations, but on the contrary, just as it emerges from capitalist society; which is thus in *every* respect, economically, morally, and intellectually, still stamped with the birth-marks of the old society from whose womb it emerges."[43] All objectionable aspects of past society do not automatically disappear under socialism; many of them will remain and a good deal of work will still be required to overcome them.

Moreover, far from the emancipation of women being automatic, *socialism* will not even be automatic. Socialism will have consciously to be built. What socialism means, for Marx, has to do much less with achieving a pat utopian blueprint, an ideal set of institutions, than it has to do with achieving a certain form of *activity.* Socialism can almost be defined as a society that begins to eliminate obstacles to *free activity.* "All-round dependence, this primary natural form of the world-historical co-operation of individuals, will be transformed by this communist revolution into the control and conscious mastery of these powers, which, born of the action of men on one another, have till now overawed and ruled men as powers completely alien to them."[44] Socialism begins to remove certain kinds of obstacles and begins to put people in the position of consciously and collectively controlling their social relations themselves. This requires certain material preconditions and certain forms of conscious activity,[45] failing which "all the old filthy business would necessarily be restored...."[46]

Thus, as they struggle to become free, these individuals themselves will have to consciously and freely set about the emancipation of women—and they could certainly fail to achieve this emancipation. In the *Economic and Philosophic Manuscripts,* Marx considers one form of communism that might arise after the demise of capitalism—what he calls "crude" communism. This communism, which Marx totally rejects, far from overcoming property, merely generalizes it and makes it the property of the community, and, along with this, it turns women into the communal property of men.[47] Far from it being the case that communism will automatically overcome the oppression of women, crude communism merely communalizes this oppression. Thus, again, very clearly, individuals will have to work consciously to build an acceptable communist society and to emancipate women within it—it is not expected to happen automatically.

For these reasons, the feminist movement and feminist theory should not subordinate themselves to the socialist movement and socialist theory. The latter certainly will not solve all problems for women and there will be much left for feminists to do in socialist society, though the socialist movement and socialist theory certainly can and should contribute to the feminist movement and feminist theory, as well as vice versa. In general, it is not fruitful to argue that one form of oppression—of women, races, or classes—is more fundamental than another, that one is the source out of which another rises, or that overcoming one will overcome the others. One form of oppression should not be reduced to another nor to one theory that will explain them all. They are different, though they can interact in complex ways. Overcoming one or developing a theory to overcome one may help in overcoming another, may remove some obstacles, but it is not likely to do so completely. It is not desirable to reduce all theories of oppression and emancipation to one theory. Pluralism is necessary and desirable here. And, as I have argued in Chapter 7, I do not think that Marx's views are incompatible with this.

II. Men, Women, and the Species

Even if I have been successful in defending Marx against claims that central and distinctive elements of his thought are incompatible or in contradiction with fundamental commitments of modern feminist theory, still, other critics might argue and have argued that what little Marx does have to say about feminist issues does not make any serious conceptual contribution to modern feminist theory and that in large part he ignores women, excludes them from, or at best considers them peripheral to, serious theory.

For example, Eisenstein says, "Marx never questioned the hierarchical sexual ordering of society. He did not see that this . . . made species life unavailable to women, and hence that its actualization could not come about through the dismantling of the class system alone."[48] It has also been argued that Marx's critique of private property fails to see that property is controlled by males,[49] and it has been claimed that Marx fails to pay enough attention to reproduction.[50] It is quite clear that Marx devotes little space to discussion of such matters, but I would like to claim that if what he does in fact say is *conceptually* unpacked and developed, then we will discover that he has a good deal to say that is relevant to modern feminist theory and that reproduction, women's relation to species life, and the oppression of women that arises from the relationship of men to private property are not at all peripheral matters for Marx.

For example, in a very interesting though rather brief passage from the *Economic and Philosophic Manuscripts,* Marx suggests that the relation of man to woman is a most fundamental species relationship and that in this relationship we find indicated most clearly the level to which the human essence has been realized. In fact, from this relationship we can judge the human species' whole level of development.[51] This passage is often referred to by feminist theorists,[52] but, as far as I am aware, it has never been conceptually unpacked. Let me begin to try to unpack it.

As we have seen, in the *German Ideology* Marx claims that the relationship of man to woman in the procreation of life is both a natural relationship and a social one.[53] He makes the same point here in the *Economic and Philosophic Manuscripts* when he says,

> The direct, natural, and necessary relation of person to person is the relation of man to woman. In this natural species-relationship man's relation to nature is immediately his relation to man, just as his relation to man is immediately his relation to nature—his own natural destination. In this relationship, therefore, is sensuously manifested, reduced to an observable fact, the extent to which the human essence has become nature to man, or to which nature to him has become the human essence of man . . . This relationship also reveals the extent to which man's need has become a human need; the extent to which, therefore, the other person as a person has become for him a need—the extent to which he in his individual existence is at the same time a *social* being.[54]

This passage clearly claims that the relationship of man to woman is natural, and it also claims that this relationship to nature or the natural "is immediately his relation to man" and that this relationship reveals the extent to which the other person "has become for him a need." In other words, it claims that this relationship is a *social* relationship, one, in fact, that reveals the extent to which the individual is a "social being." We must also see that the relationship between man and woman, for Marx, is an essential relationship—it is part of the essence of human beings. This is so for Marx because, as we have seen earlier, need indicates essence. If we need something, our need indicates that without that thing we cannot develop, become what we can be, realize our potential, or be fulfilled—in short, we cannot realize our essence. Need indicates that what we need is essentially related to us; that it is part of our essence.[55] In this way, man and woman are part of each other's essence. They need each other in the most fundamental way—to give birth to the future species and, indeed, to have been born themselves. Thus this essential relation is natural or biological; it is necessary for the biological reproduction of the species. And it is also social—each needs an other person, and other persons of past generations. Thus this relationship to nature—the natural or biological dimension of human existence—is a relation to others, a social relation; and this social relation is a natural or biological relation. We must not view the natural relation and the social relation as two different and unconnected relations. They are intimately connected, and the social, we have seen, will mediate and historically transform the natural.

To say that the human being is a social being is also to say that human beings are not radically individual, atomic, isolated beings. Human beings are by nature social beings. They are *essentially* social beings—or species beings. Other human beings are part of our essence: essential to what we are, how we develop, and what we can become. Individual human beings are socially constructed by others, by society, by culture, by the human species in general. Individuals take in the aims, values, aspirations, conceptions, perspectives, knowledge, technical know-how, strategies, and many other things, of their sociocultural world. The individual then works this over, labors upon it, perhaps develops it, perhaps comes up with something new, and then redeposits it back in culture for others to take in and repeat the process. Individuals are produced by others, by culture, by the species. And, also, individuals produce, transform, and develop others, their culture, the species: "just as society itself produces man as man, so is society produced by him."[56]

This, in rough outline, as we have seen in earlier chapters, is Marx's general view of the relationship of the individual to the sociocultural world. What we must now notice in particular is that this relationship, in which the species transforms and produces itself and its world, this species relationship, in what is one of its most fundamental and essential forms, is the relationship of *man* to *woman*,[57] a relationship from which one can judge the human species' "whole level of development." What does this mean?

In giving birth to a child, a woman and a man produce, naturally and biologically, a new member of the human species. However, it is not simply this particular man and woman who produce this particular child. We must say that the human species has produced a new individual member of the species. The particular man and woman are themselves the outcome of the species—the outcome of the species' past natural, biological, genetic development—and they pass this inheritance on to their child. Moreover, in nurturing and raising the child, in giving the child an upbringing and an education, the parents also pass on to the child the sociocultural inheritance of the species—cultural aspirations, aims, values, conceptions, perspectives, knowledge, technical know-how, strategies, and so forth. Through the relationship of man to woman, the species objectifies itself in a new member of the species. The parents mediate between the species (its past biological and sociocultural development) and the individual young child.[58] And then the child, as it grows up, will work upon this inheritance, transform it, perhaps come up with something new that can be redeposited in culture for others to take in, and perhaps the child will also pass this inheritance on by contributing to the biological reproduction of future members of the species and then their cultural upbringing and socialization as well.

Without this essential relation of man to woman, obviously, there would not be a human species, and, for Marx, individuals would not be species beings—beings who can take in and pass on, beings who can be transformed by and can transform, the biological and sociocultural inheritance of the species.[59]

But also to be a species being, for Marx, is to be able to work for the benefit of the species. And very clearly, the relation of man to woman in reproducing a child is to work for the benefit of the species. It is to produce biologically and culturally a new member of the species, who may go on to do the same for future members of the species. This relationship constitutes, as Marx says, our "natural destination"—our *"Bestimmung,"* our vocation or destiny.[60]

Moreover, to realize the species' essence we must work for the universal and must do so consciously, freely, and intentionally.[61] So also in the desire of parents for a child and in their desire to bring up a child, they transcend mere self-interest. They work for the development of the other, the child, though at the same time it is *their* child and thus in an important sense *themselves* that they work for. But despite the fact that they work for themselves in some sense, they nevertheless work for the development of another who may grow up to become a reproducer (biologically and culturally) of the further development of still other children and thus of the future species. And just as parents work to improve the conditions of their child over their own conditions, they thus work to improve the conditions of the future species. They work to satisfy the needs and develop the powers and capacities that are important for their child, but which at the same time would be important for any child, any member of the species, and which may well be passed on through their child to the future species. They thus work to satisfy needs and to develop powers and capacities that would be universalizable, that therefore, we must say, would be demanded by the categorical imperative, and in doing so they contribute to the realization of the essence of the species.

Most parents, of course, do not consciously work for the species in this way. They seek their own satisfaction and development in having and in bringing up a child, and they seek the satisfaction and well being of *their* child, which in some sense is in *their* own interest also. Perhaps they even have a natural biological drive to have and to raise a child. But, nevertheless, this biological drive, if it exists, and this self-interest (which is certainly culturally mediated and shaped, and thus is a sociocultural interest) lead to the universal—the continuance and development of the species—whether the parents realize it or not. We can say that these drives have built into them, despite the narrower and self-interested focus of the parents, a tendency to realize the essence of the species and to work for the universal, the categorical imperative.

In other words, we have here another version of what we earlier found in the "Introduction to the Critique of Hegel's Philosophy of Law." There the particular, selfish, class interest of the proletariat led unintentionally toward the universal, the categorical imperative.[62] Since the proletariat was so deprived and oppressed, its needs and interests (for food, clothing, shelter, education, general human development, and so forth) would be basic needs and interests we would be satisfied for any and all human beings, universal species needs and interests whose satisfaction would be demanded by the categorical imperative and which would be necessary for the realization of the essence of the species. And just as the proletariat, as it acts self-interestedly to satisfy its needs and interests, whether it realizes it or not, heads toward what the categorical imperative would demand, so as parents self-interestedly satisfy the needs and interests of their child, they too, whether they realize it or not, work toward what the categorical imperative would demand and what is necessary for the realization of the essence of the species.

This biological drive, if it exists, as well as the culturally mediated self-interest of the parents, can, however, become a conscious and intentional working for the benefit of the species, and for Marx it ought to become so. Individuals ought consciously to mediate between the past inheritance of the species and the future development of the species. They ought to comprehend this relationship, understand it, consciously embed it in their social, cultural, political, and familial institutions, and act on it consciously and morally in accordance with the categorical imperative and thus for the realization of the essence of the species.

It is important to see, though, that what we have here is not *merely* a *moral ought.* Biological as well as sociocultural drives are also present here and they themselves work toward the same end that morality would demand.[63] And once we see this, we can begin, consciously and morally, to guide, to hasten, these drives toward their goal. If so, then this natural biological drive (if it exists) as well as the sociocultural drive (which is also natural, at least in the sense that it occurs despite us and without our intention) can be made conscious and can be morally guided toward the realization of our essence. Thus, nature would become the essence of human beings and the human essence would become natural.

However, it is not at all the case that in all societies this natural biological and this sociocultural drive will lead smoothly toward the categorical imperative and the realization of the species essence. A great deal of alienation, oppression, and domination can be present in any given society that will frustrate this process. Marx, after all, takes up the whole discussion of the relation of man to woman and the realization of the human essence in the context of his discussion of crude communism.

Crude communism, for Marx, is communism that does not abolish private property but rather allows it to "persist as the relationship of the community to the world of things."[64] It transfers property to the ownership of the community. Moreover, along with this, crude communism institutes a community of women. Marx has in mind, perhaps, Plato's community of women or the views of some earlier utopian socialists. At any rate, crude communism rejects marriage, which, Marx says, historically was "certainly a form of exclusive private property. . . ."[65] Instead, in crude communism,

> a woman becomes a piece of communal and common property. It may be said that this idea of the community of women gives away the secret of this as yet completely crude and thoughtless communism. Just as woman passes from marriage to general prostitution, so the entire world of wealth (that is, of man's objective substance) passes from the relationship of exclusive marriage with the owner of private property to a state of universal prostitution with the community.[66]

Crude communism merely generalizes capitalist property. It makes property common or communal. It does not eliminate property. Likewise, women are still possessed, owned—they are still the property of men. It is just that they are held in common rather than privately. The oppression of women has not been eliminated. Marx says, "In the approach to woman as the spoil and handmaid of communal lust is expressed the infinite degradation in which man exists for himself, for the secret of this approach has its unambiguous, decisive, plain and undisguised expression in the relation of man to woman and in the manner in which this direct and natural species-relationship is conceived."[67]

This conception of the relationship of man to woman, the conception of women as possessions, will frustrate the realization of the human essence and make it impossible to work for the benefit of the species, the universal, the categorical imperative. It will, in fact, express the "infinite degradation" in which human beings exist for themselves because it will transform the relationship of man to woman, this species relationship, which, despite us, leads to the universal, toward the development of the species as a whole, and which should be consciously pursued as one of our highest ends. It will transform this into a mere means to satisfy the lust, the particular sexual interests, of the individual men of this crude communistic community.

For men to treat women as property, as possessions, as things to be owned, as instruments of production,[68] as means, either individually, as in past society, or collectively, as in this crude communistic society, is not only very obviously to violate the categorical imperative to treat all persons as ends in themselves, but it is to violate the very essence of the relationship of man to woman, the species essence, my essence, because the relationship of man to woman most fundamentally expresses the fact that human beings are species beings and must work for the benefit of the species. Human beings are produced by and produce (both biologically and socioculturally) the species as a whole. And for an individual to have been produced by the species, human beings in the past must have worked (even if only unconsciously) for the universal, the species. This is not only something they morally ought to have done, but something they in fact did, naturally, biologically, and culturally. If not, there would not *be* a species—I myself would not exist. To raise to the conscious, intentional, moral level this natural, biological, and sociocultural fact—to comprehend what we in fact are so as to fully and consciously become what we can be—requires that we work consciously for the universal, the species as a whole, the categorical imperative, and thus for the realization of our essence. As Marx says, for an existent to realize its essence it must live up to its concept. Just as a true friend is one who lives up to the concept, the ideal, of friendship, so the true relation of man to woman is one that lives up to the concept, the ideal, of this relation.[69]

For men to relate to women and children as possessions, to conceive the species relation is this way, to imply that the vocation of women and children is to satisfy my lusts, my particular interests, rather than to work for the universal, the species, is to violate the essence of the species, which is also my own essence; and thus is not only an infinite degradation, but it is also an absurd contradiction. In other words, the argument here is that men should not possess women because that is harmful to women, but if this is not enough to convince incorrigible men the argument further suggests that for a man to possess a woman expresses the violation of his very own essence, of what he is as a human being.

If we understand what human beings are, namely, species beings, beings that are the objectification of the species' past inheritance and that contribute to passing on this inheritance to the future species; if we see that each individual is a link in a long chain—a mediating, connecting, link—between the past and the future of the species, then we see that to claim to own, possess, control a human being—a wife or child—implies, whether I realize it or not, a claim to possess, to own, to control, the ongoing development, the process of inheritance, of the species. In claiming to possess, to own, to control my wife and child, I would be claiming to control, through my wife and child, the future species, or at least to control the relation of my wife and child to the future species. This is not only outrageous, but it is absurd—because it is impossible.

They will escape me and develop on their own. They will do so just as I did in escaping from, in transcending, the human species that produced me, in escaping my parents, my father, who produced me and would have claimed to possess, to control, to own, me. After all, I have asserted my own autonomy, my independence, from my parents. I have done so, if in no other way, at least in claiming to own, to possess, to control, *my* child or wife, and, by implication, through them future generations.

Nevertheless, it is ludicrous to think that in possessing a wife or child I can *really* control their relation to culture, that I can even control the upbringing of my child—control what my child will take in from the past social, cultural, and moral inheritance of the species. It is literally impossible to actually and fully *reduce* this transmission, this general species process, to my simple possession and control. It will always escape me. Culture is too complex to control all that the child takes in even from its parents, certainly for the father to control all that the child takes in from its mother—the mother will almost always be able to escape the control of her husband (as well as her father) at least in this way. Even for the husband to control all that the child takes in from himself, the child's father, is impossible, let alone the rest of culture that surrounds the child, and let alone the way the child will grow up to interact with this culture in the future.

Moreover, to the extent to which I try to reduce this transmission, try to make it serve my particular interests rather than the species in general, and to the extent to which I succeed, I violate, distort, frustrate, slow down the future development of the species. And those who did this in the past have violated, distorted, and frustrated my own development. Thus, the approach to woman as the spoil of lust, as possession, as property, expresses the infinite degradation in which men, who wish to possess women, exist for themselves. This desire to possess women and children expresses the degree to which I, as the offspring of previous generations of the species, have been distorted, degraded, and frustrated in my development. Thus, from the way that men and women act toward each other, the way they culturally conceive the species relationship, we can see as an observable fact the past development of the species, and we can judge the character of that development—the degree to which men and women have realized their essence or violated, contradicted, distorted, and degraded the essence of the species; thus their *own* essence, their own nature.

Moreover, as de Beauvoir put it, "the woman who enjoys the richest individual life will have the most to give her children. . . ."[70] Thus, for men to treat women as possessions, as means, to distort and frustrate their development, will distort and frustrate the development of their own children, who will, at least in large part (if not, as in the past, almost totally) be raised by women. And indeed this will have happened in the past to the man himself who was also brought up by a woman. The possession of women implies the frustration and distortion of the development even of those who come to possess women. Thus, obviously for women but also for men, the past inheritance of the species must come to be reunderstood and reconstructed from a feminist perspective. One must uncover women's history, and criticize it, discover women's real contributions, and revalue them. If not, the transmission of culture to the future species will continue to exclude crucial aspects of the species' inheritance, prolong women's silence and silencing, and prolong the species' degradation and impoverishment.

In all of this, Marx has made it quite clear that the proper relation of man to woman should not be one of possession or property (whether private or communal). Indeed, Mitchell claims that beyond this Marx never ventured.[71] But already, in unpacking and developing this section, we have seen that Marx has ventured further. We have seen that the relation of man to woman should be one that works for the universal, the categorical imperative, and the realization of the species essence. But still this does not say enough, except at a very abstract level, about what the relationship between man and woman *should* be. What this relationship should be, I think, becomes clear in the rest of the section of the *Economic and Philosophic Manuscripts* in which this discussion appears, the section entitled "Private Property and Communism." This has not been noticed either by Marx scholars or feminist theorists, I suspect, because Marx, in the rest of this section, for the most part stops referring to the relationship of man to woman. Nevertheless, in the rest of this section Marx continues to reject private property as well as the relationship of having, owning, or possessing. And that, after all, was what he was objecting to in the relationship of man to woman. Moreover, in the rest of this section Marx explicitly spells out the relationship that he thinks should replace the attitude of possession. Thus clearly this is the attitude he is also advocating for the relationship between man and woman, though he does not come right out and say so. This relationship, I have argued elsewhere,[72] as well as in Chapter 6, is an *aesthetic* relationship.

Lest calling this relationship an aesthetic relationship suggest to anyone that what is being said here is that men should relate to women as beautiful objects of desire, or as objects of sexual beauty to be possessed, let me hasten to point out that that is precisely what an aesthetic relationship *is not* for the tradition of German aesthetic theory (Kant, Schiller, Hegel) to which Marx was heir. An aesthetic relationship is explicitly contrasted to a relationship of possession or a relationship in which desire, interest, or inclination predominate.[73] An aesthetic experience, for this tradition, is, on the subjective side, one where inclination, feeling, or desire, on the one hand; and reason, our intellectual and reflective capacities, on the other, are brought into harmony and balance, where neither side predominates over the other, and thus where the whole person is brought into play. It is also, on the objective side, a relationship in which you relate yourself to the object or person for their own sake, where you appreciate them as ends in themselves, and where you open yourself to their particular, intrinsic qualities as valuable in their own right.[74]

For example, Marx says, "Private property has made us so stupid and one-sided that an object is only ours when we have it—when it exists for us as capital, or when it is directly possessed, eaten, drunk, worn, inhabited, etc.,—in short when it is used by us."[75] Instead of this, we want an open sensitivity to a rich, complex, diverse world of other people appreciated as ends in themselves. "Each of [our] human relations to the world—seeing, hearing, smelling, tasting, feeling, thinking, observing, experiencing, wanting, acting, loving . . . are . . . in their orientation to the object . . . the appropriation of human reality."[76] These sensitivities, Marx says, should "become directly in their practice *theoreticians.*" This means that they "relate themselves to the thing for the sake of the thing. . . ."[77] The term "theory" implies the contemplation of something as an end in itself. It is directly opposed to a grasping, need-driven, or possessive relationship. Marx says, "The care-burdened, poverty-stricken man has no sense for the finest play; the dealer in minerals sees only the commercial value but not the beauty and the specific character of the mineral . . ."[78] or also, I suggest, of the other person.

If a man possesses a woman, if he views her merely as his property, he will not see her as the objectification of the past inheritance of the species; he will not see her specific character, her human qualities, her intrinsic virtues. He will not see these things for two reasons. First, because women have been reduced to possessions, to things, to means for the satisfaction of men's lust, and thus have been closed off from the past inheritance of the species—it was not allowed to develop in them or it has been submerged, hidden, and distorted in them. Or, second, he will not see these qualities in her because he has not developed in himself the sensitivity to appreciate such qualities. "Just as music awakens in man the sense of music, and just as the most beautiful music has no sense for the unmusical ear—is [no] object for it, because my object can only be the confirmation of one of my essential powers—it can therefore only exist for me insofar as my essential power exists for itself as a subjective capacity; because the meaning of an object for me goes only so far as my sense goes. . . ."[79] He will not have developed this sensitivity because he is caught up in and can only understand crude possession. He is poverty stricken and can only see commercial value, in part, perhaps, because he himself was the possession of others. After all, if his mother was the possession of his father, then he, as the possession of his mother, was the possession of a possession. All of this will indicate the poverty of the species as objectified in the ongoing relationship between man and woman, their own poverty, and the poverty they will transmit to and reproduce in the future species through their child.

It is Marx's view that objects and persons themselves stimulate in us a sensitivity, a need, for those objects or persons.[80] So, if a woman, or a man, has not had the inheritance, the wealth, the powers and capacities, the diversity of the species objectified in them, or if these qualities have been distorted in them, then these qualities will not be there to stimulate appropriate responses in other persons, to call forth the capacity of others to appreciate them, or develop them for themselves. Men and women, thus, will not foster each other's development, and consequently will transmit and reproduce this poverty through their child in the future development of the species. This will certainly not produce the "rich human being . . . in need of a totality of human manifestations of life . . ."[81] that Marx is after.

Moreover, an aesthetic relationship quite clearly implies that one must not reduce the other person to an abstract category, "strip [them] of all determinateness so as to class [them] as capitalist or worker,"[82] or, we might add, men should not see women as merely wives, housewives, or objects of lust. Instead individuals must appreciate the specific qualities, the character, the concrete determinateness, of other persons.

For Marx, how we conceive the relation of man to woman, the species relation, and how we embed this conception in our social, cultural, political, and familial institutions, has to do with how we socially construct our world. Marx says that such conceptions, "feelings, passions, etc., are not merely anthropological phenomena in the [narrower] sense, but truly *ontological* affirmations of being (of nature). . . ."[83] In other words, such conceptions and feelings are not merely subjective attitudes, not merely *for-us,* or anthropological, but they affirm, reinforce, and construct reality *ontologically.* They form the future of the species, the way men and women will relate to each other, their social relations and institutions, the way they will work on their world and be formed by that world, and the way this will all be transmitted and reproduced for the future species.

Private property, money, and especially the possession of women, for Marx, fundamentally—ontologically—distort social reality:

> That which is for me through the medium of money—that for which I can pay (i.e., which money can buy)—that am I myself, the possessor of the money. The extent of the power of money is the extent of my power. Money's properties are my—the possessor's—properties and essential powers. Thus, what I am and am capable of is by no means determined by my individuality. I am ugly, but I can buy for myself the most beautiful of women. Therefore I am not ugly, for the effect of ugliness—its deterrent power—is nullified by money . . . It is the visible divinity—the transformation of all human and natural properties into their contraries, the universal confounding and distorting of things: impossibilities are soldered together by it.[84]

This, for Marx, actually overturns reality; it turns an image, a whim, a distortion, into reality. And it turns reality into a mere image, whim, or distortion:

> Money as the external, universal medium and faculty (not springing from man as man or from human society as society) for turning an image into reality and reality into a mere image, transforms the real essential powers of man and nature into what are merely abstract notions and therefore imperfections and tormenting chimeras, just as it transforms real imperfections and chimeras—essential powers which are really impotent, which exist only in the imagination of the individual—into real and essential powers and faculties. In the light of this characteristic alone, money is thus the general distorting of individualities which turns them into their opposite and confers contradictory attributes upon their attributes.[85]

Instead of this, "Assume man to be man and his relationship to the world to be a human one: then you can exchange love only for love, trust for trust, etc. If you want to enjoy art, you must be an artistically cultivated person; if you want to exercise influence over other people, you must be a person with a stimulating and encouraging effect on other people. Every one of your relations to man and to nature must be a specific expression, corresponding to the object of your will, of your real individual life."[86]

Again, concrete, specific, individual, human relations—a sensitivity to specific qualities valued as ends in themselves—must replace abstract and reductive categories, images, or distortions (like women as mere objects to be bought or possessed).

In a letter of 21 June 1856 to Jenny, his wife, Marx writes,

> I now understand how it is that even the least flattering portraits of the mother of God, the "Black Madonnas", could have their inveterate admirers—more admirers, indeed, than the good portraits. At any rate, none of these "Black Madonna" portraits has ever been so much kissed and ogled and adored as your photograph . . . Mere spatial separation from you suffices to make me instantly aware that time has done for my love just what the sun and the rain do for plants—made it grow . . . I feel myself once more a man because I feel intense passion, and the multifariousness in which we are involved by study and modern education, no less than the scepticism which inevitably leads us to cavil at every subjective and objective impression, is calculated to render each one of us petty and weak and fretful and vacillating. But, love, not for Feuerbachian man, not for Moleschottian metabolism, not for the proletariat, but love for a sweetheart and notably for yourself, turns a man back into a man again . . . In your sweet countenance I can read even my infinite sorrows, my irreplaceable losses [a reference to the death of three of the Marxes' children], and when I kiss your sweet face I kiss away my sorrow. "Buried in her arms, revived by her kisses"—in your arms, that is, and by your kisses—and let the Brahmins and Pythagoras keep their doctrine of re-birth, and Christianity its doctrine of resurrection.[87]

It is often argued by modern feminists that certain ways of experiencing the world, certain personality traits, attitudes, and feelings tend to be more characteristic of women than of men. And while these attitudes, feelings, and traits have no doubt functioned as part of the oppression of women in the past, nevertheless, in emancipating women, they should not be lost. They are most important—they should be preserved and revalued. They should contribute to women's liberation and the restructuring of culture.[88] As Gottlieb puts it, abstract reason that seeks authority in something more than the shared experience of communicating subjectivities and subjective needs, that sets itself apart from the inevitable rootedness and partiality of a particular person, group, or time, that seeks detached objectivity, are among the qualities that generally tend to characterize male attitudes. Whereas partiality, particularness, the concrete and determinate, authority rooted in communicating subjectivities and subjective needs, feeling, nurturing, and caring are qualities that generally tend to characterize female attitudes.[89]

Notice that in this letter to Jenny, Marx continuously takes the feminine side. The particular is more important than the general—this specific person, Jenny, is more important than the proletariat. Personal feelings are more important than abstractions. The subjective is more important than the objective. Partiality is more important than impartiality.

However, one must at the same time admit that men are notoriously capable of such attitudes and statements when they want to flatter, seduce, or use women; and, indeed, in this letter itself the question arises as to whether Marx's attitude toward his wife is sexist. How are we to understand his reference to the ogling and adoration of Jenny and to the fact that she causes passion to arise in him that makes him feel like a man again?

I would not want to argue that Marx's letter is *completely* free of all sexism. After all, elsewhere Marx says, upon the birth of his daughter, Eleanor, that he would have preferred a son.[90] And he is capable, though not very often, as far as I can see, of statements like the following: "If he is an idle capitalist, they only save him the labour of doing anything at all: like a slut having her hair curled or her nails cut instead of doing it herself. . . ."[91] In the letter to Jenny, Marx is trying to flatter his wife and in doing so gets caught up, to some extent, in the language of his time. He also tends a bit to put her on a pedestal. I do not think, beyond this, though, that the letter is sexist.

I do not think, for example, that Marx presents his wife as a sex object. His comparing of her to the Madonna works against such an interpretation. The kissing and ogling of Jenny's photograph is likened to the kissing and ogling of portraits of the mother of God, which certainly deemphasizes the sexual. It might not deemphasize the sexual for a believing Christian, who, as heir to the courtly love tradition, might well assimilate sexual love for a woman to love of the Madonna. But Marx is certainly not a Christian, believing or otherwise; it is not at all likely that he loves the Madonna; and thus it would be quite odd for him to chose this analogy to express sexual love for Jenny. Rather, it is clearly adoration or admiration of the Madonna, and of Jenny, that is the issue here. And this admiration of the Madonna, in the first sentence of the quotation, is clearly an *aesthetic* admiration of the Madonna as an artwork, and, as well, it is adoration as religious worship. I suggest that this admiration or adoration should be understood, as in the *Economic and Philosophic Manuscripts,* as an aesthetic contemplation of Jenny as an end in herself, an appreciation of her specific qualities, her particular virtues. And these personal qualities are much more important than abstractions like Feuerbachian man, Moleschottian metabolism, or the proletariat.

Moreover, the passion that Jenny arouses in him, and which makes him a man again, while not unsexual, I would suggest, echoes the notion in the *Economic and Philosophic Manuscripts* that the relation between man and woman, need and passion, exchanging love only for love, is what makes you truly human—in Marx's case, a man. The relation to, the need for, the passion for, the particular qualities, the specific virtues, the humanness, of the other person as an end in themself, as valuable in their own right, is likened to admiration or adoration of the Madonna. Marx does not bring in the Madonna, I do not think, to suggest anything specifically religious—after all, Jenny is more important than the doctrines of rebirth or resurrection—but to suggest that one's passion, like religious passion, is not to possess or own, because the Madonna and the Madonna's qualities are not things to be owned or possessed. They are ends in themselves, to be viewed theoretically, to be contemplated aesthetically, to be valued for their own sakes. That is precisely what brings you alive, what makes you human—what makes you, in Marx's case, a man—and realizes the human essence. And, clearly, this being brought alive is not mere sexual arousal. Rather, it echoes and is preferred to something much larger and more important than that, rebirth or resurrection, which, certainly for religious traditions, and, metaphorically for Marx, implies the highest realization of the human essence.

At any rate, I suggest that Marx wants to bring together, to balance, the masculine and feminine qualities I mentioned above. He wants to develop an abstract, general, objective, rational theory that will contribute to the realization of concrete, particular, subjective, committed, emotional affirmation between human beings. "You can exchange love only for love, trust for trust,"[92] but to do so is to contribute to the realization of the species essence, the development of the human species as a whole.

Indeed, is it not the case that Marx's thought is often accused of opposite and contradictory qualities. Marx is often accused of being overly abstract, of making unrealistic claims for objectivity and scientificity, of being unrealistically deterministic, and of overlooking concrete, specific, personal relations. But at the same time, his thought is often accused of being partial rather than impartial, committed to the cause of the proletariat rather than value-free, based on particular class interests rather than the abstract common good, based on personal vision rather than scientific detachment, and based on a particular culture's development rather than being universal. Perhaps it could even be argued, if there were time, that Marx wants to link both of these sides in an almost androgynous balance. His thought comes across as impartial, objective, abstract, and scientific, but it is an attempt to realize the concrete, partial, personal, and emotional. And, at least at times, it leans toward the latter. In the *German Ideology,* Marx says that abstract philosophy is to the actual study of the concrete world as masturbation is to sexual love.[93] And Marx continuously uses metaphors of birth, sexuality, relations between man and woman, to describe abstract, theoretical social processes; for example, he says, the proletariat "have no ideals to realize, but to set free the elements of the new society with which old collapsing bourgeois society itself is pregnant," and, elsewhere, that social theory "can shorten and lessen the birth-pangs" of the emergence of this new society. [94]

III. Housework and Alienation

For modern feminist theorists, housework and childrearing, which are centrally important matters, can be seen in different and even opposed ways. They can be seen as the most rewarding activity and they can also be seen as the greatest oppression. Rosaldo writes, "men have no single commitment as enduring, time-consuming, and emotionally compelling—as close to seeming necessary and natural—as the relation of a woman to her infant child . . . Women are felt to be close to their children; they have access to a kind of certainty, a sense of diffuse belonging, not available to men."[95] Gordon writes, "Child care, for all its difficulty, is inherently less alienated and more creative than most other work; it offers a mother at least a semblance of control over her working conditions and goals."[96] On the other hand, Ferguson and Folbre say, "Repetitive menial work becomes much more meaningful when it is part of a large task providing love and support. This is the point that the antifeminist right has pressed home again and again. Children are sometimes pictured as the reward for housework. As Phyllis Schafly points out, 'most women would rather cuddle a baby than a typewriter or factory machine.' "[97] Less ironically, Oakley, quoting the Peckham Rye Women's Liberation Group, writes, "[']The appropriate symbol for housework (and for housework alone) is not the interminable conveyor belt but a compulsive circle like a pet mouse in its cage spinning round on its exercise wheel, unable to get off . . . "Housework is a worm eating away at one's ideas." Like a fever dream it goes on and on . . . ['] The monotony of housework turns it into a mindless task."[98] However, Joseph writes, "Circumstance contributed to the autonomous position maintained by the Black woman in her 'household domain.' Being a homemaker in the slave quarter was a cultural experience that was imposed upon the slaves. In spite of the wretched accommodations available in the quarter, Black women were able to be expressive, creative, and in their autonomy, were able to continue the practice of African customs and habits."[99]

What these passages suggest is that housework and childcare can be seen as highly satisfying, as unalienated labor, but, at the same time, as the greatest drudgery and oppression—and they can even be both at the same time. Moreover, what is also suggested here is that these different outlooks are especially susceptible to ideological manipulation. One way to approach this disagreement would be to try to give more convincing and conclusive arguments as well as evidence for one side rather than the other. I would suggest that this approach, whichever side were taken, would be *one-sided*. To argue in one direction and reject the other would be to leave out something very important. Moreover, I think that Marx can give us the categories that, developed a bit, can allow us to see at least in part why housework and childcare can be both unalienated labor, perhaps even a paradigm of unalienated labor, and can also involve the greatest oppression and domination.

From the start here, we must see that alienation, in the way that it is understood by Marx (as well as Hegel), cannot *simply* be identified with oppression or domination. All forms of alienation, it is true, do involve oppression or domination. But all forms of domination and oppression do not necessarily involve alienation. One can be dominated and oppressed without being alienated. But if one is alienated, one is certainly dominated and oppressed. Thus, to say that the family, housework, and childcare can be free of alienation is *not* to say that there cannot at the same time be domination or oppression present.

Jaggar is one of the few modern feminists to see that housewives can be oppressed without being alienated.[100]

Alienation occurs when individuals engage in activity that gives rise to a product, result, or institution, which then escapes the control of the individuals involved. The results of human activity no longer appear to be so, but seem to take on an abstract life and dynamic of their own. They appear independent and autonomous, begin to turn upon these individuals, and come to control, dominate, and oppress them. Moreover, these individuals are either unaware of this domination and oppression, or, at least, they do not understand how it arose; and thus this domination and oppression appears to be normal or even natural.[101]

For Marx, perhaps the clearest example of alienation is to be found in commodity exchange. Alienation that arises from an exchange economy, Marx (at least in *Capital* and in later writings) also calls fetishism. In an exchange economy, individuals engage in the activity of producing products, but they do so separately. The producers are not associated; they do not collectively plan or control their production or distribution. They produce privately. Then they bring their goods to market, put them on the market, and abstract and impersonal market laws set in. As these products come to be regulated by the laws of the market, they come to have an abstract life and dynamic of their own that is not understood or controlled by the producers. Thus, these products and laws, this autonomous dynamic, comes to dominate, control, and oppress individuals. It determines how much they can produce, what they will receive in exchange for it, how products are distributed, and thus in a very significant way determines the lives of these individuals.

The market does this very obviously during economic crises, but it is doing it less obviously at all times, as when the cost of medical care or higher education is pushed beyond the means of certain classes, or when daycare, because it is costly and unprofitable, becomes unavailable to certain classes. Here, abstract relations between things (products regulated by market laws) come to dominate relations between persons. Moreover, all of this appears normal and even natural. It may not even seem like oppression or domination—or at least there does not seem to be an oppressor. No one notices that this alienation or fetishism is the result of a certain form of human interaction and could be changed if that interaction were changed.[102]

The concept of alienation or fetishism was developed (or, at least, once the concept was developed, it served) to illuminate a fundamental difference between feudal and capitalist society. In feudal society one finds direct, visible domination of person over person—of the feudal lord over the serf. As this sort of domination was eliminated with the rise of capitalist society, the bourgeoisie tended to congratulate itself. In ridding (at least in the socioeconomic sphere) the direct and visible domination of the sort found between lord and serf, of person over person, the bourgeoisie tended to think that it had eliminated oppression and domination per se—all domination and oppression (at least in the socioeconomic sphere). The concept of alienation or fetishism was used to burst this bubble of illusion. It is very definitely the case that in bourgeois society there is still oppression and domination; it just takes a different form. There is no feudal lord dominating serfs in the "free" market, but there certainly is fetishism or alienation present. The abstract laws of the market replace the feudal lord. And the domination and oppression of the market, while it cannot be blamed on a person, is nevertheless worse than feudal domination because it is not visible, not understood, and thus is more insidious, widespread, and penetrates social life more deeply.

It is clearly Marx's view that there was no alienation or fetishism in the feudal socioeconomic sphere. Yet there certainly was domination and oppression—direct personal domination and oppression—there. Serfs were forced to give over a portion of their production, or of their labor time, to the feudal lord and to tithe to the Church, but there was no abstract, autonomous realm of exchange. Relations remained personal relations that did not appear as relations between things.[103] As I have said, all domination and oppression are not alienation or fetishism. This is also perfectly clear in Hegel. Many people think that in the section "Lordship and Bondage" of Hegel's *Phenomenology of Spirit*, we find the paradigm of alienation. This is a serious mistake. The German words *Entäusserung* and *Entfremdung*, which are translated as "alienation" and "estrangement," never even appear in that section. The relation of the master to the slave is not alienated. There is direct, visible, personal domination of the slave by the master, but the very fact that this domination is direct, visible, and personal implies that no alienation is present. To be alienated one must engage in an activity that produces a dynamic that takes on an abstract, independent, autonomous life of its own. And the individuals must not be able to see, not understand, that they have created this abstract power that turns upon them and dominates them. This power cannot be simply the personal power of a master. The master's life and power are originally his own; they are not created by the slave. It is true that the slave's recognition and service establishes the master as master, that the slave's work feeds and supports the master, but this is perfectly visible, completely understood, and it is a direct, personal relationship, not an abstract one.

The master–slave relationship is only transformed into an alienated relationship much later in the *Phenomenology,* in the section "Self-Alienated Spirit," where Hegel no longer discusses a clear, direct, and visible relationship between two individual consciousnesses. Instead he discusses a whole cultural world, with a socioeconomic and a political realm, where the activities of individuals give rise to classes and a political state, which are the outcomes of individual activity but which do not appear to be. They take on an abstract life and dynamic of their own and domination is not the direct and visible domination of person over person. Moreover, even the sort of domination that might *appear* to be domination by a person—for example, the domination of an absolute monarch (which is really an institution rather than a person)—is still the outcome of the recognition and service of individual citizens that has taken on an abstract, autonomous, institutional form, and does not appear to be the outcome of the activity of those individuals. In short, to have alienation there must arise between the dominated and whatever dominates an abstract, independent, autonomous realm with a dynamic of its own that makes this domination possible, which is nothing but the outcome of the activity of those dominated but which is not seen to be so.[104]

All of this is especially relevant to the family and to housework. We can see that while there may not be any alienation or fetishism in the family, there certainly can be direct, visible, and personal domination of women by men. It is Marx's view that no fetishism or alienation arises within the traditional family. After explaining his concept of fetishism in the first chapter of Volume I of *Capital,* Marx goes on to give four examples of societies or situations free of fetishism. The third is the "patriarchal industr[y] of a peasant family, that produces corn, cattle, yarn, linen, and clothing for home use." There is no fetishism here because there is no exchange of commodities within the family. The members of the family do not work separately and then exchange their products among themselves as on a market. No impersonal, abstract, autonomous market laws set in or come to control them. They work together consciously, collectively, and cooperatively.[105] Much of this would also be true for the modern family in capitalist society.

Fraser, however, seems to suggest that it is wrong to claim that money and exchange have no place in the family. Studies of family decision making, finances, and wife battering, she points out, show that the family is permeated with money; and, she argues, there is an exploitative exchange of services, labor, cash, and sex in the family.[106]

The problem here is with the term "exchange." When a serf turns over a portion of grain to the feudal lord or to the Church, or when parents let their child use the car after cutting the lawn, or even when a husband turns over the paycheck to his wife, these things can be loosely called exchange, but they are not commodity exchange in the technical sense. "Exchange" for Marx means buying and selling on a market. And in a developed exchange economy, the main form of distribution of goods and services is carried out through buying and selling on a market. It is only here that the dynamic of products and market laws, relations between things, can come to dominate relations between persons. It is only here that fetishism and alienation can occur. They cannot occur between feudal lord and serf, between Hegel's master and slave, between parents and the child to whom they loan the car for cutting the lawn, or between a husband and his wife to whom he turns over the paycheck. There can very well be conflict, domination, and oppression in the family that is directly connected to finances, labor, rendering of services, and sex; and this can even lead to wife beating; but it is not due to commodity exchange that takes place within the family. Domination and oppression within the family of the sort that Fraser has in mind is very clearly domination by a person[107]—the male, the husband, the father—and it is quite direct and visible. This oppression may in part be due to the effect that commodity exchange in society has on the family, which we will have to discuss, but in a fundamental sense that cannot be overlooked this oppression in the family arises out of nonmarket relations, relations within the family, the domination of persons by persons—which is certainly oppressive, but is not alienation.

Let us look at labor within the family—housework and childcare—to see to what extent and in what ways it can be called unalienated. It might be thought that the concepts "alienated labor" and "unalienated labor," for Marx, refer exclusively to the labor involved in social production—factory work—and not to housework. After all, many people think that Marx privileges, if he does not attend exclusively to, social production. But it is quite clear that for Marx housework *is* labor and that the patriarchal industry of a peasant family; that is, housework, before the rise of capitalism, was social production.[108] And I think we can argue that housework is unalienated labor—in fact, almost an ideal model of unalienated labor.

What does it mean for labor to be alienated? In the *Economic and Philosophic Manuscripts,* Marx argues that individuals must labor upon the natural, material world; they must transform it into products that can satisfy their needs. In doing so, workers objectify themselves in their products. They pour their lives into them. The product is the objectification, the manifestation, the expression, of the workers' powers, capacities, and ideas. Yet, if labor is alienated, workers do not control their products—their products do not belong to them. The more the workers objectify themselves, the more they produce, the poorer the workers become and the richer this independent, autonomous realm of products becomes. And thus the workers come to be dominated by these products that they very definitely need but do not control.[109]

Moreover, if labor is alienated, the workers do not even control their own activity in the process of producing these products. The work is not voluntary, but coerced. It is not work directly to satisfy the needs or serve the aims of the workers themselves. The workers' activity does not belong to them; it belongs to, is controlled by, and produces a product for, another.[110] And thus the work in itself is not satisfying, certainly not as an end in itself—it is only engaged in as a means to gain a wage.

These two forms of alienation, alienation from the product and alienation in the process of production, produce a third form of alienation—alienation from the species. This, for Marx, is the key form of alienation, and it explains what is most objectionable about the first two forms of alienation. To say that workers are alienated from the species is to say that they are unable to work for the benefit of the species. If they do not control their own activity, and if they do not control their product, they will hardly be able to direct their activity or their product for the benefit of the species. Moreover, if they do not control their product or their activity, then their product and their activity will only be able to benefit individuals in opposition to the rest of the species. Their product will benefit the owner of the product— the capitalist. And their activity will gain them a wage; it will benefit the workers themselves as individuals but not the rest of the species. Instead of recognizing that human beings are species beings, beings whose needs, powers, ideas, and values—whose very essence—is formed and shaped in and by the community, and thus instead of working consciously for the benefit of the community as the only effective, long-term way to contribute to their own development, instead of working collectively for a richer sociocultural world that could be consciously regulated to support and stimulate the development of each member of the community, they turn their work, their species activity, into a mere *means* to serve the particular interests of individuals in opposition to other individuals and in opposition to the community as a whole.[111]

If individuals do not work consciously for the benefit of the species, they will produce an alienated, dehumanized world in which they cannot be at home:

> It is just in his work upon the objective world, therefore, that man really proves himself to be a species-being. This production is his active species-life... The object of labour, is therefore, the objectification of man's species-life: for he duplicates himself not only, as in consciousness, intellectually, but also actively, in reality, and therefore sees himself in a world he has created. In tearing away from man the object of his production, therefore, estranged labour tears from him his species-life....[112]

If work is unalienated, human beings will be able to see themselves in their world, see it as the outcome, the manifestation, the expression, the objectification of their own powers, capacities, purposes, and ideas. In objectifying themselves in such a world, they will humanize it and create a world where they can be at home.[113]

I think it should be clear that in housework workers would normally be in control of the product or result of their work. In washing dishes or clothes, in cleaning or cooking, in sewing clothes or quilting, the houseworker remains in control of the product or result. Certainly these products do not take on an independent, autonomous life of their own the way products do on a market. Moreover, houseworkers also remain in control of their own activity in all these tasks, and that activity can be satisfying.[114] This is not to suggest that these tasks individually or the quantity of them that pile up, are not difficult and even exhausting. Marx is quite aware that any work can be difficult and exhausting:

> Adam Smith conceives labour to be a curse... It does not seem remotely to occur to him that the individual "in his ordinary state of health, strength, spirits, skill, dexterity" also needs a normal portion of labour ... But equally A. Smith has no inkling that the overcoming of these obstacles is in itself a manifestation of freedom—and, moreover, that the external aims are [thereby] stripped of their character as merely external

natural necessity, and become posited as aims which only the individual himself posits, that they are therefore posited as self-realization, objectification of the subject, and thus real freedom, whose action is precisely work . . . Really free work, e.g. the composition of music, is also the most damnably difficult, demanding the most intensive effort.[115]

Difficult as they may be, cleaning and washing can still be satisfying. Sewing, quilting, cooking, decorating, painting, and building can not only be satisfying but creative, and can develop one's powers and capacities. Childcare can also be emotionally rewarding.

Most importantly, housework does not involve alienation from the species. Childcare, and indeed all housework, which provides an environment for the child, as well as childrearing and the educating of a child, very clearly, in working for the benefit of the child, works for the benefit of the species. This is a primary reason why housework can be meaningful and satisfying in a way that alienated factory work can never be. Both the product and the activity of housework are under the houseworker's control and can be consciously and meaningfully directed for the benefit of the child and, through the child, for the benefit of the future species.

Housework would almost be a paradigm case of objectifying oneself in the object, in the household, and of being able to see oneself in it; see it as the outcome of one's powers, capacities, ideas, purposes, and activities. Housework produces a humanized environment where one, literally, can be at home. This occurs when one builds a picnic table for the back yard, plants a vegetable or flower garden, repaints or redecorates, builds an extra room for the new baby, makes a dress for one's daughter, quilts, cooks food that the members of the family especially like, and even when one cleans or washes dishes or clothes.

However, *the* paradigm case of labor that produces a humanized object,[116] perhaps what is even in the back of Marx's mind when he speaks about this matter,[117] is the labor of childbirth and the nurturing, raising, and educating of a child. Here, in the most complete way possible, "nature appears as [your] work." You duplicate yourself not only biologically, culturally, "intellectually, but also actively, in reality . . ." and therefore you see yourself in what you have created.[118] You can contemplate yourself, your own doing, in the child. The child's biological and cultural development is the objectification of yourself in the child, and can be contemplated and appreciated as such, as well as as a contribution to the future species. Also, just slightly changing Marx's own words in another passage,

I would have been, for [my child] the mediator between [her] and the species, and therefore would have become recognized and felt by [my child] as a completion of [her] own essential nature and as a necessary part of [herself], and consequently would know myself to be confirmed both in [my child's] thought and [her] love . . . In the individual expression of my life and therefore my individual activity I would have directly confirmed and realized my true nature, my human nature, my communal nature.[119]

There is another aspect of overcoming alienated labor that we must mention. To specialize in one narrow aspect of the division of labor, to produce, as Adam Smith's classical example has it, the twelfth part of a pin, all day long, day after day, for years on end, can be absolutely deadening and even crippling. To overcome such repetition and drudgery in tasks that are not at all satisfying or creative, Marx suggests the exchangeability of function. Even if society has overcome the aspects of alienated labor discussed above, this does not mean that every single task in a factory can become satisfying and enjoyable. The solution is to rotate jobs so that one does not get stuck in an unpleasant job for long. Marx, as we have seen, expresses this notion rather fancifully in the *German Ideology,* where he says, "in communist society, where nobody has one exclusive sphere of activity but each can become accomplished in any branch he wishes, society regulates the general production and thus makes it possible for me to do one thing today and another tomorrow, to hunt in the morning, fish in the afternoon, rear cattle in the evening, and criticise after dinner, just as I have a mind, without ever becoming hunter, fisherman, shepherd or critic."[120] Marx makes this same point less fancifully in other places.[121] The point is to move around so as not to be locked into one narrow task, so as to get a broader perspective of the whole, so that you will be better able to understand and control the whole process of production, and so that you can develop different powers and capacities. Perhaps no particular job can be satisfying if you are stuck in it for too long, but rotating through many jobs can be satisfying.

As should be obvious, housework does not involve narrow specialization. The houseworker regularly rotates through a wide variety of different tasks, certainly a wider variety than the average worker in a capitalist factory. Many household tasks can be dull, repetitious, and difficult—they can be drudgery. But some household tasks are not, and rotating tasks can make the whole process satisfying while some aspects of it are less so. The point that simply must be made is that difficulty, repetition, even drudgery, by themselves do not produce alienation; they do not even produce oppression. Something else is required to produce alienation or oppression. The most unalienated work, the most satisfying work, can involve certain aspects that are simply dull, repetitious drudgery. Artistic work, the production of films, or scholarship can all involve long stretches of dull, difficult, repetitious drudgery and still be highly creative and satisfying. Moreover, overcoming such difficult obstacles can be an exercise in liberty if the work as a whole is meaningful and significant. For drudgery to become oppressive, there must be more drudgery than can be overcome by rotating tasks, and the work must lack meaning and significance, either because it is not done voluntarily but is coerced, or because it does not benefit others, the species. And, indeed, this leads us to the key to understanding how housework and childcare, which can be almost paradigms of unalienated labor, can also be the greatest oppression and slavery.

It may seem strange to claim that housework can be both an unalienated ideal and also the greatest slavery and oppression, but it is not really so strange. After all, Marx makes the very same point about labor in general. Labor is the highest human activity—it is species activity. It transforms, develops, and realizes the external world as well as the powers, capacities, and needs—the essence—of the species. And if labor is alienated it creates the greatest slavery and oppression. In fact, one has to say, both about labor in general and household labor in particular, that they can be the greatest slavery and oppression precisely because they are the highest activity. If labor in general and household labor (especially childcare) in particular were not the highest activities, then their distortion and degradation could not be the most serious form of oppression. Marx says that the semiartistic work of the medieval craftsworker, because it was so absorbing and engaging, was even more *slavish*. In other words, to make work that is inherently satisfying and emotionally engaging oppressive *increases* the oppression. If the work were not engaging, if it were not important, thus if the worker could be indifferent to it, Marx says, it would not be as slavish.[122]

As de Beauvoir puts it, "Marriage is obscene in principle in so far as it transforms into rights and duties those mutual relations which should be founded on spontaneous urge. . . ."[123] Housework and childcare can be unalienated, meaningful, satisfying, and enjoyable. But if they are *expected* of a housewife, if they are her *duty*, if she is coerced into doing them, if it is her *role,* her *destiny*, then they become slavish and oppressive. A woman may enjoy, may find meaningful and significant, may care about and be emotionally involved in, housework and childcare, but as Marx, in a slightly different context, quoting from a speech by Lord Ashly, put it, "the virtues, the peculiar virtues of the female character [are] perverted to her injury . . . all that is most moral and tender in her nature is made a means of her bondage and suffering."[124] Love should be exchanged only for love, trust for trust.[125] Such expectations should not be imposed upon you as your destined role.

A very good example of this can be found in Virginia Woolf's *To the Lighthouse*. In that novel, one of the main characters, Mrs. Ramsay, is an especially warm, generous, caring, and nurturing person. It is clear that Woolf depicts her as a woman who likes her domestic tasks and who finds them important and meaningful. Mrs. Ramsay nurtures her children, is very careful about not wounding the ego of her husband, cares for the poor and the ill, and in central scenes of the novel is engaged in organizing and preparing a large family dinner party. She is concerned that the food be cooked to perfection, that the guests be seated properly, that they interact smoothly, that the women make the men feel comfortable, that they ease them into conversation and make them feel important, and so forth. And Lily Briscoe, a younger woman, is very much impressed by Mrs. Ramsay's domestic and social abilities. She would like to be like Mrs. Ramsay, or at least thinks she *ought* to be like Mrs. Ramsay. But she finds this very difficult. At the dinner party, without anything being spoken between her and Mrs. Ramsay, it becomes Lily Briscoe's job to do what Mrs. Ramsay expects of her, to ease a particularly obnoxious and self-centered young man into conversation, to make him feel important and comfortable.

The point that slowly and powerfully emerges here is that despite the fact that Mrs. Ramsay enjoys and cares very deeply about her domestic obligations, and despite the fact that Lily Briscoe wants to become like Mrs. Ramsay, what oppresses them both is that these roles are expected of them. No one actually says they are expected, but that only makes the oppression worse. It is just assumed that these are their roles as if it were their destiny. This makes Mrs. Ramsay feel, as she puts it, like "a sponge sopped full of human emotions" which she must constantly squeeze out to those around her, especially the men. And these expectations come close to paralyzing Lily Briscoe.[126]

Here love is not exchanged only for love. Emotions and virtues that are deeply admirable are not allowed to be ends in themselves. They are expected, demanded, turned into means for the smooth functioning of domestic life and the service of men. To be expected to do what you like doing, what is virtuous and human, for it to become a role imposed upon you as a destiny, erodes and degrades its value and meaningfulness. And the more you *like* it, the more oppressive it becomes. If it were not expected, if it were not demanded as your role, it could be engaged in freely. Or if it were not enjoyable, meaningful, or important it could just be engaged in indifferently.

Honest, open feelings, relating to persons, caring about them, for their own sakes, loving them because they are lovable—this sort of open, transparent emotional situation would be the ideal. But any oppression, domination, or enforcement of roles here will turn the nurturer into a slave at the most intimate level of feelings. In working for the benefit of the species, especially in childbirth, nurturing, and childrearing, women, as de Beauvoir puts it, become slaves to the species.[127] Women are burdened by their species activity, locked into it, subordinated to it, destined to it, and thus become slaves to the species. The highest human activity becomes the most slavish and the deepest virtues a means to bondage.

However, we must focus not just upon oppression and domination, but also on alienation. Housework and childcare, we have seen, can be unalienated ideals. How then does alienation enter the home, the family, and how does it develop between men and women? All men, as well as women, are born of women. In giving birth to children, as well as in nurturing them, caring for them, bringing them up, and educating them, women objectify themselves in their children, and this objectification humanizes, encultures, the child. But from the very beginning, the child takes on a life of its own, and as the child gets older its life becomes more and more independent and autonomous. Is this not already what we have described as alienation? Not yet, I do not think. This is still just part of the humanization or socialization of the child. Humans beings *should* become independent and autonomous. A mother wants her child to become independent and autonomous. If it does not, the child will not develop fully as a human being.

However, as the child becomes increasingly independent and autonomous, the child (or the child interacting with others) can separate from, turn upon, and come to dominate and oppress the women who gave them birth. Here it is possible that we have alienation, but still it is possible that we do not yet have it—that we only have the domination of persons by persons. Many modern feminist theorists, and Marx himself (we have seen in Section I of this chapter), want to insist that the domination of women can simply arise before the rise and predominance of the economic sphere, or even before the development of any significantly powerful sphere separate from the family. It is the case, I think, that for alienation to arise for women in the family there must arise a sphere outside the family that becomes larger and more powerful than the family—a social, economic, religious, or political sphere—which then can effect alienation in the family. But personal domination can arise before the development of these spheres external to the family, and even after these spheres develop some oppression in the family can simply be personal; that is, not fully derivable from or explainable as a result of these external spheres.[128]

For alienation to be effected in the family, women must more or less remain in the family isolated from other spheres that arise and come to have a life and dynamic of their own that is independent and autonomous, which largely excludes women, which therefore women do not adequately understand and certainly do not control, and which thus gives rise to a power that comes to oppress and dominate women. This occurs as men come to engage with other men outside the family in activities and interaction that form social, economic, religious, or political spheres. As children grow up and join these existing spheres they can separate from, turn upon, and come to dominate and oppress the women who gave them birth. It is Marx's view that in early history none of this occurs. Economic production occurs largely within the family. There is little economic activity going on outside it. There is little or no barter or exchange, which, even when they do begin, take place on the borders of the community with outsiders.[129] In early society, the political sphere as a separate sphere outside the family can be nonexistent, minimal, or undeveloped. And even as it develops, it can be a sphere in which both men and women participate relatively equally, as Marx and Engels, following Morgan, think was the case with Native American tribes.[130] The religious sphere may not be separate from the family or may include women. It may even be the case that this early society is peaceful and does not engage in, or does not engage much in, military activity.

But, at a certain point, and differently in different cultures, military activity, political activity, economic activity, especially exchange, can develop as spheres in which men interact with men,[131] in which men come to be the main or the most numerous participants. This division of spheres between men and women arises out of the original sexual division of labor and personal male domination latent in the family as well as accidents. Marx says, "The slavery latent in the family only develops gradually with the increase of population, the growth of wants, and with the extension of external intercourse, both of war and barter."[132] As these separate spheres develop and take on a more complex dynamic, as they become more independent of women and the family, as they become more powerful and are able to shape the cultural world, its outlooks and values, in accord with their own dynamic, and thus as women come to have less control and understanding of this dynamic because they are excluded from it, alienation arises. Women gave birth to these men, nurtured them, raised them, but they become independent of these women, part of an autonomous dynamic, which turns upon, which dominates and oppresses, and which alienates, women.

It must also be said that as men become a part of this alien dynamic, are caught up in it, and are molded by it, they too are alienated. The more complex this dynamic becomes, the less these men can understand it or control it even though they are a part of it, even though it is their realm. They can be carried along by it more than they direct it—think of the development of a complex market or of men being swept up in patriotic or military fervor.[133]

Furthermore, as men get caught up in these independent dynamics, they can come to resent women, who, because they are excluded, do not understand these male activities, who may not approve of them, and who therefore may try to prevent or try to lure men away from these activities. Men may well come to identify themselves, identify their role, with these activities and feel that their "masculinity" is called into question or threatened by women who do not understand or approve of, or who oppose, these activities.

Moreover, this model can explain how women, excluded from these extrafamilial spheres, because they are excluded from them, may nurture, develop, and preserve, in the sphere of the family, values, attitudes, outlooks, and emotions that are more valuable and human than those that develop in these external spheres, which women develop and preserve as alternatives to or in reaction and defense against those external spheres. These qualities, because they are different, can further reinforce the desire of men to exclude women from these external spheres, to see them as inadequate to these spheres, or to be hostile to them; and this can contribute to the further oppression of women. But at the same time the very exclusion of women from these more ruthless external spheres can reinforce their attitudes, values, outlooks, and emotions, and help them to remain more human and valuable. Moreover, men, caught up in their own dynamic, developing values and outlooks of their own, can come to be alienated from these more valuable and human qualities that develop among women and the family, and men can become degraded.

This alienation model will also explain how male domination can be developed and reproduced without being fully intended by men, and also how it can be accepted by women. Men get caught up in a dynamic that they do not understand or control, a dynamic that sweeps them along, a dynamic that therefore appears normal or natural, which molds, dominates, and alienates them, and whose future consequences they cannot foresee. The development of male domination cannot be seen as an intentional conspiracy planned by men. An understanding of basic sociocultural dynamics makes such a conspiracy theory implausible. At the same time, however, *within* the parameters of this ununderstood and uncontrolled dynamic that carries them along despite themselves, men can certainly exclude, oppress, and dominate women, and they can do so *consciously* and *intentionally,* in and through legal codes, governmental policy, religious doctrine, and so forth.

Though at the same time, a good deal of this will appear normal, natural, proper, and moral to men as well as to women, again because it occurs within, fits with, and follows from this uncontrolled, ununderstood, alienated dynamic that appears normal or natural. All consciousness and intention occur within a culture and its dynamics. A fully adequate feminist theory, it seems to me, must be able to explain how women historically have been oppressed without, at least to a considerable extent, anyone, men or women, realizing women were oppressed, or consciously intending to oppress them. There is certainly a fundamental sense in which men benefit from, are responsible for, and are clearly to be *blamed* for the historical development of the domination of women, but it is not in the sense of a fully conscious, fully understood, and fully intended conspiracy theory. There is a sense in which they have been caught up in a dynamic they do not understand.

It must be noticed that there is a crucial subjective component to oppression. One may well be oppressed without being aware that one is oppressed, without *feeling* oppressed. To feel oppressed, one must come to *see* oneself as oppressed, and that is never a simple, empirical matter of just looking at one's condition. Someone else can point to aspects of your life that are oppressive, but that is not likely to be enough to make you aware of your oppression. After all you already know quite well what your life has been like; you just have never seen it as oppressive. It is just the way life is; it is normal, or bad luck, or unavoidable, or natural, or fate; how could it be changed anyway? Most women in the past have not seen themselves as oppressed, and they certainly were not unaware of what had happened in their lives—they just did not see those conditions as oppressive. And this is not just true of women—most male workers have not felt oppressed as workers. This, in fact, is the most common of attitudes. And it is not just a characteristic attitude of those "poor dupes," those "others," those of the past. It is true for all of us. If we could eliminate all oppression of women (or of any other group) that we are currently aware of, it would be a serious mistake to think that we had eliminated *all* oppression of women (or of these other groups). New oppressions that we are currently unaware of will certainly be discovered and uncovered in the future, much as they have been in the past, which is to say that all of us are *blind* to ways in which we are *currently* oppressed. The conservative is wrong in thinking that if you do not feel oppressed you are simply not oppressed, and that you only get talked into thinking you are oppressed by the radical. But, at the same time, the radical is wrong in thinking that if you are oppressed it should be obvious that you are oppressed, and that you are a reactionary if you do not see that you are.

There are many forces at work to prevent one from seeing oneself as oppressed. The first step in accepting this fact, after all, will involve actually accepting a kind of inferiority. It lowers one's self-esteem to admit that one is oppressed, and it will not at all be easy or pleasant to do so. Even for oppressors to see that they are oppressing others involves a similar acceptance of inferiority. And this, in front of someone who, in a superior tone, is earnestly telling you that you are oppressed or an oppressor, will be especially difficult. Moreover, the second step is even more painful. Accepting the fact that you are oppressed or an oppressor means that you will have to *do* something about it. And when you have no idea what to do, this can be quite confusing and frightening. When you do come to have some idea of what to do, then things become even more difficult. You will have to actually *change* things and, even worse, change *yourself*.

At any rate, pointing to empirical facts is never very likely to convince anyone that they are oppressed or an oppressor. To see this requires gaining a different paradigm, a different perspective on things, a different consciousness—it requires a revaluation of values and the development of a new theory.

Getting back to alienation, Jaggar argues that alienation is a characteristic of capitalist relations and thus that, for Marx, housewives cannot be alienated.¹³⁴ I do not think this is correct. We have already seen that alienation can precede capitalism, and, also, while it is the case that housework in the family can be unalienated, alienation can very well enter the family from outside. For Marx, as the economic sphere develops, especially as exchange and finally capitalism develop, economic factors will come to predominate in determining the other spheres of society in a way that they did not in early history. At this point the alienation involved in the economic sphere—market alienation or fetishism—can enter the family. We must now focus more carefully upon the way in which capitalism enters the family, alienates it, and oppresses it.

In capitalist society, for Marx, labor power is seen as—is *reduced to*—a commodity. It is bought and sold on the market like any other commodity. This particular commodity is produced when parents give birth to, nurture, raise, and educate a child who will become a laborer. From the capitalist perspective, then, procreation, childcare, and housework, at least for the working class, tend to be seen as—are *reduced* to—the production of labor power. How is the value of this commodity determined?

> the value of labour-power is determined, as in the case of every other commodity, by the labour-time necessary for the production, and consequently also the reproduction, of this special article. So far as it has value, it represents no more than a definite quantity of the average labour of society incorporated in it . . . Given the individual, the production of labour-power consists in his reproduction of himself or his maintenance . . . Therefore the labour-time requisite for the production of labour-power reduces itself to that necessary for the production of those means of subsistence . . . necessary for the maintenance of the labourer. [Also] the seller of labour-power must perpetuate himself, "in the way that every living individual perpetuates himself, by procreation." . . . Hence the sum of the means of subsistence necessary for the production of labour-power must include the means necessary for the labourer's substitutes, i.e., his children, in order that this race of peculiar commodity-owners may perpetuate its appearance on the market.¹³⁵

Housework and childcare, then, are necessary to produce and maintain the value of labor power.¹³⁶ The houseworker produces use values—prepares food, sews clothing, provides and maintains shelter, and contributes to the upbringing and education of the worker or future worker.¹³⁷ This labor in the family is not paid labor—it is done for free.¹³⁸ The capitalist can simply assume that it will take place in the family outside the capitalist economic sphere: the "capitalist may safely leave its fulfillment to the labourer's instincts of self-preservation and of propagation."[139]

As capitalism develops, especially as it introduces machinery that dispenses with the need for muscular power, Marx argues, it draws women and children into the factory, in fact, it brings the whole family into the factory. Thus, Marx says, the capitalist "usurp[s] the labour necessary in the home of the family."[140] This means that some of the housework, previously done by the housewife, "such as sewing and mending, must be replaced by the purchase of ready-made articles. Hence the diminished expenditure of labour in the house is accompanied by an increased expenditure of money. The cost of keeping the family increases, and balances the greater income. In addition to this, economy and judgment in the consumption and preparation of the means of subsistence becomes impossible."[141] A great deal of housework, of course, will still have to be performed, most likely by the woman, who will now have less time to do it and will be able to do it less efficiently and economically.

Moreover, Marx suggests, bringing extra members of the family into the factory will not simply multiply the income of the family by the number of new workers. He says, it "spreads the value of the man's labour-power over his whole family. It thus depreciates his labour-power. To purchase the labour-power of a family of four workers may, perhaps, cost more than formerly it did to purchase the labour-power of the head of the family, but, in return, four days' labour takes the place of one, and their price falls in proportion to the excess of the surplus labour of four over the surplus labour of one."[142] In other words, what the capitalist will end up paying these four workers (at least over time as settled by market forces) will be precisely the value of their labor power—what it costs to maintain and reproduce the laborer and the laborer's family. Some of the housework will still be done for free, but since, with the wife working, the family will now have to pay for some of the services previously performed by the housewife and other services now will not be performed as economically, this extra expenditure of money will have to be included in the increased wage that the capitalist will have to pay the whole family. But by no means must this be, nor was it historically, a simple multiple of what the male worker originally received working alone. What the family will receive in wages is precisely what it costs to produce and reproduce their labor power, which is now, with the wife working, somewhat more than before, but still requires far less than four times what the male worker originally earned.¹⁴³ The market will drive wages toward this level.¹⁴⁴

This together with the fact that the woman must now work both in the factory as well as in the home produces intense alienation. As the woman enters the factory, she directly enters the sphere of alienated labor.¹⁴⁵ Since this also means that she can do less housework than before and thus must purchase on the market certain goods and services that she previously provided herself, it will mean that alienation will also enter the household. Housework itself will come under the sway of market forces that cannot be controlled. Market forces will control the cost of goods and services that must be purchased as well as the fact that the family's wage will be depressed significantly below a multiple of the husband's original wage toward the minimum cost for the production of labor power. The fact that the family needs these goods and services, these products, but does not control them and finds them difficult to afford, gives rise to alienation from the product—makes them slaves to these products that they need but do not control. Moreover, the fact that the wife has less time to do housework, and thus will end up doing it less economically and less efficiently, means that she will also be alienated in the sense that she will lose control over her own activity. Her activity will be more frustrating, and since it is expected of her it will feel more coerced. She will be alienated in the process, the activity, of housework.

And just as alienation from the product and in the process of production give rise to alienation from the species, because one does not control and therefore cannot direct either one's product or one's activity for the benefit of the species, so also in housework and in childcare, since the housewife does not control the product or her activity, she cannot direct them for the benefit of the species. Instead, housework and childcare produce a mere commodity—they produce labor power. A woman works to prepare her child, her husband, and herself to enter the alienated realm of the factory; she thus works to distort and frustrate the development of the species. Work that could be satisfying and meaningful becomes embittering. Housework and childcare, which could be ends in themselves, are turned into means to produce a commodity that the capitalist takes advantage of, uses as a means, to gain more surplus value and to pay lower wages. Such housework does not produce a humanized environment, an environment where the family can be at home; it transforms the home into an alienated realm that turns human beings into commodities destined for the alienated realm of the factory.

The housewife who is expected to do this double work also becomes alienated from her husband. Alienated and uncontrolled market forces that drive a workman to bring his wife and child into the factory to make ends meet, Marx says, mean that the workman who previously "sold his own labour-power, which he disposed of nominally as a free agent" now "sells his wife and child. He has become a slave-dealer."[146] And if he forces his wife to do the housework at home, he also becomes an oppressor and intensifies her alienation in the home.

Such a husband clearly oppresses his wife and increases her alienation, but we cannot say that he *exploits* her, as Fraser, MacKinnon, and de Beauvoir seem to suggest he does.[147] Housework, according to the capitalist view of things, is not productive labor. To the extent that capital conquers the whole of production, including that of the home and of industry carried out in the home for self-consumption rather than for the production of commodities for sale on the market, Marx says, it transforms work in the home into unproductive labor.[148] Before this, work in the home was social production, even though it did not produce commodities for sale on the market.[149] Productive labor, Marx says, "in its meaning for capitalist production, is wage-labour which, exchanged against the variable part of capital (the part of the capital that is spent on wages), reproduces not only this part of capital (or the value of its own labour-power), but in addition produces surplus-value for the capitalist."[150]

Unproductive labor, on the other hand, is labor that produces only use values and does not produce surplus value. If an actor or a clown works for a capitalist and returns to the capitalist more than he or she receives in wages, their labor is productive. If a tailor comes to the capitalist's house, or if the capitalist's wife sews his trousers, they produce a mere use value and their labor is unproductive. The work of domestic servants is unproductive labor. The same labor, however, performed in a public hotel, if it earns profit for a capitalist, is productive labor.[151]

Unproductive labor, then, is labor that produces use values, which are simply paid for out of income—wages, profits, or revenue.[152] Productive labor, on the other hand, is labor that produces surplus value and profit for the capitalist. A productive laborer is one who works for a capitalist and produces goods that the capitalist can exchange for a value above and beyond what the capitalist must pay in the form of a wage to the productive worker for the value of the worker's labor power.[153] Exploitation is the appropriation of this surplus value. In pocketing the value that the laborer produces above and beyond what must be returned to the laborer in the form of a wage, the capitalist exploits the laborer.

Household labor, on the other hand, is unproductive labor that the working class must perform for itself,

> but it is only able to perform it when it has laboured "productively." It can only cook meat for itself when it has produced a wage with which to pay for the meat; and it can only keep its furniture and dwellings clean, it can only polish its boots, when it has produced the value of furniture, house rent and boots. To this class of productive labourers itself, therefore, the labour which they perform for themselves appears as "unproductive labour." This unproductive labour never enables them to repeat the same unproductive labour a second time unless they have previously laboured productively.[154]

It is clear that from his wife's household labor the husband receives only use values that are consumed, and whatever expenditure of money is involved is paid for out of income—wages earned in the factory. In normal, modern housework, his wife does not produce products that can be exchanged on a market for a value in excess of a wage she receives for housework, or, since she receives no wage, ought to receive; or, simply, what it costs to reproduce the family's labor power. Her household labor does, however, produce the commodity of labor power, which is exchanged for a wage. But even here no surplus value is accrued in excess of what it costs to produce that labor power. The family does not profit from the capitalist. It merely earns a wage determined by the value of labor power—a wage that is equivalent to what it costs to carry on housework and to reproduce the labor power of the family. Thus, however oppressive this is, his wife does not produce surplus value and thus the husband does not appropriate surplus value. Therefore, he does not exploit his wife. Besides working in the factory, the wife may do most of the housework involved in reproducing the labor power of the rest of the family, which is then exchanged for a wage necessary to support the family. She thus performs work that makes possible the gaining of a family wage that does not return to her in proportion to the work she contributed. This is clearly unjust, but she is not producing surplus value for the rest of her family or her husband above and beyond what it costs to reproduce their labor power and to keep them alive, and thus she is not being exploited.

The term "exploitation," of course, also simply means "taking advantage of," "benefiting unfairly from," "using a person," and so forth. In this sense we *can* say that a husband exploits his wife. But he does not do so in the technical sense—the sense in which we say that a capitalist exploits a worker—he does not appropriate surplus value.

Housework is simply unproductive—it does not produce surplus value for anyone. However, it does *save* surplus value for the capitalist. To employ laborers, the capitalist must pay the value of labor power. He must pay what it costs to maintain and reproduce labor power, and this includes the costs of housework and childcare. The capitalist puts the laborer (or the whole family of laborers) to work in his factory where they put in enough labor time (which Marx calls necessary labor time) to produce a value equivalent to what the capitalist must pay them for the value of their labor power—their wage. But they are also obliged to continue to labor far beyond that point. This surplus labor produces more for the capitalist than he must pay for the value of their labor power, their necessary labor time. This "more," this surplus labor, is the source of the capitalist's surplus value, which he exploits from the laborers and pockets himself.[155]

It is clear that even if the wife works alongside her husband in the capitalist's factory, she still must do a good deal of housework when she returns home, and she does the latter for free. If the capitalist had to pay for this free labor (labor that is *necessary* for the maintenance and reproduction of labor power), he would have to pay higher wages and this would reduce the amount of surplus value he would be able to appropriate. The fact that he does not have to pay for this free labor, therefore, *saves* his surplus value. Thus, the wife has to engage in surplus labor in the factory over and above the necessary labor needed to reproduce her wage, which surplus labor the capitalist appropriates directly, which he exploits; and she also engages in necessary labor at home (necessary to the maintenance and reproduction of labor power), which she is not paid for, and which the capitalist does not appropriate directly, but which he benefits from by saving his surplus value. Whether or not we can call this exploitation we will discuss in a moment.

At any rate, it cannot be argued that the husband exploits his wife here. It is true that by obliging his wife to do the housework, the husband saves money—he does not have to hire someone else to do the housework. But this does not produce any surplus value for the husband; it does not even save him any surplus value, because there is no surplus value involved. Even if the husband hires outsiders to do the housework instead of his wife, their work would still be unproductive labor. It would not produce surplus value, and thus could not involve exploitation. Such work is *potentially* productive labor, the source of surplus value, and thus exploitation, but if this potentiality has not been realized, it is not productive labor, the source of surplus value, or exploitation. If a husband were to hire his wife out as a domestic laborer, or were to sell clothing she had made, or food that she had prepared, and if he pocketed all or even some of the money gotten in exchange for it, then his wife's work would be productive labor, a source of surplus value to the husband, now become a capitalist, and this would be exploitation. But if he does not do this, if he just obliges his wife to work in the home, then he does not exploit her, though he may well oppress her. Even if the wife works in the factory alongside her husband, and if he keeps her wage or controls how it is spent without her voluntary consent, while this is oppression and perhaps even theft, it is still not exploitation. If I steal money as a pickpocket or if I refuse to share with my fellow thugs the loot gotten from robbing a liquor store, I am a thief and a rat, but I do not exploit them— I do not extract surplus labor and surplus value—any more than I do from my wife.

What about the capitalist? Does he exploit the labor of women that is carried out in the home? If exploitation is defined as the appropriation of surplus labor whose product is exchanged for surplus value, and if the woman working in the home produces no surplus value, then we cannot say that the capitalist exploits her either, as Morton holds he does.[156]

Why can't the housewife produce surplus value? She produces, or contributes to producing, a commodity (labor power) that is exchanged on a market (the labor market) for a wage. And just as all commodities are assumed to exchange at their value, what it costs to produce them (the socially necessary costs of raw materials, machinery, buildings, wages, and so forth), so labor power exchanges for (gains a wage equivalent to) what it costs to produce it.

The capitalist, however, has the power to make the laborer engage in surplus labor whose product the capitalist can exchange on the market for surplus value, which he pockets himself. The houseworker in the home is not in the position to produce surplus value. The commodity that she produces (labor power) exchanges for a wage that is simply equal to what it costs to produce it. Why can't she produce surplus value? For example, what if she works harder or longer to better nourish and educate her family, or what if she has more children? Couldn't this generate surplus value? To see this, imagine that she were *only* to nourish her family to the point where they could engage in necessary labor time, the amount of labor time required to reproduce their wage, and then they simply collapsed from exhaustion such that the capitalist could not get them to engage in any surplus labor at all that could be exchanged for surplus value on the market. Well, the capitalist would simply fire these workers, or, if all workers available were like this, the capitalist would go out of business and cease to be a capitalist. What then if this woman decided to work harder and longer hours to produce a better commodity (or more of them) so that they would be capable of engaging in surplus labor for the capitalist and he can gain surplus value. Doesn't this woman, then, perform surplus labor, labor above and beyond the minimum labor necessary to produce the commodity labor power capable of lasting through necessary labor time and then collapsing? And if she does this surplus labor, isn't it her work that allows the capitalist to gain surplus value by exploiting in his factory the surplus labor of the workers made possible by the surplus labor of the wife in the home? And if so doesn't the capitalist appropriate the wife's surplus labor and thus her surplus value—doesn't he therefore exploit her?

No, not from the capitalist perspective. The surplus value involved here does not belong to the wife, but to the capitalist. If our capitalist purchases iron from another capitalist who produces it, that iron will contain surplus labor that was already objectified in it in the ironworks. Our capitalist will purchase the iron on the market at its value, and it will rightfully belong to our capitalist. He will then set his own laborers to work on it, and gain his own surplus value by selling on the market the commodities they produce. This surplus value belongs to our capitalist, not to the capitalist who owns the ironworks, and the latter is in no way exploited—he was paid the value of his iron. In just the same way, our capitalist pays the family the value of their labor power. The fact that he exploits the family in his factory does not mean that he exploits the wife at home any more than he exploits the owner of the ironworks whose iron he makes use of in the process of seeking his own profit. Our capitalist has paid the value of the iron as well as the value of labor power.

But if the wife works hard (engages in surplus labor) in the home to allow her family to be able to engage in surplus labor in the factory, if she produces a commodity (labor power) that exchanges on a market (the labor market), and if she produces a better (harder-working, longer-lasting) product, doesn't she produce surplus value that the capitalist appropriates? No, not from the capitalist perspective. She is incapable of producing surplus value. Even if she works harder and longer to produce a harder- and longer-working laborer, the market and competition will see to it, sooner or later, that she receives only what it costs to produce labor power. She will never gain surplus value. Perhaps, until the market adjusts, the family members, if they work harder and better, can get a raise in pay, or if the wife has more children, the family will earn more, but sooner or later competition will cause the market to adjust and the average family wage will equal the cost of producing labor power.

But why can the capitalist, then, gain surplus value by exchanging commodities on the market while the houseworker cannot? Why won't the market adjust so that what the capitalist's commodities will exchange for will equal his costs of production—eliminating his surplus value? The market will certainly tend in this direction. Struggle by labor for a shorter workday and higher wages will tend to reduce the amount of surplus labor time the capitalist can demand and the surplus value he can appropriate (especially if the capitalist cannot pass these higher costs on to the consumer in the form of higher prices because of the pressure of competition from other firms).

But the fact is that if the surplus value of a particular capitalist shrinks too far, the capitalist will simply quit business. Long before this happens, however, the capitalist will begin threatening his workers. If they expect him to stay in business, if they hope to keep their jobs, they will have to accept reduced wages, longer hours, harder work, and so forth. And so wages will be pushed back toward subsistence level. No surplus value will accrue to the family as it exchanges its commodity (labor power) on the labor market for a wage. After all, this is the necessary condition that allows the capitalist to gain surplus value for *himself*, and the capitalist is more powerful here.

Thus, it is just a fact of life in capitalist society that the houseworker cannot produce surplus value in the home, and the capitalist can in the factory. After all, Marx argues, if wages were to rise above the costs of reproducing labor power, capitalism would fail to reproduce capitalist relations of production. This can be seen most clearly in colonies where, if wages exceed the costs of reproducing labor power, laborers will soon be able to set themselves up as individual peasant farmers, and capitalists will find it difficult or even impossible to keep laborers.[157] But at any rate, if the houseworker cannot produce surplus value in the home, then the capitalist cannot exploit the houseworker as houseworker. Just as if the ironworks from which I buy iron is for some reason not capable of selling it at a profit, I do not exploit them by buying their iron on the market at the normal market price and turning it to the production of surplus value in my own factory. However, the ironworks, at that point, will go out of business. The family is not in a position to go out of business when the value of labor power is pushed (as it is normally pushed) to subsistence level. To go out of business for the family is to die. The owner of the ironworks, after going out of business, can clip his coupons or invest in a better industry.

It is deeply ironic that the capitalist oppression of the housewife cannot even be called exploitation. This is not to suggest, however, that capitalism is simply innocent. Capitalism has a remarkable and mysterious ability to establish moral categories in a way that allows it to avoid being blamed by anyone using those categories. Far from this exonerating capitalism, however, it makes capitalism even worse—if, that is, we are able see behind the mystification.

Moreover, the distinction between productive and unproductive labor, it should be unnecessary to say, is *not* something Marx approves of or accepts, as some modern feminist theorists seem to think.[158] Marx presents this distinction as an ugly fact generated by capitalist society and, indeed, as a fundamental critique of capitalist society. Unproductive labor produces use values and productive labor exchange values. And it is absolutely clear that Marx deeply objects to the fact that in capitalist society the realm of exchange value predominates such that to realize something as a use value it must first be realized as an exchange value.[159] In other words, all use values, to be realized in consumption, to satisfy human needs, must first be realized as exchange values—that is, exchanged, sold, on the market. And, of course, this market produces alienation or fetishism. Even to be able to afford to produce human beings—develop their powers and capacities—they, or at least their labor power, must first be sold as a commodity on the market in exchange for a wage. This is certainly not something Marx accepts. It is clearly Marx's goal to eliminate exchange value[160] as well, of course, as market exchange and thus alienation or fetishism. And if this occurs, the capitalist distinction between productive and unproductive labor would disappear. Without exchange and thus exchange value, there could be no productive labor in the capitalist sense, no labor that produces commodities, which, when exchanged on the market, could produce surplus value for the capitalist.

For Marx, it should be clear, "productive" labor is not truly productive. It produces surplus value only for the capitalist and impoverishes, alienates, and degrades the wage worker and the houseworker.[161] "Unproductive" labor, on the other hand, not only produces use values, which are real wealth, but it also produces human beings, their powers and capacities, and thus is truly productive labor, labor that can enrich and develop the human species. As capitalism is replaced by a socialist community for which all production is collectively and democratically controlled production of use values for consumption by the whole community as well as the production of human beings (the development of the powers and capacities of individuals), the capitalist distinction between productive and unproductive labor will disappear. "Unproductive" labor will become truly productive and the private appropriation of "productive" labor in the form of surplus value and thus exploitation will disappear.

IV. The Family and Community

There is another matter that we must discuss here. Capitalism, for Marx, alienates the political state from civil society. This is a form of alienation that did not always occur in precapitalist society. For example, in feudal society, one's socioeconomic position was simultaneously one's political position.[162] To be a duke or an earl was to hold a political title and a political position, but one was also, say, the Duke of Burgundy or the Earl of Gloucester, which is to say that one held a landed estate and thus a socioeconomic position. In capitalism, the economic sphere of civil society has been separated from the political state. The political state crystalizes as a power that stands outside and dominates civil society. Individuals perhaps vote every four years for political representatives, but other than this the political state is a distant, alien realm. The individual is locked into civil society, the realm of particular, selfish, economic interests and is cut off from the collective, universal concerns of the political community.

So also, capitalism separates and alienates the family from civil society. Again, this separation did not exist, or did not exist so sharply, in precapitalist society. The home, the family, was the locus of work that was social production.[163] Work for the feudal serf, for example, was carried on in the family, by the family, and on the family's plot. Family and society, or family and social production, were one. Capitalism draws workers out of the family, and the locus of social production becomes the factory in civil society. All productive labor takes place in civil society, in the factory, and what work is left in the home, housework, becomes unproductive labor.[164] Moreover, the houseworker, the wife, if she has not been drawn into the factory, is locked into the home, isolated from the larger world of economic interests and social production in civil society, which in turn is isolated from the common, collective, universal concerns of the political state.

As capitalism develops, especially as it introduces machinery, it also draws women and children out of the home and into the factory. As it does so, it increases the oppression of women who now have double work—in the household and in the factory. However, this does draw women into the larger world of civil society, of economic concerns, and of social production. This is not, however, a stable situation for women. Capitalism, for Marx, needs an industrial reserve army. In times of economic expansion, capitalism needs a pool of laborers who are not working, or whose work can be dropped, so that they can be drawn into work where it is needed by the expanding economy. Then when this economic expansion ceases, begins to shrink, or when crises occur, these laborers are dumped back into the industrial reserve army.[165] Women constitute an important part of this reserve army. Thus, they oscillate between double work (in the home and in the factory) and thus double oppression, on the one hand, and, on the other, exclusion from civil society, social production, and isolation in the narrow confines of the home. Moreover, the male worker oscillates between drawing his wife and child into the factory beside him and thus becoming a slave dealer[166] and, on the other hand, wanting women and children excluded from the factory. This is due either to a humanitarian concern for women and children, whom they do not want subjected to the miserable conditions of the factory,[167] or, instead (or perhaps at the same time), to maximize their competitive advantage, so that their own wages are not lowered in having to compete with lower-paid women and children. Thus, the male worker oscillates between doubly oppressing women (who have to work in the factory as well as the home) and isolating them in the narrow confines of the home and away from the larger world of civil society.

The emancipation of women, Engels argues, is impossible if they are isolated in the home and excluded from the sphere of society and social production.[168] This is so, Jaggar theorizes, because only in society and social production can women gain a sense of independence, equality with men, and class consciousness.[169] Yet including them in production, Engels realizes, will involve increased oppression of women. Marx argues, for example, that despite the oppression and slavery produced in the family, despite the destruction of the family, by capitalism, nevertheless capitalism lays the foundation for a higher form of the family and of relations between the sexes by drawing women into social production beside men and thus including women in the larger sphere of social production.[170] For Engels, the double work and thus double oppression of women, brought about when they enter the factory, can be eliminated in socialist society by industrializing housework—making it a public industry.[171]

Housework, we have said, does involve exchangeability of function, the rotation of tasks, but still the range of this exchangeability is narrow and it is also alienated from the autonomous spheres that develop outside the family. The rotation of tasks should also involve rotation to tasks outside the home; it should involve rotation into the larger social realm where women can develop a larger range of powers, capacities, and ideas, where they can gain a larger view of the whole of their world, and where they can thus begin to exert some control over it.

The family and civil society are very different realms and very much opposed to each other. Civil society is competitive, antagonistic, and fetishized. It is the realm of self-interest and of the aggressive pursuit of these self-interests. The family, on the other hand, is more cooperative and less competitive. It is a realm of common concerns more than a realm of self-interest. It can also be a realm of nurturing, support, and caring—a realm of reciprocal affirmation and reinforcing emotions.[172] It is a small community, a *Gemeinschaft,* which is quite unlike the *Gesellschaft* of civil society. This is not to paint an idealized, romanticized, or ideological picture of the family, as if there were no troubles, disagreements, or oppression within it. The best of friends, the tightest-knit communities, after all, can disagree. Moreover, disagreements among those who are close to each other can often times be far more intense and bitter than among those who are strangers. Furthermore, community, bonds of feeling, nurturing, caring, and support do not rule out oppression. Many people seem to think that love can only take place between equals who respect each other as equals. That is romantic illusion. It is quite possible to love, to deeply and seriously love, someone you consider your inferior. And it is quite possible to love someone while what you expect of them oppresses them. You can, after all, love your dog. This is not to say, however, that love is not of the highest value. Love *ought* to be exchanged only and equally for love. The point is to remove the oppression and realize the love.

For Hegel, too, the relationship of the family to civil society is similar to the one that we have described. For Hegel, civil society is a competitive realm of self-interest alien to the emotional bonds and the cooperative community of the family.[173]

If civil society and the family are so radically opposed to each other, there would seem to be two possibilities with respect to the liberation of women. First, women, along with men, could evacuate the family and enter civil society. And to avoid the double oppression this would involve for women, we could, as Engels suggests, industrialize housework and childcare. But if civil society and the family are so radically opposed, then as both parents enter the alienated, competitive, antagonistic, self-interested, and grueling realm of civil society, they will bring that alienation, antagonism, and so forth along with them back into the family when they return to the home at the end of the day. This will erode the family. At the end of the work day, with their nerves frayed and on edge, they will find it much more difficult to maintain the communal, caring, and emotionally supportive realm of the family. This will tend to weaken the family and dissolve it. Many modern feminists would simply say good riddance to this oppressive institution. And it would be impossible to disagree, at least with the end of the oppression that has historically been involved in the family.

But, at the same time, certain other things would be lost: that aspect of housework, now industrialized, that can be an unalienated ideal and that humanizes the environment of the home; working for the benefit of the species in raising a child yourself; the caring, nurturing, emotionally supportive, and communal dimension of the family; and the cultivation and preservation of valuable human emotions, attitudes, outlooks, and values. All of these qualities and activities have certainly been wrapped up with and inseparable from the historical oppression of women in the family, but this is not to say that when the oppression of women is overcome these qualities and activities should not be seen as of the highest value, and that it would not be a serious loss if they disappeared.

The only way to support the family, the second possibility here, it would seem, would be to keep one adult in the family. It could be *either* the husband or the wife. In the past it has almost always been the wife, and in the future, in most cases and for the foreseeable future, it will probably still be the wife. If one person remains in the family isolated from the competitive, antagonistic, aggressive, fetishized, self-interested realm of civil society, this person could keep alive the emotional, supportive, nurturing, caring, and communal realm of the family and counterbalance the negative elements of civil society brought home into the family at the end of the day by the other person. The family could be preserved, but the preserver would lose the development and scope of the larger world of civil society, would be locked into the family and into expected roles, and would be oppressed.

Thus, it would seem that we must choose between liberating women and losing the family (and all that is valuable in it) or preserving the family but giving up the liberation of women and accepting their oppression. It *seems* that we must choose, but I would suggest that there is a third way—a way that is at least implied in Marx's thought. The third way is to do away with *civil society*. Marx, after all, wants to eliminate the competitive, antagonized, self-interested, fetishized realm of exchange—the market or civil society—and transform it into a community where individuals consciously cooperate and work intentionally for the benefit of the species. This would be a realm where common, universal, communal, species concerns, now isolated at the realm of the political state, would be brought down to, realized, and embedded within the everyday activity of society. This would be a realm where individuals work consciously and collectively for the universal, the common good, the species, in their everyday activity in the social community. It would be a realm of friends who support each other—a realm of communal solidarity.

Moreover, it is the view of many modern feminist theorists that the best condition for women is one where the separation between family and society, the private and the public sphere, is minimized.[174] If society becomes communal, it will not be antagonistic to the family, which itself is a small community. To take a simple example, think of a frontier farming family. Here there would be no alienation between civil society and the family. There would be no civil society (no market, competition, exchange, or fetishism), or this realm would be far enough away as to have little effect on the family. Moreover, there would be few spheres that exclude women (or they would be undeveloped) for the man to get caught up in. The family works in common, collectively, and its labor is social production. Here the work of the women is of major importance for survival. Its importance cannot be distinguished from the importance of the man's labor. There may be a division of labor. The man might plow, take care of the livestock, do the building, and the woman might prepare the food, sew most of the clothes, quilt, care for the children, but *all* of this is work that is crucial to the survival of the family. Without any of it, the family would suffer. The woman's work is important—as important as her husband's work. Her work is *objectively* important even if her husband, *subjectively,* is reluctant to say so or to recognize its importance. The objective importance of her work is visible, manifest.

Moreover, her work need not be confined to the house. She can also work outside the house in the fields. Even grandparents, children, and grandchildren can work in the fields; they can work long hard hours, and they can do so *without* eroding the family, without eroding the valuable qualities nurtured in the home. Indeed, generations upon generations have thought that such work tends to reinforce the valuable qualities nurtured in the family. In other words, because both the home, narrowly conceived, and the world of work, conceived as larger than the work going on in the house, are both communal, part of one cooperative group, because there is no antagonistic, competitive, fetishized realm of civil society, productive work does not erode the home. It is part of the home and reinforces it.

Well, obviously, the modern feminist movement is not about to return to the frontier homestead. That is not the point here. The point is to eliminate civil society and locate the family in a community that will not erode it. That is the possibility that Marx's thought opens up for us. If we can break down, blur, the difference between family and society, if we can surround the family with a neighborhood community, so that the immediate community becomes an extension of the family, so that the family moves out into the immediate community, and so that the further reaches of society are communal, more like the family, then the liberation of women without the destruction of the family will be eased.

The immediate neighborhood community could be responsible for childcare, and not in a distant and impersonal, but in a familiar and personal, way, something like an extended family. Also, the neighborhood community could be responsible for a good deal of housework. Engels suggests that housework should be industrialized. Exactly what this means is not clear. If it means that an industrial organization of strangers enters your home to work, that is not especially appealing. Moreover, if it means that housework becomes the ongoing profession of a class, this could create (or perpetuate) a class of menial laborers. It might be much better to have a good deal of housework, as well as childcare, done by the immediate community on a basis of rotation (with the help of some professionals). All, including men, would take part in it, and do so as a part of social production. They would get time off from their other work, not do it in their free time, and it would be part of the work expected for earning one's share of social production. After all, housework and childcare contribute to the maintenance and reproduction of labor power as well as of the future species. If it were done in free time, it would save the community surplus labor and thus perhaps be an exploitation of individuals by the community.

Moreover, organized neighborhood communities, with women having a significant voice and being an active force in these communities, might well be the only effective way to stop things like wife battering—something legal agencies seem powerless to stop in our society. Neighbors, with the communal responsibility to do so, could keep an eye out and listen in for wife beating, then intervene and put peer pressure on this person, make it clear that there will be no public invisibility, no private realm, for wife beating. Similar peer pressure could be brought to bear on tyrannical husbands, and could very possibly be effective in reducing rape and in making the streets safe for women and children, as well as men.

At the same time, it would not be acceptable merely to eliminate private life and the privacy of the home. A balance would have to be struck. There should be a private realm of the home, and certain activities in the home should remain private. Even some housework and childcare, which can be satisfying, could be left to individuals in the home. This realm of privacy and intimacy is necessary to cultivate valuable attitudes, outlooks, and emotions—attitudes of caring, nurturing, and support. It is necessary as a realm in which love is exchanged only for love, and trust for trust. It is necessary as a realm to nurture the intimate, the personal, and the particular as equally important to the communal, the general, and the common. It is necessary to have a realm, as Marx put it in his letter to Jenny, where Jenny (or Karl) is more important than the proletariat.

Moreover, certain ways in which society enters the home, for example, through television and television commercials, which in our society bring alienated, competitive, consumerist, and often sexist values into the home, values that especially affect children and thus the future of the species, could well be controlled by the larger community. This aspect of present-day society could be excluded from the home. On the other hand, it would be possible to integrate nonhousehold work with the home. This already occurs to some extent today. University professors, scholars, journalists, people who work with computers or in electronics industries, as well as many others, can often do a part of their professional work at home. As society becomes increasingly computerized, this should become increasingly possible.

Or, it could be possible, besides having childcare available in the immediate neighborhood community, to have it available at work, if work is far from one's home, and to allow time for interaction between parent and child during the workday and at the workplace. Community planning could also try to better integrate residential neighborhoods, shopping areas, and workplaces so that they can be closer to each other and linked in various ways. The point is to break down the isolation of the home from the larger realm of the social community, to end alienation in society by making it more communal, and yet preserve a realm of privacy and intimacy in the home.

Such changes could eliminate, or at least seriously reduce, the structural oppression of women—the oppression that arises from, or is reinforced by, social, economic, and political forces. What would remain would be the personal oppression of women. This would have to be worked on by a community that communicates with itself, that creates a common arena of discourse, or of different and diverse discourses, that works to discover and uncover further oppression, which it then confronts by persuading others of its existence, by trying to change attitudes, and thus eliminating this oppression.

At any rate, it seems to me that Marx's thought does have something valuable to say to modern feminism and can be used to develop feminist theory.

Notes

1. Balbus, 33–36. Baudrillard, 59, 65–67, 83–88. Sahlins, vii–viii, 3, 34, 127–28, 168.

2. See, for example, Z.R. Eisenstein, "Developing a Theory of Capitalist Patriarchy and Socialist Feminism," in *Capitalist Patriarchy and the Case for Socialist Feminism* (hereafter *CPCSF*), ed. Z.R. Eisenstein (New York: Monthly Review Press, 1979), 11–13. L. Nicholson, "Feminism and Marx: Integrating Kinship with the Economic" in *Feminism as Critique*, eds. S. Benhabib and D. Cornell (Minneapolis: University of Minnesota Press, 1987), 16–30. J. Flax, "Postmodernism and Gender Relations in Feminist Theory," in *Feminism/Postmodernism*, ed. L.J. Nicholson, (New York: Routledge, 1990), 46–47.

3. S. Harding, "What is the Real Material Base of Patriarchy and Capital?" in *Women and Revolution*, ed. L. Sargent (Boston: South End Press, 1981), 143–44.

4. E.g., Eisenstein, 9–14. "Simone De Beauvoir questions Jean-Paul Sartre," trs. J. Howe and R. Mulvey, *New Left Review*, 97 (1976), 74.

5. M.Z. Rosaldo, "Woman, Culture, and Society: A Theoretical Overview," in *Woman, Culture, and Society,* eds. M.Z. Rosaldo and L. Lamphere (Stanford: Stanford University Press, 1974), 17–19. Also, S.B. Ortner, "Is Female to Male as Nature Is to Culture?" in *Woman, Culture, and Society,* 67–87.

6. Some feminists would disagree with this; see, for example, E. Reed, *Women's Evolution* (New York: Pathfinder Press, 1975). Also R. Rohrlich-Leavitt, B. Sykes, and E. Weatherford, "Aboriginal Women: Male and Female Anthropological Perspectives," in *Toward an Anthropology of Women,* ed. R.R. Reiter (New York: Monthly Review Press, 1975), 111.

7. M.Z. Rosaldo, "Woman, Culture, and Society," 22–23.

8. Balbus, 82 n. Eisenstein, 13.

9. *Capital,* I, 82 n and *MEW,* XXIII, 96.

10. As is claimed by Balbus, 33–34; Sahlins, 3, 128, also 34, 127; and Baudrillard, 83–88.

11. *Grundrisse, MECW,* XXVIII, 46–47 and *MEGA,* II, 1.1, 44–45.

12. *Grundrisse, MECW,* XXVIII, 37 and *MEGA,* II, 1.1, 35–36.

13. *GI, MECW,* V, 31 and *MEW,* III, 20–21.

14. *GI, MECW,* V, 44 and *MEW,* III, 31.

15. Ibid. See also *Capital,* I, 351, also 78 and *MEW,* XXIII, 372, 92.

16. *GI, MECW,* V, 32–33 and *MEW,* III, 22. See also *CPE, MECW,* XXIX, 275 and *MEW,* XIII, 20–21.

17. *GI, MECW,* V, 42–43 and *MEW,* III, 29.

18. *Origin,* 5–6 and *MEW,* XXI, 27–28. Meillassoux (*Maidens, Meal and Money,* xi) defends placing production and reproduction on the same level, and he points out that the reproduction of human beings is the production of labor power.

19. *Origin,* 6 and *MEW,* XXI, 28.

20. *GI, MECW,* V, 46, also 33 and *MEW,* III, 32, 22.

21. *Origin,* 42, 49–50, 58, 147 and *MEW,* XXI, 53, 60–61, 68, 157–58. In the *Ethnological Notebooks* (121), it is possible that Marx shifts a bit in Engels's direction. There Marx does speak of the greater freedom and influence of women at an early stage of history that was still reflected in goddesses like Juno and Minerva. But, on the other hand, perhaps this *greater* freedom and influence is not incompatible with the "slavery latent in the family [which] develops *gradually* with the increase of population, the growth of wants, and with the extension of external intercourse, both of war and barter" (*GI, MECW,* V, 33 (my italics) and *MEW,* III, 22). Perhaps such slavery just had not developed enough to eliminate a freedom and influence greater than that which exists in the modern period.

22. C.A. MacKinnon, *Toward a Feminist Theory of the State* (Cambridge, Mass.: Harvard University Press, 1989), 13–14. See also B. Thiele, "Vanishing Acts in Social and Political Thought: Tricks of the Trade," in *Feminist Challenges: Social and Political Theory,* eds. C. Pateman and E. Gross (Boston: Northeastern University Press, 1987), 36. Also, Harding, 146.

23. See G. Rubin, "The Traffic in Women: Notes on the 'Political Economy' of Sex," in *Toward an Anthropology of Women,* 157–210.

24. Marx says, "there springs up naturally a division of labour, caused by differences of sex and age, a division that is consequently based on a purely physiological foundation . . ." (*Capital,* I, 351 and *MEW,* XXIII, 372).

25. *GI, MECW,* V, 43 (my italics) and *MEW,* III, 29. On this same page Marx makes it clear that the family is also a social relation; in fact, to begin with it was "the only social relation." Meillassoux mistakenly thinks that Marx, unlike Engels, was influenced by bourgeois ideology in thinking the family natural (Meillassoux, *Maidens, Meal and Money,* 3).

26. *Capital,* I, 372 n and *MEW,* XXIII, 393 n.

27. *Theories of Surplus Value* (hereafter *TSV*), ed. S. Ryazanskaya (Moscow: Progress, 1963–68), Part III, 294–95 and *MEW,* XXVI, Teil III, 289.

28. *Capital,* I, 609 n and *MEW,* XXIII, 637 n. See also, *EPM, MECW,* III, 303, 305, see also 295–96 and *MEW,* suppl. I, 543, 546, 535.

29. *Grundrisse, MECW,* XXVIII, 29–30 and *MEGA,* II, 1.1, 28–29.

30. *GI, MECW,* V, 256 n and *MEW,* III, 238 n.

31. *EPM, MECW,* III, 301–2 and *MEW,* suppl. I, 541–42.

32. *EPM, MECW,* III, 295–96 and *MEW,* suppl. I, 535.

33. Rubin, 158. *Wage-Labour and Capital, MECW,* IX, 211 and *MEW,* VI, 407.

34. Balbus, 63–66.

35. *Manifesto, MECW,* VI, 491 and *MEW,* IV, 469.

36. See also, *Capital,* I, 394–95, 461 and *MEW,* XXIII, 416–17, 485.

37. *Manifesto, MECW,* VI, 502 and *MEW,* IV, 478–79. *EPM, MECW,* III, 294–95 and *MEW,* suppl. I, 534–35.

38. *Capital,* I, 396 and *MEW,* XXIII, 418, Also *Origin,* 64 and *MEW,* XXI, 74.

39. *Capital,* I, 489–90 and *MEW,* XXIII, 514.

40. E.g., Eisenstein, 9–10. B. Weinbaum, *The Curious Courtship of Women's Liberation and Socialism* (Boston: South End Press, 1978), 51, 56–57. "Simone De Beauvoir questions Jean-Paul Sartre," 74.

41. *Origin,* 148 (my italics), also 66 and *MEW,* XXI, 158, 76.

42. *Origin,* 73 and *MEW,* XXI, 83.

43. *Gotha, MECW,* XXIV, 85 (my italics) and *MEW,* XIX, 20.

44. *GI, MECW,* V, 51–52 and *MEW,* III, 37. Also, *Capital,* I, 78–81 and *MEW,* XXIII, 92–95.

45. *GI, MECW,* V, 87–88, 48–49 and *MEW,* III, 67–88, 34–35.

46. *GI, MECW,* V, 49 and *MEW,* III, 35.

47. *EPM, MECW,* III, 294–95 and *MEW,* suppl. I, 534–35.

48. Eisenstein, 9–10.

49. N.C.M. Hartsock, *Money, Sex, and Power: Toward a Feminist Historical Materialism* (New York: Longman, 1983), 146. L.M.G. Clarke and L. Lange, *Sexism of Social and Political Theory* (Toronto: University of Toronto Press, 1979), x–xi.

50. M. O'Brien, *The Politics of Reproduction* (Boston: Routledge & Kegan Paul, 1981), 18, 24, 35. R. McDonough and R. Harrison, "Patriarchy and Relations of Production," in *Feminism and Materialism,* eds. A. Kuhn and A. Wolpe (London: Routledge & Kegan Paul, 1978), 27–28.

51. *EPM, MECW,* III, 295–96 and *MEW,* suppl. I, 535.

52. E.g., S. de Beauvoir, *The Second Sex,* tr. H.M. Parshley (New York: Bantam, 1961), 689 and, for the French, *Le deuxième sexe* (hereafter *DS*) (Paris: Gallimard, 1949), II, 504. Hartsock, 145–46. J. Mitchell, *Woman's Estate* (New York: Pantheon, 1971), 110. O'Brien, 35. B. Ollman, *Social and Sexual Revolution* (Boston: South End Press, 1979), 159.

53. *GI, MECW,* V, 43 and *MEW,* III, 29.

54. *EPM, MECW,* III, 295–96 (my italics) and *MEW,* suppl. I, 535. The connection that Marx establishes in this passage between women and nature might be thought to be objectionable. S. Ortner (67–87) suggests that universal, cross-cultural devaluation of women is connected with the distinction between nature and culture, the identification of women with nature, and the fact that all cultures devalue nature; that is, consider nature lower than culture. I suggest that far more historical evidence would have to be presented to sustain her argument, which seems to me to be the projection of a very modern, Lévi-Straussian perspective on the relationship of nature to culture back onto all past cultures. It seems to me that many past cultures, perhaps even most traditional cultures, believed the exact opposite. They did not at all think of nature as inferior to culture. Instead they thought of nature as constituting a norm, even a moral norm, to which culture ought to accord and that, in general, culture, or convention, was inferior to nature. It may well be that deeper studies of cultures that do not devalue nature but do devalue women, yet identify them with nature, might show that women are not devalued in all ways—that the positive valuation of nature carries over to women in certain respects. The universal, cross-cultural devaluation of women, argued for by Ortner and Rosaldo, need not mean that women are devalued in *all* ways. It may well be the case, however, that women are associated with physical or biological nature more than with rational or intellectual nature and thus are devalued in this way. But it would still not follow from any of this that Marx, who operates with a concept of nature, and who even thinks that the relation of man to woman is a relationship to nature, would be devaluing women, despite himself, just because he is committed to a traditional concept of nature. Marx certainly would not accept the devaluing of nature in general, nor would he even accept the devaluing of physical nature as opposed to intellectual nature, as should be obvious by the importance he grants to labor. At any rate, the connection among women, nature, and devaluation, it seems to me, requires much greater historical evidence before it becomes convincing, and certainly before one would have to conclude that there is something objectionable about Marx's use of the concept of nature.

55. *EPM, MECW,* III, 336–37 and *MEW,* suppl. I, 578. *CM, MECW,* III, 218–20 and *MEW,* suppl. I, 452–54.

56. *EPM, MECW,* III, 298 and *MEW,* suppl. I, 537.

57. In considering Marx's views here, the question arises as to whether or not he is heterosexist. This is a very difficult question. I have no way to prove that he was not. In fact, he very probably was. In the middle of the nineteenth century in Marx's world, as far as I can see, the concept "heterosexism" simply did not exist. All, including those who were not heterosexual, were most likely heterosexist. Engels, for example, speaks of the Greeks who "fell into the abominable practice of sodomy and degraded alike their gods and themselves with the myth of Ganymede" (*Origin,* 57 and *MEW,* XXI, 67). Nevertheless, I think that whatever suggestions of this sort one might find embedded in Marx's thought can be rejected and the core of his argument will stand. See also note 59 below.

58. *CM, MECW,* III, 228 and *MEW,* suppl. I, 462.

59. The biological relation of man to woman (or at least of sperm to ovum) is fundamental and necessary. It cannot be replaced, or at least modern science has not yet been able to do so. The sociocultural relation of man to woman in raising a child, while historically the ideological social norm up to recent times, is, of course, not at all necessary. Children can be brought up by single parents, parents of the same sex, extended families, communities, individuals involved in group marriages, and so forth. When Marx describes the relation between man and woman as an essential relation, I do not think his point is to prescribe this relation universally and eternally. After all, to say that something is essential or natural is *not,* as we have seen, to say that it is eternal or unchanging for Marx. Whether Marx would personally object to relations that are not heterosexual, I simply do not know; but conceptually they are not ruled out here.

Marx wants to argue for an essential relation between men and women because, as I will try to show, he wants to construct an especially powerful argument against the domination of women by men, an argument that tries to do more than merely appeal to the good will of men. He tries to show that men violate their own essence in dominating women, and thus he must show that men and women are part of each other's essence. In other words, the claim that there is an essential relation between men and women is a necessary one if Marx is to hold that it violates a man's essence to dominate women, but this claim does not imply that all other relationships besides that of man to woman are ruled out as against one's essence or against nature. To put this another way, human beings can, in male-female relationships, develop their powers, capacities, and essence in very significant ways; but they can obviously do so, for Marx, in other ways also—simply consider his whole discussion of labor.

60. *EPM, MECW,* III, 295 and *MEW,* suppl. I, 535. For a most interesting discussion of similar matters that goes much further, see O'Brien, 19–64.

61. *EPM, MECW,* III, 275–76 and *MEW,* suppl. I, 515–16.

62. *CHPLI, MECW,* III, 182–87 and *MEW,* I, 385–91.

63. They do so much as in Kant's "Idea for a Universal History"; see above Chapter 4.

64. *EPM, MECW*, III, 294 and *MEW*, suppl. I, 534.
65. Ibid.
66. *EPM, MECW*, III, 294–95 and *MEW*, suppl. I, 534. See also *Manifesto, MECW*, VI, 502 and *MEW*, IV, 478–79.
67. *EPM, MECW*, III, 295 and *MEW*, suppl. I, 535. *JQ, MECW*, III, 172 and *MEW*, I, 375.
68. *Manifesto, MECW*, VI, 502 and *MEW*, IV, 478.
69. "Debates on Freedom of the Press," *MECW*, I, 154 and *MEW*, I, 50. "Divorce Bill," *MECW*, I, 308–9 and *MEW*, I, 149–50.
70. de Beauvoir, *The Second Sex*, 495 and *DS*, II, 200.
71. Mitchell, 110.
72. *Schiller, Hegel, and Marx*, Chapter 3. Also, *Marx and Ethics*, Chapter 2.
73. *CJ*, 38–44 and *Ak*, V, 204–10.
74. Schiller, "The Moral Utility of Aesthetic Manners," *EAP*, 126–32 and *SWN*, XXI, 28–34. Also, "On Grace and Dignity," *EAP*, 209 and *SWN*, XX, 287.
75. *EPM, MECW*, III, 300 and *MEW*, suppl. I, 540.
76. *EPM, MECW*, III, 299–300 and *MEW*, suppl. I, 539–40.
77. *EPM, MECW*, III, 300 and *MEW*, suppl. I, 540.
78. *EPM, MECW*, III, 302 and *MEW*, suppl. I, 542.
79. *EPM, MECW*, III, 301 and *MEW*, suppl. I, 541.
80. Ibid. *Grundrisse, MECW*, XXVIII, 29–30 and *MEGA*, II, 1.1, 28–29.
81. *EPM, MECW*, III, 304 and *MEW*, suppl. I, 544.
82. *EPM, MECW*, III, 317, also 285 and *MEW*, suppl. I, 557, 524.
83. *EPM, MECW*, III, 322 and *MEW*, suppl. I, 562.
84. *EPM, MECW*, III, 324 and *MEW*, suppl. I, 564–65.
85. Ibid.
86. *EPM, MECW*, III, 326 and *MEW*, suppl. I, 567.
87. "Marx to Jenny Marx on 21 June 1856," *MECW*, XL, 54–56 (passage in brackets is my addition) and *MEW*, XXIX, 532–36. The term "Black Madonna" refers to early wood carvings of the Virgin Mary.
88. See, for example, M. Markus, "Women, Success and Civil Society," in *Feminism as Critique*, 97.
89. R.S. Gottlieb, *History and Subjectivity: The Transformation of Marxist Theory* (Philadelphia: Temple University Press, 1987), 106.
90. "Marx to Engels on 17 January 1855," *MECW*, XXXIX, 508–9 and *MEW*, XXVIII, 423.
91. *Economic Manuscripts of 1861–63, MECW*, XXXI, 194 and *MEGA*, II, 3.2, 614.
92. *EPM, MECW*, III, 326 and *MEW*, suppl. I, 567. See also *CM, MECW*, III, 227–28 and *MEW*, suppl. I, 462–63.
93. *GI, MECW*, V, 236 and *MEW*, III, 218.
94. *CWF, MECW*, XXII, 335 and *MEW*, XVII, 343. *Capital*, I, 10 and *MEW*, XXIII, 16. Also see *Gotha, MECW*, XXIV, 85 and *MEW*, XIX, 20.

Chapter Eight

95. M.Z. Rosaldo, "Woman, Culture, and Society," 24, 26.
96. L. Gordon, "The Struggle for Reproductive Freedom: Three Stages of Feminism," in *CPCSF*, 125.
97. A. Ferguson and N. Folbre, "The Unhappy Marriage of Patriarchy and Capitalism," in *Women and Revolution*, 320.
98. A. Oakley, *The Sociology of Housework* (New York: Pantheon, 1974), 80.
99. G. Joseph, "The Incompatible Menage À Trois: Marxism, Feminism, and Racism," in *Women and Revolution*, 95.
100. A.M. Jaggar, *Feminist Politics and Human Nature* (Totowa, N.J.: Rowman & Allanheld, 1983), 218.
101. *EPM, MECW*, III, 272–77 and *MEW*, suppl. I, 511–17. *CM, MECW*, III, 224–27 and *MEW*, suppl. I, 459–61. *Capital*, I, 71–76 and *MEW*, XXIII, 85–90. Also *Schiller, Hegel, and Marx*, Chapters 2–4.
102. *Capital*, I, 72–79 and *MEW*, XXIII, 86–93. *CM, MECW*, III, 224–27 and *MEW*, suppl. I, 459–61.
103. *Capital*, I, 77 and *MEW*, XXIII, 91–92. It is Jaggar's view that "[m]arriage is . . . a relation that is remarkably similar to the feudal relation of vassalage . . ." (Jaggar, 217, also 219).
104. *PS*, 111–19, 294–321 and *PG*, 141–50, 347–76. For further discussion of Hegel's concept of alienation, see my *Schiller, Hegel, and Marx*, Chapter 2.
105. *Capital*, I, 77–78 and *MEW*, XXIII, 92. Also, in early history, exchange or barter, for Marx, had no place within primitive society or the patriarchal family. It begins on the border of the community with other communities, and then begins to affect the community and the patriarchal family; *Capital*, I, 87 and *MEW*, XXIII, 102. *CPE, MECW*, XXIX, 275–77 and *MEW*, XIII, 20–22.
106. N. Fraser, "What's Critical about Critical Theory?: The Case of Habermas and Gender," in *Feminism as Critique*, 37–38.
107. When I call this oppression personal, I only mean that it does not have its source in, is not determined by, economics or biology. I definitely do *not* mean to say the this oppression is not caused or influenced by anything other than some mysterious inner person. I simply think that Marx has no theory of where this oppression comes from and thus leaves plenty of room for different theories about what determines this "personal" behavior—psychological theories like Chodorow's, a theory of sexuality/power like that of MacKinnon, or other possible theories.
108. *CPE, MECW*, XXIX, 275 and *MEW*, XIII, 20. *Capital*, I, 78, 395, 395 n and *MEW*, XXIII, 92, 416, 416–17 n.
109. *EPM, MECW*, III, 271–74 and *MEW*, suppl. I, 511–14.
110. *EPM, MECW*, III, 274–75 and *MEW*, suppl. I, 514–15.
111. *EPM, MECW*, III, 275–76 and *MEW*, suppl. I, 515–17.
112. *EPM, MECW*, III, 277 and *MEW*, suppl. I, 517.

113. *EPM, MECW,* III, 301 and *MEW,* suppl. I, 541.

114. It may seem that there would be aspects of housework where the houseworker is not in control—when the dishwasher or the water heater breaks down, when the houseworker must deal with the plumber or repair person, or simply when purchasing any store-bought goods. It is quite clear that alienation can enter the family from the alienated sphere of civil society that surrounds it—it can do this through technology, market exchange, or through the need for and dependence on produced goods. And as civil society grows more powerful, so will alienation within the family. At any rate, this sort of alienation is brought to housework from *outside* (and we will discuss this when we get there). But if we are trying to identify the *source* of alienation, we must say that housework itself can be free of alienation, if we can separate it from the effects of civil society (and perhaps in our world we can do that only in thought). Nevertheless, it might also be objected that houseworkers, in bringing up their children, often, at a certain point, are unable to control them. This may be true, but unless it is a specific kind of loss of control, again produced by forces outside the family (I will argue below), it is not alienation. After all, human beings (certainly at a certain age) should *not* be controlled. Part of what alienation or fetishism means is that what are really relations between persons come to appear as abstract relations between things. The point is to return them to relations between persons. Relations between persons may not be unproblematic, but they are the paradigm of unalienated relations for Marx. This is to say that the concept of alienation, for Marx, is not a catchall that includes all ills, everything that is undesirable, such that when alienation is overcome all will be perfect. If alienation is overcome, there will still be many ills that need to be remedied, but they are different ills and must be understood and treated differently. Moreover, Marx's concept of alienation does not include the modern notion of psychological alienation.

115. *Grundrisse, MECW,* XXVIII, 529–30 and *MEGA,* II, 1.2, 499.

116. As I have argued elsewhere, Marx uses the term "object" in an unusual way. To say that humans are our object is *not* to say that they are things or may be used as things. For Marx, we are essentially related to objects; they are parts of our essence; and they are ends in themselves; see *Marx and Ethics,* 58 ff.

117. I say this because of Marx's constant use of childbirth as a metaphor for social transformation; for some examples, see note 94 above.

118. *EPM, MECW,* III, 277 and *MEW,* suppl. I, 517.

119. *CM, MECW,* III, 228 (passages in brackets are my addition) and *MEW,* suppl. I, 462.

120. *GI, MECW,* V, 47 and *MEW,* III, 33.

121. *Poverty of Philosophy, MECW,* VI, 189–90 and *MEW,* IV, 156–57. *Capital,* I, 421, 487–88 and *MEW,* XXIII, 443–44, 511–12.

122. *GI, MECW,* V, 66 and *MEW,* III, 52.

123. de Beauvoir, *The Second Sex,* 418 and *DS,* II, 48.

124. *Capital*, I, 402 n (translation altered) and *MEW*, XXIII, 425 n.
125. *EPM, MECW*, III, 326 and MEW, suppl. I, 567.
126. V. Woolf, *To the Lighthouse* (New York: Harcourt Brace Jovanovich, 1927), 51, 137–40, 154–55.
127. de Beauvoir, *The Second Sex*, 223–33 and DS, I, 62–76.
128. This involves a very difficult issue. Here and in the previous paragraph I am speaking as if one can neatly separate the child's growing up and developing as a human being from an undesirable separate process of alienation. Marx would, I think, be willing to accept the notion that in alienated societies, growing up and developing would be wrapped up with alienation, but he would always want to insist that growing up and developing should and could be separable from alienation; that is, that they could be unalienated in an unalienated society. For many modern theorists, especially those influenced by Foucault, it is not clear that this is possible. In reading MacKinnon (especially Chapter 7), for example, the development of one's sexuality (certainly part of developing as a human being), given the way sexuality is constructed in a male-dominated culture, seems inseparable from power and the oppression of women. Simply to develop as a human being in a specific culture is to dominate or be dominated. To develop as a human being is inseparable from alienation. Or perhaps the term alienation is no longer appropriate if it can never be avoided. However, it is not clear how sexuality gets constructed for MacKinnon. Is it influenced by external spheres such that if they were changed sexuality could develop without alienation? At any rate, it is my contention that Marx has no theory of how male domination develops in the person—that is left open for others to fill in.
129. *Capital*, I, 87 and *MEW*, XXIII, 102. *CPE, MECW*, XXIX, 290–91 and *MEW*, XIII, 35–36.
130. *Ethnological Notebooks*, 144–50, 162–63, 172–73. *Origin*, 76–77 and *MEW*, XXI, 86–87.
131. See also Rubin, 168.
132. *GI, MECW*, V, 33 and *MEW*, III, 22.
133. For Marx, it is clear that even the capitalist, who is also caught up in the dynamic of capitalist society, is alienated, not just the proletariat; see *HF, MECW*, IV, 36 and *MEW*, II, 37.
134. Jaggar, 218, also 307.
135. *Capital*, I, 170–72, also 395 and *MEW*, XXIII, 184–86, 417.
136. There has been an extensive discussion of housework and unproductive labor; for some examples, see M. Benston, "The Political Economy of Women's Liberation," *Monthly Review* XXI, No. 4 (1969), 13–27. M. Dalla Costa and S. James, *The Power of Women and the Subversion of the Community* (Bristol, England: Falling Wall Press, 1972). W. Secombe, "The Housewife and Her Labour Under Capitalism," *New Left Review* 83 (1973), 3–24. P. Smith, "Domestic Labour and Marx's Theory of Value," in *Feminism and Materialism*, 198–219. J. Gardiner, "Women's Domestic Labor," in *CPCSF*,

173–89. M. Molyneux, "Beyond the Domestic Labour Debate," *New Left Review* 116 (1979), 3–27.

137. *Capital,* I, 171–72 and *MEW,* XXIII, 184–86.

138. *Capital,* I, 395 and *MEW,* XXIII, 417.

139. *Capital,* I, 572 and *MEW,* XXIII, 598. This chapter is not intended as a contribution to the already extensive domestic labor debate but rather as a broader discussion of housework, alienation, and oppression. Nevertheless, in touching on some of the issues central to the domestic labor debate, I hope I have been able to slide around some of the objections that have been made to the claim that the housewife's labor produces the value of labor power (see also notes 141 and 144 below). Smith, for example, wants to distinguish between and oppose: (1) housework as a set of services that merely produce use values for immediate consumption, and (2) housework as the production of a definite product, labor power, which is a commodity (P. Smith, 201). I do not see that these two can be separated. In capitalist society, labor power simply becomes a commodity. It is bought and sold on a market, and to stay alive, laborers must compete to sell this, their only commodity. Furthermore, it is quite clear that labor power is neither produced nor maintained without housework and childcare. Housework as a set of services that produce use values for consumption is *necessary* to produce and maintain labor power. But even further, housework is necessary to allow workers to *compete* in selling their labor power. No ordinary laborer earns enough of a wage simply to pay for all the housework that needs to be done. Efficient housework may well mean the difference between a well-fed, strong, and healthy worker who is able to compete and one who is not. Under such conditions generated by capitalism, housework becomes the efficient production of the commodity labor power, which must be exchanged on the market to keep the laboring family from starving.

140. *Capital,* I, 394–95, 395 n and *MEW,* XXIII, 416–17, 416–17 n.

141. *Capital,* I, 395 n and *MEW,* XXIII, 417 n. Gardiner (181–82) holds that the value of labor power is determined only by the cost of means of subsistence (food, clothing, shelter, and so forth) necessary to maintain labor power, and not by housework. But again I do not see how these two can be separated. The cost of necessary means of subsistence is in very significant part *determined* by housework—determined by how much or how little housework the houseworker is able to do and determined by how efficient the houseworker can be (both of which in turn depend on whether the houseworker works in the factory full time, part time, or only works in the home). Again, the working-class family cannot afford to purchase all the goods and services it needs to stay alive. Housework is necessary to keep the cost of producing and maintaining labor power down.

142. *Capital,* I, 395 and *MEW,* XXIII, 417.

143. The value of labor power does involve a historical and moral element. "The number and extent of his so-called necessary wants, as also the modes

of satisfying them, are themselves the product of historical development, and depend therefore to a great extent on the degree of civilization of a country, more particularly on the conditions under which, and consequently on the habits and degree of comfort in which, the class of free labourers has been formed. In contradistinction therefore to the case of other commodities, there enters into the determination of the value of labour-power a historical and moral element. Nevertheless, in a given country, at a given period, the average quantity of the means of subsistence necessary for the labourer is practically known" (*Capital,* I, 171 and *MEW,* XXIII, 185).

144. Both Gardiner and Smith seem to assume that, on the view they oppose, housework would have to create a value that is added to the value of labor power over and above the cost of subsistence. As Smith says, the value of labor power "would be equivalent to the value of the means of subsistence bought with the wage *plus* the value said to be created by the domestic labour" (P. Smith, 202. Gardiner, 181–82). And, for Smith, since this extra value created by domestic labor would not be paid (the family's wage is only enough to cover subsistence), labor power then would be sold below its value. Moreover, it would be the only commodity sold below its value and thus would totally disrupt Marx's whole theoretical system where all commodities sell at their value. Smith, I think, is quite mistaken. We are trying to understand and explain the value of labor power here. It would thus be circular and absurd to say, as Smith in effect is saying, that the value of labor power is determined by the value of labor power. Smith is saying that the value of labor power (sold to the capitalist for a wage and put to work in the factory) is determined by the value of (the housewife's) labor power (added, of course, to the cost of means of subsistence). We cannot appeal to the value of labor power to explain the value of labor power. This just pushes the question back a step.

Marx, I think, approaches things quite differently. If the laborers are not homeless and starving, then they are receiving from the capitalists the value of their labor power—which is determined by what it costs to produce and reproduce labor power. This requires enough to purchase what has to be purchased to survive, but at the same time requires a good deal of housework. The value of labor power, the wage, is not high enough to allow the family to purchase everything it needs. A great deal has to be done by the houseworker and real efficiency is necessary. From the capitalist perspective, housework is not paid below its value, as Smith suggests. Labor power does not have a set value. What would it be, $4.25 an hour because that is where the minimum wage has been set? Where does that come from? We are back here trying to understand the value of labor power upon which minimum wage laws would have to be built. Labor power is paid at its value—its value is what it costs to keep the laboring family alive and reproducing laborers. Housework is paid at its value, not below its value.

Smith thinks that there is something wrong with saying that the value of housework is only what it costs to purchase means of subsistence, that there is no "plus," no extra, no surplus for the extra value created by domestic labor. But what is so surprising about this? The wage of the factory worker too only covers means of subsistence. The factory worker receives no plus, no extra, no surplus—that is pocketed by the factory owner. Labor power—the labor power expended in the factory together with the labor power expended in the home to make it possible to expend labor power in the factory—is paid at its value. The wage is equivalent to the value of labor power. Given capitalist market forces, that value tends toward the subsistence level. Very clearly, any plus, extra, or surplus would have to come out of the capitalist's surplus—which the capitalist will fight. There will be a struggle between capital and labor over this surplus. The fact that capital wins is what makes the system capitalist. The fact that the laborer loses is what reproduces laborers.

145. *Capital*, I, 645 and *MEW*, XXIII, 674–75.
146. *Capital*, I, 396 and *MEW*, XXIII, 418.
147. Fraser, 37. MacKinnon, 67–68. See also "Simone de Beauvoir questions Jean-Paul Sartre," 76–77. Also Meillassoux, *Maidens, Meal and Money*, 77. However, Secombe (11) argues that the housewife is not exploited.
148. *TSV*, Part I, 159 and *MEW*, XXVI, Teil I, 129. *Origin*, 65 and *MEW*, XXI, 75.
149. *CPE, MECW*, XXIX, 275–76 and *MEW*, XIII, 20–21. *Capital*, I, 77–78 and *MEW*, XXIII, 92. *Origin*, 65 and *MEW*, XXI, 75.
150. *TSV*, Part I, 152 and *MEW*, XXVI, Teil I, 122.
151. *TSV*, Part I, 157–59 (passages in brackets are my addition), also see 160 and *MEW*, XXVI, Teil I, 127–29, 130.
152. *TSV*, Part I, 159–60 and *MEW*, XXVI, Teil I, 129–30.
153. *TSV*, Part I, 156, 160 and *MEW*, XXVI, Teil I, 126, 130.
154. *TSV*, Part I, 166 and *MEW*, XXVI, Teil I, 136.
155. *Capital*, I, 217–18 and *MEW*, XXIII, 230–32.
156. P. Morton, "Women's Work is Never Done," in *The Politics of Housework*, ed. E. Malos (London: Allison & Busby, 1980), 148.
157. *Economic Manuscripts of 1861–63, MECW*, XXX, 115–16 and *MEGA*, II, 3.1, 102.
158. McDonough and Harrison, 27–28. A. Kuhn, "Structures of Patriarchy and Capital in the Family," in *Feminism and Materialism*, 47. E. Zaretsky, *Capitalism, the Family, and Personal Life*, revised edition (New York: Harper & Row, 1986), 9–10.
159. *CPE, MECW*, XXIX, 283–84 and *MEW*, XIII, 28–29.
160. *Gotha, MECW*, XXIV, 85 and *MEW*, XIX, 19–20.
161. *Capital*, I, 573 and *MEW*, XXIII, 598.
162. *JQ, MECW*, III, 165–66 and *MEW*, I, 367–68.
163. *Capital*, I, 77–78 and *MEW*, XXIII, 92. *CPE, MECW*, XXIX, 275–76 and *MEW*, XIII, 20–21.
164. *TSV*, Part I, 159 and *MEW*, XXVI, Teil I, 129.

165. *Capital*, I, 478, 487 and *MEW*, XXIII, 502, 511.
166. *Capital*, I, 396 and *MEW*, XXIII, 418.
167. *Capital*, I, 498–99 and *MEW*, XXIII, 522–23.
168. *Origin*, 148 and *MEW*, XXI, 158.
169. Jaggar, 66.
170. *Capital*, I, 489–90 and *MEW*, XXIII, 514; this passage has already been quoted above at note 39 of this chapter.
171. *Origin*, 148 and *MEW*, XXI, 158.
172. There are, of course, families that are not nurturant and caring. I certainly do not want to suggest that if we could eliminate alienation all families would simply become nurturant and caring. Capitalism is obviously not responsible for all ills in the world and alienation is not a catchall containing everything undesirable; such that if alienation were overcome everything would be perfect. I have been trying to delimit alienation in this chapter: to show how it involves but cannot simply be identified with all forms of domination and oppression, and to show that it is a specific ill, not a catchall for all ills. Marx has a very powerful analysis of certain forms of alienation and oppression. But once alienation is overcome, other human difficulties will remain to be dealt with. And there are many such difficulties that Marx has little or nothing to say about—like personal oppression or psychological alienation. That is left to other theorists.
173. *PR*, 110, 112, 114, 148 and *GPR*, 149, 151, 154–55, 198.
174. M. Z. Rosaldo, "Woman, Culture, and Society," 36, 41. L. Lamphere, "Strategies, Cooperation, and Conflict Among Women in Domestic Groups," in *Women, Culture, and Society,* 100, 111. R. R. Reiter, "Men and Women in the South of France: Public and Private Domains," in *Toward and Anthropology of Women,* 253, 282. J. Evans, "Feminist Theory and Political Analysis," in *Feminism and Political Theory* (London: Sage Publications, 1986), 103–19.

Bibliography

Works by Marx and Engels

Marx, K., and F. Engels. *Marx Engels Collected Works.* New York: International, 1975 ff.

———. *Communist Manifesto,* in *Marx Engels Collected Works,* VI.

———. *German Ideology,* in *Marx Engels Collected Works,* V.

———. *Holy Family,* in *Marx Engels Collected Works,* IV.

———. *Marx and Engels Selected Correspondence.* Tr. I. Lasker. Moscow: Progress, 1965.

———. *Marx Engels Gesamtausgabe.* Berlin: Dietz, 1975 ff.

———. *Marx Engels Werke.* 41 vols. Berlin: Dietz, 1972 ff.

———. "Anglo-Chinese Treaty," in *Marx Engels Collected Works,* XVI.

———. "Berlin *National-Zeitung,*" in *Marx Engels Collected Works,* VIII.

Marx, K. "British Politics," in *Marx Engels Collected Works,* XII.

———. "British Rule in India," in *Marx Engels Collected Works,* XII.

———. *Capital.* Ed. F. Engels. 3 vols. New York: International, 1967.

———. "Capital Punishment," in *Marx Engels Collected Works,* XI.

———. "Chinese Affairs," in *Marx Engels Collected Works,* XIX.

———. *Civil War in France,* in *Marx Engels Collected Works,* XXII.

———. *Class Struggles in France,* in *Marx Engels Collected Works,* X.

———. "Comments on James Mill," in *Marx Engels Collected Works,* III.

———. "Comments on the Latest Prussian Censorship Instruction," in *Marx Engels Collected Works,* I.

———"Comments on the North American Events," in *Marx Engels Collected Works,* XIX.

———. "Commissions of the Estates in Prussia," in *Marx Engels Collected Works*, I.

———. "Communist Trial in Cologne," in *Marx Engels Collected Works*, XI.

———. "Critique of the Gotha Program," in *Marx Engels Collected Works*, XXIV.

———. *Critique of Hegel's Philosophy of Law*, in *Marx Engels Collected Works*, III.

———. "Critique of Hegel's Philosophy of Law: Introduction," in *Marx Engels Collected Works*, III.

———. *Critique of Political Economy*, in *Marx Engels Collected Works*, XXIX.

———. "Debate on Jacoby's Motion," in *Marx Engels Collected Works*, VII.

———. "Debate on the Law on Thefts of Wood," in *Marx Engels Collected Works*, I.

———. "Debates on Freedom of the Press," in *Marx Engels Collected Works*, I.

———. *Difference Between the Democritean and Epicurean Philosophy of Nature*, in *Marx Engels Collected Works*, I.

———. "Dissertation Notes," in *Marx Engels Collected Works*, I.

———. "Divorce Bill," in *Marx Engels Collected Works*, I.

———. *Economic Manuscripts of 1861–63*, in *Marx Engels Collected Works*, XXX–XXXII.

———. *Economic and Philosophic Manuscripts*, in *Marx Engels Collected Works*, III.

———. *Eighteenth Brumaire of Louis Bonaparte*, in *Marx Engels Collected Works*, XI.

———. "Elections," in *Marx Engels Collected Works*, XI.

———. "English," in *Marx Engels Collected Works*, XIX.

———. "English Atrocities in China," in *Marx Engels Collected Works*, XV.

———. *Ethnological Notebooks of Karl Marx*. Ed. L. Krader. Assen: Van Gorcum, 1972.

———. "Future Results of British Rule in India," in *Marx Engels Collected Works*, XII.

———. "General Council of the IWA to the Central Bureau of the International Alliance of Socialist Democracy," in *Marx Engels Collected Works*, XXI.

———. *Grundrisse*, in *Marx Engels Collected Works*, XXVIII–XXIX.

———. "History of the Opium Trade," in *Marx Engels Collected Works*, XVI.

———. "Inaugural Address of the Working Men's International Association," in *Marx Engels Collected Works*, XX.

———. "Indian Revolt," in *Marx Engels Collected Works*, XV.

———. "Industrialists of Hanover and Protective Tariffs," in *Marx Engels Collected Works*, I.

———. "Instructions for the Delegates," in *Marx Engels Collected Works*, XX.

———. "Investigation of Tortures in India," in *Marx Engels Collected Works*, XV.

———. "Justification of the Correspondent from the Mosel," in *Marx Engels Collected Works*, I.

———. "King of Prussia and Social Reform," in *Marx Engels Collected Works*, III.

———. "Latter-Day Pamphlets," in *Marx Engels Collected Works*, X.

———. "Leading Article in No. 179 of the *Kölnische Zeitung*," in *Marx Engels Collected Works*, I.

———. "Letters from the *Deutsch-Französische Jahrbücher*," in *Marx Engels Collected Works*, III.

———. "Marx to 'Otechestvenniye Zapiski' in Nov. 1877," in *Marx and Engels Selected Correspondence*. Tr. I. Lasker. Moscow: Progress, 1965.

———. "Marx to F. Domela-Nieuwenhuis on 22 February 1881," in *Marx and Engels Selected Correspondence*. Tr. I. Lasker. Moscow: Progress, 1965.

———. "Marx to Feuerbach on 11 Aug. 1844," in *Marx Engels Collected Works*, III.

———. "Marx to Jenny Marx on 21 June 1856," in *Marx Engels Collected Works*, XL.

———. "Marx to Lassalle on 10 June 1858," in *Marx Engels Collected Works*, XL.

———. "On the Jewish Question," in *Marx Engels Collected Works*, III.

———. *Poverty of Philosophy*, in *Marx Engels Collected Works*, VI.

———. "Provisional Rules of the Association," in *Marx Engels Collected Works*, XX.

———. "Record of Marx's Speeches on General Education," in *Marx Engels Collected Works*, XXI.

———. "Record of Marx's Speeches on Landed Property," in *Marx Engels Collected Works*, XXI.

———. "Record of Marx's Speeches on the Seventh Anniversary of the International," in *Marx Engels Collected Works*, XXII.

———. "Reflections of a Young Man on the Choice of a Profession," in *Marx Engels Collected Works*, I.

———. *Revelations of the Diplomatic History of the 18th Century*, in *Marx Engels Collected Works*, XV.

———. "Review," in *Marx Engels Collected Works*, X.

———. "Reviews from the *Neue Rheinische Zeitung*," in *Marx Engels Collected Works*, X.

———. "Revolution in China and Europe," in *Marx Engels Collected Works*, XII.

———. *Revolutionary Spain*, in *Marx Engels Collected Works*, XIII.

———. "Sicily and the Sicilians," in *Marx Engels Collected Works*, XVII.

———. *Texts on Method*. Tr. T. Carver. New York: Barnes and Noble, 1975.

———. *Theories of Surplus Value*. Ed. S. Ryazanskaya. 3 vols. Moscow: Progress, 1963–68.

———. "Vienna and Frankfurt," in *Marx Engels Collected Works*, IX.

———. *Wage-Labour and Capital*, in *Marx Engels Collected Works*, IX.

Engels, F. "Democratic Pan-Slavism," in *Marx Engels Collected Works*, VIII.

———. *Origin of the Family, Private Property, and the State*. New York: International, 1942.

———. "Principles of Communism," in *Marx Engels Collected Works*, VI.

General Works

Adamson, W.L. *Marx and the Disillusionment of Marxism*. Berkeley: University of California Press, 1985.

Adler, M. *Kant und der Marxismus*. Berlin: E. Laub'sche Verlagsbuchhandlung, 1925.

Adorno, T.W. *Negative Dialectics*. Tr. E.B. Ashton. New York: Seabury, 1973.

Althusser, L. *For Marx*. Tr. B. Brewster. London: NLB, 1977.

———. *Lenin and Philosophy and Other Essays*. Tr. B. Brewster. New York: Monthly Review Press, 1971.

———. *Politics and History*. Tr. B. Brewster. London: NLB, 1972.

———, and É. Balibar. *Reading Capital*. Tr. B. Brewster. London: NLB, 1970.

Amariglio, J.L. "Economic History and the Theory of Primitive Socio-economic Development." Doctoral Dissertation. University of Massachusetts, 1984.

Amariglio, J.L., S.A. Resnick, and R.D. Wolff. "Class, Power, and Culture," in *Marxism and the Interpretation of Culture*. Eds. C. Nelson and L. Grossberg. Urbana: University of Illinois Press, 1988, 487–501.

Aristotle. *The Complete Works of Aristotle*. Ed. J. Barnes. 2 vols. Bollingen Series LXXI. Princeton: Princeton University Press, 1984.

Aronowitz, S. *The Crisis in Historical Materialism*. New York: Praeger, 1981.

Ashcraft, R. Locke's "Two Treatises of Government." London: Allen & Unwin, 1987.

———. *Revolutionary Politics and Locke's "Two Treatises of Government."* Princeton: Princeton University Press, 1986.

Augé, M. *The Anthropological Circle: Symbol, Function, History*. Tr. M. Thom. Cambridge: Cambridge University Press, 1982.

Avineri, S. *Hegel's Theory of the Modern State*. Cambridge: Cambridge University Press, 1972.

———. *The Social and Political Thought of Karl Marx*. Cambridge: Cambridge University Press, 1970.

Balbus, I.D. *Marxism and Domination*. Princeton: Princeton University Press, 1982.

Barker, E. "Introduction" to *Social Contract*. London: Oxford University Press, 1960.

Bauer, O. "Marxismus und Ethik," *Die Neue Zeit* XXIV (1905–6), 485–99.

Baudrillard, J. *The Mirror of Production*. Tr. M. Poster. St. Louis: Telos Press, 1975.

Beck, L.W. *A Commentary on Kant's Critique of Practical Reason*. Chicago: University of Chicago Press, 1960.

Benhabib, S., and D. Cornell, eds. *Feminism as Critique: On the Politics of Gender*. Minneapolis: University of Minnesota Press, 1987.

Benston, M. "The Political Economy of Women's Liberation," *Monthly Review* XXI, No. 4 (1969), 13–27.

Berger, P.L., and T. Luckmann. *The Social Construction of Reality*. Garden City, N.Y.: Anchor, 1967.

Berlin, I. "Does Political Theory Still Exist?" in *Concepts and Categories*. Ed. H. Hardy. London: Hogarth, 1978.

———. "Two Concepts of Liberty," in *Four Essays on Liberty*. Oxford: Oxford University Press, 1969.

Booth, W. J. *Interpreting the World: Kant's Philosophy of History and Politics*. Toronto: University of Toronto Press, 1986.

Brien, K.M. *Marx, Reason, and the Art of Freedom*. Philadelphia: Temple University Press, 1987.

Burman, S., ed. *Fit Work for Women*. New York: St. Martin's, 1979.

Callincos, A. *Is There a Future for Marxism*. London: Macmillan, 1982.

Cassirer, E. *Rousseau, Kant, and Goethe*. Trs. J. Gutman, P.O. Kristeller, and J.H. Randall, Jr. Princeton: Princeton University Press, 1945.

———. *The Question of Jean-Jacques Rousseau.* Tr. P. Gay. Bloomington: Indiana University Press, 1963.

Cassirer, H.W. *A Commentary on Kant's Critique of Judgment.* New York: Barnes and Noble, 1970.

Chodorow, N. *The Reproduction of Mothering.* Berkeley: University of California Press, 1978.

Clark, L.M.G., and L. Lange, eds. *Sexism of Social and Political Theory.* Toronto: University of Toronto Press, 1979.

Clifford, J. *Person and Myth: Maurice Leenhardt and the Melanesian World.* Berkeley: University of California Press, 1982.

———. *The Predicament of Culture.* Cambridge, Mass.: Harvard University Press, 1988.

Clifford, J., and G.E. Marcus, eds. *Writing Culture.* Berkeley: University of California Press, 1986.

Cobban, A. *Rousseau and the Modern State.* Hamden, Conn.: Archon Books, 1964.

Cohen, G.A. *Karl Marx's Theory of History.* Princeton, N.J.: Princeton University Press, 1978.

Cohen, T., and P. Guyer, eds. *Essays in Kant's Aesthetics.* Chicago: University of Chicago Press, 1982.

Cole, G.D.H. "Introduction" to *The Social Contract and Discourses.* New York: Dutton, 1950.

Colletti, L. *From Rousseau to Lenin.* Trs. J. Merrington and J. White. New York: Monthly Review Press, 1972.

———. *Marxism and Hegel.* Tr. L. Garner. London: NLB, 1973.

Collins, J.L. "Unwaged Labor in Comparative Perspective: Recent Theories and Unanswered Questions," in *Work Without Wages: Domestic Labor and Self-Employment within Capitalism.* Albany: SUNY Press, 1990, 3–24.

Collins, J.L., and M. Gimenez, eds. *Work Without Wages: Domestic Labor and Self-Employment within Capitalism.* Albany: SUNY Press, 1990.

Connolly, W.E., ed. *The Bias of Pluralism.* New York: Atherton Press, 1969.

Cranston, M. "Introduction" to *The Social Contract.* Harmondsworth: Penguin, 1968.

Crawford, D.W. *Kant's Aesthetic Theory.* Madison: University of Wisconsin Press, 1974.

Crocker, L.G. "Introduction" to *The Social Contract and Discourse on the Origin and Foundation of Inequality Among Mankind.* New York: Washington Square Press, 1967.

———. *Rousseau's Social Contract.* Cleveland: Case Western Reserve University Press, 1968.

Dahl, R.A. *Democracy and Its Critics.* New Haven, Conn.: Yale University Press, 1989.

———. *Democracy, Liberty, and Equality.* Oslo: Norwegian University Press, 1986.

———. *Dilemmas of Pluralist Democracy.* New Haven, Conn.: Yale University Press, 1982.

———. *Pluralist Democracy in the United States.* Chicago: Rand McNally, 1967.

———. *Who Governs? Democracy and Power in an American City.* New Haven, Conn.: Yale University Press, 1961.

Dalla Costa, M., and S. James. *The Power of Women and the Subversion of the Community.* Bristol, England: Falling Wall Press, 1972.

de Beauvoir, S. *Le deuxième sexe.* 2 vols. Paris: Gallimard, 1949.

———. "Simone de Beauvoir questions Jean-Paul Sartre." Trs. J. Howe and R. Mulvey. *New Left Review* 97 (1976), 71–80.

———. *The Second Sex.* Tr. H.M. Parshley. New York: Bantam, 1961.

Derrida, J. *Of Grammatology.* Tr. G.Y. Spivak. Baltimore: Johns Hopkins University Press, 1976.

Dews, P. *Logics of Disintegration.* London: Verso, 1987.

Dickey, L. *Hegel: Religion, Economics, and the Politics of Spirit 1770–1807.* Cambridge: Cambridge University Press, 1987.

Dunn. J. *The Political Thought of John Locke.* Cambridge: Cambridge University Press, 1969.

Dupré, L. *Marx's Social Critique of Culture.* New Haven, Conn.: Yale University Press, 1983.

Durkheim, E. *Division of Labor in Society.* Tr. G. Simpson. New York: Free Press, 1964.

———. *Socialism.* Tr. C. Sattler. New York: Collier Books, 1962.

Einaudi, M. *The Early Rousseau.* Ithaca: Cornell University Press, 1967.

Eisenstein, Z.R., ed. *Capitalist Patriarchy and the Case for Socialist Feminism.* New York: Monthly Review Press, 1979.

———. "Developing a Theory of Capitalist Patriarchy and Socialist Feminism," in *Capitalist Patriarchy and the Case for Socialist Feminism.*

———. *The Radical Future of Liberal Feminism.* New York: Longman, 1981.

Ellenburg, S. "Rousseau and Kant: principles of political right," in *Rousseau After Two Hundred Years.* Ed. R.A. Leigh. London: Cambridge University Press, 1982.

———. *Rousseau's Political Philosophy: An Interpretation from Within.* Ithaca: Cornell University Press, 1976.

Elster, J. *Making Sense of Marx.* Cambridge: Cambridge University Press, 1985.

Evans, J. "Feminist Theory and Political Analysis," in *Feminism and Political Theory*. London: Sage Publications, 1986.

Fabian, J. *Time and the Other: How Anthropology Makes Its Object*. New York: Columbia University Press, 1983.

Feinberg, J. *Social Philosophy*. Englewood Cliffs, N.J.: Prentice-Hall, 1973.

Ferguson, A., and N. Folbre. "The Unhappy Marriage of Patriarchy and Capitalism," in *Women and Revolution*. Ed. L. Sargent. Boston: South End Press, 1981.

Firestone, S. *The Dialectic of Sex*. New York: Morrow Quill, 1970.

Flax, J. "Postmodernism and Gender Relations in Feminist Theory," in *Feminism/Postmodernism*. Ed. L.J. Nicholson. New York: Routledge & Kegan Paul, 1990.

Foucault, M. *Language, Counter-Memory, Practice*. Trs. D.F. Bouchard and S. Simon. Ithaca, N.Y.: Cornell University Press, 1977.

———. *Power/Knowledge*. Trs. C. Gordon, L. Marshall, J. Mepham, and K. Soper. New York: Pantheon, 1980.

———. *The History of Sexuality, Volume I*. Tr. R. Hurley. New York: Vintage, 1978.

Fox Bourne, H.R. *The Life of John Locke*. 2 vols. New York: Harper & Brothers, 1876.

Franklin, J.H. *John Locke and the Theory of Sovereignty*. Cambridge: Cambridge University Press, 1978.

Fraser, N. "What's Critical about Critical Theory?: The Case of Habermas and Gender," in *Feminism as Critique*. Eds. S. Benhabib and D. Cornell. Minneapolis: University of Minnesota Press, 1987.

Gardiner, J. "Women's Domestic Labor," in *Capitalist Patriarchy and the Case for Socialist Feminism*. Ed. Z.R. Eisenstein. New York: Monthly Review Press, 1979.

Geras, N. *Marx and Human Nature: The Refutation of a Legend*. London: NLB, 1983.

Gimenez, M. "The Dialectics of Waged and Unwaged Work: Waged Work, Domestic Labor and Household Survival in the United States," in *Work Without Wages: Domestic Labor and Self-Employment within Capitalism*. Albany: SUNY Press, 1990, 25–45.

Glazer, N. "Servants to Capital: Unpaid Domestic Labor and Paid Work," in *Work Without Wages: Domestic Labor and Self-Employment within Capitalism*. Albany: SUNY Press, 1990, 142–67.

Godelier, M. "On the Definition of a Social Formation: The Example of the Incas." *Critique of Anthropology* I (1974), 63–73.

———. *Perspectives in Marxist Anthropology.* Tr. R. Brain. Cambridge: Cambridge University Press, 1977.

Goldmann, L. *Immanuel Kant.* Tr. R. Black. London: NLB, 1971.

Gordon, L. "The Struggle for Reproductive Freedom: Three Stages of Feminism," in *Capitalist Patriarchy and the Case for Socialist Feminism.* Ed. Z.R. Eisenstein. New York: Monthly Review Press, 1979.

Gottlieb, R.S. *History and Subjectivity: The Transformation of Marxist Theory.* Philadelphia: Temple University Press, 1987.

Gough, J.W. *John Locke's Political Philosophy.* Oxford: Clarendon Press, 1973.

Gould, C.C., and M. Wartofsky, eds. *Women and Philosophy: Toward a Theory of Liberation.* New York: Perigee, 1980.

Gramsci, A. *Selections from the Prison Notebooks.* Trs. Q. Hoare and G.N. Smith. New York: International, 1971.

Guardian, Vol. 43, No. 28 (May 22, 1991).

Guyer, P. *Kant and the Claims of Taste.* Cambridge, Mass.: Harvard University Press, 1979.

Habermas, J. *Legitimation Crisis.* Tr. T. McCarthy. Boston: Beacon, 1975.

———. *The Theory of Communicative Action.* Tr. T. McCarthy. 2 vols. Boston: Beacon, 1984–87.

Harding, S. *The Science Question in Feminism.* Ithaca: Cornell University Press, 1986.

———. "What is the Real Material Base of Patriarchy and Capital," *in Women and Revolution.* Ed. L. Sargent. Boston: South End Press, 1981.

Hartsock, N.C.M. *Money, Sex, and Power: Toward a Feminist Historical Materialism.* New York: Longman, 1983.

Hegel, G.W.F. *Aesthetics.* Tr. T.M. Knox. 2 vols. Oxford: Clarendon Press, 1975.

———. *Gesammelte Werke.* Hamburg: Felix Meiner, 1968 ff.

———. *Grundlinien der Philosophie des Rechts.* Ed. J. Hoffmeister. Hamburg: Felix Meiner, 1955.

———. *Hegel's Philosophy of Nature.* Tr. M.J. Petry. 3 vols. London: Allen and Unwin, 1970.

———. *Lectures on the History of Philosophy.* Trs. E.S. Haldane and F.H. Simson. 3 vols. London: Routledge & Kegan Paul, 1968.

———. *Lectures on the Philosophy of World History: Introduction.* Tr. H.B. Nisbet. Cambridge: Cambridge University Press, 1975.

———. *Natural Law.* Tr. T.M. Knox. Philadelphia: University of Pennsylvania Press, 1975.

———. *The Logic of Hegel.* Tr. W. Wallace. Oxford: Oxford University Press, 1968.

———. *Phänomenologie des Geistes.* Ed. J. Hoffmeister. Hamburg: Felix Meiner, 1952.

———. *Phenomenology of Spirit.* Tr. A.V. Miller. Oxford: Clarendon Press, 1977.

———. *Philosophy of History.* Tr. J. Sibree. New York: Dover, 1956.

———. *Philosophy of Right.* Tr. T.M. Knox. Oxford: Clarendon Press, 1967.

———. *Sämtliche Werke.* Ed. H. Glockner. 26 vols. Stuttgart-Bad Cannstatt: Frommann, 1964, 1927–40.

———. *Vorlesungen über die Philosophie der Weltgeschichte.* Ed. G. Lasson. Hamburg: Felix Meiner, 1968, II–IV.

———. *Vorlesungen über die Philosophie der Weltgeschichte.* Ed. J. Hoffmeister. Hamburg: Felix Meiner, 1955, I.

Heller, A. *The Theory of Need in Marx.* New York: St. Martin's, 1976.

Hess, M. *Moses Hess: Philosophische und Sozialistische Schriften.* Eds. A. Cornu and W. Mönke. Berlin: Akademie, 1961.

———. "The Philosophy of the Act," in *Socialist Thought.* Eds. A. Fried and R. Sanders. Garden City, N.Y.: Doubleday, 1964.

Hindess, B. *Philosophy and Methodology in the Social Sciences.* Sussex: Harvester Press, 1977.

Hindess, B., and P. Hirst. *Mode of Production and Social Formation.* Atlantic Highlands, N.J.: Humanities Press, 1977.

———. *Pre-capitalist Modes of Production.* London: Routledge & Kegan Paul, 1975.

Hirshman, A.O. *The Passions and the Interests.* Princeton: Princeton University Press, 1977.

Hobbes, T. *The English Works of Thomas Hobbes.* Ed. W. Molesworth. 11 vols. Darmstadt: Scientia Aalen Verlag, 1962.

———. *Answer to Bishop Bramhall,* in *English Works,* IV.

———. *Considerations Upon the Reputation of Thomas Hobbes,* in *English Works,* IV.

———. *A Dialogue between a Philosopher and a Student of the Common Laws,* in *English Works,* IV.

———. *De Cive or Philosophical Rudiments Concerning Government and Society,* in *English Works,* II.

———. *De Corpore Politico, or the Elements of Law,* in *English Works,* IV.

———. *Human Nature,* in *English Works,* IV.

———. *Leviathan,* in *English Works,* III.

———. *Liberty, Necessity, and Chance*, in *English Works*, IV.

———. "Short Tract on First Principles," in *The Elements of Law*. Ed. F. Tönnies. Cambridge: Cambridge University Press, 1928.

Hoffman, J. *Marxism, Revolution, and Democracy*. Amsterdam: Grüner, 1983.

hooks, b. *Yearning: Race, Gender, and Cultural Politics*. Boston: South End Press, 1990.

Hountondji, P.J. *African Philosophy: Myth and Reality*. Trs. H. Evans with J. Rée. Bloomington: Indiana University Press, 1983.

Howard, D. *The Development of the Marxian Dialectic*. Carbondale: Southern Illinois University Press, 1972.

Hundert, E.J. "The Making of *Homo Faber*: John Locke Between Ideology and History," *Journal of the History of Ideas* XXXIII (1972).

———. "Market Society and Meaning in Locke's Political Philosophy," *Journal of the History of Philosophy* XV (1977).

Hyppolite, L. *Genesis and Structure of Hegel's Phenomenology of Spirit*. Trs. S. Cherniak and J. Heckman. Evanston, Ill.: Northwestern University Press, 1974.

Jaggar, A.M. *Feminist Politics and Human Nature*. Totowa, N.J.: Rowman & Allanheld, 1983.

Joseph, G. "The Incompatible Menage À Trois: Marxism, Feminism, and Racism," in *Women and Revolution*. Ed. L. Sargent. Boston: South End Press, 1981.

Kain, P.J. "Kant and the Possibility of Uncategorized Experience," *Idealistic Studies* XIX (1989).

———. *Marx and Ethics*. Oxford: Clarendon Press, 1988.

———. *Marx' Method, Epistemology, and Humanism*. Dordrecht: D. Reidel, 1986.

———. "Nietzsche, Skepticism, and Eternal Recurrence," *Canadian Journal of Philosophy* XIII (1983).

———. *Schiller, Hegel, and Marx*. Montreal: McGill-Queen's University Press, 1982.

Kant, I. *Critique of Judgment*. Tr. J.H. Bernard. New York: Hafner, 1966.

———. *Critique of Practical Reason*. Tr. L.W. Beck. Indianapolis: Bobbs-Merrill, 1956.

———. *Critique of Pure Reason*. Tr. N. Kemp Smith. New York: St Martin's, 1965.

———. *First Introduction to the Critique of Judgment*. Tr. J. Haden. Indianapolis: Bobbs-Merrill, 1965.

———. *Foundations of the Metaphysics of Morals*. Tr. L.W. Beck. Indianapolis: Bobbs-Merrill, 1959.

———. "Idea for a Universal History," in *On History.* Ed. L.W. Beck. Indianapolis: Bobbs-Merrill, 1963.

———. *Kant's Gesammelte Schriften.* Ed. Königlich Preussischen Akademie der Wissenschaften. Berlin: de Gruyter, 1910 ff.

———. *Metaphysical Elements of Justice: Part I of the Metaphysics of Morals.* Tr. J. Ladd. Indianapolis: Bobbs-Merrill, 1965.

———. On the Common Saying: "This May be True in Theory, but it Does Not Apply in Practice," in *Kant's Political Writings.* Ed. H. Russ, Cambridge: Cambridge University Press, 1971.

———. *On History.* Ed. L.W. Beck. Indianapolis: Bobbs-Merrill, 1963.

———. *Perpetual Peace,* in *On History.* Ed. L.W. Beck. Indianapolis: Bobbs-Merrill, 1963.

———. *Religion Within the Limits of Reason Alone.* Trs. T.M. Greene and H.H. Hudson. New York: Harper and Row, 1960.

———. "What is Enlightenment?" in *On History.* Ed. L.W. Beck. Indianapolis: Bobbs-Merrill, 1963.

Kelly, G.A. *Hegel's Retreat from Eleusis.* Princeton: Princeton University Press, 1978.

———. *Idealism, Politics, and History.* London: Oxford University Press, 1973.

Kiss, A. *Marxism and Democracy.* Budapest: Akadémiai Kiadó, 1982.

Kittay, E., and D. Meyers, eds. *Women and Morality.* Totowa, N.J.: Rowman and Allenheld, 1986.

Kojève, A. *Introduction to the Reading of Hegel.* Tr. J.H. Nichols, Jr. New York: Basic Books, 1969.

Kontopoulos, K.M. *Knowledge and Determinism: The Transition from Hegel to Marx.* Amsterdam: Grüner, 1980.

Kuhn, A. "Structures of Patriarchy and Capital in the Family," in *Feminism and Materialism.* London: Routledge & Kegan Paul, 1978.

Kuhn, A., and A. Wolpe, eds. *Feminism and Materialism: Women and Modes of Production.* London: Routledge & Kegan Paul, 1978.

Kuhn, T. *The Structure of Scientific Revolutions.* 2nd edition. Chicago: University of Chicago Press, 1970.

Lamphere, L. "Strategies, Cooperation, and Conflict Among Women in Domestic Groups," in *Women, Culture, and Society.* Eds. M.Z. Rosaldo and L. Lamphere. Stanford: Stanford University Press, 1974.

Larkin, P. *Property in the Eighteenth Century.* Dublin: Cork University Press, 1930.

Lash, N. *A Matter of Hope: A Theologian's Reflections on the Thought of Karl Marx.* Notre Dame, Ind.: University of Notre Dame Press, 1981.

Leacock, E.L. "Introduction," to F. Engels, *The Origin of the Family, Private Property and the State.* London: Lawrence & Wishart, 1972, 7–67.

Levine, A. *Liberal Democracy: A Critique of Its Theory.* New York: Columbia University Press, 1981.

———. *The Politics of Autonomy.* Amherst: University of Massachusetts Press, 1976.

Lévi-Strauss, C. *The Savage Mind.* Chicago: University of Chicago Press, 1966.

Locke, J. *Essays on the Law of Nature,* Ed. W. von Leyden. Oxford: Clarendon Press, 1954.

———. *Fundamental Constitutions of Carolina,* in *The Works of John Locke,* IX.

———. *A Letter Concerning Toleration,* in *The Works of John Locke,* V.

———. *Two Treatises of Government.* Ed. P. Laslett. New York: Mentor, 1965.

———. *Some Considerations of the Consequences of the Lowering of Interest, and Raising the Value of Money,* in *The Works of John Locke,* IV.

———. *The Works of John Locke in Nine Volumes.* 12th edition: London: Rivington et al., 1824.

Lomasky, L.E. *Persons, Rights, and the Moral Community.* New York: Oxford University Press, 1987.

Lovejoy, A.O. *Essays in the History of Ideas.* Baltimore: Johns Hopkins Press, 1948.

Lukes, S. *Marxism and Morality.* Oxford: Clarendon Press, 1985.

———. *Power: A Radical View.* London: Macmillan, 1974.

Machiavelli, N. *The Prince.* Tr. T.G. Bergin. New York: Appleton-Century-Crofts, 1947.

MacIntyre, A. *After Virtue.* Notre Dame, Ind.: University of Notre Dame Press, 1981.

———. *Whose Justice? Which Rationality?* Notre Dame, Ind.: University of Notre Dame Press, 1988.

MacKinnon, C.A. *Toward a Feminist Theory of the State.* Cambridge, Mass.: Harvard University Press, 1989.

Macpherson, C.B. *Democratic Theory: Essays in Retrieval.* Oxford: Clarendon Press, 1973.

———. *The Life and Times of Liberal Democracy.* Oxford: Oxford University Press, 1977.

———. *The Political Theory of Possessive Individualism.* Oxford: Clarendon Press, 1962.

Malos, E., ed. *The Politics of Housework*. London: Allison & Busby, 1980.

Markus, M. "Women, Success and Civil Society," in *Feminism as Critique*. Eds. S. Benhabib and D. Cornell. Minneapolis: University of Minnesota Press, 1987.

Masters, R.D. *The Political Philosophy of Rousseau*. Princeton: Princeton University Press, 1968.

McBride, W.L. *The Philosophy of Marx*. New York: St. Martin's, 1977.

McCarthy, G.E. *Marx and the Ancients*. Totowa, N.J.: Rowman and Littlefield, 1990.

———. *Marx' Critique of Science and Positivism*. Dordrecht: Kluwer, 1988.

McDonough, R., and R. Harrison. "Patriarchy and Relations of Production," in *Feminism and Materialism*. Eds. A. Kuhn and A. Wolpe. London: Routledge & Kegan Paul, 1978.

Meillassoux, C. *Anthropologie économique des Gouro de Côte d'Ivoire*. Paris: Mouton, 1964.

———. "From Reproduction to Production: A Marxist Approach to Economic Anthropology," in *The Articulation of Modes of Production: Essays from "Economy and Society."* Ed. H. Wolpe. London: Routledge & Kegan Paul, 1980, 189–201.

———. *Maidens, Meal and Money: Capitalism and the Domestic Community*. Cambridge: Cambridge University Press, 1981.

Miliband, R. *Marxism and Politics*. Oxford: Oxford University Press, 1977.

Mill, J.S. *Considerations on Representative Government*. Ed. C.V. Shields. New York: Liberal Arts Press, 1958.

———. *On Liberty*. Ed. C.V. Shields. Indianapolis: Bobbs-Merrill, 1956.

———. "The Subjection of Women," in *Essays on Sex Equality*. Ed. A.S. Rossi. Chicago: University of Chicago Press, 1970.

———. *Utilitarianism*. Ed. O. Piest. Indianapolis: Bobbs-Merrill, 1957.

Miller, R.W. *Analyzing Marx*. Princeton, N.J.: Princeton University Press, 1984.

Mitchell, J. *Psychoanalysis and Feminism*. New York: Pantheon, 1974.

———. *Woman's Estate*. New York: Pantheon, 1971.

Mitias, M.H. *Moral Foundation of the State in Hegel's "Philosophy of Right."* Amsterdam: Rodopi, 1984.

Molyneux, M. "Beyond the Domestic Labour Debate," *New Left Review* 116 (1979), 3–27.

Moore, S. *Critique of Capitalist Democracy*. New York: Paine-Whitman, 1957.

———. "Hobbes on Obligation, Moral and Political: Parts I and II" in *Journal of the History of Philosophy* IX (1971) and X (1972).

———. *Marx on the Choice between Socialism and Communism.* Cambridge, Mass.: Harvard University Press, 1980.

———. *Three Tactics: The Background in Marx.* New York: Monthly Review Press, 1963.

Moraga, C. *Loving in the War Years.* Boston: South End Press, 1983.

Morton, P. "Women's Work is Never Done," in *The Politics of Housework.* Ed. E. Malos. London: Allison & Busby, 1980, 130–57.

Negri, A. *Marx Beyond Marx.* Trs. H. Cleaver, M. Ryan, and M. Viano. South Hadley, Mass.: Bergin and Garvey, 1984.

Nelson, C., and L. Grossberg, eds. *Marxism and the Interpretation of Culture.* Urbana: University of Illinois Press, 1988.

Nicholson, L. "Feminism and Marx: Integrating Kinship with the Economic," in *Feminism as Critique.* Eds. S. Benhabib and D. Cornell. Minneapolis: University of Minnesota Press, 1987.

———. *Gender and History: The Limits of Social Theory in the Age of the Family.* New York: Columbia University Press, 1986.

Oakley, A. *The Sociology of Housework.* New York: Pantheon, 1974.

Oakeshott, M. "The Moral Life in the Writings of Thomas Hobbes," in *Hobbes on Civil Association.* Berkeley: University of California Press, 1975.

O'Brien, M. *The Politics of Reproduction.* Boston: Routledge & Kegan Paul, 1981.

Okin, S.M. *Women in Western Political Thought.* Princeton: Princeton University Press, 1979.

Olivecrona, K. "Locke's Theory of Appropriation," *Philosophical Quarterly* XXIV (1974).

Ollman, B. *Social and Sexual Revolution.* Boston: South End Press, 1979.

Ortner, S.B. "Is Female to Male as Nature Is to Culture?" in *Woman, Culture, and Society.* Eds. M.Z. Rosaldo and L. Lamphere. Stanford: Stanford University Press, 1974.

Pateman, C., and E. Gross, eds. *Feminist Challenges: Social and Political Theory.* Boston: Northeastern University Press, 1987.

Paton, H.J. *The Categorical Imperative.* London: Hutchinson, 1965.

Patton, P. "Marxism and Beyond: Strategies for Reterritorialization," in *Marxism and the Interpretation of Culture.* Eds. C. Nelson and L. Grossberg. Urbana: University of Illinois Press, 1988.

Peters, R. *Hobbes.* Harmondsworth: Penguin, 1956.

Plamenatz, J. "On le Forcera d'Etre Libre" in *Hobbes and Rousseau: A Collection of Critical Essays.* Eds. M. Cranston and R.S. Peters. Garden City, N.Y.: Anchor, 1972.

Plant, R. "Economic and Social Integration in Hegel's Political Philosophy," in *Hegel's Social and Political Thought*. Ed. D.P Verene. Atlantic Highlands, N.J.: Humanities Press, 1980.

———. *Hegel: An Introduction*. Oxford: Basil Blackwell, 1983.

Plato, *The Collected Dialogues*. Eds. E. Hamilton and H. Cairns. Bollingen Series LXXI. New York: Pantheon, 1961.

Polanyi, M. *The Great Transformation*. New York: Rinehart, 1944.

Poulantzas, N. *State, Power, and Socialism*. Tr. P. Camiller. London: NLB, 1978.

Putnam, H. *Reason, Truth and History*. Cambridge: Cambridge University Press, 1981.

———. *The Many Faces of Realism*. Lasalle, IL: Open Court, 1987.

Rawls, J. *A Theory of Justice*. Cambridge, Mass.: Harvard University Press, 1971.

Reed, E. *Women's Evolution*. New York: Pathfinder, 1975.

Reiss, H., ed. *Kant's Political Writings*. Cambridge: Cambridge University Press, 1971.

Reiter, R.R. "Men and Women in the South of France: Public and Private Domains," in *Toward an Anthropology of Women*.

———, ed. *Toward an Anthropology of Women*. New York: Monthly Review Press, 1975.

Resnick, S.A., and R.D. Wolff. *Knowledge and Class: A Marxian Critique of Political Economy*. Chicago: University of Chicago Press, 1987.

Rey, P.P. "The Lineage Mode of Production." *Critique of Anthropology* III (1975), 27–79.

Riemer, N. *Karl Marx and Prophetic Politics*. New York: Praeger, 1987.

Riley, P. *Kant's Political Philosophy*. Totowa, N.J.: Rowman and Littlefield, 1983.

———. *Will and Political Legitimacy*. Cambridge, Mass.: Harvard University Press, 1982.

Rohrlich-Leavitt, R., B. Sykes, and E. Weatherford. "Aboriginal Women: Male and Female Anthropological Perspectives," in *Toward an Anthropology of Women*. Ed. R.R. Reiter. New York: Monthly Review Press, 1975.

Rorty, R. *Philosophy and the Mirror of Nature*. Princeton: Princeton University Press, 1979.

Rosaldo, M.Z. *Knowledge and Passion*. Cambridge: Cambridge University Press, 1980.

———. "Woman, Culture, and Society: A Theoretical Overview," in *Woman, Culture, and Society*. Eds. M.Z. Rosaldo and L. Lamphere. Stanford: Stanford University Press, 1974.

———, and L. Lamphere, eds. *Women, Culture, and Society.* Stanford: Stanford University Press, 1974.

Rose, M.A. *Marx's Lost Aesthetic.* Cambridge: Cambridge University Press, 1984.

Rousseau, J-J. *Discourse on the Origin of Inequality,* in *The First and Second Discourses.* Ed. R.D. Masters. Trs. R.D. Masters and J.R. Masters. New York: St. Martin's, 1964.

———. *Discourse on the Sciences and Arts,* in *First and Second Discourses.* Ed. R.D. Masters. Trs. R.D. Masters and J.R. Masters. New York: St. Martin's, 1964.

———. *Emile.* Tr. A. Bloom. New York: Basic Books, 1979.

———. *Government of Poland.* Tr. W. Kendall. Indianapolis: Bobbs-Merrill, 1972.

———. *Œuvres complètes.* 4 vols. Paris: Gallimard, 1959 ff.

———. *On the Social Contract.* Ed. R.D. Masters. Tr. J.R. Masters. New York: St. Martin's, 1978.

Rowbotham, S. *Women's Consciousness, Man's World.* Harmondsworth: Penguin, 1973.

Rubin, G. "The Traffic in Women: Notes on the 'Political Economy' of Sex," in *Toward an Anthropology of Women.* Ed. R.R. Reiter. New York: Monthly Review Press, 1975.

Ryan, A. "Locke and athe Dictatorship of the Bourgeoisie," *Political Studies* XIII (1965).

Ryan, M. *Marx and Deconstruction: A Critical Articulation.* Baltimore: Johns Hopkins University Press, 1982.

Sabine, G.H. *A History of Political Theory.* 3rd edition. London: G.H. Harrap, 1963.

Sahlins, M. *Culture and Practical Reason.* Chicago: University of Chicago Press, 1976.

———. *Stone Age Economics.* Chicago: Aldine-Atherton, 1972.

Said, E.W. *Orientalism.* New York: Random House, 1978.

Saitta, D.J. "Marxism, Prehistory, and Primitive Communism." *Rethinking Marxism* I (1988), 145–68.

Saner, H. *Kant's Political Thought.* Tr. E.B. Ashton. Chicago: University of Chicago Press, 1973.

Sargent, L., ed. *Women and Revolution.* Boston: South End Press, 1981.

Schiller, F. *Letters on the Aesthetic Education of Man.* Trs. E.M. Wilkinson and L.A. Willoughby. Oxford: Clarendon Press, 1967.

———. "On Grace and Dignity," in *Essays Aesthetical and Philosophical.* London: Bell, 1879.

———. "The Moral Utility of Aesthetic Manners," in *Essays Aesthetical and Philosophical*. London: Bell, 1879.

——— *On Naive and Sentimental Poetry*. Tr. J.A. Elias. New York: Ungar, 1966.

———. *Schillers Werke: Nationalausgabe*. Eds. J. Petersen and G. Fricke. 43 vols. Weimar: Böhlaus, 1943 ff.

Schwartz, J. *The Sexual Politics of Jean-Jacques Rousseau*. Chicago: University of Chicago Press, 1984.

Secombe, W. "The Housewife and Her Labour Under Capitalism," *New Left Review* 83 (1973), 3–24.

Seigel, J. *Marx's Fate: The Shape of a Life*. Princeton: Princeton University Press, 1978.

Seliger, M. *The Liberal Politics of John Locke*. New York: Praeger, 1969.

Shaw, W.H. *Marx's Theory of History*. Stanford: Stanford University Press, 1978.

Singer, P. *Marx*. New York: Hill and Wang, 1980.

Skinner, Q. *The Foundations of Modern Political Thought*. 2 vols. Cambridge: Cambridge University Press, 1978.

Smith, A. *The Wealth of Nations*. Ed. E. Cannan. New York: Random House, 1937.

Smith, P. "Domestic Labour and Marx's Theory of Value," in *Feminism and Materialism*. London: Routledge & Kegan Paul, 1978.

Spivak, G. "Can the Subaltern Speak?" in *Marxism and the Interpretation of Culture*. Eds. C. Nelson and L. Grossberg. Urbana: University of Illinois Press, 1988.

Stephen, L. *Hobbes*. London: Macmillan, 1904.

Stern, R. "Unity and Difference in Hegel's Political Philosophy," *Ratio* II (1989).

Talmon, J.L. *The Origins of Totalitarian Democracy*. London: Secker and Warburg, 1952.

Taylor, A.E. "The Ethical Doctrine of Hobbes," in *Hobbes Studies*. Ed. K.C. Brown. Cambridge, Mass.: Harvard University Press, 1965.

Taylor, C. *Hegel*. Cambridge: Cambridge University Press, 1975.

———. *Philosophy and the Human Sciences: Philosophical Papers 2*. Cambridge: Cambridge University Press, 1985.

Terray, E. *Marxism and "Primitive" Societies*. Tr. M. Klopper. New York: Monthly Review Press, 1972.

Thiele, B. "Vanishing Acts in Social and Political Thought: Tricks of the Trade," in *Feminist Challenges: Social and Political Theory*. Eds. C. Pateman and E. Gross. Boston: Northeastern University Press, 1987.

Thompson, J. "Women and Political Rationality," in *Feminist Challenges: Social and Political Theory.* Eds. C. Pateman and E. Gross. Boston: Northeastern University Press, 1987.

Todorov, T. *The Conquest of America: The Question of the Other.* Tr. R. Howard. New York: Harper & Row, 1984.

Tucker, D.F.B. *Marxism and Individualism.* Oxford: Basil Blackwell, 1980.

Tully, J. *A Discourse on Property.* Cambridge: Cambridge University Press, 1980.

Van Leeuwen, A.T. *Critique of Earth.* New York: Scribner's, 1974.

———. *Critique of Heaven.* New York: Scribner's, 1972.

Vaughan, C.E. "Introduction" to *The Political Writings of Jean Jacques Rousseau.* 2 vols. Cambridge: Cambridge University Press, 1915.

von Leyden, W., ed. *Essays on the Law of Nature.* Oxford: Clarendon Press, 1954.

Vorländer, K. *Kant und der Sozialismus.* Berlin: Reuther und Reichard, 1900.

Warrender, W. *The Political Philosophy of Hobbes.* Oxford: Clarendon Press, 1957.

Watkins, F. "Introduction" to *Rousseau: Political Writings.* Edinburgh: Thomas Nelson & Sons, 1953.

Watkins, J.W.N. *Hobbes's System of Ideas.* London: Hutchinson, 1965.

Weinbaum, B. *The Curious Courtship of Women's Liberation and Socialism.* Boston: South End Press, 1978.

Williams, R. *Marxism and Literature.* New York: Oxford University Press, 1977.

Wolin, S. *Politics and Vision.* Boston: Little, Brown, 1960.

Wolpe, H. *Race, Class & the Apartheid State.* London: James Curry, 1988.

———, ed. *The Articulation of Modes of Production: Essays from "Economy and Society."* London: Routledge & Kegan Paul, 1980.

Wood, N. *John Locke and Agrarian Capitalism.* Berkeley: University of California Press, 1984.

Woolf, V. *To the Lighthouse.* New York: Harcourt Brace Jovanovich, 1927.

Wright, E.H. *The Meaning of Rousseau.* London: Oxford University Press, 1929.

Yovel, Y. *Kant and the Philosophy of History.* Princeton, N.J.: Princeton University Press, 1980.

Zaretsky, E. *Capitalism, the Family, and Personal Life.* Revised edition. New York: Harper & Row, 1986.

Index

abolitionists, 10
absolute, 15, 140, 143, 208, 210; government, 38–39; knowledge, 158–59, 283; sovereign, 19, 23–25, 30, 35n35, 65–66; spirit, 192
Adamson, W.L., 287–88
adoration, 341
Adorno, T.W., 254
aesthetic, 202, 204–6, 297, 336–37, 341; education, 206; judgment, 112, 120n43; state, 219–20
aesthetical ideas, 121n43
aesthetics, German, 336
Africa, 260, 343
age, 323, 378n24
agriculture, 84, 86, 130, 277, 284, 296, 318
AIDS, 184
air travel, 252
Akbar, 278
alchemists, 183
alienated labor, 347, 351, 361
alienation, 4, 9, 130, 136–38, 140–42, 146–47, 151n46, 161, 166–74, 177, 179, 184–85, 188–92, 194–99, 203, 205, 208, 211–13, 217, 222, 245, 248, 257–58, 268, 295–96, 317, 325, 331, 342–59, 362, 368–76, 382n104, 383n114, 384n128, 384n133, 385n139, 388n172; from the product, 161–62, 188, 348, 361; from the species, 162, 348, 350, 361; in the process of production, 161–62, 348, 361; *see also* estrangement; fetishism
all-round individual, 248–50, 270
Althusser, L., 283, 292, 305n121, 306n122
altruism, 81, 164, 178–79, 189, 199, 201
America, 38, 43, 48, 260, 264, 271, 277, 298, 300n6
American "savages," 17, 33n3
Amish, 262
anarchists, 239–40
ancient world, 126, 133, 135, 142, 207, 232n172, 262, 282, 287, 290, 295–97, 315–17
androgyny, 342
animals, 84, 161, 252, 317, 321
anomalies, 284
anomie, 9
anthropology, 209, 288, 298, 314, 338
anti-Semitism, 273
antipluralism, 2
ape, 288
Appolonian, 211
arbitrator, 24

409

Archimedean point, 192
architect, 308n154
architectonic, 109, 111
aristocracy, 26, 155
Aristotle, 49, 76, 79, 118n3, 165, 172, 203, 220–23, 281–83; *Politics,* 49
arithmetic equality, 172, 222–23
armed people, 257
army. *See* standing professional army
Aronowicz, S., 279
art, 181, 188, 203, 231n129, 251–52, 262, 268, 339, 341, 352; Greek, 291–92, 295, 297, 315
artificial person, 21
artisan, 79, 203
Ashcraft, R., 48, 50, 53–54
Ashly, Lord, 353
Asia, 273, 296
assimilation, 132, 298–99
astronomy, 288, 312
Athens, 258–59, 290–93, 315
Augé, M., 298
authoritarianism, 143–44
authority, 12, 18, 21, 23, 26, 39, 44, 51, 56–57, 60n14, 63n55, 66, 74, 77, 87, 101, 115–17, 146–47, 173–74, 214, 219, 222, 237, 289, 323, 340; parental, 276, 323–24; religious, 10, 12; scientific, 12; traditional, 10
autocrat, 114, 117, 119n22, 144–45
automatic workshop, 269
autonomy, 76, 128, 173–74, 193, 291, 334, 343–49, 354–56, 371
avarice, 99
Avineri, S., 143

Bacon, F., 211, 297
Balbus, I.D., 279, 312, 323
banishment, 94n43
barbarism, 96n75, 132, 265, 271, 278, 296, 299
barter, 42, 44–46, 289, 318–19, 355–56, 382n105

Baudrillard, J., 279, 312
Bauer, B., 273
beautiful world, 7, 109, 112–13, 202, 204, 206–7, 211, 220
beauty, 112–13, 120n43, 121n43, 202, 204–5, 207, 211, 251–52, 297, 336–38; as symbol of the morally good, 121n43, 205, 207
bees, 308n154
benevolence, 220
Berlin, I., 235, 299n1
Bestimmung, 329
Bildung, 132
biology, 286, 316, 320–22, 328–31, 333, 350, 379n54, 380n59, 382n107
birth, 98, 218, 328–29, 340, 342, 354–56
Black Madonnas, 339, 381n87
blacks, 12, 262, 264, 273, 300n4, 322, 343
blueprint, 12, 325
Bonaparte, L., 173
bondage, 132, 353–54
bourgeoisie, 154, 172, 178, 181, 212, 218–19, 223, 228n75, 243, 254, 256, 265, 270–71, 273, 275, 277, 282, 284, 287, 289, 295–99, 342, 345
bricolage, 262
Brisco, Lily, 353
British, 273–77, 297; East India Company, 274, 278; rule in India, 273, 275, 277
bureaucracy, 225n9

California, 269
canon, 14
capitalism, 10, 12–14, 50, 161, 166, 178, 218–19, 223, 239, 243–44, 264–77, 279, 281–87, 290–92, 296–99, 306n123, 313–14, 322–25, 332, 336–37, 340, 345–48, 351, 358–71, 384n133, 385n139,

386n144, 388n172; agrarian, 50; manufacturing, 50; mercantile, 50
caprice, 134
Carey, H., 277
caring, 340, 353–54, 371–72, 375, 388n172
Cartesian break, 1
caste, 274
categorical imperative, 3–4, 70–71, 94n32, 102–4, 114, 118n22, 122n53, 123–24, 134, 148n1, 153–55, 158, 161–64, 167, 173, 175, 181–82, 190–91, 195, 202–4, 260–62, 330–35
categories, 280–87, 305n116, 306n123, 313, 315, 337, 339, 343, 368
Catholicism, 282, 290, 292–93, 315
causality, 20, 121n43, 127, 129, 191
censorial tribunal, 78, 83
censorship, 264
certainty, 139
Charlemagne, 278
chattel, 322
Chicana, 255
childbirth, 314, 350, 354, 383n117
childcare, 263, 342–43, 347, 350–54, 359, 361, 364, 372, 374–76, 385n139
childrearing, 314, 350, 354
children, 182, 202, 219, 266, 276, 297, 313, 318–19, 323–24, 329–43, 347, 350–51, 354–55, 359–62, 365–67, 370, 372, 374–76, 380n59, 383n114, 384n128
chimeras, 338
China, 260, 271, 276–77, 299, 305n109
Chodorow, N., 382n107
Christianity, 282, 284, 339–40
Church, 10, 132, 345, 347
citizen militia, 7, 89, 122n53, 158, 172, 213, 256–57
city state, 49, 118n3
civil: disobedience, 25, 33; laws, 18–19, 22–23, 25, 28, 30, 36n52, 114, 129, 176, 184; religion, 79, 83, 94n43; servants, 225n9; society, 4, 46, 124–25, 132–34, 141–45, 147, 150n36, 166–67, 169, 177, 194–96, 199, 215, 217, 227n59, 369–74, 383n114; war, 17
civilization, 84, 271, 275–76, 278–79, 287, 296–99, 386n143; Western, 275–76, 278
class: conflict, 163–64; struggle, 157, 163; *see also* propertied class; propertyless class; ruling class; working class
classes, 25, 156, 172, 175–76, 199, 213, 219, 243, 245, 249, 254, 256–58, 267, 270, 272, 297, 313, 320, 326–27, 342, 344, 346, 370, 374; polarization of, 144
Clifford, J., 298–99
Colletti, L., 230n124
colonies, 367
commensurable, 281
commerce and trade, 4, 42–43, 79–80, 82, 86, 101, 106, 123, 131–35, 142, 144–47, 166, 177, 195, 239, 241–42, 273
commercials, 375
commodities, 166, 266, 271, 281, 299, 306n123, 344, 359, 361–68, 385n139, 386n143, 386n144
commodity exchange, 247, 289, 344, 347
common good, 3–4, 66–67, 69–73, 75, 77–82, 84, 106, 108–9, 111, 124, 131, 133–35, 145, 147, 160, 164–66, 219, 235–36, 242, 373
commonwealth, 32
communal individual, 5, 176, 196, 223, 230n124, 245, 296
communal property. *See* property, communal
communication, 9, 77, 84, 166, 249–250, 253, 255, 258–59, 264, 271, 296, 340, 376

communism, 7–8, 13, 159, 170–71, 178, 201, 218, 228n75, 238, 240, 244, 247, 250, 268–69, 277, 298, 326, 331, 335, 351; crude, 247, 326, 331–32; stage one of, 172, 218–20, 222–23, 325; stage two of, 172, 218–20, 222–23
Communist party, 157, 160, 254
community, 3–5, 9–13, 52, 54, 71, 73–76, 78, 81–82, 90–91, 120n41, 123–24, 128, 130–31, 135–36, 150n36, 153, 157, 163–71, 175–79, 181–84, 189, 195–202, 212–18, 222–24, 232n172, 238–40, 244, 246, 249–60, 264, 267, 270, 272, 274, 289, 296, 331–32, 348–49, 355, 369, 371–76, 380n59, 382n105; of women, 332
compact, 27–29, 32, 39, 60n6; tacit, 28–30
comparison, 280–82, 285, 287
compassion, 222
competition, 10, 81, 99, 105–6, 125, 133, 157, 160, 163, 194, 222, 367, 370–74, 385n139
computers, 375
concrete, 281, 287, 293; for thought, 281, 293, 315
conqueror, 27–30, 32, 51
conscience, 10, 19, 22, 28, 165–66
consent, 17–18, 21, 26, 39, 44–49, 52, 62n36, 134, 158, 239; tacit, 14, 46
conservative, 358
consumerism, 375
consumption, 200–202, 251, 270, 291, 321, 360, 362–63, 368–69, 385n139
contemplation, 188–89, 197–99, 205–6, 216, 336, 341, 350
contract, 22, 25–28, 36n54
contradiction, 19, 22, 47, 71, 94n32, 103, 115–17, 155, 157, 174, 185, 255, 272, 274–75, 277, 282, 294, 311–12, 326, 333, 335, 338, 342

corporations, 147
correct scientific method, 281
Corsica, 86
coup, 114, 157
courtly love tradition, 340
covenant, 19, 27–28, 36n54
creativity, 200–202, 342–43, 350–52
credit, 166
criticism, 144, 158–60, 268, 282–84, 351
cunning of reason, 125
custom and tradition, 3–4, 9, 53, 73, 75–86, 95n54, 96n75, 123–24, 128–35, 140, 142–46, 164–65, 175–79, 181, 223–24, 245–46, 256–58, 262, 302n53, 343

Darwin, C., 14, 321
daughter, 340, 350
de Beauvoir, S., 335, 352, 354, 362
death, 90, 94, 98, 255, 259, 269, 368; penalty, 90–91, 94, 96n91
deductive: method, 23, 29, 31; science, 31
degradation, 332–35, 357, 369
Deity, 242
delegate, 170–71, 198
deliberations, 71–72
democracy, 4–5, 7–8, 23, 26, 153, 163–64, 168–70, 174, 194, 196, 228n83, 256–59, 369
deputies, 7, 89, 96n85, 168–71, 197–200, 255–57
Derrida, J., 302n36
Descartes, R., 1
despotism, 278
destiny, 99, 273–74, 320, 322, 327, 329, 352–54
determinant in the last instance, 292, 306n121
determinism, 159, 180, 192–93, 265, 303n67, 312, 342; biological, 320
devils, 104
dialectic, 13, 136–37, 140, 192–93,

200, 254, 292–93, 311; method, 286
Diet, 89–90
dietine, 89–90
difference, 12, 238–55, 258, 260–70, 280, 284–85, 287, 296–98, 302n36, 320
differentia specifica, 267
dignity, 98, 221
dilettante, 270
discipline, 4, 126, 132–37, 142–43, 177
discourse, 246, 259, 263–64, 376
disinterested, 205–6
dissent, 143
dissolution: of government, 40; of society, 40
distribution, 58–59, 165, 178, 199, 218, 222–24, 256, 344, 347
diversity, 11, 245–70, 296, 301n29, 314, 336–37
Divine, 143, 148, 338; laws, 34n26
division of labor, 80, 84, 105, 150n36, 228n75, 243, 245, 248–49, 267–71, 317–20, 351, 373, 378n24; gendered, 312–13, 316; sexual, 316–23, 355
dogma, 158–60, 200
domestic labor, 365, 386n144; debate, 385n139; industrialization of, 324
domestic servants, 262
domination, 2, 10, 137, 161–62, 165, 170–71, 175, 178, 188, 205–6, 254, 257, 259, 261, 264, 315–19, 325, 331, 343–47, 354–57, 380n59, 384n128, 388n172; *see also* male domination
Don Quixote, 125
drudgery, 343, 351–52
duelling, 297
Duke of Burgundy, 369
Dunn, J., 41, 50, 52–53
Durkheim, E., 150n36

Earl of Gloucester, 369
East, 271
ecology, 228n75
economic crises, 156, 344, 370
education, 14, 59, 98, 107, 132, 134, 136–37, 173, 187, 206, 236, 245, 248, 253, 262–63, 271–72, 329–30, 339, 344, 350, 354, 359, 365; American, 271
egoism, 191, 289
Einaudi, M., 81
Eisenstein, Z.R., 327
electric telegraph, 275, 291
electricity, 208–10
Elster, J., 178, 189, 199–202, 279
emancipation, 5, 10–13, 132, 154, 156, 167, 219, 223, 250, 255, 264, 267, 273, 323–26, 339, 370
empirical, 282, 285, 287, 306n123, 357
empiricism, 139–41, 155, 207–8, 210
employee, 25, 177
employment, 236
empowerment, 257–58
enfranchisement, 89
Engels, F., 247, 267, 277, 314, 318, 324–25, 355, 370–72, 374, 377n21, 378n25, 380n57; *Origin of the Family,* 319
England, 156, 244, 267, 273, 275–77
enjoyment, 165, 203, 206, 267
Entäusserung, 345
Entfremdung, 345
epic: Greek, 291–92, 297; poetry, 297
epistemology, 24, 139–40
equal property. *See* property, equal
eros, 252
essence, 130, 135–43, 146–47, 162–63, 165, 170, 176–77, 179, 182, 184–216, 222, 230n102, 230n104, 251–52, 254, 260, 267, 301n29, 302n37, 303n64, 322, 327–35,

341, 348, 351–52, 380n59, 383n116; existence corresponding to, 184–89, 204, 254, 333; *see also* species, essence
essential powers, 321, 337–38
estates, 43, 51–55
estranged labor, 349
estrangement, 136–38, 140–42, 147, 151n46, 161–62, 165–66, 178, 192–93, 208, 222, 265, 345; *see also* alienation; fetishism
ethical universalism, 235
ethnic minority groups, 11, 236, 261, 263, 300n4, 300n6
ethnocentrism, 2, 13–15, 270, 272–44, 277–80, 283–84, 296, 298
Europe, 10, 14, 86, 275, 278, 285; Eastern, 7–8
evolution, 285–86, 296, 308n162
exchange, 42, 44, 47, 150n36, 163–67, 172, 177–78, 181, 188, 195, 218, 266, 281, 306n123, 319, 344–47, 355, 362–68, 373, 382n105, 383n114
exchange value, 218, 265, 289, 368
exchangeability of function, 268–69, 351
executive, 53, 79, 117, 171, 173–74, 255
exploitation, 50, 247, 267, 270, 276, 289–91, 323–24, 347, 361–69, 375, 387n147

Fabian, J., 283, 298–99
factions, 35n44, 68, 72, 77, 79, 89, 102, 242
Fama, 292
family, 42, 49, 60n6, 84, 107, 196, 249, 263, 276, 312–13, 316–20, 323–24, 331, 338, 343, 346–47, 350, 353–74, 377n21, 378n25, 383n114, 385n141, 386n144, 388n172; first form of property, 319

farming, 79, 367, 373
fascists, 239–40
fatal accident, 84, 86
fate, 358
Feinberg, J., 220–22
feminism, 5, 10, 13, 255, 262–63, 311–14, 320, 322, 324, 326–27, 335, 339, 342–44, 354, 357, 368, 372–76, 377n6
Ferguson, A., 342
fetishism, 232n170, 266, 297, 306n123, 344–47, 359, 368, 371–74; *see also* alienation; estrangement
feudalism, 10, 282, 284–86, 289, 296–97, 345, 369, 382n103
Feuerbach, L., 339, 341, 352
fiction, 18–19, 28–29, 31–32
Filmer, R., 44, 56
final purpose, 111–13, 120n41, 121n43, 123, 159
Folbre, N., 342
Foucault, M., 235
France, 173, 212, 216, 249, 269
Franco-Prussian War, 170
Fraser, N., 346–47, 362
free: forced to be, 65, 73–74, 174–75, 185; markets, 238, 240, 345; rider, 183–84; thinker, 272; time, 374–75; trade, 156, 277, 289; will, 98, 265
freedom, 9–11, 45, 74–75, 77, 85, 88, 90, 96n75, 102, 104–5, 110–13, 120n41, 127, 129–30, 133, 135, 139–43, 162, 173–74, 176, 179–80, 185, 190–93, 195, 200, 203–6, 212, 233n190, 235, 264, 289, 297, 325, 330, 349–50, 354, 377n21; of speech, 143, 212; of the press, 143, 155, 157, 160, 275; rational, 3–5, 123–24, 129, 176
freedom-from, 10–11
French: peasantry, 258, 296; Revolution, 135

Freud, S., 14
friendship, 165, 220–21, 223–24, 333, 371, 373
frontier, 373–74
fundamentalists, 262

Ganymede, 380n57
Gemeinschaft, 75–78, 165, 168, 371
gender, 245, 314, 320; roles, 314, 320, 322
general interest. *See* interests, general
general will, 3–4, 24, 65–83, 86–91, 92n8, 94n32, 95n54, 108, 118n22, 123–24, 131, 134–35, 141, 148n1, 163, 173–77, 194–95, 199–200, 214, 219, 235, 242
genetic, 329
geological, 316
geometric equality, 172, 222–23
geometry, 29
Germany, 17, 33n3, 132, 155, 277, 345
Gesellschaft, 75–78, 165, 168, 371
Glaucon, 100–101
God, 19, 27, 34n26, 39, 41, 44, 46–49, 59, 62n42, 102, 110–12, 137, 140, 143, 158–59, 192, 204, 300n3; mother of, 339–40
goddesses, 377n21
Godelier, M., 306n121
gods, 380n57
gold, 41, 44, 265, 322
Gordon, L., 342
Gottlieb, R.S., 339
government, 3–4, 24–26, 30, 37–39, 43, 46, 50–56, 62n37, 63n55, 64n71, 82, 86–89, 92n8, 95n54, 115–16, 144–46, 149n36, 156–58, 166, 171–72, 212, 214, 216, 222, 237, 249, 255–56, 272, 297–98, 357; absolute, 40; limited, 40
grammar, 272
grandchildren, 374

grandparents, 374
gratitude, 221–22
great books, 14
Greek *polis,* 76, 128, 165, 205, 220
Greeks, 78, 281, 291–93, 297, 380n57
Gyges' ring, 100

habit, 76–77, 128, 132–33, 302n53, 343
happiness, 77, 84, 99, 110–13, 120n41, 202–4, 206–7, 211
Harding, S., 313
having, 303n64, 335
Hegel, G.W.F., 2–5, 31, 75–76, 80–81, 123–51, 153, 158–60, 163–64, 168, 172, 176–77, 179, 190–200, 203, 207–8, 210–11, 215, 225n9, 226n27, 235, 257, 265, 283, 287, 303n64, 336, 343, 345, 347, 371–72, 382n104; *Encyclopaedia,* 139; *Phenomenology of Spirit,* 125–27, 129, 136–38, 345–46; *Philosophy of History,* 132; *Philosophy of Right,* 125, 132–33, 141
Hermes, 292
heroes, 270
Hess, M., 233n182
heteronomy, 103, 130, 135, 137, 141–43, 162, 173–74, 188, 190, 192–93, 215, 233n182
heterosexism, 380n57
heterosexual, 380n57, 380n59
hierarchy, 254, 259, 263–64
highest good, 7, 109–13, 115, 120n41, 121n43, 202–4, 207, 211, 220
highway robbery, 30
Hindess, B., 293
Hindostan, 273–75
Hirst, P., 293
historical materialism, 156, 159, 180, 279, 316

history, 4, 14–15, 19, 28–33, 46, 81, 88, 98–99, 102, 106, 108–9, 112–14, 120n41, 121n43, 123–25, 128, 130, 132–33, 136, 142, 144–45, 154–60, 178, 180–82, 184, 187, 189, 192, 194, 197, 202, 204–5, 207, 209, 245, 252, 254, 273, 275, 279–90, 293, 297–99, 306n123, 311, 315–18, 321–22, 324, 335, 355, 357, 372, 377n21, 379n54, 380n59, 382n105, 385n143; of ideas, 1; of philosophy, 139; stages of, 279, 284, 286–87, 296–97; universal, 106
Hobbes, T., 2–3, 17–37, 39–40, 43, 45–47, 50, 56–59, 62n36, 65–66, 74, 76, 82–84, 98, 100–101, 108, 114–16, 144–45, 179, 214, 235–37, 241, 256, 300n2; *De Cive*, 26, 28, 32; *Elements of Law*, 26, 28; *Leviathan*, 18, 25–26, 28, 32
homemaker, 343
honor, 166
hope, 7
Hountondji, P., 298
household, 361
housewife, 337, 344, 358, 360, 362, 365, 368, 386n144, 387n147
housework, 320, 325, 342–43, 346–64, 370, 375, 383n114, 384n136, 385n139, 385n141, 386n144; industrialized, 371–72, 374
houseworker, 359, 365, 367, 369, 383n114, 385n141
housing, 236
hubris, 254
human nature, 45, 49, 76, 88, 165, 182, 267, 321–22, 351
humanism, 210
humanities core courses, 14
Hungary, 8
hunger, 251, 321
husband, 319, 347, 353, 361–65, 374–75; and wife, 39
hypothesis, 45

Idea, 124, 146, 150n36, 158–59, 196, 215
idea: for a universal history, 159, 204, 207; historical, 109, 111–13; of reason, 109, 121n43; regulative, 109, 159, 207, 211
ideal, 3, 8, 78, 84, 165, 169–70, 189, 203, 205–6, 213–14, 224, 254, 333, 348, 352, 354, 372; community, 12, 119n24, 123, 176, 255, 270; of labor, 228n75; society, 4–7, 81, 87, 92n8, 107, 111, 133, 147, 153, 160, 163–64, 168, 177–78, 194, 213, 224, 228n75, 232n172, 245, 250, 267, 297; state, 97–98, 108, 113–14, 118n3, 123, 131, 134, 145
idealism, 6, 196, 210–11
identity, 254, 284
ideology, 10, 12–13, 92n21, 155–56, 240–41, 272, 289, 306n121, 343, 371, 378n25
idiocy of rural life, 271
Illinois, 270
image, 338–39
imagination, 8, 121n43, 126, 291–93, 308n154, 315–16, 318, 338
imitation, 76, 128
immisseration, 144–45, 147
imperialism, 278, 280, 299
inalienable, 166
inclinations, 74, 77, 99, 103–5, 110–13, 127, 129, 135, 162, 173, 190–91, 202–5, 219–20, 336
income, 362–63
India, 273–77, 280
individual, 179–83, 191, 196, 201, 212, 230n124, 245–47, 249, 255–56, 295, 328, 349; consciousness, 4–5, 127, 135, 140–41, 143, 153, 179, 194–95, 207–8, 210; isolated, 169, 196, 216; liberty (*see* liberty, individual); self-consciousness, 137–38, 140–41, 143

individualism, 50, 75, 77–78, 90–91, 142, 246
individuality, 126, 134, 148, 169, 179, 260, 267, 338
industrial reserve army, 370
inertia, 262–63
inferiority, 358
infrastructure, 294, 306n121
inheritance, 319, 329, 331, 333–37
injustice, 100, 104, 117
intercourse, 156, 247, 249–50, 271, 273, 317, 319, 356, 377n21
interdependence, 80–81, 101, 105–6, 124–25, 134, 150n36, 182, 253
interests, 111, 127, 130, 135, 142, 147, 162, 180–81, 194, 199, 204–5, 238–39, 243–44, 254, 258, 290, 330, 336; class, 4, 25, 154–57, 163, 175, 177, 213, 243, 247, 330, 342; common, 67, 73, 106, 108, 156–57, 160, 176, 199–200, 255; conflicting, 3–4, 160, 163, 177–78, 190; corporate, 68, 72, 242; general, 67–74, 78–79, 81, 92n8, 106, 108, 154–55, 157, 166, 175–76, 199, 235; individual, 127, 133–34, 141; long-term, 28–29, 35–36n35, 70, 73, 75, 104, 108; national, 101; particular, 3, 4, 10, 67, 69–103, 106–9, 111, 113, 123–29, 131–35, 141–42, 144–47, 153–61, 163, 165–67, 174–79, 181, 185, 190, 194–95, 204, 206, 212–19, 235, 242, 330, 333–34, 342, 349, 369; private, 67–68, 80, 87, 125, 182, 185; self, 21–23, 28, 35n35, 70–81, 85, 90–91, 97–98, 100–102, 105–9, 124, 126, 131–32, 135, 141, 154, 161, 164, 179, 183, 189–91, 260, 289, 330–31, 369, 371–73; *see also* property, interest
internalization, 180–82, 190, 192, 201
international law, 98, 101, 124

International Working Men's Association, 243–44, 263, 277
intimacy, 354, 375–76
intolerance, 10, 240, 242
invisible hand, 81, 106, 124, 133, 160, 164, 172, 177, 179, 194–95, 215, 219
Ireland, 277
iron, 265, 366–68
ironworks, 366–68
irony, 368
Islam, 239
Italians, 275

Jagger, A.M., 344, 358, 370
Jameson, F., 1
John Bull, 267
Joseph, G., 343
journalist, 7, 92n21
Judaism, 239, 262, 273
Judeo-Christian morality, 14
judgment, 111–12; reflective, 111; teleological, 121n43
Juno, 377n21
Jupiter, 292
juryman, 54
justice, 18, 22, 31, 45, 66, 72, 85, 97–108, 115, 150n36, 157, 220–24, 238, 250, 277, 305n111; distributive, 218; Rawls's two principles of, 238

Kant, I., 2–6, 8, 19, 31, 33, 70–71, 75–76, 81, 93n26, 94n32, 97–129, 133–35, 139–41, 144–45, 153–64, 176–77, 191, 202–11, 225n2, 261, 265, 336; *Critique of Judgment,* 111–12, 205; *Critique of Practical Reason,* 109–12, 162, 203, 205, 207; *Critique of Pure Reason,* 109, 111; *Foundations of the Metaphysics of Morals,* 205; "Idea for a Universal History," 98, 110, 206; *Metaphysical Elements of Justice,* 117; *Perpetual*

Peace, 104; *Theory and Practice*, 111, 115
Kanuman, 274
kinship, 306n121, 319
Kuhn, T., 283

labor, 38, 42, 44, 48, 60n6, 79, 172, 180, 185–89, 192, 195, 206, 208–12, 218, 228n75, 265–66, 269, 276, 281, 284, 290, 308n154, 319, 321–24, 328, 343, 347–49, 351, 359–61, 363, 365, 373, 379n54, 380n59; abstract, 265; agricultural, 284; certificates, 172; market, 365–67; power, 323, 359–68, 375, 377n18, 385n139, 385n141, 385n143, 386n144; time, 171, 219, 222, 281, 345, 359, 364, 366; unions, 240; *see also* domestic labor; productive labor; unproductive labor; workers
laborers, 48, 55, 147, 324, 359–60, 363–64, 366–67, 370, 374, 386n143, 386n144
laboring class, 63n63
land, 38, 40, 42, 48, 53, 85–86; enough and as good, 38, 43, 48
landed estates, 369
language, 84, 87, 181, 188, 222, 340
law: of gravity, 174; of nature, 18–19, 21–22, 25, 27–28, 34n26, 41, 43, 47–49, 55, 59, 70, 175 (*see also* natural law); rational, 4, 142, 175, 185, 194
Leacock, E.L., 308n162
league of nations, 98, 101, 104–5, 108, 124, 155
left Hegelians, 159
legislator, 65, 87–88, 96n78, 117, 170, 184
legislature, 53–55, 64n75, 68, 78, 89, 91, 117, 147, 256–58
legitimacy, 18–19, 29–31, 36n52, 44–45, 47–49, 59, 62n48, 76, 114–16, 168–73, 171, 175, 197–200, 237
legitimate revolution, 5, 26–27, 31, 40, 54, 56, 114, 116
Leibniz, G.W., 253, 267
lesbian, 255
Levellers, 53
levelling, 163, 247
Lévi-Strauss, C., 262, 296, 379n54
liberalism, 5, 10, 75, 90–91, 141, 179, 182–83, 189, 201, 235–36, 239, 244, 260, 266–67, 278, 300n3, 302n53, 320
liberation, 10–13, 15, 311–12, 339, 372–74
liberty, 51–55, 64n71, 75–76, 278, 302n53, 352; individual, 3, 10, 65, 67, 75, 83, 88, 90–91
liberum veto, 90, 96n90
license, 85
limited government, 3, 23–24, 37, 50, 54–55, 57, 82, 144
limited sovereignty, 58, 82
Lincoln, A., 270
linear accelerators, 181
Locke, J., 2–5, 17, 20, 25, 33, 37–65, 76, 82–83, 94n43, 118n3, 144–45, 147, 172, 179, 238–39, 241–42, 244, 257, 300n3; *Considerations of the Consequences of the Lowering of Interest*, 55, 57; *Essays on the Law of Nature*, 47; *Fundamental Constitutions of Carolina*, 53; *Two Treatises of Government*, 37, 47
locomotives, 291
logic, 287
lord and serf, 345, 347
love, 165–66, 221–22, 252, 265, 267, 336, 339, 341–42, 351, 353–54, 371, 375; sexual, 340–42
lust, 332–34, 337

Machiavelli, N., 31, 97, 107–8
MacIntyre, A., 259

MacKinnon, C.A., 320, 362, 384n128
Macpherson, C.B., 41, 50, 52–54; *Political Theory of Possessive Individualism,* 50
Madonna, 340–41
magicians, 183
magistrate, 87
majority vote, 26, 67, 69–71, 78, 94n32
male: domination, 312–14, 316, 319–20, 323, 357, 384n128; supremacy, 325
Malthus, T.R., 277
mandat impératif, 170
marbles, 25, 32, 39–40, 144
Marcuse, H., 1
market: forces, 360–62, 387n144; laws, 165, 178, 344–47
markets, 7, 81, 101, 105, 124, 165–66, 177–78, 205, 217, 222, 224, 239, 344, 346–47, 349, 356, 359, 361–68, 373, 383n114, 385n139
marriage, 98, 219, 266, 319, 325, 332, 352, 382n103; monogamous, 319
Marx, E., 340
Marx, J., 339–41, 375
Marx, K., 1–16, 19, 25, 31, 39–40, 59, 75, 82, 89, 96n85, 98, 109, 113, 116, 144, 147, 150n36, 153–388; *Capital,* 247, 253, 256, 266, 269, 276, 285–86, 289, 314, 320–23, 344, 346; *Civil War in France,* 255–56; "Comments on James Mill," 197; Communist Descartes, 1; *Communist Manifesto,* 1, 156–57, 160, 178, 181, 289, 323; "Critique of the Gotha Program," 172, 217–18, 256, 266, 325; *Economic and Philosophic Manuscripts,* 160, 186, 327, 335, 341, 348, 365; *Eighteenth Brumaire,* 173, 249, 258; *German Ideology,* 156, 175–76, 213, 216–17, 265, 269, 273, 316, 318, 320–22, 327, 342, 351; *Grundrisse,* 280, 282, 291, 293, 306n122, 315–17, 321; *Holy Family,* 156; "Introduction to the Critique of Hegel's Philosophy of Law," 153, 156, 330; "On the Jewish Question," 216–18, 273–74 ; *Poverty of Philosophy,* 164, 269; *Theories of Surplus Value,* 321
master, 85, 249, 346; and servant, 39, 42; and slave, 174, 345–47
masturbation, 342
material conditions, 160, 175–76, 180, 199, 202, 243, 279, 290, 292–93, 314
mathematics, 181, 288, 312
maxims, 103, 114–16, 142, 157, 162
meaning, 252, 265, 294, 298, 337
medical care, 344
medieval: craftsworker, 352; world, 203, 207
Melon, J.F., 81
merchant's capital, 285
metallurgy, 84, 130
metaphysics, 139–41, 143, 207–8, 210–11, 265
method, 280–81, 285–88, 293, 296, 306n122, 315–16
methodological individualism, 201
Mexicans, 304n96
Middle Ages, 132, 290, 292–93, 315
Middle East, 182
military, 354–55, 363
Mill, J.S., 63n63, 278–79; *On Liberty,* 278
Minerva, 377n21
miracles, 254
Mitchell, J., 335
modernity, 10
Moleschottian metabolism, 339, 341
monad, 216, 253
monarchy, 17, 23, 26, 29, 106, 115–16, 146, 151n66, 346
money, 38–49, 51, 61n28, 62n49,

107, 165–66, 247, 300n3, 338, 347, 360, 363–65
money making, 62n49
monotony, 343
Moore, S., v, xi, 91n1
Moraga, C., 255
moral: constraints, 219–20, 223–24, 267; law, 19, 25, 103–4, 110–13; obligation, 8, 18–32, 35n35, 36n52, 47, 49; prescription, 22, 29, 38; truth, 24
Moralität, 76–77, 128–29, 133, 148
More, T., 6, 97, 102, 106–8
mores, 77
Morgan, L., 298, 308n162, 355
Morton, P., 365
murder, 86
music, 252, 257, 337, 350
myth of Er, 76
mythology, 291–92, 315–16, 318, 380n57; Egyptian, 292; Greek, 292

Native American, 355
natural: law, 22–23, 25, 41, 47, 50, 62n42, 62n49, 174 (*see also* law of nature); right, 38, 55; science, 20
naturalism, 210
needs, 79–80, 85, 99, 105, 125, 132, 150n36, 154–56, 161–65, 167–73, 178, 185–93, 195, 197–98, 201, 203–9, 216, 219–20, 222–23, 228n75, 244, 250–53, 255, 257, 261–62, 265–67, 291, 317–18, 321, 327–28, 330–31, 336–37, 341, 348, 352, 361, 368, 383n114, 386n144
negative rights, 216–18
negro, 322
New York Tribune, 277
news media, 7
Nietzsche, F., 14, 211
nihilism, 211
nonviolence, 239

noumena, 120n41, 129, 140, 191–93
nuclear power, 210
nurture, 314, 329, 340, 350, 353–54, 356, 359, 371–72, 374–75, 388n172

Oakley, A., 343
objectification, 4, 136–38, 141–43, 184, 186–200, 205, 208, 210, 216, 246–47, 253, 257–58, 260, 265, 329, 333, 336–37, 348–50, 354, 366
observation, 281, 336
office, 21, 24
ogle, 339–40
oligarchic party, 259
ontology, 9, 209–10, 338
opinion, 77, 89, 92n21, 134, 178
oppression, 2, 9–11, 13, 59, 157, 167, 236, 242, 259, 263, 295, 313, 323–27, 330–32, 339, 342–45, 347, 352, 354–58, 362–63, 365, 368, 370–73, 376, 382n107, 384n128, 385n139, 388n172
Orient, 274, 282
original position, 61n36, 238
Ortner, S.B., 379n54
"Otechestvenniye Zapiski," 285
others, 127, 130, 137, 142, 165, 181–82, 189–91, 193, 195, 197, 200, 202, 223–45, 358
ought, 97, 126–29, 164, 189, 191, 331, 333, 353, 371; implies *can,* 8; versus *is,* 126–29, 134
ovum, 380n59

pagan idol, 273, 275
painting, 268–69
paradigm, 282–88, 293–94, 315–16, 343, 350, 352, 358, 383n114
paradox, 98
parents, 318, 329–31, 334, 347, 359, 372, 376, 380n57
Paris Commune, 170, 213, 254, 256

Index   421

parliament, 53–54, 63n63, 171, 173, 239–40, 243, 246, 249
particular interest. *See* interests, particular
party, 68, 72, 92n21, 200, 254–56, 272
passions, 18, 21, 35n27, 69, 124–27, 133–34, 141–42, 158–59, 209, 338–41
paternalism, 278
patriarchy, 274, 289, 318–19, 346–47, 382n105
patriotism, 77–80, 82, 131, 356
Patton, P., 263
paupers, 144
peace, 85, 98–99, 101–2, 104–5, 109, 119n24, 124, 156
peasant, 248–49, 271, 296, 299, 346–47, 367
Peckham Rye Women's Liberation Group, 343
people, 25–27, 36n52, 43, 46, 52–53, 56–58, 69, 71, 87–89, 96n78, 105, 115–17, 138, 143–46, 168, 171–72, 175, 214, 229n83, 237, 255–57, 273
perception, 251
perfection, 111, 121n43, 160, 204–6
phenomena, 111, 121n43, 129, 140, 191, 196
phenomenalism, 210
philosophy, 10, 23, 30–31, 33, 76, 86, 97–98, 107, 139–40, 155, 158–59, 207, 231n129, 254, 342; of history, 3–6, 19, 29, 31, 98, 102, 110–12, 118n3, 120n41, 120n43, 122n45, 123–25, 127, 133–34, 153, 158, 160, 163, 177, 205, 226n27; of science, 282, 315
physics, 174, 181
pickpocket, 365
pity, 221
place, 9, 11, 300n4
planning, 157, 170, 198, 218, 240, 248, 344, 376

Plant, R., 149–50n36
plants, 186, 209, 321, 339
Plato, 6, 31, 76, 79, 97, 100, 102, 106–8, 252, 332; *Republic*, 97, 100
play, 252
playboy bunny, 322
pleasure, aesthetic, 112, 120n43
plebeian, 270
pluralism, 2, 5, 11–13, 143, 235–48, 250, 254–55, 258, 260–64, 267–68, 270, 273, 299n1, 300n3, 300n6, 305n111, 326
Poland, 89–90, 168, 172, 198
polarization of classes, 145, 147
political: economy, 12, 166, 288; rights, 216–18, 223–24; society, 43, 45, 49, 52, 58, 60n6; theory, 2, 6, 9, 17, 25, 29, 31, 37, 39, 56, 60n14, 97–98, 106, 108–9, 113, 118n3, 123, 144, 153, 230n124, 241, 312
political state, 166–67, 194–95, 199–200, 212–13, 255, 257–58, 346, 369–70, 373; alienated from civil society, 167–68, 171, 176, 195, 198, 212, 214, 217, 369; dominating civil society, 167–68, 171, 212, 222, 255–57, 297, 369; estranged from civil society, 166; standing over civil society, 167–68, 212, 222, 297; withering away of (*see* state, withering away of)
poor-law reform, 51, 63n55
Popkin, R., 1
population, 84, 98, 317–19, 377n21
positive rights, 216
possessions, 39, 41–44, 51, 58, 60n6, 85, 241, 332–38; women as, 323, 332–37, 339
possessiveness, 178–81, 199, 205–6
postulates of practical reason, 109–13, 203, 207, 211
power-over, 146, 258
powers and capacities, 99, 156, 185–

90, 197–98, 201, 204, 208–9, 245, 250, 253, 257–58, 261, 265, 267, 270, 330, 337, 348–49, 350–52, 368–69, 371
practical reason, 109–11, 129, 207
pregnant, 254, 342
premodern, 3, 10, 131, 144, 292, 315
price, 360, 368
"primitive" society, 80, 84, 86, 88, 279, 287, 289, 298–99, 382n105
prince, 79, 106–8
prisoner of war, 19
privacy, 375–76
procreation, 321, 327, 359
production, 187–88, 198–99, 201, 218, 248, 251, 256–57, 268, 270, 280–81, 284, 286, 289–92, 294–96, 312–14, 317–19, 321, 324–25, 332, 344–45, 349, 351, 355, 359, 362, 366, 368–70, 377n18; bourgeois mode of, 271; forces of, 156, 159, 160, 164–65, 172, 228n75, 247, 279, 291, 293, 313; instruments of, 178, 247, 271; means of, 240; mode of, 249, 285, 290, 299; relations of, 160, 178, 279, 293, 306n121, 312, 367
productive labor, 362–63, 365, 368–69; *see also* unproductive labor
productivism, 279, 288–90, 305n121, 312–13
profit, 105, 362–63, 366–67
projects, 193, 260–61
proletariat, 4, 10, 153–56, 160, 167, 172, 175, 213, 216, 243, 254, 275, 330–31, 337, 340–42, 375
propertied class, 3, 33, 51–55, 57, 59, 64n75, 82, 144, 241–42, 244
property, 3–4, 25, 37–40, 42, 51–54, 56–59, 60n6, 73, 79–80, 82–85, 131, 134, 142–46, 241–42, 295, 320, 323, 326, 334–35; common, 332; communal, 43–44, 55–57, 79, 271, 280, 282, 298, 326, 332, 335; equal, 38–44, 48, 55–57, 73,

79; interest, 3, 25, 40–41, 57–59, 82–83, 144–45, 239, 241–42; landed, 284–85, 295; natural right to, 38; private, 79, 85, 107, 129, 163–64, 172, 177, 188, 212, 227n73, 239, 280, 319, 327, 331–32, 335–36, 338; qualifications, 53–54, 147; rights, 57–58; title, 39, 43; tribal, 318; unequal, 3, 38–50, 55, 58–59, 61n36, 65, 79, 82, 84–85, 131, 144, 239, 242, 300n3; women as, 323, 326, 332, 334–36
propertyless class, 3–4, 33, 50, 52–55, 57–59, 73, 82, 144
prophecies, 102
prostitution, 322, 332
Protestantism, 10, 262, 282, 284
providence, 102
psychology, 316, 382n107
public opinion, 78, 267
public person, 21
public versus private, 373, 375
publicity, principle of, 114–15, 157–58
punishment, 21, 40, 51, 63n55, 89, 117, 265
purposiveness, 99, 112–13, 120n41, 120n43, 126, 165, 205–7, 211, 216, 220
Pythagoras, 339

rabble, 57, 144
race, 266, 326
racial differences, disappearance of, 273
racial minority groups, 11, 236, 261, 263, 300n4
racism, 14–15, 273, 304n96
radicals, 235, 254–55, 358
Ramsay, Mrs., 353
ransom, 19, 28–30, 36n55
rape, 375
Raphael, 201, 269–70
rationality, 20–22, 70, 100–101, 104, 128, 130, 137, 140–46, 160, 162,

175–76, 185, 194, 202, 206, 219–20, 241, 341
Rawls, J., 18–19, 30, 45, 61–62n36, 94n32, 238–40, 300n3
reactionary, 358
reason, 10, 18, 21, 34n26, 53, 76–77, 86–88, 103–6, 109–10, 112–13, 121n43, 142–43, 146–48, 155, 159, 173–74, 176, 205–6, 219, 287, 336, 340; *see also* practical reason; theoretical reason
rebirth, doctrine of, 339, 341
recall, 7, 255
recognition, 9, 39, 43, 136–38, 142, 147, 165, 194, 199, 264, 346, 351, 374
reconciliation, 138, 195, 207
reform, 114, 159
regulative idea. *See* idea, regulative
reincarnation, 76
relations, 178, 189, 281, 289, 295, 313, 321, 328–29, 336, 339, 345; between men and women, 322, 324, 327–29, 331–33, 335–38, 341–42, 371, 379n54, 380n59; between things, 344–45, 347, 383n114; essential, 328–29; species, 327, 329, 331–32, 334, 337–38
relative autonomy, 305n121
relativism, 300n3
religion, 9–10, 50, 73, 75–76, 94n43, 132, 137–38, 140, 143, 238–39, 242, 245, 262, 272–74, 282, 288–89, 295–96, 300n6, 341, 355, 357; disappearance of, 273–74; *see also* civil religion
Renaissance individuals, 248
rent, 277, 285, 287
representation, 53, 59, 121n43, 146–47, 168–71, 175, 196–99, 202, 230n124, 231n129, 249
representatives, 7, 21, 27, 32, 54–55, 68, 78, 80, 89, 154, 168–71, 196–98, 266, 369

reproduction, 313–14, 316, 318–19, 322–23, 327, 329–30, 337–38, 357, 359–64, 366–67, 375, 377n18, 386–87n144
republicanism, 104, 114, 119n22, 145, 174
respect, 55–56, 144
resurrection, 339, 341
revenue, 362
revolution, 4–6, 25, 29, 33, 40–41, 59, 60n13, 82, 84–85, 102, 113–15, 122n53, 153–60, 164, 166, 180–81, 214, 216, 233n174, 255, 273–75, 277, 291, 298, 325; bourgeois, 154, 181
proletarian, 153–54, 181
Rey, P.P., 293
Ricardo, D., 227n59, 277
right: prior to the good, 300n3; to a citizen militia, 217; to a free press, 212–13, 217, 233n174; to free speech, 212, 217; to privacy of correspondence, 213, 233n174; to property, 41, 51, 55, 58, 63n55, 212; to revolution, 25, 29, 33, 41, 54–56, 64n71; to vote, 55, 63n66, 170
rights, 39, 57, 65, 67, 115, 141, 155, 212–24, 233n182, 239, 266–67, 297, 300n4, 352; of man, 212; transcended, 219, 223–24
ritual, 261
robber, 19, 28
Roman Church, 10
Rome, 290–93, 315
Rosaldo, M.Z., 314, 320, 342, 379n54
Rousseau, J-J., 2–6, 18–20, 24–25, 30, 43–46, 56, 59, 62n36, 65–97, 106, 108, 114–16, 118n22, 123–24, 130–35, 141, 144–45, 147–48, 149n34, 153, 158, 163–64, 168, 171–76, 181, 194–200, 214, 227n59, 230n124, 235–36, 242, 256–58; *Constitutional Project for*

Corsica, 86; *Discourse on Inequality*, 83, 85–88, 130; *Emile*, 69–70, 174; *Geneva Manuscript*, 68–70; *Government of Poland*, 75, 88–89; *Social Contract*, 68, 75, 77, 80, 83, 85–90, 106, 168, 173, 175, 217
Rubin, G., 322
rule egoism, 35n35
ruling: class, 171, 173, 243; ideas, 243
Russia, 8, 285, 296, 299
Ryan, M., 254

Sabbala, 274
Sahlins, M., 279, 290, 292, 312, 315; *Culture and Practical Reason*, 279
Salamanasser, 46
San Francisco, 269
savagery, 84, 87, 296
scarcity, 20, 48, 84
Schafly, P., 343
Schiller, F., 113, 205–6, 219–20, 336; *Letters on the Aesthetic Education of Man*, 219
science, 9–10, 12, 23, 30–31, 107, 181, 183–84, 188, 272–73, 275, 279, 281, 283, 288, 290, 293, 315, 342, 380n59; normal, 283–84; of politics, 23
scientific crisis, 284
scientific deduction of sovereignty by institution, 19–20, 23, 24n27, 29, 35n35, 100, 237
scripture, 34n26
sculptor, 268
second-class citizens, 52
security, 20–22, 28, 34n26, 40–41, 100–101, 108, 143, 233n174, 240
seduce, 340
self-authorized laws, 21–22, 28
self-determined, 21, 28, 74, 103, 127, 129, 142–43, 146–47, 168, 173–74, 176, 190–92
self-esteem, 221, 358

self-preservation, 20–21, 58, 100–101, 360
self-seeking, 80–81, 102, 106, 124–25, 132–33
self-sufficiency, 79, 249, 271
selfishness, 20, 99–100, 102, 104–5, 160, 178, 181, 193
Senator, 270
sensation, 20, 139, 205–6, 209, 252, 321–22, 337
sensitivities, 251, 258, 336–37
Sepoy revolt, 274
serfdom, 132, 347, 369
servants, 43, 53, 61n23
service, 125, 136–38, 197, 346–47, 354, 360–61, 385n139
sex object, 336, 340
sexism, 2, 14–15, 313, 340, 375
sexuality, 255, 266, 276, 314, 317, 320–23, 327, 332, 341–42, 347, 378n24, 382n107, 384n128
Shakespeare, W., 267, 291
shame, 221–22
shoemaker, 169–71, 198, 248
silver, 41, 44
Sismondi, J., 277
Sittlichkeit, 76–77, 124, 126–34, 136, 142, 144–48
skepticism, 339
slave dealer, 323, 362, 370
slavery, 10, 12, 52, 61n23, 74, 78, 132, 203, 206, 268, 274, 281, 318–19, 322, 324, 343, 345, 352, 354, 361, 370, 377n21; to the species, 354
slut, 340
Smith, A., 80–81, 105–6, 149n36, 124–25, 133, 135, 141, 145, 160, 164, 177, 227n59, 349, 351
social: cohesion, 3–4, 25–27, 39–41, 47, 57–58, 82, 116, 144–46, 150n36, 239–43, 246, 257–58; compact, 40; contract, 20–22, 25–26, 45, 47, 76–77, 85–86, 100–101, 108, 227n59, 238; theory, 2–

4, 25, 37–41, 50, 56–57, 59, 60n14, 76, 81–82, 116, 144–45, 179, 189, 312; transformation, 5–6, 33, 114, 155, 180, 383n114
social contract theory, 18, 41, 43, 45–46
socialism, 8, 10, 239, 241, 279, 296, 299, 311, 314, 323–26, 369, 371
socialization, 314, 329, 354
Socrates, 76, 128, 258
sodomy, 380n57
solidarity, 57, 77, 81, 150n36, 220, 224, 373; mechanical, 150n36
Soltykov, Prince, 275
sophists, 358
sovereign, successor of, 35n35, 40
sovereign body, 68–69, 71–72, 92n8, 93n21, 167, 195–96, 198
sovereignty, 2–3, 18–19, 21–27, 32, 35n26, 36n52, 39, 43, 47–48, 56–59, 65–67, 74, 82–83, 88–89, 101, 105, 113–17, 119n22, 143–46, 147, 171, 214, 223, 237–38, 241, 255–57, 274, 289, 300n3; absolute, 2–3, 82–83, 144–45, 214; by acquisition, 17, 19–20, 25, 27–33, 35n35; by institution, 17, 19–20, 23, 29–32, 36n52; dissolution of, 3, 5, 256, 258; limited, 24, 83; of the people, 3, 32, 54, 56–58, 116–17, 144–45, 147, 255–56; *see also* supreme power
Soviet Union, 7, 224
soviets, 240
Sparta, 258, 262
specialization, 268–71, 283, 351
species, 14, 161–69, 177–78, 181–83, 189–98, 200, 202, 204, 207–8, 214–16, 222, 245–46, 250, 260, 262, 273, 318, 322, 326–37, 348, 350–54, 361, 369, 372–73, 375; activity, 162, 169, 204, 217, 349, 352, 354; being, 160–61, 166–67, 169, 182, 188–89, 191–93, 196, 328–29, 333, 348–49; essence, 7, 212, 216, 330–35; life, 327, 349
sperm, 380n59
spirit, 4–5, 77, 87, 124, 126–28, 130, 132, 135–38, 141–43, 145–46, 153, 155, 173, 177, 179, 194–96, 208–11, 253, 257, 264, 290–91
spoilage, principle of, 38, 41–42, 48
St. Mary's College, 1
standing professional army, 7, 89, 122n53, 158, 172, 213, 256–57
starving, 252, 255, 265
state: bureaucratic, 7; destruction of, 171; standing over society, 7, 12, 150n36, 172, 175, 199, 213; withering away of, 3, 25, 39–40, 82, 116, 144, 150n36, 230n124
state of nature, 3, 17–32, 33n3, 35n35, 36n52, 37–51, 57, 60n6, 62n37, 62n48, 77, 83, 84–88, 95n66, 96n78, 100–101, 108, 144, 179, 227n59, 237–42, 300n2
statesman, 149n36
stealing, 103–4; *see also* theft
Stern, R., 149n36
Steuart, J., 133, 149n36, 177, 231n129
subsistence, 48, 55–56, 367–68; means of, 359–60, 385n141, 386n143, 386n144
suffrage: popular, 147; universal, 64n71, 170–71, 270; universal manhood, 53, 64n71
sun, 186, 209, 339
supersensible, 111, 120n41
superstructure, 290, 294, 306n121
supreme power, 26, 52, 56, 64n75
surplus, 387n144; labor, 256, 290, 360, 364–66, 375; labor time, 367; production, 41–42, 84, 130; value, 361–69
Switzerland, 277

symbolic, 121n43, 207, 211, 279, 289–98, 305n121, 315–16
synthetic, 203

talent, 166, 245, 247, 249, 261, 268; artistic, 268
tariffs, 156, 277
taxes, 53, 59, 63n63, 117
technology, 180–81, 184, 187, 258, 279, 383n114
teleology, 112, 120n41, 120n43, 283–84, 286–87, 296
television, 375
theft, 70, 72–73, 80, 155, 365; *see also* stealing
theology, 102
theoretical: knowledge, 109, 112, 291; reason, 109–10, 207
thing in itself, 129, 140, 191, 207–10, 230n119, 254
Third World, 255
Thrasymachus, 97, 100
Thucydides, 97
time, 298
tithe, 245, 287
Todorov, T., 298
toleration, 143, 235–36, 238–41, 243–44, 278, 305n111
Tönnies, F., 75
tools, 105, 187
Tory, 272
totalitarianism, 3, 5, 10–11, 65–66, 73, 75–76, 78, 83, 87–88, 91, 94n43, 96n91, 143–44, 235–36, 242
totality, 109, 137, 140, 143, 146, 247–48, 251, 287
totalizing, 2, 11, 235, 254–55, 263, 288
trade, 4, 40, 48, 62n49, 79, 156; *see also* commerce and trade
tradition, 1–2, 5, 11, 15, 177, 259–61, 274, 289, 336, 341; *see also* custom and tradition

transcendental self, 129, 191–93
transcendental unity of self-consciousness, 139
tribe, 318, 355
Tribunate, 96n90
tribute, 287
trust, 64n75, 339, 341, 353, 375
trustworthiness, 166
truth, 138, 159, 210, 254, 277, 305n111
Tully, J., 50, 53
Turks, 305n109
tyrant, 76

umbrella agreement, 235, 238–46, 255, 259–60, 263, 300n3, 300n4
unalienated, 354, 359, 383n114; labor, 347–49, 352, 372
understanding, 112, 120n43, 301n29
unemployed, 51
union, 92n21, 157, 263
United States, 12, 14, 236, 241, 244, 272, 297, 300n4
universal class, 225n9
universalization, 94n32, 103–4, 116, 155, 161–62, 174, 185, 190, 194, 196, 198, 214, 260–61, 263–64, 330
University of California, San Diego, 1
unjust, 114–16, 119n22, 157, 363
unproductive labor, 362–65, 368–70, 384n136
unsocial sociability, 99, 101
upbringing, 76, 202, 329–330, 334, 354, 359
Ure, A., 269
use value, 265, 289, 362–63, 368–69, 385n139
utilitarianism, 203, 265
utility, 104, 290–91, 265
utopian, 3, 5–6, 8, 12, 31, 33, 80–81, 83, 86–87, 91, 92n8, 97, 106–7, 109, 123, 131, 133–34, 148,

159, 163–64, 175–76, 178, 189, 201, 224, 228n75, 241, 254, 269, 325
utopian socialists, 332

value, 42, 166, 205, 281, 283, 359–60, 362–66, 385n139, 386n144
variable capital, 362
vassalage, 382n103
veil of ignorance, 94n32
Vergegenständlichung, 186
veto, 90–91
Vico, G., 321
violence, 158
Virgin Mary, 381n87
virtue, 77, 98, 107, 110–12, 125–27, 129, 134, 165–67, 190, 202–4, 207, 215, 221–22; and the way of the world, 125–28, 130, 135, 141, 179, 190, 289, 353–54
vocation, 333
volition, 104, 110
voting instructions, 168, 197–98, 200, 255–56
Vulcan, 291–92

wage, 43, 48, 161, 203, 306n123, 323, 348, 360–68, 385n139, 386n144; labor, 306n123, 362, 369
war, 29, 84, 86, 99, 101–2, 104–6, 109, 120n41, 156, 158, 318–19, 356; of all versus all, 25, 84–85, 100

Washington, D.C., 298
way of the world. *See* virtue and the way of the world
weapons, 183
West, 271, 279, 285, 298, 305n116
Western Marxists, 7
Whig, 53
wife, 319, 322, 333–34, 337, 347, 362–67, 370, 372; battering, 347, 375
will of all, 67, 72
witchcraft, 297
women, 10–12, 236, 247, 261–64, 276, 278, 297, 311–76, 377n21, 379n54, 384n128
women's roles, 320–21, 352–54
Wood, N., 50
Woolf, V., 353
workers, 11–13, 236, 248, 250, 261, 263, 265–66, 269, 323, 337, 348, 358, 361–62, 364, 366–67, 370, 385n139
working class, 10, 12, 160–61, 166, 170–71, 203, 206, 218–19, 243–44, 254–55, 323, 359, 363, 385n141
world: literature, 271; market, 270, 273
World Spirit, 158
worship, 341

Xerxes, 46

Yankee, 277

About the Author

Philip J. Kain was born in San Francisco, California, on May 21, 1943. He received a B.A. in philosophy from St. Mary's College of California and a Ph.D. in philosophy from the University of California at San Diego. He has taught at the University of California at Santa Cruz, Stanford University, and is presently an associate professor and the chair of the Philosophy Department at Santa Clara University. He has written three previous books on Marx: *Schiller, Hegel, and Marx* (1982), *Marx' Method, Epistemology, and Humanism* (1986), and *Marx and Ethics* (1988). He is presently at work on a book on Hegel.